H.P. Blavatsky
THE SECRET DOCTRINE DIALOGUES
H.P. Blavatsky Talks With Students

H.P. Blavatsky

THE SECRET DOCTRINE DIALOGUES

H.P. Blavatsky Talks With Students

THE THEOSOPHY COMPANY
LOS ANGELES, CALIFORNIA
2014

First Edition 2014

The Theosophy Company
Los Angeles, California

ISBN 978-0-9898541-0-8

Contents

Introduction   I

The Stanzas of Dzyan   V

Original Manuscript Page 1 A photocopy.   XIV

1. Meeting January 10, 1889   1
Stanza 1, Slokas 1-2:
Parabrahm, Ain-Soph; Laya centers; protyle and *hyle;* time, space and duration; Sat, "Be-ness"; the nature of intelligence and consciousness; the logoi.

2. Meeting January 17, 1889   27
Stanza 1, Slokas 3-4:
Universal mind; consciousness; the Ah-hi; cosmic ideation; deep sleep; Buddhi and Mahat; four truths of Buddhism; the Nidanas and Maya; dreams; instinct; the cerebrum and the cerebellum.

3. Meeting January 24, 1889   59
Stanza 1, Slokas 5-8:
Buddhism; space; Darkness and Light; Father-Mother-Son; Laya; Parabrahm, the causeless cause, Sat, rootless root; dreamless sleep; the senses; clairvoyance; light, sound and color.

4. Meeting January 31, 1889   95
Stanza 1, Slokas 6 & 9; Stanza 2, Slokas 1-2:
Dhyan-Chohans, Planetary spirits; planets; the Builders; Dhyani-Buddhas, Manus and Rishis; the Sephiroth; Alaya and Jivatma; Planetary chains; Rishis and Manus; water, fire and occultism; modern science and hypotheses; induction and deduction.

5. Meeting February 7, 1889   129
Stanza 2, Slokas 3-4:
Three logoi; the point in the circle; the Mundane, Solar and

Universal Eggs; potentiality and potency; Fohat, "Pho"; Astral Light; Pythagorean geometry, numbers; Triangles and Pyramids; the Tetragrammaton and Tetraktys; "Yod-he-va," the Elohim.

6. Meeting February 14, 1889   153
Stanza 3, Slokas 1-3:
The first Logos; Duration and Time; radiation and emanation; Akasa and Astral Light; early Christianity; noumena and phenomena; Dhyan-Chohans and Dhyani-Buddhas; Manu; Manvantaras; cosmic elements and elementals; the fate of mediums; Water; the Virgin-Egg; language; thought and ideas.

7. Meeting February 21, 1889   191
Stanza 3, Slokas 2-4:
Vibration and germ; Pythagorean triangle; "Radiant Essence"; Paramatma and Jivatma; atoms and molecules; ether and Akasa; elements; "world-stuff"; war in heaven; 14 Manus; seven rays; numbers and principles; colors and prisms; Ralston Skinner and the Kabalah; the pyramids.

8. Meeting February 28, 1889   223
Stanza 3, Slokas 5-9:
The Root; the Milky Way and "world-stuff"; Light and Time; "knots" of Fohat; the Sun; nebular theory; sun spots; Fire; weight and gravity; Water; numbers and colors; Kwan-shai-yin and Kwan-yin; Oeaohoo; the veil of reality; Electricity and Fohat; the kama-rupa of amber and electricity; the ant; organic and inorganic matter; Fire; Keely's inter-etheric force; Thompson and Crookes; suns and planets; the atmosphere.

9. Meeting March 7, 1889   257
Stanza 3, Slokas 10-11:
Æther and Akasa; ether and Astral Light; the circle; the Web of the Universe; the Monad; planets and gravity; one absolute force; the Absolute.

10. Meeting March 14, 1889 295
Stanza 4, Slokas 1-5:
"Sons of the Fire"; Nirvana; Father-Mother; Kabalistic permutation; the Alhim (Elohim); the Logos; "god geometrizes"; suns, comets, meteors and planets; the Pleiades.

11. Meeting March 21, 1889 323
Stanza 4, Sloka 6; Stanza 5, Slokas 1-3:
The Lipika, Æons, the Syzygies of Simon Magus; Word, Voice and Spirit; "the rejected Son"; Mahat; the Absolute; the atoms; "Sons of Fohat".

12. Meeting March 28, 1889 341
Stanza 4, Sloka 5; Stanza 5, Slokas 1-5:
The Sun and planets; comets, cosmic dust and nebula; Fohat; atoms; electricity; the Caduceus of Mercury; the Hindu trinity; the four corners; magnetic influences.

13. Meeting April 4, 1889 371
Stanza 5, Sloka 6; Stanza 6, Slokas 1 & 3-4:
Personal Ego and Impersonal Self; Atma-Buddhi-Manas; Vach; Laya centers; Fohat and the Mayavi-rupa; pralayas; Atoms; Force; Light and Heat; Nirvana and Parinirvana; Globes, Rounds and Races; the Moon Chain; Keely's telescope.

14. Meeting April 11, 1889 403
Stanza 6, Sloka 4:
Atmospheres and elements; meteors; minerals; atoms and molecules; Laya centers and primordial substance; Fohat, electricity and Energy; influence of the Moon; magnetism; Mars, Mercury.

15. Meeting April 18, 1889 429
Laya centers, matter and substance; seven planes of substance; triangle and square; classes of Monads; perfection in evolution; Mt. Meru; the Sishtas; anthropoids; populations; the Todas and Mulakurumbas of India.

16. Meeting April 25, 1889 457
Stanza 6, Sloka 5:
The moon and earth; motion; Fohat; Lunar Pitris; Rounds, globes and principles; karma of civilization; Nature; Kama Rupa and Prana.

17. Meeting May 2, 1889 491
Stanza 6, Slokas 5-6:
"The Dragon"; Saturn; cosmic "seats"; Kabalah; Cosmic Consciousness; seeds and atoms; Chaos and Eros; the struggle for existence; selfishness; elliptic and parabolic orbits; states of matter.

18. Meeting May 9, 1889: Transcription missing.

19. Meeting May 16, 1889 523
"The Key to Theosophy"; practical theosophy; Father Damien and Labro; altruism; growth of the Theosophical Society; pseudo-Theosophists; influences of planets and color; Theosophists and Mystics; basic theosophy.

20. Meeting May 30, 1889 549
Stanza 7, Slokas 1-3:
Prana, Jiva and Monads; the Unknown and the Unknowable; Manas; the brain; Karma and heredity; the Fourth Round.

21. Meeting June 6, 1889 575
"The Key to Theosophy"; Karma, unmerited suffering; Devachan; free will; memory; reincarnation.

22. Meeting June 20, 1889 607
Materialism and understanding; natural forces and hierarchies; Theosophy and fanaticism; intuition; Atma, Buddhi and Manas; Jiva and Prana.

No evidence exists that meetings were held May 23 or June 13, 1889.

Appendix 1 635
Possible missing fragment from Meeting 1, page 4.

Appendix 2 636
"Appendix on Dreams" from *The Transactions of the Blavatsky Lodge*.

Appendix 3 655
Blavatsky Lodge Meetings:
Participants and the meetings they attended.

Appendix 4 659
The Secret Doctrine: A Paper read before the Blavatsky Lodge of the T.S. by William Kingsland, President.

Index 665

Introduction

The modern Theosophical movement, inaugurated in 1875 by H. P. Blavatsky and others with the formation of the Theosophical Society, had nearly perished by the time HPB moved to London in May of 1887. Although a worldly success, attacks from without and a lack of support from within had rendered the Society almost lifeless. Psychic phenomena, and a general misunderstanding of the nature of the "masters" and the principle of Universal Brotherhood – the fundamental purpose of the Movement – had distracted both the Society and the world's attention from the deeper teachings.

Retreating to Europe to regain her health and to re-group among friends, HPB had left India in 1885, ill, exhausted, near death in fact, yet determined to carry on with the work her teachers had set for her. At last, she was able to gather about her a revitalized nucleus of workers, which came to be called the Blavatsky Lodge. The next four years produced a flourish of wonderfully productive activity, beginning with a new magazine, *Lucifer,* in the fall of 1887. The additional helping hands allowed HPB to focus upon and complete *The Secret Doctrine* by 1888, and *The Key to Theosophy* and *The Voice of the Silence* the following year.

Once published, *The Secret Doctrine* proved to be a tremendous catalyst for serious student inquiry. Questions about the book and its subjects, particularly cosmogenesis, were the topic of the weekly meetings of the Blavatsky Lodge, held at HPB's home on Lansdowne Road. Students of Theosophical history will no doubt recognize many of the names of prominent Theosophists of the day who attended. In a letter to her sister, Vera, HPB gives a behind-the-scenes glimpse of those proceedings:

> Every Saturday we hold a reception and every Thursday a meeting, with all its scientific questions, with shorthand writers at my back, and with a couple of reporters in corners. Does not all this take time? I have to prepare myself for every Thursday, because the people who attend these meetings are not ignoramuses, but men

such as Kingsland, the worker in electricity, as Dr. William Bennett, and the naturalist, Carter Blake. I have to be ready to defend the theories of occultism against those of applied sciences so that it will be possible to print them straight away from the shorthand reports in our new special monthly magazine under the title of *Transactions of the Blavatsky Lodge*.

The first installment of the *Transactions* was published a year later, in 1890, carrying a note that the printed version was "somewhat condensed from the original discussions," and presenting the material in an anonymous question and answer format. Another volume shortly followed, and though others were indicated, nothing further appeared. The recorded weekly meetings were held from January 10 to June 20, 1889, but the published accounts only covered the meetings up to March 14. Two meetings also took place in December, 1888, and resulted in the Appendix on Dreams included in the first volume, and included here as Appendix 2, making the present work a complete record of the dialogues H. P. Blavatsky held with her students over a seven month period.

This material, 21 handwritten folios of over 30 pages each, provides a useful commentary on the ideas expounded in *The Secret Doctrine*. As much as possible, it is a word-for-word transcription from the original handwritten reports of the meetings (A sample, page one of the original MS, follows.) The report of the first meeting of January 10, 1889 is unique in that it bears HPB's handwritten editorial changes, which differ from the version published at the time. Among the many changes made to the first dozen or so pages was her crossing out "Madame Blavatsky" and inserting "HPB." Her preference for the latter designation is well-known, and most participants in the dialogues reported herein so referred to her, but we have maintained the former designation when it was used by the stenographers. At the meeting of May 16 and after, the discussions turned to a new project HPB was working on, *The Key to Theosophy*, and karma, reincarnation, and the after-death states were among the topics covered. Students will find in these dialogues a faithful account of HPB speaking clearly and providing much food for thought.

The sentence structure of the reports has been maintained as recorded, wherever possible. Only minor editing has been done for uniformity of punctuation and spelling of words, which are left in the original British English used by the stenographers. Any additions, which are few and provided for the sake of readability, are indicated by the following parentheses { }. Sometimes the text of the handwritten reports contains a blank space where the stenographer was unable to get a word or term, and this is indicated by brackets [ ]. Occasionally, parts of the MS text were crossed out, perhaps by HPB herself, and have been included in brackets [thus]. All footnotes are by the transcribers. Sanskrit terms are given as closely as possible to those used by HPB, who followed the forms generally in use in her time.

This volume is intended neither to replace nor to correct the existing *Transactions of the Blavatsky Lodge*, but may be viewed as a companion work. A comparison with the *Transactions* immediately shows how much HPB edited the latter, yet these transcriptions provide a powerful, first-hand introduction to HPB in discussion. We are treated to her broad, philosophical and penetrating mind, her biting wit, her gentle and not-so-gentle impatience with human foibles, and her self-deprecating willingness to inquire into ideas and engage the minds of others.

These are real dialogues, based on the most difficult, abstruse material of the early pages of *The Secret Doctrine*: the nature of reality, the substance of the universe, the basis and nature of consciousness, mind and matter. The questions come from some of the best, open young minds of the time, and anticipate many still pondered today. Here is HPB direct – wise, articulate, grumpy, sharp, raw, unedited – and we are given a "fly-on-the-wall" ear to the world's first study class in *The Secret Doctrine,* with the author, or writer, rather, HPB herself presiding!

COSMIC EVOLUTION.

In Seven Stanzas translated from the Book of Dzyan.

STANZA I.

1. The eternal parent wrapped in her ever invisible robes had slumbered once again for seven eternities.

2. Time was not, for it lay asleep in the infinite bosom of duration.

3. Universal mind was not, for there were no Ah-hi to contain it.

4. The seven ways to bliss were not. The great causes of misery were not, for there was no one to produce and get ensnared by them.

5. Darkness alone filled the boundless all, for father, mother and son were once more one, and the son had not awakened yet for the new wheel, and his pilgrimage thereon.

6. The seven sublime lords and the seven truths had ceased to be, and the Universe, the son of Necessity, was immersed in Paranishpanna, to be outbreathed by that which is and yet is not. Naught was.

7. The causes of existence had been done away with; the visible that was, and the invisible that is, rested in eternal non-being—the one being.

8. Alone the one form of existence stretched boundless, infinite, causeless, in dreamless sleep; and life pulsated unconscious in universal space, throughout that all-presence which is sensed by the opened eye of the Dangma.

9. But where was the Dangma when the Alaya of the universe was in Paramartha and the great wheel was Anupadaka?

STANZA II.

1. . . . Where were the builders, the luminous sons of Manvantaric dawn? . . . In the unknown darkness in their Ah-hi Paranishpanna. The producers of form from no-form—the root of the world—the Devamatri and Svâbhâvat, rested in the bliss of non-being.

2. . . . Where was silence? Where the ears to sense it? No, there was neither silence nor sound; naught save ceaseless eternal breath, which knows itself not.

3. The hour had not yet struck; the ray had not yet flashed into the Germ; the Matripadma had not yet swollen.

4. Her heart had not yet opened for the one ray to enter, thence to fall, as three into four, into the lap of Maya.

5. The seven sons were not yet born from the web of light. Darkness alone was father-mother, Svâbhâvat; and Svâbhâvat was in darkness.

6. These two are the Germ, and the Germ is one. The Universe was still concealed in the Divine thought and the Divine bosom. . . .

STANZA III.

1. . . . The last vibration of the seventh eternity thrills through infinitude. The mother swells, expanding from within without, like the bud of the lotus.

2. The vibration sweeps along, touching with its swift wing the whole universe and the germ that dwelleth in darkness: the darkness that breathes over the slumbering waters of life. . .

3. Darkness radiates light, and light drops one solitary ray into the mother-deep. The ray shoots through the virgin

egg, the ray causes the eternal egg to thrill, and drop the non-eternal germ, which condenses into the world-egg.

4. Then the three fall into the four. The radiant essence becomes seven inside, seven outside. The luminous egg, which in itself is three, curdles and spreads in milk-white curds throughout the depths of mother, the root that grows in the depths of the ocean of life.

5. The root remains, the light remains, the curds remain, and still Oeaohoo is one.

6. The root of life was in every drop of the ocean of immortality, and the ocean was radiant light, which was fire, and heat, and motion. Darkness vanished and was no more; it disappeared in its own essence, the body of fire and water, or father and mother.

7. Behold, oh Lanoo! The radiant child of the two, the unparalleled refulgent glory: Bright Space Son of Dark Space, which emerges from the depths of the great dark waters. It is Oeaohoo the younger, the * * * He shines forth as the son; he is the blazing Divine Dragon of Wisdom; the One is Four, and Four takes to itself Three,[1] and the Union produces the Sapta, in whom are the seven which become the Tridasa (or the hosts and the multitudes). Behold him lifting the veil and unfurling it from east to west. He shuts out the above, and leaves the below to be seen as the great illusion. He marks the places for the shining ones, and turns the upper into a shoreless sea of fire, and the one manifested into the great waters.

8. Where was the germ and where was now darkness? Where is the spirit of the flame that burns in thy lamp, oh Lanoo? The germ is that, and that is light, the white brilliant son of the dark hidden father.

---

1 In the English translation from the Sanskrit the numbers are given in that language, *Eka*, *Chatur*, etc., etc. It was thought best to give them in English.

9. Light is cold flame, and flame is fire, and fire produces heat, which yields water: the water of life in the great Mother.

10. Father-Mother spin a web whose upper end is fastened to Spirit—the light of the one darkness—and the lower one to its shadowy end, matter; and this web is the universe spun out of the two substances made in one, which is Svâbhâvat.

11. It expands when the breath of fire is upon it; it contracts when the breath of the mother touches it. Then the sons dissociate and scatter, to return into their mother's bosom at the end of the great day, and re-become one with her; when it is cooling it becomes radiant, and the sons expand and contract through their own selves and hearts; they embrace infinitude.

12. Then Svâbhâvat sends Fohat to harden the atoms. Each is a part of the web. Reflecting the "Self-Existent Lord" like a mirror, each becomes in turn a world.

STANZA IV.

1. . . . Listen, ye Sons of the Earth, to your instructors—the Sons of the Fire. Learn, there is neither first nor last, for all is one: number issued from no number.

2. Learn what we who descend from the Primordial Seven, we who are born from the Primordial Flame, have learnt from our fathers. . . .

3. From the effulgency of light—the ray of the ever-darkness—sprung in space the re-awakened energies; the one from the egg, the six, and the five. Then the three, the one, the four, the one, the five—the twice seven the sum total. And these are the essences, the flames, the elements, the builders, the numbers, the arupa, the rupa, and the force

of Divine Man—the sum total. And from the Divine Man emanated the forms, the sparks, the sacred animals, and the messengers of the sacred fathers within the holy four.

4. This was the army of the voice—the divine mother of the seven. The sparks of the seven are subject to, and the servants of, the first, the second, the third, the fourth, the fifth, the sixth, and the seventh of the seven. These "sparks" are called spheres, triangles, cubes, lines, and modellers; for thus stands the Eternal Nidana—the Oeaohoo, which is:

5. "Darkness" the boundless, or the no-number, Adi-Nidana Svâbhâvat:—

    I. The Adi-Sanat, the number, for he is one.
    II. The voice of the Lord Svâbhâvat, the numbers, for he is one and nine.
    III. The "formless square."

And these three enclosed within the ◯ are the sacred four; and the ten are the arupa universe. Then come the "sons," the seven fighters, the one, the eighth left out, and his breath which is the light-maker.

6. Then the second seven, who are the Lipika, produced by the three. The rejected son is one. The "Son-suns" are countless.

STANZA V.

1. The Primordial Seven, the First Seven Breaths of the Dragon of Wisdom, produce in their turn from their Holy Circumgyrating Breaths the Fiery Whirlwind.

2. They make of him the messenger of their will. The Dzyu becomes Fohat, the swift son of the Divine sons whose sons

are the Lipika, runs circular errands. Fohat is the steed and the thought is the rider. He passes like lightning through the fiery clouds; takes three, and five, and seven strides through the seven regions above, and the seven below. He lifts his voice, and calls the innumerable sparks, and joins them.

3. He is their guiding spirit and leader. When he commences work, he separates the sparks of the Lower Kingdom that float and thrill with joy in their radiant dwellings, and forms therewith the germs of wheels. He places them in the six directions of space, and one in the middle—the central wheel.

4. Fohat traces spiral lines to unite the sixth to the seventh—the crown; an army of the Sons of Light stands at each angle, and the Lipika in the middle wheel. They say: This is good, the first Divine world is ready, the first is now the second. Then the "Divine Arupa" reflects itself in Chhaya Loka, the first garment of the Anupadaka.

5. Fohat takes five strides and builds a winged wheel at each corner of the square, for the four holy ones and their armies.

6. The Lipika circumscribe the triangle, the first one, the cube, the second one, and the pentacle within the egg. It is the ring called "Pass Not" for those who descend and ascend. Also for those who during the Kalpa are progressing towards the great day "Be with us." Thus were formed the Rupa and the Arupa: from one light seven lights; from each of the seven, seven times seven lights. The wheels watch the ring. . . . .

STANZA VI.

1. By the power of the Mother of Mercy and Knowledge—

Kwan-Yin—the "triple" of Kwan-shai-Yin, residing in Kwan-yin-Tien, Fohat, the Breath of their Progeny, the Son of the Sons, having called forth, from the lower abyss, the illusive form of Sien-Tchang and the Seven Elements:[2]

2. The Swift and Radiant One produces the Seven Laya Centres, against which none will prevail to the great day "Be-with-Us," and seats the Universe on these Eternal Foundations surrounding Tsien-Tchan with the Elementary Germs.

3. Of the Seven—first one manifested, six concealed, two manifested, five concealed; three manifested, four concealed; four produced, three hidden; four and one tsan revealed, two and one half concealed; six to be manifested, one laid aside. Lastly, seven small wheels revolving; one giving birth to the other.

4. He builds them in the likeness of older wheels, placing them on the Imperishable Centres.

How does Fohat build them? he collects the fiery dust. He makes balls of fire, runs through them, and round them, infusing life thereinto, then sets them into motion; some one way, some the other way. They are cold, he makes them hot. They are dry, he makes them moist. They shine, he fans and cools them. Thus acts Fohat from one twilight to the other, during Seven Eternities.

5. At the fourth, the sons are told to create their images. One third refuses—two obey.

The curse is pronounced; they will be born on the fourth, suffer and cause suffering; this is the first war.

6. The older wheels rotated downwards and upwards. . . . The mother's spawn filled the whole. There were battles

---

[2] Verse 1 of Stanza VI. is of a far later date than the other Stanzas, though still very ancient. The old text of this verse, having names entirely unknown to the Orientalists would give no clue to the student.

fought between the Creators and the Destroyers, and battles fought for space; the seed appearing and re-appearing continuously.

7. Make thy calculations, Lanoo, if thou wouldest learn the correct age of thy small wheel. Its fourth spoke is our mother. Reach the fourth "fruit" of the fourth path of knowledge that leads to Nirvana, and thou shalt comprehend, for thou shalt see . . . . .

STANZA VII.

1. Behold the beginning of sentient formless life.
First the Divine, the one from the Mother-Spirit; then the Spiritual; the three from the one, the four from the one, and the five from which the three, the five, and the seven. These are the three-fold, the four-fold downward; the "mind-born" sons of the first Lord; the shining seven.
It is they who are thou, me, him, oh Lanoo. They, who watch over thee, and thy mother earth.

2. The one ray multiplies the smaller rays. Life precedes form, and life survives the last atom of form. Through the countless rays proceeds the life-ray, the one, like a thread through many jewels.

3. When the one becomes two, the threefold appears, and the three are one; and it is our thread, oh Lanoo, the heart of the man-plant called Saptaparna.

4. It is the root that never dies; the three-tongued flame of the four wicks. The wicks are the sparks, that draw from the three-tongued flame shot out by the seven—their flame—the beams and sparks of one moon reflected in the running waves of all the rivers of earth.

5. The spark hangs from the flame by the finest thread of

Fohat. It journeys through the Seven Worlds of Maya. It stops in the first, and is a metal and a stone; it passes into the second and behold—a plant; the plant whirls through seven changes and becomes a sacred animal. From the combined attributes of these, Manu, the thinker is formed. Who forms him? The seven lives, and the one life. Who completes him? The five-fold Lha. And who perfects the last body? Fish, sin, and soma. . . . .

6. From the first-born the thread between the Silent Watcher and his Shadow becomes more strong and radiant with every change. The morning sun-light has changed into noon-day glory. . . . .

7. This is thy present wheel, said the Flame to the Spark. Thou art myself, my image, and my shadow. I have clothed myself in thee, and thou art my Vahan to the day, "Be with us," when thou shalt re-become myself and others, thyself and me. Then the builders, having donned their first clothing, descend on radiant earth and reign over men—who are themselves. . . .

The Theosophical Society.

Meeting on Wednesday, January 10th 1889
at 17 Lansdowne Road. W.

Harbottle Esq., — President.

Mr Keightley (Secretary): In the Proem to the "Secret Doctrine" Vol I pp 8 & 9, speaking of space, this is said (reads quotation). That is just the few words on the subject of space in the abstract: but the first sloka of the first stanza runs as follows: "The Eternal Parent (space) wrapped in her ever invisible robes had slumbered once again for 7 eternities" and on this the first question that strikes one to ask is why is the Eternal Parent, or space, called feminine here?

Mad. Blavatsky "H.P.B.": Perhaps it is a mistake to do so; but since it is impossible to define Parabrahm, or that which is beyond human conception, therefore once that we are speaking of that first something which can be conceived, we had better say "She"; it is the In all the cosmogonies goddess & goddesses, the former becoming the goddess that comes first, the immaculate mother, from wh. proceeds the God. Therefore we have to adopt one of the other two genders, and we cannot say it, because from it nothing can proceed, strictly speaking, neither a radiation nor an emanation.

Mr Keightley: So that the Egyptian Neith

1.
The Theosophical Society.
Meeting on Wednesday {Thursday}, January 10, 1889 at 17 Lansdowne Road, W.

{Thomas B.} Harbottle Esq. — President.

Mr. {B.?} Keightley (Secretary): In the Proem to *The Secret Doctrine*, speaking of space, this is said (reads quotation, Volume I, pp. 8 *et seq.*[1]). That is just the few words on the subject of space in the abstract: but the first Sloka of the first Stanza runs as follows: "The Eternal Parent (Space), wrapped in her ever invisible robes, had slumbered once again for seven eternities," and on this the first question that strikes one to ask is why is the Eternal Parent, or Space, called feminine here?

Mme. Blavatsky: Perhaps it is a mistake to do so. But since it is impossible to define Parabrahm, or that which is beyond human conception, therefore once that we speak of that first something which *can be* conceived, we had better say "She." In all the cosmogonies it is the goddess and goddesses that come first, the former one becoming the all immaculate mother from which proceed all the gods. We have to adopt either one or the other gender, as we cannot say IT. From IT nothing can proceed, strictly speaking, neither a radiation nor an emanation.

Mr. Keightley: Is that the Egyptian Neith?

Mme. Blavatsky: In truth, it is beyond Neith. But it is Neith in one sense.

---

[1] "Space is called in the esoteric symbolism 'the Seven-Skinned Eternal Mother-Father.' It is composed from its undifferentiated to its differentiated surface of seven layers. 'What is that which was, is, and will be, whether there is a Universe or not; whether there be gods or none?' asks the esoteric Senzar Catechism. And the answer made is — SPACE."

Mr. Keightley: Then the IT itself is not the seven-skinned Eternal Father-Mother in this Stanza?

Mme. Blavatsky: Assuredly not. The IT is the beyond, the *meta*, the Parabrahm. This which is, is the female aspect of Brahmâ, the male.

Mr. Keightley: And that is what is spoken of in the Proem that I read as the "seven-skinned Father-Mother"?

Mme. Blavatsky: Yes, it becomes that at the first flutter of differentiation. Then the subjective proceeds to emanate—or falls into the objective and becomes what they called the Mother Goddess, from which proceeds the Logos or Father God, the unmanifested. For the manifested Logos is quite a different thing again and is called the "Son" in all the cosmogonies.

Mr. Keightley: Is the first differentiation from the absolute IT female always?

Mme. Blavatsky: It is sexless; but the female aspect is the first it assumes. Take the Jewish Kabalah. You have "Ain-Soph" which is also the IT, the infinite, the endless, the boundless, the adjectives used in conjunction with IT being negatives of every kind of attributes. From IT the negative, the zero, 0, proceeds number One, the positive which is Sephira or the Crown. The Talmudists say it is the "Torah," the law, which they call the wife of "Ain-Soph." Now see the Hindu cosmogony. There you find that Parabrahm is not mentioned; but only Mulaprakriti: there is Parabrahm and there is Mulaprakriti, which latter is the lining so to say, or the aspect of Parabrahm in the invisible universe. Mulaprakriti means the root of matter, but Parabrahm cannot be called the "root," for it is the rootless root of all that is. Therefore, you must begin with Mulaprakriti, the veil of Brahma as they call it. Take any cosmogony in the world: you will always find it begins thus; the first manifestation is the Mother Goddess, the reflection, the root or the first plane of substance. From, or rather in that Mother Goddess is formed the unmanifested Logos her son and husband at once, as he is called the Concealed Father; and from these two the manifested Logos which is the Son itself—

the Architect of all the visible universe.

Mr. Keightley: The second question is, "What aspect of space, or the unknown deity 'That,' of which you speak further on, is here called the Eternal Parent"?

Mme. Blavatsky: Well it is just this androgynous something; the *Svabhavat* of the Buddhists. It is non-differentiated, hence—an abstraction. It is the Mulaprakriti of the Vedantins. If you proceed to make it correspond with the human principles it will be Buddhi; Atma corresponding to Parabrahm. Then comes Mahat which corresponds to Manas.

Mr. Keightley: And so on downwards.

Mme. Blavatsky: Yes.

Mr. Keightley: Then what are the seven layers of space? You speak in the Proem of the "seven-skinned Father-Mother."

Mme. Blavatsky: It is what Aristotle called the *privation* of matter; that which will become the seven planes of Being, beginning with the spiritual and passing through the psychic till it comes down to the material plane. Then there

[Page missing in original. See Appendix 1. p. 635]

has named the *protyle*; that which he would like to find, which he does not find, and which he certainly cannot find on this plane or earth. It is the first non-differentiated substance or *spiritual matter.*

Mr. Keightley: Is it *Laya*?

Mme. Blavatsky: "Robes" and *all* are in the Laya condition, up to that point from which the primordial substance begins to differentiate, and thus gives birth to the universe and all in it.

Mr. Keightley: Are they called "invisible" because they are not objective to any differentiation of the consciousness?

Mme. Blavatsky: Say rather "invisible" to consciousness, if any differentiated consciousness were possible at that stage of evolution. Most assuredly it cannot be seen. Do not you see in the book that even for the Logos Mulaprakriti is only a veil? And it is a veil that the Logos sees, this veil or the robes in which the Absolute is enveloped, but cannot perceive the latter.

The President: Is it correct to call it Mulaprakriti?

Mme. Blavatsky: If you speak to a Hindu you will find that what a Vedantin calls Mulaprakriti is called Aditi in the Vedas. The Vedanta philosophy means, literally speaking, "the end of all knowledge." The great difficulty in studying the Hindu systems esoterically is that in India alone there are six schools of philosophy. Now if you analyse these you will find that they agree perfectly in substance. Fundamentally they are identical; but there is such a wealth of names, such a quantity of side issues, of all kinds of details and ornamentations; of sons being their own fathers, and fathers born from their own daughters, that you become lost in all this, as in a jungle. State anything you will from the esoteric standpoint to a Hindu, and if he only wants to he can contradict and prove you in the wrong, from the standpoint of his own particular sectarian view, or the philosophy he accepts. Each of the six schools of India has its own views and its own (to it) peculiar terms. So that, unless you hold strictly to some one school and say so, your special terminology is sure to be misunderstood. It is nothing but splitting hairs, and quarreling about things that have no importance in reality.

Mr. Keightley: Then the same term identically is used in quite a different sense by different philosophies: for instance Buddhi has one meaning in the esoteric philosophy, and a different meaning in the Sānkhya?

Mme. Blavatsky: And quite a different meaning again in the *Vishnu Purāna* in which there are seven Prakritīs that come from Mahat and the latter is called Maha-Buddhi.

Mr. Keightley: That is again quite different.

Mme. Blavatsky: No it is not; fundamentally it is perfectly the same thing, though in every philosophy you will have some other name and meaning given to it.

Mr. Kingsland: Yet we must call it something. Are we to have our own terms?

Mme. Blavatsky: I think the best thing you could do would be to coin new English words. If you want to ever become Western philosophers, you had better not take from the Hindus, who will be the first ones to say: "Behold, these Europeans! They take from us all they can, disfigure everything and do no good." Find equivalents for all these terms, coin new English words, and do not depart from them; and then there will be no confusion.

Mr. Kingsland: Does *protyle* come near the term *Laya*?

Mme. Blavatsky: There it is. You are obliged to throw yourself on the tender mercies of ancient Greek and other ancient languages, but the modern languages are really too materialistic and I doubt whether you can get any words to express that which you need.

Mr. Ashton Ellis: We may as well get it from the Greek as the Anglo-Saxon; all our scientific words are coined either from the Greek or the Latin, and become English only by use. Such a word as *protyle* is not really English at all.

Mr. Keightley: It is just adopted.

Mme. Blavatsky: How long? Hardly two years ago?

The President: If we have one word that answers the purpose, why not use it? Mr. Crookes[2] probably used the word *protyle* on the most materialistic plane of all.

Mme. Blavatsky: What he means by it, is primordial homogeneous matter.

---

2 William Crookes, English physicist, 1832-1919, who coined the term protyle for a hypothetical primordial substance.

Mr. Ashton Ellis: Perhaps, just when it is about to enter into the state of differentiation.

Mme. Blavatsky: Then certainly it is not "the robes" that he will ever discover, because they are on the seventh plane of matter and he is searching on this one, which is the lowest.

Mr. Keightley: His protyle is "pre-hydrogen."

Mme. Blavatsky: Nothing else, and yet no one will ever be able to find it. How many times have the scientists been disappointed. How often have they thought they had come at last to a real atom, protylic and homogeneous, to find it each time a compound thing of two or three elements! But let us go on.

Mr. Keightley: Is there, so to speak, on each of the seven planes, homogeneous matter relatively to that plane? Is it the root of every particular plane?

Mme. Blavatsky: There is; only it must be homogeneous only for that plane of perception and for those who are on that plane. If Mr. Crookes is ever able to find the protyle he is after it will be homogeneous for only him and us. The illusion may last for some time, until the Sixth Race perhaps, when mankind will be entirely changed. Humanity is ever changing, physically and mentally and perfecting itself with every Race more, as you know we are acquiring learning, perception and knowledge that we did not have before. Therefore, the science of today is the ignorance of tomorrow.

Dr. Williams: I should think it would be a great mistake to adopt any word that has been already adopted by a scientist with another meaning. Protoplasm had once come almost to mean the same thing as protyle does, but they have now narrowed it down.

Mme. Blavatsky: And quite right; because protyle, after all, comes from the Greek word ὕλη {*hyle*}, and the Greeks used it certainly not as a word belonging to this plane. Besides which it was used in the Chaldean cosmogony, before the Greeks.

The President: And yet is not ὕλη {*hyle*} used to mean "the root of matter" by certain writers?

Mme. Blavatsky: It is; but these writers are not very ancient.

The President: No, but they used it in a sense which rather transcends that. The word ὕλη {*hyle*} is now used really as giving very much the same idea that we endeavoured to give when we used the word Mulaprakriti.

Mme. Blavatsky: Well, I do not know. There's Doctor Lewins,[3] who calls himself a Hylo-Idealist, if you please; so there is the metaphysical meaning of the word desecrated entirely. So you certainly had better use another term. *Laya* does not mean anything in particular, on that plane or the other, but means a state, a condition. It is a Sanskrit word conveying the meaning of something entirely undifferentiated and changeless, a zero-point wherein all differentiation ceases. That is what it means and nothing else.

Mr. Kingsland: The first differentiation would represent matter on the seventh plane?

Mme. Blavatsky: I believe, you can say so.

Mr. Kingsland: That is to say, I suppose that Mr. Crookes' ideal protyle would be matter on its seventh plane.

Mme. Blavatsky: I do not know Mr. Crookes' ideas about that. I am not sure, but what I understand he wants to find is simply matter in that state which he too calls the "zero-point."

Mr. Keightley: Which would be so to speak the Laya point of this plane.

Mme. Blavatsky: I doubt whether he has any idea about other planes at all, and suspect he is perfectly satisfied with this one. What he wants to find here is the protyle atom, this is plain. But what

---

3 Robert Lewins, developer of the philosophical movement Hylo-Idealism, described as material idealism; hence, Hylo-Idealist.

can even he or any one else know of atoms, something that no one has ever seen. What is an atom to scientists but another "working hypothesis" added to all the rest? Do you know, Dr. Williams?

Dr. Williams: No, indeed I do not.

Mme. Blavatsky: But, as a chemist, you must know what they mean by it?

Mr. Kingsland: It is a convenient definition of what they think it.

Mme. Blavatsky: But surely they must have come now to the conclusion that it is no convenient definition, no more than their *elements* are. They speak about some sixty or seventy elements, and laugh at the old honest nomenclature of the four and five elements of the ancients, and yet where are their own elements? Mr. Crookes has come to the conclusion that strictly speaking there is no such thing known as a chemical element. They have never arrived yet at a simple or single molecule, least of all, at an atom. What is it then?

Mr. Kingsland: An atom is a convenient term to divide up a molecule.

Mme. Blavatsky: If it is convenient to them I have no objection to it. You call also iron an element, don't you?

Mr. Ashton Ellis: I think we ought never to forget that it is called the atomic *theory*. It has never been claimed as anything more.

Mme. Blavatsky: Aye, but even the word "theory" is now used in a wrong sense, by the modern schools, as shown by Sir W. Hamilton.[4] Why should they, once they laugh at metaphysics, use a purely metaphysical term when applying it to physical science? And there are those to whom theory and axiom mean the same thing. So long as their pet theory is not today upset—which happens more often than the leap year—they regard it as an *axiom*; and woe to him, who dares doubt or even touch it, outside the sacred precincts of the fanes of science!

---

4 Sir William Hamilton, Scottish metaphysician, 1788-1856.

Mr. Ashton Ellis: It is its inventor, Dalton,[5] who called it atomic theory.

Mme. Blavatsky: Well, let us proceed.

Mr. Keightley: You speak of seven eternities. What are the seven eternities, and how can there be such a division in Pralaya when there is no one to be conscious of time?

Mme. Blavatsky: The modern astronomer knows "the ordinances of heaven" still less than his ancient brother did. Yet the fact, that if asked whether he could bring forth Mazzaroth[6] in his season, or was with "him" who spread out the sky—the astronomer would reply in the negative—prevents him in no wise from speculating about the ages of the sun, moon, and geological times, when there was not a living man with or without consciousness on earth. Why could not the ancients speculate or cognize *backward* and forwards as moderns do?

Mr. Keightley: Why should you speak of seven eternities? Why put it that way?

Mme. Blavatsky: Because of the invariable law of analogy. As Manvantara is divided into seven periods so is Pralaya; as day is composed of twelve hours, so is night. Shall we say because we are asleep during night and are not conscious of time, that the hours do not run the same? They pass on and the clocks strike though we may not hear or count them. Pralaya is the "Night" after the Manvantaric "Day." There is no one by and consciousness is *asleep* with the rest. But since it exists and is in full activity during Manvantara, and that it is fully alive to the fact that the law of analogy and periodicity is immutable, and being so that it must act equally at both ends, why cannot the sentence be used?

Mr. Ashton Ellis: I should want to know how you can count an eternity.

---
5 John Dalton, English physicist, 1766-1844, noted for his ideas about atomic theory.
6 Mazzaroth, mentioned in Job 38:32, interpreted as the constellations.

Mme. Blavatsky: Here we are! Because we Westerners are foolish enough to talk about and to speculate on something that has neither beginning nor can end, therefore the ancients must have done the same! I say they did not. No people in days of old has ever meant by "Eternity" beginningless and endless duration. Take the Greeks, speaking of Æons. Do these mean something eternal? No more than their *Neroses*[7] did. They had no word for eternity in the sense we give it. *Parabrahm* and *Ain-Soph*, and the *Zeruana Akerne*[8] of the Avesta represent alone such an eternity—all the other periods are finite. All these were astronomical, moreover, based on tropical years and other enormous cycles—withal, finite and therefore, they are not eternities, but a way of speaking of eternity. It is the word Æon in the Bible that was translated as eternity; and yet it is not only a period but means an angel and a being as well.

The President: But is it not true to say in Pralaya there is the Great Breath?

Mme. Blavatsky: Assuredly, for the "Great Breath" is ceaseless; it is the universal *perpetuum mobile*.

The President: If so, it is not possible to divide it into periods. It does away with the idea of absolute and complete nothingness. It does seem incompatible that you should speak of any *number* of periods; but if you have the Great Breath you might say there are so many indrawings and outdrawings of the Great Breath.

Mme. Blavatsky: And this would make away with the idea of absolute rest, were not this absoluteness of rest counteracted by the absoluteness of motion. Therefore, one is as good as the other. There is a magnificent poem on the Pralaya. I forget the name of its Hindu author. It is written by a very ancient Rishi and he writes and compares that motion of the Great Breath during the Pralaya to the rhythmical motions of the ocean. It is a most magnificent picture. It is the only reference on this subject that I know or ever heard of.

---

7 Neros, a cycle of 600 years.
8 Zeruana or Zervana Akerne, Persian: boundless, limitless time.

Mr. ——: The only difficulty is when the word eternity is used instead of the word Æon.

Mme. Blavatsky: Why should I use the Greek word when I can use an English one? I give the explanation in *The Secret Doctrine* by saying the ancients had no such thing as eternity—as commonly understood.

Mr. ——: Still, Æon, to the ordinary English reader, would not mean eternity.

Mme. Blavatsky: We have quite enough of foreign words; I have tried to avoid and put them into English.

The President: Æon, to most European Christian readers, does mean eternity, as they have translated it as "for ever and for ever."

Mr. A. Ellis: That always involves a beginning at least.

The President: No, "for ever and ever" backwards and forwards.

Mr. Ellis: It is sempiternal. It has a beginning, but it has no end. If you make a thing plural you divide it. There you make a point of beginning and a point of end. You will always make a division.

The President: Then you agree with the seven eternities.

Mr. Ellis: I think it is only a word that may be taken up by one of the daily papers. I do not think there is any difficulty in the least. The meaning of it is that there are seven concurrent phases, going on at the same time. It is division of time laterally. That is what I meant, if you can understand it. That is what I wanted to know, if you count it in that way.

Mme. Blavatsky: I count it in such a way as to translate as best I can the real meaning of a very difficult and abstruse text, and then to give the interpretations that I was taught and have learned. It is just as you say; because if you read my explanations, there you will find the same thing.

Mr. Keightley: Before we leave the subject, I would ask, is the relation of Pralaya and Manvantara strictly analogous to the relation between sleeping and waking?

Mme. Blavatsky: In a certain sense only, of course. It has that relation, if you take it in the abstract. During night we all exist and we are, though we sleep and may be unconscious of so living. But during Pralaya everything disappears from the phenomenal universe and merges in the noumenal. Therefore *de facto* there is a great difference.

Mr. Keightley: You remember you gave us a very remarkable thing about sleep, saying that "it was the shady side of life." Then is the Pralaya the shady side of cosmic life?

Mme. Blavatsky: You may call it so. It is a time of rest. Even cosmic matter, indestructible though it be in its essence, must have a time of rest, its Laya condition notwithstanding. The absoluteness of the eternal all-containing one essence has to manifest itself equally, in rest and activity.

Mr. Keightley: The next question is on Sloka 2. "Time was not, for it lay asleep in the infinite bosom of duration." The first point is what is the difference between time and duration as here used?

Mme. Blavatsky: Duration *is*: it is neither a beginning nor an end, nor time, as its very name implies, though we may divide it into Past, Present and Future. What is time? How can you call that "time" which has neither beginning or an end? Duration is beginningless and endless; time is finite.

Mr. Keightley: Duration is the infinite, and time the finite conception?

Mme. Blavatsky: Time can be divided, duration cannot; therefore the word duration is used.

Mr. Kingsland: The only way you can define time is by the motions of the earth.

Mme. Blavatsky: But, you can define time in your conception also, can't you?

Mr. Kingsland: Duration, you mean?

Mme. Blavatsky: No, time; for as to "duration" there is no such thing as splitting it, or putting landmarks on it. It is impossible.

Mr. Kingsland: But we can define time by certain periods.

Mme. Blavatsky: But not duration, which is the one real eternity. In this finite and phenomenal universe, of course you can. All you can do is to divide time in duration and take illusions for realities.

Mr. Kingsland: But without that you would not be able to define time at all.

Mme. Blavatsky: Why not? The natural division of time is night and day.

Mr. Kingsland: The essential idea of duration is existence, it seems to me.

Mme. Blavatsky: Existence has limited and definite periods, and duration is a thing which has neither a beginning nor an end. While it is something perfectly abstract and contains time, time is that which has no duration. Duration is just like space. Space as an abstraction is endless; but in its concreteness and limitation, space becomes a representation of something. Of course you can call space the distance between this book and that table or between any two points you may imagine. It may be enormous, or it may be infinitesimal, yet it will always be space. But all such specifications are divisions in human conceptions. In reality, space is what the ancients called Deity itself.

Mr. Keightley: Then time is the same as space. They are one in the abstract.

Mme. Blavatsky: As two abstractions they may be one; yet I would say duration and space, not time and space.

Mr. Keightley: You get time and space with differentiation, time being the subjective character corresponding to space, the objective, one being the objective and the other being the subjective side of all manifestation.

The President: They are the only attributes of the infinite, really. But attribute is a wrong word, inasmuch as they are coextensive with the infinite; but then that is also a difficult word.

Mr. Ellis: How can you say that? They are nothing but the creations of your own intellect. They are nothing but the forms in which you cannot help conceiving things. How can they be called attributes? Take cause and effect, they are nothing but the way in which you think of things. If you had a different brain you would think about things in a different way.

Mme. Blavatsky: And now you speak as a Hylo-Idealist would. We do not speak of the phenomenal world, but of the noumenal universe. It is without space and time, but still there is duration and abstract space. In the occult catechism it is asked: "what is the thing which always *is*, which you cannot imagine as not 'being', do what you may." The answer is—Space. For, there may be not a single man in the universe to think of it, not a single eye to perceive it, not a single brain to sense it, but still space *is*—and you cannot make away with it.

Mr. Ellis: Because you cannot help thinking of it.

Mme. Blavatsky: My or your thinking has nothing to do with it. Space exists there where there is nothing and must exist in full vacuum as elsewhere.

Mr. Ellis: The philosophers have reduced it to this. They say they also are nothing but attributes, nothing but accidents.

Mme. Blavatsky: Buddha says better than this still. He says speaking of Nirvana, that Nirvana, after all, is also an illusion.

Mr. Ellis: You would not call eternal space and duration the only attributes of the Infinite?

Mme. Blavatsky: I would not give to the Infinite any attributes at all. That only which is finite and conditioned can have attributes.

Mr. Keightley: You touched upon a question that is put here. Time and space in modern philosophy are conceived of, as you said, simply as forms of the human physical brain, and as having no existence apart from human intellect, as we know it. Thence arises this old question: "We can conceive of no matter that is not extended" (in consequence of that faculty or that peculiarity of mental faculty), "no extension that is not extension of something. Is it the same on the higher planes, and if so, what is the substance that fills absolute space, and is it identical with that space?" You see, that brings to a focus the question.

Mme. Blavatsky: "Is it the same on another plane?" Now how can I answer your query? I never travelled in absolute space, as far as I know. All I can give you, is simply the speculations of those who had a thousand times more brains than I, or any of you have. Some of you would call them vagaries. We don't.

Mr. Ellis: Does not he answer his own question in the question itself?

Mme. Blavatsky: How?

Mr. Ellis: He presupposes that that is the only way in which the intellect can think.

Mr. Keightley: I say on this plane our intellect is limited. In this way we only conceive of matter extended.

Mr. Ellis: If your soul or anything else could conceive, we will imagine for a moment, in another form. You cannot get an answer in words to that, can you? Your intellect has to understand those words. Therefore intellect, not being able to conceive in any other way, cannot get an answer in any other way.

Mme. Blavatsky: On this very same plane, there are not only the intellects of men. There are other intellects, and intelligences, call them whatever you like. The minds of animals, from the highest to the lowest, from elephant down to the ant. I can assure you that the ant has in relation to its own plane just as good an intellect as we have. If it cannot express it to us in words, it yet shows high reasoning powers, besides and above instinct, as we all know. Thus finding on this plane of ours so many and such varied states of consciousness and intelligences, we have no right to take into consideration or account only our own human consciousness, as though there were no other. Nor can we, beyond accepting it as a fact, presume to decide how far animal and insect consciousness goes.

Mr. R. Hall: Why not? Natural science can find it out.

Mme. Blavatsky: No, it cannot. It can speculate and guess but will never be able with its present methods to acquire any certitude for such speculation. If Sir John Lubbock[9] could become an ant for awhile, and think as an ant, and remember it when returning to his own sphere of consciousness then would he know something for certain; not otherwise.

Mr. Keightley: The ant's conceptions of time and space are not our own conceptions.

Mme. Blavatsky: And therefore, if we find such conceptions that are not our conceptions and that are entirely on another plane, we have no right to deny *a priori* the existence of other planes of which we may have no idea but which exist, nevertheless, planes higher and lower than our own by many degrees.

Dr. Williams: May I suggest on that point that every animal is more or less born with its faculties. Man is born the most helpless and ignorant of all and progresses, so far as we know, forever, in the acquisition of the enlargement of his intelligences. That seems to be

---

9 Sir John Lubbock, English politician, banker and archeologist, 1834-1913, was also author of the popular book, *Ants, Bees, and Wasps*, 1882, which was reprinted again in 1888.

the most practical difference between the intelligence of all animals and man.

Mr. Ellis: Have you ever seen a dog taught to sit on its hind legs?

Dr. Williams: Whenever animals are put beyond the influence of civilization they always return without exception to the primitive and prior condition into which they were born. This shows that they have no capability of holding on longer than they are under the influence of civilization.

Mr. Ellis: They would lose a great deal. But how are we to know they have not developed before? If they were put in different circumstances, of course they would lose a great deal.

Dr. Williams: So far as our experience goes, we know the terms on which they were, and very clearly too.

Mr. Ellis: We know they can be taught, therefore they resemble man. If we put man back out of civilization what does he become? Nothing but the animal.

Mme. Blavatsky: To say that animals have no intelligence is the greatest fallacy in the world. How shall science explain to us the facts that there is no animal or insect which cannot be taught to remember, to obey the voice of the master. Why, take a flea. He will fire a gun, and he will draw water, and he will do all kinds of tricks.[10] If a flea has an intellect, what must it be with others which are more developed? How can we say that the animals have got no intellect?

Mr. ——: They have not got the quality of thinking.

Mme. Blavatsky: They have not got the quality of reasoning, and yet they have.

Mr. ——: A horse will pull a string and fire off a cannon, but he does not know anything about the objects of it.

---

10 "Flea circuses," where trained insects played instruments and moved objects, were a great attraction of the nineteenth century.

Mme. Blavatsky: This is a question that has never been satisfactorily answered, because it is simply our organization and our human conceit that causes us to make of man a king of all the animals. I say there are animals compared to which a mortal man is the lowest of the animals. There is not a dirtier animal in the world than man, and I say it is a great insult to any animal to go and compare him to a man. I would object if I were an animal. You cannot find any man who is as faithful as a dog. It shows feeling and affection. It does not show reasoning power, but it does show intelligence, feelings and memory. It is just the same as a man.

Mr. ——: Look at the birds that pull up their own water.

Mr. ——: But you cannot compare that with human intelligence.

Mme. Blavatsky: I think in all probability an ant has a thousand times more intellect than a man, if we take the proportionate size.

Mr. ——: It is well known that any intelligent donkey, if he is left with only a door between him and the garden where he can get the things he might have to eat, will open it; he will pull down the handle of the door. Again, look at the way cats that are out at night act. In many a house that I have been in, the cats knock at the windowpane with their heads on the balcony in front; and look at the way dogs will pull the bell sometimes. Surely that is reasoning enough.

Mme. Blavatsky: Go and compare a child and a kitten, if you please, when they are born; what can a child do? And a cat, immediately it stands on its legs, goes eating.

The President: That is, I think, what Dr. Williams meant just now when he said, "The animal is born more or less with all its faculties, and generally speaking does not gain on that, while man is gradually learning and improving." Is not that really the point?

Dr. Williams: That is exactly the point.

Mme. Blavatsky: Of course man is a perfected animal. He is a progressive animal.

Mr. Ellis: Is not it a question of degree and surroundings?

Mme. Blavatsky: We look upon the animals, as the men of science look upon us.

The President: I think it is fair to say that the animal intelligence cannot be denied, and simply to add that the intelligence of the animal is of a different plane to anything we humans can appreciate. And so will it go higher and higher. That which transcends the human intelligence we cannot pretend to understand in any way. That answers that question as put there.

Mr. ———: But does not one of the great distinctions between the animal and the human intelligence be in the fact that human beings can, to some extent, work with abstract thought, while the animal can only work in the concrete? That is to say, that the animal can largely be taught and apparently will reason from it in conjunction with the fact that it may get food or something that it likes; whereas a human being can actually argue from facts and by means of imagination create the surroundings.

Mr. Ellis: How do you teach a child? By giving it a lump of sugar stick, or else smacking it. The child passes as you know by physiology through all the stages of every other class of animals, and therefore they are passing through the same stages as the animals are in now.

The President: We have rather wandered from the point I think.

Mr. Keightley: The question is, is there any consciousness or conscious being to cognise and make a division of time at the first flutter of manifestation?

Mme. Blavatsky: I should think not.

Mr. Keightley: In the way that Subba Row[11] speaks of the first Logos

---

11 T. Subba Row, influential South Indian Theosophist, 1856-1890, wrote on the metaphysical aspects of the *Bhagavad-Gita*.

he implies——

Mme. Blavatsky: That the Logos kept a diary, or what?

Mr. Keightley: He implies both consciousness and intelligence.

Mme. Blavatsky: Well I am not of Subba Row's opinion. You forget one thing, he spoke about the Logos without saying whether it is the first or second he spoke about, the unmanifested or the manifested Logos. Several times he calls it Iswara, so it is not the unmanifested Logos, because Iswara was never Narayana. You may call it whatever you like, but it is not the highest Logos, because that from which the manifested Logos is born is that which is translated by me there "the Eternal Father-Mother." In the *Vishnu Purana* they call it the egg of the world, and this egg of the world is surrounded by seven skins or layers or zones—call it whatever you like—it is that which is given in the Purana as the Golden Egg. This is the Father-Mother, and in this Golden Egg is born Brahmâ, the male, which is in reality the second Logos, or the third, according to the enumeration adopted, not the highest—that is to say the point which is everywhere and nowhere. Mahat comes afterwards. Mahat is something between the third and fourth, it fluctuates, you understand, because it contains the physical germs in it and the whole roots of all the physical universe. At the same time it is a universal Divine Mind.

Mr. Keightley: It is the first manifestation, then?

Mme. Blavatsky: It is the 3rd but it overlaps the 4th.

The President: Then the first Logos is the first point within the circle.

Mme. Blavatsky: The first point, because there is the circle, the circle which has neither limit nor boundaries, nor can it have a name nor attributes, nor anything, and this point which is put there, is the unmanifested Logos. Which is simultaneous with that line you draw across the diameter. The first line is the Father-Mother and then comes from that Father-Mother the second Logos, that is to say, the manifested word. For instance in the Hindu Puranas, it is said (and the Orientalists have said a good deal about that also) that the first production of Akasa is sound. Now Akasa is just what is called there the Mother or the Father-Mother (call it whichever you like), and sound means there simply speech or expression of the unuttered thought; and it is the Logos, that which the Greeks and Platonists called the Logos, and is just that which is sound and which made Dr. Wilson[12] and many other Orientalists say, "What fools these Hindus are!" They speak of Akasa, which is, according to our showing, Chaos, and from this Chaos they make sound proceed. It means just that which was adopted subsequently by St John, the Evangelist, who speaks about the Logos, saying just the same thing in other words.

Mr. Keightley: On the subject of time this question has been put "What is the consciousness which takes cognizance of time?" Is the consciousness of time limited to the plane of waking physical consciousness or does it exist on higher planes? Is the consciousness or sense of succession, limited purely to our present plane? Or does it exist on higher planes?

Mme. Blavatsky: Whose consciousness? Why, you must tell me, of whom you are talking—whose consciousness is limited?

Mr. Keightley: Our own. All our consciousness is succession. We have a succession of ideas or succession of thought. Haven't we?

Mme. Blavatsky: Then who is there to think like that?

Mr. Keightley: You speak of time. "Time was not." Time to our minds conveys this idea of succession.

Mme. Blavatsky: And if time *was not*, it can convey no such idea. Time was not means that there was duration only and not time, because no one was there to make time or the division of time. That which was not, how can it have any consciousness or any aspect of consciousness? What does it mean, all this?

---

12 Probably Horace Hayman Wilson, English Orientalist, 1786-1860, whose translation of the *Vishnu Purana*, Mme. Blavatsky used.

Mr. Keightley: This question really applied to a later subject. You speak thus of time: "Time is only an illusion produced by the succession of our states of consciousness as we travel through eternal duration, and it does not exist where no consciousness exists." Then the question which is put is, is the consciousness of time, in our sense of the word, limited only to our present plane of waking consciousness, or does it exist on any other planes?

Mme. Blavatsky: It cannot exist because even in sleep it does not exist. You have been answering it to yourselves how many times, when we have been talking about dreams.[13]

Mr. ——: Seeing that the "Gods" have a beginning and an ending, they must exist in time.

Mme. Blavatsky: They exist in space and time. Duration cannot be divided.

The President: But the word succession applies to them.

Mr. ——: But is there not a consciousness which can take cognizance of it?

Mme. Blavatsky: Certainly the universal mind can.

Mr. ——: Then the idea exists there.

Mme. Blavatsky: I don't think so. In the Absolute there cannot exist the same division of time as in our conception. I would say there is a consciousness there, but I don't think time has got anything to do with it. Can you say that the sea has also a conception of time in its rhythmical striking of the shore, in the movement of the waves and so on? To my mind, the Absolute can have no consciousness, or not a consciousness such as we have here, and that is why they speak as they do about the Absolute. It has neither consciousness, nor desire, nor wish, nor thought, because it is absolute thought,

---

13 The preceding meetings in December 1888 had dealt with the subject of dreams and can be found as an Appendix to *Transactions of the Blavatsky Lodge*, Part 1, 1890. See Appendix 2.

absolute desire, absolute all—just what the *Daily News*[14] laughed at from not understanding the true definition of the Absolute. They said—I don't remember how the phrase went there in the *Daily News,* do you, Miss ——?

Miss ——*:* I do not.

Mme. Blavatsky: They laughed at "Be-ness" and yet there is no other way in this world of translating the word *Sat* but by Be-ness, because it is not existence, for existence implies something that feels that it exists. Existence must give you the idea of having a beginning, a creation, and an end, it is just what Gautama Buddha says about Nirvana—or if not Buddha, it is {Nagasena?}. He says Nirvana does not exist, but it *is.* Try to make what you can of this Oriental metaphysical conception. Still it is there, it exists and all the philosophy is built on it.

Mr. Ellis: The Hebrew Jehovah was "I am."

Mme. Blavatsky: He calls himself so. So is the Ormuz{d} of the Persians, too. Every one of us is {Ehyeh asher Ehyeh?} the "I am that I am."

Mr. Duncan: Be-ness has some connection with the word "to be."

Mme. Blavatsky: Yes, but it is not that. No word, my dear Mr. Duncan, can apply better than that, better than the word Be-ness. It is a word we have coined, and we have coined it correctly, I think. It is the only thing that renders the Sanskrit word *Sat.* It is not existence, it is not being, it is absolute Be-ness.

The President: It is both being and non-being.

Mme. Blavatsky: Well then, how can you explain that better? We cannot conceive it. Our intellects are limited and finite and language is far more finite and conditioned than we are. So how can we explain that which we can only conceive by our highest intuition?

---

14 The London *Daily News* of January 10th had just published a notice of *The Secret Doctrine* as "The Secret of all Things."

Mr. Ellis: The Germans understand it at once because they have a word they use every day, that is the word "sein." "Sein," of course, means "to be," and "das sein" means, of course, what you mean by the word Be-ness. I am sure nobody would have said that was absurd, only you cannot use German words. No German would call this word absurd, but a frivolous Englishman would.

Mme. Blavatsky: Well now, you Englishmen invent a word that would answer to that "sein" there.

Mr. Ellis: One is constantly meeting with the absolute poverty of our language for purposes of translation. In German one or two words may require twenty for perfect translation.

Mme. Blavatsky: Now look at Max Müller.[15] Why, he makes a mess of it positively, as the English language must have at least 40 or 50,000 words more invented or coined to express a part of that which the Sanskrit language expresses.

Mr. Ellis: We have no methods of doing what they do in the Sanskrit. They couple two words together and you have the whole meaning of a sentence. If we want to express that same quality I have found over and over again you have to put about twenty words. You cannot do it in one or two.

Mr. Duncan: I think that last question had reference to the consciousness of time.

Mme. Blavatsky: Oh, this is all finite beginning and ending, so you cannot find any correspondence between that and real duration or real abstract space, for it is not, it cannot be localized. There is such a thing as time; it has a beginning and an end.

Mr. ———: Yes but are we conscious of it?

Mme. Blavatsky: No, even the Devachanee is not conscious of it.

Mr. ———: But he is conscious of a succession of states of

---

15 Friederich Max Müller, German Orientalist, 1823-1900, editor of the 50-volume *Sacred Books of the East* series.

consciousness.

Mme. Blavatsky: No, all is present to the Devachanee. There is no past, because he would recall it and regret it, and there is no future because he would be anxious to have it. Devachan is a state of bliss in which everything is present; that is why they say the Devachanee has no conception and no idea of time; to him everything is just a real and vivid dream.

Mr. ———: He can have no idea of time in as much as there is nothing to measure it by.

Mme. Blavatsky: To him it is not a dream, but to us it is a dream. When we dream everything is present and we enjoy the greatest bliss.

Mr. ———: In a dream also we may dream a lifetime in half a second, yet we are conscious of succession of states of consciousness. Events take place one after the other.

Mme. Blavatsky: After the dream, not during the dream. During the dream you will be conscious of nothing of the kind. You will perhaps forget there is such a thing as succession of states of consciousness. You will forget it surely.

Mr. Ellis: If you were describing a picture to somebody you could not give him all that picture at once, you have to give him first one part of the picture then another, although you have it all in your mind.

Mme. Blavatsky: Yes, you have it all before you all the time.

Mr. Keightley: That is the last question.

2.
The Blavatsky Lodge of The Theosophical Society.
Meeting held January 17, 1889.

Mr. A. Keightley: Stanza 1 continued, Sloka 3: "Universal mind was not, for there were no Ah-hi to contain it."[1] This Sloka seems to imply that the universal mind has no existence apart from the Ah-hi, but in the commentary you state that during the Pralaya, "the 'universal mind' remains as a permanent possibility of mental action, or as that abstract absolute thought, of which mind is the concrete relative manifestation," and that the Ah-hi are the vehicle for divine universal thought and will. "They are the intelligent forces that give to Nature her 'laws,' while themselves acting according to laws imposed upon them by still higher powers…(they are) the hierarchy of spiritual beings through which the universal mind comes into action."[2] This commentary suggests that the Ah-hi are not themselves the universal mind, but only the vehicle for its manifestation.

Mme. Blavatsky: Universal mind and absolute mind are one. Are they not? Very well, that only implies that as there are no finite differentiated minds during Pralaya, therefore it is just as though there were no mind at all, if there is nothing to contain it, or to perceive it. That is the meaning. There is nothing to reflect or contain the ideation of the absolute mind, therefore *it is not*, because everything outside of the absolute and immutable Sat, or the Be-ness, is necessarily finite and conditioned, since it has a beginning and end, and here is something with no beginning and no end. Therefore since the Ah-hi *were not*, there was no universal mind, because you must make a distinction between the absolute mind

---
[1] *The Secret Doctrine* I:37.
[2] *The Secret Doctrine* I:38.

which is ever present, and its reflection in the Ah-hi at the first flutter of Manvantara. The Ah-hi are on the highest plane; they are those who reflect the universal mind collectively, and begin the work of evolution of all the lower forces until they come, throughout the seven planes, down to our lowest plane.

Mr. A. Keightley: Then the Ah-hi and the universal mind are necessary compliments of one another?

Mme. Blavatsky: Not at all. Universal mind, or absolute mind, always *is*, whether during Manvantara or during Pralaya; it is immutably one. But since the term Ah-hi means the highest Dhyanis—the Logoi perhaps—those which begin, which are the creation—or evolution, not creation, because everything is an emanation; since the Ah-hi were not, there was no universal mind, because it was the absolute dormant, latent mind, and it was not differentiated in the collectivity of these Dhyanis.

The President: It was, rather, absolute consciousness.

Mme. Blavatsky: It was absolute consciousness which is not consciousness. What is consciousness? Further on you make a question: "Can consciousness exist without any mind?" But it will come in time. You had better proceed, unless you have some other questions to ask. For instance, let us represent to ourselves, if you can do such a thing, that universal mind is a kind of vacuum, but vacuum with latent consciousness in it. You just suppose you pump out all the air you can from some vessel, there is a vacuum. You cannot represent yourselves in that particular vessel as a vehicle: there is the vacuum; but break these vessels that contain this *soi-distant* vacuum; where shall you look for it? It has disappeared, it is everywhere and nowhere. It is something, yet it is the absence of something. It is entirely a homogeneous thing. This is what is supposed to be a vacuum, I think. Dr. Williams, how would you describe vacuum?

Dr. Williams: Absolute vacuum is a figment, really.

Mme. Blavatsky: It is a figment which is a negative thing. It is the supposed place where nothing exists.

Dr. Williams: It is absence of air, I should think.

Mme. Blavatsky: You break those vessels and nothing exists, therefore universal mind is not, because there are no vehicles to contain it.

Mr. A. Keightley: The first question is, can you give us a definition of the universal mind, which will solve the difficulty?

Mme. Blavatsky: Well, I think I have just done so.

Mr. A. Keightley: Quite so. Then number 2. "What are the higher powers which condition the Ah-hi?"

Mme. Blavatsky: Well I don't call them powers at all; it is simply a manifestation of the periodical law, the universal law, which becomes by turns active or inactive. This is that law of periodical manifestation which creates them, which emanates them. I always use the word create, which is a very bad and wrong word to use, for there is no creation.

Mr. A. Keightley: Then the power, which is higher than the Ah-hi, is the law which necessitates manifestation.

Mme. Blavatsky: Just so; periodically, when the hour strikes, it comes, and they appear into manifestation. They are on the first rung of manifestation, after which it goes on gradually shaping itself more and more.

Mr. B. Keightley: It should really be THE law, and not A law.

Mme. Blavatsky: The law and not a law. I give it {to} you from the standpoint of esoteric, or eastern teaching. If physical science objects, just say so, and I will try to repent. Who of you has an objection to make?

Mr. Kingsland: The grand difficulty is to account for this law.

Mme. Blavatsky: You want to go beyond even the first manifestation, beyond what they call the Supreme Cause; you want to go beyond that. You try to understand first the Supreme Cause, as they call it, and I can assure you, you won't understand it; it is all a figment, all our imagination. We try to do the best we can, but it does not stand to reason at all. We do not even approach this absolute, this merely logical speculation which dates from thousands and thousands of years. If physical or modern science can say or invent something better, let it do so, but it has not done it yet. There are gaps and flaws everywhere, and at every moment one thing breaks its nose, and another comes, and then they jump over the wall and imagine some other speculation; that again in its turn breaks its nose, and that is all it is.

Mr. Kingsland: Would not cosmic mind be a better term than universal mind in this case?

Mme. Blavatsky: No; cosmic mind would take in the third degree. Cosmic mind is simply confined or limited to the manifested universe.

Mr. Kingsland: Quite so. In that sense it seems the passage is intended.

Mme. Blavatsky: Cosmic mind is quite a different thing from universal ideation. It is just the manifestation of that mind during the Manvantaric period of activity. But universal ideation knows no change. It was, always was, is, and will be. I never said it does not exist: it does not exist for our perception, because there were no minds to perceive it. Universal mind was not because there was no one to perceive it. One is latent and the other is active. One is a potentiality.

Mr. Kingsland: The universal mind was in the absolute, but it was cosmic mind that was not.

Mme. Blavatsky: Yes, but we speak here about manifestation. I cannot go and invent things; I am obliged to translate just as the

Stanzas give it in the book.

Mr. Kingsland: That is the manifestation.

Mme. Blavatsky: Well, let us call it cosmic mind, if you like it better.

Mr. Kingsland: I only think there is a confusion between universal mind and absolute mind.

Mme. Blavatsky: If you say universal mind, it is absolute, but if you say cosmic mind, that is another thing.

Mr. Kingsland: Then you can't say that it was not.

Mme. Blavatsky: Cosmic ideation was not, but universal mind was.

Mr. Kingsland: Quite so.

Mme. Blavatsky: How can I put that it was not? I am obliged to translate as it is, and then to give all the commentaries. I didn't invent them. If I were inventing it, I might put it otherwise.

Mr. Kingsland: If you say universal mind was not manifested, you get over the difficulty.

Mme. Blavatsky: Those who have written this do not concern themselves with the manifested universe. This relates to the highest, and does not deal yet with the universal matter, it deals with the universe of ideation of consciousness and so on.

Mr. Kingsland: It deals with the first manifestation.

Mme. Blavatsky: You had better send your protest to those who have written this thing, because I can't help it.

Mr. Kingsland: No, it is the English translation. Do you see what I mean, Harbottle?

The President: I see what you mean.

Mr. Mead: It is the same thing looked upon from different points of view.

The President: I think we are apt to use the word cosmic as applied to the manifested universe in all its forms. This does not touch anything of the sort. This is the first absolute consciousness or non-consciousness, and I think it really does mean that the absolute consciousness could not be that universal mind because it was not to be expressed, it could not be expressed, there was no expression for it. That is what I take to be the meaning of it.

Mr. Kingsland: There was no expression for it; but it was there.

The President: It was there and it was not there.

Mme. Blavatsky: Because the Ah-hi were not, to the persons who can conceive of it; since there was nothing and no one to conceive of it, how could it be? It was not. You must remember the peculiar mode of expression used by the Easterners. They express it always allegorically, always figuratively. You cannot ask them to express in scientific language which says so much and means so little.

Mr. Kingsland: When you say it was not, you mean it was not in the absolute.

Mme. Blavatsky: I beg your pardon. I say it was not, simply.

The President: If you can say it was, that would be taking a very one-sided view of what we mean by *Sat*. That would be equivalent to saying that *Sat* was being.

Mr. Mead: I think the question hangs on the time referred to altogether. It involves the question of time, and no time then existed.

The President: I think it goes even farther back than that. I think it is all inherent in the meaning we attribute to the word *Sat*, which is as I say both being and non-being.

Mr. Kingsland: I don't think there is any confusion in our minds, it is in the terms.

Mme. Blavatsky: Just read this over again, will you?

Mr. A. Keightley: "What are the higher powers which condition the

Ah-hi?"

Mme. Blavatsky: No, no, not that. I mean the thing to which Mr. Kingsland takes objection.

(Mr. A. Keightley then read the passage: *Secret Doctrine*, Stanza 1, Sloka 3 and commentary.

Mme. Blavatsky: It ought to be higher "power" not "powers."

Mr. Kingsland: First you say it was, and then it was not.

Mme. Blavatsky: I didn't say that. The Absolute must be always, it is a perfect impossibility for it to be otherwise. The Absolute is a thing which must be taken tacitly. If there is such a thing as absolute something and not something, an absolute unknown or unknowable, then it must always have been and always be. It is impossible it should go out of the universe. This is a tacit assumption.

Mr. Kingsland: But if you take it as it is written there, "universal mind was not," it treats of it as if it were a manifestation, but mind itself is not a manifestation.

Mme. Blavatsky: Mind is a manifestation, universal mind is not the same thing; let us call it an ideation. Cosmic ideation was as soon as the Ah-hi appeared and continues throughout the Manvantara. But this is universal absolute ideation, and *is* always and cannot get out of the universe, whereas cosmic ideation was not and the only mistake is that I did not put cosmic. But why should I? I cannot put things out of my own head; I just translate as it is. There are many, many verses that come between, that I have left out altogether. It may be this would be better.

Mr. B. Keightley: Also, I think the term cosmos is used almost throughout *The Secret Doctrine* in reference chiefly to the solar manifested universe, and is not taken in the sense as referring to that which precedes.

Mme. Blavatsky: I think we shall only deal with "cosmos" as our solar system. I think I say it in some place there, at least I so remember. I have a recollection that I have been writing about it.

Mr. A. Keightley: I think I see Kingsland's objection, he means to say this expression is liable to cause a certain amount of confusion because, just as Madame Blavatsky has now expressed it, the universal mind always *is* and never can be. But that which is identical with what we call cosmic ideation was not, because the Ah-hi were not there to perceive it.

Mme. Blavatsky: And, as there was no manifestation, it was an impotentiality.

Mr. A. Keightley: First you say universal mind was not and then you say universal mind is always a permanent thing and always is.

Mme. Blavatsky: Because I try to explain the Stanza. I know the meaning, I know the spirit too, not the dead letter, I don't take the dead letter; I give it as it is, and then I give the spirit of it.

Dr. Williams: Does not the expression, "universal mind," convey, itself, that idea?

Mr. B. Keightley: I think it is implied in the word, "mind."

Mme. Blavatsky: We are obliged to use it.

The President: Unless you call it consciousness.

Mme. Blavatsky: It is absolute consciousness. But it is not consciousness as we understand it.

Dr. Williams: If you get rid of all predicates, everything has been done that can be done. You say the Absolute is. If you say more than that you approach perception, and that is manifestation.

The President: You cannot attribute mind to the Absolute until you have got something capable of perception radiating from the Absolute, in which case it is correct to say that the universal mind was not.

Mr. Kingsland: It is correct in one sense but creates confusion.

Mme. Blavatsky: But what can we do? Do you want to change it? Now it is printed, what can you do?

Mr. Kingsland: We cannot do anything, now it is printed.

Mme. Blavatsky: Then why do you break my heart? (Laughter)

The President: You asked him to object, really.

Mme. Blavatsky: But what can we do now? I think about 20 persons have broken their heads about it when they were preparing the thing, even the great metaphysical Fawcett,[3] because I have been asking all of them. Is there anything according to Herbert Spencer[4] or any of your scientists which you can object to? "No," they said "it is perfect," and now you find flaws! Well, let us pass on.

Mr. A. Keightley: "To what cosmic plane do the Ah-hi here spoken of belong?"

Mme. Blavatsky: To the first, the second, and the third. Because it is a triad, a manifested triad, a reflection of the non-manifested. Taking the triad in the sense that Pythagoras gives it, it disappears in the darkness and the silence. Taken in this sense it is the only thing, as there is Atma, Buddhi, Manas—well, all, the first, second and third planes—the Ah-hi belong to these planes.

Mr. A. Keightley: That is to say the Ah-hi belong to the cosmic planes which correspond to Atma, Buddhi, Manas.

Mme. Blavatsky: Just so, they correspond.

Mr. B. Keightley: Then this question cannot arise, that Atma,

---

3 Edward Douglas Fawcett, 1866-1960, English journalist who helped HPB with *The Secret Doctrine* and went on to write on metaphysics. He was the brother of Col. P. H. Fawcett, the explorer, who left to discover a lost city in the Amazon in 1925 and never returned.
4 Herbert Spencer, English philosopher and sociologist, 1820-1903, who posited the "Unknowable" as the basis underlying the phenomenal world.

Buddhi, Manas——

Mme. Blavatsky: I know, the two are on the same plane.

Mr. B. Keightley: They are successive emanations; you get the Atma, Buddhi in man, before Manas makes its appearance.

Mme. Blavatsky: But we do not speak of man now, if you please, we speak in general that these correspond. Don't you go and mix up man with it now. We speak of the macrocosm simply, at the beginning when there was the first flutter of Manvantaric dawn, and then evolution begins.

Mr. B. Keightley: The question I want to put exactly is this: Are those three planes simultaneous emanations or do they emanate one from the other?

Mme. Blavatsky: I suppose one from another, but I could not tell you that. Don't ask me questions I cannot answer.

Mr. B. Keightley: That is the question that is now meant here.

Mme. Blavatsky: Do you really want to apply mechanical law to cosmogony as it is in the metaphysical minds of the Orientals? You won't get much if you come to apply space and time because there was no space and no time, so how can you ask me this question?

Mr. B. Keightley: Well, then, that settles the question.

Mme. Blavatsky: After this comes the question of the reflection of the triad in space and time, therefore, how can you apply anything mechanical?

Mr. B. Keightley: That is what I wanted you to say. I got what I wanted.

Mr. A. Keightley: Question 4. "Have these Ah-hi been men in previous Manvantaras or will they become so?"

Mme. Blavatsky: They will become men in subsequent Manvantaras.

Mr. A. Keightley: Then do they remain permanently on this very exalted plane during the whole period of the Manvantara?

Mme. Blavatsky: Of the 15 figures?[5] No, they pass through all the planes until they become on the third plane Manasaputra, the sons of Manas or mind. They are arupa. On the highest plane these Ah-hi are arupa, that is to say formless, bodiless, without any substance, without anything, they are breaths. On the 2nd plane they first approach to *rupa* or to form. Then on the third they become Manasa-rupa, those who become incarnated in men.

Mr. A. Keightley: Then is that stage taken in one Manvantara or are those various stages?

Mme. Blavatsky: It is. It is all the same thing, only a distinction is made. On every plane they reach they are called by other names.

Mr. A. Keightley: Quite so.

Mme. Blavatsky: There is more and more differentiation because what we talk about is the homogeneous substance, which we call substance from our conceit, because it cannot be any substance which we can conceive of. Later they become substance, if you like.

Mr. A. Keightley: Then the Ah-hi of this Manvantara——

Mme. Blavatsky: They do not exist any more, if you please. They have become long ago [   ].[6] Read *The Secret Doctrine*, you will see the thing there.

Mr. A. Keightley: I understood you to say they did not become men in this Manvantara.

Mme. Blavatsky: The 15 figures apply to the solar system. The first answers relate to the beginning of the whole objective universe, but after that, when you begin to speak about the Father-Mother, then it

---

5 The Manvantaric life cycle relating to the solar system, "a duration of time which extends over fifteen figures."
6 This passage is left blank in the original. The published version of the *Transactions* gives "Planetary, Solar, Lunar, and lastly incarnating egos."

relates to our objective universe and to the solar system only because our teaching does not busy itself at all with things outside. At least those things that I have selected. I could not go and select the whole thing. I have only taken that which relates to our solar system. I have just taken two or three just to show the general idea, and then skipped over whole Stanzas and came to the point. I have said there are some 60 Stanzas passed over. I would have had compliments from the *Daily News* if I had translated the whole of it.

Mr. B. Keightley: Then on the re-awakening, will the men of one Manvantara have to pass through a similar stage to the Ah-hi stage in the next Manvantara?

Mme. Blavatsky: In many, many Manvantaras at the end of the tail of the serpent; when the tail will be in the mouth of the serpent, I might say. What have you got the ambition of becoming? An Ah-hi, or what? You will have time, my dear fellow, to do many things before you become an Ah-hi.

Mr. A. Keightley: "A man can choose what he shall think about, can the analogy be applied to Ah-hi?"

Mme. Blavatsky: No, because a man has free will and the Ah-hi have no free will. They have a collective will. They are obliged to act simultaneously. It is one law that gives them the impulse and they have to act just according to that law. I do not call it free will. Free will can exist only in man, in a man who has a mind with consciousness, which acts and makes him perceive things not only within himself but outside himself also. These Ah-hi simply are forces; you don't take them to be men, do you? They are not human beings.

Mr. A. Keightley: No, but I take them to be conscious agents in the work.

Mme. Blavatsky: Conscious in so far that they act within the universal consciousness. The Manasaputra is a different thing when they come on the third plane.

Mr. Hall: Can the Ah-hi be said to be enjoying bliss?

Mme. Blavatsky: Why should they enjoy bliss or enjoy non-bliss? What have they done to do so? I don't think they enjoy anything of the kind. They cannot smoke cigarettes, even, when they like. Why should they enjoy bliss? What extraordinary ideas you have! You can enjoy bliss only when you have known what suffering is.

Mr. Hall: I was making a distinction in my mind between bliss and happiness.

Mme. Blavatsky: I thought it was the same thing; you can have neither happiness nor bliss if you have not known suffering and pain.

Mr. Hall: I was thinking of bliss as the state of the Absolute.

Mme. Blavatsky: You suppose the Absolute is bliss? The Absolute can have no condition, no attribute, nothing at all. The Absolute is conditionless; that is the first thing to learn about the Absolute. It is only that which is finite and differentiated which can have some attribute or something of the kind.

Dr. Williams: How can they be said to be conscious intelligences in as much as intelligence is such a complex thing?

Mme. Blavatsky: Because the English language does not furnish us with a better word. I admit the word is very inadequate, but the English language is not the Sanskrit language. If it were written in Sanskrit you would not find a single objection, but what can you do with the English language or any other European language?

Dr. Williams: There may not be one word, but I should think a collection of words would express anything.

Mme. Blavatsky: Oh, then try, if you please, to do so!

Dr. Williams: It seems to me from what I can gather from your elucidation that it really means a force which is a unity, not a complex action and reaction of several forces—which would be implied in the word intelligence or anything which implies complexity—but rather it is that simple force, almost. The noumenal, the aspect of phenomenal force, would at least express better what is meant by that.

Mme. Blavatsky: Well, I don't know. You take one flame and represent yourselves a flame and it will be unity; but the rays which will proceed from that flame, they will become complex and do all kinds of things and will be seen to act each one on its own line.

Dr. Williams: But they only become complex when they find receptacles in lower forms.

Mme. Blavatsky: Just what they do find. The lower they descend the more they find it. But it is all one; it is simply the rays which proceed from one; and more and more do they proceed to differentiate until they become fully conditioned and fall down here in this world of ours, with its thousands and millions of inhabitants—as Carlyle[7] said, "most of them fools."

Dr. Williams: Well, the Ah-hi, then, considered as a primary essence, would be a unity.

Mme. Blavatsky: Certainly, because they proceed from unity. It is the first of the seven rays, as they call it.

Mr. A. Keightley: Then they are the reflection of unity.

Mme. Blavatsky: What are the prismatic rays, if you please, if not one single white ray? From the one they become three, from the three they become seven, because there is a prismatic scale of colours.

Mr. A. Keightley: Seven, but they are still one when they are moving rapidly over each other.

Mme. Blavatsky: To our perception, quite so. They become seven just in the same way, there if you please take the analogy.

Mr. A. Keightley: Next question. You say that during deep sleep "mind is not" on the material plane; but it is implied that during this period mind is active on another plane. Can you give us a definition

---

7 Thomas Carlyle, English author, 1795-1881.

of the characteristics which distinguish mind in the waking state from mind during the sleep of the body?

Mme. Blavatsky: Well, I suppose there is a great difference between the two. You see, the reason in higher minds sleeps, but the instinctual mind is awakened. That is the difference. The reason of the higher mind, in the physical man, is not always the same. Today I have been looking at a book and I learnt at last the great difference between cerebrum and cerebellum. I was always mixing them up in my mind, I was not sure of them, and this morning I on purpose went to look and I at last learnt that this is the cerebellum (pointing to the head) and this the cerebrum. The one sleeps when the other is awake, and if you ask an astrologer, he will give you a magnificent idea. I don't know where it is stated, but the brain is all in 7, and he separated them and put all the planets that answer to those portions. Now here you will find the earth, the sun, and the moon, here at the back of the head; and this part sleeps and rests when the other is awake.

Mr. A. Keightley: Then what do you mean by instinctual mind?

Mme. Blavatsky: You see, it passes from a plane which we regard as an illusion. Now, for instance, this plane in which we are proceeding is called reality; we call it illusion, but we say that this part going to sleep, and this part of the brain having no more a definite function, it is the other one that begins and carries away man on the Astral— which is still more deceptive, because it is all the emanations of everything that is bad. It preserves no record. The great serpent, it is called. Now if the higher mind sleeps there you will have a perception of the dreams and you can bring back when you awake the recollection of them—this pretence of dreams, but I think we have been discussing dreams quite enough—and unless it is that, you will have all these chaotic dreams because you have all these dreams with this peculiar part of your brain, the cerebellum.

Mr. B. Keightley: One thing that question was meant to cover was this: for instance, the fundamental conditions of the mind in the waking state are space and time.

Mme. Blavatsky: Yes.

Mr. B. Keightley: Do they exist for the Manas, the mind, during the sleep of the physical body?

Mme. Blavatsky: No.

Mr. B. Keightley: So there you get at any rate one very marked distinction between the manifestation of man on the two planes of consciousness.

Mme. Blavatsky: There may be something approximate, some hallucination of space and time; but certainly it is nothing real. We have been talking about it many times, and have seen that in one second you may live through the events of thirty years, as some dreams prove to you. Therefore there is no conception, no possibility of conceiving of division of time.

Mr. B. Keightley: Or of space.

Mme. Blavatsky: They are both in duration or eternity; they are not in time.

Mr. A. Keightley: Next question: It has been stated that Manas (mind) is the vehicle of Buddhi, but the universal mind has been spoken of as Maha Buddhi. Can you define for us the distinction between Manas and Buddhi as applied in a universal sense, and Manas and Buddhi as manifested in man?

Mme. Blavatsky: Well, cosmic Buddhi is the vehicle of Mahat, that is to say, in the sense of Buddhi being Prakriti and this is Prakriti; at least it descends in the seven planes, that is the difference, and the Buddhi of man proceeds from the highest Akasa. He does not go on the highest plane until he comes to the most objective plane. Maha-Buddhi is used there in the same sense as Prakriti in its seven manifestations.

Mr. B. Keightley: But is the vehicle of Mahat, the universal mind? Does the Manas in man proceed from the universal mind too?

Mme. Blavatsky: Yes it proceeds from Akasa—Buddhi, I mean, or Manas. The Manasa-Dhyanis are the same Ah-hi I just told you of on a lower plane.

Mr. B. Keightley: Because, of course, one would naturally think, as Mahat is the universal mind, that Manas in man proceeds from the universal mind.

Mme. Blavatsky: It is just the same Prakriti in its last manifestation. It is what in the Kabalah is called Malkuth, the Bride of Heavenly Man—well, earth, everything earthly, or atomic.

Mr. B. Keightley: *i.e.*, the plane of objective consciousness, in fact, waking consciousness.

Mr. A. Keightley: Question 8. "Can there be consciousness without mind?"

Mme. Blavatsky: There we come to the great question. Consciousness—what is it? It is only the faculty of the mind, is not it? It is that which permeates the mind or the Ego, and causes it to perceive that such a mind has action, that such a thing is so—is not that it? How do you explain it otherwise? Consciousness is not a thing *per se*. It is a faculty of the mind. That is what Hamilton will tell you and what all the Eastern idealists will tell you. They cannot tell you anything else. It is a thing inseparable from mind—unless it is the mind of an idiot, of course you won't have any consciousness.

Mr. A. Keightley: You say the fashion now-a-days amongst philosophers is to speak slightingly—

Mme. Blavatsky: We know that, of course.

Mr. A. Keightley: —of the idea of making mind an entity.

Mme. Blavatsky: Of course, but mind is still the soul. It is perfectly synonymous with soul. Those who don't believe in soul certainly will tell you that there is no such thing as consciousness apart from brain, and once the brain is dead and the man is dead, there is no consciousness. The Nihilists, the Atheists and the Materialists will tell you so. If you believe in mind, mind is the soul or the Ego. What kind of a soul is that if it has not any consciousness?

Mr. A. Keightley: But they accept consciousness.

Mme. Blavatsky: But not after the death of man, while we accept consciousness after death, and say the real consciousness and the real freedom of the Ego or the soul begins only after the physical death of man. It is then that it is no longer impeded by terrestrial matter that it is free, that it can perceive everything.

Mr. A. Keightley: Because they confine their consciousness to the sense of perception.

Mme. Blavatsky: That is what they do, and we don't. It is the difference between us.

Mr. Hall: When you say the physical death of man, do you mean the permanent death?

Mme. Blavatsky: What other death is there for a man?

Mr. Hall: I don't know whether it is the fact that you meant us to take it that after each death the soul is free and can proceed without being hampered by the body.

Mme. Blavatsky: You make a too subtle distinction. What is it you are talking about?

Mr. Hall: If you mean when a man ceases to incarnate, that is another thing.

Mme. Blavatsky: When does he cease? When he becomes Nirvanee, when you are dead and no Hall will exist any more, but your Ego will. The Roger Hall will have become one of the dresses that your Ego has thrown off to assume another in a certain time.

Mr. Hall: But then why should the Ego be anymore able to perceive things than it is at present?

Mme. Blavatsky: Because it is not impeded by matter, by gross matter. Can you see what is behind that door unless you are a clairvoyant? There, there is no impediment of matter and the soul sees everything. It goes into Devachan, its own place, and afterwards it must reincarnate. But there are cases when they don't go into Devachan, that is what we are fools enough to believe in.

Mr. Hall: It would not apply to every physical death.

Mme. Blavatsky: We do not speak about exceptions, they only prove the rule; we speak about the average death.

Mr. B. Keightley: There is a moment of freedom of that mind, I take it, between the actual death and the time when the Ego proceeds to the Devachanic state.

Mme. Blavatsky: We can only go by analogies. When I am dead, I will come and tell you, if I can. I do not think I will, but there are others who have been in trances, which is just as good as death, and there are those yogis who were, for instance, 40 days buried.

Mr. Hall: Those yogis are exceptions.

Mme. Blavatsky: There, consciousness can live and the body is—I do not say dead, but any doctor will tell you, it is dead.

Mr. Hall: But all these are exceptions. I was asking whether it applied to every physical death, because if at the ordinary physical death of ordinary man his Ego must go along of itself, then it is not impeded in Devachan by the illusory bliss as it is by the illusory matter.

Mme. Blavatsky: Don't let us mix up these things or we will never end here.

Mr. A. Keightley: Then we come to the 4th Sloka. "The 7 ways to bliss were not. The great causes of misery (Nidana and Maya) were not." The question is, what are the 7 ways to bliss?

Mme. Blavatsky: Well, they are practically faculties, of which you will know more later on, perhaps, if you go a little deeper into esotericism.

Mr. A. Keightley: Then the 7 ways are not actually mentioned?

Mme. Blavatsky: No, they are not mentioned in *The Secret Doctrine*, are they? They are not, I should say not.

Mr. A. Keightley: I don't think they are. Then the question is: "Are the 4 truths of the Hinayana School the same as the 4 truths mentioned by Edwin Arnold in his book *The Light of Asia?*"[8]

Mme. Blavatsky: Almost the same. He mentions something which is somewhat different from it.

Mr. A. Keightley: The first is of sorrow, the 2nd is of sorrow's cause, the 3rd of sorrow's ceasing and the 4th is the way.

Mme. Blavatsky: What do you understand by Edwin Arnold's explanation?

Mr. B. Keightley: Read the passage please, Arch. (Mr. A. Keightley then read the passage indicated, *The Light of Asia.*)

Mme. Blavatsky: All this is theological and all this exoteric; this is what you can find in all the volumes that any Buddhist priest will give you; but there is far more explanation, of course, in Aryasanga's[9] works, though that is the esoteric too. Arnold took it from the Singhalese Buddhism.

Mr. A. Keightley: Then do these four truths: the first of sorrow, the second of sorrow's cause, the third sorrow ceasing and the fourth the way, do they represent the four noble truths esoterically?

---

8 Edwin Arnold, 1832-1904, author of the popular life of the Buddha in verse, *The Light of Asia.*
9 HPB indicates in *The Secret Doctrine* that there were two Aryasangas: one a pre-Christian adept, the other, the Buddhist philosopher, known as Asanga, connected with the formation of the Yogācāra school during the fourth century of our era. See *Secret Doctrine*, I:49-50 fn.

Mme. Blavatsky: Yes, I think they do. You will find Buddhism all about them.

Mr. B. Keightley: What do they really stand for?

Mme. Blavatsky: It would take too long and it has no relevancy to this Sloka. It would take much too long. It is impossible to tell you now. It would take several evenings to explain to you one of them thoroughly.

The President: Then we will put them down for the future.

Mr. B. Keightley: I am not sure it would not be a profitable thing to take up next time.

Mme. Blavatsky: I am not sure that it would be. You had better follow the Slokas. You are not going to follow that, because the four noble truths meant one thing for the priests of the yellow robes, and meant different things to the mystics. The one acts on the dead letter, just the same as our priests will act on the canons of the Church, and the mystics have got nothing to do with it.

Mr. A. Keightley: Can you give us any idea for the moment?

Mme. Blavatsky: I cannot, I am not an exoteric Buddhist. Ask Olcott.[10] He is the man to know all these things. He is a very pious Buddhist and I am not. I am nothing pious.

Mr. A. Keightley: Then I put this question now, "Is the eightfold path the same as the 7 ways to bliss?"

Mme. Blavatsky: Yes.

Mr. A. Keightley: "Are Nidana and Maya the (great causes of misery) aspects of the absolute?"

Mme. Blavatsky: Is that number 4?

---

10 Henry Steel Olcott, President-Founder of the Theosophical Society, 1832-1907. Olcott had publicly converted to Buddhism on a tour of Sri Lanka in 1880, and had written an influential *Buddhist Catechism* for the schools there.

Mr. A. Keightley: That is number 4.

Mme. Blavatsky: Now what can Nidana, I ask myself, and Maya have to do with each other? Nidana means the concatenation of cause and effect. The twelve Nidanas are the enumeration of the chief causes which produce material for Karma to strike you very heavily. Maya is simply an illusion. Now what has Nidana to do with Maya? I cannot understand what analogy, what idea one has in common with the other. If you take the universe as an illusion, a Maya, then certainly the Nidanas as being in the universe are included in the Maya, but apart from that, what has one thing to do with the other?

Mr. B. Keightley: Then why do you class them together in that way?

Mme. Blavatsky: They are two distinct things. Maya is an illusion. You think yourself a very grand fellow, that you can go and compete with any Ah-his, and any of the [ ]. But you make a fool of yourself and then comes Nirvana and shows it to you. It is just then, I think, that the man cannot take into his own head that he is not separate from the one and he goes and thinks himself a very great man in his own individuality, and he is nothing at all. He is still one in reality. It is nothing but Maya, an illusion; but taking this Maya, it is illusion or ignorance that brings us to commit all the acts which awaken the Nidanas, which produce the first cause of Nidana; this cause having been produced, the effects follow and there is Karma. Of course Nidanas and the production of bad Karmic effects and Maya are at the root of every evil. If we knew what we are we would not do such things. Everyone of us thinks he or she is a unit and something very grand in the eyes of all the authorities upstairs that you may think of; we are simply a drop of water in the ocean, not to be distinguished from another drop in the ocean, that is all we are. This sense of separateness is at the root of all evil. You know, there is no correspondence, no analogy, except the one I gave just now.

{The} President: The only possible analogy is that they both of them are synonymous with manifestation, inasmuch as there cannot be any manifestation without the production of Nidanas on the one

hand and Maya on the other.

Mme. Blavatsky: You think you can produce something but in reality you cannot produce anything at all.

The President: The instant one single chain of a causation is started by any manifestation whatever, there is the Nidana.

Mme. Blavatsky: Now let us say: I have dressed myself in a red dress, I go out and because I am dressed in a red dress I have produced a cause, and a bull goes for me because I irritated his nerves; there is the Maya of the bull and there is the Nidana I have produced. So you can put two and two together. It is just an illusion which makes us produce the most Nidanas.

The President: "Are Nidana and Maya aspects of the absolute," is the exact form of the question.

Mr. B. Keightley: The question really ought to be separated; the question is to ask, first of all, is Maya an aspect of the Absolute?

Mme. Blavatsky: It cannot be an aspect of the absolute. It is {an} aspect of the differentiation, if you put it this way. If Maya means an illusion, everything that is differentiated is an illusion also, but it cannot be an aspect of the absolute.

The President: Maya is a manifestation surely.

Mme. Blavatsky: Certainly; the absolute cannot have any manifestation whatever, it can have reflection at best.

Mr. B. Keightley: In one of the old articles in *The Theosophist*, Maya is described as the cause of manifestation. I forget by who.

Mme. Blavatsky: Perhaps by some Hindu.

Mr. B. Keightley: By some good Hindu metaphysician. I am not sure if it was not Subba Row himself. He describes Maya as the cause of differentiation.

Mme. Blavatsky: If there were no Maya, there would be nothing—

no differentiation.

The President: But if there were no differentiation, there would be Maya so you cannot put one before the other, can you?

Mr. B. Keightley: But you are taking Maya as the cause of differentiation, therefore the moment you get behind differentiation, where is the Maya? Mme. Blavatsky said that even Nirvana is a Maya.

Dr. Williams: Maya is a collective term meaning all manifestation.

Mme. Blavatsky: Certainly; they say that every thing is an illusion, because, first of all no two persons in the world see things in the same way. They may see it alike on general principles, but they won't see it altogether in the same way, and secondly, that which has a beginning and an end is not a reality, and, being less than the wink of the eye, it is an illusion, a momentary deception of the senses. This is why they call it an illusion. They call reality only that which ever was, is, and will be, which cannot be, now, that absolute consciousness or what they call Parabrahm, or what in Kabalah is called Ain-Soph.

Dr. Williams: The term, it seems to me, applies to the complex points of differentiation. Differentiation applies to the unit and the other term applies to the collection of units.

Mr. B. Keightley: Yes, that is the way to explain it.

Mme. Blavatsky: Now I must ask Mr. Kingsland to bring in his objections.

Mr. Kingsland: It is Dr. Williams' turn.

Mme. Blavatsky: Do make it a little lively. Don't go to sleep, all of you. This won't be any illusion.

Dr. Williams: I notice one thing as you passed along the explanation. I do not quite understand what the idea was at the back of it. I think the expression would lead to a misunderstanding of what the real facts are. That is with reference to the cerebellum and cerebrum as being, respectively, the organ of the higher mind and lower mind.

Mme. Blavatsky: I never said higher mind and lower mind. I said this one acted during the waking hours; for instance, with everyone of us now, what acts is the front part—I think you call it cerebrum. Well, the other is active simply when this part sleeps and rests and becomes, so to say, inert—well, it is paralyzed. Then the dreams begin and the mind begins to live and to feel and to be conscious with that part of the brain that is astrologically. I don't know if it is so, scientifically, and I don't presume to say, because there is no atom of science in me; I simply say that which the Occultists say and which the Kabalists say, and all kinds of hallucinated lunatics in general. That is what I tell you.

The President: You have described the back part as the instinctive.

Dr. Williams: That is the word I wanted.

Mme. Blavatsky: "Instinctual." Yes.

Dr. Williams: Of course, I want to avoid if possible making the appearance of any discrepancy. I stand as a go-between, between the two to reconcile, if possible, the two statements. Leave that for a moment or so and take an animal. An animal is supposed to have an instinctive mind, but the cerebellum is the organ of vegetative life. It simply controls the functions of the body, nothing more.

Mme. Blavatsky: But yet it acts during sleep.

Dr. Williams: The sensual mind is the mind to which the senses open, and there can be no thought, no ideation, no anything of which we predicate intellect or instinct anywhere, except in that part of the brain into which the senses do go, and that is the cerebrum.

Mme. Blavatsky: I said it is the organ of instinctual animal function and these functions will reflect themselves in the dreams to produce the dreams, and unless the higher Ego takes in hand the plane of the material [ ] the dreams will have no sequence, even, because those dreams that we remember and that really have something in them are produced by the vision of the higher Ego. They are not produced by anything else. Every dog dreams, and certainly we cannot say a dog has prophetic dreams.

Mr. A. Keightley: Is not the cerebellum what you may call the organ of habit?

Mme. Blavatsky: Well, if I say instinctual, it comes to the same thing.

Mr. A. Keightley: Except that habit is very often referred to what we may call the present phase of existence and instinct to a past phase of existence.

Mme. Blavatsky: Whatever its name, the only thing that functions during night is cerebellum and not the cerebrum, because the dreams or the emanations—I don't know how to express it—well, those instinctive feelings which are felt here are just recollections of what took place. I told you my dream the other day. The thing gets distorted, and at the moment you awake you have a dream, and you have a thing that is half mixed up with all those feelings that were acting during sleep, and so on. If this part (the front brain) acted during sleep, then we would have consecutive dreams, because now we sit here we do not dream. We think, you understand, and we have all kinds of dreams awake, but there is some consecutiveness in them; we can think what we like and just make it clear. We can invent pictures, or, for instance, a man will be writing a novel; but in a dream you don't do that, just because it is *that* part which acts.

Dr. Williams: The consecutiveness is brought about entirely by the coordinating faculty. I do not know that scientific men have attempted to determine what part of the brain it is.

Mme. Blavatsky: It does not act in sleep.

Dr. Williams: But the cerebrum certainly does act, and the proof of it is this: that the nearer we approach the waking sleep, the more vivid our dreams become.

Mme. Blavatsky: Just so; *when* you are awakening, but not before.

Dr. Williams: When we are awakening, it is cerebrum which is coming into consciousness.

Mme. Blavatsky: It is just like something that has been very much heated during the day and which will emanate or irradiate during the night, but not at all because there is something acting there; it is the energy of the brain that comes out unconsciously.

The President: Didn't you describe it just a moment ago as being that portion of the brain which received the impression of the senses? Is not it exactly during sleep when we receive such impressions? The reception of a very vivid impression.

Dr. Williams: Of course, you cannot reproduce anything except from that portion of the brain where it has been registered. The cerebellum does not receive and register impressions through the cerebrum.

The President: It is because the senses are producing no impressions at all that we sleep, really.

Mr. B. Keightley: Not quite "no impressions at all," because if you make a noise over a sleeping man he will awake, and very likely will be able to trace his dream to the sense of oppression which awoke him.

The President: Don't you think that seems to show, from the very fact that brain activity is required to register it, that the brain must be brought into activity again? Or in other words, he must be woke up.

Dr. Williams: All that you are describing is the function of the cerebrum.

Mme. Blavatsky: You have no consciousness of the activity of the cerebrum and it acts mechanically.

Mr. B. Keightley: One notices it often in ordinary life.

Mme. Blavatsky: In dreams, in the same way the memory comes into play. You must have a memory and perception of this thing, and if you catch one glimpse of it, maybe you will be able to reconstruct the dreams. I knew persons who could reconstruct their dreams in the most extraordinary way; if they only caught one little bit, it was enough. They would just throw themselves into a kind of negative state, and little by little it would come to them again, so that they could pump out again these things that were present unconsciously; but those persons are very rare. The average person dreams what is perfect nonsense, dreams of digestion, of nervous disturbances, etc., but I speak with respect to dreams that really are dreams.

Dr. Williams: It cannot be a matter of any importance. Still, I think if it should go out as it is, it would be very severely criticized. Whether this is a matter of any consequence, I don't know.

Mme. Blavatsky: If we were to write like all the blessed sages in the world, we should be pitched into. "The Theosophical Society," they say, "is absurd." It is a jumble, it has hallucinations, it is this, that, and the other; what can you do?

Dr. Williams: I suppose the Theosophical Society and yourself, as well, desire so far as possible to avoid giving them occasion for such remarks.

Mme. Blavatsky: It is no use to sit under an umbrella the whole of your life.

Mr. A. Keightley: One does not want to give them a handle they can seize hold of.

Mr. B. Keightley: Your old simile for the sleep of the brain was a very good one, the flickering embers of the fire just dying down. If you reverse that and suppose a current of air passes over the slumbering embers—

Dr. Williams: That would be a beautiful illustration of it.

Mr. B. Keightley: That is the true analogy; then you get it.

Mme. Blavatsky: I do not know if this is put down.

Mr. B. Keightley: The point of it is this: you get a factor or two, as it were. These waking sparks in the cerebrum, the brain, just beginning to awake, combined with the activity that has been going on all night in the cerebellum, which in its turn is fading below the plane of consciousness.

Mme. Blavatsky: Were you here, Dr. Williams, when we talked about that? I have it all in the little book. I have been writing considerably in it. It is not notes such as I have taken here. There I have been writing whole pages.

Mr. A. Keightley: Does the cerebellum ever permanently stop working?

Mme. Blavatsky: No, but it is perfectly lost in the functions of the cerebrum, which is, just as Dr. Williams says, connected more with—what do you call it—vegetative life.

Mr. B. Keightley: The stimuli which proceed from the cerebellum during waking life fall, all of them, below the waking consciousness. The field of consciousness being entirely occupied by the cerebrum till it goes to sleep, when the stimuli from the cerebellum begin to form the field of consciousness.

Dr. Williams: You say all consciousness must necessarily reside in the cerebrum. I am speaking now of the ordinary dream state, that the ordinary dream state must always be connected with more or less activity of the cerebrum. Of course, when we say it sleeps, there is not an absolute paralysis, there is circulation of the blood. It is simply the withdrawal of the ordinary, normal amount of blood that occupies it during waking hours. Just in that state there are a great many stages.

The President: Then if dreams are the beginning and the end of sleep, they occur practically at the particular moment when the cerebrum is going to sleep, and deep sleep is temporary paralysis.

Mr. B. Keightley: I don't think it is strictly true that the cerebrum is the only seat of consciousness.

Mme. Blavatsky: No, but it is that which polishes the ideas and makes them perfect—coordinates them, but the other does not. It simply gives conscious desires and so on.

Dr. Williams: They say a sensitive plant has consciousness. I meant coordinating consciousness.

Mr. B. Keightley: Du Prel[11] cites some very curious experiments showing there is a kind of local consciousness.

Dr. Williams: That is what they call reflex connection?

Mr. B. Keightley: He goes further than that in the cases of clairvoyants who perceive through the stomach. He cites a number of well authenticated cases that were experiments of his own, in that direction, in which he shows that the threshold of consciousness is capable of a very wide range of variation, very much wider than we are accustomed to attribute to it, both upwards and downwards.

Mr. A. Keightley: The point I was about to raise is this. You get your cerebrum acting from the point of your consciousness at the beginning and end of sleep. Very well then, in the intervening period, a period of deep sleep, the consciousness of the man is not lost; that goes on.

Mr. B. Keightley: The consciousness of the man is then inherent in the higher Ego.

Mr. A. Keightley: But the brain is not a sufficiently sensitive registering organ under those circumstances.

Mr. B. Keightley: No; except what is impressed upon it at the moment of awakening, and that is liable, of course, to get mixed up with the suggestions and stimuli and sensations that have been going

---

11 Baron Carl Du Prel, German philosopher, 1839-1899, who was a member of the Theosophical Society.

on during the night in the cerebellum.

Mr. A. Keightley: Now, query: The cerebellum has sometimes been called the coordinating organ of the physiological senses.

Mr. B. Keightley: Of the sense of sight, do you mean?

Mr. A. Keightley: Coordinating organ—I want to query whether it is possible for the cerebrum to be the coordinating organ of ideas?

Mr. B. Keightley: As opposed to sensations?

Mme. Blavatsky: Sensations. I suppose the animal also will have its sensations coordinated. If you give it a name in man, it is a different thing. In man there are the ideas, whereas an animal has nothing of the kind. It is simply an instinctual feeling; the animal does not think.

Mr. A. Keightley: Well, but roughly speaking, you have the animal with his sensation, which sensation is transmitted to the brain, if there is anything to be done with it for the first time. That process is repeated, until finally there is a sort of course of action determined, giving a repetition of the sensation. Ultimately, the end of it is that the cerebellum appears to act as an organ which will entail a definite course of action following a similar sensation without the creature taking a conscious part in the process. Is not that supposed to be the function of the cerebellum?

Dr. Williams: Yes.

Mr. A. Keightley: Then, you see, the cerebrum has taken its part and the cerebellum takes its part during the waking hours. Very well then; then we come to another part of it. Is it possible for the cerebrum to be a coordinating organ of ideas, as the cerebellum is a coordinating organ of action?

Mme. Blavatsky: Well, really, I don't know physiology enough for it, I can tell you. I don't know all the scientific things and I have read a good deal of what Huxley[12] was saying about the evidence of one lobe and another lobe. I say he has a theory which I cannot make head or tail of, just to reconcile it with occult theories, with what we are taught.

Dr. Williams: I don't think you could understand him. I think Huxley is ultra materialistic.

Mme. Blavatsky: He speaks about things most peculiarly. I read him several times and I think if I read it ten times, I could not understand it either. It may be very scientific physiologically, but in reality, as well as I could check it by my own experience in dreams, all that I see in sleep etc., I could not make head or tail of it. I don't see it is that at all.

Mr. B. Keightley: If you tickle a sleeping man gently, he will make a movement to brush it away, but without waking. Therefore the stimulus goes to the cerebellum and the mechanical action is produced. Arch's point was this: does the cerebrum, the forebrain, act in the same way with regard to the ideas? Does that establish a coordination between ideas?

Mme. Blavatsky: I believe it does. It cannot be otherwise.

Dr. Williams: I should say it could not be otherwise.

The President: Well I think we might make it now general.

---

12 Thomas Henry Huxley, English biologist, 1825-1895.

3.
Blavatsky Lodge of
The Theosophical Society
Meeting January 24, 1889
at 17 Lansdowne Road, W.

Mr. A. Keightley: The first question arises from what was stated at a previous meeting, when you said that it would take too long. We want to know if you will give us some explanation of the four and seven truths, even if it takes all the evening, as you said it would be too large a subject to deal with at the same time as others.

Mme. Blavatsky: Well, I will answer as follows: Everything about the four truths you can find in the *Buddhist Catechism*[1] or any of the exoteric books, but I do not think you are ready, anyone of you, for the esoteric explanation of them; therefore I had better ask you to postpone this.

Mr. A. Keightley: Can anything that is esoteric be found in these exoteric books?

Mme. Blavatsky: You can find it in any manual of Buddhism; in Olcott's book, for instance. There is nothing occult about it.

Mr. A. Keightley: Then how far is that exoteric side to be taken for anything real?

Mme. Blavatsky: It is real, because in the Buddhist church they practice it, and certainly the high priests know the truth about it,

---

1 H. S. Olcott's *A Buddhist Catechism, according to the Canon of the Southern Church*, a discussion in question and answer form of the basic tenets of Buddhism, was originally printed in Ceylon in 1881 in English and Sinhalese for use in Buddhist Schools. It was reprinted ca. 1888/89 by the Theosophical Publishing Society of London.

and they do not take the exoteric forms literally. As to the small fry and the laymen, they do.

Mr. A. Keightley: Then how far has that any value?

Mme. Blavatsky: It has a great value, because it is a discipline and it helps them to lead a good life and to have their mind fixed always on the spiritual.

Mr. A. Keightley: Then we pass on. *The Secret Doctrine*, Stanza 1, Sloka 5. "Darkness alone filled the boundless All." Is "darkness" the same as the "Eternal Parent: Space," spoken of in Sloka 1?

Mme. Blavatsky: How can it be the same thing? To me, Space is something already with attributes, at least in potentiality; it is differentiated matter, and "darkness" is something of which no attributes can be predicated, surely, for it is chaos; it is the Absoluteness. How can it be the same?

Mr. A. Keightley: But then is "darkness" there used in the sense of the opposite pole to light?

Mme. Blavatsky: Yes, the opposite pole to manifestation. "Darkness" means something that is perfectly void of any attributes or qualities—all negative.

Mr. B. Keightley: It is not opposed to light, then, but opposed to differentiation?

Mme. Blavatsky: There is no light yet.

Mr. B. Keightley: But it is really taken as the symbolism of negativeness.

Mme. Blavatsky: It is taken as that which you can find in the Bible, the void, "Tohu-va-bohu"[2] as they call it, the "chaos"; as it is said: "everything was darkness, and on the darkness the spirit of God was." Just the same as in that sense. There was nothing in it—in the

---

2 Genesis, 1:2, "And the earth was without form, and void."

Universe.

Mr. Kingsland: Is it that there is no light, or simply nothing to manifest it?

Mme. Blavatsky: There is nothing to manifest it. It is not darkness as absence of light, but it is darkness as Absoluteness in the absence of any manifestation.

Mr. Kingsland: Quite so; just the same as the Universal Mind we were discussing last time?

Mme. Blavatsky: Just so.

Col. Chowne: Then it says: "Light proceeds from Darkness."

Mme. Blavatsky: After that. First comes light. Light is the first Logos—call it whatever you like—it is the non-manifested Logos. In the second Logos it is not the Creator, but the light. In the *Vishnu Purana* they do not call it even Brahmâ, because Brahmâ is an aspect of Vishnu in the *Vishnu Purana*. What they say is, it is Vishnu—all. Vishnu *is* and *is not*.

Mr. A. Keightley: Then what is the difference there between the derivations of Vishnu and Brahmâ, the spreading and the pervading?

Mme. Blavatsky: In the *Vishnu Purana* you will find Vishnu spoken of as the Absolute "No-Thing," as the Ain Soph, that which is perfectly unknown, endless and incomprehensible. The Heavenly Man is its vehicle to manifest itself in the Universe when the Ain Soph becomes that celestial man. Just in the same way we deal with Vishnu in the *Vishnu Purana*, who will be spoken of as the Absolute; and then one of his aspects will be Brahmâ, the male, not the neuter, and after that he becomes everything. In the Veda you won't find Vishnu prominently mentioned, nor Brahmâ. Vishnu is named in the Veda, but is not mentioned as anything of a high order. As to Brahmâ, he is not mentioned at all.

Mr. A. Keightley: Then that quotation, "For Father, Mother and

Son were once more One"?

Mme. Blavatsky: Means that all *that*, the creative forces and the causing forces—if I may use the expression—and the effect of this cause is the Universe. Again, in the undifferentiated condition all was merged into one and was One. The Absolute is during the Pralaya, always.

Mr. A. Keightley: Second. What are the different meanings of the terms: Father, Mother and Son? For in the Commentary you explain them (a) as Spirit, Substance, and the Universe; (b) as Spirit, Soul and Body; (c) as the Universe, the Planetary Chain, and Man.

Mme. Blavatsky: Well, so they are. I think I have explained entirely. What can I say more? Unless you anthropomorphize them and make ideals of them, and deities, and put them as the Father, Mother and Son, as put all kinds of goddesses and gods. I do not see how I can explain it in any other way.

Mr. A. Keightley: Then take the last items of the series: I suppose "Son," "Substance," "Body" and "Man" correspond?[3]

Mme. Blavatsky: Certainly they do.

Mr. A. Keightley: Then why are "Father-Mother" linked together? And then the correspondence comes, "Spirit and Substance"; "Spirit and Soul"; and the "Universe and the Planetary Chain"; and the third term in the series seems to proceed from the other two.

Mme. Blavatsky: I put all the examples because it can be applied to anything. It can be applied to a planetary chain, it can be applied to the solar system, it can be applied to the whole Cosmos or anything you like. It is simply a figure of speech—a metaphor.

Mr. A. Keightley: But I think the point that I was meaning was this: you have Father and Mother and then you have the Son. The sentence seems to mean that the Son is distinct from the Father and the Mother, and that ultimately, in Pralaya, the Son is merged back

---

[3] Given as "Son, Universe, Man, Body" in *Transactions*, p. 37.

again into the Father and Mother in a closer union.

Mme. Blavatsky: Remember, I do not speak about the period preceding what they call in common parlance "Creation." I speak about the time after matter was differentiated, but before it began to assume form. I say in *The Secret Doctrine* I do not touch the thing which was pre-natal—if you can say that of the Cosmos. I do not touch this at all. Father-Mother simply means here the differentiated primeval substance, protyle, when it began to differentiate and became positive and negative, the active and the passive, and the Son, the production of the two, is the Son of the Universe, that is to say, of the universal forms.

Mr. A. Keightley: Then the ultimate state is the Laya state of Father, Mother and Son?

Mme. Blavatsky: Laya is that which remains during Pralaya, but also that which, in the manifested universe, is at the terminus of all matter. It is the zero-point. Now ask Mr. Bulaki Rama what Laya means. He knows and will explain it to you a great deal better than I. I say it is non-differentiated matter, the zero-point, as Crookes calls it. I don't know how to describe in any other way, that point where indestructible substance becomes homogeneous, entirely and absolutely homogeneous, that is to say, and not objective.

Mr. A. Keightley: Then is that the point you are speaking of here, just at the time when the Father, Mother and Son become once more One?

Mme. Blavatsky: Yes, but I don't know, I don't think it is in *The Secret Doctrine*. I simply make reference to that which was before the Father-Mother period. If there is Father-Mother, then certainly there is no such condition as Laya.

Mr. B. Keightley: Father-Mother are later than the Laya condition.

Mme. Blavatsky: Certainly, individual objects may be in Laya, but the universe cannot be in Laya when Father-Mother appear there, as it is said in this Stanza.

Mr. A. Keightley: That is the point I was meaning. Where the Son and the Father and the Mother reunite, there can be no differentiation at all.

Mme. Blavatsky: Certainly, it is the Laya, but not at that point you are talking about.

Col. Chowne: You explained it once as the essence.

Mme. Blavatsky: It is the essence, it is that which exists and does not exist, it is space. Now, for us, space is a word which has no meaning unless we limit and condition it; but in reality, space is the most abstract thing, and space containing all is just that unknown deity which is invisible and which we cannot understand, which we can but intellectually sense. What do they call it in Sanskrit, "dis," isn't it? The "ten divinities" that are in space. It is written "dis."

Mr. Bulaki Rama: "Desha," you mean, the "Ten Divinities" of space.

Mme. Blavatsky: It is just what I have been talking about. They pronounce like "sh" what we pronounce as "s," for instance, they would say "shloka" for what we call "Sloka."

Mr. B. Keightley: Is Fohat one of the three—Father, Mother, and Son—or what is it?

Mme. Blavatsky: Fohat is a manifestation. You mix up in the most extraordinary way the first Logos and the second Logos. The first is the unmanifested potentiality of Father, Mother and Son and of everything. It makes a triangle, that which is so dealt with by the Pythagoreans. You mix up the second Logos, which is the collectivity of the creators, or what they call in Greek Demiurgi, the builders of the universe, or simply the masons.

Mr. B. Keightley: I only want to get as clear as we can the sense in which the term is used in *The Secret Doctrine*.

Mme. Blavatsky: I use it in many senses in *The Secret Doctrine*. If you ask me such a thing I cannot remember in what sense I use it in such and such a page, but I can tell you in general what it means.

Mr. A. Keightley: Question 3. Can you give us the equivalents of these terms (Father, Mother and Son) in (a) the Vedāntic, and (b) in the Sankhya phraseology?

Mme. Blavatsky: No, Sir, I do not teach you the Vedanta or the Sankhya. It will only confuse you, and make matters worse. Let us hold to the esoteric philosophy, without mixing up the Sankhya and other philosophies with it. There are many things which are identical, but now, since we learn Occultism, I do not see why I should go and speak on it. This is, I know, a knotty question. I am perfectly sure of it.

Mr. A. Keightley: Question 5. During Manvantara, when the "Son" is in existence or awake, do the Father and Mother exist independently, or only as manifested in the Son?

Mme. Blavatsky: This is a thing which tickled me very much when I read it. I cannot understand, unless you want to become polytheists and idolaters, how anyone can offer such a question as that. How can a Father and Mother be independent of the Son? Are the Father and Mother two entities of the male and female persuasions and the Son the product of these two entities? Why, it is all one, it seems to me. How can we anthropomorphize in such a way in metaphysical questions? Well, look here, I cannot tell you any better than this, that they are, if you like, centripetal and centrifugal forces. This is the Father-Mother. That which they produce is the Son. I cannot say any better, because this gives you the whole thing.

Mr. B. Keightley: And that is the point; because in our mental conceptions we had conceived of the centripetal and centrifugal forces as existing independently of the effects they produce. We regard the effects in ordinary thinking as secondary to these two forces.

Mme. Blavatsky: Well, you are very wise in the West. You are great pundits, a thousand times more so than any of these benighted pundits in the East. (I am not one of them, but I am very near to them in my heart.) But still you do not know anything about it, and you cannot bring me any of your Herbert Spencers, or your other scientists, who know anything about it. They do not understand the thing as we do; they do not understand it aright, because you think about centripetal and centrifugal forces not as to any effect they produce. Therefore you think when there are no effects they will exist the same, do you, and they will produce no effect? They will be effectless. But why should you go and conceive a thing upside down? If these centripetal and centrifugal forces exist they must be producing effects, because there is nothing aimless in nature, and if they exist they produce effects. When there are no more effects the Forces do not exist either.

Mr. Kingsland: They exist as separate entities for mathematical purposes.

Mme. Blavatsky: Oh, for mathematics, but in nature and in science it is a different thing. We divide also a man into seven principles. We do not mean that in man there are seven skins or seven entities, or seven souls or, as Gerald Massey[4] thought, seven devils. They are only aspects of the one and nothing else. It certainly does not mean that. I see that you have been reading a good many books in your British Museum, but you are not accustomed to the way of expression—well, to this metaphorical form of speech of theirs. I do not know how it is, but I have been brought up from childhood in this way; and in the Georgian and Armenian times there was always this metaphorical mode of expression. In Persia they won't say a single word.

Mr. A. Keightley: Then we pass on to Sloka 6. "The universe, the Son of Necessity, was immersed in Paranishpanna. The causes of existence had been done away with."[5] If the "causes of existence" had

---

4 Thomas Gerald Massey, English poet and writer, 1828-1907, who argued for ancient Egypt as the homeland of western civilization.
5 The second sentence is quoted from Śloka 7.

been done away with, how did they come into existence again? For you state in the Commentary that the chief cause of existence is the desire to exist, and it has been just stated that the Universe is the Son of Necessity.

Mme. Blavatsky: What a contradiction indeed; it is extraordinary. "The causes of existence had been done away with" refers to the past Manvantaras or age of Brahmâ, but the cause which makes the wheel of Time and Space run into eternity, which is out of time and space (now try and understand me) has nothing to do with finite cause or that which we call Nidanas. What has one thing to do with the other? That is a little bit of criticism which I could not understand. I received it very humbly with very great gratitude, but I thought to myself of the person who wrote it. I do not think he will ever be a rival to Schopenhauer,[6] or anyone like him. That was my intimate opinion. What is contradictory there.

Mr. A. Keightley: Nobody has said it is a contradiction.

Mme. Blavatsky: But read it, if you please. It is a very great contradiction. I want all of you to remark that.

Mr. A. Keightley: It is the contrast here. If the causes of existence had been done away with, how did they come into existence again? And there you answer that by saying that one Manvantara had disappeared into Pralaya and that the cause which led the previous Manvantara to exist is behind the limits of space and time, and therefore causes another Manvantara to come into being.

Mme. Blavatsky: Yes, because that cause is immutable and has nothing to do with the *causes* of this terrestrial plane produced by finite and conditioned being, and we say *that* cause is immutable and it can be in no sense a finite consciousness or desire. It postulates an absurdity to give to the Absolute desire or consciousness or necessity. If you don't understand it, read it, and you will see it is so. I say it is no more natural to predicate of the Absolute, or to charge the

---

6 Arthur Schopenhauer, German philosopher, 1788-1860.

Absolute with desire or thought, than it is to say, for instance—how did I put it here—than the striking of the hours in a clock proves the desire of the clock to strike. Now you say: "Yes, the clock is wound up." I say the universe is wound up. The only difference is that this one is wound up in space and time, and the other is out of space and time, that is to say, in eternity; therefore, it is one and the same thing. Whoever has something to say against it, let him come and say it, and I will see what objection there is. There I am charged positively with the most absurd idea, as if the Absolute could have any desire or feel necessity, is not it so? Read it all over again.

Mr. A. Keightley: Well, it is divided into two or three different headings (reads again).

Mme. Blavatsky: Well I don't find "the blind will" of Schopenhauer so very stupid; it is a thousand times more philosophical than the philosophy of the ruler who created man. Doesn't it accuse me of contradiction? Well, not me, but the Sloka there.

Mr. B. Keightley: No, I don't think so. It seems to me to ask for an explanation.

Mme. Blavatsky: How can I explain why, when I am sitting down, I am not standing up? What can I say?

Mr. A. Keightley: It practically reduces the whole matter to "what is the cause in the Absolute of differentiation?"

Mr. B. Keightley: The difficulty is you cannot postulate—

Mme. Blavatsky: Ah! It is a very easy question to ask, you understand. I know you don't ask, but many ask. Fawcett asked it. He wants to ask what is the cause that propels or compels Parabrahm to create. Parabrahm is not a cause. It is not even the Absolute, as I say, but Absoluteness. Now, how can we know the cause that propels Parabrahm to create? That which is behind all the veil of matter is incomprehensible, and no finite intellect can conceive it. Well, we can perhaps have a slight conception in our hazy ideas that there may be such a thing, but we don't understand it, and to come and ask for the cause is perfectly ridiculous. Look at what Subba Row says in his lectures; it is perfectly true. He says that even the Logos—the first, not the second—cannot see Parabrahm. He sees simply the veil of matter, Mulaprakriti. So you see what it must be; then how can you know the cause, when we have no idea of Mulaprakriti, even? It is simply a conception, and it is just as Buddha said: "What is Nirvana? It is nowhere." "Then it is not, it does not exist?" "No, it does not exist, but it *is*." Well, just the same with that. Nirvana itself is a Maya. You will come always to the old question, unless you can conceive of such a thing as an eternal, endless, perpetual motion machine which you will call the universe—though properly we cannot call it a machine. We cannot call that a machine which is unlimited, limitless; but if you can conceive even of such an idea, you will never conceive of the Absolute in the way you do. You just try to imagine space in nature without giving it limits or form or anything. Understand my idea, and just try to imagine two forces: the centripetal and the centrifugal, which periodically must emanate from IT. Just as the clock must strike so this strikes and emanates periodically. When it has done striking it goes to sleep again. Try to imagine that and then you will have perhaps a notion. I tell you what was in my conception in the beginning. I had the perpetual motion machine. Mind you, it is not that I say, and certainly not that I would go and advocate, the automatic creation of the materialists; never. But it is for the purpose of giving a shape to it, and to allow people to conceive of it, because otherwise, you cannot.

Mr. B. Keightley: It is a peg to hang your mind upon.

Mme. Blavatsky: Yes, you must have a peg; therefore, imagine a perpetual motion machine which has no form and which is endless. Well, you can, with a little imagination, have these two forces which appear and disappear periodically.

Mr. Gardner: What portion of the machine is Parabrahm?

Mme. Blavatsky: What! Put him to bed! Please give him a pillow! Mr. Gardner, my dear man! Shame him, if you please, let him blush—Parabrahm, why, it is all. If there is one mathematical point in the universe where Parabrahm is not, then you had better go to bed, because it does not exist. It is not the present it is eternal. Oh! Do explain, somebody else, will you, please? Tell him some verses from the Veda to refresh him—anything you like.

Mr. A. Keightley: Supposing you take your conception of a machine. If ultimately you work out your conception of the universe, you bring yourself back to plain, simple, centrifugal and centripetal forces.

Mme. Blavatsky: With intelligence, *plus* intelligence; that will be another kind of "machine."

Mr. A. Keightley: Very well, call that the primary differentiation, and get that back to Parabrahm.

Mme. Blavatsky: Why should it get back to Parabrahm? It will get back to Parabrahm when the universe has finished its Age of Brahmâ, its cycle.

Mr. A. Keightley: Very well, then, you get your primary differentiation, and you postulate then that you must have a cause, the great first cause, the Absolute.

Mme. Blavatsky: No, I beg your pardon. The great First Cause is not the Absolute, never call it that; the great First Cause is the first unconscious radiation or emanation. Call it what you like, you know English better than I do. That which periodically manifests itself as light.

Mr. B. Keightley: The unmanifested Logos, in fact.

Mme. Blavatsky: Yes, the unmanifested Logos, if you like, but never Parabrahm. It is the causeless cause of all, and Absoluteness cannot be a cause. That is the great difficulty.

Mr. B. Keightley: Look at the paradox. You will say on the one hand that Absoluteness cannot be a cause, and you call it in the same breath a causeless cause.

Mme. Blavatsky: Because, in the first place, the English language is very poor, and in the second place, human language is almost as poor. And then, with our finite language, our finite brains, our finite conception, it is impossible to put in form that which is formless. How can you go, and presume to put it in language? Look at Herbert Spencer, he also calls it the First Cause, and he mixes it up with Absoluteness. Why, this is a very great philosophical mistake, at least in the eyes of the Vedantins. Certainly it is the greatest mistake.

Mr. A. Keightley: What I am getting towards is this, that you get back to your unmanifested Logos, and behind that, whatever attribute you chose to apply, you have Parabrahm.

Mr. B. Keightley: As the root.

Mme. Blavatsky: Look here, if you want to have the Vedantin theory, there is Parabrahm and Mulaprakriti. They are the same; only, Mulaprakriti is an attribute—it is a primordial, undifferentiated matter. We can conceive of such a thing, knowing there is such a thing, if we take it a little limited, that is of limited size or space; but we cannot conceive of that which is beyond that matter, that is to say, which is not even spirit, which is metaspirit, and is a thing inconceivable to the human intellect, and we can only barely sense it in our conceptions. We cannot put it in any definite words. This is the thing I want to impress upon you. Now Mr. Gardner thought Parabrahm was *some*thing; Parabrahm is *no thing*. Not *nothing*, it is Ain-Soph, the Endless. It is not *a thing* which is all and nothing, for it is Be-ness, and not non-being. Now try to understand this philosophically.

Mr. Kingsland: But it is still the First Cause, isn't it?

Mme. Blavatsky: It is the root of all, the causeless cause, the root of everything, and the First Cause, the unmanifested Logos, is that which will be the cause of everything in the universe.

Mr. Kingsland: You don't use the term "causeless" in the sense of cause-that-is-not-a-cause for anything else, but you use it in the sense of a cause that has not a cause behind it.

Mme. Blavatsky: It is a universal potentiality of that which will become potency. That is to say, if there is a difference in the English language between potentiality and potency. Is there?

Mr. B. Keightley: Certainly there is, distinctly.

Mr. Kingsland: That overcomes your objection, then.

Mr. B. Keightley: Yes, I only put it as a paradox of expression.

Mme. Blavatsky: They call it the rootless root; that is to say, it has no root because it is causality itself—causation.

Mr. Kingsland: It has no root, but it is the root of everything.

Mme. Blavatsky: It is the spiritual basis of all cause, which Mulaprakriti certainly is not. They say Ākāśa has only one attribute, and it is sound, in the *Vishnu Purana*. What is sound? It is Logos, that is to say, the sensuous representation of something. You see, it is very difficult for me to tell you. I speak English like a Spanish cow, and I am very sorry for it, but I cannot speak better, though I try to explain it as well as I can.

Mr. A. Keightley: Is it possible, as a speculation, as an entirely speculative thing, to conceive that after the universe has gone back into the Parabrahmic condition, that there should be to that Parabrahmic condition a ParaParabrahmic.

Mme. Blavatsky: It is what they say—ParaParabrahmic, that is the expression they use in philosophy. Don't they?

Mr. Hall: It is the old story about veil behind veil.

Mme. Blavatsky: No, it is not that. It is {that} nothing is behind the veil but nothingness—the root of all.

Mr. A. Keightley: Otherwise, you don't get back to infinity.

Mme. Blavatsky: Well, infinity is Sat, and Sat is Parabrahm, and

Parabrahm is Absoluteness; it is immutability.

Mr. B. Keightley: You see, you can't have the fallacy of an endless chain of the hen from the egg, and the egg from the hen and so on backwards. You must come to a stopping point somewhere.

Mr. A. Keightley: Must you? That is the question.

Mme. Blavatsky: You can conceive of it. If you train your intellect to be always aspiring and striving after the beginning of things, then you can.

Mr. B. Keightley: Can you go back?

Mme. Blavatsky: If you take the Aristotelian method you cannot go on, and you will be lost in a maze of all kinds of speculations which will be fruitless. But if you begin with the universals, taking the method of Plato, then I think you can, because then having once traveled on that road you can far more easily backtrack, and beginning from the particulars ascend to the universals. Then your method will be splendid; not quite on the lines of the men of science, but still it is good for something.

Mr. B. Keightley: But what I understand Arch was putting was this: behind that cause you have one cause, and behind that another cause, behind that another, and so on ad infinitum.

Mme. Blavatsky: Is it so, Arch?

Mr. A. Keightley: It is partly that. Well it is this: the subject seems to me so big that you can't get the right expression.

Mme. Blavatsky: But "causeless cause" puts a stop to it, because that means there is no cause behind it and that it had no cause, because it is cause itself. Why, for instance, do we say that the Absolute cannot think, nor can it desire, nor can it have attributes? Why, I have been saying to you a thousand times it has no consciousness. It has no desire because it is absolute desire; "IT" being the Absoluteness. How can you have the smallest thing that is not in IT? But we can't say that anything is an attribute of IT.

Mr. B. Keightley: Certainly not.

Mme. Blavatsky: Because an attribute is something finite, and this is infinite. So a stop is put to our speculations, by these words: "causeless cause" and "rootless root." And I think it is the most remarkable, suggestive and graphic expression I ever saw.

Dr. Williams: I think it says everything that can be said.

Mme. Blavatsky: Take the Vedanta. I don't know of any philosophy in the world higher than that philosophy.

Mr. A. Keightley: Then we come to section b, question 6.

Mr. B. Keightley: I think you can pass over those; they have been practically dealt with. We have just been discussing them. Pass on to the next one.

Mme. Blavatsky: Oh no, he has not done. There is a, b, c, and d of that.

Mr. A. Keightley: (Reads) "To conceive of either a necessity or a desire in the Absolute is to destroy the Absoluteness of the Absolute, or to reduce it to the 'blind will' of Schopenhauer."

Mme. Blavatsky: Well, I have answered that question. It is not at all to reduce it to the 'blind will' of Schopenhauer, but the "blind will," as far as I can express it, it is expressed perfectly; that which appears to us as "blind will" is absolute—well, not intelligence; but yes, absolute intelligence, absolute wisdom or knowledge, or absolute consciousness.

Mr. A. Keightley: (b) "If this desire is attributed to the Logos, it can only exist subsequent to the emergence of the Logos."

Mme. Blavatsky: I say no desire is attributed to Logos number one. That is what I said to you before.

Mr. A. Keightley: (c) "If it is said to exist as a latent potentiality in the Logos during Pralaya, then there must be a cause that makes it pass from latency into activity. Whence then the impulse to manifestation?"

Mme. Blavatsky: That is the old original question. We come again to the first principles. It is old Fawcett, who wants absolutely that someone should leave their visiting card at the door of Parabrahm and ask him what impels him to such capers, to create the universe. How can we answer that? It is a perfect impossibility. The potentiality, it says, if it exists in the Logos, it exists in everything. It exists in you, it exists in this fan and everywhere. Once we have approached the Pralaya—well, certainly we are in it, and it exists everywhere—but why should "the impulse" be absolutely limited to the Logos? There is again a thing which shows he has not been thinking on these Eastern lines.

Mr. A. Keightley: "The visible that was, and the invisible that is, rested in eternal non-being, the One Being." Question 7. What is the meaning of the expression, "the visible that was, and the invisible that is"?

Mme. Blavatsky: "The visible that was" means the universe of the past Manvantara, which had dropped into eternity and was no more. Very well; and "the invisible that is" means the eternal, present and ever invisible deity. It is abstract space, absolute Sat, and then we go over again what we have been talking about. It is very simple that; I don't see why the question is asked.

Mr. B. Keightley: It was really to find out from what point of view you were speaking in that Sloka, whether of the past Manvantara or not.

Mme. Blavatsky: Certainly, the past Manvantara. "The visible that was," was no more, "and the invisible that is" in this is certainly that which was, and that which will be in everything.

Mr. A. Keightley: Then we get to Sloka 8. "Alone the one form of existence stretched boundless, infinite, causeless, in dreamless sleep;

and life pulsated unconscious in universal Space, throughout that All-Presence which is sensed by the opened eye of the Dangma." Does then this "eye" open upon the Absolute, or is the "one form of existence" and the "All Presence" here mentioned other than the Absolute?

Mme. Blavatsky: Well, but the eye of Dangma being open and all that—I suppose everyone ought to see that it is again a metaphorical way of expressing the thing. You may open your eyes, and anyone can open his eyes on the Absolute, but the question is, "shall we see It"? It is not said that the eye saw, it says it "sensed." Now, if it is said that on opening the eye Dangma saw the Absolute, then it would be a fallacy and an absurdity, but it is said "sensed," if you please.

Mr. B. Keightley: It is not taken in that sense. What was meant by the question was, is it through this open eye that we do receive such sense, or such feeling, or such consciousness, whatever you take it to be?

Mme. Blavatsky: Do you take it for your own eye?

Mr. B. Keightley: No, for the highest spiritual faculty.

Mme. Blavatsky: There was no Dangma at that time, therefore nobody could see it. What other questions have you, then?

Mr. A. Keightley: What is "dreamless sleep"?

Mme. Blavatsky: "Dreamless sleep" is a sleep without dreams, I suppose. I certainly cannot give you a better definition than that. Who can?

Mr. A. Keightley: What does it mean?

Mme. Blavatsky: A dreamless sleep means a sleep without dreams.

Mr. B. Keightley: But that simply describes its state in relation to waking consciousness.

Mme. Blavatsky: In what particular is it? What is it about the dreamless sleep? I would like to know to what page it refers, what I have been talking about.

Mr. B. Keightley: It is part of that Sloka.

Mme. Blavatsky: I remember very well. I use the expression, only I don't see what there is. It means that there can be no presentation of the objects you can see in the universe, and therefore it is a "dreamless sleep."

Mr. B. Keightley: What you say here is this (reads passage from *The Secret Doctrine*, I:47).

Mme. Blavatsky: I think that I have explained it, and what can I explain more?

Mr. Kingsland: It implies there is something very active going on in that state of dreams. I think what you want to know is, what is that which is active going on?

Mr. B. Keightley: A greater degree of activity.

Mr. Kingsland: What they want to get at is, what is that activity?

Mme. Blavatsky: I surely cannot give you what is the activity of the causeless cause. I can tell you what is the activity in man. Therefore I am obliged to say I did not graduate as high as that. Man is a microcosm of the macrocosm. It means all the spiritual faculties behind matter. Matter being asleep and resting, we are more active than ever, though we cannot see with our spiritual eyes. But this belongs to the question of dreams, it does not belong at all to this series of questions.

Mr. B. Keightley: It is deeper than a state of dreams; it is further back still.

Mme. Blavatsky: There are no dreams on the physical plane. I said to you here that it is when we do not dream about anything that we dream the most. Not only that, but we act the most, and we live on an entirely different plane from this one, and our life is a thousand times more active. Our existence, rather, is a thousand times more varied; and it would be a nice thing if we could bring it back.

Mr. Kingsland: How do we act?

Mme. Blavatsky: We cannot take it, certainly, as we act on a physical plane, since that plane we are then on is Arupa, when here we are Rupa.

Mr. Hall: Do we generate Karma in that condition?

Mme. Blavatsky: No, we do not. A man generates Karma every time he moves, with the exception {of} the activity of his highest faculties.

Mr. Hall: Therefore it is the higher faculties which operate.

Mme. Blavatsky: And therefore you come to the dreams again. If you dream, for instance, you slew somebody, and you slew him asleep, that even affects your idea, and you dream you are killing a man. Do you know, it may so happen that you will really kill a man, and the man will die, if you see it in the dream. Don't try it, because you may do a nice little bit of black magic if it succeeded. If you had success, it might kill the man.

Mr. Kingsland: Now we are speaking about dreams that come back to consciousness?

Mme. Blavatsky: No, you can begin in consciousness and end unconsciously. The more it goes into the regions of the spiritual, the more it will be potent, and the easier you will kill the man.

Mr. B. Keightley: And the less you will remember about it.

Mr. Kingsland: Do you mean to say you can dream you have murdered a man, and not remember it at all, and that dream would be a potential force which might make you murder the man?

Mme. Blavatsky: It is your desire in the dream to hurt somebody. If you are neither an adept nor a black magician nor anything of the kind, nor a Jadoo,[7] you cannot do it while you are awake, but in the dream life you are no more impeded by the limits of matter and of your senses, and that which limits you when you are awake. Then you can produce effects just the same as a hypnotizer could kill one of his subjects. You have such a potency in you that you can kill a man at a distance, by thinking you are killing him.

Mr. Hall: But he must be asleep.

Mme. Blavatsky: Not a bit of it. *You* must be asleep, not he.

Mr. Kingsland: Then the question is whether those actions produce Karma.

Mme. Blavatsky: That is what I say. On the lower plane, they will produce Karma; but if you are in your higher spiritual senses, you won't kill a man at all. There you have not got those passions, and where you have not got them, by wanting to kill a man in the high spiritual regions you would kill yourself—because you are not separate from any man in creation, as your mind is not separate from the ALL.

Mr. Kingsland: In these dreamless sleeps it is only the higher principles which are active.

Mme. Blavatsky: We are talking about what Hall asked about, potentiality.

Mr. Kingsland: In every case we were referring to dreamless sleep.

Mme. Blavatsky: Dreamless sleep you may not remember, but from the next lower state you may remember, and do a good deal of mischief.

Mr. A. Keightley: Then, question 10. What portion of the mind and what principles are active during dreamless sleep?

Mme. Blavatsky: Now, please, leave this. This will make us go on till twelve o'clock, wool gathering. It belongs, my dear fellow, to

---

7 Hindi term for magic or wonderworking, usually applied to traveling conjurers.

these other things. We discussed dreams for four or five evenings, you know.

Mr. A. Keightley: We have no record of it.

Mme. Blavatsky: I have a record, excuse me. I can repeat it to you. I will take the same things and answer you.

Mr. A. Keightley: Then that closes these questions.

Colonel Chowne: There is one thing you talked about: you said there was no other way of expressing how light came except by a cause, and that cause was darkness.

Mme. Blavatsky: Darkness so far that we don't know anything about it, and it is perfect darkness for us; we cannot discern anything behind that, it is impossible.

Colonel Chowne: But how does the light come?

Mme. Blavatsky: In consequence of an immutable law which manifests itself periodically. Just as I say the clock strikes and shows the hours without being conscious of it at all. Now, the clock is an automatic thing, and the other is a thing which has absolute consciousness. Therefore, to us it is no better than clockwork, because we cannot see how the intellect works.

Mr. A. Keightley: Then darkness and light in that Stanza are not used as pairs of opposites.

Mme. Blavatsky: No, no; I use darkness because there is no other word suitable. If you say chaos and take that, immediately you create all kinds of confusion. Immediately you will have thoughts of chaotic matter and all kinds of anomalies. Therefore, I use the word darkness, which is a great deal better.

Colonel Chowne: The light that you refer to is not the physical light that we think of?

Mme. Blavatsky: Oh, no! The light means, well, the first potentiality of all—the first flutter in undifferentiated matter which throws it into objectivity and into a plane which is nearer to manifestation than the other. That is the first light. Light is figuratively used.

Mr. A. Keightley: But then, also later in *The Secret Doctrine*, in the more scientific part, you state that light is only made visible by darkness, or rather darkness is the original thing and light is the result of the presence of objects in the objective world.

Mme. Blavatsky: If there is no sun, there would be no light, certainly, in the objective world.

Mr. A. Keightley: But I mean if there were no objects, there would be nothing to reflect the light.

Mme. Blavatsky: Take two rays of light, and they will produce darkness.

Mr. A. Keightley: Take a globe of water and pass an electric beam through it. The electric beam is perfectly dark, unless there are objects in the water, in which case you get specks of light.

Mme. Blavatsky: Yes, that is a good illustration.

Mr. B. Keightley: You cannot see the light, it passes through the water perfectly invisible.

Mr. Kingsland: You cannot see light itself. But light may be manifested to another sense, as something quite different, may it not?

Mr. B. Keightley: Yes, because, after all, the light is only differentiation of vibration.

Mme. Blavatsky: You can have the sense of light in the taste or hearing; in all your senses you can have it, or you can, for instance, in the hearing have the sense of taste and have the sense of seeing; why, look at the clairvoyants, they are perfectly asleep. They are in a trance, moreover, and they {you} come and put a letter {upon them} and the clairvoyant reads {it}. How is that?

Mr. A. Keightley: That is an extra sense.

Mme. Blavatsky: It is not an extra sense. It is simply that the sense of seeing can be shifted. It passes into the sense of touch.

Mr. A. Keightley: Is not the sense of perception the beginning of the sixth sense?

Mme. Blavatsky: Oh, yes, but that goes a little further. This is simply the shifting of the physical sense of sight into the sense of touch, nothing else. Now those clairvoyants will, blindfolded, read to you a letter; but if you ask them what will be the letter that I will receive tomorrow, that is not written yet, the clairvoyant will not tell you. But the sense you are talking about (the sixth sense) will, because it is there before you. That is quite a different thing. One is manifestation on the physical plane, and the other on the spiritual plane.

Mr. B. Keightley: You have an instance of this shifting of one sense into a another when you happen to take some very fiery extract into your mouth. It will produce the sense of a flash of light before your eyes.

Mr. A. Keightley: For instance, if you put the two poles of an electric battery together in your mouth, you will get a flash of light in your eyes and you get a metallic taste in your mouth.

Colonel Chowne: If you knock your head against a wall, you get a flash of light in your eyes, too.

Mr. A. Keightley: That is the sense of touch transferred into the stimulation of the optic nerves.

Mme. Blavatsky: This is very interesting, and you ought to collect as many facts as you can about those phenomena on the physical plane. Then you could go higher and use the phenomena which are in correspondence. You know what I mean, until we come to the highest that we can have.

Mr. B. Keightley: Now a blind man, too, gets practically the sense of sight transferred into the sense of touch, and besides that, he develops a very definite sense of locality which is independent of the sense of touch. For instance, he will find his way about a town or about a house which he knows without touching the objects to localize himself.

Mme. Blavatsky: Certainly, he sees by the other senses.

Mr. B. Keightley: But how does he see? Which of the senses helps him to get at it?

Mr. A. Keightley: But even when in possession of all the senses, physiologists have worked on the idea of a sense of direction.

Mr. Hall: Yes. There certainly must be one.

Mme. Blavatsky: Dr. Williams, what do you say to that?

Dr. Williams: I don't know anything about the sense of direction. I have not heard anything of it.

Mr. A. Keightley: It is supposed to refer to the semi-circular canals in the ear.

Dr. Williams: Senses of direction—that one might hear a sound, do you mean?

Mr. A. Keightley: No. Suppose that part of the brain is removed in an animal. As long as the animal is standing still and not moving, every function goes on perfectly naturally. If it once begins to move, even in places where it is most familiar, the idea of direction is lost. For instance, a canary in which this has happened, or there is some disease of the semi-circular canals, or any, will not be able to find its way to its food if these canals have been interfered with. The sense of direction is entirely lost.

Mr. B. Keightley: But all the control over the muscles is perfectly intact; it does not stagger about.

Mr. A. Keightley: No; it simply cannot go straight. That is very interesting. You will find it, really, in any physiological book of late years which deals with the functions of the brain.

Mr. B. Keightley: Where are they situated?

Mr. A. Keightley: Close behind the ear.

Mr. B. Keightley: Then it must be connected with the sense of hearing.

Mme. Blavatsky: I am afraid physiology is very much at sea as to the most elementary questions about the senses and so on; it goes and denies *à priori* the possibility of super-senses, if I may call them so, and does not know a single thing about the most simple matters, about that which one has experience of every day of one's life. It does not know anything about the touch and the sight.

Mr. A. Keightley: Don't you think it would be a thing for some future Thursday, if you would take the senses and give us some principles to work upon?

Mme. Blavatsky: I would have all the physiologists sitting on me, if I did. Not in public you know.

Mr. A. Keightley: But you are not in public. You are only in Blavatsky Lodge.

Mme. Blavatsky: I am not learned enough to undertake such a thing as that.

Mr. B. Keightley: I think you could do it, if you tried. We should be content with the little elementary things, but I think you could give us the others, if you tried.

Mr. A. Keightley: At present, one works blindly in connection with these things, and often sets about working on matters which really are of no use, and have to be completely unlearned again.

Mme. Blavatsky: What does physiology say about it? You see, I am more capable of detecting mistakes if I see them; if I read a book on physiology, or if I hear somebody talk. It is a great deal easier for me to find the mistake than to come and tell you anything about the thing, because not knowing physiology or your technical terms, and not being sure how far they have progressed with their illusions and hallucinations, I do not know where to begin.

Mr. A. Keightley: I shall be very happy to supply you with books.

Dr. Williams: He can supply illusions enough.

Mme. Blavatsky: Can you tell me, Dr. Williams, what they say in physiology about it?

Dr. Williams: They say a great deal.

Mme. Blavatsky: Do they say anything about this?

Dr. Williams: The only thing they say worth consideration is—or rather the deduction that may be made from what they do say is—every sense may be resolved into the sense of touch. You may call that the coordinating sense, and the deduction is made from their embryological investigations, which show that the sense of touch is the first and primary sense, and that all others have been evolved from that, since sight and sound and taste, everything, are simply more highly specialized or differentiated forms of touch. I know of nothing worthy of consideration.

Mme. Blavatsky: If you go to the trouble of reading the *Anugītā*[8] and the conversation between the brahmin and his wife, I can assure you, he teaches very good things to his wife there, and very philosophically. You won't lose your time. He (Mr. Keightley) can lend it to you, if you like. Really, it is worth reading, and the brahmin speaks there about the seven senses. All the time he talks about the seven senses. It is translated by Max Müller.[9] "Mind and Understanding" are the two extra senses, and I say it is very badly

---

8 The *Anugītā* is a discourse between Krishna and Arjuna that forms part of the *Mahabharata*, and was delivered after the great battle described therein.
9 Edited by Max Müller, it was translated by Kashinath Trimbak Telang as Volume 8 of *The Sacred Books of the East* (1882).

translated, because it does not mean that in Sanskrit at all. I think the first sense, you understand, is sound, on the top of the ladder, on the last rung on the terrestrial plane. Maybe they will win their case by touch, but I do not think it is so.

Mr. B. Keightley: By touch they mean skin, sensibility.

Mme. Blavatsky: Do they call skin, also, the eye that sees?

Mr. B. Keightley: No, they say the eye that sees is formed of one of the nerves of the skin.

Mr. A. Keightley: No, the eye is the outgrowth of the brain.

Mme. Blavatsky: And that is all that they say, the physiologists. They do not make much progress, it appears.

Dr. Williams: I meant that that to me seems to be the only thing worth thinking very much about. That deduction is founded on the beginning of the very lowest forms of life, the first differentiation of that which results in the organ of sight, a simple pigment cell which is more sensitive to light than the other cells. I am not sure that there is no harmony between the most advanced physiology and that proposition of yours.

Mme. Blavatsky: The sense of sound is the first thing that manifests itself in the universe. Then after that, sound, certainly, is in correspondence with colours or sight; that is the second thing. Well, I think you have got enough for tonight.

Dr. Williams: I think the sense of sound always passes into the sense of sight. I do not think we can have any conception of anything unless it does.

Mme. Blavatsky: If you could only see clairvoyantly a person playing a piano, you would see the sound as plainly as you hear it. If you allow yourself to sit there in your own normal state and listen, of course you will hear the sound, but if you only can concentrate your ideas; just paralyze your sense of sound—you can even put cotton in your ears —you will see the sound and how much better you can see it, and detect every little note and modulation that you could not do otherwise. You cannot hear at a distance, but you can see at a distance.

Dr. Williams: Do you mean you see it as a sort of rhythmic movement?

Mme. Blavatsky: You see it if you are accustomed to it. Now let us take an illustration. For instance, to hear a person sing on the stage, you must be within a limited distance from the stage, in a place where the acoustic properties are good and where the sound travels freely. But now you just imagine yourself that you have a very good sight, and you sit there and a *prima donna* will sing, say in Kensington Gardens; you can see it if there is no impediment. You will hear it with your sight better than you will see with your ears. That is paradoxical, but it is perfectly occult and true. Note this.

Mr. B. Keightley: Supposing you stop your physical ears and watch clairvoyantly the plane, and allow your clairvoyant hearing, so to speak, to operate at the same time. Clairvoyant sight would translate itself into hearing on the same plane.

Mme. Blavatsky: One would merge into the other. You can taste sound, if you like, too. There are sounds which are exceedingly acid, and there are sounds which are exceedingly sweet, and bitter, and all the scale of taste, in fact. This is no nonsense, I say it seriously, and you will find it so if you want to know about the super-physical senses.

Mr. A. Keightley: Then, do you get the same extension of smelling into touch?

Mme. Blavatsky: Yes, you may reverse entirely and shift one sense into the other, and you may make it a great deal more intense and do anything you like. Now in the Vedas it is said—or is it in the Upanishads, I think it is the Upanishads—they speak about seeing a sound. I don't know if I did not mention it in *The Secret Doctrine*. Oh!

I wrote an article in *The Theosophist*[10] about it. There is something either in the Upanishads or the Vedas.

Mr. Bulaki Rama: Yes, there is several times a mention of seeing a sound, but we think it is in the metaphorical sense.

Mme. Blavatsky: Now you want to take it so, because you are in the England universities.

Mr. B. Keightley: Instead of being the sons of Brahmâ!

Dr. Williams: I wonder if anyone has read a story in the last number of *Harper's Magazine*,[11] a story of a sailor who had been cast away on an island in one of the Archipelagoes, in the South Seas, and finds a race of people who have entirely lost the art of talking. They understand each other and see what they think, but they regard sound as a very gross way of communicating thought. It is a very interesting little sketch.

Mme. Blavatsky: It would be a "Palace of Truth." You could not say then, "How happy I am to see you," and send them to all kinds of disagreeable places in your mind. They communicated in such a way as that in the olden times. Their thoughts took objective form.

Mr. A. Keightley: They hit each other in the eye with the thought.

Dr. Williams: He says he found it a powerful incentive to moral elevation (laughter).

Mme. Blavatsky: They could not fib, then. You could not say a falsehood. How nice it would be to go into a drawing room of Mrs. Grundy's[12] and just to know that they must communicate their thoughts. It would be the sweetest thing in the world! How many compliments would be exchanged! Well gentlemen, what else? Once

---

10 "Occult or Exact Science?" *The Theosophist*, vol. 7, April, May 1886, where she quotes the Book of Kiu-te that "sound is seen before it is heard." See also *H.P. Blavatsky - Theosophical Articles*, II:46.
11 "To Whom This May Come" by Edward Bellamy, *Harper's New Monthly Magazine*, vol. 78 (February 1889), pp. 458-466.
12 Mrs. Grundy was a personification of British propriety during HPB's time.

I am dead I won't be worth much, so take your last chance before I die. Gardner has subsided.

Mr. Gardner: No, I was thinking, "before you took your dreamless sleep."

Mme. Blavatsky: We should know more about the senses and could just exchange thought and all kinds of things simply by scratching our noses. We would understand each other. This business would be thought transferring. It would be a very nice thing.

Mr. B. Keightley: It is a very curious thing, that transference of sense localities in parts of the body. For instance, as a rule, with the mesmeric clairvoyant, the sense of sight is transferred to the pit of the stomach and it won't operate in any other part of the body. Though sometimes it is at the back of the head.

Colonel Chowne: There is some centre of nerves there.

Mme. Blavatsky: You will learn that.

Mr. Gardner: Sometimes it works through the forehead.

Mr. B. Keightley: Generally the pit of the stomach or the back of the head.

Mme. Blavatsky: They never tried it here, at the back of the head (pointing).

A Lady: They tried it through the feet.

Mr. B. Keightley: I never heard of seeing through the feet, though certainly the sense of sight is one they have experimented with the most.

Colonel Chowne: You mean a blind man is supposed to read colours. I do not see how he distinguishes red from blue.

Mme. Blavatsky: The colours, you see, he can know. For instance, a deaf man can be looking at the sounds; he can see because it gives him a kind of sound. Of course he does not hear it as a sound, but it is transferred to his mind as a something that is sound, really. Though it cannot be expressed. You could not understand it, of course.

Mr. Hall: Deaf and dumb people very often like to put their hands on a piano while it being played, so that the vibration may be communicated to their brains.

Mr. B. Keightley: Then there is the well-known case of a blind man, who always associated sounds with colours. He had a conception, red, which he associated with brass instruments, the trumpet particularly. Red always suggested to his mind the trumpet.

Mme. Blavatsky: It is extremely interesting, this association of sounds and colours by vibration, and then it is a very scientific thing, as I think somebody speaks about it. Now, for instance, the sounds have got so many modulations and vibrations. And light is just the same way.

Dr. Williams: Sound begins at fifteen vibrations a second and runs through a very limited scale, so far as the ear is capable of conceiving it. The vibrations increase in intensity, and then comes the sense of heat. The different senses seem to take up one scale of vibration, of which all these different manifestations consist. You go on with the sense of heat until you get a dull redness, and there you get light, and so you run through the whole gamut. It passes out of light, then call it the chemical rays that passes beyond colour and produces chemical changes.

Mme. Blavatsky: Isn't there a difference in the prismatic colours? They are 7, and then there is something, I forget how they call it, a measurement.

Mr. B. Keightley: A wavelength.

Mme. Blavatsky: I don't know how they call it. There are only five of them seen, or three. Is it an instrument that was invented, that these seven colours reduce themselves to five, then to three and then one?

Mr. B. Keightley: No, there are three primary colours. These other seven are formed from combinations of those. First you get five—

Mme. Blavatsky: No, I speak about some instrument.

Mr. Kingsland: Perhaps the spectroscope.

Mme. Blavatsky: No, not that. I read that they had invented an instrument which could give not only the radiation of colours but the reduction of colours, and that seven colours passed through some 77 shades until merged into one white, you know.

Mr. Hall: Is that the helioscope?[13]

Mr. Kingsland: It is only a matter of combining again after they are once dispersed by means of the prism.

Mme. Blavatsky: Oh, but it is the seven colours, where in their, so to say, gradation or shading, instead of being seven they become perhaps 77 times seven?

Dr. Williams: I think it was some adaptation for showing the ratio, rather, of wavelength and colour to rate vibration. That would be an almost indefinite number of vibrations, of course.

Mme. Blavatsky: But they must be counted. I speak about that because it will always come back to the 3 and the 4 and the 7.

Mr. Hall: Some people associate the different kinds of colour with different kinds of pain.

Mme. Blavatsky: It is very easy. When you have neuralgia, there must be some colour you cannot look at without terrible pain.

Dr. Williams: Insane persons are treated sometimes by means of colour.

Mme. Blavatsky: Now did you ever think why bulls are irritated at the red colour? Do you know it gives them terrible pain? It enters

---

13 An instrument used for observing the sun.

somehow or other through their sight into the brain, and makes them perfectly crazy. It gives them physical pain.

Mr. Gardner: Is that why they wear red coats in hunting?

Mr. Kingsland: They don't hunt bulls!

Mr. Gardner: Oh! I thought you said "wolves."

Mme. Blavatsky: Some colours do give pain. There are some sensitive persons who cannot look at very bright colours, they feel positively nervous at some combinations of colours, they cannot bear it.

Dr. Williams: I think it is the most interesting question of science.

Mme. Blavatsky: But I think the far more interesting question is to see the result of various combinations in the occult spheres. Now you will see one result on the terrestrial plane; but if you were to follow it up and see what are the results produced in the invisible sphere, well, it is invisible but still, some of the effects will become objective. Though the causes which are set in motion will be invisible, you will see the effects.

Dr. Williams: It is always far more interesting to investigate any question from the point of view of principles before descending into particulars.

Mme. Blavatsky: I believe the only exact science that you have is mathematics, and mathematics proceeds in this way.

Dr. Williams: Yes, from first principles to details.

Mme. Blavatsky: Certainly, it is not quite the Aristotelian way that you can use in mathematics.

Dr. Williams: I do not think science would object to this more than this: "Be sure of your first principles. If you know what they are, then there would be no difficulty."

Mme. Blavatsky: But how about they who don't know what they see before their noses? They only see that which they think they see, and then they are obliged to give them up, because they see they are mistaken. Why are the men of science so very, very conceited?

Dr. Williams: Well, I think it all grows out of the idea that man in a certain way creates everything from himself, that he has no relation to any higher power than himself, and he regards himself as the highest power in the universe.

Mme. Blavatsky: Is it conceit?

Dr. Williams: I should say almost supreme conceit.

Mme. Blavatsky: How about our grandfathers? For the scientists want us to have a grandfather common with the ape; that is supreme degradation.

Mr. B. Keightley: No, they may think this: "Look how gloriously we have progressed in a few thousand years."

Mr. Hall: Like a self-made man who is always referring to the time when he came to London with twopence in his pocket.

Mme. Blavatsky: How do you know there are not self-made apes in the forest? We do not know anything about it. I have seen apes who are very wise. I have seen many; I love apes. I have a great tenderness for them, and I think they are better than men are. It is a fact.

(The proceedings then came to a close.)

4.
The Theosophical Society. Meeting at Blavatsky Lodge on Thursday, January 31, 1889.

Mr. A. Keightley: The first question is in connection with śloka 6, Stanza 1 (reads passage from *The Secret Doctrine*). Now, with reference to the "Seven Lords," question 1 runs: "Since confusion is apt to arise in the correct application of the terms, will you please distinguish between Dhyan-Chohans, Planetary Spirits, Builders and Dhyani-Buddhas?"

Mme. Blavatsky: Yes; but you know, really, it will take a volume if you want to know all the hierarchies and every distinct class of angels among the Dhyan-Chohans, the Planetary Spirits, the Dhyani-Buddhas, the Builders, etc. Now, Dhyan-Chohan is a generic name for all Devas, or celestial beings. They are one and all called Dhyan-Chohans. Now, a Planetary Spirit is the ruler of a planet, a kind of personal God, but finite; that is the difference you see. A Planetary Spirit is the one that has to rule and watch over each globe of a chain, or every planet, and there is some difference between those who are over the great sacred planets, and those over small chains like ours, because the earth has never been one of the sacred planets—never. It was simply taken as a substitute, like the moon and the sun, because the sun is the central star, and the moon has never been a {sacred} planet. It is dead long ago.

Mr. A. Keightley: But does the earth belong to a chain which belongs to the train of one of the sacred planets?

Mme. Blavatsky: Oh no, not at all. The earth has its own chain. Then there are six companions which are not seen, which are on three different planes.

Mr. Kingsland: Are none of those other six, one of the sacred planets?

Mme. Blavatsky: No, sir, not one, and it is not feasible.

Mr. Kingsland: Then how are we to distinguish between them?

Mme. Blavatsky: The seven sacred planets of antiquity were the planets which astrologers take now, minus the sun and the moon, which are substitutes.

The Chairman {T.H. Harbottle}: And plus two that we do not know.

Mme. Blavatsky: Yes, of which one is an intra-Mercurial planet, which they are trying to find and cannot. They wanted to call it Vulcan, or to give it a name before it was found out; they think they have found it, but they are not sure. Some say there are several, others one, but they do not know. When they find out they will know that it is one of the secret {sacred?} planets, and the other one is what I cannot explain. It was as the substitute of this planet that the moon was taken, and it was seen at a certain hour of the night just as though it was near the moon, but it was not; it is this planet which was not known at all. I think sometimes they do not give the name, but as to my astronomical ideas, I would not trust them.

The Chairman: It is not Herschel,[1] is it?

Mme. Blavatsky: I thought it was at one time, and yesterday evening I was thinking a good deal about it, but I am not sure. If I were to see, or if it were possible to have a planisphere[2] of the heavens to see at certain hours of the night, as astronomers must have it, I would have recognized it; but if it is not Herschel, I could not tell you.

The Chairman: But the modern astronomers say about Herschel that it is a planet which has an almost unexpected and what we should call an occult influence upon things; and they, having recently

---

1 The planet Uranus was at one time referred to as "Herschel's planet" after its modern discover, the English astronomer, William Herschel, 1738-1822.
2 A star chart.

discovered Herschel, assign exactly the sort of attributes to Herschel in astrology that one should expect of the secret planet.

Mme. Blavatsky: That is why I thought it was so, but I am not sure, and I cannot tell you until I have seen the planispheres, but as far as the name is concerned, you cannot go by the Sanskrit in order to know what is the name. I do not know well enough beyond this, that it is an occult planet, which is seen at a certain hour of the night, directly, as though near the moon.

Mr. Kingsland: Every night?

Mme. Blavatsky: I am not sure whether it is every night. I know it was so, and that it had a sacred day, also.

Mr. Gardner: It moves very slowly.

Mme. Blavatsky: And, mind you, the motion is retrograde. Therefore I do believe it is Herschel; but I would not swear to it.

Mr. B. Keightley: If you do away with the moon as one of the astrological planets, you would have to attach to one of the others the influence which is at present ascribed to the moon, and the question is, whether that can be done.

Mme. Blavatsky: What is said is this, that the influence of this secret planet passes through the moon, i.e., the occult influence of this secret planet; but whether it passes so that it comes in a direct line, or how, I cannot explain. That is for you mathematicians to know better than I can.

The Chairman: Then, if that were so, you would find the influence of Herschel would be very strong indeed when it was in conjunction with the moon, as the astrologers call it.

Mr. Kingsland: Are these seven planets all on the same plane as ourselves?

Mme. Blavatsky: Certainly.

Mr. Kingsland: Then I presume there is a separate plane belonging to each of those.

Mme. Blavatsky: Yes, you find it in *The Secret Doctrine*.

Mr. A. Keightley: Are there minor chains belonging to these sacred planets? You say the earth has never been one of the sacred planets, and it has a chain.

Mme. Blavatsky: It has a chain and many others have chains, which have not been discovered, but will be discovered just as much as the earth's. That is one of the smallest planets, as you know yourselves.

Mr. Kingsland: What makes the others sacred or secret?

Mme. Blavatsky: I suppose because they have occult influences.

The Chairman: But then the seven are on a different hierarchy, as it were, to the planetary spirit of the earth?

Mme. Blavatsky: Oh, yes. The planetary spirit of the earth is what they call the terrestrial spirit and is not very high. The planetary spirit has nothing to do with the spiritual man. It has to do with the things of matter with the cosmic beings—they are cosmic rulers, so to say, and they form into shape and fashion things. They have everything to do with matter, but not with spirit. With spirit it is the Dhyani-Buddhas who have to do. It is another hierarchy that has to do with that, and I am explaining it to you here.

The Chairman: These seven planetary spirits, as we should use the phrase, have really nothing to do with the earth, except incidentally.

Mme. Blavatsky: They have everything to do with the earth, materially.

Mr. Kingsland: They have to do, in fact, with man in his higher part.

Mme. Blavatsky: They have nothing whatever to do with the spiritual man.

Mr. Kingsland: Have they anything to do with the fifth principle?

Mme. Blavatsky: They have something to do with the fourth principle but with the three higher principles they have nothing to do whatever. I have not finished yet. You asked me what were the things, and I tell you. First, Dhyan-Chohans was a generic name for all the celestial beings. Second, the Builders are a class called by the ancients Cosmocratores, the builders. They are builders simply, like the celestial masons who shape under the orders of the architect, so to speak. They are but the masons to the grand architect of the universe.

Mr. Kingsland: Are they not the planetary spirits, then?

Mme. Blavatsky: What, the Builders? Well, they are, but of a lower kind.

Mr. A. Keightley: Do they act under the planetary spirit of the earth?

Mme. Blavatsky: Well, no. The planetary spirit of the earth is not a bit higher, unless he is one who has attained his rank, so to say, earlier than the others, and therefore he is considered the chief of them. Mind you, I tell you that which is said not in the exoteric religions (though in some, of course, you may learn it), but in the esoteric teaching.

The Chairman: But are not the Builders of various classes when considering the solar system or the universe as a whole or any one particular planet? I mean, are there not Builders absolutely terrestrial, in the same way that there are builders of the solar system and the universe?

Mme. Blavatsky: Most assuredly.

Mr. Kingsland: Then the terrestrial Builder is a planetary spirit?

Mme. Blavatsky: Yes, but a very low kind. What is our earth compared to Jupiter, for instance (well, we won't speak of the solar angels)? It is nothing but a speck of dirt or mud.

The Chairman: But it has its hierarchy.

Mme. Blavatsky: Of course it has, all of them have. This will be shown to you here. They are reflected in the intelligence of the G.A.O.T.U.,³ which is simply Mahat, the Universal Mind. There comes again the third. Well it is said distinctly, the planetary spirits are those who watch over planets and globes of a chain such as that of our earth. Now, fourth, you spoke about Dhyani-Buddhas. They are the same as the higher Devas. In India they are what are called Bodhisattvas in the Buddhist religion, but exoterically they are given only as five whereas there are seven. Why they do so is because exoterically they take it "*à la lettre,*" but they represent the Seven, and it is also said in *The Secret Doctrine,* "the five Buddhas who have come, and two who are to come in the Sixth and Seventh Races." Now, esoterically, their president is {Vairocana?},⁴ and he is called the Supreme Intelligence, and the Supreme Buddha, and [ ]⁵ which is again higher than the [ ], because he is as much above [ ] as Parabrahm is above Brahmâ or Mahat. It is the same difference. Or as, for instance, the Dhyani-Buddha is higher than the Manushi Buddha, the Human Buddha—which is the same difference. The Dhyani-Buddhas are one thing exoterically and another thing in occultism. Exoterically, each is a Trinity. (continues reading from her own notes.) That is the difference between Dhyani-Buddhas and the others. The Dhyani-Buddhas are those who remain from a previous Manvantara on a planet which is not as high as ours, which is very low; and the others have to pass through all kingdoms of Nature, through the mineral kingdom, the vegetable kingdom, and the animal kingdom.

Mr. Kingsland: Then the Dhyan-Chohan is prehuman, and the Dhyani-Buddha is posthuman.

Mme. Blavatsky: They are all Dhyan-Chohans.

---

3 The Masonic formula meaning "Grand Architect of the Universe."
4 The published *Transactions* gives Vajrasattva, though stating this is exoterically so.
5 *Transactions*: Vajradhara.

Mr. A. Keightley: Well, the planetary spirit.

Mme. Blavatsky: That is a creature in this period.

Mr. A. Keightley: Prehuman?

Mme. Blavatsky: How do you mean prehuman?

Mr. A. Keightley: Will be a human.

Mr. Kingsland: Dhyani-Buddhas have been men.

Mme. Blavatsky: And the Dhyani Buddhas were before, and they will not be men on this, but they will be something higher than men, because at the end of the Seventh Race it is said they will come and incarnate on earth.

Mr. Kingsland: Will they be what corresponds to man on a higher plane?

Mme. Blavatsky: I don't know, but they will come in the Seventh Round, because all humanity will then become Buddhas, or Devas. They are the emanations or the reflections of the Manushi Buddha, the Human Buddhas. Not necessarily Gautama Buddha, for he is a Manushi Buddha, a human Buddha, a saint—whatever you like to call it.

Mr. A. Keightley: Question 2. "Does the planetary spirit in charge of a Globe go into Pralaya when his Globe enters Pralaya?"

Mme. Blavatsky: The planetary spirits go into Pralaya at the end of the Seventh Round, not after every one of the rounds, because he is in charge of the Globe, and has to watch the workings of the laws even during the *statu quo* condition of the Globe when it goes into its time of rest, that is to say, during its inter-planetary Pralaya. I explain everything in *The Secret Doctrine*, and this is explained somewhere there.

The Chairman: I don't remember it.

Mr. B. Keightley: I don't think you put it in print.

Mme. Blavatsky: Maybe. Then they must have left it out. Or perhaps it is the third or fourth volume. I remember I have written it. There is the third volume; it is full of the Buddhas, Devas, and things.

Mr. A. Keightley: Well then, if anything is missed out of *The Secret Doctrine*, we will say it is in the third volume.

Mme. Blavatsky: No, really, I could show it to you, it is in the third volume. I know I have written it.

Mr. A. Keightley: Then Question 3. "Does the Dhyani, whose province it is to watch over a Round, watch over, during his period of activity, the whole series of Globes, or only over a particular Globe?"

Mme. Blavatsky: I have explained this just now. Each of them has his own Globe to watch, but there are seven planetary spirits, and it is Dhyani-Buddha. You make a mistake there.

Mr. A. Keightley: I said Dhyani.

Mme. Blavatsky: Here it is said when the All and planetary, and the Dhyani-Buddhas and all who will appear on earth in the Seventh Round when all humanity will have become Buddhas {and} Devas, their sons, and they will be no more trammeled with matter, there is a difference between planetary and the other (continues reading from her own notes). Mind you, in the Kabalah you will see always mention of the three higher planes, of which they speak with great reluctance. Even there they will not go as far as that, they simply give you the Triad: Chochmah (or whatever they call it) and Binah, the male and female intelligence, or wisdom and intelligence. And this Binah in the Kabalah is called the Jehovah, and a female, if you please.

Mr. Kingsland: It says here that the Dhyani is to watch successively every one of the rounds. A little confusion arose there.

Mme. Blavatsky: But Dhyani is a generic name, as I said to you. It is an abbreviation of Dhyani-Chohans, that is all, but not of Dhyani-

Buddhas. Dhyani-Buddhas are quite a different thing. If I said it, it is a very great mistake, a *lapsus linguae* to which I plead guilty very often—as I have just said 28 was 5 times 7.

Mr. A. Keightley: Question 4. Is there any name which can be applied to the "Planetary Spirit," which watches over the entire evolution of a planetary chain?

Mme. Blavatsky: Which one is it?

Mr. A. Keightley: Number 4.

Mme. Blavatsky: I had two or three pages written out, but perhaps it is better that I should not read it. There is nothing at all, it simply explains why we do not worship them.

The Chairman: Well, let us have it; it is a very interesting point, that.

Mme. Blavatsky: This is why we go against the idea of any personal extra-cosmic god. You cannot worship one such god, for "the gods are many," is said in the Bible. Therefore you have to choose either to worship many, who are all one as good, and as limited, as the other, which is polytheism and idolatry; or do as the Israelites have done——choose your one tribal god. (continues reading from notebook.) Now this, in the Bible, is what is said: "The gods are many, but the God is one."[6] Why? Because it is their own god that they have chosen. With the end of Pralaya he disappears, as Brahmâ does, and as all other Devas do. That is to say, he is merged in the Absolute, because he is simply one of the rays, which, whether the highest or the lowest, will all be merged into the Absolute, and therefore we do not worship and we do not offer prayers to them, because if we did we should have to worship many gods; and if we address our prayers to the one Absolute, then I do not think the one Absolute has got ears to hear us. That is my opinion. It may be atheistical and I may appear a very great infidel, but I cannot help it.

---

6 This is a paraphrase of 1 Corinthians 8:5-6.

Mrs. Williams: What objection would there be to worshipping many gods?

Mme. Blavatsky: I do not see any objection, but it would be a tiresome thing. You would not have time to pay them all compliments. It would be rather a monotonous thing.

Mrs. Williams: You spoke of it as being idolatrous. I wanted to find out whether in your mind it was so.

Mme. Blavatsky: Not at all. I say if we have to offer prayers to some personal god, then we must believe in many gods, and we must offer prayers to many or to none, because why should we have a preference? We do not know whether it is the best or the worst we may fall upon. It may be one who is not at all very perfect.

Mr. B. Keightley: Besides, we should make the others jealous.

Mme. Blavatsky: Besides, we have a god within us, every one of us. This is a direct ray from the Absolute; every one of us is the "celestial ray from the one — ", well, I do not find any other word but the Absolute and the Infinite. Now then, number 4.

Mr. A. Keightley: Is there any name which can be applied to the Planetary Spirit, which watches over the entire evolution of a Planetary Chain?

Mme. Blavatsky: No name, unless you make of it the generic name since he is not alone but seven. (Continues reading from her notebook.) If you give him this name it will be a very good name, I think. It will be scientific and it will answer the purpose, but you are at liberty to give any name you like. What is in a name? "Choose you the daily gods you duly worship," says Joshua.[7]

Mr. A. Keightley: Is there any name applied to it in the Sanskrit?

Mme. Blavatsky: Look here, the Vaishnavas worship Vishnu, the Saivas worship Shiva, the other—how do you call them?—the [ ]

---

7 This is a paraphrase of Joshua 24:15.

worship Krishna, and so on. Everyone has a god of his own. Everyone chooses his own tribal god, or anything they like, or their racial god, and they are happy.

The Chairman: But such a god as Vishnu is the synthesis of the seven.

Mme. Blavatsky: One is the creator, so called, though he certainly did not create matter out of nothing, but the universe out of something. The other is a preserver and the third is a destroyer; but being that, he is the highest, because that which destroys, regenerates, and because you cannot have a plant growing without killing the seed. Therefore, he destroys to give a higher form, you understand.

Mr. A. Keightley: Then these three questions: the name of the "Planetary Spirit," and "Is there a name which can be applied to the Planetary Spirit watching over a Round?" Also, "Is Brahmâ the correct term to use concerning the Planetary Spirit of one Globe during one Round, or would Manu be the more correct term?" In this sense is Manu identical with Brahmâ?

Mme. Blavatsky: You have jumped to number 6.

Mr. A. Keightley: I put those three together, because they really practically come together. We wanted to distinguish a Planetary Spirit in a Chain of Worlds from the Planetary Spirit over one Globe, which really rules one Globe, and thirdly to ask whether Brahmâ is the correct term to use.

Mme. Blavatsky: Of the universe they would never say Brahmâ. They would say Manus, and they are the same as Brahmâ; and then the rest of them, sometimes they are reckoned the seven, sometimes ten, according to what they are talking about, and this is in the esoteric meaning in the Puranas.

Mr. A. Keightley: There is a special class of Planetary Spirits which deal with a Chain.

Mme. Blavatsky: There are Rishis, and the Manus are those who are over every Round.

Mr. A. Keightley: Then are the Manus and the Rishis the same?

Mme. Blavatsky: They are just the same—Rishi or Manu. What is Manu? Manu comes from Man, to think—the thinking intelligence. Now just the same as this [   ], which is the intelligence, or this [   ] is considered the supreme intelligence, and he and Brahmâ are one. Take the *Vishnu Purana;* take any Purana which will give you exoterically these things. They give the real thing, and they invent many things just as blinds. But you will find a good many things which you will never find in the other scriptures. They will come and ornament things, and yet the fundamental truths are there.

Mr. A. Keightley: I want to avoid, if possible, all these blinds with regard to these names.

Mme. Blavatsky: The Brahmins will pitch into us after that. Why shall I give them names? Am I a Roman Catholic priest, to come and baptize them, and give them all different names? For me they are ideations. I am not going to give them names. If I told you the real occult names, it would not make you any the wiser. You are sure to forget them the first moment.

The Chairman: But it helps us to place them.

Mme. Blavatsky: Then let us take the Prismatic Idea: let us call them the Red God and the Orange God and the Yellow God and the Blue and the Green.

The Chairman: Very well, but in regard, for instance, to that seven in one, what relation do they bear to the Sephiroth?

Mme. Blavatsky: They are three and seven. They are ten in all, but the higher is considered the greatest, and the seven, the god descending into matter.

The Chairman: What relation is there between that seven and the seven we were speaking of?

Mme. Blavatsky: The Planetary Spirits? None.

The Chairman: Are they the Planetary Spirits?

Mme. Blavatsky: Well, I would not call them that. You never find a single name which is not Angelic. Take the Kabalah. They call it the third Sephiroth, as being intelligence; his angelic name is {Zaphiel?}, and he is called Jehovah, and this, that and the other, and the book goes on and gives the thing. How it is called, you cannot understand it. But, you see, all of them start from one point, and make a kind of broken ray, coming from one focus. Shall we then in this way give names to all of them?

The Chairman: No, but I think we might understand what they are, and what relation they bear to names which we do know at present. The Sephiroth is a name which is particularly familiar, and if one can have an idea that they are in the seventh Sephiroth, we might know.

Mme. Blavatsky: They are just the Cosmocratores on a higher plane, but yet the last hierarchy, Malkuth coming to earth, and this is the perfect hierarchy.

The Chairman: Then the sevenfold or prismatic gods which preside over the Planetary Chains will be something lower.

Mme. Blavatsky: Certainly they will; because they are not the Watchers, you know.

The Chairman: I have got what I wanted.

Mme. Blavatsky: If you tell me what you want, I will say, but why are you so inquisitive, tell me?

The Chairman: Only because I think one looks for these analogies all through, and when the analogies do not seem to fit, you are puzzled. The only way to attempt to understand them is to see one analogy running through them.

Mme. Blavatsky: Do you want to compare them with the Kabalah?

The Chairman: Yes, but not in detail, because I do not know enough about its details. One wants to know the relation, as it were, of the Planetary Chain to the Cosmos, and secondly, of the spirits ruling the Planetary Chains to the spirits of the Cosmos, and so on.

Mme. Blavatsky: It is the [ ] in its collectivity, and this includes the seven lower Sephiroth. And it becomes another thing, for it becomes the bridegroom of the bride, Malkuth.

Mr. A. Keightley: Then we pass on to the Stanza following: "But where was the Dangma when the Alaya of the Universe (Soul as the basis of all, Anima Mundi) was in Paramartha (Absolute Being and Consciousness which are Absolute Non-being and Unconsiousness) and the Great Wheel was Anupadaka?"[8] Does Alaya mean that which is never dissolved, being derived from "a" and "Laya"?

Mme. Blavatsky: [Well, in this book they are very rough. I have just strung them together. They are simply notes.] Alaya is the living sentient or active Soul of the World (Continues reading from her notes.) Now, the Alaya {Laya} means the negation or Layam, as they call it, because it is that which is perfect non-differentiation. It is perfectly homogeneous and it is negative, inactive, and has no attributes, and Alaya is the Soul of the Universe.

Mr. A. Keightley: Then practically this Stanza means "Where was the Dangma, when the Alaya of this universe was in Laya."

Mme. Blavatsky: There is Bulaki Rama, who will give you the true explanation. Because I give you the Hindu things simply on analogy. I do not profess to teach it. What I give is occultism and the occult doctrine and I try to make, for example, to the Hindus and those who have read Hindu books, the thing more clear. I just give you the analogy, but there is a Sanskrit scholar. How would you explain it?

Mr. Bulaki Rama: Laya means that which is absolutely nothing, from the root (la?) {li}, to disappear, and Alaya means not alive.

---

8 *The Secret Doctrine* 1:47 (Stanza I, Śloka 9).

Mme. Blavatsky: Just what I give you here. One is manifested and fully active and the other has disappeared from the realm of manifestation and fallen into Non-Being. So, then, I have given them correctly.

Mr. A. Keightley: Then it is different exactly from what we put down in the question as being, e.g., never dissolved.

Mme. Blavatsky: Certainly not, because it is non-differentiation. Alaya means latent. At the end of Manvantara, when Pralaya sets in, certainly the Alaya will become Laya and fall into nothing. There will be the one Great Breath only. It is most assuredly dissolved. It *is* eternally, throughout the Manvantaras, but the Laya is nothing, it is the thing which is a negation of all. Just the same as the Absolute, the Parabrahm; it is and it is not.

Mr. B. Keightley: Alaya is simply two negatives put together to make a positive. You can get at it in that way.

Mr. Bulaki Rama: Laya means to disappear forever, and therefore it is not negative.

Mme. Blavatsky: That is to say, it is nothing; it is just like Ain-Soph. What is Ain-Soph? No-thing. It is not a thing; that is to say, it is nothing, the zero point.

The Chairman: It is neither negative nor positive.

Mme. Blavatsky: Hence Alaya is the one active life in Jivatma, while Laya is the life, latent. One is absolute life and Be-ness, and the other is absolute non-life and non-Be-ness. So you see it is perfectly the opposite.

Mr. A. Keightley: Then the next question is asked in these words, "Page 50, Alaya is the one life, the one life is Jivatma. Are then Alaya and Jivatma identical?"

Mme. Blavatsky: I should say that they were. I do not see any difference. Anima Mundi—that is Jivatma, the Soul of the World, the living soul. Jiva is life. For the matter of that, every life has got its Jiva, but this is the Jivatma, the one Universal Soul. I think so, at least. May be you will tell me otherwise, but it seems to me that Alaya and Jivatma are one.

Mr. Bulaki Rama: Certainly.

Mme. Blavatsky: How would you translate "Atma"?

Mr. Bulaki Rama: Well, it means that which is present.

Mr. A. Keightley: What is the difference between Atma and Jiva?

Mme. Blavatsky: Jivatma is the life everywhere, that is, Anima Mundi, and Atma simply is—well, as he explains it.

Mr. B. Keightley: It is your All-presence.

Mr. Kingsland: Then it can only be Jivatma during Manvantara.

Mme. Blavatsky: Certainly. At least, the Vedantins say so; after that all becomes Parabrahm, and Parabrahm is beyond our conception. It is something we cannot certainly go and speculate about, because it has no attributes. It is all and nothing, nothing in our conceptions, or our ideas.

Mr. A. Keightley: Stanza 2: "Where were the Builders, the luminous sons of Manvantaric Dawn? In the Unknown Darkness in their Ah-hi (Chohanic Dhyani-Buddhic) Paranishpanna. The producers of form (rupa) from no form (arupa), the root of the world—the Devamatri and Svabhavat, rested in the bliss of Non-Being." Question 9. "Luminous Sons of Manvantaric Dawn." Are these the perfected human spirits of the last Manvantara or are they on their way to humanity in this or a subsequent Manvantara?

Mme. Blavatsky: They are the primordial seven rays from which will emanate, in their turn, all the other luminous or non-luminous lives, whether angels or devils, men or apes. These are the seven rays from which will come all the flames of being and everything in this world of illusion. The seven logoi.

Mr. A. Keightley: Yes, exactly. Then question 10.

Mme. Blavatsky: There you go again. Because I wanted to explain to you here that some are this and some are something else. "Some have been, others will become." (Continues reading from her notebook.) Everything, therefore, is there in the seven rays. You cannot say which, because they are not yet differentiated and therefore are not yet individualized.

The Chairman: And within these are both prehuman and posthuman.

Mme. Blavatsky: Exactly. That is a very much earlier stage. This belongs all to the precosmic times, it does not belong to the after state. It is precosmic, before there was a universe.

Mr. A. Keightley: What puzzles one is talking of the negation, [ ], first of all, and then speaking of the luminous sense. One gets accustomed to the recurrence of terms which are intracosmic, in contradistinction to precosmic.

Mme. Blavatsky: It is only after the differentiation of the seven rays and after the seven forces of Nature have taken them in hand and worked on them that they become one, the cornerstone of the temple; the other the rejected stone of clay or piece of clay. After that begins the shifting and the sifting and the differentiation and everything, and the sorting of things, but this all belongs to the precosmic period, therefore it is very difficult. These answers are for those who are perfectly familiar with the occult philosophy, and as they proceed, I do not take them one after the other. There are breaks of forty Stanzas, and there are Stanzas that I would not be permitted to give. What can I do? I do the best I can. There are things they would not permit for anything to be translated. I wish I could. It is no fault of mine. Therefore are our teachers called egoists, and selfish, because they do not want to give the information to the Fellows of the Royal Society, who would appreciate it so much! Who would sense it, and who would drag it in the mud, and laugh at it as they do everything else. Now then, question 10.

Mr. A. Keightley: "Builders—our Planetary System." By our Planetary System, do you mean the solar system, or the chain to which our Earth belongs?

Mme. Blavatsky: The Builders are those who build or fashion things (Continues reading from her notebook.) By Planetary System, I mean the solar system. I suppose it is called the solar system. I would not refer thus {to} that {as} the Planetary Chain. I would call the latter simply a chain and if I say Planetary System, it is the solar system; if I say Planetary Chain, it is the Chain of Worlds. I do not know whether I am right in so using it. This one is our planet, the root, the lowest one, but the others are not, because they are not seen. They are spheres, globes; they are not on our plane

Mr. B. Keightley: It is the old mistake about Mars and Mercury.

Mme. Blavatsky: My dear sir, I have shown it in *The Secret Doctrine*. If Mars and Mercury belonged to our chain, we would not see them, we would not know anything about them. How could we see that which is not on our plane? It is perfectly impossible. Now, then comes a thing which pertains more to physics and chemistry and all that than anything else, but still you can, I suppose, learn something from that.

Mr. A. Keightley: Stanza 2. In reference to what is said on page 54 of oxygen and hydrogen combining to form water, would it really be correct to say that what we perceive is, in reality, a different "element," if the same substance? For example, when a substance is in the gaseous state, it is the element of air which is perceived; and when combined to form water, oxygen and hydrogen appear under the guise of the element of water. Would it be correct to say that when we get it in the solid state—ice—we then perceive the element of earth? Would a clairvoyant perceive oxygen and hydrogen separately in the water?

Mme. Blavatsky: There are two or three things I do not recognize at all. It must be Mr. Harte,[9] who has put his finger in the pie. You remember at the beginning you wanted to make it more plain, and I have been crossing it out as much as I could. I can recognize in a minute what is mine and what is not. He begins to make comparisons, and I don't see at all the object of the comparison. I think it is all correlations, and I don't see how we can say this or the other. They have made a most absurd objection to calling the earth and water and fire and air elements, because they say they are composed of elements. Now they begin to find out that they do not approach even to an element in their chemical analysis, and that such a thing as an element can only exist in their imagination. They cannot get at an element which is really an element. Do what they will, they will find more and more that the element of today will become the two elements of tomorrow. This is a world of differentiation; therefore, if we call water an element, we have a perfect right so to do, because it is an element. It is something which does not resemble anything else, it is not like fire or air or earth. These are all the states of one and the same element, if you like, of the one element in Nature. These are various manifestations in various aspects, but to our perceptions they are elements. Now they go and quarrel: "Shall we call it an element?" and then they say that oxygen and hydrogen do not exist any more, since they have correlated and become something else; but if you go and decompose water, immediately you have the two elements reappearing. Do they pretend to create something out of nothing?

Mr. B. Keightley: No, they say they do not understand.

Mme. Blavatsky: It proves that they are latent, and it is a fallacy to say they do not exist. They disappear from our plane of perception, from our senses and sight, but they are there. There is not a single thing that exists that can go out of the universe.

Mr. Kingsland: Oxygen and hydrogen are all differentiated states of

---

9 Richard Harte, an American member who was one of Mme. Blavatsky's many helpers with *The Secret Doctrine*. He left to work at the headquarters in India in October, 1888.

something. When they are combined to form water we lose sight of them as distinct differentiations, but if we could follow them with our inner sight, should we still see them?

Mme. Blavatsky: Most assuredly, because the test gives it to you. Not a very experienced person is required to test water, and if that person knew something of oxygen and hydrogen, that person would tell you immediately which predominates; that is the test which will give you the real thing, but of course it must be an occultist. But they are there. They may be all the same—but they are not, if you please. They will take a drop of water and decompose it and they will find so and so, but then the analysis or instrument cannot detect which is more intense than the other. The proportion will become the same, but it won't be the same in the intensity or taste. This is an occult thing—I mean the intensity of one thing or the other. An occultist, if he were really so, would tell you even the plane from which it comes, too. Well, I don't want to tell you more, because it would seem like a fable, and you would not understand.

Mr. Gardner: For instance, the water when I was going up Snowdon[10] tasted very pure.

Mme. Blavatsky: Most assuredly, that water which you will get on the Himalayas will be quite different from the waters you drink in the valleys and the plains. There is nothing physical without its subjective moral and spiritual aspects, and so on.

Mr. Kingsland: We cannot decompose the water without getting a definite quantity of oxygen and a definite quantity of hydrogen. You say one may be more intense than the other.

Mme. Blavatsky: Intense in quality, not in quantity.

Mr. Gardner: The quality of the oxygen?

Mme. Blavatsky: Yes, sir.

Mr. Kingsland: But that is not perceived.

---

10 The highest mountain range in Wales, with numerous footpaths.

Mme. Blavatsky: You don't perceive the presence of the soul in man, at least the men of science don't, but we do; that is the difference. How can you go and argue with a man of science?

Mr. Kingsland: We are dealing with the most physical plane.

Mme. Blavatsky: Never mind. The physical plane cannot exist nor give you any correspondence nor anything without having the spiritual mixed with it, because otherwise you cannot go to the root of things. When your men of science tell me they are acting on the physical plane, and say metaphysics is all nonsense, I see that their science is really perfectly honeycombed with metaphysics. The scientists cannot go beyond matter; beyond the things they perceive, it is all speculation,

The Chairman: The reason we cannot distinguish in this way as to quality and intensity is because we have no perception of the three higher elements. If we had, we should at once distinguish.

Mme. Blavatsky: Certainly. Mr. Harbottle has just hit the nail on the head. I don't want to enter into it, because I shan't be understood.

Mr. Gardner: What do you mean by the term intensity?

Mme. Blavatsky: I mean intensity.

Mr. B. Keightley: You know whether a taste is intense or not.

Mme. Blavatsky: Now, you will take a drop of vinegar—let us come on the lowest plane—and you will know this vinegar weighs so much. You will take the same weight of another vinegar, and it will be quite different, but the weight will be the same.

Mr. Gardner: Well, the strength.

Mme. Blavatsky: Call it strength, if you like. I call it intensity.

The Chairman: It shows itself in the absence or presence of the essence.

Mr. Kingsland: That can be analyzed chemically.

The Chairman: Yes, but there is something behind that.

Mr. Kingsland: There is nothing corresponding to that intensity in the molecule of oxygen and hydrogen, in the case of these we can analyze with our chemical methods.

Mme. Blavatsky: I will tell you a better thing yet, if you go on the occult principle. We are not Christians, we do not believe in the doctrine of transubstantiation as it is taught in the church, we are occultists, and yet, I say there is such a thing as transubstantiation on the occult plane, and that if it comes to this, if the priests, the Roman Catholic priests, were not such stupid fools, they would give a very good reply. They would say: "We take bread and wine, and we say that it changes by a kind of miracle or a mystery into the flesh and blood of Christ." Very well, then; once they take Christ to be one with the Absolute (which they do, I don't know how they arrange it), then they are perfectly right. In this bread and wine there is as much of the Absolute, and I tell you that in every drop we swallow, and every morsel we eat, there is as much of Parabrahm as there is in anything, because, everything coming from the one Absolute it is impossible it should not be there. Transubstantiation is that which takes away for the time being—whether on the plane of illusion, or on the plane of senses—which takes away one quality of a thing, and makes it appear as though it were another. The bread and wine changes, and becomes flesh and blood. With a hypnotized person, you may give him a tallow candle and he will exclaim, "What delicious chocolate." The hypnotized person does not believe. If he were not hypnotized, he would be choked unutterably. And if we go on to the plane of realities, then really, once they say their Christ is one with the Absolute, they are logical in maintaining the doctrine of transubstantiation, for the bread and wine becomes his flesh, because it is flesh and blood; if you want to anthropomorphize. Certainly a Vedantin would not say such a thing, but they act very logically, and that is all. Now I have told you a thing of which I did not like to speak, because I may hurt the feelings of any Roman Catholic who may be among you. I don't like to hurt the feelings of anybody. [Bert looks very pale, you see].

Mr. A. Keightley: Is this question possible to answer? Is it utterly nonsensical to say, when you speak of a gas, you perceive the different elements in that gas, as distinguished from its liquid condition?

Mme. Blavatsky: It is in the liquid condition, and yet you detect the gas in this liquid condition, you detect it clairvoyantly.

Mr. A. Keightley: For instance, oxygen ordinarily is in a gas; by various processes it is reduced to a liquid and solidified. The question really means this: when you find it in the gaseous condition, is it the element of air in the oxygen, the occult element of air which is perceived; and again the occult element of water which is perceived in the liquid condition, and the occult element of earth in the solid?

Mme. Blavatsky: Most assuredly. You have first of all fire—not the fire that burns there, but the real fire that the Rosicrucians talk about, the one flame, the fire of life. On the plane of differentiation it becomes fire in whatever aspect you like; fire from friction or whatever it is, it is fire. Very well, after that it produces the heat in the liquid and then you pass through the element of water and from the liquid it becomes gas. You must know better than I, speaking of the physical things. Then from the gas, the two gases mix up and produce water. You take simply a drop of water and follow it. When solid it becomes ice. When ice is liquefied it becomes water, this water becomes vapor, ether, anything you like; and then it entirely disappears in the universal flame, which of course you physicists won't speak about. The universal flame—you call it inter-ether, but follow it like that and there it is. It is the element which appears to you here, and to say that this gas is not there or these two are not there I should say is a fallacy. The only thing we can say is that the gases have passed from the plane of the objective into the plane of the subjective.

Mr. Kingsland: It seems to me that it is only possible with the physical senses to see one element at a time, and therefore we are quite right to say if anything is in a liquid state that what we perceive is the element of water.

Mme. Blavatsky: Perfectly. There you are perfectly right, and an occultist will answer you so. He will say as I tell you: it has disappeared from the plane of the objective and appeared on the plane of the subjective.

Mr. A. Keightley: Then all substances on the physical plane are really so many correlations or combinations of these elements and ultimately of the one element.

Mme. Blavatsky: Most assuredly, if you only realized this: how many times I have spoken to you about this, that the first thing to realize is the existence of One and only One, i.e., of the Absolute. You have to start from universals to the particulars. You cannot proceed on your Aristotelian system, you will never come to anything. You will come to grief and confusion, and you will be always knocking your heads against stone walls, and your heads will come out second best. [How can you come and begin a thing? On its appearance you have to go to the primal motor and beyond that to the spiritual cause.]

Mr. Kingsland: How could we do that before we are initiates?

Mme. Blavatsky: I beg your pardon, there is no need to become initiates. There is something beyond matter, but the men of science laugh at metaphysics, and they say, "fiddlesticks for your metas," and yet I say they are always dealing with metaphysics; that is what they do.

Mr. Kingsland: You can start with that hypothesis.

Mme. Blavatsky: If you permit metaphysics in your hypothesis, and you do not believe in metaphysics, what is your hypothesis worth? Take, for instance, ether. Now, in *Webster's Dictionary*, what do they call it? "A problematical or hypothetical agent of so and so, which is not yet believed in." They take it as just a necessity, and yet you build on that ether the whole theory—axiomatic, mind you, your axiomatic teachings of light, and your vibrations. What right have you to do it? If you base yourself on a phantom of your imagination, a physical consciousness that it is such a thing, I call it humbug and sham.

Mr. Kingsland: You want us to go further back.

Mme. Blavatsky: I want men with something like brains, but not men with brains only on the physical plane that they cannot see beyond. They have not got feelers or antennae.

Mr. Kingsland: How can you, by getting a something which is hypo-hypothetical, so to speak, arrive at more knowledge by working on what you do not know?

Mme. Blavatsky: You don't work on your own inventions, you work on the wisdom of the ages, and if during these 100,000 years or so all the men of the best intellects said all the same and found out this, and their adepts and their wise men said the same thing over and over again, there must be more truth in that than in the speculations of the few.

Mr. B. Keightley: I think the position is summed up in this way. Physical science is—

Mme. Blavatsky: Nothing but a conceit.

Mr. B. Keightley: The whole basis of occultism lies in this, that there is latent within every man a power which can give him true knowledge, a power of perception of truth, which enables him to deal first hand with universals, if he will be strictly logical and face the facts and not juggle with words. Thus he can truly proceed from universals to particulars by the effect of the innate spiritual power which is in every man, and with certainty, not as a hypothesis. It is a hypothesis only as regards our physical senses.

Mr. Kingsland: But how is he to get at that except through initiation?

The Chairman: A man has consciousness, or has not.

Mme. Blavatsky: He has it inherent in him, it is simply the method of your education together with these ideas that they took into their heads "that we will not proceed in such a way, that we will take the Aristotelian method and the Baconian method, and there never was a man in antiquity who was capable or worthy of untying our shoestrings." And therefore you see they do take one hypothesis after the other. There is not a single thing that will be said in science that is not purely hypothetical. From your Sir William Thomson,[11] who said of something: "I have come to the conclusion that it does not exist more than 50,000,000 years ago," and then said: "I am of opinion it existed 80,000,000 {years} ago." Between 80 and 50,000,000 there is a difference. Huxley goes and says a certain thing takes 1000 years; another one will go and say something else, while another says, "I am not disposed to admit such a thing." Why, my dear sir, Plato was a match for any one of your greatest philosophers of the day. Such sages as Plato— I don't speak about Socrates, but I think Plato could beat all the Schopenhauers, and Herbert Spencers, and Hartmanns[12] and all the *tutti quanti* that the nineteenth century is so proud of. And if he proved that you could not get at knowledge unless you began from universals and speculated down to particulars, and found the thing on the terrestrial plane, I suppose he was more right than you are. We had intelligence, we had knowledge, we had most extraordinary knowledge before. What have we got now?

Mr. Kingsland: It is only in the last few years that we have had the privilege of learning this.

Mme. Blavatsky: You had the privilege nearly 1,900 years ago. You knew it all. It was only in the fifth century that you succeeded in destroying every temple. You have been hunting the occultists and have been acting so that those who knew went away, hid themselves and never came near the civilized minds. Everything was destroyed; your poor scientists are nothing but the children of the reaction, and the men of science who have eyes will not see, and will not permit that anyone in antiquity was greater than themselves. You go and read your best men from Oxford and Cambridge. When they

---

11 Sir William Thomson, Scottish physicist, 1824-1907, raised to the peerage in 1892 as Lord Kelvin. There is an extensive footnote about him in *SD* II:10.
12 A reference to the German philosopher, Eduard von Hartmann, 1842-1906.

speak about Plato, they say, "Oh! He did not know anything about the circulation of the blood. Pythagoras—well, he knew a little bit of arithmetic, but we are the kings, you know, and the gods in the nineteenth century." And it has led to something very beautiful, your civilization—the highest morality, to begin with.

Mr. B. Keightley: The whole point lies in this: as to the way you are going to set to work to build your hypothesis. Suppose you are hypothesis building, which I don't expect. I am quite sure, not by the physical senses, but by the use of strict logic and strict reasoning, you can form a basis of thought. If you look at Schopenhauer and read him carefully, and Hartmann and others, you will find that step-by-step they have come to the same bases of thought as have been adopted in India, particularly in the Vedantin system.

Mr. Kingsland: By the inductive method.

Mr. B. Keightley: No, though they pretended to do it by the inductive method. They started by an intuition. Schopenhauer got the idea, it came upon him like a flash. He then set to work, having got his hypothetical idea and started with the broad basis of facts. He got his facts together, and so, you reading his book are nicely led up to reach the point which came to him as a flash, but he did not get it by the inductive method. He says he did not.

Mme. Blavatsky: Every fact you get you do get by intuition, you get it by a flash.

Mr. B. Keightley: Every scientist of the nineteenth century, from the time science has become anything like science, has said the same thing, that he has made his great discoveries not by a system of classifying facts in the nice Baconian method, but by having the facts in his mind.

The Chairman: Darwin especially says so. He gives you the moment at which the idea first occurred to him, and it was in comparing some of the physical flora and fauna.

Mr. Kingsland: But they had been working for years, if the idea came to them apparently in the form of intuition—

The Chairman: But they might have been quite unconsciously working up to it in various ways. If you read what Darwin says himself, you will come to the same conclusion as I did, that the thing came to him almost as a finished idea.

Mme. Blavatsky: All of them come just in that way: intuitionally.

The Chairman: I cannot quote it, I wish I could, but I will turn it up.

Mme. Blavatsky: There is somewhere a book which says that all the greatest discoveries that have ever been made in the world came just like flashes of lightning, everything, even to the law of gravitation. How did Newton discover that? Through the apple.

Mr. Kingsland: If you have no knowledge of universals, how are you to proceed from universals to particulars? What knowledge of universals has this century, we will say? They have got no knowledge of the law of God, that is the highest ideal of the universe.

Mme. Blavatsky: A very high one, yes.

Mr. B. Keightley: But they have not carried out the canon which was laid down, that their ideas should be tried by strict logic.

Mr. Kingsland: Excuse me, Herbert Spencer does not.

Mme. Blavatsky: Herbert Spencer calls it the First Cause, and he calls it the Absolute and I will show it {to} you in his *First Principles*.[13] He calls the Absolute "the First Cause" in three lines. Well, the First Cause cannot be the Absolute because the First Cause is the first effect.

Mr. Kingsland: That only proves to me that a man who may be considered to be one who has the highest intellect has no knowledge

---

13 *First Principles* (1862) was the first volume of what would become a nine-volume work under the title of *A System of Synthetic Philosophy* covering biology, sociology, ethics and politics.

of universals.

Mme. Blavatsky: Because he has been made to study on your methods.

Mr. Kingsland: How can the poor fellow help that?

Mme. Blavatsky: You take Solomon Ben Judah,[14] the great philosopher, who was a Jew, one of the greatest men living, he whose works have been refused by the French Academy—I don't know what you call it, the French University. They proclaim them heretical, because they say he was an Aristotelian, and Aristotle was not then in odor of sanctity. This Aristotelian has more spirituality in him than any of the great men of science that I ever read about. Because he explains Kabalah just in the way that *The Secret Doctrine* would explain it. [The "Secret Doctrine" of the East]. In the most spiritual way he explains it, and yet he is called an Aristotelian, and why? Because he had an intuition. He is one of the greatest of the poets.

Mr. Kingsland: But you are not really answering my objection. There may be a man here and there who has this intuition, but the ordinary mortals who treat of our political economy, and our methods of improving our dwellings and all the rest of it, how can they obtain the knowledge of these particulars, when they have practically no idea of universals?

The Chairman: It seems to me that the real objection to the lines adopted by modern science lies in the fact that in every case when they make a so-called discovery, they jump at it. They go a long way ahead and argue downwards, and they are very often completely wrong. What I mean is this, most of their detail work comes after the idea of their main scheme has occurred to them, and they then make the details fit in if they won't do so of themselves. Instead of taking the logical test and commencing with universals and then

---

14 Eleventh century Spanish Jewish philosopher and poet, known also as Solomon ibn Gabirol or Avicebron. His works being interdicted by the University of Paris is mentioned in Isaac Myer's *Qabbalah*, 1888, p. 9.

seeing if it agrees with the particulars, they work backwards and they make the particulars agree with the false conception, and they won't permit anybody to start a little higher up and argue down to them, and according to their particulars. That is really why occultism and science are at loggerheads.

Mme. Blavatsky: The thing that they say is: "Oh! look at science; everything they have said is perfectly correct. Everything is brought there and the cases are shown and so on and they are dovetailed together"—I say because they are syllogisms. They began, if you please, by inventing a proposition; they will come to the conclusion that it is dovetailed, but it is not. That the first proposition is the correct one. It may be anything. I may come and say: "a horse has the head of a serpent, therefore all horses are with serpent's heads," and it would be a scientific proposition because I put it myself, which is perfectly incorrect.

The Chairman: You see, they, most of them, start with a universal, only it happens to be a negative.

Dr. Williams: I think Mr. Kingsland's point is this, that while it is a perfectly true principle, yet before the mind is open to receive universals, it must have facts as a basis for the universals, otherwise it could not exist.

Mme. Blavatsky: Well, mind being a microcosm, I suppose he would have some means of getting to the macrocosm.

Dr. Williams: It seems to me that the two go always hand in hand.

Mme. Blavatsky: I touch this thing. Why do I touch it? Because I have a hand. What makes the hand to move? Will power, whatever you like. From where does it come? Go and follow it out in that way, and if you follow from these particulars to your own universals, then after a few times you will be perfectly able to begin and take first the universals, and then having come to something, make your hand the head of it.

Dr. Williams: That is what I say: you first have to trace your hand

and from that you may predict many things; but you must have your facts first. If you begin with a child, you do not begin teaching him as the very first thing some universal fact, because you cannot.

Mr. Kingsland: You see, HPB blames the scientists of today. I instance Herbert Spencer as a man who has got as near the Absolute as any of our modern men, and she is down on him; if a man like he is so far wrong, what are all the rest of us to do?

Mme. Blavatsky: Shall I tell you, and give you good advice? Try to be a little less conceited, you men of science, that is the way to begin. Try not to think yourselves the only intelligences that have ever been developed in this universe and that all the rest are fools, and that the ancients did not know anything at all, and don't go and consult what the ancients said, because they study classics very well. How many ideas have I traced in your modern science which have never been acknowledged to their proper source and which were stolen bodily from ancient science? I could write, if they only took one of my articles, in one of your great reviews, I can assure you, and I would put them to shame. I have traced five or six modern inventions which I can trace as easily as you like to the old men of science who existed thousands of years ago.

The Chairman: There is a great deal in Lucretius.[15] Lucretius is full of modern science.

Mr. B. Keightley: I think the practical answer to your question is this: not to deny with quite such dead certain as your modern men do.

Mr. Kingsland: I do not say they could not find universals if they tried to look for them.

Mme. Blavatsky: Let them be agnostics, but don't let them be bigots.

---

15 Probably Titus Lucretius, the first century B.C. Roman poet known for *De rerum natura* (On the Nature of Things).

Mr. B. Keightley: You take a man like Huxley. The first thing he will say is: "I know that that is not so." You say to him anything—that, for instance, in every material thing we see there is a psychic side; in another way, that the thing exists on a different plane of consciousness. He will say, "I know that is not so" before you have got the words out of your mouth, almost.

Mme. Blavatsky: There is a man of science—and he is a great man of science in America—who pitches into me in the *American*.[16] He says it is all chaos, and he goes on and he is obliged to say: "Yes, it is true, but why does she show such animus to the men of science, if she quotes them?" But I quote them just to break their heads with the weapons furnished by the older men of science. He sends to us the most stupid things. He sends his journal in which he speaks about it. Some men of science who write in the journal wanted, it may be, that I should be exposed, but they only showed their own ignorance.

Mr. A. Keightley: Does not the difference between the men of science who talk about the particulars and you who talk about universals consist in this: that the man of science, as a general rule, depends purely upon his reason and his observation to deal with the facts of his physical consciousness? The practice of working from universals depends upon the intuition, which proceeds from a higher plane of consciousness, but as the man of science declines to admit anything but that which he can touch with his physical senses, he will insist on negativing anything else.

Mme. Blavatsky: He steps off from the platform of agnosticism, which is perfectly his right, but he has no right to come and dogmatize on his own plane of matter. If he said: "It is not the province of physical science to go beyond physicals; it may be, or it may not be on the physical; to every appearance it is so and so," then we should say: "Very well; we bow to you; you are a very great man; you find every faculty in the hind leg of a frog, and all sorts of things"; but why does he say: "There is nothing beyond that," and everyone who

---

16 Probably *Scientific American*.

comes and says beyond that there is knowledge he will come and pitch into? Mind you, I had a very great respect for science when I was in my green age, between twenty and thirty. The men of science were then my gods.

Dr. Williams: I do not think the great representative men of science take that ground. They did in the past, and there are some who occupy a lower sphere who do today. Spencer, for instance, whenever he is brought face to face with {a} thing which may be true or not true simply says, "it may be."

Mme. Blavatsky: But you take the best of them. He certainly is one of the greatest intellects; I do not mean to say at all because he says something flapdoodle somewhere that he is not a great man of science—he is. But when you say that Huxley does this thing or Tyndall,[17] or when you say any fellow of the Royal Society, I say no, I have seen a good many of them, and with the exception of Crookes and of Wallace[18] I never found one who would not call the other a madman. Do you suppose the others do not call Crookes a madman? They say: "He is cracked on one point." So they say about Wallace. Have they the right to say that of such a man of science, that he is cracked because he believes in things beyond matter? They have no such right at all.

Dr. Williams: I do not know what the smaller men say because I never care to read what they write.

Mme. Blavatsky: Look at Huxley; look at the tone of regret he adopts. Didn't they say that Zöllner[19] died a madman? Look at the French scientists, they all say he did. All the Germans say the same: "Softening of the brain." "He died in consequence of the fact that he happened to believe in the phenomenal form."

---

17 John Tyndall, Irish physicist and popular writer and lecturer on science, 1820-1893.
18 Alfred Russel Wallace, English naturalist, 1823-1913, who like William Crookes had advocated for a scientific investigation of spiritualism.
19 Johann Zöllner, German scientist, 1834-1882, who took an interest in trying to validate mediumistic phenomena and whose career suffered accordingly.

Mr. Kingsland: But that is something like blaming a schoolboy for not applying the calculus.

The Chairman: That is equivalent to saying that the scientists are deficient in principles.

Mr. B. Keightley: They are only that because they choose to make themselves so, and they choose deliberately to be dogmatic.

Mr. Kingsland: The best of them do not deal in dogmatic negatives.

Mme. Blavatsky: I do not know. Look at Huxley and such men. They deal greatly in dogmatic negatives. I do not call Tyndall a very great man of science. He is a popularizer and a compiler. I call Huxley a great man of science, and there is not one more bitter than Huxley, not one.

(These remarks closed the proceedings)

5.
The Theosophical Society.
Meeting held at Blavatsky Lodge
on February 7, 1889.

Mr. A. Keightley: Sloka 3, Stanza 2. "The hour had not yet struck; the ray had not yet flashed into the Germ; the Matri-Padma had not yet swollen." "The ray of the 'Ever-Darkness' becomes, as it is emitted, a ray of effulgent life or light, and flashes into the 'Germ'—the point in the Mundane Egg, represented by matter in its abstract sense." {Question} 1. Is the point in the Mundane Egg the same as the point in the circle—the unmanifested Logos?

Mme. Blavatsky: Never; the point in the circle is that which we call the unmanifested Logos. The manifested Logos is the triangle, and I have said it many times. Does not Pythagoras speak of the never manifested Monad which lives in solitude and darkness, which, when the hour strikes, radiates from itself number 1? This number 1, descending, produces number 2, and number 2, number 3, the three forming a triangle, the first full geometrical figure in the world of forms. It is this triangle which is the point in the Mundane Egg, and which, after gestating, starts from the egg and forms a triangle and not the point in the circle, for the point in the circle is the unmanifested Logos.

Mr. A. Keightley: That is what I thought.

Mme. Blavatsky: Brahmâ-Vâch-Vîraj in the Hindu philosophy, and it is Kether, Chochmah and Binah in the Sephirothal tree. The one Logos is the potential, the unrevealed cause; the other the actus, or in other words, the Monad evolving, from its invisible self, the active effect which in its turn becomes a cause on a lower plane. Now discuss the matter. Who has any objections? Collect your combativeness and go on, gentlemen. Has no one any objections to offer? Do ask, Mr. President.

The President: Well, in a sense, the second question bears upon it, because it illustrates, or at least it will settle the question, as to the exact plane of differentiation with which the whole of this Sloka is dealing as I take it. Ask the second question.

Mr. A. Keightley: 2. "What is the Ever-Darkness, in the sense used here?"

Mme. Blavatsky: Ever-Darkness means the ever-unknowable mystery, behind the veil even of the Logos.

Mr. A. Keightley: Parabrahm, in fact.

Mme. Blavatsky: Parabrahm; even the Logos can see only Mūlaprakriti. It cannot see that which is beyond the veil; that is the "Ever-Unknowable Darkness."

Mr. A. Keightley: What is the ray, then, in this connection?

Mme. Blavatsky: The plane of the circle whose face is blank {black} and whose point in the circle is white; but white figuratively, because certainly it has no colour. The first possible conception in our minds of the invisible Logos. Ever-Darkness is eternal and the ray is periodically flashed out of its central point through the germ. The ray is withdrawn back into the central point and the Germ grows into the second Logos, the triangle within the Mundane Egg. If you don't understand still, you just offer me any questions, and I will try to answer them.

The President: The difficulty we were all in when we were reading this Sloka the other day and considering it was, that we were doubtful whether it really referred to the same epoch of manifestation as the earlier portion, as the first Stanza, for instance.

Mme. Blavatsky: There is the beauty of these Stanzas, and I will tell you afterwards, later in the questions.

The President: I may say, I think most of these questions are intended to bring out this point, that is to say, whereabouts we are.

Mr. B. Keightley: Because the Mundane Egg seems to be really the third stage, at any rate not earlier than the third.

Mme. Blavatsky: The first stage is when the point appears within the dark circle, within that unknowable darkness.

The President: May I interrupt you for one moment—that point being the unmanifested Logos?

Mme. Blavatsky: Yes. The second stage is when, from that white point, proceeds the ray which darts and produces the first point, which in the Zohar is called Kether or Sephira, then produces Chochmah and Binah, the first triangle, which is the manifested Logos. And yet, from this manifested Logos will go the seven rays, which in the Zohar are called the lower Sephiroth, and which in our system are called, well, the Primordial Seven, from which there will proceed innumerable series of hierarchies. They simplify the thing and take simply the four planes and the worlds and so on. That is all. This does not explain anything.

Mr. Kingsland: What you say is that the triangle is what you here refer to as the Germ in the Mundane Egg?

Mme. Blavatsky: Yes.

Mr. B. Keightley: The Mundane Egg being used in a very much wider sense than that of terrestrial—being the Universal Egg, so to speak.

Mme. Blavatsky: There is the Universal Egg and the Solar Egg; they refer to it, and of course you must qualify it and say what it is.

Mr. B. Keightley: Abstract form is the same, whatever scale you take it on.

The President: Being the eternal feminine, really.

Mme. Blavatsky: No, no. There is no eternal female principle, and there is no eternal male principle. There is the potentiality of both in one only, a principle which cannot be even called spirit.

The President: Put it thus, then: abstract form being the first manifestation of the female principle.

Mme. Blavatsky: The first manifestation, not of the female principle, but of the ray, that proceeds from the central point, which is perfectly sexless; this ray produces first that which is the potentiality united of both sexes, but is not yet either male or female sex. That differentiation will come later when it falls into matter, when the triangle becomes a square. The first tetraktys.

The President: Then the Mundane Egg is as sexless as the ray?

Mme. Blavatsky: It is undifferentiated primordial matter.

The President: One is in the habit of associating matter with anything to which the name of female is applied.

Mme. Blavatsky: Matter certainly is female, because it is receptive of the ray of the sun which fecundates it, and this matter produces everything that is on its face; but that is quite a different thing. This is on the lowest plane.

The President: This is substance, rather than material.

Mr. B. Keightley: And substance is of no sex.

Mme. Blavatsky: Do you know what is matter? The synonym of matter is mother, and mother comes from matter, they are interchangeable.

Mr. A. Keightley: Then what I want to understand is this: You have the ray, which ultimately starts the manifested Logos, or the Germ within the Mundane Egg. Does the Mundane Egg exist, then, in any way, excepting potentiality, before this first triangular—if you may call it so—Germ is started by this ray?

Mme. Blavatsky: What is the egg, the Mundane Egg, or Universal Egg, call it whatever you like, whether on the principle of universality, or on the principle of a solar system? The egg means the ever-eternal, existing, undifferentiated matter, which is not strictly matter as we ordinarily use the term, but which, as we say, is the atoms. The atoms are indestructible; and matter is destructible in *form*, but the atoms are absolutely indestructible.

Mr. Gardner: Do you mean to say that the atoms are not yet crystallized?

Mme. Blavatsky: I do not speak about chemical atoms. I speak about the atoms of occultism, which certainly no chemist has ever seen. They are mathematical points. If you read about the Monads of Leibniz,[1] you will see what it is, this atom.

Mr. A. Keightley: Then may one say the Germ is the active point within the Alayic condition of substance?

Mme. Blavatsky: The Germ is simply a figurative way of speaking. The Germ is everywhere. Just as when one speaks of the circle whose centre and circumference is everywhere and nowhere; because, given the proposition that the circle is endless, surely it is infinite, and you cannot place the circumference anywhere, or put any centre to that which is limitless. It is simply a way of talking, just to bring to your conception something more clearly than you could otherwise imagine it. Just the same with the Germ. They call it the Germ, and the Germ is all the Germs, that is to say, the whole of Nature: the whole creative power that will emanate, that they call Brahmâ or any name you like, for on every plane it has got another name.

Mr. A. Keightley: Then you practically answer the third question. "What stage of manifestation is symbolized by the Mundane Egg?"

Mme. Blavatsky: I say the Mundane Egg is on the plane of

---

1 Gottfried Leibniz, German philosopher and polymath, 1646-1716. His 1714 work, *Monadologie*, outlined his thesis of the monad as the ultimate unit that is a free, independent agent.

differentiation, the first stage if you like; but from the plane of non-differentiation it is the third, as I just told you. The Egg represents the just differentiated cosmic matter in which the vital creative Germ receives its first spiritual impulse, and potentiality becomes potency. I think that is answered.

The President: Yes.

Mr. B. Keightley: That is a very good phrase, "potentiality becomes potency"; it just expresses the difference between the first and the second Stanzas.

Mme. Blavatsky: That is my difficulty, you see, I don't know English well enough to come and explain it to you.

Mr. A. Keightley: Question 4. "Is the Matri-Padma here spoken of the eternal or the periodical Egg?"

Mme. Blavatsky: The eternal, of course; it will become periodical only when the ray from Logos number one will have flashed from the latent Germ in the Matri-Padma, which, you understand, is the Egg, the womb of the universe, as it is called. You would not call eternal the physical germ in the female, but rather the latent spirit of the Germ concealed within the male cell in Nature. In all the creations of plants or animals, it is just the same. Take it on analogy or on the method of correspondence, it is just the same.

Mr. B. Keightley: Sloka 4. "But, as the hour strikes and it becomes receptive of the Fohatic impress of Divine Thought (the Logos or the male aspect of the Anima Mundi, Alaya)—its heart opens." Question 5: Does not "Fohatic impress of Divine Thought" apply to a later stage of differentiation, strictly speaking?

Mme. Blavatsky: Now look here, this involves a very difficult answer. I wish you would give all your attention to it. Understand once for all, for if you understand clearly this thing, it will prevent your putting many, many questions which are perfectly useless, and you will understand them better also. You see, I have explained to you as well as I can, now try and correct me, if you please, if I don't explain clearly. They want to say that Fohat is a later manifestation. Very well. I answer that Fohat is, as a full-blown force or entity, a later development. Fohatic as an adjective may be used in any sense, Fohat as a noun springs from a Fohatic attribute. Do you understand this now? No electricity will be developed or generated from something where there is no electric power. But before electricity, or a certain kind of electricity, is developed, you can speak about the electric impulse and electric impress, cannot you? I say Fohatic, because Fohatic has got a special meaning in the esoteric teaching; and I will first give you the meaning here. It comes afterwards, you know. The Divine Principle is eternal and gods are periodical.

Mr. B. Keightley: In other words, the Fohatic principle—to translate it into a different term—the Fohatic principle is eternal, but Fohat is an entity or a god.

Mme. Blavatsky: Or, as a synthesis of this force on our plane of differentiation, it is periodical and is limited, and it comes later.

The President: The Fohatic principle produces Fohat instead of arising from it.

Mme. Blavatsky: It is the Śakti or Force of the Divine. Fohat and Brahmâ are all one thing. They are various aspects of the Divine Mind.

Mr. B. Keightley: Have you written nothing more about that there?

Mme. Blavatsky: Not here. It is too easy a thing to write anything about. It comes in the next question.

Mr. A. Keightley: "In the commentary on Stanza 2, is it not your aim to convey some idea of the subject by speaking of the correspondences on a much later stage of evolution? For instance, is not 'Fohat' in the sense used here the synthesis of the primordial seven, and therefore appearing at a much later stage than that of the first manifestation of the Alaya?"

Mme. Blavatsky: It is so, most assuredly; but then you were told more than once that the commentaries busy themselves but with the evolution of our solar system in this book. The beauty and the wisdom of the Stanzas are in this, that they may be interpreted on seven different planes, the last reflecting in its grossly differentiated aspect, and copying on the universal law of correspondences, or analogy, all that it sees before in the beginning. Every plane is a reflection and a copy of another plane. As it took place in the definite, undifferentiated plane, so it took place on the second, on the third, on the fourth, and so on. Now these Stanzas represent all of them, and the student who understands well the gradual development, so to speak, and the progressive order of things, will understand perfectly to which it applies. If we talk about the higher divine world, we shall talk just in the same way, because in *The Secret Doctrine* that I give to the world and to your great critics, I certainly give it as applied to the solar system, and even this they do not understand. They call it idle talk, so why shall I go and bother my brains to go into something more on the higher plane? This is not for the profane, let us make a difference, we must draw a line of demarcation somewhere.

Mr. Forsyth: Then are we to understand, Madame, that the whole of the writing in *The Secret Doctrine* has reference only to the solar system, as we understand the solar system?

Mme. Blavatsky: It has reference to that chiefly. The second volume is simply the development of life on our earth, not even in the solar system, for the thing is so tremendous that it would require 100 volumes to write all this. Sometimes I make remarks about larger questions, but as a whole the exposition begins and ends on this earth and with the development of life from the first day of Manvantara. You see how they are confused even on this terrestrial plane; so what would it be if I mixed up the evolution of life on Neptune, or beyond the solar system? Why, they would not understand a word. The esoteric doctrine teaches all that, but then it is not in a few months you can learn. You have to study for 20 or 30 years, and according to your capacity it will be given to you, because a man may be spirit-blind just as he is colour-blind on this plane, and I know unfortunately too many of those who are perfectly spirit-blind.

The President: But yet the Stanzas up to the point we have reached them do deal with the awakening from the Pralaya.

Mme. Blavatsky: Most assuredly; but after that, when I come and say that so many Stanzas are left out, then it begins with the solar system.

The President: That is really the point I wanted to get at, whether the second Stanza was still entirely dealing with that awakening from the Maha Pralaya. We have not come to the point you mention yet, have we?

Mme. Blavatsky: Certainly not, but as it deals with this awakening on all the planes, you can apply it to any plane, because one covers the other.

The President: Because, we are feebly and vaguely attempting to apply it to the highest plane of which we have the faintest idea.

Mr. B. Keightley: There is also this, that the Stanzas deal with the abstract, and the commentaries are applied more particularly to the solar system.

Mme. Blavatsky: But the Stanzas contain seven meanings, and every one of them may be applied to the highest, and the second, the third, and so on to the seventh plane of matter. But certainly I speak more about the four lower planes. As you will see there, when we come to the part about the moon and the evolution of the stars and so on, there I speak more about the solar system. I limit myself to that in the commentaries. Not in the Stanzas, because I have rendered them just as they are.

Mr. Kingsland: I think we are making a little mistake in this way. Instead of following the process entirely out on the first plane, and then taking it on to the lowest plane, we are supposing it takes place on the higher plane, and we immediately jump down on the lower, instead of following the whole process on one plane.

Mme. Blavatsky: Perfectly so; but it did not begin on a Thursday, and it won't end on a Thursday. The creation began on Monday, didn't it—because Sunday is the day of rest?

Mr. B. Keightley: Because he took his day off on Sunday.

Mme. Blavatsky: Sabbath breaking, I call it.

The President: No, Sabbath is Saturday.

Mme. Blavatsky: You call it Sabbath, it is no fault of mine. Well, then, we will go on. Moreover, you have to learn the etymology of the word Fohat. There is where it becomes difficult to understand. It is a Turanian compound word. "Pho" is the word. "Pho" was once and is derived from the Sanskrit "bhu," meaning existence, or rather the essence of existence. Now, "Swayambhū" is Brahmâ and man at the same time. "Swayambhū" means self-existence and self-existing; it means also Manvantara. It means many, many things according to the sense in which you take it, and one must know exactly whether the accent is on the "m" or on the "u", or where it is, for therein lies the difference. Take "bhu." It means earth, our earth. Take "Swayambhū." It means divine breath, self-existence, that which is everlasting, the eternal breath. To this day in China, Buddha is called "Pho."

A Lady: Is not the first meaning, breath?

Mme. Blavatsky: It is not. It is self-essence. It is very difficult for me to translate it to you. Look at the Sanskrit dictionaries. They will give you 100 etymologies, and they won't know what it is. It is existence, it is self-evolution, it is earth, it is spirit, everything you like. It depends on the accent, and how it is placed. That is a very difficult thing. In this sense, certainly it comes from bhu and sva. Now, they don't pronounce the "b" generally, it is "Pho", which is bhu or Budha, which means wisdom. Fohat comes from Mahat, and it is the reflection of the Universal Mind—the synthesis of all the seven and the intelligences of all the seven creative builders or kosmocratores. Hence the word, you understand—for life and electricity are one in our philosophy. I told you, I think, Mr. Kingsland, that they say life is electricity, and the one life is simply the essence and the root of all the electric phenomena that you have in this world on this manifested plane.

The President: If "Sat" is the potentiality of being, "Pho" is the potency of being—the very next thing.

Mme. Blavatsky: That is very good. Just repeat it.

The President: If "Sat" is the potentiality of being, "Pho" is the potency of being itself, the next to "Sat."

Mme. Blavatsky: That is so, and it is a very good definition indeed.

Mr. A. Keightley: Can you explain more fully the process by which Horus or any other god is born *through* and not *from* an immaculate source? Can you render in clearer language the distinction between "through" and "from" in this sense? The only explanation given is rendered in the unintelligible mathematics of the *Source of Measures*.[2]

Mme. Blavatsky: If mathematics is unintelligible, what can my poor, unfortunate English teach you better? Because mathematics alone can express that which it is impossible to express in words, in such poor words as mine are.

Mr. B. Keightley: I think I should prefer your words to the mathematics.

Mme. Blavatsky: That is a compliment, of course.

Mr. B. Keightley: I quite agree with it.

Mme. Blavatsky: The author of the *Source of Measures* is a very great Kabbalist. I have got a very great regard for him, and he is one of my pupils, and he knows a thousand times more than I do. In mathematics I am the biggest fool that ever was created. Two and two will seem to me five. I labored under the impression that 5 times

2 *The Key to the Hebrew-Egyptian Mystery in the Source of Measures*, Cincinnati, 1875, by James Ralston Skinner, 1830-1893.

7 was 28.

Mr. Kingsland: Then do not be surprised if we cannot make anything of it.

Mme. Blavatsky: I get mixed up sometimes on this plane, but you have not got always to pull yourselves down by the tail as I have. I have got my own region. Now listen to this, and I will try to give it as well as I can. On the first plane of differentiation there is no sex, but both sexes exist potentially in the primordial matter, as I have before explained to you. Now that mother which I just told you was the same as matter is not fecundated by any act in space and time, but fertility or protectiveness {productiveness?} is inherent in it. Therefore, that which emanates or is born out of that inherent virtue is not born *from* but *through* it. That is to say, that virtue is the sole cause that the something manifests through it as a vehicle, whereas on the physical plane the mother is not the active cause but the passive effect, rather, and the agent of an independent cause. Now listen: even in speaking of the mother of their God, Christians will show her first fecundated by the Holy Ghost and say Christ is born from her, whereas Christ is not born "from" but "through" her. Lightning may manifest itself through a board, pass through it, but the chip of wood from the hole made by the thunderbolt proceeds from the wood plank. Do you see the difference? "From" implies and necessitates a limited and conditioned object *from* which it can start, *from* which something starts, this act having to take place in space and time. "Through" applies to eternity as much as to anything else, as much as to something limited. The Great Breath, for instance, thrills *through* space, which is endless, and is "*in*" not "*from*" eternity. Do you understand the difference?

Mr. Kingsland: Would not a good illustration be the case of a ray of light passing through a crystal and becoming seven colours? You say it is an immaculate medium?

Mme. Blavatsky: It is an immaculate medium. It is not that this medium is fecundated, it is not that, it passes through, it is the vehicle, therefore the Matri-padma; the first scene is called born from an immaculate matter, which is the root of the immaculate conception in the Christian religion, because it is taken from that the immaculate matter. He is not born *from* her but *through* her, and Christians if they understand well their own dogmas would not say he is born *from* the Virgin Mary, but *through* her, if they wish to make an incarnation of Jesus; there is the great difference. But, for instance, the Roman Catholics have materialized the idea in such a way that they positively made a goddess of her, and drag her at the same time in the mud; and made of her a simple woman, instead of explaining. They don't preserve the original idea. They do not say, as they should, that she was such a virtuous woman that she was chosen to be the mother of that in which God incarnated. But by saying she is a goddess, they imply a false idea, and that they do consider her as a goddess is shown by their adoration. And as a goddess, what merit has she got? No merit at all. She need be neither virtuous, good, bad, nor indifferent. It is supposed that she gives birth to gods. I say the religions have materialized this divine abstract conception in the most terribly materialistic way. Speaking of spirituality, there is nothing more materialistic and coarse in this world than the religions, Christian, Brahmanical, anything—except the Buddhist, which is not a religion but a philosophy. They have all dragged down divinity to the lowest depths of degradation. Instead of trying and rising to a divinity, they try to drag down the Logos, just as in America I have seen the negroes in Methodist Churches get into such a state of excitement that they will jump up and do all kinds of things, and then with their umbrellas they will try to catch Jesus and say, Come here, Jesus! Come here, Jesus! It is positive blasphemy. I have seen it once, and it disgusted me.

Mr. Forsyth: And they fall down on the floor.

Mme. Blavatsky: Oh! You have seen it too. I am very glad you can corroborate my statement.

Mr. Forsyth: Yes, they fall down and foam at the mouth.

Mme. Blavatsky: Now comes a question, gentlemen, a strange question, a mathematical one.

Mr. A. Keightley: "How does the triangle become the square; and how does the square become the six-faced cube?"

Mme. Blavatsky: In occult Pythagorean geometry, the tetrad is said to combine within itself all the materials of which Cosmos was produced[3]; that is the Pythagorean rule. The point or 1 extends to a line that make 2, the line to a superficies, 3; the superficies or triad or triangle is converted into a solid or 4 or the tetrad, by the point being placed over it.

Mr. B. Keightley: A pyramid, it is a four-pointed figure.

Mr. Kingsland: It is a four-sided figure.

The President: It is a four-sided figure.

Mr. ———: Is it pyramidical?

Mme. Blavatsky: Yes, but it must have something on it. We will see how it is transformed into the pentagon and the pentagon into the six. The square becomes after that a cube, and so on.

Mr. A. Keightley: But a pyramid is not a square.

Mme. Blavatsky: The base of it is.

The President: No, it is a triangle turned into a pyramid.

Mme. Blavatsky: Excuse me, there are four faces. My dear sir, I don't speak to you about the figures. They asked me about the square. They do not speak about the cube here, they speak about the cube afterwards.

Mr. Kingsland: Isn't it built on a square, and then it becomes the four things.

Mr. Gardner: The four sides coming up to the apex.

---

3 *Transactions*, p. 88 reads: "…from which Kosmos is produced".

The President: You may have a three-faced pyramid.

Mme. Blavatsky: I don't speak here of that, it will come later. You can take Pythagoras by the beard if you can get him.

Mr. Kingsland: Do you mean a triangle becomes a tetraktys?

Mme. Blavatsky: I say it becomes the tetraktys because matter is square always. It is always a plane square, and once that the triangle falls into it, you have the seven. Allow me a pencil and I will draw it for you. There is the triangle, and it is inscribed between four lines.

Mr. B. Keightley: We shall see as we go on. You get a plane square, then the moment you add another point, a fifth point outside that, you get your pyramid or square-based pyramid.

Mr. Kingsland: We want to know how you get your square, first.

Mr. ——: How do you get from the triangle to the square?

Mme. Blavatsky: I can't show it to you, but in mathematics it exists. It is not on this plane of matter that you can square the circle. We know what it means to square the circle, but the men who spent years trying to square the circle are shut up in lunatic asylums. On this plane you cannot think of squaring the circle, but we can. It is quite a different thing.

The President: Eliphas Lévi[4] takes it in this way: he takes the first eternal as representing the triangle, and the synthesis of the three forming a fourth point; but I don't see myself how that brings one any nearer to matter. I think he puts it that way in his works. Does he not?

Mr. B. Keightley: The point becomes the line two, the line becomes a plane superficies three, then you have the triangle or the first plane figure.

Mme. Blavatsky: And the superficies or triangle is converted into a solid of four, or the tetrad, by the point being placed over it.

---

4 Pen name of Alphonse Louis Constant, French occult writer, 1810-1875.

Mr. B. Keightley: Then that is the triangular pyramid.

Mme. Blavatsky: But then it becomes again another thing to make the cube out of the square. It will become a triangular pyramid, but it will come on the base of the square.

The President: At the same time, what one wanted to get at was that the first four stages ought to have produced, and according to that process did produce four dimensions—if you take the point, line, superficies, and solid, you have 1, 2, 3, and 4. But, of course, if you take the ordinary plane square, you are simply altering a mathematical figure, still of the same dimensions.

Mme. Blavatsky: You can't understand the thing unless you have this conception very clearly in your mind: that the first real figure that you can conceive of and that can be produced in this world of ours is a triangle. The point is no figure at all, nor the "2," for which the Pythagoreans had the greatest contempt, because it cannot form any figure. You can do nothing with them, you cannot make of two lines a figure. The first one then is the triangle, and this is taken as a symbol of the first manifested Logos; the first in this world of manifestation. I think this is as plain as can be.

The President: And further; the first possible solid is the four-sided figure with four angles, four sides, each plane side contained by three lines. It is not the square, it is the pyramid; it is the three-sided pyramid.

Mme. Blavatsky: {Sephira?} which is the point by itself {Kether?} produces, or is one.[5] It goes to the left or the right, it produces Chochmah, the wisdom. He makes this plane, which is a horizontal plane of matter, and produces intelligence, Binah, or the Mahat, and then returns back into the first. There are the four, if you like. It is not the concrete quaternary; I don't know these names. It is still the tetraktys, and this is called the Tetragrammaton in the Kabalah. It is called that, because it is the first thing. The triangle falling into

---

5 See p. 131 and *Transactions*, p. 84.

matter, or standing on matter, makes the four, that is to say, spirit, matter, male and female. That is the real significance of it. This number contains both the productive and {the} produced numbers; this is why it is sacred. Now, it is the spirit, will, and intellect which form the triangle animating the four lower principles, and then come the seven principles which we speak of in Theosophy. They are the same that Pythagoras spoke about, the seven properties in man, and even the Rosicrucians took it. The square becomes the cube when each point of the triangle becomes dual, male and female. The Pythagoreans said once 1, twice 2, and there ariseth a tetrad having on its top the highest unity, which becomes the pyramid whose base is a plane tetrad; divine light resting on it makes the abstract cube. Now take six solid or concrete squares, they make a cube, don't they? And the cube unfolded gives you the cross or the vertical four, barred by the horizontal three. Four here and three will make seven, because you count again the central square, as you know (I have given it in *The Secret Doctrine*), making our seven principles or the Pythagorean seven properties in man. And this is the cross, the symbol of Christianity, which is the vertical male and the horizontal female. It is spirit and matter, and at the same time it is the most phallic symbol there is.

Mr. B. Keightley: Isn't that rather excluded, because the vertical is four, while the horizontal is three?

Mme. Blavatsky: My dear sir, that which is above is itself below, but the below is seen as in a looking glass reversed. I told you it is four and divine; on the divine plane it becomes four, and material on the plane of matter, for matter is four also. That which is three and divine here is, for instance, the three higher principles in man becoming the nothing yet. It is nothing yet, it is simply the first thing which will become something. You must always take this, that it will be reversed and will be like the reflection in the looking glass, for your right arm will appear to you your left.

Mr. B. Keightley: Therefore you get your three and your four interchanged.

Mme. Blavatsky: Just so.

Mr. B. Keightley: Question 9: "What is meant by Astral Light in the middle paragraph of page 60?"

Mme. Blavatsky: It means an infernal misprint of the printer, who just put "has" instead of "lies," and also carelessness of the bright but not quick-eyed editors. They just ask in the most innocent way what it means. It means an infernal mistake of the printer and an oversight on your part for which I ought to have skinned you if I had seen it.

Mr. B. Keightley: You saw the proofs too; you are in the same boat.

Mme. Blavatsky: Read it; see if it has any sense.

Mr. A. Keightley: (reads the passage: *Secret Doctrine*, vol. 1, p. {60}.)

Mr. B. Keightley: That *has* means *lies*, that is what it is.

Mr. A. Keightley: But "has" has distinctly a meaning.

Mme. Blavatsky: It has not, because Astral Light expands. What is "has," then, if you please?

The President: You can say a thing has something between it and another thing.

Mr. Forsyth: What do you wish to say then, madam?

Mme. Blavatsky: I would say it expands. It is a misprint, I can assure you. Look at my manuscript.

Mr. Forsyth: I would like you to think of a word and let us know decidedly what word it is.

Mme. Blavatsky: If they say it is correct, they are English and I am not.

The President: "Is spread." It has that meaning to me.

Mme. Blavatsky: Will you kindly read this, Mr. Forsyth, because I take it for a misprint, and I know I would never put this sentence.

Mr. B. Keightley: You would often say this room has a door between it and the next.

Mme. Blavatsky: But there is nothing there relative to "has."

Mr. B. Keightley: The Tetragrammaton.

Mr. Forsyth: "Has" means possession.

The President: We did not ask that question.

Mme. Blavatsky: What is meant by Astral Light is explained in questions 10 and 11. Why are you so very impatient, all of you?

Mr. Kingsland: I don't think we misunderstood the meaning of that.

Mme. Blavatsky: Oh you are very, very pundit-like, all of you.

The President: I don't understand what it means, but I understand what you mean to convey.

Mme. Blavatsky: What can be meant by Astral Light? The Astral Light is the great deceiver.

Mr. B. Keightley: We seem to have gone suddenly from the stage of the first manifested Logos, and landed ourselves on the other side of the plane of Astral Light and Tetragrammaton.

Mme. Blavatsky: Now, what do you mean? Allow me. "Thus is repeated on earth the mystery enacted, according to the seers, on the divine plane." (continues reading from passage in *The Secret Doctrine*.) That is to say, the second Logos becomes a Tetragrammaton, the triangle and the four. I think it is as plain as can be. "It is now in the 'Lap of Maya' or illusion and between itself and the Reality HAS the Astral Light," etc. Now, why did you come and pitch into me in my old age and dishonour me? I believe this thing is the most clear of all the blessed paragraphs that are here in the book. Is it, or not? I put it to the justice of those here. You see how I am ill-treated.

Mr. Forsyth: It is a shame, madam. I think your interpretation, "lies" in place of "has," has a somewhat different meaning to the general reader. It certainly to me has a slightly different meaning.

Mme. Blavatsky: Maybe it is more English, but I would not put it.

Mr. Forsyth: If you put it in classic English, "has" is strictly a matter of possession.

Mme. Blavatsky: I suppose they understand it just as it is. What is it Mr. Kingsland just proceeded to scold me for?

Mr. Kingsland: I do not think it has been perfectly made clear yet how the three becomes the four.

The President: Yes, I think it has. I think the explanation of that is that the "four" really and truly means what we call the third dimension of space, and consequently is Maya—the Tetragrammaton, in one sense. You mean a different sort of four, and if it can do that, obviously there is Maya and the highest triangle. It answers itself, that use of the pyramid to explain the four.

Mme. Blavatsky: Just so.

Mr. Kingsland: Is the Astral Light used there in the sense of Maya?

Mme. Blavatsky: Most assuredly. When you come there to a certain passage where I speak of the seven principles and the moon and all that, I show there are only four planes, that the three which are above do not belong to our terrestrial chain or to the chain of any planet. You do not know anything about it. You can't speculate. I am not a high adept. I am a poor old woman very ill-treated here. We speak only of the four planes that we can conceive.

Mr. B. Keightley: We apologize to you, but the explanation of the whole thing is the pyramid.

The President: It explains it all, because we get in that four what we could not see at all, the third dimension of space, and consequently Maya. One is apt to look on the Tetragrammaton as above Maya.

Mme. Blavatsky: Did you read my article in *The Theosophist* on the Tetragrammaton?[6] The Kabbalists say something else, but in my sight the Tetragrammaton is not very high. I have been just answering Mr. Subba Row. He said: "How can it be seven principles?" I said: "I am not going to worship the Tetragrammaton. I do not see why I should. I do not worship differentiated things." "I know only of the Absolute and perfectly homogeneous. I can invent for myself any kind of conceptions and flapdoodles." The tetraktys by which the Pythagoreans swore was quite a different kind of tobacco, if you please, quite another thing. You just take the third chapter of Genesis and the beginning of the fourth and you find there the Tetragrammaton. You find Eve and Adam and Jehovah, who becomes Cain. That is what you find. There is the Tetragrammaton. That is the first one which is symbolized. Then comes at the end of the fourth chapter already the human conception, and there is Enoch and there is Seth, and to him was born a son, Enos. And it is written in the real Jewish scrolls, "From that time man began to be male and female," and they have translated it in the authorized—James's version—"From that time man began to call upon the Lord." I ask you if you can translate it like that, when in the real Hebrew you see men began to be called "Jod-he-vah." That is always so, you know. They say one thing in the Hebrew scriptures and they translate it as another. They do not take into consideration the fact that the people had all symbolical and figurative language. Then they will never come and see this difference: it is always "Lord God," or "God," or "Jehovah" and all that, nothing else, and even "Jehovah" says to Moses that he never was called by the name Jehovah. Centuries and thousands of years before that there is Abraham, who builds an altar to "Jehovah." Is it so, or not?

The President: In the revised version, they translate Elohim as "Lord" in the first chapter.

Mme. Blavatsky: They have no right to translate Elohim as "God" in the singular. It means "Lords" and "Gods." Everything there is in

---

6 Blavatsky, "Tetragrammaton," *The Theosophist*, November 1887, pp. 104-116.

the plural. They cannot go against the facts. They translate Abel and say it is the "son of Eve." I say fiddlesticks! I say it was a daughter of Eve for Abel is the female aspect of Cain. When they separate, the first separation is shown in the first verse of the fourth chapter, when Cain was born unto Eve, and she said there, it is translated: "I have gotten a man from the Lord," though it doesn't mean this. It means what Ralston Skinner showed perfectly; it means Jehovah, male and female kind. Abel comes afterwards and is female, and then comes the separation of sexes. And then they say he kills Abel, and he doesn't kill him at all—he marries him. That is the whole of it. I am obliged to tell you these things, if you are to learn. History is history and facts are facts.

Mr. A. Keightley: How does Astral Light come between Tetragrammaton and "reality"?

Mme. Blavatsky: How do I know? It is there. That is answered.

Mr. A. Keightley: What is "reality" in this context?

Mme. Blavatsky: That which has neither form, colour, limitation, attributes, nothing. A number that is nothing, it is all; it is the Absolute. Now, this, if I have not said it 120 times, I have not said it once.

The President: The whole of these questions have arisen out of a misunderstanding of the word Tetragrammaton. Now I think we understand what Tetragrammaton is.

Mr. B. Keightley: It is simply humanity, as far as I know it. Man.

Mme. Blavatsky: No, it is rather different—I do not call it so. It is Malkhut, when the bridegroom comes to the bride on earth; then it becomes humanity.

Mr. B. Keightley: After the separation.

Mme. Blavatsky: The seven lower Sephiroth must be all passed through. The Tetragrammaton becomes more and more material.

Mr. B. Keightley: And then after the separation he is completely Tetragrammaton.

Mme. Blavatsky: Then he becomes an M.P. or a Grand Master of all the Masons.

Mr. Kingsland: In one sense the Astral Light is between the four lower planes and the three higher ones.

Mme. Blavatsky: Between Tetraktys and Tetragrammaton there is an immense difference. The difference is because Pythagoras swore by the Tetraktys of the invisible Monad, which comes and having produced the first point and the second and the third retires afterwards into the darkness and everlasting silence, i.e., into that of which we cannot know anything. It is the first Logos, and this is the Tetraktys. There is the point. The point comes, that is 1. He produces the first point, the second, third, and fourth. Or if you take it from the point of matter, there is the horizontal plane of the triangle and there is the second side, the third and the point. Eliphas Lévi says many things to which certainly I will never consent, and he knew very well he was bamboozling the public. He simply laughed at people.

The President: At the same time he gives that idea of the formation of the four, inasmuch as he suggests it is the first triangle and the synthesis of it. You may perfectly well take the Monad which forms the 1, the 2, the 3 and retires into the darkness. At any rate it is not a great extension of the idea, and therefore I say he is really describing the tetraktys.

Mme. Blavatsky: And I just showed it to you. You take the point in the circle and you proceed and make a triangle from the lower point and take the plane of matter and you proceed like that, it becomes the reverse. He takes it on a lower plane.

Mr. B. Keightley: That is how the confusion has arisen in our minds. Eliphas Lévi is speaking of the tetraktys as the Tetragrammaton.

Mme. Blavatsky: In the preliminary rules to the Esoteric Section[7] I said: "please, all those who want to study the eastern esoteric science, have the kindness not to belong to any society except the Masonic societies, which are perfectly harmless, to the Masonic societies or to the Odd Fellows, but you must not belong to any of the occult societies, that teach you after the western methods." Very well; this morning I received an insult. Mr. Westcott[8] writes to me and says: "I am a fellow of the Theosophical Society, and am I going to be blackmailed and sent like a black sheep out of the fold because I have belonged to a society." I said: "My dear fellow, I have got nothing to do with you. You don't belong to my Esoteric Section; you are welcome to belong to anything you like." Now you see the enormous confusion it produces in you, simply because you have read Eliphas Lévi. What shall it be with others who study in other societies, which will go and say that the Tetragrammaton is the highest divinity? You will have such a confusion that you will never learn anything of the one or the other, and the consequence will be that you will be in the most fearful state of confusion. I said you may belong to the Masonic societies, but not to the occult societies. I am perfectly sure I have got enough to do. Whether there are 300 members or 30, I don't care. It will be useless trouble to teach and teach and find they won't understand it.

The President: We have no more formal business tonight.

---

7 HPB founded the Esoteric Section in London, October 1888, as an inner section of the Theosophical Society for those wanting to make a greater commitment to the movement.
8 William Wynn Westcott, 1848-1925, Freemason, hermeticist, and one of the founders in 1888 of the occult group, the Hermetic Order of the Golden Dawn.

6.
The Theosophical Society.
Meeting of the Blavatsky Lodge,
Thursday, February 14, 1889.

Mr. Kingsland (in the absence of Mr. Harbottle) took the Chair.

Mr. A. Keightley: The first verse, Stanza 3. "The last vibration of the seventh eternity thrills through infinitude. The Mother swells, expanding from within without like the bud of the lotus." (Commentary, the first three sentences.[1]) Question 1. Does the commencement of time as distinguished from Duration correspond to the appearance of the second or manifested Logos?

Mme. Blavatsky: Is it the first question, this?

Mr. A. Keightley: Yes.

Mme. Blavatsky: You see, it was not there. I answer the question which was written there. It doesn't seem to meet it. You say: "How is it that the mother swells," and so on, if there is a difference between Duration and time, or to what time it corresponds, to what period? That is the question isn't it?

Mr. A. Keightley: (reads question again.)

Mme. Blavatsky: Certainly it does not correspond, because you see that when the Mother swells, it is a good proof that the differentiation has set in; and while, when Logos number one radiates through primordial or undifferentiated matter in Laya, there is no action in chaos. Thus there is a great difference between those. There is no time at this stage. There is no time. There is neither space nor time when the first thing begins, and it is all in space and time once

---
1 *The Secret Doctrine*, I:62.

it is differentiated. The last vibration of the seventh eternity is the first one announcing dawn, and it is this last vibration which is the synonym of the unmanifested Logos at the time of the primordial radiation. It is Father-Mother, potentially; and when the second Logos emanates the third, has it become the Virgin Mother: then only. Do you understand the difference?

Mr. A. Keightley: I understand the difference between these two, but I do not see how it applies to time and Duration.

Mme. Blavatsky: When the first Logos appears, there is neither time nor space. Duration is always; it is eternal; but there is neither time nor space; it is outside time and space. This last, seventh vibration means just the same as if it was said: the first Logos radiated. That is to say, the ray emanated from the Absolute—or radiated rather, because nothing emanates from the Absolute. Therefore, this term, the last vibration of the seventh eternity, applies to the moment or period, whatever it is, when the first Logos appears, when the first light appears. Therefore it is certainly not the time of the second Logos.

Mr. B. Keightley: The question as put there was whether time appears; whether you can speak of time from the moment when the second Logos, the unmanifested-manifested Logos, appears.

Mme. Blavatsky: Most assuredly, because then time begins. It is what he told me that made me answer, because I could not understand your question when I read it first. I thought you meant that the word "time" could not be applied to the seventh vibration, or you mixed up the first and the second Logos. It was written in a way that I could not understand. Certainly there is an immense space of time between the two. One is just at the last moment when it ceases to be outside of time and space, and the second is when space and time begin—periodical time.

Mr. B. Keightley: Space and time as periodical manifestations begin with the second Logos.

Mme. Blavatsky: When it is said the Mother swells like the lotus or the bud, it means that it has begun already—because it could not have happened before. Before there is no action possible and no quality applied to anything. It is impossible to see it here, at least in our philosophy. The divine ray, Logos number one, is the abstract parent, while Logos number two is at the same time his mother's son and her husband. Now, if you go and study the cosmogonies and the theogonies of all the peoples you will find in the Egyptian, in the Indian and the Chaldean, everywhere, that the second Logos, the creative Logos, is spoken of as his mother's husband and his mother's son. Now, for instance, Osiris is the son and husband of Isis, and Horus is the son and the husband and the father too. It is all interchangeable. Just the same with Brahmâ; Brahmâ is the father, the husband and the son of Vach. You understand the difference—when he differentiates.

Mr. A. Keightley: That is to say, that the first differentiation is everything, practically.

Mme. Blavatsky: Most assuredly. It is only on the second plane that this Mother becomes the Virgin Mother, because before that it has no qualification, none whatever, no adjective.

Mr. Kingsland: In other words, you would say there is no differentiation with the first Logos. The differentiation only begins with the second, and therefore the first Logos is outside of time and space, and time and space begin with the second.

Mr. A. Keightley: The second question refers to the words: "One is the abstraction or noumenon of infinite time (Kala)." Is this the "Duration" referred to in Stanza 1: "Time...lay asleep in the infinite bosom of Duration," or is it the potentiality of time?

Mme. Blavatsky: I have been just explaining it. Duration has always potential time in it, in itself. Duration is Eternal time which had neither beginning nor end. Time is something, and that is why they say in the eastern philosophy, "Time is the son of Duration, its child."

Mr. A. Keightley: Yes, exactly.

Mme. Blavatsky: Infinite time.

Mr. A. Keightley: At once with the second Logos you proceed out of Duration into time, and time is therefore periodical, while Duration is eternal.

Mme. Blavatsky: Just so, as I have just been saying. Periodical time is the child of eternal Duration. Well, has anyone questions to ask? Let them ask, if they have anything, because after that it won't be understood again. Have you anything to ask, Mr. Kingsland?

Mr. Kingsland: No, I think I have not.

Mr. Scott-Elliot: You mentioned radiation and emanation. One has never any distinct idea. What is the difference between radiation and emanation?

Mme. Blavatsky: Enormous. Radiation is the unconscious action, so to say, of something from which something radiates, but emanation is—well, it supposes already something that emanates out itself consciously. Now radiation can come from the Absolute; emanation cannot. Nothing can emanate from it.

Mr. Scott-Elliot: Radiation comes from the Absolute.

Mme. Blavatsky: Yes, the first radiation, when the Logos radiates. The first ray, that of which it is said in the Bible: "Let there be Light, and Light was."[2] The first divine light, this is radiation. It radiates; but emanating means emanating one from the other—how shall I say—from one being to another being, that is the difference. I make this difference because I do not know how to translate it in any other way. We have a word for it in the occult language, but it is impossible to translate it into English.

Mr. Scott-Elliot: Then there is a closer connection between that which has emanated and that from which it emanates than there is

---

2 Genesis, 1:3

between that which radiates and that from which the radiation takes place.

Mme. Blavatsky: No. You see, the radiation—if it radiates, it is sure, sooner or later, to be withdrawn again. Emanation emanates and may run into other emanations and it is separated; that is a different thing. It may be, of course, that at the end of the cycle of times it will also be withdrawn into the one Absolute, but meanwhile, during the cycle of changes and the cycle of change of forms, this will be an emanation, and it is in my mind the same as evolution—of course, in another sense, but it is exactly the same thing. One thing evolves from the other and one thing emanates from the other, with the change of forms and substance and so on.

Mr. A. Keightley: Number 3. Page 63, line 5 {of *The Secret Doctrine*}. Is not Astral Light used here in a different sense from that on page 60, line 22? Please enlarge upon this idea of prototypes existing, before becoming manifest upon the material plane.

Mme. Blavatsky: Yes, certainly. Well, Astral Light is a very wide term. As I said, I use this because to use another would be to make the book still more incomprehensible, and heaven knows that they are complaining quite enough of its being very difficult to understand already. I have tried to avoid all such words, and I have put Astral Light in general. Now suppose I had said and given to you the difference—that Astral Light is used here as a convenient term for one very little understood, "the realm of Akasa or primordial light manifested in the divine ideation." Now, suppose I had to use this very long phrase. Very few would understand it, I would have to explain what is divine ideation, I would have to explain what is the Akasa; I would have to explain the difference between Akasa and Ether, and so on. Therefore, I use it simply as a term that everyone understands. Astral Light is everywhere. It may be from the highest plane to the lowest plane, it is always Astral Light, at least according to the Kabalists. All the Kabalists call it so, from the days of the alchemists and the Rosicrucians. Astral Light must be accepted here as a generic term for universal and divine ideation reflected in the waters of space or chaos, which is the Astral Light proper. That is to say, the Astral Light is like the mirror of the highest divine ideation, but it is all reversed, because it is a plane of illusion and everything is topsy-turvy there. In the divine thought everything exists and there was no time when it did not so exist, so that it is impossible to say that anything came out, because this divine mind is Absoluteness and everything was, is, and will be in it. At least, according to our philosophy, it is the undifferentiated—I will not say field—but the noumenal abstract space which will be occupied, the field of primordial consciousness. It is the field, however, of latent consciousness which is coeval with the Duration of the first and unmanifested Logos—which is the light which shineth in darkness, which is in the Gospel, is the first word used there; which comprehends it not. When the hour strikes for the second Logos then from the latent potentiality radiates a lower field of differentiated consciousness, which is Mahat. It is called Mahat in the *Vishnu Purana* and all the other Puranas, or the collectivity of those Dhyan-Chohans of which Mahat is the representative. Now do you understand the thing that you have been asking the last time?

Mr. Kingsland: Not altogether. What is the relation between Astral Light used in that sense and Fohat?

Mme. Blavatsky: Fohat is in the Astral Light because it is everywhere until the fourth plane, but the Astral Light doesn't go to the fifth plane. Then begins the Akasa. You see, we call Astral Light that which mirrors all the upper planes of consciousness, matter, being, call it whatever you like.

Mr. Kingsland: When you say that the Astral Light contains the prototype of everything, does it contain not only the prototype, but does it contain it in a sequence of events in the same way that we have sequence of events on the physical plane?

Mme. Blavatsky: There is a great difference between how this Astral Light reflects all kinds of things and how the other reflects them, because the first ones, the highest ones, are eternal. The Astral Light is periodic. It changes not only with the great Manvantara but it changes with every period, with every cycle. The Astral Light will change with every tropical year,³ if you like.

Mr. Kingsland: Then everything that exists on this plane exists first of all in the Astral Light?

Mme. Blavatsky: No, it exists, first of all, in divine ideation on the plane of divine eternal consciousness and nothing can exist or take place on this plane if it does not exist there.

Mr. Kingsland: And then, further, it is reflected on the Astral Light.

Mme. Blavatsky: But it is reflected topsy-turvy; that is why we call it illusion. It is from the Astral Light that we take our prototypes. The evolution takes its prototypes from the Astral Light, but the Astral Light takes its representation from the upper ones and gives them entirely upside down. Just like a looking-glass, it will reverse everything, therefore we call it illusion.

Mr. Kingsland: Therefore, both we ourselves and Nature get our ideas from the Astral Light in whatever we produce?

Mme. Blavatsky: They cannot get them, and those who go mentally beyond the Astral Light, those are they who see the truth and can sense it, otherwise they will never see it. If they do not go beyond the Astral Light they will be always in that ocean of illusion or deception, of self-ideation which is good for nothing, because once we begin to think we see things really with our eyes of senses, with our physical eyes, we won't see anything at all.

Mr. B. Keightley: There really seem to be three stages. First, divine ideation reflects itself in [ ], the highest Akasa beyond the Astral Light.

Mme. Blavatsky: Which is the eternal, full of divine consciousness, which being Absolute consciousness cannot differentiate, cannot have any qualities, cannot act, but it is only that which is reflected from it or mirrored that can act, because the unconditioned and the infinite

---

3 Sidereal year, a cyclic period of 25,868 years, *SD*, II:505.

can have no relation with the finite and conditioned. Therefore it is our medium from which we take our "middle Heaven," as the Gnostics called it, the middle space, on which is Sophia Achamoth. The Gnostics all spoke about the middle space, which was the region of Sophia Achamoth, not the Sophia the Divine Sophia, but the Sophia Achamoth, the mother of all the evil spirits, the seven spirits, the builders of the Earth. And the Gnostics said it was these ones that built, and that therefore the God of the Bible was one of those wicked spirits. This is what they said, the Gnostics, Valentinus and Marcion and so on.

Mr. B. Keightley: They had three heavens, then?

Mme. Blavatsky: I wish somebody could translate this thing. I have it entirely in Latin. It is the Pistis of Sophia.[4] If only somebody could translate this!

Mr. B. Keightley: I think Roger Hall knows it.

Mme. Blavatsky: But it must be given entirely in the Kabalistic language. You know nothing of the Kabalah, and you won't be able to do it; it wants somebody who knows Kabalah well. I can't ask Mathers[5] to do it, because he will do it in his own Kabalistic way. There will be eternity in the way and there will be St Joseph and everything; therefore I can't give it to him. I must get somebody who knows Latin and at the same time who knows Kabalah well enough to translate. There you will see this middle space and the upper middle space and the seven heavens that they spoke about. You see, if you only study the early Christian Fathers and compare that with what is said now with the theological teachings, why, you see there is just the same difference as there is between the teachings

---

4 *The Pistis Sophia* (the faith of Sophia), an important Gnostic text that was partially translated in Mme. Blavatsky's magazine, *Lucifer*, Volumes 6, 7 and 8 from 1890 to 1891.
5 Samuel Liddell "MacGregor" Mathers, English occultist, 1854-1918, one of the founders of the Hermetic Order of the Golden Dawn.

of Ammonius Saccas[6] and the teachings of Mr. Spurgeon.[7] They believed in the seven heavens and the seven planes, they talked about the incarnation. I will show it to you in the teachings of the Church Fathers, beginning with Alexandrinus[8] and ending with any of them. Then, after the sixth century, there begins our own flapdoodle church, theology which disfigures everything, which becomes more and more Pagan, which takes not, mind you, the Pagan ideas of the higher initiates, but of the mob, the rabble. You see they always come and say I go against Christianity. I never go against Christ or the teachings of Christianity of the first centuries, but I go against this terrible perversion of all the truths. There is not a single thing they have not disfigured, and in such a way that you cannot name a rite, whether in the Roman Catholic or the Episcopal or Protestant Churches, that cannot be traced directly back to the rites of the pagan mob. Not at all of the mysterious initiates, but the pagan mob, simply, at the time when they were so persecuted, and when they wanted to save the scriptures of the initiation, and they had to compromise and come to terms, and they had come to terms with the Fathers of the church, who were very ignorant. They were either very learned or very ignorant. Now let us take Augustine; they call him the greatest man and the wisest. I say he is as ignorant as can be, and then they went and made a kind of *olla podrida* out of these Pagan rites and the little things of the initiations. I am going to give it all in *Lucifer*,[9] the rites of ritualism in masonry and the church, and I am going to give it in five or six numbers. I think it will be very interesting for the masons, and for others too, because I show the origin, and I show it on the authority of the manuscripts and the old classics, and they cannot say I have invented it.

Dr. Williams: I was talking with a bishop of the Church of England

---

6 Ammonius Saccas, third century A.D. Greek philosopher in Alexandria, Egypt, who as the teacher of Plotinus, influenced the development of Neoplatonism.
7 Charles Haddon Spurgeon, English Baptist preacher, 1834-1892.
8 Clement of Alexandria, leader of Christians in Alexandria, c. 150-c.215.
9 "The Roots of Ritualism in Church and Masonry," *Lucifer*, March, May 1889. The May installment ended with the words "To be continued" but never was. See also *H.P. Blavatsky - Theosophical Articles*, III:203.

last week, and he admitted that if the Church wanted to continue its integrity it would have to go back to the teaching of the early Christian fathers.

Mme. Blavatsky: But they will have to give up the temples and everything. The early Christians until the beginning of the third century would not hear of temples, or rites, or ceremonies, or churches or anything of the kind. That which is called a church in Paul is simply a gathering and an assembly in a room; there were no churches, no rites, nothing at all. You know what this {Minucius} Felix says: he says, "you say that we are not pious because we have not temples, and this, that, and the other, but we cannot have a temple, for where is the temple that is large enough to contain the Almighty and the Absolute?"[10] This is his argument, that went dead against the temples; therefore, if your bishop wants to return, he will have to make away with every church and temple, and every chapel. They have to go to the endowment of Jesus. When you pray, don't go into the synagogues and do as the Pharisees do, go into the room and pray. This is the meaning of it. Surely there is not the slightest comparison between what Jesus or Christ taught you, and what the Church is doing, not the smallest similitude. It is like two different things, it says one thing and you do another; and you call yourselves Christians, when you are all nothing but the most paradoxical people in creation. I mean all Christendom, I don't mean only England.

Dr. Williams: I think the world is coming to it very fast now.

Mme. Blavatsky: If I can help it a bit, I am perfectly ready to do anything. I can assure you I am perfectly ready to do anything, even to be cut into a thousand pieces, I don't care; for this is the curse. It is Church cant!

Mr. Kingsland: They would have to have meetings on the model of the Blavatsky Lodge.

Mme. Blavatsky: Well, at the Blavatsky Lodge they don't teach

---

10 These words are a paraphrase of the third century Roman Christian apologist Minucius Felix's *Octavius*, 32.1.

anything but good. They don't teach you anything of the vices. It is not a self-admiration society. At the Blavatsky Lodge you hear from me very disagreeable truths, but I think they do not do you any harm, do they? I say I am a very poor specimen of anything good, but I will say as the Lutheran preacher did: "do as I tell you, don't do as I do."

Dr. Williams: What is the first manifestation of the Astral Light proceeding downward toward matter?

Mme. Blavatsky: From the Astral Light? Already it will be on the fourth, third and second planes—from which of the planes do you mean? You take *The Secret Doctrine* and you see the four planes. It is useless to speak about that which cannot be given in any language.

Mr. Kingsland: I think what Mr. Williams means is, what is that which makes the reflection become potentiality?

Mr. Williams: What is the first manifestation proceeding out from the Astral Light toward the plane of manifestation? I mean manifestation on the material plane.

Mme. Blavatsky: My dear Dr. Williams, I must ask you first, do you speak about theogony? Do you speak about the physical forces? On what plane do you want me to tell you this? Because, if you speak about the theogony, I may say there are all the builders that proceed from it, the builders of the cosmic terrestrial world.

Dr. Williams: But the different planes are all inter-reality are they not?

Mme. Blavatsky: Certainly, but what is this Astral Light? All these intelligences, which are already from the sun {son?} of chaos, in matter and all these builders of the lower world proceed from it. All the seven elements, of which you know only five so far, or four.

Mr. A. Keightley: Then, there you are speaking of two distinct planes: the cosmic plane, and that which applies particularly to our earth. I suppose you would say, then, there were as many divisions of the Astral Light, if one may so speak of it, as there are planetary systems.

Mme. Blavatsky: Most assuredly.

Dr. Williams: Did you use the term there in our abstract sense, in the sense of unity?

Mme. Blavatsky: I use terms mostly in that sense, at least, in my mind it all comes to that, I am afraid. But when we begin talking about the plane of differentiated matter and the evolution on earth, of course I am obliged to go into details.

Dr. Williams: Really, the idea at the back of the question was whether it manifests simultaneously in many different ways, or whether there is some sort of emanation from the Astral Light which constitutes a higher degree of potentiality from which various forms in the physical universe proceed, or the physical forces proceed. Or whether they proceed simultaneously in many different forms from this unity.

Mme. Blavatsky: I think the question will be answered in the following question.

Mr. B. Keightley: I think it is covered by the question of the prototypes.

Mme. Blavatsky: Now, question 4 is answered in the third.

Mr. A. Keightley: Question 4 is: "Is there an evolution of types through the various planes of the Astral Light or do all possible types exist in the Divine Thought?"

Mme. Blavatsky: Certainly, no possible types, nothing can be there, that does not exist in the Divine Thought.

Mr. A. Keightley: In that case (that there is an evolution) would it be correct to say that actual Astral prototypes of physical forms only exist on the lowest plane of the Astral Light?

Mme. Blavatsky: Yes, because this is the world of forms, and there there are no forms. You cannot come and make the comparison there. It is the world of forms, and there is the world Arupa.

Mr. B. Keightley: You have not read the keynote of the thing.

Mme. Blavatsky: Number 4 is answered in the third. Number 5 is answered here. The existence of physical forms on the Astral plane—their prototypes can best be compared to the noumenal germ from which will proceed the phenomenal germ which will finally become the acorn. Now, do you understand this thing?

Dr. Williams: No, I am afraid I do not.

Mme. Blavatsky: That first it can be compared to a noumenal germ; from the noumenal germ there comes the phenomenal germ and that germ becomes the acorn. Now, just to show you the different prototypes on different planes and how one thing is evolved from the other. From the acorn will grow an oak and this oak as a tree may be of a thousand forms, all varying from each other. You see, all these forms are contained in the acorn, and yet from the same acorn the form that the oak will take depends already on extraneous circumstances, on physical forces at work, and all kinds of things. You know it is impossible to speak about this. The germ is there, but you cannot speak about form, and it is contained in the phenomenal germ and the noumenal germ.

Dr. Williams: Does the noumenal germ exist in the Astral Light? Can that in any way be said to be an emanation from the Astral Light?

Mme. Blavatsky: It is. The noumenal germ does not exist in the Astral Light but beyond, above. It is already a physical germ that exists in the Astral Light, the physical germ. That is to say, the prototype, what Aristotle calls the privation of matter.

Dr. Williams: Do you understand this prototype of the developed oak tree exists or does it develop with the physical oak tree? And is not the development of the physical oak tree the result of the developed prototype?

Mme. Blavatsky: Surely it is, but we cannot give it a form and expression here. We know that nothing can be here unless it is found in another higher plane, and from one plane to another it must proceed. From the highest it comes to the lowest and must have its development; only here it has its last consolidation of forms and development of forms. And this I tell you further: it is such a difficult subject that I do not think any one of you, even those who study Occultism, can understand it, and this is that the real Vedāntin philosopher will tell you that even the oak or the tree that grows from the germ has its karma, and that whatever way it grows it is the result of karma. Now, try to understand that.

Mr. A. Keightley: Does that mean, then, that supposing you have an oak tree, the privation of the oak tree is a perfect example of a tree growth?

Mme. Blavatsky: Yes; but who had done the privation; who has traced it out?

Mr. A. Keightley: That is the Divine Thought, as I understand it.

Mme. Blavatsky: I beg your pardon. It is the Dhyan-Chohan, the builders on the lower plane, and as they draw it, it is their karma for having drawn it.

Mr. A. Keightley: But I thought they could not draw, apart from the natural evolutionary law.

Mme. Blavatsky: It is sometimes in such extraordinary forms that it is a thing of intention. We can't see it, but it is so.

Mr. Kingsland: Do you mean they actually draw it as it will be when the tree is full grown, before the tree is full grown?

Mme. Blavatsky: Just so, as the astral body of every man, woman, and child must exist before the physical body grows over it, and the physical body takes the shape of the astral form. The Hindus will tell you the gods, Brahmâ, Vishnu, Siva are all under karmic law. They all say the same. You read the Hindu books, you will find it. All that which is at the end of Pralaya to die, so to say, to end in a certain form, is under karmic law.

Mr. Kingsland: That is closely connected with the phenomena of prediction. How is it that somnambulists are able to predict certain events that take place?

Mme. Blavatsky: Because they see it in the Astral Light.

Mr. B. Keightley: You get this state. The Dhyan-Chohan first of all takes that, the noumenal idea of it, or reflects it from the Divine Mind, as I understand; that, of course, is perfect in the Divine Mind, it is perfection. But as the Dhyan-Chohan takes it or reflects it in himself and transmits it again in the astral plane he modifies it, of course, either intentionally or otherwise—according to what I do not know, but either intentionally or otherwise—so that you get then the oak tree modified somewhat from perfection.

Mme. Blavatsky: This is why the Rosicrucians and all the Kabalists of the Middle Ages spoke about spirits, that every species, every tree, everything in nature, every kingdom of nature has its own elements, its own Dhyan-Chohans, or what they call the elemental spirits.

Mr. Hall: Would the Dhyan-Chohans be the Hamadryads?[11]

Mme. Blavatsky: It is the Greeks who call them so.

Mr. B. Keightley: Then, when you have, for instance, oaks, you have many different variations of oaks, each differing very considerably from each other. Are they, so to speak, differentiations of a single idea in the Divine Mind, differentiated in a thousand forms?

Mme. Blavatsky: They are the broken rays of one ray, and on every plane they are broken. As they pass through the seven planes they are all broken on each plane into thousands and millions, until they come to the world of forms; and every one breaks into an intelligence

---

11 Spirits of trees in Greek mythology.

on its own plane, because every plant has an intelligence. It is no use to come and say that there are only sensitive plants which feel, and all that. If botanists could have the slightest—we won't say Kabalistic ideas, but real clairvoyant powers or intuition—they would see that there is no plant that has not got its own intelligence, its own purpose of life, its own free will. It cannot, of course, walk or perambulate or move, but it has its own purpose of life. It can do this, the other, or the third. It can be receptive or non-receptive. It can close its petals or unclose them, it has its own ideation—each little blade of grass.

Mr. B. Keightley: Its own intelligence on its own plane.

Mme. Blavatsky: And this intelligence is not the plant, it is that Dhyan-Chohan, or let us call it elemental, that incarnates in it. It all seems as though we are a pack of fools, believing in all this. The Kabalists laugh at this belief of nymphs and sylphs and gnomes and all that, but this is perfectly true, this is an allegorical way of talking; there is not a thing in this universe that is not animated, and all these atoms go to form a thing. They are the product of a kind of intelligence of its own, a cosmic intelligence that acts.

Mr. Hall: I think botanists practically admit all that.

Mme. Blavatsky: Only for the sensitive plants.

Mr. Hall: Look at the way they admit plants will grow towards the light; that implies it.

Mme. Blavatsky: Look at the great piety of the solar flower—of the sun-flower. It will always turn to the sun. Why, it is considered in the East a very pious yogi among the flowers, especially as it is clothed in yellow, and they have a great respect in some parts for it.

Mr. Scott-Elliot: But surely the words Dhyan-Chohan and elemental are not convertible. We have always understood Dhyan-Chohan as referring to the providers of the whole system.

Mme. Blavatsky: Dhyan-Chohan applies to everything. You call it Dhyan-Chohan, but you cannot call them Dhyani-Buddhas.

Mr. Scott-Elliot: I have always understood it to be a Dhyani-Buddha.

Mr. Kingsland: We had it all explained last Thursday.

Mr. Scott-Elliot: Then these elementals, all the creation, are they on their way to animal life, those that animate plants, say?

Mme. Blavatsky: Just the same, and the animals are on their way to humanity, and humanity on their way to Devas or the highest Dhyan-Chohans. We have used the words promiscuously because no one has taken the trouble to learn it from the A.B.C. to the last letter. We always have spoken of the Dhyan-Chohans without going into details, and these are the details that will give you the correct idea, otherwise you will be at sea, and you will never understand it.

Mr. A. Keightley: Then I suppose you can speak of evolution from the prototypal world, through the elemental kingdom up to minerals and animals and human beings in the elemental world, as well as on the other parts.

Mme. Blavatsky: Just the same below, so it is above.

Mr. A. Keightley: But at the same time, are they separate or are they one and the same thing?

Mme. Blavatsky: Well, they are separate as you are separate from another man who may be walking now in Regent Street.[12]

Mr. Hall: Is it not that we are just the material shadows of our astral prototypes?

Mme. Blavatsky: We are; and the astral prototypes are the shadows of their higher prototypes, which are the Dhyans, up to the Dhyani-Buddha.

Mr. A. Keightley: Could you use the term in this way: that there is an elemental which is connected with us in the astral world, we ourselves being separated from that elemental in the astral world;

---

12 Fashionable thoroughfare in London's West End.

that the elementals are represented in this astral world, and so are we, but we are in addition represented in the physical?

Mme. Blavatsky: We are in the Divine World also.

Mr. B. Keightley: No, I will tell you how it is. Our body—the cells of our physical body—have of course their astral correspondence, which you might call elementals. Those are not ourselves, but we must have as human beings our humanity, so to speak, on the astral plane, apart from the animal elementals which are the correspondencies of the physical body.

Mr. A. Keightley: That is what I meant.

Mr. B. Keightley: The animal elementals on the astral plane.

Mme. Blavatsky: These are questions of immense difficulty. They are such abstruse questions that one answer will elicit another question and then this question elicits ten questions more. It is a thing to which you Europeans are not at all accustomed. It is a train of thought that you could not follow unless you began from the beginning, and were trained as the Eastern people are trained, especially now the yogis, who begin a systematic course of training for the development of metaphysical ideas, and so on. It is a very difficult, abstruse subject, this. You see, it is not enough to come and have a very flowery tongue, and to express yourself well and to have a flow of language. You must first of all pass into the heads or the brains of those who listen to you a clear representation of what a thing is in reality. Unless you do that you will be listening to a very nice metaphysical speech, as I know many friends of ours have done and get nothing out of it. You have to know and understand everything and how it stands in relation to another thing, and you have to begin from the beginning and proceed from the universals to particulars. And then it will be extremely difficult for you to understand anything on the higher planes. This is a question that we had already.

Mr. A. Keightley: There is another question arising out of that that

I wanted to ask you. I was talking to a man not very long ago who said that there had been a communication from a sort of intelligence which signed itself "Chela," and it was written by means of a medium. That medium, according to the intelligence, was not very amenable. It varied, the condition varied, and so did the communications, but one sentence which was used struck me as rather curious. It said: "First of all you have to get the brain in a proper receptive condition, then when that brain is in a proper receptive condition, it stimulates the muscles of the hand to follow out the letters which are traced in a subtle medium." Probably he meant the letters in the Astral Light; that is to say, there seemed to be a double action. First, there was a tracing of the letters. Secondly, there was an impression on the brain to stimulate the nerves and the muscles and all the rest of it, to follow the tracings with pen and ink or pencil of that which was traced in the Astral Light. Is that a true representation of the way such things are done?

Mme. Blavatsky: When you trace it from the Astral Light, your brain may go to sleep, and need simply have the will to copy that without giving it a thought, whether it is good, bad or indifferent, wise or foolish.

Mr. A. Keightley: But that is an actual thing. Supposing for instance that this physical writing here was previously traced in the Astral Light. Were I a medium, my hand would follow the tracings with the pencil in the Astral Light with the physical pen and ink.

Mme. Blavatsky: Most assuredly, but certainly you must see it, and seeing, of course you must have a certain process going on in your brain.

Mr. A. Keightley: According to this explanation, apparently there was the double process going on—not only the sight but the stimulation of the brain to follow this tracing.

Mme. Blavatsky: "Stimulation"—I don't understand the use of it. If you don't want to do it, then perhaps your brain would be stimulated to do it. I cannot understand it.

Mr. A. Keightley: That was the explanation of the medium not being particularly amenable.

Mme. Blavatsky: Well, let us have question 6.

Mr. A. Keightley: Page 63, line 22 {of *The Secret Doctrine*, Vol. I}. "Is Manu a unity of human consciousness personified into one human comprehension, or is he the individualization of the Thought Divine as applied for Manvantaric purposes?"

Mme. Blavatsky: Oh! It is about the root Manus and the Seed Manus. It is about the fourteen you are talking.

Mr. A. Keightley: (repeats the question.)

Mme. Blavatsky: Well, didn't we speak of it last time, or the time before last? You asked me, I think, whether Manu and those builders were the same. That is at least the spirit, and whose duty it was to watch over the planet; and I told you then there were seven of them. Don't you remember this? It is just the same. Well, do you want to know what Manu is, and what he represents, or do you want simply, metaphysically, to know what kind of consciousness he has or how many consciousnesses he represents? Again, I don't understand that.

Mr. A. Keightley: It means this—is Manu what you may call the primary thought, which is separated into a variety of intelligences in the physical world? That is to say, is Manu the thing from which intelligences proceed on earth in diversity, or is he the synthesis of divers intelligences?

Mme. Blavatsky: He is not. He is the beginning of this earth; from Manu humanity is born. He was the only one who remained, and the others, who came with him, they have gone somewhere else, and, you see, he creates humanity by himself. He creates a daughter to himself, and from this daughter there is the evolution of humanity of the soul, mankind. Now, Manu is a unity, which contains all the pluralities and their modifications. The name "Manu" comes from the word "man," to think; it is a Sanskrit word, and thought in its actions and human brains is endless. So it is Manu which is and contains in itself all these forms that will be developed on earth from the particular Manu. Every Manvantara has its own Manu. Every [ ] has its own Manu. From this Manu the Manus of all the Kalpa Manus will be such.

Mr. A. Keightley: Then, practically, Manu is in the position with regard to humanity as a prism is to a single ray of white light.

Mme. Blavatsky: I would call it the white light which contains all the other lights, and then passes through the prism of differentiation and evolution.

Mr. A. Keightley: Then, that is the decomposing prism. Then, Manu has no relation to a uniting prism, if we may so use it, the prism of re-union.

Mme. Blavatsky: Going to one Manu, no. The Manu is simply the Alpha of something differentiated, which, when it comes to the Omega, that something disappears. It is Omega, and then you pass onward.

Mr. A. Keightley: Then, that is practically what I mean.

Mme. Blavatsky: Except, perhaps, Swayambhu.

Mr. Kingsland: Can't you say it stands in relation to each Manvantara the same as the first Logos?

Mme. Blavatsky: Yes, on the physical plane it is just in the same relation as if you take it on this, on the physical plane. It will be just that as it stands on {the} universal plane.

Mr. B. Keightley: Now, look at it for a moment. From the side of consciousness, you may say all the cells of the human body have each their own individual consciousness, but yet there is the unit of consciousness which is the man—well, is the analogy applicable to the Manu?

Mme. Blavatsky: I think it is—very well.

Mr. B. Keightley: Is the Manu a unit of consciousness which remains a unit?

Mme. Blavatsky: It is the latent, or it contains in itself all that.

Mr. B. Keightley: Which remains a unit in spite of differentiation. There is the unit of consciousness in a man, but still there are all the cells of his body which are individualized to a certain extent. But the unit of consciousness of man still persists.

Mme. Blavatsky: Yes, just that. I think it is a very good analogy.

Mr. B. Keightley: Because I want to get at the point whether the Manu represents a single consciousness—if I may make the phrase, one, a unit.

Mme. Blavatsky: But do you suppose that your consciousness is a single consciousness? Why, your consciousness is a reflection of thousands and millions of consciousnesses.

Mr. B. Keightley: But still it is united in a focus.

Mme. Blavatsky: But still this contains all consciousnesses which you have absorbed, and no one has got one alone. I don't know what you mean by that, that your brain is a focus. Of course, it is there. Manu is, as I say, meaning to think. It is the thinking man.

Mr. Hall: Has Manu, then, an individuality?

Mme. Blavatsky: Well, I don't know. It has no individuality in the abstract sense.

Mr. Scott-Elliot: All the consciousnesses that you have been talking about, are they the hosts of the Dhyani-Buddhas who are concentrated in the ray of the one man?

Mme. Blavatsky: Oh, no. The Dhyani-Buddhas are on the higher plane. They have nothing to do with our dirty household work of our earth. It is just as you will put, for instance, somebody as a great governor in the house, and then this governor will have nothing to do with the work of the kitchen maids. Of all that, he does not know anything. He governs simply a place. Or let us take the Queen, if she were not a constitution, or anyone, an emperor. In such an example, that is the thinking man, it has nothing to do with what the subalterns do. If you understand me, this is a thing which belonged to that mind. To that ruler, they are under the sway of that ruler, and yet that ruler is not cognizant of them. So it is with the Dhyani-Buddha that has come and emanated from him and all that. But he has nothing to do with them. It is just like the millions of cells that do something automatically or the foot which steps there without thinking about it. Every one thing has got its allotted duty to perform, but the Dhyani-Buddha is the supervisor. I gave it all to you about two Thursdays ago.

Mr. B. Keightley: Not quite what you have given now.

Mme. Blavatsky: Very well, then. Of course, if we go on with the conversation you will hear new things for 365 days in the year, because the subject is immense. I cannot express myself. My dear Mr. Scott-Elliot, I tell you, as I grow older the worse I begin speaking English. I begin to be in despair. I have the more thoughts in my head and I can express them less and less. It is very difficult for me to express it. I can write it but to speak it is very difficult.

Mr. A. Keightley: Then Manu is a unit of consciousness which differentiates into a multitude.

Mme. Blavatsky: It is.

Mr. A. Keightley: Then is Manu pre-Manvantaric? What I am wanting to get at is this.

Mr. Kingsland: What becomes of Manu at the end of the Manvantara?

Mme. Blavatsky: Manu is not individuality. It is not one. It is the whole {of} mankind.

Mr. Scott-Elliot: The whole of mankind?

Mme. Blavatsky: Certainly, it is not an individual. The Hindu will come and tell you man {Manu ?} is an individual, but I say it is perfect nonsense. Manu is that, the forefathers, the Pitris, the progenitors of mankind, as it is called.

Mr. B. Keightley: In other words, it is a name applying to the Monads which come from the Lunar Chain.

Mme. Blavatsky: Why are they called the Lunar? Because the moon is said—of course, in defiance of all astronomy—to be the parent of the Earth; and these are the Monads. They progressed and passed through the First Round, and then it is they who, having become the first men, the Manus give birth to others by evolving their astral selves. They give birth to humanity, they give birth to the animals, and to all kinds of things. So in the Puranas they say for instance such and such a high yogi gave birth to all the serpents or all the birds— this, that, and the other—you see it there.

Mr. Scott-Elliot: What I wanted to express was the perfected humanity of one Round becomes the Dhyan-Chohans, or the Dhyani-Buddhas of the next Manvantara, and are the guiding rulers of the universe.

Mme. Blavatsky: But what do you call Manvantara? We call Manvantara seven Rounds; and this is a small, little Manvantara, of our globe.

Mr. Scott-Elliot: What bearing has Manu on the hosts of the Dhyani-Buddhas?

Mme. Blavatsky: He has no bearing at all. The hosts of the Dhyani-Buddhas evolve a lower set of Dhyani-Buddhas, these Dhyani-Buddhas a third, and so on. There are seven of them, though in Tibet they take only five Buddhas—after that they begin to be Cosmocratores, the builders (call them whatever names you like, they have all got special names in the Sanskrit)—then the builders of the Astral Light; and it is an endless hierarchy of one kind of Dhyanis evoluting another kind of Dhyans. Every one becomes more consolidated, more material, until it comes to the builders of this universe, some of which are Manus, the Pitris and the Lunar ancestors. It has a task, to give birth to men; and they give birth by projecting their astral shadows, and the first humanity (if humanity it can be called) are those Chayas of those Lunar ancestors over which physical nature begins building the physical body, which first begins to be formless; then the Second Race begins to be more and more {formed}. Then they are sexless; then they become bisexual; and then hermaphrodites, and then they separate and go all kinds of ways for the propagation of mankind. This is all given in *The Secret Doctrine*.

Mr. Scott-Elliot: Then, talking of Manvantara, the Manvantara is the period which is embraced by the seven rounds of seven planets.

Mme. Blavatsky: The Manvantara of our planetary chain.

Mr. Scott-Elliot: But I see you talk in *The Secret Doctrine* of a minor Manvantara.

Mme. Blavatsky: There is a minor Manvantara, and there is a major Manvantara, and there are various kinds of Manvantaras.

Mr. Scott-Elliot: Or rather, I thought Manvantara meant the circle, a single round of the seven worlds, and that Kalpa represented the total seven rounds of the seven worlds.

Mme. Blavatsky: Minor Manvantara means between two Manus, but as I show also there, there are fourteen Manus in reality. There are seven Root Manus at the beginning of the round and Seed Manu, as it is called, at the end of the round. Therefore they make fourteen. There are two Manus for each round, but these Manus are simply figures of speech—they are symbols {of} the beginning of humanity and the end, and the Manus are simply synonymous with the Pitris, the fathers, the progenitors of mankind, the Lunar ancestors. These are Manus.

Mr. Scott-Elliot: What would you call the duration of a minor Manvantara?

Mme. Blavatsky: If you take the exoteric duration, it is one thing. I could not tell you.

Mr. B. Keightley: Manvantara simply means the period of activity. You may speak about it as twelve hours of daylight and Pralaya of the night, or you may speak of Manvantara as the individual life of man.

Mme. Blavatsky: There are seven kinds of Pralaya and seven kinds of Manvantara, and they are all mentioned, from the *Vishnu Purana* to the last ones; all kinds of Pralayas and Manvantara also.

Mr. B. Keightley: It simply means a period of activity and it is not limited in any of the Theosophical writings. It is never used in a definite sense as meaning a definite period of years; you have to gather from the context what period is spoken of a specific period of time.

Mr. Scott-Elliot: During which the rays circle round the seven globes.

Mr. B. Keightley: You have to gather from the context what the extent of the Manvantara that is spoken of is, but you cannot go very far wrong, because what applies on one scale applies to the smaller scale, just as you take it.

Mr. A. Keightley: Question 7, page 64, second paragraph. "Is 'water' as used here purely symbolical or has it a correspondence in the evolution of the elements?"

Mme. Blavatsky: I speak about the water here simply in this way. You see, you make a great mistake, all of you, in confusing the universal elements with the terrestrial elements. Now, again, I do not speak about the chemical elements, I speak simply about the elements as they are known here, that we have been talking the last time about. We had a long conversation about it. But the universal elements, I would call them the noumena of the terrestrial elements. They are cosmic elements. Cosmic does not apply to our little solar system. Cosmic is infinite. I have in my head always the infinitude.

Dr. Williams: Are they identical with the elementals, or is that something entirely different?

Mme. Blavatsky: Elementals are simply the creatures produced for the various species in differentiation. That is to say, every differentiation of matter produces and evolves a kind of a force of an intelligence—well, anything you like—that which the Kabalists and the Rosicrucians called elemental spirits, nature's spirits. They chronologised those things, but we say there is an intelligence, in every one there is a force. Hartmann[13] there writes about undines, and he believes they are real creatures. It is a little bit too much to believe in sylphs, they are creatures of our imaginations, and they do not exist by themselves.

Mr. Hall: Would not they exist to the person who believes in that seriously?

Mme. Blavatsky: Every one of us can believe in elementals which they create for themselves. There are some who create this or that. This is what the spiritualists do, if you please. You can create an elemental, but this elemental will have no existence outside your vitiated imagination. It will be an intelligence, but the form you will give it, and the attributes you will give it, will be of your own creation, and this is the horrible thing.

Mr. Hall: And it weakens you physically.

Mme. Blavatsky: It will make a lunatic of you. It evaporizes you. This is why most mediums end in the lunatic asylums or get drunkards for life. Look at Kate Fox.[14] Look at Charles Foster[15] and all the great mediums, in fact. They are all half crazy.

---

13 Franz Hartmann, German Theosophical writer, 1838-1912. He dealt extensively with the creatures of the elements, and especially with the female water-spirits, the undines, in his 1887 life of Paracelsus, and *An Adventure Among the Rosicrucians*.
14 Kate Fox, one of the American pioneers of mediumship, 1837-1892, who ended her days as an alcoholic.
15 Charles H. Foster, American medium, 1838-1888, whose alcoholism led him to the insane asylum and a vegetative state.

Mr. A. Keightley: But then there, "water" is used as actually the first cosmic element.

Mme. Blavatsky: It is. It is called water, darkness; chaos is called water. "The waters of space" means you can have water. What is water? What is matter? Matter is in one of the three states: solid, fluid or gaseous. Very well, and in occult things there are four states more, there are seven states. But if you only speak and you say I shall limit our conversation only to this plane, if you take it as water in three states, as matter in its three states, you will understand perfectly what I mean.

Mr. A. Keightley: But what I am working at is this: water is used as the one element originally in the cosmic sense, and then finally on the terrestrial plane, water is preceded by ether, fire and air.

Mme. Blavatsky: But ether contains in itself fire and water and air and everything, all the elements, all the seven, and this ether which is the hypothetical agent of your physical science is the last form of Akasa. Therefore you can judge.

Mr. B. Keightley: But the point, really, of that question was this: as to whether the term water is applied to the cosmic, first matter, apparently from which everything evolves.

Mme. Blavatsky: Because it is not yet solid matter. That is why, as we know it, we cannot go and speak about that if we do not show it on this plane—something that we know, that we can conceive and understand. Now, space instead of water in the scriptures of any Bible some other word was used that we cannot understand, some word that has no meaning to us. That is why they call it water, because it has not the solidity of matter.

Mr. B. Keightley: Supposing that we knew anything about ether, it might just as well be called ether.

Mme. Blavatsky: Most assuredly, the moist principle—what is it the philosophers call it? "The hot and moist principle," from which proceed all things. "The waters of space"—you read this expression in all the scriptures and the Puranas and even in the Bible, and everywhere it is the same thing.

Mr. B. Keightley: It is from the "waters of space" that the Sophia Achamoth proceeds.

Mme. Blavatsky: It proceeds from this Astral Light.

Mr. B. Keightley: Sophia Achamoth proceeds from the "waters of space."

Mme. Blavatsky: Moses says it requires earth and water to make a living soul. Understand it, if you like—and it is very easy—that is to say that man is a living soul, that the Nephesh is of a dual element. It partakes of the middle pre-astral of the psychic and of the metaphysic.

Mr. B. Keightley: It is really, then, the root, the Astral Light.

Mme. Blavatsky: That which is all the prototypes of everything on earth.

Mr. A. Keightley: Verse 2 {3}, Stanza 3. Are the virgin-egg and the eternal-egg the same, or are they different stages of differentiation?

Mme. Blavatsky: In its prototypal form as the eternal-egg and not the virgin-egg, the virgin-egg is already differentiated.

Mr. A. Keightley: You say in one sense it is absolute eggness.

Mme. Blavatsky: In one sense it is, but not in another sense. In this sense of the inner nature of its essence, it is the eggness, just as I say; but in the sense of its form in which it appears for its purposes of differentiation and evolution, it becomes a virgin-egg. It is all a metaphorical way of speaking. I say it is just the same. The eternal-egg is a pre-differentiation in a Laya condition; at that moment (before differentiation) it can have neither attributes nor qualities. The virgin-egg is already qualified, therefore differentiated, but it is the same, just as I told you. Everything is the same, nothing is separated from the other in its abstract essential nature. But in the world of illusion, in the world of forms, of differentiation, we seem all to be various persons and to be different things and all kinds of subjects. Well, whoever has got questions to ask, let them. I think there are many questions, I think, that you ask me over and over again, questions from another aspect; and it is the same aspect.

Mr. A. Keightley: When we ask you questions from the different points of view, it all serves to explain things. Then we are able to put them before you in the light in which we may understand them.

Dr. Williams: When you were speaking of writing from an appearance which is the Astral Light, can you explain anything more of that phenomena? If there is a writing in the Astral Light from which the medium writes, does not that imply form in the Astral Light?

Mme. Blavatsky: No, I would not say it is a form. It is something that assumes a form for the time being and takes a form which is comprehensible to the medium.

Dr. Williams: The medium sees or perceives something, otherwise there would be nothing from which he would write.

Mme. Blavatsky: Most assuredly, it takes that. The potential energy, the essence of the thing, assumes a form which {is} comprehensible to the medium.

Mr. Hall: It assumes form in his own brain only.

Mme. Blavatsky: And he sees it. Now, for instance, a sentence will be uttered in a language which is perfectly unknown to the medium, which the medium has never heard. This medium will see the thing repeated in the Astral Light not in the language that he or she does not understand, but in the language which is its own language. When two persons speak, let us say an adept speaks with his chela, that chela does not understand the language of the adept or the adept the language of the chela on the physical plane, yet they understand each other because every word that is uttered is impressed on the brain, if you like—no language, the language of thought.

Mr. Scott-Elliot: No language is necessary.

Mr. Hall: You ask anybody who knows one or two languages equally well, you nearly always find he is unable to tell you in which he thinks.

Mme. Blavatsky: I am perfectly unable to say in what language I think sometimes. Very likely I can just perceive, you know, that I think in some language.

Dr. Williams: Is not that a lack of concentration upon the subject of thought itself? If one were to concentrate their minds it seems to me they must inevitably think in one or other of the languages in which they are equally familiar.

Mr. B. Keightley: No, because the more concentrated your thought, the less you think in words.

Mr. Hall: It is only when the man reflects afterwards, and then he has to give a certain form to his thoughts, and then he takes one of the languages which he knows.

Dr. Williams: Is thought anything until it assumes form?

Mr. B. Keightley: You can certainly have formed thought apart from words.

Mme. Blavatsky: How do the dumb and the deaf think, in what language?

Dr. Williams: Well, there is something which stands with them for words. The signification in their minds is precisely the same.

Mme. Blavatsky: Sometimes deaf and dumb persons will be taught a language by the process that they have invented, and after that, when they are able to communicate their thoughts to people, they cannot say in what language they thought. They had no guide.

Dr. Williams: But words are simply symbols to express qualities. We perceive the qualities in various ways and the words simply stand as symbols for the qualities. Now, they have another set of symbols and those symbols convey to their consciousness the same qualities that words do to ours, so that it actually comes to the same thing.

Mme. Blavatsky: But you said one must think in a special language.

Dr. Williams: And they think by their sign language.

Mr. Hall: I think not, because you cannot think the language until you have formed it.

Mme. Blavatsky: When you speak, do you follow the ideas that take form in your thinking? You don't think, you just speak as it comes to you, especially a man who is accustomed to speak easily.

Mr. Kingsland: You generally think too rapidly for speech at all.

Mme. Blavatsky: But this thinking does not at all take place in a language.

Dr. Williams: Do we think at all, then?

Mme. Blavatsky: We could not speak and give expression to thought if we did not think.

Dr. Williams: That is what I am trying to analyze. There is something which precedes, and speech is the external symbol which first exists in the mind.

Mr. Hall: That is the real thought.

Mme. Blavatsky: It is abstract thought.

Mr. Hall: A man would never have to look for words. When he thoroughly understands his subject, he knows all the things he wants to talk about; and then he is at a loss for words to translate the idea.

Miss Kenealy: Speech is precipitated thought, just as one may have chemical solution, and thought is that solution. Speech is solution precipitated.

Mme. Blavatsky: I think this is a good definition.

Miss Kenealy: One thinks ideas, not words.

Mme. Blavatsky: What form do these thoughts take in the brain? I know I could not follow, I could not say what I think. I think and I will say it, but I cannot say in what form they have come in my brain.

Mr. A. Keightley: Then you don't think in symbols?

Mme. Blavatsky: If I want to think something, I want to meditate it, but when I talk simply, as I talk now, I don't give a thought to that—thought!

Dr. Williams: I don't mean that you watch the mechanical processes that are going on in your brain, but I mean thought must take a concrete form until it is used in speech; otherwise, naturally, there could be no speech.

Mme. Blavatsky: I can only judge by my own experience.

Mr. Kingsland: But when you are meditating—for instance, without any attempt to put them into words—when you simply think about a thing, meditate about it—that is the question.

Dr. Williams: Then I should say we are thinking or we are not thinking. We may make the mistake that was attributed to a certain extent to Washington, who went always about with his head down and his hands behind his back. Somebody said he was a very deluded man, he thought he was thinking, and it seems to me we are either thinking or not thinking, and in meditation we either have thoughts or we do not have thoughts. Now the moment we have a thought, that is a concrete form in the mind, but it is, as the lady remarked, a precipitation, so to say, from the realm of ideas. An idea is not a thought, it is something entirely different; and ideas precipitate themselves into thought.

Mr. B. Keightley: But I think you can certainly have thought that is not expressed in words.

Dr. Williams: I don't think you can. The moment ideas are precipitated into thought, then you can speak. We fail to distinguish between the realm of feeling and emotion and thought. Feeling and emotion is only one of the sources. They are really identical. Feeling is only one of the sources of ideas which are precipitated into thought.

Mr. Hall: {Dr. Williams?} takes entirely a different idea of what thought is from what I think the rest of us would take it.

Mr. Kingsland: You classify thought in a different way.

Mr. B. Keightley: (to Mme. Blavatsky) When you are thinking out an article, do you think it out in words?

Mme. Blavatsky: Never.

Dr. Williams: If you don't think in words, where do the words come from?

Mr. B. Keightley: They come afterwards.

Dr. Williams: From what do they come?

Mr. B. Keightley: For instance, Mme. Blavatsky writes an elaborate article like one she has been writing now. Well, I know from the way in which that article was written, the draft of that article, the outline of it, the distinct sequence of the ideas and so on must have existed in her mind—not in words, before she put pen to paper.

Dr. Williams: Oh, of course. I understand there exist in memory the materials.

Mr. B. Keightley: No, no. The plan, the idea of the article—how it was to be put, what facts were to be brought in—but not if you asked her to write down on paper the plan on which she was going to write her article.

Mr. Kingsland: Dr. Williams wants to draw a distinction between an idea and a thought.

Dr. Williams: I have something else, that was simply this—there is a time in the evolution of thought when things become manifested to consciousness; now what exists prior to that? That was the point I was after all the while. Prior to anything taking form in human consciousness, can we predicate anything of it at all?

Mme. Blavatsky: Well, let us say I am a carpenter, and I want to build or construct something—well, let us say a cabinet—how do I do it unless I am told to do so and so? If I am left to my own resources, I begin thinking it will be so and so, but this thought is not created in my brain; it is that I have put myself *en rapport* with a certain current which makes my thought draw from that privation of the thing which I am going to do in the Astral Light. Now, do I express it so that you understand it?

Mr. Kingsland: Supposing a person finishes his argument. You know in a moment what you are going to say. You know exactly what it is, though you take five minutes to answer it, you thought it in five seconds.

Dr. Williams: Thought is instantaneous. You have got to go through what takes time when it precipitates itself, so to say, in the realm of space and time. Then the movements of the mouth take the time.

Mr. Kingsland: But surely you knew in a moment what answer you were going to give.

Mme. Blavatsky: Dr. Williams, believe me, perhaps I will say a very great absurdity, and perhaps not. As I understand the thing, it seems to me that thought is a perfect sponge, and that it imbibes into itself from the Astral Light, and the more the capacity of this sponge to imbibe, to absorb ideas that are in the Astral Light, the more you will have ideas. Now, persons who are dull, it is because their brains are not sponge-like as that of others. They are very hard sponges through which it passes with great difficulty, but our thoughts—we call them our own, it is only the form into which you put them that is our own—but the beginning, the origin of that thought, has existed from all eternity. It must be somewhere either in this or on the plane of divine ideation. We cannot invent anything that was not or is not.

Mr. Kingsland: It is just that your brain has managed to catch it.

Mme. Blavatsky: A man who is very intelligent and a man who is very stupid, it is simply the capacity of his physical brain; and he is capable to start his ideas. I am speaking now occultly.

Dr. Williams: What then would be your definition of a thought?

Mme. Blavatsky: You must ask me something easier. I am not a speaker, I cannot give it to you in good language. I see it and understand it, but I cannot express it.

Miss Kenealy: Thought is a faculty of the higher brain and speech is a faculty of the lower brain, to a great extent automatic and mechanical.

Mme. Blavatsky: Yes, but there is something beyond that. It is the definition on the physical plane. But you must go beyond.

Mr. B. Keightley: You get to this question: what is the power in speech which makes it convey ideas? Because it actually exists. I know in reading other languages, and you might see it in English. It often happens to me in reading German. If I am reading German, particularly out-of-the-way books, I come across a word I have never seen before. It is not a compound of any words that I know, yet in reading that I shall get an accurate idea of the word. I have often tested it by hunting it up and found I have got from the word itself—

Miss Kenealy: A sort of correspondence.

Mr. Kingsland: It is the word standing in the context.

Mme. Blavatsky: Tell me another thing. How is it that a person of average intelligence, or very intelligent, who will be able to speak and write and all that, comes to an illness, there comes something—well, physiological reasons, and the brain is so plugged up that it is impossible—it cannot evolute a single idea, the person can neither think nor write nor express anything. That shows there is something, that there is a physiological reason which shuts up the avenues through which all the ideas from the Astral Light pass. Is it so or not? I ask these ladies who have been studying physiology.

Mr. B. Keightley: Everyone feels sometimes that one's brain is packed with cotton wool, and there is not an idea of any kind in it.

Dr. Williams: I remember several years ago an article of mine was criticized by a scientific materialist, and he said it made him feel as though ants were crawling through his brain. It must have been congested through his effort to understand it.

Mr. Hall: Don't you think when a person sees a word which he does not know, and yet gets a clear idea of it, that it is because he is in a certain way in a magnetic rapport?

Mme. Blavatsky: With the man who wrote, or what?

Mr. Hall: With the ideas of the man who wrote it; and that he gets it from the Astral Light.

Mme. Blavatsky: But as Mr. Kingsland says just now, it is perhaps because of what precedes and follows. The general sense of the sentence makes one guess at the word.

Miss Kenealy: Is there not a direct correspondence between thought and words? I think there is.

Mr. B. Keightley: Between thought and sound. Not necessarily between thought and words, as there is an element of the arbitrary in words.

Mme. Blavatsky: You see, this is why I say that human testimony is such an unreliable thing. For instance, we are talking and there are two persons in the room. A person may be saying to me something. In 99 cases out of a 100 that person will be saying to me one thing and I will understand it in my own way, and though perhaps I will understand the thing and remember, yet there will be something that will not represent in my brain that which that person said. That is why it is impossible to go and repeat what another said to you, because you will not repeat the very words, which you do not retain in the memory; but you repeat simply the suggestions of your own thought, with variations.

Dr. Williams: Some individuals remember words and repeat them verbatim. They used to do that in the ages past much more than they do now, the necessity for that having passed away. We remember now the first principles which underlie communications, and we may use different words in expressing those principles, but yet we do correctly convey the principles which were communicated to us. I think it has grown out of the necessities of the times, of the changed way in which we acquire knowledge and communicate it. But I think the test of every human mind, the test of truth, must come back to a knowledge of its own constitution. I do not say any other possible test for the truth to the individual mind, except a greater or less degree of knowledge of its own constitution, and this very subject of thought and mind seems to me goes right back to the very root of it all. If we listen to beautiful music or if we look at a beautiful picture, we may not have a thought about them; and yet we are thrilled, and that is all emotional, that is pure feeling, and so I think it is very often we mistake a thrill of feeling for a thought, or a series of thoughts. So I would make that distinction between feeling and thought and between ideas and thought. The moment anything comes into thought, the mind having coordinated the material out of which that comes into thought, then it takes form; and then it {is} capable of speech, and therefore, when we think anything, we can express it in speech.

7.
The Theosophical Society.
Meeting of the Blavatsky Lodge
at Lansdowne Road. Holland Park
on Thursday, February 21, 1889.

Mr. Harbottle in the Chair

Mr. B. Keightley: First are some additional questions on some points that we just touched upon last time. Stanza 3, Sloka 2: "The vibration sweeps along," etc. (Reads from {*The*} *Secret Doctrine*.) The first question is: How are we to understand the expression that the vibration touches the whole universe and also the germ? For does not the germ mean the germ of the universe not yet called into existence?

Mme. Blavatsky: Now, will you put me this very long speech in very short sentences, for I don't understand what you mean here. Maybe I have misunderstood you far more than you have misunderstood me.

Mr. B. Keightley: Not having put the question, I cannot say.

Mme. Blavatsky: Whoever has put the question, let him rise and explain.

Mr. Kingsland: I think the question has reference to the explanation with reference to the germ, that the universe has not yet come into existence, because the germ being only the germ in the primordial triangle—

Mme. Blavatsky: Then what do you mean when you say the unmanifested universe? Is not the universe eternal?

Mr. Kingsland: We do not use the term here—unmanifested

universe.

Mme. Blavatsky: Do you say manifested? No.

Mr. Kingsland: We do not use either.

Mme. Blavatsky: If you do not use either, it means unmanifested universe, for here both are purely abstract terms. The universe does not mean the Kosmos or world of forms, but the formless space, the future vehicle of the universe which will be manifested. Otherwise how could we speak, as we do, of the unmanifested universe? The same for the germ. The germ is eternal and must be so if matter—or rather the undifferentiated atoms of future matter—are said to be indestructible and eternal. That germ therefore is one with space, as infinite as it is indestructible, and as eternal as abstract space itself. Now do you understand? The same again for the word vibration. Who can imagine that the term is meant here for a real audible sound? Why, it is figurative.

Mr. Kingsland: Yes, but is it not figurative in the same sense that the emanation from the first triangle is figurative?

Mme. Blavatsky: Not at all. It is figurative; but speaking of the universe, how can I say anything else? Shall I say, "the space in which will be the universe"?

Mr. Kingsland: Does not the vibration correspond to the point, the unmanifested Logos?

Mme. Blavatsky: It does. But it is from darkness, which means here the "beyond," beyond the first Logos, even. That is what it means.

The President: Is it the ray from the eternal Logos that is the vibration?

Mme. Blavatsky: No, no, no. Read the thing again and it will make them understand.

Mr. B. Keightley: The first Sloka was this (reads again from *The Secret Doctrine*, Stanza 3, Sloka 2).

Mme. Blavatsky: Well, all this is figurative.

Mr. Kingsland: And the whole Sloka refers to the period before there is any manifestation whatever.

Mme. Blavatsky: Most assuredly. It refers to the abstract things, to the potentiality of that which will be. Space is eternal, as is repeated many times in *The Secret Doctrine*. Space is something that will be whether there is a manifested universe or an unmanifested universe. This space is synonymous with the universe. It is synonymous with the "waters of space," with everything, with eternal darkness and with Parabrahm, so to say.

Mr. Kingsland: Then this vibration is before even differentiation begins.

Mme. Blavatsky: There I am just telling you. You read this second question.

Mr. B. Keightley: Question 2. Is not the germ here, the point in the circle, the first Logos?

Mme. Blavatsky: Precisely, and the central point being everywhere, the circumference of the circle is nowhere. This means that all such expressions are simply figures of speech. I think this proves it.

Mr. B. Keightley: Is that all you have?

The President: I think one sometimes does not quite see how apparently fresh terms are to be referred back to the old ones; but I think that explains it.

Mr. Kingsland: It seems to be jumping back a little bit. Whereas we began to be catching on to differentiation, now we seem to go back.

The President: The first Stanza is negative and the second positive, in a sense. Almost the whole of the first Stanza says: "There was not this, there was not that, nor the other. It is simply a description of the nothingness or the all"; whereas with the second Stanza we begin at once with that which precedes differentiation, the first movements as it were.

Mr. B. Keightley: Speaking of that which *will be* positive, in fact.

The President: Is not it rather that?

Mme. Blavatsky: Most assuredly. Perfectly so, just so, that is what I have been saying.

The President: But it really refers to the same points.

Mr. B. Keightley: Then the third Sloka: "Darkness radiates light." Question 3. Is this equivalent to the first Logos becoming the second Logos?

Mme. Blavatsky: Now, you see this question, if you only look back over the transactions, has been answered more than once. Darkness as a general rule refers only to the unknown totality, the absoluteness. It is all a question of analogy and comparisons. Contrasted with eternal darkness, the first Logos is light certainly; contrasted with the second, or manifested, Logos, the first is darkness and the second is light. All depends upon where you locate that or another power, on what plane and so on. Now, is this clear?

Mr. B. Keightley: Yes, and I am very glad the question has been asked because it has brought a general explanation.

Mme. Blavatsky: If I were to answer from every standpoint, it would not be 2 but 22 volumes. How is it possible to answer more than in general terms?

Mr. B. Keightley: Question 4. The phrase is: "Darkness radiates light, and light drops one solitary ray into the waters." Why is light represented as dropping one ray? How is this one ray represented in connection with the triangle?

Mme. Blavatsky: Because howsoever many powers may appear to us on this plane, brought back to their first, original principles they will all be resolved into unity. We say seven prismatic colours, don't we, but they proceed all from the one white ray and they will be drawn back into this ray, and it is this one solitary ray which expands into the seven rays on the plane of illusion. It is represented in connection with the triangle, because the triangle is the first geometrical figure on the third dimensional plane; and we cannot come and give figures which can only be represented on planes of which we have no conception or idea. Therefore we are obliged to take that which has a certain aspect here on this plane. It is stated in Pythagoras, as also in the oldest Stanzas, that the ray which Pythagoras called the Monad descended from no place, *a-loka*, like a falling star through the planes of non-being into the first world of being, and gave birth to number 1. Then, descending to the right following an oblique direction, it gives birth to number 2. Then, turning at a right angle, it begets number 3, and from thence re-ascends at an oblique angle (do I make use of the right expression?) to number 1 back again; from whence it disappears once more into the realm of non-being. These are the words, I do not know how to translate better—that is to say, it starts, it shoots, then having passed through innumerable worlds of non-being and formless worlds, where no form can exist, it proceeds and creates the point first. Then it proceeds to the right in an oblique direction and creates number 2, and having created number 2 it returns and creates number 3, and thence returns to number 1, and from this it disappears into non-being again.

Mr. B. Keightley: Where does the right angle occur?

The President: Is there a right angle? It is an equilateral triangle.

Mr. Kingsland: It is an acute angle.

Mme. Blavatsky: What do you call, if you please, a horizontal like that (drawing with pencil on a sheet) when it arrives here (indicating), is it not a right angle? I meant that obliquely. I had in my mind a different thing.

Mr. Gardner: It would be 45 degrees.

Mme. Blavatsky: (Describes the angle meant with a pencil on paper.)

Mr. B. Keightley: The point really to get at is this: in the conception of it, are the sides of the triangle imagined as being equal, so that it is a perfectly symmetrical triangle?

Mme. Blavatsky: It is a triangle just as Pythagoras gives it.

Mr. B. Keightley: It is rather an important point, because you know that the right angled triangle is a very important figure in geometrical science, and Pythagoras was the discoverer of that very wonderful proposition.

Mme. Blavatsky: Of the hypotenuse, but that is not this. Then we will please put horizontal instead of right.

Mr. Hall: But horizontal what? You cannot have an imaginary horizontal.

Mme. Blavatsky: In this I cannot follow you. I am no pundit in geometry, mathematics, or anything like that.

Mr. Kingsland: It is a line at right angles to the radius, starting from the point.

Mr. Hall: Is it an equilateral triangle?

Mr. Kingsland: Yes.

Mr. B. Keightley: The moment you think of a point and the line descending from it, you have an imaginary horizontal right angle to the first line.

Mr. Hall: Then this ray first of all descends.

Mr. B. Keightley: Not vertically.

Mme. Blavatsky: First of all it descends vertically. It shoots like a falling star, as is said, and then it goes in the oblique direction; and then it goes in the horizontal direction, and then it returns like that, obliquely, as he says, and rises again.

Mr. Hall: I understand that.

Mme. Blavatsky: That is just what Pythagoras gives in the old books, for Pythagoras studied in India and he was called the Yavanacharya.[1] All the books are full of the traditions of the Greek teacher, because he was a teacher in many things for them also and he learned with the Brahmins, with the initiated, and he taught the uninitiated a good deal. Everyone says it was Pythagoras. Many traditions speak of him as going again into the country and the west and teaching this, that, and the other. I have been reading many things. He is called the Yavanacharya, the Greek teacher.

Mr. Kingsland: Then do you say when this one ray forms a triangle that it has begun to differentiate?

Mme. Blavatsky: Most assuredly. The triangle is the first differentiation, of the one ray. Certainly, it is always the same ray, and from this ray come the seven rays; and the seven may be as the one that started from the unknown to the known, and then produced the triangle.

Mr. Kingsland: After it has got to the apex and formed a triangle, do you say it has begun to differentiate?

Mme. Blavatsky: Then it begins to differentiate.

Mr. Kingsland: Then the one solitary ray here is simply equivalent to the point.

Mr. Hall: I want to put one question. You say: "all the planes of non-being"; how can there be planes in non-being?

Mme. Blavatsky: There are, but it is too long to explain it now. There are planes of non-being. I understand your objection perfectly, but it is so.

Mr. B. Keightley: Then again in a sense there is something (of course quite in a different sense from what we use the word here), something you can call differentiated, though not as we know the term.

---

1 Sanskrit: "The Ionian Teacher."

Mme. Blavatsky: I understand that is the whole question. It is not "differentiated," but yet there are planes. To us, the lowest appear differentiated, but there, it is just that which is non-being to us, which is being and matter to others. It is all analogies. We cannot come and reach with our finite intellect that which is pure, undifferentiated first principle. It is perfectly impossible, not only on this plane, but on the 77th plane.

Mr. Hall: Then you can say in an instance of this kind, you never can reach any plane where there would not be a higher.

Mme. Blavatsky: I can assure you, you won't. You must get disembodied first, and then you must be again embodied 77 million times. I would like to know, how can something finite understand that which is infinite? It is all human speculation, my dear sir, let there be the highest intellect in the world, the highest initiated adept. It is as Masters said: that the highest Dhyan-Chohans of the solar system can have no conception of what is in the higher systems—in those still higher than our solar system. It is a perfect impossibility, because, however high they may be (we may call them personal gods and far more than personal gods), still they are finite. They are not the unity—the Absolute, and the time will come when they have to dissolve, in whatever manner they may do so, whether cremated or buried, I don't know, but there will be a time when the end comes for them.

Mr. Hall: Then, is there a finite point you might call, in a sense, the absolute finite point of the journey of all?

Mr. B. Keightley: Final point? You see, you cannot bring in any way whatever the Absolute in connection with the finite.

Mme. Blavatsky: It makes me despair that most of them must go beyond, they must touch, they must hear, they must sense, and in a way conceive it with one of their five physical senses, otherwise very few will understand. It is, my dear sir, the effect of your education from your childhood. All of you are brought up in a kind of material atmosphere, and you must have everything put before you so that it speaks to one of your senses, otherwise you cannot understand it. Even the God you believe in, you make something finite, you make him feel anger, you make him feel goodness, you make him smell sweet, and you make this, that, and the other of him and all kinds of things, just as though this God was a gigantic man and nothing more.

Mr. Hall: I mean this: when at the end of the Manvantara for the whole universe, so to speak, when everything gets reabsorbed into the Absolute, then when Maha-Pralaya is over, and a fresh Maha-Manvantara begins, might you not say in a sense there was, if I may use the term, a special point?

Mme. Blavatsky: But all this depends on which Maha-Pralaya you speak of. Is it that which refers to this little speck of dirt which we call our planetary chain, or is it the Maha-Pralaya of the whole universe?

Mr. Hall: Of the whole universe.

Mme. Blavatsky: What do we know of it? Why, in comparison with the Hindus, nothing. They just put 15 zeroes to show it.

Mr. B. Keightley: How can you answer the question? How can you ask it?

Mr. Kingsland: Have you read this last pamphlet on Parabrahm?[2]

Mr. Hall: No.

Mr. Kingsland: You would not ask it if you had. Read that and then you have the question answered. It is all there.

Mr. B. Keightley: Yes, it is all there.

Mme. Blavatsky: Let us hold to that which we can conceive. Don't let us go beyond the limits, not only of the universe, but the Kosmos; and let us hold to our solar system, and that is more than

---

2 *Parabrahm* by Amaravella (Edouard Coulomb), translated from *Le Lotus* by G.R.S. Mead. London: Theosophical Publishing Society, 1889. Vol. 1, no. 18 of *Theosophical Siftings*.

we can understand or conceive of in all our lives. As everything is "as below, so above," and as this is the first axiom in the occult sciences, therefore you can draw your analogies as much as the power of every man will allow him. That is all the advice I can give you. Some may go far beyond this, others cannot go as far as that. Everyone can conceive, but let us hold to this solar system, and it will be enough for the time being, otherwise we will go wool-gathering, and nothing will come out of it.

Mr. Kingsland: After this last pamphlet, I really think we ought to draw a line at this particular subject.

Mme. Blavatsky: Because the first thing will be that some of you gentlemen will have brain fever, and then I shall have the misery of seeing some of you shut up in a lunatic asylum. I can assure you it is so, and this thing can happen.

Mr. B. Keightley: I will give Hall a prescription. If he wants to understand the meaning of his own question, I will ask him to sit down for half an hour and write the figure one, and then go on for half an hour making zeroes after it. When he has done that I will ask him to state in words the figures he has written down, and when he has done it, I will tell him that is the first and second Maha-Manvantara he is talking about.

Mr. Hall: But in theory would not there be—

Mme. Blavatsky: Oh, theory! There you are.

The President: Take analogies, not theory.

Mr. B. Keightley: Sloka 4 (reads from *The Secret Doctrine*). Question 5: "Is the 'Radiant Essence' the same as the Luminous Egg? What is the root that grows in the Ocean of Life"?

Mme. Blavatsky: You see, this is again the same thing. You don't make the slightest allowance for the metaphorical mode of expression. You are all the same, if you please. There must be a certain solidarity. What one says, another will say. I don't make any distinction whatever there, so you are answerable one for the other. Of course the Radiant Essence is the same as the radiant or Golden Egg of Brahmâ. "The Root that grows in the Ocean of Life" is the potentiality that transforms into objective differentiation, like the universal, subjective, ubiquitous, undifferentiated germ, or the eternal potency of abstract nature. Now, is it so? Is it plain? And the "Ocean of Life" is the "One Life," "Paramatma" when the transcendental supreme and secondless soul is meant. "Jivatma" when we speak of the physical and animal, or rather, differentiation of Nature's soul—expressions all found in the Vedantin philosophy. Now try to remember, Paramatma and Jivatma are the same identically, and even the soul of a man and of an animal, a Nephesh, is just the same; but there is a distinction. One is the supreme subjective soul of the secondless, and the other is already in the manifested universe. Jivatma, that is to say, is the life that gives being to the atom, and the molecule, and the man, and everything in creation—plant, mineral, and so on.

The President: And the other is the potentiality; potency and potentiality express the difference.

Mr. B. Keightley: Then you say in the commentary, speaking about the Radiant Essence: "from an astronomical point of view," etc. (reads from *The Secret Doctrine,* page 67, b). Question 6. "Is the Radiant Essence, Milky Way, or World-Stuff, resolvable into stars or atoms, or is it non-atomic?"

Mme. Blavatsky: In its precosmic state, of course, the Radiant Essence is non-atomic, if by atoms you mean molecules or compound units, for where have you seen a real atom that you could show me? An atom is simply a mathematical point with regard to matter. It is what we call in occultism a mathematical point.

Mr. B. Keightley: It has position, it has location.

Mme. Blavatsky: It has location, certainly, but not a location as you understand it, because a real atom cannot be on this plane.

Mr. B. Keightley: That I understand.

Mme. Blavatsky: Then how can you ask? Just when you go on to this plane, you must go outside time and space.

Mr. Kingsland: An atom cannot, but a molecule can.

Mme. Blavatsky: What do you chemists call an atom?

Mr. Kingsland: This ought to be "resolvable into stars or molecules," not "into atoms." Now if you read it in that sense it will be all right.

Mr. B. Keightley: Then: "is it resolvable into stars or molecules, or is it non-molecular?"

Mme. Blavatsky: Most assuredly, because this world stuff from one plane to another goes and forms everything that you see, all the stars and all the worlds, and so on.

Mr. Kingsland: Then when may it be said to be sufficiently differentiated to call it molecular?

Mme. Blavatsky: Molecular, as you call it, is only simply on this our globe; it is not even on the other globes of our planetary chain, it does not exist in the same way. The others are already on another plane.

Mr. Kingsland: Is not the ether, for instance, molecular?

Mme. Blavatsky: I don't know. It may be molecular; yes, in its lower or lowest strata, then it may be, but the ether of science, that science suspects, is the grossest manifestation of Akasa. When it penetrates something, or forms something, it may be molecular, because it takes on the shape of it. Now, remember that ether is in every blessed thing that you can think of; there is not a thing in the universe where ether is not. Therefore we say it takes a shape, but not outside of the gross matter, which is also that ether, only crystallized. What are we, what is matter, but crystallized ether? This is what matter is.

Mr. Kingsland: Then the ether is on its way to a lower differentiation, on its way from Akasa, and it will become ether in this Manvantara or a future Manvantara—what we now know as the physical atoms.

Mme. Blavatsky: Most assuredly that is so, but not in this Manvantara.

Mr. B. Keightley: I don't know if I am right, but the difference as I understand it between atom and molecule, strictly speaking, is this: that a molecule must be composed of several atoms. The idea it conveys to one is that.

The President: It need not, there are also non-atomic molecules.

Mr. Kingsland: That is only a chemical term.

Mr. B. Keightley: And an atom is only one.

Mme. Blavatsky: May I tell you a thing and try to impress it upon you? You take a molecule, and fancy to yourselves that this molecule is an independent being *per se*. The seventh principle of every molecule will be the atom of which you speak. But you cannot catch it in your scales or your retorts or your chemical combinations. Now do you understand what we mean by atom? The atom is the seventh principle of every molecule, the finest, the smallest that you can find in this world. Why, what is one of the names of Brahmâ? It is "atom". He is called atom, and at the same time that he is an atom, he is the whole.

Mr. Gardner: Is it Atma?

Mr. Kingsland: Now you are saying it in a purely metaphysical sense. It is very important it should be distinguished from the way in which chemists use it.

Mme. Blavatsky: But you are all taking your ideas and the correctness of your language from how the chemists use it. I am the biggest ignoramus in the world in regard to chemistry. Why should I go and stuff my head with the speculations of today, when tomorrow I may have to throw them off, and take up some other speculations? You have {not} come to that point that there is one single thing you can feel perfectly sure of, that it is there, and that the truth will remain. It is an axiom that the truth, or the axiom of today, is the error of tomorrow.

Mr. B. Keightley: I think it would be a good thing if you can give us—not from our standpoint, but from the occult standpoint—the definition of atom and molecule, simply that we may understand.

Mme. Blavatsky: Look here, to do such a thing as that you have to make a glossary and dictionary of occult terms. For instance, such a glossary as we have now, trying to give some correct conception of words which the Orientalists use without knowing what they mean; and therefore enlarge the ideas, giving them more definitions, more meanings, and trying to do something for the better and clearer comprehension of the people. But if we began now to use the terms from the occult standpoint, none of you would understand a word, because you have not got a conception of the thing itself. You have to study first the science and just penetrate yourself with all these things that do really exist on the occult side of Nature, before you can understand those terms. What is the use? Now give one question please, and let me try to see if I can answer you, so that I may see whether you understand it or not. What is it that you want?

Mr. B. Keightley: We want to know about this atom.

Mme. Blavatsky: I am quite ready.

Mr. Kingsland: If the atom is such an abstract metaphysical conception of a single metaphysical point, how is it that we can speak of molecules as being composed of atoms?

Mme. Blavatsky: I never said that. A molecule, one of these that you speak of, is composed of an enormous quantity of other molecules that you cannot see, and each one is composed of as great a number again and the atom is—that which you call atom, I don't know in what sense, is some fiction of your imagination, but what we call an atom is simply the seventh principle of the molecule, as of everything else—of the smallest molecule you can find.

Mr. Kingsland: On this plane, take one of the metals, take iron. There is such a thing as the smallest molecule of iron, that is to say, a thing which cannot be divided without losing its molecular properties.

Mme. Blavatsky: What does it become, and why do you call iron an element? Why do you cheat the public and call it an element?

Mr. Kingsland: What does it become?

Mme. Blavatsky: If it loses its molecular property and becomes something else, what is that something else?

Mr. Kingsland: I suppose—

Mme. Blavatsky: But science must not suppose. I ask science.

Mr. Kingsland: No, no, we are talking occultly, we are trying to get at what occultism teaches.

Mme. Blavatsky: When it becomes non-molecular, it becomes resolved into one of its principles, of which you know nothing. There is not the smallest speck in this world, which has not got its seven principles. Mind you, what for us is the smallest atom on the plane of reality is something very objective indeed.

Mr. B. Keightley: You see, the scientific idea of atom or molecule, particularly of a molecule (because the idea of atom is very vague), has not got anything to do with bulk, whether it is visible under a microscope or not. Their definition is this: if you break up a molecule of iron, it will no longer show the properties on the physical plane that we know have characterized it. It enters a certain chemical combination in a particular way.

Mme. Blavatsky: Certain, certain and certain, that is all.

The President: Because they do not know.

Mme. Blavatsky: Then why should they go and dogmatize? We say it is the principles; let us say the astral body.

Mr. B. Keightley: I am not speaking of what happens beyond.

Mme. Blavatsky: The chemists will not see the astral body of that which is not molecular.

Mr. B. Keightley: The chemical idea of the thing is entirely—and we understand it to be entirely—limited to this point. They do not know what happens to the thing afterwards, and that is what I am trying to get some idea of, what occultism says about it, because there science simply folds her hands and says, "I don't know."

The President: Isn't it just as much a death of the molecule of iron as the losing of the physical body is called death on the physical plane? The remaining principles being there all the same, but minus the body. So the molecule is the earthly principle.

Mr. B. Keightley: Iron is not itself properly and occultly an element at all. It does not deserve the name.

The President: It is an element in one sense. It is not an element in the sense in which we speak of the four or seven elements. It is an element in the sense in which Crookes uses it. It is an element in the scientific sense—formed of the protyle or the undifferentiated matter. In that sense it is an element because it has certain definite properties.

Mme. Blavatsky: It is the elemental principle; therefore it is that they do not go beyond that. If you told me at once that they analyze or break up any molecule of iron and that it becomes two other things, that you could call elements. I would say: very well then, we have only to give a name, and then you will have something to speak about. But if they come and tell me it becomes nothing, why, go to bed!

Mr. B. Keightley: So far, science has not succeeded in breaking up the molecule of iron.

Mme. Blavatsky: Then if it has not succeeded, why then does it speak about it? They don't do so, and they speak of what could be done.

Mr. B. Keightley: Crookes says there is a probability that some day or another they will succeed.

Mme. Blavatsky: Then we will talk of it. So far they have not done it, and why should we talk about it?

Mr. Kingsland: Occultism says it is possible to do it; we want to know what will become of it when it is done?

Mme. Blavatsky: It won't be one principle; it will be several principles. It passes from the plane of objectivity to the plane of subjectivity.

The President: The molecule is the final production in the differentiation of matter, and if you can destroy that said molecule, in the sense in which the scientists would use that phrase, you are simply going back into the undifferentiation.

Mme. Blavatsky: Take the smallest grain of sand and try to break it up and see what it is. You cannot get at the first principles and the origin of things on this plane, and Crookes will be looking for it for 30,000 years, and he won't be able to find anything, for it is impossible to see anything of the kind on this plane.

The President: It cannot be done on this plane. You must be on another plane before you can do it. What Crookes has done with certain other metals is a very different thing. He has simply found there that people have been mistaken in thinking they were homogeneous, that is a very different thing.

Mr. B. Keightley: No, no! His theory—whether it is true or not I have no means of judging—goes a great deal further than that. He says that what are called elements—iron and so on, oxygen, hydrogen and so on—are, if I may use the phrase, points of stable equilibrium in the differentiation of protyle. He gives that curved picture, and he shows how all these elements representing different stages of more or less stable equilibrium succeeding each other in density or in some property come one after the other. Then the question is, what idea is it proper to attach to these points, which go at present in chemistry by the name of elements, looking at them in Crookes' sense? That is to say they are not elemental bodies, but they represent these points of stable equilibrium, certain stages in the evolution of matter on this plane.

Mme. Blavatsky: I am not able to coin a word.

The President: You said something to us about the three first gases the other day, some little time ago, which may bear upon it. There is something in *The Secret Doctrine* about it.

Mr. B. Keightley: We want to agree upon some word we can apply to these things that at present are called elements.

Mme. Blavatsky: Shall we call it Anu? That means atom, but it is the name of Brahmâ.

Mr. B. Keightley: What I want is to name these bodies which exist on this physical plane which possess these characteristics.

The President: If you call them chemical elements, that answers the purpose.

Mme. Blavatsky: I think so; what name can we give? People will say we have a jumble.

The President: If we say chemical elements, we know perfectly well we don't mean fire, water, earth and air.

Mr. B. Keightley: As long as it is said that the term chemical elements is not used with any idea that they are elemental bodies, but simply these stages of evolution, according to Crookes' view; we can adopt that phrase.

Mme. Blavatsky: They are the false noses of the molecule.

Mr. B. Keightley: That is rather an idea, that.

The President: You could not exactly call them the false noses of the elements.

Mme. Blavatsky: Well it is not a mask, it is a false nose.

Mr. B. Keightley: The whole position is that we don't know what they are.

Mr. Hall: They are considered apparent, anyway, by chemists.

The President: I think the phrase best for them is, "chemical elements."

Mr. B. Keightley: Have you got any more about the radiant essence, or did you read it all?

Mme. Blavatsky: Yes, I read it all. It is number 7 already we are at.

Mr. B. Keightley: You refer here, speaking about the World-stuff and the primordial matter, to the Hindu allegory of the "Churning of the Ocean of Space." Question 7. Can you give us an idea of how the analogies of "churning the ocean," "the cow of plenty," and "the war in heaven" are related to each other and to the cosmogonic process?

Mme. Blavatsky: Now fancy only this: I have got to give a thing which begins at non-being and ends at the end of the Maha-Pralaya, and I have got to give it in one of the séances at the Blavatsky Lodge in five minutes. How is it possible to put such a question as that? If you gave me one-twentieth part of the first question, I may be able to do it. In the first place, do you know what the "churning of the ocean" means with the Hindus?

Mr. B. Keightley: I know the story, the allegory.

Mme. Blavatsky: But what does it mean in reality? It simply means an allegorical representation of the unseen and the unknown primeval intelligences, the atoms of our occult science, fashioning and differentiating the shoreless ocean of the radiant essence. It means that it is the atoms which are churning the ocean, and that they are differentiating the matter. It is simply an allegorical representation.

Mr. B. Keightley: It refers also to a process you mention later on, of the vortical movements.

Mme. Blavatsky: Most assuredly; but this is one of the details. I speak of the general aspect of the thing. This is the allegorical representation of that period. Now to give the analogies between the "churning" and "war in heaven" is rather difficult. This war began at the first vibration of Manvantaric dawn and will end at the blast of the last trumpet, that is to say, the "war in heaven" is going on eternally. Theologians may have taken one period and made of it all kinds of things, e.g., the fall of man— the picture that is given in the Revelation, which has entirely another meaning in reality—but this war in heaven is going on eternally.

The President: As long as there is differentiation, there must be war.

Mme. Blavatsky: You cannot say otherwise. It is just as light and darkness fighting and trying each to overcome the other. Differentiation means contrast, and contrasts will be always fighting.

The President: But there are various stages of the war in heaven, referred to under different names.

Mme. Blavatsky: Most assuredly, there is the astronomical and the physical, and the war in heaven, when the first Manvantara begins in general; then for everyone every time there is a war in heaven. There is a war in heaven of the 14 Manus who are supposed to be the presiding genii of our Manvantaric plane, the Seed Manus and the Root Manus. The war in heaven means that there is a struggle and an adjustment, because everything tends to harmonize and equilibrate; everything must equilibrate before it can assume any kind of shape. The elements of which each one of us is composed are always fighting, one crowding out the other; and we change every moment, just as some of your men of science say. Or as one says when he is sick: "I am not anymore the man I was; I am quite a different man." It is quite true. We change every seven years of our lives, sometimes becoming worse than we were before.

The President: Then there really does not seem to be much analogy between that churning and the other, because that is a special process.

Mme. Blavatsky: It refers to the churning by the Gods, when the Nagas came and some of them stole of the Amrita, and there was war between Gods and Asuras, and the Gods were worsted. This refers to the first portion, to the extension of the universe and the differentiation of primordial, primeval matter.

Mr. Hall: Even literally, "churning" means differentiation.

Mme. Blavatsky: Oh, my dear Hall, you are a pundit! But churning means also something else. There are seven symbolical meanings to everything, not one. This is only cosmogonically speaking, that is what it refers to, but there are others, too. You can remember in Revelation that there is a thing in the 12th or the 8th chapter when the woman comes.

Mr. B. Keightley: Yes, and Saint Michael and the dragon.

Mme. Blavatsky: This I do not want to deal with now. Ask as many questions as you like.

Mr. B. Keightley: Question 8. In what sense can numbers be called entities?

Mme. Blavatsky: When there is no intelligence, when they are meant for digits, then certainly they are nothing but symbols, signs to express an idea. They must be intelligent entities, then what is your idea of asking this? What did you think about it?

Mr. B. Keightley: I don't know who put the question, really.

Mme. Blavatsky: Whose question was that?

Mr. Coulomb: Mine. I wanted to know what was the meaning of numbers.

Mme. Blavatsky: Why don't you look at the fingers of your hand? You would see that you had five on one hand and five on the other.

Mr. Coulomb: But they are not intelligent. (Laughter)

Mme. Blavatsky: You do lose your time in making useless questions.

Mr. B. Keightley: Those are all the written questions.

Mr. Hall: I should like to know how you vivify numbers.

Mme. Blavatsky: I do not vivify them at all. That is how I vivify them.

Mr. Hall: How do you attract the intelligence into them?

Mme. Blavatsky: Ask another time, early in the morning. No doubt there are many things you would like to know.

Mr. Hall: That can be done.

Mme. Blavatsky: How they do like to ask questions that are positively—well, they begin nowhere and end nowhere!

The President: I fancy Mr. Hall wants to know wherein lies the occult value of numbers.

Mme. Blavatsky: Have patience, and you may learn it.

Mr. Hall: I did not ask so much as that.

The President: But you expressed your question in that direction. That is a very interesting question.

Mme. Blavatsky: You had better go and begin by the A.B.C. of the question, and just ask the first questions, and I will answer you. Don't come and ask me right in the middle of a thing. You must ask me in order, and I am perfectly ready to answer you.

The President: Are all numbers that we have or can get all to be reduced to their various relations to the first seven rays? They all do fit in, don't they, in some way?

Mme. Blavatsky: All, yes, all; because the seven are seven principles, but the first one counts for ten. So it is with the Sephiroth; if you take the seven lower Sephiroth and the three higher, it makes ten, that is the perfect number.

The President: So that all those combinations, all possible combinations, will belong to one or other of the rays.

Mme. Blavatsky: Surely, the white ray, and then after that, its gradations come and form the first one. You take the prism; in what order do you have the colours, do you remember? The colours are given. So it begins and you can see how it is.

Mr. Kingsland: Why is the radiant essence here spoken of as seven inside and seven outside?

Mme. Blavatsky: Because it has seven principles on the plane of manifestation and seven principles on the plane of non-manifestation. Can I say to you anything better? What cross-examiners you are.

Mr. Kingsland: Not *cross*!

Mme. Blavatsky: No, *cross-examiners*.

Mr. B. Keightley: There you get back to the planes of non-being.

Mme. Blavatsky: I can assure you if you only took the trouble to read the things and immediately form a conception in your head, it would bring you to the correspondences and analogies, and you would understand it without putting any of these questions; because, as I say, it is an axiom and a rule you must not depart from: as below so it is above, as above so it is below. Only put it on another plane and it comes to the same thing.

Mr. B. Keightley: To my mind this idea has become absolutely plain, that what we refer to as non-being and non-manifestation is to be understood as only referring to our intelligence and our intellect and to us. It is very evident you cannot speak of and you don't refer in *The Secret Doctrine* to *absolute* non-being and *absolute* non-manifestation at all.

Mme. Blavatsky: I refer to absolute non-being from the standpoint of our finite and relative intellects. This is what I do, but not at all what it would be, because that which is for us absoluteness, perhaps if you go on the plane higher, it will be something relative for those on the plane above.

Mr. B. Keightley: And if you go more above, it will become something more relative. In fact, with our intellects we are in too great a hurry to get to the Absolute and so draw a line.

Mme. Blavatsky: You are all in too much of a hurry, and if you go on splitting hairs your brains will become like a homogeneous jelly. It is a very dangerous thing, this. Try to go one after the other and not miss any of the rungs of the ladder, or else it will lead you into some very extraordinary places.

Mr. Kingsland: I was wondering how far that would apply to the molecules that we were just discussing.

Mme. Blavatsky: It applies to the molecules just the same. The lowest one will apply to that plane where the molecules are seen and tested by your chemists.

Mr. Kingsland: But the seven outside would not refer only to this plane of matter.

Mme. Blavatsky: It does, and the seven inside, those that are beyond are beyond. We might just as well say 49, or multiply the seven *ad infinitum*. It is simply said to cover the ground, and so there are seven outside and seven inside—seven outside, that is to say, those that go down below; and seven inside, those we are not concerned with, because we would not understand much, because we do not know anything about them, but it does not at all limit the thing to 14. (after a pause) Well, everyone waits and nobody speaks.

Mr. Johnston: I did not clearly understand what was meant by the war in heaven. Can there be something in a place of bliss which can amount to war?

Mme. Blavatsky: War in heaven means simply in space. If you talk of heaven from the Christians standpoint, of course, it will be heaven and the golden harp.

The President: Or if you take even the Latin caelum.

Mr. Hall: Or take the original vehicle—it means space.

Mr. B. Keightley: It is only in England, particularly in the churches, that the idea of heaven as a place of bliss exists. The word itself has no such meaning attached to it.

Mme. Blavatsky: Why, the Most High in heaven means simply the sun. It has meant it before *Christianity*, and it meant it after *Christianity*. For four or five centuries they had no higher idea of God, I can assure you, than the sun. Let them come and say now that it was a symbol and a visible sign and so on. I say that they had no higher conception. I do not mean the initiates, I mean the people—the hoi polloi—the masses. There is no fitter symbol in the world than the sun; the sun gives life and radiance and everything, light and being and health, and it is the Most High in heaven.

Mr. Johnston: I thought it referred to the Christian conception.

Mme. Blavatsky: After that the sky, which is the Dyaus, the Sanskrit Dyaus, became the God, and this God was as the Lawgiver. The Son and the sun in the heavens became the Father in heaven, while "Heaven" became the abode of the Father, and he was humanized or anthropomorphized.

Mr. Johnston: I see now in what sense it is used.

Mr. B. Keightley: You will find all about the war in heaven in *The Secret Doctrine*, second volume.

Mme. Blavatsky: You will see what it is, because it has great reference to the evolution of mankind, of the intelligence of mankind, when man sprang from the animal—not from an animal, I mean not from one of the Darwinian ape-ancestors, but simply from an instinctive mass of matter—and when he became endowed with intellect. Then you will see the meaning of the war in heaven, when it is said that the angels fought, or in other words, they incarnated in humanity.

The President: Now you have a special aspect of it, one of the many.

Mme. Blavatsky: Yes, the metaphysical aspect, one of the seven. There is the astronomical aspect and all kinds of aspects. Why is it, if you please, that they give in the churches bread and wine? Why is it that you have the Communion of bread and wine? Simply because it was an offering to the sun and to the earth. The earth was supposed to be, metaphorically speaking, the Bride or the wife of the sun and the sun fecundated the earth, and there was the wine and the bread. It is one of the oldest pagan ceremonials and festivals, which finally came to be adopted by the theologians in the church. It was a purely pagan festival. It was in one place called the mysteries of Proserpine, and in another place called by another name and so on, and then it came and landed in the church, and became a sacrament. There is the sun, there is the earth, there is humanity—the humanity which is not sun but son, which is the third, and there they made all these ceremonials and these mysteries. I am going to give in *Lucifer* the roots of ritualism and modern masonry, on church ritualism and modern masonry, and you will read it all in the next *Lucifer*. I begin a series of articles.

Mr. Gardner: Do you mean the sun represented it?

Mme. Blavatsky: No, I don't mean that at all. The sun represented the father and the moon the mother, and after that humanity represented the Son and the wine and the bread were productions of the earth and were made sacred, if you please, in those solar ceremonies. They were offered to all the solar gods, to Bacchus and to Apollo and to everyone; "this is my flesh and this is my blood," and so it is. Perhaps I hurt the feelings of some Christians here.

Which of you is a Christian? I think you are all blue infidels, as far as I can see, and nobody is hurt much. Speak, any of you who feel hurt in their Christian feelings.

Mr. Hall: No, there is no Peter here.

Mme. Blavatsky: Because you ask me and I am obliged to tell you what I know. If there was a clergyman, here perhaps I would abstain. No, I don't think I would, because he has no business to come here if he does not want to hear things not to his advantage.

Mr. Gardner: There is a question I should like to ask you. You referred to it in the second volume of *The Secret Doctrine*, on the Pyramids.

Mme. Blavatsky: The Pyramid again has something to do with the Son.

Mr. Gardner: You say man is represented by 113, numerical value. Do you mean that is the Hebrew of the word man?

Mme. Blavatsky: Yes, in the Kabalah, it is. It is Kabalistically the value of the Hebrew characters.

Mr. B. Keightley: According to Mr. Ralston Skinner.

The President: But 113 adds up to 5; and the five-pointed star represents man always.

Mme. Blavatsky: It represents man by the letters, because the Hebrew word means man; if you take every letter and if you take the corresponding number and if you put these numbers together, it gives you 113.

Mr. Gardner: The numerical value of the Hebrew letters.

Mme. Blavatsky: Certainly, of the Hebrew letters. It does not mean at all the Sanskrit letters. I never said it did. Every system has got its own calculation. In Hebrew it is quite a different thing. If you take all the signs of the Zodiac and if you put them together and sum up the numbers, every sign of the Zodiac will give you a name of the 12 sons of Jacob.

Mr. Gardner: It is man in Hebrew. It is not man in English.

Mme. Blavatsky: No, but the English language has not invented the language of the Kabalah. It takes the property of other persons and then sets itself up as very high.

Mr. Gardner: And then I fancy there is a misprint here. You say 113 over 2. It has got 133 over 2.[3]

Mme. Blavatsky: Maybe there is a misprint. I am not answerable for that.

Mr. Keightley: I think it is in a quotation from Ralston Skinner.

Mme. Blavatsky: Ralston Skinner is a Mason and an extraordinary Kabalist.

Mr. B. Keightley: It is a mistake reproduced from a mistake of his.

Mme. Blavatsky: Just as I have taken it, so it is. If I had paid attention to it, I would not have done it.

Mr. Gardner: Then you take from the top of the great step to the ceiling {of the Great Pyramid}.

Mme. Blavatsky: These you can all find from Smyth.[4] Ralston Skinner has elaborated it, but yet Ralston Skinner is perfectly mistaken in this, because he speaks of things as though really such a thing as the temple of Solomon ever existed, or the ark of Noah, and so on. Why, it never existed in those measurements.

Mr. Gardner: And that coffer in the King's Chambers has never been removed.

Mme. Blavatsky: I saw it there a few years ago. It is one with the floor as far as I could see. I am not sure, though.

---

3 *The Secret Doctrine*, II:466.]
4 Charles Piazzi Smyth, 1819-1900, Astronomer Royal of Scotland.

Mr. Gardner: And do you know whether that is anything occult, that niche in the Queen's Chamber?

Mme. Blavatsky: Everything has got its significance and everything relates to mysteries, to the mysteries of initiation. It was the great temple of the official initiation.

Mr. B. Keightley: Smyth's opinions are completely knocked on the head. They are not correct because of Petrie,[5] who was rather a pyramidalist before he went out there, spent months most carefully verifying all Piazzi Smyth's measures, and he knocked them on the head by proving all the measurements are wrong.

Mme. Blavatsky: But Ralston Skinner does not take Smyth, and I have taken him out of it. For the last three years I have been in correspondence with him, and I said take care. It is so and so. I gave him the correspondences as it was in the Chaldean and as it was really in the Indian teaching, and he took my suggestions and he found three or four mistakes, and I have got any quantity of his manuscripts in which he gives his ideas; but he is not sure of his facts, and he is carried on by an idea. Now he has changed his ideas in the new book that he wants me to write an introductory chapter to.

Mr. B. Keightley: You see, all these fellows are very apt to get crazy after a fixed idea.

Mme. Blavatsky: You cannot learn anything unless you are perfectly impartial and have not got a hobby. Otherwise you are sure to get mixed up and you will come and not bring your speculations to fit your facts but your facts to fit your speculations.

Mr. Gardner: Isn't it true that some of these men were seeking to find out other chambers in it, and one of them held up a light in such a position that no breeze from outside could touch it, and yet the candle flickered and he came to the conclusion that there must be other chambers, and shortly afterwards a message came from the

---

5 William Flinders Petrie, English Egyptologist, 1853-1942.

Khedive[6] to tell him to discontinue his researches.

Mme. Blavatsky: The Khedive is a donkey in these sciences; he is not even a Mason. He is a very nice young man.

Mr. Gardner: He might have the idea of doing so.

Mme. Blavatsky: The idea of what?

Mr. Gardner: These ideas coming at the right moment.

Mme. Blavatsky: I knew him when he ran about without trousers, a child of five years. I know him perfectly well. He was a very nice child, and he is become a very nice young man. But I can assure you he has nothing mystical in him.

Mr. Hall: I think Mr. Gardner means he might have been put up to do it by somebody.

Mme. Blavatsky: His father, yes. His father with all his great vices, with all his immorality, Ismail Pasha,[7] was a man who had a streak of mysticism in him. He always had the Bedouins with him and the monks, and he knew some men who were extremely learned. But this one knows nothing; he was brought up by English and French nurses in the harem of his several mothers.

Mr. Kingsland: And he is not even a Mason.

Mr. B. Keightley: It is an interesting question to know this, whether these secret places, these chambers, do exist underneath the Pyramids.

Mme. Blavatsky: Certainly they do.

Mr. B. Keightley: They must be protected in some way.

Mme. Blavatsky: They are protected in all kinds of ways. They are protected by the greediness of the Arabs and they are protected in many, many ways, and the thing is that unless they go and turn off

---

6 Title of the ruler of Egypt, meant here for Tewfik Pasha, 1852-1892.
7 1830-1895, deposed in favor of his son in 1879.

the Nile at a certain spot, they will never get to them. They have to turn off the Nile and get to the iron door that exists to the present day, and has not been opened for two thousand years. There is a Mason that knew it, a Mason named [ ], who was the Venerable of the Lodge.

Mr. Gardner: At the Cairo Lodge.

Mme. Blavatsky: One of your Lodges, your real true blue Masonic Lodges.

Mr. Hall: How could an iron door last 2,000 years?

Mme. Blavatsky: Why could not an iron door last not only 2,000 years, but 20,000 years?

Mr. Gardner: Would not it rust?

Mme. Blavatsky: It would not rust. Perhaps there are several incredulous; I say it exists.

Mr. B. Keightley: His point is any iron door however thick would {have} rusted through in a thousand years.

Mme. Blavatsky: It would not be destroyed.

Mr. B. Keightley: Yes, eaten through, perfectly porous.

Mme. Blavatsky: My dear sir, I tell you it is protected, it is not a door of such iron as you would take from a smith. Just as they do with their mummies, if mummies have lasted, then I suppose an iron door could.

Mr. B. Keightley: What is interesting is that the others are so infernally greedy; if they knew anything about it they would go for the things that are there.

Mme. Blavatsky: They do not know it. I spoke to Maspero;[8] he is a Fellow of the Theosophical Society. I passed the whole day with

---

8 Gaston Maspero, French Egyptologist, 1846-1916.

him in Cairo. I asked him about all the papers that he ever found. Maspero is the Director of the Boulaq Museum.[9]

Mr. B. Keightley: Which, by the by, is to be no more at Boulaq.

Mme. Blavatsky: He was there, then, and we sat there between the tombs and the old mummies, and he was telling me of some of the things he has discovered, and he said, "never could I give it to the world, because I would lose my situation." Because Marriette Bey[10] tried to do it, and he was not listened to, and the academy said some very disagreeable things about all kinds of secrets that are there. He found a whole room, he told me—and this thing is known, by the by—and this room was full—Maspero discovered it—it was full of all kinds of retorts and alchemical things and those utensils that the alchemists used; and several parchments he found that he has read and deciphered; enough to see that they had all these alchemical secrets, and he found even some powders and things that he feels sure was the powder to make gold. He found it in this room which exists there to this day. I was going there, only Mrs. Oakley[11] could not stop.

Mr. Gardner: That is near Luxor.

Mr. B. Keightley: What is he going to do with all his collection when he dies?

Mme. Blavatsky: He is a very young man about 38 or so. He is no more than 38 years of age.

Mr. Gardner: What post does he hold over there?

Mme. Blavatsky: Director of the Museum at Boulaq in Cairo. He is one of the most learned of the Egyptologists.

Here the proceedings closed.

---

9 The former home of the Museum of Egyptian Antiquities, located in the district of Boulaq in Cairo.
10 Auguste Mariette, French Egyptologist, 1821-1881.
11 Isabel Cooper-Oakley, 1854-1914, English Theosophist who accompanied HPB to India in 1884.

8.
The Theosophical Society.
Meeting of the Blavatsky Lodge,
at 17 Lansdowne Road, Holland Park, W.
on Thursday, February 28, 1889.

Mr. Harbottle in the Chair

Mr. B. Keightley: Stanza 3 continued, Sloka 5. "The root remains," etc. (Reads from *The Secret Doctrine*.) What is meant by saying that these remain?

Mme. Blavatsky: I beg your pardon. Those are Mr. Kingsland's. Well, let them be first. It is Mr. Kingsland who asks this, and I am going to answer him first. All right, let them be. Now, "that these remain." It means that whatever is, and whatever the plurality of the manifestation is, is all one element, one, that is what it means. It is always summed up in one.

Mr. B. Keightley: It really means they are different aspects of the one element.

Mme. Blavatsky: Of the one, certainly.

Mr. Kingsland: It would appear from that that it means almost that they remain without differentiation.

Mme. Blavatsky: Oh, no, don't pitch into the style if you can't say anything better. You see, I tried to translate as well as I could, you know, as close to the original as possible.

Mr. B. Keightley: Then speaking in the Commentary of Curds you say: "The curds are the first differentiation," etc. (Reads from *The Secret Doctrine*.) Are we to suppose that the Milky Way is composed of matter in a state of differentiation other than that with which we are acquainted?

Mme. Blavatsky: Most assuredly it is; it is the storehouse of the materials out of which the new stars, planets and all bodies are produced. You cannot have matter in that state on earth here. It is impossible; it is quite a different kind of matter.

The President: It is protyle.

Mme. Blavatsky: Oh, no, it is not protyle, it is less but it is quite different. It is positively a storehouse of all kinds of materials, which when it comes on to the earth, let us say, or into our solar system, it is entirely differentiated. Besides that, the matter that you have beyond the solar system is entirely in a different state of differentiation.

Mr. Kingsland: The matter we see here we see entirely by reflected light. Do we see the Milky Way by the light we make ourselves?

Mme. Blavatsky: Most assuredly; you cannot see otherwise; it is impossible, you cannot. When they come and take the measurements of stars, and the distances, and all that, I say it is impossible it should be correct, because you must always allow a certain margin for the effect of optical delusions and so on.

Mr. Gardner: Refraction.

Mr. Kingsland: Then from an astronomical point of view is the Milky Way outside altogether of the stellar system?

Mme. Blavatsky: It is really and entirely another state of matter, and matter is, as I say to you, the material out of which everything will be made.

The President: But outside as regards state, not as regards position?

Mme. Blavatsky: No.

Mr. B. Keightley: Because, for instance, they have just been making very wonderful photographs of the nebulæ, the great nebula of

Andromeda, etc.

Mr. Kingsland: Is that matter in the same state as the Milky Way?

Mme. Blavatsky: I could not tell you; I am not learned enough for it. But it is quite a different state of matter altogether.

Mr. Gardner: What about the planets?

Mme. Blavatsky: Oh, the planets are a different thing. You cannot find anything in the planets that there is not on earth.

Mr. Kingsland: Then the Milky Way, we may take it, radiates its own light. It is analogous to the state of matter that is in the sun.

Mme. Blavatsky: It is the "World-stuff," as I call it. You cannot call it by any other name. I say to you again I am not learned enough to tell you the difference. I do think there is a difference between the nebulæ and the real Milky Way which you see, just as though it was like a highway of dust, like a film.

Mr. Kingsland: In other words, the nebulæ are more differentiated.

The President: But some of the nebulæ are resolvable.

Mr. B. Keightley: But they are clusters of stars; they are not true nebulæ at all.

The President: It has never been proved there is no nebulæ.

Mr. B. Keightley: The Andromeda.

The President: In other words, you have not yet succeeded in resolving it.

Mme. Blavatsky: Well, yes; but I cannot believe in it. I think if it is not today, tomorrow it will be proven that it has not been resolved or resolvable. It seems to me it is all simple theory—that it turns out something else, as many times we have been mistaken already.

Mr. B. Keightley: Then this matter, "Radiant and Cool"?

Mme. Blavatsky: You just forgive it, if you please.

Mr. B. Keightley: As it stood originally, it is "This matter, which, according to the revelation received in the primeval Dhyani-Buddhas," etc. (Reads).[1]

Mme. Blavatsky: "Radiant" it ought to be, and it is put "radical." They have made of primordial matter something political. They have got politics on the brain! I never put "radical." I put "radiant and cool," I can assure you. I could find the manuscripts and I could show you it is so. It is one of these mistakes of the printers and sub-editors and so on. There is another thing I wish to ask. Why does Mr. Kingsland say this was seen probably by the First Race, and so on?

Mr. B. Keightley: He says—this matter appearing "when seen from the earth," etc. (*The Secret Doctrine*)—Mr. Kingsland asks: Would not this be to the perception of the First Race and not to our present physical senses?

Mme. Blavatsky: I say no.

Mr. Kingsland: No; that is answered now by the first question.

Mme. Blavatsky: Certainly, because we see just in this way.

Mr. B. Keightley: Then Sloka 6. "The root of life," etc. (Reads *The Secret Doctrine*.) The first question put is: "What are the various meanings of the term 'fire' on the different planes of Kosmos?"

Mme. Blavatsky: Now, you see, there is a question again that they put me! I have to give about {the} 49 fires on every plane, and there are seven times seven—seven planes. I have got to give this very *easy* explanation, if you please. Now, how is it possible? Hold to something and ask a definite question. Fire is the most mystic of all elements, as the most Divine, and to give even a small percentage of its meanings in their various applications on even one plane, let alone on the different planes of Kosmos, is perfectly impossible.

---

1 *The Secret Doctrine*, 1:69.

Now, shall I give you on one plane, in the solar system?

Mr. B. Keightley: Please.

Mme. Blavatsky: Very well; take, for instance, the solar fire on our plane alone. Fire is the father of light, light the parent of heat and of air, vital air, says the occult book, and the absolute deity can be referred to as darkness, the dark fire. Then the first progeny of Light is truly the first self-conscious God, for what is light but the world-illuminating and life-giving deity? Light is Time, what from an abstraction has become a reality. Now, this is which you could not understand. Do you understand the meaning of it? Light is Time, which Time from an abstraction has become a reality. If there were no light you would not have time.

Mr. B. Keightley: Because you would have no point.

The President: Darkness is duration.

Mme. Blavatsky: And there is no time in duration except in Manvantaras. No one has ever seen real primordial light, the one true light, but what we see is only its broken rays or reflections, which become denser and less luminous as they descend into form and matter. Do you really think with the physicists that it is the sun which is the cause of Light? We say (see *The Secret Doctrine*) that the sun gives nothing from himself, because he has nothing to give. He is a reflection and no more; a bundle of electro-magnetic forces, one of the countless milliards of knots of Fohat. Now, I want you to remember this expression, "knots." Fohat is called the thread of primordial light, the thread of Ariadne,[2] indeed, in this labyrinth of chaotic matter. This thread runs down and down through the seven parent planes and ties itself occasionally on its way into knots. This is how they explain it in the occult books. Every plane being septenary—hence the 49 mystical and physical forces—the big knots form stars and suns and systems, the smaller planets. It is, of course, a metaphor, but the electro-magnetic knot of our sun and its forces are

---

2 Daughter of King Minos of Crete who gave Theseus the thread that led him out of the Labyrinth.

neither tangible nor dimensional, nor yet material or even molecular, as, for instance, common electricity is. Now, saying not molecular, I say that which Helmholtz[3] says, but I will just say what we mean by saying electricity is molecular. It is a reflection, as I say the sun is; the sun absorbs, psychicises, and vampirises his subject within his system. He gives out nothing *per se*. Now, how unutterably foolish it is to say that the solar fires are being consumed or extinguished. Were it so, would not the sun, while losing its heat and flames, be also losing something of its dimensions or magnitude? Do you think so? Is it possible? Must we think, then, that the sun is at the bottom a kind of round disc, made of some inconsumable asbestos, which, once the pitch around it is consumed, will get extinguished? Why, it would be that. If the solar fires were to go out you would see the sun shrinking or diminishing.

Mr. Kingsland: We need not necessarily suppose that would take place within any observable time.

Mme. Blavatsky: I do not know if they say it goes with such rapidity as that. Listen to Sir Wm. Thompson[4] and you will learn what he says. The sun, it is said, does not give out anything, it doesn't take anything; it feeds and works within its own system; it vampirises from all the planets and from everything that comes within it, and sometimes very likely it is almost impossible that anything should come into the sun from without the solar system. This is what is taught now. I do not give you my ideas; they are very heterodox, they are perfectly unscientific. I show you what the Occult Sciences say. They do not allow that the planets have been formed or ejected out of the sun, as the modern theory goes. They say it was not so, that the sun is not even what they say. There are no fires, there is nothing tangible in it; it is merely a reflection, a reflection of this. It is called a bundle of magneto-electric forces.

Mr. ———: Do not the occultists accept Laplace's theory?[5]

---
3 Hermann von Helmholtz, German physicist, 1821-1894.
4 Sir William Thomson (Lord Kelvin), 1824-1907, British mathematical physicist.
5 Pierre-Simon Laplace, French mathematician and astronomer, 1749-1827,

8. MEETING FEBRUARY 28, 1889

Mr. B. Keightley: That the solar system is originally a nebula, more or less, an enormous spherical mass of very diffuse matter which is revolving round its axis at a very great rate. There are differences, because according to Laplace's theory, you get this globular mass spinning very fast. In consequence of its rotation it breaks up into rings. Gradually, owing to small changes, those rings get condensed and form planets. If they do not form planets they form meteors.

Mme. Blavatsky: Do you mean to say he says it is from that Milky Way we have been talking about just now? Then it is the "World-stuff," and it goes into eternal rotation. It begins by suns and after having made the big knots it comes in the smaller ones, and so on.

Mr. B. Keightley: The point of that theory is that all these planets round the sun are formed from these rings; but elsewhere, in *The Secret Doctrine*, you state that before a heavenly body of any kind settles down to sober family life as a planet it is first a comet and goes careering through space. Well, that is quite contrary to Laplace altogether.

Mme. Blavatsky: Laplace is not an occultist, but yet there is something very near what you state. I never studied Laplace in my life.

Mr. ———: This is the nucleus of the whole system.

Mr. B. Keightley: No, no, no, that is not Laplace's theory.

Mr. ———: Yes, he thought all those rings were thrown out from the periphery of the mass.

Mr. B. Keightley: No, in consequence of the rapid rotation. There are points of minimum and maximum velocity. These are not shown mathematically. There are certain points at which the strains (?) {rings?} are unequal. The space between two rings is left void by this process of condensation. Then if there is anything of that kind which disturbs the equilibrium of one of those rings it will gradually break

---

famous for his probability theory.

up, but there is no idea of things being thrown off from the sun.

Mr. ——: I do not mean it exactly in that sense; I meant outside.

The President: May I ask one question which I think bears upon that? Does the sun survive several series of planetary existences? For instance, in *The Secret Doctrine* you say that the present earth is the daughter of the moon.

Mme. Blavatsky: Daughter, yes. I know what you want to say; of course it is. Our Pralaya is quite a different thing, a very different one from the Solar Pralaya, of course.

The President: Because that, in itself, answers the suggestions that the present planets are thrown off from the sun during the formation of the sun itself, and is itself a contradiction of Laplace's theory.

Mme. Blavatsky: I say that Laplace's theory looks like ours, because we say everything comes from the Milky Way, and that it begins when the Manvantaric dawn of the solar system begins, and that it goes on. And they show Fohat running like a thread; and these threads sometimes get entangled in a knot, and the central star, the solar system, begins the little knots, and so on.

The President: Then the theory must be taken very generally, and certainly not specifically, as applied to our solar system as it at present exists. In that case that would simply mean the sun was, so to say, slightly older than the rest of the planets.

Mr. B. Keightley: It is said elsewhere that all the planets have been comets. I am not sure, but there is a suggestion, and I am not certain how far it is intended to go, that all the planets have been suns before they settled down to planetary life.

Mme. Blavatsky: And every planet will become that which the moon has become now, and every time it will become like the moon: it will shoot out its principles and make another planetary chain as ours is. Our earth is very, very young, and such moons as ours there are but we don't see them because they are nearly faded out.

This one is already quite old. When they come and tell me that that moon is a bit of the earth, and that it was shot out, I say it is perfect nonsense. "When the day was only two hours old," I think that is what they say, and now they have been making the calculation that to make the day 23 hours instead of 24 would require something like 600,000,000 of years.

Mr. Kingsland: You say the electromagnetic emanation from the sun is neither molecular nor dimensional.

Mme. Blavatsky: I will just explain this here. The sun has but one distinct function. He gives the impulse of life to all that moves and breathes and has its being within its light. It is stated in *The Secret Doctrine* that the sun is the throbbing heart of the system. You remember, each throb is an impulse, very well, but this heart is invisible: no astronomer will ever see any more than you, I, or anyone else, that which is concealed is that heart, and that which we see and feel are simply the apparent flames and fires, and they are only the nerves that govern the muscles of the solar system. Now, did I express myself well? They are not the muscles, they are the nerves, the impulses. This is a real occult theory.

Mr. Kingsland: But now there must be the material base in the sun.

Mme. Blavatsky: There is, but we do not see it. The sun as we see it is simply the reflection. It is simply the reflection of that which exists, a bundle of electromagnetic forces—whatever it is. You see, they call it the heart, but it is not the heart, the heart is concealed. What we see is simply—well, let us say all the planets and everything are the muscles, and that which we see are the nerves that give the impulse, you understand.

The President: Actually, we don't see the material core, the centre, but simply, its surroundings, its envelope.

Mme. Blavatsky: Just so, the radiance that it throws off, but we can never see the real thing.

Mr. Gardner: And the sun spots?

Mme. Blavatsky: That I have explained in *The Secret Doctrine*. Now, for the impulse; I speak of it not as a mechanical impulse, but a purely spiritual one. What I would call nervous impulse, if I make use of the right word.

Mr. B. Keightley: Yes, that is to say, not an impulse thought of as a vibration on the physical plane, of the physical nerve fibre, but that which underlies that in the same way that a sound is different from the vibration.

Mme. Blavatsky: Now you ask about the various meanings of the term "fire" in *The Secret Doctrine*. Under this term the occultists comprehend all. Fire is the universal deity and the manifesting God life; fire is ether, and ether is born of motion, and motion is the eternal, direct, invisible fire. Again, light sets in motion and controls all in nature, from that highest primordial ether down to the tiniest molecule in space. Remember this occult axiom: motion is the Alpha and the Omega of that which you call electricity, galvanism, magnetism, sensation, moral or physical thought, and even life on this plane. It is motion which is the Alpha and the Omega of all that, and motion is simply the manifestation of fire, what we call the dark fire. All cosmical phenomena were therefore referred to by the occultists and the Rosicrucians as animated geometry. You will find it always referred to as animated geometry—every cosmic phenomenon, every polar function is only a repetition of primeval polarity. Every motion begets heat, and ether in motion is heat. When it slackens its motion, then cold is generated, for cold is ether in a latent condition. Mind you I give you the Kabalistic terms and simply translate the things. Within the seven principal states of nature are the three positive and three negative principles synthesized by the primordial light. They are six states. The three negative states are: first, darkness, second, cold, third, vacuum or the nothing. The three positive states are: first, light on our plane, second, heat, third, all nature or everything in nature. Thus fire is the unity of the universe. Pure fire without fuel is Deity at the upper rung. Cosmic fire or that which calls it forth is every body and atom of nature in the manifested nature. Name me one thing which does not contain latent fire in itself, and then you can contradict me. Everything is fire, but fire under various forms.

Mr. Kingsland: In fact, it has as many differentiations as matter.

Mme. Blavatsky: Because fire you can never come and analyze as you do with air and water and say that is composed of such and such things. You know, broadly speaking, it is combustion, but fire is the one great mystery of this universe, and it is everything, and this fire is what they call Deity, and I say that the fire worshippers who worship the sun are a thousand times more philosophical than we, for this is the one great symbol that can be understood. I do not say the sun is such a very great unity in the universe, but in our solar system it is the ambassador, the representative of the real creative force or Deity, principle, call it whatever you like; you understand my meaning. Now listen: when we say that fire is the first of the elements, it is only the first in our visible universe; this fire of which we speak, which everyone of us knows under its various forms, and that fire that we all know even on the highest plane of our solar universe, the plane of globe A and G. In one respect fire is only the fourth, for the occultists say, and even the medieval Kabbalists say, that to our human perception and even that of the highest angels or Dhyan-Chohans, the universe, deity, is darkness, and from this darkness the first appearance of Logos is—what do you think? It is not light; it is weight, air, or ether, the first thing that weighs, that cannot be seen, and yet it weighs in its primordial state. Then the second is light, the third, heat, and the fourth, fire. The fire that we know, mind you; I don't speak about the universal fire, that is a different thing. Now, will you please put the questions plainly, because I am rather tired of them. I want really serious questions. I get mad over these questions and I want to put things that I can only put when I am mad.

Mr. B. Keightley: Now that question of weight suggests a thing that would be very interesting. It is said over and over again in the [ ] theosophy that the scientific theory of gravity is untrue. Well now what do you mean, what does an occultist mean when he speaks of weight? Does he mean attraction?

Mme. Blavatsky: Well I don't know, weight is weight, how can I explain it otherwise?

The President: Does weight exist without gravity?

Mme. Blavatsky: Well it is gravity in the occult sense; it is not gravity as you call it on the Newtonian principle. We can explain it and do simply as attraction and repulsion. This weight is all because it throws out, it goes in circuit and absorbs again and it all proceeds to create all the universe and everything that is below. It always is this weight which you cannot say is above or below or on the right side or the left. This weight is something within but not within as to size, but within as to perception, differentiation and everything.

Mr. Kingsland: It is the same thing as we had previously, the expanding from within, without.

The President: The real point seems to be that if gravity is simply attraction and repulsion, that it must be the first of the attributes, so to say, of any differentiation whatever. As soon as you have two things, they must be pulverized.

Mme. Blavatsky: Surely.

The President: And therefore they may {be} pulverised in darkness.

Mme. Blavatsky: How can you explain otherwise the comets that go against the law of gravitation, how can you? It has been seen hundreds of times, comets in most cases go with their tails right against gravitation.

Mr. B. Keightley: They go and flap their tails in the face of the sun, in fact.

Mme. Blavatsky: It is an insult to the sun and the sun sits quiet.

Mr. ———: I thought those tails were a certain gas.

Mme. Blavatsky: Even gases have some weight. I know it from the blood poisoning. Well, what is the fourth question?

Mr. Gardner: I should like to ask about the question of weight with regard to that triangle. You told us—

Mme. Blavatsky: This is out of the programme.

Mr. B. Keightley: Number 3, you have practically answered. It is this, what are the meanings of "water" in the same applications?

Mme. Blavatsky: Well, water being composed of 1/9 of hydrogen (a very inflammable gas, as we are told, and without which no organic body is found), of 8/9 of oxygen (which we are told produces combustion when too rapidly combined with a body), what is water but one of the forms of primordial fire, in a cold or latent and fluidic form? It is nothing else. This is in reality what water is.

Mr. B. Keightley: It is the cold state.

Mme. Blavatsky: The cold and fluidic state of fire. It is the female aspect of fire, as matter is the female aspect of spirit.

Mr. Kingsland: Is there any connection between the numbers?

Mme. Blavatsky: Most assuredly. Numbers and colours, everything is connected. This, if you please, is esoteric.

Mr. B. Keightley: Question 4. Are fire and water the same as Kwan-Shai-Yin and Kwan-Yin?

Mme. Blavatsky: Reverse the question and ask are Kwan-Shai-Yin and Kwan-Yin the same as fire and water, or rather are the latter the symbols of these, and I will say yes: but what does it mean? The two deities in their primordial manifestation are the Diadic or dual God, the sexual nature and Prakriti.

Mr. B. Keightley: Then Sloka 7: "Behold O Lanoo," etc. (reads from *The Secret Doctrine*). The question is number 5. Will you give us the terms corresponding to the three Logoi amongst the words Oeaohoo, Oeaohoo, the younger, Kwan-Shai-Yin, the Kwan-Yin, father-mother, fire and water, bright space and dark space?

Mme. Blavatsky: No I won't (laughter). Have you not just read it is Oeaohoo, the younger, the three stars? Why did I put the three stars "whom thou knowest now as Kwan-Shai-Yin"? You know it is that, well enough—or shall I give you a series of quadruple stars? If I put three stars it is not that I did not know the things, it is because I cannot give it. What is the end of Sloka 7, Stanza 3 (reads passage from *The Secret Doctrine*), the one manifested into the great waters? Think over it and you will understand all that is permitted to you to understand here, is there. Fire is spirit-matter. This water stands for matter. Fire stands for the solid spirit, water for the one manifested element. Fire is heat, water, moisture; you understand the difference between heat and moisture. One is male, the other, female, the creative element here on earth, or the evolutive principles within, or the innermost principles. "Within," we say; all of you illusionists would say above, I just said to you there is no above. I believe the qualificative terms, dark space and bright space, give you the key quite sufficiently. I cannot give you any more, therefore there are the stars. I don't know it myself.

Mr. B. Keightley: Question 6. What is the veil which Oeaohoo the younger lifts from East to West?

Mme. Blavatsky: The veil of reality. The honest and sincere curtain or act drop-lifted or made to disappear in order to show the spectators the illusion we call stage scenery, actors and all the paraphernalia of the universe, which is a universe of illusion. Is this clear?

Mr. B. Keightley: The veil of Maya, in other words.

Mme. Blavatsky: I beg your pardon. It shows us Maya and lifts up and shows us the veil of reality. He makes it disappear, just to show us the illusions that are on the stage. Mr. Smith playing Othello or anything else is a sham; it is only illusion and nothing else. I think this perfectly clear.

Mr. B. Keightley: Question 7. What is the "upper space" and "shoreless sea of fire"?

Mme. Blavatsky: The "upper space" is the space within, as I just said, or the universe as it first appears from its Laya state, a "shoreless" expanse of spirit or "sea of fire."

Mr. B. Keightley: Question 8. Are the "great waters" here the same as those on which "darkness moved?"

Mme. Blavatsky: Well, I wish to say one thing, that "darkness moved," you put here in quotes. I don't remember to have put anywhere that darkness moves. I don't know on what darkness can ever move. I don't know what they have been doing. I have heard of a darkness which was upon the face of the deep or the great waters, but even in Chapter 1, Genesis it is distinctly stated, verse 2, that darkness was, and that that which moved upon the face of the waters was not darkness but the Spirit of God. Now see esoterically the meaning of these two verses in Genesis. They mean that in the beginning, when Kosmos was yet without form, and chaos, or the outer space, that of illusion, was still void, darkness alone was. Now if you take Kalahamsa, the dark swan or the swan of eternity (it is interchangeable), and at the first radiation of the dawn the Spirit of God, which means Logos number 1, began to move on the face of the great waters of the deep; therefore, if we want to be correct, and if not clear, let us ask are the great waters the same as the darkness spoken of in *The Secret Doctrine*? I will answer in the affirmative. Kalahamsa reads in a dual manner. Now, exoterically, if you speak about Kalahamsa, I took them to task in *The Secret Doctrine* (and I was perfectly right) for putting such a thing as that, that Kalahamsa was Parabrahm. It is not so, but esoterically it comes to that. Exoterically it is Brahmâ, which is the swan or the vehicle in which darkness manifests itself to human comprehension, but esoterically it is darkness, itself the ever unknowable absoluteness which becomes the vehicle of Brahmâ the manifested. For under the illusion of manifestation—that which we see and feel and which comes under our sensuous perception, as we imagine—is simply that which we neither hear, feel, see, taste or touch at all: a gross illusion and nothing else. Now, is this too metaphysical?

Mr. B. Keightley: I follow it.

Mme. Blavatsky: But I want the others to follow it. You are here always.

Mme. Tambaco: I think it seems clear.

Mr. B. Keightley: Question 9. In what sense can electricity be called an entity?

Mme. Blavatsky: In what sense shall I explain once for all so as not to have the same question repeated over and over again every Thursday? In what sense can I explain it to you? How many times have I explained it, and yet you come back? Electricity in a lamp is one thing. Fohat is the cause of that one spark in its millions of aspects, or the said spark in the lamps is quite another thing. Which do you want me to explain? Fohat is not electricity and electricity is not Fohat. Fohat is the sum total of the universal cosmic; electricity is an entity, because entity is that which is from the word [ ][6] to be and which exists for us, if not independently, by itself, apart from us. Fohat is an entity, but electricity is a mere relative signification. If taken in the usual scientific sense, Fohat is spoken of as cosmic electricity—as the sun is said to get in one's eyes or face or in one's garden, but surely it is not the sun that gets into one's eyes or face. The sun is an entity, and you would hardly call the effect of one of its beams an entity. Electricity is the molecular principle in the physical universe, and here on earth, because, being generated as it is in every disturbance of molecular equilibrium, it then becomes, so to say, the kama-rupa of the object in which such disturbance takes place. Rub amber and it will give birth to a son whose name is Fohat, if you like it, on the lower plane, because in one sense Fohat means birth or life from an apparently inanimate object. Rub a nettle between your thumb and finger and you will obtain by the grace of Fohat an effect or a son in the shape of boils and blisters on them. That is also Fohat. All is electricity, it is all an electric thing, from the nettle

---

6 The published version of the *Transactions*, p. 120 gives: "Entity comes from the Latin root *ens*, "being," of *esse*, "to be".

up to the lightning that kills you, it is just the same. It is simply the aspect of that one universal fire, and this one aspect is electricity. It is everything, but in various shapes.

Mr. ──: Do you mean to say there is only one force in Nature?

Mme. Blavatsky: In reality there is only one, and on the manifested plane it shows itself in millions and millions of various forms.

Mr. Gardner: Is the electricity in the nettle the same as what we have in the batteries?

Mme. Blavatsky: Most assuredly not.

Mr. Kingsland: The electricity that you generate, for instance, in rubbing amber, would you say that was both molecular and dimensional?

Mme. Blavatsky: Well, it is molecular, because it is the kama-rupa of the amber that acts; and certainly if it is to produce some distortions of the equilibrium it must produce something, because you cannot produce something in nothing. Mind you, electricity you will call an effect. I say the effect is molecular.

Mr. Kingsland: On the amber?

Mme. Blavatsky: Very well; but electricity, what is it? It is the effect of that which is molecular by itself. It is an entity, for electricity is the whole world of atoms in a certain state and under certain conditions.

Mr. Kingsland: Is there, for instance, emanated from the amber, matter in any state of differentiation?

Mme. Blavatsky: That which emanates from the amber is that which, unfortunately, your microscope won't see. But it *is* molecular.

Mr. B. Keightley: But it is visible to the appropriate senses.

Mme. Blavatsky: Positively. It is estimated that there are some insects that would see it and you would not. If you had, for instance, the white ants[7] that are in India, the most impudent of all creatures—and nothing in the world will make them get out of your way—they immediately will scatter like I don't know what, because they perceive that.

Mr. Gardner: Simply rubbing a piece of amber?

Mme. Blavatsky: Or there is a tree in India which you will rub, and if you rub it, they will never approach it.

The President: If you can describe it as a kama-rupa, that answers the question.

Mme. Blavatsky: I cannot explain it in any other way; it is the kama-rupa, the disturbing influence which comes and disturbs the equilibrium. I cannot explain it any better than that.

Mr. Gardner: You mean the astral envelope of the amber?

Mr. B. Keightley: No, no, the fourth principle. Now, question 10. "You say that 'Fohat is cosmic electricity' and the son. Is electricity, or Fohat, then, the same as Oeaohoo the younger, or the third Logos?"

Mme. Blavatsky: Electricity is the work of Fohat, but Fohat is not electricity. The throwing in one shape or the other of molecules into new combinations of forms into new correlations or disturbances of the equilibrium, as you call it, in general is the work of Fohat, the emanation of the seven sub-logoi. I advise you not to talk much of the seven-voweled deity. I am sorry I wrote and published it at all, I am very sorry, for there they began to tear it to pieces and speak about it just as though it were a potato. It is the combined active principle, the electric force, life, everything that comes out and emanates from those entities.

Mr. B. Keightley: Question 11. Sloka 8: "Where was the germ," etc. (reads from *The Secret Doctrine*). The question is: "Is the spirit of the flame that burns in thy lamp our Heavenly Father or Higher Self?"

---

7 Termites.

8. MEETING FEBRUARY 28, 1889

Mme. Blavatsky: It is neither the Heavenly Father nor the Higher Self. "The spirit of the flame" is simply speaking about the real bona fide lamp, and not at all metaphorically. It is neither one thing nor the other. He asks simply, the teacher, "where is the spirit of the flame that burns in thy lamp"—in any lamp, but not of gas, certainly.

Mr. B. Keightley: Now question 12. "Are the elements the bodies of the Dhyan-Chohans?"

Mme. Blavatsky: It is a perfectly useless question, because, read the symbolism in *The Secret Doctrine* and you will find the question. I cannot give it to you in talking as well as I have written it. Why don't they read it; why come and ask this?

Mr. B. Keightley: Then Question 13. "Are hydrogen, oxygen, ozone and nitrogen the primordial elements on this plane of matter?"

Mme. Blavatsky: They are. On other planes, even volatile ether, I think you call it that—never mind. I want to show that which is the most volatile would appear as the mud at the bottom of the River Thames, or on the bridges. Every plane has its own colours, sounds, dimension of space, etc., etc., quite unknown to us on this plane, and as we have, for instance, the ants, they have quite other perceptions of colour and sounds. Those who are intermediary creatures, a kind of transitional state between two planes, so on the plane above us, there are creatures, no doubt with senses, and faculties unknown {known?} to the inhabitants there, but {un?}known to us. They will probably play the same part as the ants play here, because the ants come from a lower sphere.

Mr. B. Keightley: Just emerging.

Mme. Blavatsky: Yes.

Mr. B. Keightley: That is the last of these questions.

Mr. Kingsland: Does not the perceptive power of the ant—for instance, the way in which it differs from our perceptive powers of colour—simply depend upon conditions, physiological conditions?

Mme. Blavatsky: It may be, but the wise people say otherwise. They say they can hear sounds we can certainly never hear; therefore, physiology has nothing to do with it whatever, because they do not hear with the ears as we do.

Mr. B. Keightley: They haven't got any.

Mr. ———: You can scarcely say they hear them, they sense them.

Mme. Blavatsky: They have a perception of that which we have not, on whatever plane it may be, whatever thing it may be.

Mr. Kingsland: Then we have a perception of that which they have not.

Mme. Blavatsky: Most assuredly, you are higher than they, but I say we will be the ants on the sphere above.

Mr. Kingsland: But how do you use the terms higher and lower in that sense, if they see and hear something that we do not, and we see and hear something that they do not?

Mme. Blavatsky: I mean high in general. I do not say in this particular instance. I simply say we are higher in general, that the earth is on a higher plane than the one from which the ants come.

Mr. Kingsland: Are they not on the same plane?

Mr. B. Keightley: I think it simply means earlier and later in the history of the evolution, a later and in one sense more advanced stage of evolution. The ants will pass through a stage, passing through the human stage we are in now, whereas we shall not. In that sense we are higher.

Mme. Blavatsky: I think that for you gentlemen who are electricians it is the most interesting thing, occultism, on account of its suggestiveness. It gives you ideas that you can never get from physical science.

Mr. Kingsland: I thought you meant that the ants might have the perception of a higher plane than we have.

Mme. Blavatsky: I never said that. I said they had perceptions of sounds which may be perhaps—well, I won't say how many millions, but which are within—which are not at all on our plane, which we could not hear under any circumstances.

Mr. B. Keightley: But I think we might follow up that amber and the idea of electricity as a particular state of matter. It throws a great deal of light on the subject.

Mr. Kingsland: Well, of course there is a molecular disturbance of the amber.

Mr. B. Keightley: That is to say, of the molecules on the physical plane.

Mr. Kingsland: But then, electricity to be manifested must be manifested outside the molecular substance of the amber.

Mr. B. Keightley: That is a point that is rather curious to get at. We imagine we create the electricity by rubbing the molecules of a physical piece of silk against the molecules of a physical piece of amber; that is the way we look at it.

Mme. Blavatsky: We simply give the conditions to the electricity, which is latent in it, to come out.

Mr. Kingsland: Is there anything corresponding to an emanation from amber?

Mme. Blavatsky: There is.

Mr. Kingsland: Or is it a molecular disturbance causing a molecular disturbance in the aura of the amber?

Mme. Blavatsky: No. I say it is latent in amber as it is latent everywhere, and giving it certain conditions, that which is within and which is latent in the amber will get into a fight with the electricity which is outside, and then there will be a disturbance produced. You simply change the conditions.

Mr. Kingsland: Is the electricity intermolecular, and is it manifested in the same way that you could have a sponge which is perfectly molecular? Does the amber contain electricity in the same sense?

Mme. Blavatsky: I am afraid to answer. I don't understand the question. I cannot answer you. I cannot take it in well.

The President: It seems if you use the phrase, kama-rūpa, that would be the best. I should consider that would be the same thing as saying it was intermolecular.

Mr. B. Keightley: But, you see, you have got your sponge and water—both matter on the same plane—but your electricity and your amber are matter on three different planes apart. That is to say, if you take the physical molecules of your amber as the first or lowest, the molecules of your electricity are on the same plane.

Mme. Blavatsky: Certainly, the kama-rupa, the fourth plane, that is what I tried to explain to you: kama-rupa. I am not a scientist, I am not at all an electrician or anything of the kind.

Mr. Kingsland: I thought you were using kama-rupa metaphysically.

Mme. Blavatsky: Not at all; perfectly physically.

Mr. B. Keightley: The great difference that I notice in the whole view of physical phenomena taken by occult science as distinguished from physical science is this: that in ordinary physical science we are in the habit of looking for the cause of things that we see. We rub a piece of amber and electricity is produced. The occult science will say by rubbing a piece of amber you produce conditions through which electricity, which exists latent and ready to manifest itself, can manifest itself on your physical plane.

Mme. Blavatsky: I find a far greater mistake that you all make in science, and it is the most vital mistake. It is by dividing animate from inanimate things and saying that there is such thing on the earth as a perfectly inanimate object. There is not an atom which is inanimate, not one. It is simply the most vicious kind of expression that I ever heard.

Mr. Kingsland: It is a very sensible distinction on our plane.

The President: Organic and inorganic.

Mme. Blavatsky: But there is nothing inorganic in this world; {in?} organic from your point of perception, but it is occultly speaking.

Mr. B. Keightley: Let us go into that question. What is the scientific definition or distinction drawn by science between organic and inorganic?

Mme. Blavatsky: Occultism would say to you, a dead man is more alive than ever.

Mr. B. Keightley: Please don't suggest to Kingsland.

Mr. Kingsland: Ask Dr. Williams.

Dr. Williams: I think he wants to get Mr. Kingsland's idea of the matter. I suppose he has got some particular motive.

Mr. Kingsland: But it is all *pro bono publico*.

Dr. Williams: I don't know but what you thought he had some personal idea.

Mr. B. Keightley: I thought he probably had some clear notion in his mind.

Mr. Kingsland: If you carry it down to the lowest forms, one shades into the other.

Mr. B. Keightley: Is there any definition to be given what distinguishes it? What is the characteristic according to modern science?

Mr. Kingsland: What is the characteristic between you and a lump of wood?

The President: You take the two extremes. Science has to admit there is the possibility of an entity or a substance to which they cannot assign either of the words with confidence. I say entity or substance.

Mr. B. Keightley: The only distinction I have ever heard put forward is this, the distinction of nutrition. Science will generally show—Mr. Williams, will you correct me if I am wrong?

Dr. Williams: That is purely an arbitrary one.

Mr. B. Keightley: But simply, the only criterion that is put forward as really distinguishing organic from inorganic is the function of nutrition.

Dr. Williams: I think the latest scientific views recognize no dividing line anywhere. There is no place where you may draw the line, and so this belongs on one side and that on the {other}.

Mr. B. Keightley: Even if you go down into the mineral kingdom, because you find in the phenomena of producing crystals you get some which is to all intents and purposes nutrition.

Mme. Blavatsky: I should like to know, if there was no nutrition for the inorganic substances, how they could change. The fact of their changing and crumbling down shows to you there is a growth, and that it is perfectly organic, as organic as anything else, only under other conditions. Have you ever thought that on this plane of ours there are seven planes? It is subdivided. This perhaps you have never been taught yet, that even on this plane of physical perception there are seven planes.

Mr. Kingsland: There are seven planes of matter?

Mme. Blavatsky: I define it so in the mineral kingdom and in the animal kingdom. There are planes for all. Just as I spoke of the ants, just in the same analogy there are the other things. When they come and speak to me about inanimate things, I say fiddlesticks, there is no such thing as that, it is impossible, because there is not a thing in this world that is perfectly inorganic—I don't say it in the dogmatic sense, I mean inorganic—that is not susceptible to decay and ending. Everything grows and everything changes. Everything that changes is organic; it has the life principle in it, and it has all the potentiality of the higher lives.

Dr. Williams: That certainly seems to me to be the universal idea, that there are various manifestations of life on the physical plane, and the quality of that manifestation depends entirely on the molecular relationship of the matter itself. There is no such thing in any abstract sense, as putting matter in one plane under one condition and in another plane under another condition.

Mme. Blavatsky: What is matter? Matter is simply a form of more or less crystallized and objective spirit, that is all, nothing else; and what is spirit? There is neither spirit nor matter there. They are all kinds of aspects of one and the same element in this life, if life is universal, I say there is not a point in the shoreless universe. How can there be such a thing as an inorganic atom or anything. I think Kant[8] says perfectly correctly—he is one of the physiologists I prefer the most, because he is so very fair in his matters, he opens so many doors to everything, to the possibilities. There is nothing dogmatic about him. I read very little of him, but the little makes me think he is one of the fairest I know—when he speaks about the distinctions between organic and inorganic. He says just as we occultists say, that there is no such thing in this world as something inorganic. And you take, if you please, Huxley or any of the big bugs of science, and they will come and talk about the organic and inorganic, just as though they were the fathers of everything and they had created the universe. It is perfectly ridiculous.

Dr. Williams: What would you say was the relationship of fire on the different planes? Could you say anything of the relationship which fire on the lowest plane bears to fire on the highest?

Mme. Blavatsky: It is beyond our fine perceptive faculties. There is an unbroken relation, because one proceeds from the other. It is a

---

8 Immanuel Kant, German philosopher, 1724-1804.

falling into matter and a forming into density.

Dr. Williams: That is precisely the point I was after, if the one was the inner essential life of the other. If fire on the fourth plane was the inner essential life of fire on the third plane, and so on downwards.

Mme. Blavatsky: If you speak on the planetary chain, then it will be the seventh on our plane, that it to say, it will become the Atma. It corresponds to Atma on our plane, and we cannot see Atma, but if you can imagine yourself living on the A and B planets, so it is on the spheres A and Z, then it will become Pho {four}.

Dr. Williams: I was thinking more especially of the seven planes into which human life was divided.

The President: Speaking with reference to what was said about electricity being the fourth principle; the kama-rupa of the amber.

Dr. Williams: Yes.

The President: There one would say the change from planet to planet was a molecular change, probably.

Mme. Blavatsky: Then the molecules of the change also on the other planes.

Mr. B. Keightley: There is a great deal of that in Keely's inter-etheric ideas.[9]

Mme. Blavatsky: He cannot bring it out altogether, because he is neither an occultist nor an orthodox scientist, and he will keep to his own prejudices, but otherwise he is a very grand man and discoverer. What do they say of him, Mr. Fullerton,[10] in America?

Mr. Fullerton: There have been difficulties growing out of the constitution of his company, and various things of that kind which led to a suspicion of dishonesty. That is the popular impression.

---

9 John Worrell Keely, U.S. inventor, 1827-1898, who claimed to have discovered a new form of energy or force.
10 Alexander Fullerton, American Theosophist, 1841-1913.

Mme. Blavatsky: He was too sanguine in his expectations. He thought he could just take Parabrahm by the coat-tails and show him to the public. It is a perfect impossibility. I said it from the first, it could not be. I said it always, it was perfectly useless.

Mr. Gardner: He won't stick to one thing.

Mme. Blavatsky: He wants to go on too much and too high, and therefore he will have failures always, because if he were to hold only to those few things he has found out, really he would have the greatest success, and he could bring to himself and on his side all the men of science, but he won't do it. He wants to go so much into the metaphysical that although the physicists don't want to confess it, they cannot follow him on to the plane of science. It is impossible, because then they will become Roger Bacons,[11] not Crookeses.

Mr. B. Keightley: He says if you make the proper conditions, you can cause the manifestation of something which lies concealed between the molecules of the most attenuated physical bodies, and then he gets a series of these attenuations with this matter, whatever it is, which is inter-molecular, for physical matter is molecular itself, and between its molecules there is again something which is also molecular.

Mme. Blavatsky: Ad infinitum.

Mr. B. Keightley: And so you get exactly what we say about the ether; that is four stages up his ladder, and the conditions we produce in the manifestations of ordinary electricity are simply parallel to those he employs for his.

Mme. Blavatsky: Unfortunately for us, the physicists will not accept anything of the kind, otherwise, they have only accepted the possibility that there must be something so attenuated and so invisible to our objective eyes that goes on living after us. Then they would see how very easy it is to conceive of those astral bodies who live in their astral body, and live just as much as we do, and

---

11 Roger Bacon, Franciscan friar, 1214-1294, known for his scientific approach.

they have all their principles put together and they can travel very easily to the fourth plane and act in this little universe of ours just as easily as we do without any body, and I can assure you it is the most blessed condition in the world, for there you have neither gout nor rheumatism nor anything.

Mr. B. Keightley: Nor clothes, nor breakfast to eat, nor anything.

Mme. Blavatsky: And every time that there are mediums, as the spiritualists say, they are really not so. I can assure it is, because there will be Nirmanakayas and then they will know the truth. But here they are a little bit perplexed and they will go into their own habits and so on. It is physical matter which is in their way. It is the easiest thing to understand, this.

Dr. Williams: Has not Sir William Thompson got very near Keely's idea in his "Extra Mundane Corpuscles"?

Mme. Blavatsky: Yes, he has read a very great deal of the ancient and Greek classics, but he wants to bring them all to his own ideas, to his own established theories. You see, the trouble with him is he jumps from one conclusion to another. Today he says the incrustation of the earth begins 15,000,000 ago; after tomorrow he will come and say something else, and laugh at himself. I judge from lectures. I never read yet three consecutive lectures without Sir William Thompson contradicting himself on every point. Is that exact science? I call it exact flapdoodle. It is not exact science at all.

Dr. Williams: It always seems interesting when such a man gets hold of such a simple truth.

Mme. Blavatsky: He disfigures it in such a way, and he wriggles it so that he distorts it out of recognition. Crookes is a thousand times more hopeful than he. Crookes is magnificent as a man of science.

The President: Crookes doesn't really speak out. For the scientists he has to dress up in materialistic language what is to him something very much metaphysical.

Dr. Williams: I have no doubt about that.

The President: If one reads those lectures of his, especially "The Genesis of the Elements" and others, with a little insight into it and into his own way of thinking, you see that at once.

Mme. Blavatsky: I am very sorry we separated without any cause; but you see there is a black cat between us, a black cat on two legs, and I know him. Crookes has been giving ideas that are not quite orthodox about me. He says: "Oh, the old lady is getting old and is falling into her dotage. She used to know something, but now she has given out everything and knows nothing." I am very glad he thinks so, because he would otherwise have bothered me out of my life. I made him ring the two astral bells himself. Just the last time I touched him myself. He had his hand in the glass that stood there and they produced two distinct astral bells, and therefore he knows this thing which he can do also, but he wanted me to give him the key to it. I said: "If you behave yourself, I will," but he did not behave himself, and so he did not get it. And on that he was made to believe—

The President: That you hadn't got a key?

Mme. Blavatsky: That I was a poor medium.

Mr. B. Keightley: Did you ever see, Dr. Williams, those illustrious Elihu Vedders?[12] Do you remember that frontispiece, that great wall? Does it suggest the idea of the knots of Fohat?

Dr. Williams: Yes; it was not so much a wall as a skein.

Mr. Keightley: It was the quatrains of Omar Khayyam.

Mme. Blavatsky: This is an occult thing, about the knots.

Mr. Keightley: The frontispiece is a great skein.

---

12 Elihu Vedder, an American symbolist painter, 1836-1923. His illustrations refered to are for the 1884 edition of Edward FitzGerald's translation of *The Rubaiyat of Omar Khayyam.*

Dr. Williams: I think I could draw it for you. (Draws the "skein.")

Mme. Blavatsky: It is something like centripetal and centrifugal action.

Dr. Williams: I daresay the nebulæ do assume the same forms, but he has taken that as the author of an opera does. It runs through the poem as the *motif,* so to say.

Mr. B. Keightley: An extraordinary effect it produces, drawn with a beautiful sweep.

The President: Curiously enough, it is the ordinary Japanese representation, in their rough sketches, of cloudscapes; single lines running into a sort of knot, both in carving and in drawing. I have plenty of their woodcarvings, in which a bank of clouds is given in that way.

Mme. Blavatsky: It is the old occult idea, what we called Fohat; they give it another name, and the Parsis give it another name, but he is the knot-tier. When he has made the Laya point, he begins in another place; and all the visible universe is formed like that, and all come dragging from that Milky Way, all this world-stuff dragging out, and beyond the Milky Way they say it is the Father-Mother.

Mr. Kingsland: Does that Milky Way stuff get drawn into our stellar system, that being more differentiated in forming new systems?

Mme. Blavatsky: It is the inexhaustible storehouse, and this cannot be exhausted.

Mr. Gardner: The quantity is a constant one?

Mme. Blavatsky: Always. There is not a given quantity, but it is inexhaustible, for it has neither beginning nor end.

Mr. B. Keightley: It emerges at one side to Father-Mother.

Mme. Blavatsky: All these are words, but if we speak from the physical standpoint, it is everywhere—not above our heads, our globe revolving. We say it is everywhere.

Mr. B. Keightley: Why do we see it as a limited thing running across a particular tract of the sky?

Mme. Blavatsky: Because we see that which can be seen; that and the other exists nevertheless; we see that which is more contracted, and the rest we do not see, because it is lost in such immensity that certainly no eye—even of a Dhyan-Chohan, or one of the Salvation Army that has a golden harp and plays—can see; no one.

Dr. Williams: Did I understand you correctly in speaking of the sun and the planets and the moon? At one time you spoke of them all in connection, that the planets had at some time been in the same condition that the sun is now in, and that they would at some time be in the condition that the moon is now in.

Mr. B. Keightley: They pass through the sun stage, then they become comets, then planets, then dead bodies, etc.

Dr. Williams: That would give the idea that the sun itself is approaching the state of the planet, and by and by it would reach the condition that the moon is in, and really lose its heat.

Mme. Blavatsky: The sun is not a planet, it is a central star.

Mr. B. Keightley: It is a different stage of things altogether.

Dr. Williams: Then the planets were really not suns in the same sense that our sun, the centre of our solar system, is a sun?

Mme. Blavatsky: There were suns, but it is a different kind of suns. This one is a reflection, simply.

Dr. Williams: If you were considering the close of the solar Pralaya might it not be that as it approached the consummation of that period it might be effected in that way?

Mme. Blavatsky: Most assuredly, it will. It will begin by getting less and less radiant and giving less and less heat; and it is not that which we see. That will lose fire, but it will be that behind, and these are the flames and the nerves, which is merely a reflection, and they will die out and disappear, because it has no consistency, the sun. It is nonsense to come and speak about the sun in this way; it is perfect fancy, because we see simply a reflection of all kinds of electromagnetic forces. The real furnace of the solar system, where all the fires are, and these forces, are Life, and Light, Heat, Electricity and everything, all the different correlations, that which we give different names to. This is one thing. They are just the same as the one thing of the whole universe is there. This is only in our solar system.

Dr. Williams: They must be evident, certainly.

Mr. B. Keightley: After the next solar Pralaya, that which now is the sun will, if I understand *The Secret Doctrine* correctly, become in a following Manvantara of some kind, a comet.

Mme. Blavatsky: Yes, in the following Pralaya, but it will never become a comet during the life of our little planetary chain.

Dr. Williams: The point I was after was that this outbreathing and inbreathing is not sudden, but a gradual process. There is no point between the beginning of the outbreathing and the end of the inbreathing, and therefore the sun might approach to the fullness of its forces and then would begin a gradual decadence of its forces.

Mme. Blavatsky: There is a magnificent thing described in the *Vishnu Purana*. It is an exoteric thing, full, of course, of allegories, which on their face show themselves very ridiculous and absurd, but it is full of very philosophical meaning, and this thing—when the Pralaya comes and when the seven rays begin to be absorbed—it is described in the most superb way. I wish somebody would translate it into English verse. Wilson gives it, but he makes the most terrible mistakes, and such that poor Fitzedward Hall,[13] his editor, gives more footnotes than text. "Dr. Wilson's mistakes, but he didn't have the benefits in his time that we have," and this, that, and the other,

---

13 Fitzedward Hall, American Orientalist, 1825-1901. He edited Horace Hayman Wilson's five-volume translation of the *Vishnu Purāna*, published 1864-1877.

and certainly being a Reverend he could not do it otherwise. He had always to fight for his Jehovah.

Dr. Williams: Well, there is, is there not, matter in its elementary state?

Mme. Blavatsky: Behind, not in what you see; that is merely a reflection. Well, imagine yourself that this cannot be seen, and you see only the reflection in the looking-glass.

Dr. Williams: In star analysis they get the lines showing—I do not know how many—elements they have succeeded in isolating in the sun, but a certain number.

Mr. B. Keightley: That question was answered by saying it was the effect of the atmosphere of finely divided cosmic dust, which has now been recognized by science as falling gradually to the earth, and which acts upon the light of the sun; that according to Occult Science the formation of the solar lines takes place in the earth's atmosphere and is not a phenomenon due to the sun at all.

The President: Would not the same thing apply to every star spectra?

Mr. B. Keightley: Certainly, all round.

Mr. Gardner: But they differ very much.

Mr. B. Keightley: As far as I understand what was said in those letters, they do not say that the emanation, whatever it is, the vibrations proceeding from the sun and the stars are of the same nature, but they say that the phenomena that we take to prove the presence of iron and sodium in the sun are not due to the presence of those substances in the sun, as we know them, but due to the action upon the sun's rays of the atmosphere, of cosmic dust which surrounds the earth. That is the point that is meant.

Mme. Blavatsky: Because they say this atmosphere is three miles forming.

Mr. B. Keightley: Three hundred.

Mme. Blavatsky: Oh! I imagined it was two or three miles.

Mr. B. Keightley: I tell you how they have got to that. They find the meteorites are at least 200 miles.

Mme. Blavatsky: Oh, it is three miles where you can breathe, I think, three miles of breathable air, but not atmospherical. When it approaches it, of course it differentiates and it gives quite different optical illusions. This I remember.

Mr. B. Keightley: They say they do not know quite what the atmosphere is, but it is at least 200 miles, because these meteorites get inflamed. It is very difficult to see where the boundary line really is.

The President: It depends upon what you mean by atmosphere.

Mme. Blavatsky: I thought the atmosphere was what you could breathe. What is the other?

Mr. B. Keightley: All that they say is that these meteorites are observed to take fire at a certain height, at least 200 miles above the surface of the earth, that means to say there is something that produces friction; they rub against something.

Mme. Blavatsky: Too much Fohat.

Mr. B. Keightley: That would be another way of explaining the same thing.

Mr. Kingsland: Then it is pure hypothesis that it is the friction of the atmosphere?

Mr. B. Keightley: Purely, but that is the accepted hypothesis at the present moment.

Mme. Blavatsky: For today, and on Saturday it will be changed.

Mr. B. Keightley: That one has been held the longest.

9.
The Theosophical Society.
Report of the
Weekly Meeting of the Blavatsky Lodge
held at 17 Lansdowne Road, W.
March 7, 1889.

President: Mr. Harbottle

The President: Stanza 3, Sloka 10. "Father-Mother spin a web," etc. (Reads from *The Secret Doctrine*.)

Mr. A. Keightley: Question 1. "You state that Spirit and Matter are the opposite ends of the same web; last Thursday you spoke about such opposites as light and darkness, heat and cold, void and space and fullness of all that exists. In what sense are these three pairs of opposites associated with matter and spirit?"

Mme. Blavatsky: I think in that sense everything in the universe is in association with it, with every spiritual matter, because there is always either one or the other that predominates in every subject that you can think of.

Mr. A. Keightley: Then do light, heat, and void correspond with matter, darkness, cold, etc.?

Mme. Blavatsky: What is it, which question do you put now?

Mr. A. Keightley: The first question.

Mme. Blavatsky: Pure matter is pure spirit. It cannot be understood even if admitted by our finite intellects. Of course you cannot see other {either} pure matter or spirit, because they are perfectly one in occultism.

The President: They are the noumena of the opposites.

Mme. Blavatsky: There is but one thing, call it element, force or god, anything you like, it is always one. This is what occult science teaches; and after differentiation come all and everything that is. With regard to this question I can only say that neither light nor darkness as optical effects are matter, nor are they spirit, but both are the qualities of ether, the intermediate agent in the manifested universal universe, for ether is dual. Ether is not as science knows it, but ether, as it really exists—that ether of which the ancient philosophers speak—is dual, because it is the earliest differentiation on our plane of manifestation of consciousness. It is dual in the objective, and dual as the middle Akasa in the subjective universe. In the former case, it is pure differentiated matter; in the latter, elemental. In other words spirit becomes objective matter, and objective spirit eludes our physical senses—

Mr. A. Keightley: Are the other elements beyond ether more differentiated than ether? Are they triple and quadruple?

Mme. Blavatsky: What {do} you call beyond ether? Ether is universal.

Mr. A. Keightley: For instance, the five elements are ether, air, fire, water and earth.

Mme. Blavatsky: The ether which is an element is certainly not the ether that science speaks about.

Mr. A. Keightley: No, I am not alluding to science in this particular. You stated there are five elements developed in accordance with the races.

Mme. Blavatsky: Yes. The fifth is not developed yet, that which the ancient Greeks called Zeus, that they call the deity of all. Of course, if they spoke in one sense, it was; if in another sense, it was not. Now, the Zeus of Homer certainly was not Akasa in all his Don Juanic peregrinations.

The President: Isn't it rather true to describe those elements as the different stages?

Mme. Blavatsky: Of course. Now that physical science has given the name of elements to everything it believes to be homogeneous and finds after a time it is esoteric, of course this is different; but otherwise I don't see it. The elements are those which are manifested here as the element of fire, the element of water, or the element of earth and so on. They are certainly elements because they are entirely distinct from each other, though there is not an element that has not got some other element in it. It is simply that one aspect predominates.

Mr. A. Keightley: That is the point I was meaning. Are there three main aspects, say, in fire?

Mme. Blavatsky: What three main aspects? You may make three. Ether is dual, certainly, because ether is the first differentiated celestial fire, as we call it.

Mr. A. Keightley: Is there a triple aspect in the element next below ether in differentiation?

Mme. Blavatsky: You must not mix ether with the others. Ether is an element which follows the four elements that we admit and accept, and the aether is its abstract or general sense. One you will spell "ether" and the other "aether."

The President: When you speak of the dual ether, you speak of the Æther of the Greek.

Mme. Blavatsky: Certainly. That is why they made all the other gods androgynous. They made the god or the goddess just as the Hindus had: it is the two aspects of the deity, and every one of them is certainly or does certainly belong to ether. You may call them solar or lunar gods; they are the gods of the ether. They all return to that first element, to the god of Brahmâ, from which they emanated.

Mr. Kingsland: Do you call that dual because it is the middle point, so to speak, between spirit and matter that is mentioned in the Stanza?

Mme. Blavatsky: Yes, because otherwise it will be no more on the higher planes, it will become Akasa.

Mr. Kingsland: It is exactly the intermediate point.

Mme. Blavatsky: Yes. It plays the same relation between the cosmos and the moon, our little earth, as Manas plays between the Monad and the body, just in the same way as it is mentioned in *The Secret Doctrine*.

Mr. B. Keightley: Then what were you driving at about the triple aspect?

The President: That was only, I think, because Arch was somewhat misunderstanding the way in which HPB was using the word ether.

Mme. Blavatsky: You look at the Orientalists—they translate invariably Akasa as ether. I say nothing can be more erroneous than that, because ether is something which science suspects of being particled or something equivocal. What do they call it? Some strange name—"hypothetical agent" and so on. And of course it must be something particled, since it says if it were not matter it could not do the functions that it does in the eyes of science, and Akasa is a perfectly homogeneous thing, it is the rootless root of all, it is Mulaprakriti, it is the rootless root of Nature, that which is perfectly unknown to us.

Mr. A. Keightley: That is the Akasa in its highest aspect.

Mme. Blavatsky: Yes, but not ether. Ether is the Astral Light of the Kabalists; it is devilish infernal sight, as they call it, it is Astral Light in its earliest aspects.

The President: Arch is confusing again aether and ether.

Mr. A. Keightley: No, I am not. There we get a distinction between ether, the fifth element of those five.

Mme. Blavatsky: It is not yet developed, and therefore you can hardly call it an element. It is to be developed with the Fifth Race.

Mr. Kingsland: Then that is the lowest aspect of Akasa.

Mme. Blavatsky: Yes. It is the lowest aspect to us who are the lowest aspect of all kinds of beings and of the celestial aristocracy. Of course it appears very grand, because as the proverb says: "a little eel by itself imagines itself a Himalaya." So we do in our conceit, but it is a very low thing.

Mr. Kingsland: But that ether you were speaking of is actually what science calls the hypothetical medium which transmits light.

Mme. Blavatsky: Yes, and poor science does not know whether to believe it or not.

Mr. Kingsland: Still, there it is.

Mme. Blavatsky: Well, what is question 2?

Mr. A. Keightley: In Stanza 3, Sloka 10, it is said: "Brahmâ as 'the germ of unknown darkness' is the material from which all evolves and develops." Goethe is quoted as expressing the same idea in the lines "Thus at the roaring loom of Time I ply, and weave for God the garment thou see'st him by."[1] It is one of the axioms of logic that it is impossible for the mind to believe anything of that of which it comprehends nothing. Now, if this "material" above mentioned, which is Brahmâ, be formless, then no idea concerning it can enter the mind, for the mind can perceive nothing where there is no form. It is the "garment" or the manifestation in form of God which we see or perceive, and it is by this and this alone that we can know anything of him. Question 2: What is the first form of this material which human consciousness can recognize?

Mme. Blavatsky: Well, do you direct the question psychically or physiologically, or as a question coming from materialistic science,

---

1 Goethe's lines quoted are from his *Faust*, and would have been familiar to readers of Thomas Carlyle's *Sartor Resartus*, where it was cited.

physical science?

Dr. Williams: Purely as a question of no significance to me, whatever materialists or any sect believe. I use the word materialists in quotation points, desiring you to use the word just as you did in your own sense.

Mme. Blavatsky: In my sense I would not pay the slightest attention to materialistic science. I do not believe in this materialistic science. I say they are very great in small details, but on the whole they do not satisfy anyone.

Dr. Williams: I don't use the word material in the sense in which Huxley uses it, or any of those.

Mme. Blavatsky: I want you to say in what sense you use it. I say the first sense in which we can imagine matter, or that which is in our conception of matter, that is to say, the most refined of all, the mother as we call it, the primordial. I will say it is a circle, because in all the occult books, in all the teachings and philosophies, it is impossible to imagine one's self any other first form than that of a circle. It is impossible in the Aristotelian logic, it would be a [ ] of that; but as we deal with metaphysics, and from the standpoint of the adepts in the occult sciences, then I must answer you just as occultism says. If you take, for instance, in the physical science, we will say the first geometrical figure is a triangle, but this is on the manifested plane, it is not in the world of abstraction. The first thing that you see is certainly a circle. Now this circle you can either limit or take it just according to the capacities of your conceptions and of your intuition, and you can make it limitless, all depends upon your powers of conceiving things. You can expand it *ad infinitum*, make of it a limitless circle—not only in words, in which you will say a circle is something, the circumference is everywhere and so on, you know the well-known saying—but I don't use any other figure than that. Does that satisfy you? They make us conceive of a circle first of all, and this circle which is all, and embraces all and has no plane. Let us imagine something that is—well, as large as we can imagine it—and you might expand and extend ad infinitum. If we contract it to our conceptions, it is because we want to make it conceivable to the finite intellect.

Dr. Williams: I suppose it would be a safe thing to say that the finite intellect cannot conceive of anything except what is finite.

Mme. Blavatsky: I beg your pardon: there are moments that you can conceive far beyond that, which your physical brain can conceive. Certainly you cannot conceive it if {you} simply hold to the matter and to this manifested universe, but there are moments that you can conceive far more; in your dreams you can conceive of things that you cannot when you are awake.

Dr. Williams: I understand that, but my point was after all it would be a finite conception, because the conception of a finite being.

Mme. Blavatsky: No, because this circle of light and of everything is not a being; and then you can conceive it limitless, certainly. If it is limitless you can go and search for limits, but you can conceive it is limitless. Let us say it will only apply to the manifested universe, to the objective; even that, certainly, to the astronomer must appear limitless, if they are accustomed to look through their telescopes, and do as they have to do. It must appear limitless to them.

Dr. Williams: They always think from the standpoint of space and time. That is why they say it is not limitless.

Mme. Blavatsky: That is where they limit their intellect. Once they go beyond that, they break their noses and nothing comes out of it.

Dr. Williams: When you get beyond space and time, have not you got beyond all circles of form?

Mme. Blavatsky: Most assuredly. Then you have no need for symbols and signs. Everything is in such a way then that it is impossible to express it in words.

Dr. Williams: Then that just brings us right back to the point of the question, and that was what the first form was which comes within the range of human consciousness and finite consciousness. It is not, it seems to me, so much a question of what we may imagine as what we are bound to think by the loss of the constitution of the human mind.

Mme. Blavatsky: It is a circle, I say again. It is proved Kabalistically and occultly that the first thing you may imagine when you want to imagine something is a circle.

Dr. Williams: That is exactly the point I wanted to reach.

Mme. Blavatsky: Those who tell you the biggest absurdity in science tell you you can square the circle, positively square it, and make of it any figure you like for it's in all in all.

Mr. Kingsland: Isn't it a sphere, rather than a circle?

Mme. Blavatsky: Circle or sphere, call it what you like. Of course it is a sphere—it has circumference but no plane.

Mr. A. Keightley: Then what is the next figure you get after the circle?

Mme. Blavatsky: If you begin, the first figure will be a triangle.

Mr. B. Keightley: The circle is the central point first; then the triangle.

Mme. Blavatsky: The first figure is no figure: the circle with the point; it is simply primeval germ, and it is the first thing you imagine at the beginning of differentiation, but the triangle is the one you have to conceive of, once that matter begins to differentiate, once you have passed the zero point, the Laya. It is this I wanted to say, it is just this. Brahmâ is called an atom, Anu, because atom could not be an atom, because it is for us an atom that we don't see, we simply imagine it is a kind of mathematical point and so on, but in reality an atom can be extended and made absoluteness. It is the germ, it is not the atom from the standpoint of the physicists or the chemists, it is from the occult standpoint, it is the infinitesimally small and totallic {totally?} Brahmâ. It may be the unknown limited quantity, a latent atom during Pralaya, active during the life cycles, but one which has neither circumference or plane, only limitless expansion. Therefore also the circle is but the geometrical symbol in the subjective world and it becomes the triangle in the objective. That is my answer, and it is finished. So do you understand now?

Mr. A. Keightley: I don't see how it becomes a triangle in the objective. That is what puzzled me always.

Mme. Blavatsky: If that circle is limited it would be a very difficult thing. Then there would be two things having no relation to each other, unless you put the triangle in the circle.

Mr. A. Keightley: That of course is a figure one has always seen.

Mme. Blavatsky: How is it in *The Secret Doctrine*? It is a circle, and the point then becomes the plane and with that the triangle; and this plane has nothing to do with what we imagine. It is that boundary from which begins the manifested universe. When you want to follow into cosmogony and theogony then you have to imagine the triangle, because from this first triangle, if you take this Pythagorean definition, it begins descending, as I explained to you last time, then coming back on itself, making the plane and then going up again and disappearing in darkness. That is it.

Mr. A. Keightley: Then Sloka 11, question 3. Is the word "expand" here used in the sense of differentiating or evolving, and "contract" in that of involution? Or do these terms refer to Manvantara and Pralaya? Or again, to a constant vibratory motion of the world-stuff or atoms? Are this expansion and this contraction simultaneous or successive?

Mme. Blavatsky: It is translated word for word, this, and it is all certainly figurative, metaphorical, and so on, and therefore you must not take in the literal sense everything; because you must allow something for the Eastern way of expressing it. Their Stanzas are as old as man, but this is thinking man.

Mr. A. Keightley: (Reads question again.)

Mme. Blavatsky: The Web means here, the ever existant primordial matter—pure spirit to us—the matter out of which the objective universe or universes are evolved. It means that when the breath of fire of father is upon it, it expands. That is to say, a subjective material, it is limitless, infinite, eternal and indestructible. When the breath of the mother touches it, when the time for manifestation comes, and it has to come into objectivity and form, it contracts, for there is no such thing as something material and with a form, and yet limitless. You understand, the fire, it stands here for father. It is that ever unknowable principle, which fecundates that matter, this primordial matter or the mother, and then taking a form—of course it will take a form and become limited. The universe is limitless, but yet everything that has form in it is finite. Well, this is why it is said to contract, contract—that is to say, become something less—maybe the expression is not a happy one.

Mr. B. Keightley: It means to become limited.

Mme. Blavatsky: That is what I want to say. *Now*, the critics are many, but the helpers were few when I wrote the thing. That is the mischief of it.

Dr. Williams: It is not the literal interpretation of any of the Stanzas, but only the ideas that are underneath them that we want.

Mme. Blavatsky: Oh, yes, the literal; I try to translate word for word.

Dr. Williams: But it is not that I insist upon, at all; it is the ideas that are underneath that.

Mr. Kingsland: What we took it for is this, that when the breath of mother touched it, then the sons dissociated and scattered, and returned to the bosom, the end of Pralaya; but it is the opposite way about.

Mme. Blavatsky: You can take it in any way. You can take it as the end of Pralaya, or the other way.

Mr. Kingsland: It is when the breath of mother touches it they contract and come into manifestation.

Mme. Blavatsky: Yes, and at the end of Pralaya they contract again and become less and less and less, and then they become dissociated and disintegrated and they fall into that which they were at first.

Mr. Kingsland: Wouldn't you say at the end of Pralaya they expanded?

The President: The "contraction" here is the same thing as scattering.

Mme. Blavatsky: I always took it in one sense.

Mr. Kingsland: We thought dissociating and scattering referred to the Pralaya.

Mme. Blavatsky: Oh no, it refers to the differentiation.

Mr. B. Keightley: "To return into their mother's bosom at the end of the great day."

Mme. Blavatsky: You see, you have to know the inherent powers of every atom, you have to know what really matter is on this plane, and what matter is before it is differentiated. Now, there; I have tried to give you the explanation. I don't know whether I have succeeded or not. Now, for instance, take that proposition of Sir Isaac Newton, *viz.*, that every particle of matter has the property of attraction for each other particle, etc. You know the well-known proposition. Very well. It is correct from one aspect. Then also there is Leibniz. He speaks about the Monads and says every atom is a universe in itself, which acts through its own inherent force. This is also true, but one speaks from the standpoint of psychology, and the other from that of physical science; and both say that which has neither beginning nor end, because it does not explain anything. It is a perfect impossibility. It is only occultism that comes and reconciles the two and shows that there is something else in it. They are incomplete. Man also is an atom having attraction and repulsion in him, because he is the microcosm of the macrocosm. But would it be true to say that because of that force he moves and acts independently of every other, or could act and move, unless there were a greater force and intelligence than his own to allow him to live and move? I speak about that high element of force and intelligence, that is to say, your physical science says that every atom has its inherent force in itself, and that there is no extra cosmic matter—a thing for which you pitch into me, Dr. Williams, because you say science will not allow the extra cosmic force.

Dr. Williams: I didn't mean to put it in that sense.

Mme. Blavatsky: No, but you will read it afterwards. Your physical scientists, as far as I understand them—it seems to me I understand them to say that every atom has its own inherent force in itself, and this is what makes Haeckel[2] say, for instance, that matter has created itself, that it gave itself a kick and did everything by itself. There is nothing else. Very well, I have no objection to that, but there is something else, therefore there is a force inherent in the atom, and one which acts on the atom, and this is that which I wanted to explain to you. Now one of my objects in *The Secret Doctrine* is to prove that planetary movements cannot be accounted for satisfactorily by the sole theory of gravitation, and this leads me to say that besides force acting in matter there is also that other force which acts on matter. Take, for instance, a sponge (Maybe the sponge will be a very bad simile, but still it will give the idea of what I want to show.) Take a sponge, it is soaked through and through in seawater. Every atom of it is, so to say, a dried atom or particle of seawater, yet the waves around it will toss and guide it. Now these waves are the same as those inside it, as those which created it, and which even have created that sponge which has become objective matter and perfectly specific matter. It is just the same with every atom in the universe. What I seek to express then is this: when we speak of modified conditions of spirit-matter, which is in reality

---

2 Ernst Haeckel, German biologist, 1834-1919.

force, and call them by various names, such as heat, cold, light, darkness, repulsion, attraction, electricity, magnetism and so on, all these for the occultists are simply names and expressions of difference in manifestation of one and the same force, which is always dual, at least in differentiation, but not in specific differences of force. For all such differences in the objective world result only from the peculiarities of the differentiation of matter on which the one free force acts, helped in this by that portion of its essence which we call imprisoned force. Now I must tell you that the force is one, but it differs in its aspects according to whether it is on the manifested plane, where it is encased and imprisoned in an atom or in any form that you can imagine, or whether it is this free force which I have just tried to show you, as in the illustration of the sponge. There is the other force which is absolute totality, that force is not a force only, it is all, it is life, it is consciousness. But all this is absolute, and all this not having any relation to the finite, certainly, of course, we cannot regard it or compare it with the things that we see in the manifested universe. You understand my idea, Dr. Williams?

Dr. Williams: Yes, I think I do. This is rather anticipating the questions which are to follow.

Mme. Blavatsky: That is not my fault.

Dr. Williams: But how are we to know anything about the universal force which lies behind or above or outside of them?

Mme. Blavatsky: We can never know it on the physical plane.

Dr. Williams: How are we to get any idea of it?

Mme. Blavatsky: Study occultism.

Dr. Williams: That is it. What has occultism to say about it?

Mme. Blavatsky: It says that everything you see around, that you can comprehend or conceive of, all this comes from that one absolute force. You have either to believe in a personal God who does so and so—well, of course, as the good clergyman teaches—or you have to believe that there is one absolute totality, incomprehensible, which Herbert Spencer calls the unknowable and refers to it as "He" and the "just cause" (Which is very philosophical!), or you have to choose. Logically, it cannot be anything else, because nothing can come out of nothing; everything must come from something. This something cannot be limited; if it were, it would be a personal God.

Mr. B. Keightley: It would come from something itself.

Mme. Blavatsky: It would just be the fairy hen that lays the egg, and the egg has existed before that hen, and it has produced that hen. Go on if you can understand that.

Dr. Williams: I quite see the logic of that, and I also see that it is absolutely necessary to postulate the "Absolute," something which is back of all manifestation which has no relation to us; but having postulated that, how is it possible to go any further than that? Because the moment we go further than that we begin to talk about manifestation. We can postulate an Absolute of which we can conceive absolutely nothing.

Mme. Blavatsky: Philosophy postulates nothing. It postulates its existence, not its being. It does not say it exists, it does not say it is a being, it simply says it is. Now remember what {Nagasena?} said to the king, that great [   ] when he asked him about Nirvāna. He said it is nowhere. It exists nowhere. What is Nirvāna? It is nothing. Then Nirvāna, he says, does not exist. No, it does not. Then, he says, what are you talking about? He said it is, but it does not exist, it is a state; imagine one absolute state, and this is that consciousness.

Dr. Williams: I see that as a necessity of logic when it applies simply and solely to the Absolute, or to that which forever transcends human consciousness, but the moment we leave that it is different. I want to know how it is possible to talk about the condition of a thing which is not a thing. That is what I cannot comprehend.

Mme. Blavatsky: "Nights and days of Brahmâ," have you ever studied them?

Dr. Williams: Yes.

Mme. Blavatsky: Very well. How do you imagine, for instance, a dark night and a man or men sleeping in a kind of dead sleep—let us say that dead men are like that, let us leave aside all other men. Let us say that a man is like in a dead faint, in one of those swoons; there is no remembrance. You may be five or six hours and it appears one second. Let us think of that, and yet there it comes: there is no consciousness, nothing at all, but from that consciousness of non-being a man becomes and begins thinking immediately what he is. Can you imagine that? It is very unsatisfactory analogy, but there is something in it.

Dr. Williams: Yes, I can imagine anything which comes within the range of human consciousness, but that does not seem to me to touch the point at all. We first postulate an Absolute, of which we admit we can have no conception whatever; then we begin to talk about qualities—of this which transcends human consciousness.

Mme. Blavatsky: No, we do not begin to talk about that at all; it is that absoluteness, according to the Eastern philosophy. It is that absoluteness, which, when the hour strikes of the life-cycle of the day of Brahmâ, which has qualities which were latent in it, and dormant, which were in the Laya condition, at the zero point of everything, all negative, which awaken, so to say, and from that they begin gradually one after the other to form the one whole what we call the divine ideation. We call it the divine thought, that which Plato called the eternal idea. Then after that there begins the differentiation. How many times have I been explaining it is not one? That is why the Brahmins, who are certainly the greatest philosophers in the world, postulate seven creations and at the end of the seventh begins that which I tried to explain to you here, and they have a name for every creation. I speak of those in *The Secret Doctrine* on all the planes and through all the planes of consciousness, and until it comes there—and then you may say from the seventh creation, our creation (I call it creation, it ought to be called evolution.)—then, only begins the differentiation and the fall of spirit into matter. But this goes on gradually, millions and millions of years; and when they come and speak to me about seven thousand years, I say fiddlesticks, and that is all I can say, because seven times seven millions would not cover it.

Mr. B. Keightley: It strikes me, Dr. Williams, that the logic of the position is this if the Absolute is the abstract totality in some form or another. Every object of our consciousness, whether, so to speak, an idea or anything else, must have its root in that Absolute, must come from that, in some way or another. Therefore, ultimately there must be latent, or merged in the Absolute during the time of Pralaya, the essential roots of everything which ever is, has been, or will be manifested.

Dr. Williams: Oh, I quite grant all that.

Mr. B. Keightley: Then comes in what HPB was saying, that you take up the first thing of those qualities. Behind that manifestation you cannot say anything at all.

Dr. Williams: Is not that just what has been done all through *The Secret Doctrine*? Are not there postulates made there of that which has no form, of that which is above form and yet which is in the first absolute, the Absolute?

Mme. Blavatsky: Most assuredly, I speak of it as eternal darkness, then on the second plane begins the motion; this is right that motion begins something else, and so on, until it descends, until the seven. Finite intellect cannot reach that; therefore, it has to come to begin on that stage when the first flutter of differentiation begins in the primordial matter, which is eternal.

Dr. Williams: That is the point: what the first manifestation was, and how we came to have any consciousness of it, and how it is possible to have any consciousness.

Mme. Blavatsky: It is the experience of ages and ages, of all the seers. Either you have to admit that there are such people in the world as seers or there are not. If there are, then the experience of one checks the other. They never said to each other how it was. Those who had the capacities of seers were put to the test, and if they happened to say in their utterances that they know how to produce it, and if the later one happened to say just the same things as the other said, I suppose there is some probability that it is so.

Dr. Williams: I am quite willing to admit that there is not much that comes within the range of my consciousness, but that which does, if I would be honest with myself, I must hold to, quite irrespective of what anybody has said about it.

The President: It seems to me the difficulty in these intermediate stages is this: in a sense, they are positive conceptions. The conception of the Absolute is a negative one, and therefore, it is comparatively easy to us. The intermediate stages are not within the range of our finite intellect, but nevertheless they are positive conceptions.

Mr. Yates: Everything which is within the range of the Absolute must be within our consciousness?

Dr. Williams: Yes, that is exactly the point. The gentleman has stated it.

Mme. Blavatsky: Of course, you don't study here the esoteric things, but those who study the esoteric instructions[3] will understand what I mean. Isn't it said, if we go on a lower analogy—the birth of a child, if you take, or the birth of any animal—take this and you will find it corresponds admirably. There is not a missing link. It corresponds with things which are known to science—you understand what I mean—and these are facts which are not to be gainsaid. It is impossible; it is a perfect proof because it dovetails with every{thing} that science has so far had any proofs of.

Mr. Kingsland: It seems to me that Dr. Williams' questions amounts to this: he wants to know how we can get at or appreciate what it is that acts upon matter.

---

3 The instructions issued to members of HPB's Esoteric Section, of which Instruction No. 1, dated January and February 1889, had just come out.

Mme. Blavatsky: It is the inherent force which covers the whole ground of consciousness and life and everything that you can think of; and at the same time there is a consciousness which acts on it. And these are the things I am going to give you the proofs of, now that your science is at loggerheads with itself.

Dr. Williams: Here is another way of putting it. We have to begin at the beginning, at the Absolute. Then we have next the manifestation of the Absolute. The moment you have the manifestation of anything, you have an idea, you can predicate something about it; but if you go back to anything in which you can predicate nothing, you will never come to the Absolute. Now how is it possible to say anything or predicate a condition of that which transcends consciousness?

Mme. Blavatsky: But we don't postulate anything about it. We say this transforms itself through the planes, the various planes of manifestation, until it reaches this plane of objective scientific perception—even scientific—and that those things that you know are forces in nature, as they can prove to you. There is something beyond; and this is proven by that that even the laws of Newton and Kepler[4] can be perfectly contradicted and proven to be wrong. And this is what I have been preparing here, because with your question I felt like an old war-horse that gets the smell of powder, and I just put to you the explanation.

Mr. Kingsland: I think Dr. Williams seems to suppose that if you pass our plane of consciousness you get to the Absolute.

Mme. Blavatsky: Oh, no, not at all. This passes through a plane that we can have some idea of. For us it is perfectly invisible. The men of science don't want to admit it, just because they cannot smell it or touch it, or hear it, or bring it to be perceived with their senses.

Dr. Williams: I daresay the following question will help us somehow.

Mme. Blavatsky: This imprisoned force and the free force—the worker, within, or the inherent force—ever tends to unite with its

---

4 Johannes Kepler, German astronomer, 1571-1630.

parent essence, that which is outside, and thus the mother acting within causes the web to contract, and the father without to expand. That is another explanation to you; this it is which your men of science call gravity, and we men of ignorance, or fellows, call the work of the universal life-force, spirit-matter, which is one outside space and time, and dual within space and time. This is work of eternal evolution and involution or of expansion and contraction. There: I answer every one of your objections and your questions. Do I or not? This is that dual force; and then you will come to the centripetal and centrifugal forces, which will prove to you it must be so, simply because I base myself on the mistakes of science, which are glaringly demonstrated by all the astronomers and physicists, and yet they won't admit them, but they are, if you please, like the Church clergyman—they know the mistakes and the impossibilities, but won't admit them. So your men of science, they find something that does not dovetail that upsets entirely their theory. But they are too lazy to go and invent another theory. It is very comfortable to go and invent some flapdoodle and then go on ad infinitum. Anything they say of course the hoi polloi will swallow.

Mr. A. Keightley: Then question 4.

Mr. B. Keightley: Before you pass on to that there is this. You say the inner force, the imprisoned force, causes contraction, and the father or external force, expansion.

Mme. Blavatsky: That is to say, that force which works inside or something which has form works, and has always to unite itself with that other force which is absolute; and therefore this force tends to take a form. By that action it assumes a form, whereas the other tries to expand and has no form.

Mr. Kingsland: Would not a very good example be the case of a lump of ice in water? It is an expansion of the same material as the water, but the force makes it contract and form into ice, which is something in the manifested plane; and it is always tending to go back again.

Mme. Blavatsky: And what forms the ice, your scientists don't say. They are right in the detail, but not in the general explanation.

Mr. A. Keightley: (Reads again question 4.)

Mme. Blavatsky: That is a nice question, "when." When the imprisoned force and intelligence inherent in every atom of differentiation—as of homogeneous matter—arrives at a point when both become the slaves of that intelligent force which we call Divine free-will, represented by the Dhyani-Buddhas. When the centripetal and centrifugal forces of life and being are subjected to by the one nameless force, which brings order in disorder and establishes harmony in chaos then. I cannot tell you anything else. How can I name to you the precise hour and time in a process, the duration of which is perfectly, and which the Hindus and the Buddhists, as you know, put in figures.

Mr. A. Keightley: The object of the question was at what stage of the process. Now, question 5. What is meant by the web becoming radiant when it cools?

Mme. Blavatsky: Just that which is said in the paragraph two of the comments which follow the Stanza. (The President reads the passage from *The Secret Doctrine*.)

Mr. A. Keightley: Then, question 6. Stanza 3, Sloka 11. The first paragraph of the commentary needs elucidating in reference to the part which heat plays in the forming and breaking up of the element, and also of the worlds in globes. In it is stated first that "great heat breaks up the compound elements and resolves the heavenly bodies into their one primeval element."[5] This heat apparently is already existing in a "focus or centre of heat (energy) of which many are carried about to and fro in space." What are these centres of heat? Are they visible or invisible in our plane of matter? What is the "body" referred to, which may be either "active or dead?" Is the disintegration by heat, here referred to, that which takes place in our

---

5 *The Secret Doctrine*, I:83-84.

plane and with which we are familiar in chemistry?

Mme. Blavatsky: Then you see I went to the other thing, and then I answered Dr. Williams entirely on that—the thing where you say something that is in your question 6. That is what I say you have mixed up. You go on to the end, and it will be a great deal better—to the end of that number 6.

Mr. A. Keightley: That is the end of number 6.

Dr. Williams: I think it has relation to Fohat.

Mme. Blavatsky: (After reading question 6.) No, it is not that which I answered. There is the confusion that I spoke of to you, because I know I speak of science here.

Dr. Williams: It is the second statement, Madame, that you refer to. I remember it.

Mr. A. Keightley: (Reads the second statement.)

Mme. Blavatsky: I have just answered till then. I say that science is so afraid to raise her theories into her axioms; and why does she play Penelope[6] and do today that which she would not do yesterday? Show to us that the law holds good with regard to the entirety of planetary representatives, and that they can be and are produced in accordance with the law, and then I may say that you are right. We maintain that in this case neither the laws of Newton nor of Kepler will hold good. Take the first and second law of Kepler[7], communicated in the Newtonian law as given to us by Herschel, as just stated. He says that under the influence of such attractive force you will urge two spherical gravitating bodies towards each other; they will, when moving to each other and each other's neighborhood, be deflected into an orbit concave to each other and describe, one about the other regarded as fixed, or both around the common centre of gravity,

---

6 The faithful wife of Odysseus in Homer's Greek epic, the *Odyssey*.
7 Kepler's First Law of planetary motion states: "The orbit of every planet is an ellipse with the Sun at one of the two foci." His Second Law states: "A line joining a planet and the Sun sweeps out equal areas during equal intervals of time."

curves, whose forms are those figures known in geometry by the general name of conic sections. It will depend upon the particular circumstances of velocity, distance and attraction which of those curves shall be described—whether an ellipse, a circle, a parabola or a hyperbola—but one of these it must be. Now, there is one of the theories of science which you have raised into an axiom. Now this axiom of science can be upset in the most easy way possible, by proving that of these things that take place in the phenomenon of the planetary motion, that everything goes against that. This will make you smile, of course, but when everything is given to you and proven to you, you will say this is not a vain boast but it is perfectly that which occultism claims. Now, what science says is that the phenomenon of the planetary motion results from the action of the two forces, the centripetal and the centrifugal. Is it so? And they assure us that a body falls to the ground; first, in a line perpendicular to still water; and secondly, it does so owing to the law of gravity or centripetal force. Do they say so? Now, I am going to prove to you this axiom—to prove to you what a fallacy it is. Now, a very learned occultist shows the following: that if we trust these laws, we shall find as obstacles in our way among other things, first, that the path of a circle is impossible in the planetary motion—perfectly impossible, if left to that inherent force. Second, that the argument as to the third law of Kepler[8], namely, that the squares of the periodic atoms {times} of any two planets are to each other in the same proportion as the cubes of their mean distances from the sun, gives rise to this curious result of the permeated {permitted} libration on the eccentricities of planets. Now, the said forces remaining unchanged in the nature, this can only arise, as he arose {says}, from the interference of an extraneous cause. He also proves that the phenomenon of gravitation or of falling does not exist except as the result of a conflict of forces. It is not gravity, it is a conflict of forces. It can only be considered as an isolated force by way of mental analysis. He asserts moreover that the planet's atoms or particles of matter are not attracted towards each other in the direction of right lines connecting their centres,

---

8 Kepler's Third Law of planetary motion states: "The square of the orbital period of a planet is directly proportional to the cube of the semi-major axis of its orbit."

but rather forced towards each other in the curves of spirals closing upon the centres to each other; also that the tidal wave is not the result of attraction, but simply of this conflict of forces. All this, as he shows, results from the conflict of imprisoned forces, from that which in the eyes of science is antagonism, and what is affinity and harmony to the knowledge of the occultists. Now, these things, if you wanted me to prove them, would take me about two days to prove, but I will draw for you all the geometrical things to prove to you that these things are not rare exceptions, but that they form the rule in the planetary motions. Where is, after that, your Newtonian and your Kepler propositions?

Mr. Kingsland: Is that esoteric, or is that public.

Mme. Blavatsky: Not at all; some of the things may be exoteric.

Mr. Kingsland: Is it sufficiently exoteric to be proved to the satisfaction of a man of science.

Mme. Blavatsky: The men of science laugh at it, and won't accept it. I think I have given it quite enough in *The Secret Doctrine*.

Mr. Kingsland: Can it not be demonstrated mathematically?

Mme. Blavatsky: Mathematically, I think it can. Look at those proofs I have given in my "tugs of science" in *The Secret Doctrine*. Have you read them all?

Mr. B. Keightley: You have not given a detailed proof of that, of this particular point; it would be an awfully good thing to do.

Mme. Blavatsky: Oh, thank you! If I were to give you all the proofs I could give, life would not be sufficient.

Dr. Williams: I think {you} misunderstood my position; I quite understand why you got mad now.

Mme. Blavatsky: I thought you laughed at me, saying science would say so and so.

Dr. Williams: I am not here for that. I don't care what any astronomer thinks. I know very well they quarrel among themselves.

Mme. Blavatsky: I quarrel not with you, but with science. It was what was suggested to me by you. You say so coolly, science will say this or that. I say fiddlesticks to science.

Mr. A. Keightley: You have not answered Dr. Williams' question at all.

Mme. Blavatsky: My dear sir, I tell you, you have mixed up the things. I have answered the whole of it. I felt very much excited and mad. Very well now, put the question.

Mr. A. Keightley: This is question 8. Statement to this question: In the commentary on Sloka 11 of the same Stanza, it is stated that: "Fohat, gathering a few of the clusters of Cosmic matter (nebula) will, by giving it an impulse, set it in motion anew, develop the required heat, and then leave it to follow its own new growth." Such a statement as this makes it necessary for us to abandon all of those great generalizations or conclusions which modern science prides itself upon having reached, viz: the persistence and uniformity of force and the consequent orderly changes in the universe by antecedent and sequence. Science would say that it is inconceivable that an extra-cosmic force, that is, a force not forever imminent {immanent} within matter, should break into the cycle of evolution on any point, and after a period of activity, again leave matter to its own devices. Science would say that creation, or the bringing of form within the range of our conscious perception, is the result of that something to which it has given the name Force. It would further say that the force which first brought matter within the range of perception must persistently remain within that matter as its sustaining and actuating principle, otherwise it would instantly pass from the range of perception or cease to be, so far as we are concerned. If it is once admitted that there is such a force imminent in matter, then the introduction into it of that which has not always been within it is an inconceivability of thought. Moreover, such an hypothesis would be wholly unnecessary, because all of the movements and activities of matter are completely understood without it. Question 8. Is Fohat to be understood as synonymous with force, or that which causes the changing manifestations of matter? If so, how can Fohat be said to "leave it to follow its own new growth," when all growth depends upon the indwelling force?

Mme. Blavatsky: All growth depends upon the indwelling force, because on this plane of ours it is this force alone which acts consciously in our senses. The universal force cannot be regarded as a conscious force, because you would forthwith make of it a personal God. It is only that which is enclosed in form, and limited as to form and matter—I don't know how to express myself well—which is conscious of itself on this plane. That which is limitless and absolute, as this free force or will is, cannot be said to act understandingly, but has but one sole and immutable law of life and being. Fohat is therefore spoken of as the synthetic motor power of all the imprisoned life forces put to give a medium between the Absolute and the conditioned forces. He, so to speak, is the cement between the two, as Manas is the connecting link between the gross matter of the physical body and the Divine Monad which animates it. It is powerless to act upon it directly in the First Race.

Dr. Williams: That bears directly upon the question.

Mme. Blavatsky: Very well, now, 9.

Mr. A. Keightley: Are you not going to touch upon number 6, then?

Mme. Blavatsky: 6 I have been alluding to all the time.

Mr. A. Keightley: (Reads question 6 again.)

Mme. Blavatsky: No sir, it is not that. It is a thing which cannot be explained to you. On the things that take place here, it is a perfect impossibility.

Mr. A. Keightley: Then what are those centres of heat?

Mme. Blavatsky: They are the centres, those from which, for instance, Keely draws his inter etheric force, Laya centres. Heat is paradoxical. It would not be heat to us. There is the negation of heat.

Mr. Kingsland: I thought they might be related to the knots of Fohat that you spoke about last time.

Mme. Blavatsky: This is quite a different thing. Now, 9.

Mr. A. Keightley: Will you do anything with question 7?

Mme. Blavatsky: I gave you all this about question 7.

Mr. A. Keightley: This is question 7. Could extreme cold produce the same dissociating effect as extreme heat, as Mr. Sinnett seems to convey in *Esoteric Buddhism*, page 200? I will read the passage in *Esoteric Buddhism*. (Reads passage, page 200.)

Mme. Blavatsky: Well, this is correct enough.

Mr. A. Keightley: The question actually is, "would the effect of cold be sufficient to cause a conglomerated mass like the earth to fly apart into separated particles."

Mme. Blavatsky: No, it would not.

Mr. B. Keightley: It is not a question of cold but a question of death—loss of life.

Mr. A. Keightley: That is Flammarion[9] whom Mr. Sinnett quotes as being correct.

Mme. Blavatsky: Correct in some things, but I remember perfectly well that the Master said he was not correct in other things, but Sinnett wants to bring all under the sway of science; and Flammarion, perhaps, is more for him than anyone else. I have been answering this question that he has been asking about Sinnett. It is question 11, because I find it 11 here on your type thing. Now you must go to 9. This will lead to eternal confusion.

---

9 Camille Flammarion, French astronomer, 1842-1925.

Mr. B. Keightley: All these things must be put into the report.

Mr. A. Keightley: (Statement to question 9.) Following out the thought already presented in the foregoing statements that Force is unity or One manifesting in an unlimited variety of ways, we find it impossible to understand another statement in the commentary, viz: that "there is heat internal and heat external in every atom," or as it is sometimes spoken of, latent and active heat, or dynamic kinetic heat. From my own standpoint these terms involve a contradiction. We have a perception of matter actuated by force in a peculiar way and to this particular phenomenon we have given the name *heat*. Heat, then, on the physical plane, is simply matter in motion. But there is heat in a more interior or occult sense. Yes, and how is it perceived on these higher planes of consciousness? By virtue of the same law which prevails here, because the truth of the unity of force is a universal truth, and therefore perceived in the same or similar way on all planes of consciousness. If there be heat in a more interior or occult sense than physical heat, it must be perceived by some higher or more interior sense than over present physical senses, and it must be perceived *by virtue of its activities on whatever plane it manifests*. That there may be activities and perception of activities on any plane there must be both percipient and objective *forms*. We thus see that the law of heat, on any plane of existence, is the same. Three conditions are necessary, viz., the actuating force, the form which is actuated, and that which perceives the form in motion. The terms latent heat, potential heat, or dynamic heat are misnomers, because *heat*, whether on the first or on the seventh plane of consciousness, is the perception of matter or *substance* in motion. Question: Is the discrepancy between the above statement and the teaching in *The Secret Doctrine* apparent or real? If real, at what point in the scientific teaching does the error come in?

Mme. Blavatsky: He who offered this question, and regards them as contradictions and discrepancies, can certainly know nothing of occult sciences. Why should heat be on another plane than ours, the perception of matter or substance in motion? Why should an occultist accept the conditions as a sine qua non? First of the actuating force, second the form which is actuated and third that which perceives the forming motion, as this of heat? All this is Spencerianism,[10] pure and simple. An occultist would say on the seventh plane the form will disappear, and there will be nothing to be actuated upon. The actuating force will remain in solitary grandeur—that is to say, according to the Spencerian phraseology. It will be at once the object and the subject, the perceiver and that which is perceived. How can you imagine on the seventh plane it would be the same thing? The terms used are no discrepancies or contradictions, but so many symbols borrowed from physical science in order to render all the processes more clear to the student. I am sorry I cannot go into this tonight, or any Thursday night, but a practical occultist will understand well my meaning. These questions are, I suppose, met before the end of *The Secret Doctrine*. In the third part I explain everything and if you read this, all these questions will be answered. They are met before you come to the third part; there I answered them entirely. There is no error at all there. Those who understand the symbols used know well what is meant; in fact, all the speculations of heat and force relate to and correspond with every principle in man, and this is why I brought them. Because every one of them corresponds with one of the principles, and I use them simply as symbols. Because if I used other expressions, nobody would understand me.

Dr. Williams: Very well. Of course, connected with every expressed word or thought, there are certain ideas, and it is only the ideas which underlie them that I want. I don't care for the form of expression at all. It is only the idea that underlies the words I wanted to get at. Let us take the fourth or fifth plane, there is something which corresponds to heat on the material plane.

Mme. Blavatsky: As you go and descend {ascend} on the planes, you find that everything merges more and more into unity, and

---

10 The system of thought developed by Herbert Spencer, setting forth the idea that evolution is the passage from the simple, indefinite, and incoherent to the complex, definite, and coherent.

therefore on the fourth or fifth plane certainly there is no such thing as heat and no contrast between heat and cold. Because it becomes more and more one; it tends to unity.

Dr. Williams: You speak of heat centres.

Mme. Blavatsky: Now, for instance, when I speak of heat centres, they are the centres which in the physical science would be the zero point, the negation. It would be nothing, and yet these are just that, because they are spiritual, because it is spirit.

Dr. Williams: Well, on whatever plane we speak of anything, it does not make any difference; we speak of it because we perceive something that we know; if we don't perceive it, we have nothing to say about it.

Mme. Blavatsky: Which changes entirely.

Dr. Williams: Is there anything on the third plane which anyone can perceive, which the occultist will perceive?

Mme. Blavatsky: With his mind's eye; and then he will need no form and no symbol or objective thing, because he does not see objectively; he sees only the essence and the root of things, and with senses that do not pretend to this plane. Those are the senses that I have been speaking about, when we spoke about dreams.

Dr. Williams: I admitted all the third, that the perception of anything on any plane above matter must proceed on some sense which is higher than matter.

Mme. Blavatsky: The word "perceived" is a word which conveys the wrong impression. It is "sensed" and not "perceived."

Dr. Williams: Do you wish me to understand it is impossible to gain any idea?

Mme. Blavatsky: On the physical plane, no; but if you go one plane higher, then you will perceive in another way. On the third plane you will "sense" the thing with those senses that you have no idea of on the fourth, and so on, until you come to the last plane where the higher {highest?} adept cannot penetrate.

Dr. Williams: I can perceive things which have no relation to this plane at all; but anything I can perceive, I can predicate something of, but it has no relation to space and time.

Mme. Blavatsky: Most assuredly it has none, and yet it {is} linked, it is united and linked indissolubly with this plane—that which has no relation to space or time.

Dr. Williams: Well, the apparent discrepancy—to go back a little into the second statement of the question—is this: there is brought before the mind's eye the beginning of the creation of the physical universe; there is matter in a homogeneous condition, and it was brought into that homogeneous condition because of an actuating force, otherwise it never could have reached that condition. Let us make a comparison. Let us suppose I have a trough or groove constructed for the rolling of a billiard ball, and I know if I strike with a mallet on that which would turn the scale at two ounces, it is sufficient force to send that ball eight feet. What is the necessity of our introducing as an explanation any force—which I compare to an extra-cosmic force—to that which has already received an impulse which will send it eight feet?

Mme. Blavatsky: And do you suppose it would proceed to act in this way if it did not have an inherent force which you represent, and which has an analogy to the force outside?

Dr. Williams: But you speak there of Fohat coming in at that point, and doing something and then leaving.

Mme. Blavatsky: I have no right to say more. There are things I cannot explain, which I try to make you understand—that there is force outside and a force inside; that no billiard ball is just that.

Mr. Kingsland: Is that force outside acting continuously?

Mme. Blavatsky: Most assuredly. If you leave a billiard ball, and if it is there three or four years, I don't think you would find much of it at the end.

Dr. Williams: In our conception of the universe, and it seems through all the investigations of the ages, this one thing remains true, because it is a universal truth—it has no reference whatever to the discrepancies of science, it is a universal truth—and that is this: the persistence of force, that force is everywhere persistent, though you never get the manifestation.

Mme. Blavatsky: This proves what we say, because it is absolute, because it is ever present, but they don't know the force, they don't know what it is. Can they explain to you what is force? If they want to gainsay what we say, let them explain what is force. Let them explain why their theories are a bundle of contradictions.

Dr. Williams: I am only speaking self-evident truth.

Mme. Blavatsky: That is that they will come and speak to you about the persistence of force—which no occultist will deny—but what is that force? They are perfectly unable to tell you. Before it was all matter, matter reigned supreme. After that, matter has been kicked out—there was a revolution, if you please, among the scientists. They rebelled and they enthroned "Force," and now they look at force and say, "Who are you?"

Mr. Kingsland: The occultists will say: "Force is not persistent on this plane." Speaking of science, he says that science says, force is persistent on this plane.

Mme. Blavatsky: It is persistent, certainly, because it is eternal and absolute; and it is given here under various forms and aspects, but it is not the force as it is on the seventh plane, but it certainly is persistent. But what is that force, I ask you? We say what it is. It is an absolute totality; it is the "unknowable" of Herbert Spencer, but then you see science will not admit that there is a force which acts outside of the atom, that there is an intelligent force; they will say it is all blind force. This is what they will say—force inherent, a mechanical force.

Dr. Williams: I cannot conceive of anything blind, or intelligent force, but I must conceive of force acting on matter.

Mr. B. Keightley: But that is not the point Dr. Williams was after. Dr. Williams is still troubled about the statement in *The Secret Doctrine*:[11] if Fohat leaves the nuclei, the nebulous masses, to follow their own growth.

Mme. Blavatsky: This is the fault of your learned brother. I have got the things here, and I answer it.

Mr. Kingsland: Fohat will set it in motion anew, and then leave it to follow its own growth.

Mr. B. Keightley: That Doctor Williams understands to be in contradiction to the law of forces.

Mme. Blavatsky: I tell you, all the questions here are mixed up, and I cannot find where it is. But I can tell you without looking because I know very well what I have been writing about. It is not a contradiction at all, it leaves everything. How is it expressed? It leaves the—

Mr. Kingsland: It leaves it to follow its own growth.

Mme. Blavatsky: Well, I must show it to you, because I have been writing it. All growth depends upon the indwelling force, because on the plane of ours it is this force alone—it is not that it leaves them to themselves, but Fohat acts consciously, and it is only that which acts in the inherent force which acts consciously. It cannot be expressed in any other way. It is not that the forces ceases to act, but it is that one acts consciously and the other unconsciously. The universal force cannot be regarded as a conscious force, because it would forthwith make of it a personal God. It is only that which is enclosed in form and a limitation of matter, which is conscious of itself on this plane of ours. That which, limitless and absolute, has the free force, or will,

---

11 *The Secret Doctrine*, I:84.

cannot be said to act understandingly, but has one immutable law of life and being, and therefore it is said that Fohat leaves them alone to do as they please. That is to say, that they will henceforth—this force acting in every atom will be in the eternal conflict with the force outside—well, not conflict, but harmony, as we would call it. Therefore, there is no discrepancy at all.

Dr. Williams: I did not say there was.

Mr. B. Keightley: When Fohat gives them an impulse and leaves them to themselves it means, in other words, that the outside force, or Fohat, the universal force, becomes limited in form.

Mme. Blavatsky: It does not become limited in form.

The President: It becomes differentiated.

Mme. Blavatsky: The universal force cannot be said to act consciously because it acts everywhere as an immutable law. Therefore they are said to act for themselves. I don't know how the expression goes—"the indwelling force."

Mr. B. Keightley: The phrase used is, that Fohat gives them an impulse.

Mme. Blavatsky: Yes, it is the atom, the medium between that unconscious force and that conscious force. Having established the centripetal and centrifugal forces, he leaves them. Now, this is no discrepancy; without Fohat, it is impossible, because one is the absolute, and the other is the limited. They are the two extremes—there would be no connection, and Fohat connecting, being the universal force of life in that which puts into motion the things, and gives the impulse, he is said to come. You must make some allowance for the Eastern mode of expression. I tell you I have been translating word for word.

The President: But Fohat is not the absolute immutable force, it is the synthesis of the seven rays.

Mme. Blavatsky: Not at all; he is the connecting medium between the absolute and that, since he represents all the Divine mind.

Mr. Kingsland: I asked that question; whose agent is Fohat in this case? The agent of the law. He is the representative of that, of all these Dhyan-Chohans as we call them, the Manasaputra, which means the eternal mind.

The President: It is quite clear but difficult to express, and not very easy to see.

Mme. Blavatsky: Well, it is my unfortunate English, but I defy any man with the greatest command of the English language even to come and express these abstruse things so that people could understand them.

Mr. A. Keightley: Statement to question 10. It is then further stated in the commentary that under the influence of Fohat "the required heat" is developed in order to give "*it*" the necessary impulse to follow a new growth. If "*it*" has already been dissociated by heat, how does it require more heat for the new growth? What is this new growth? What is the "*it*" here referred to, is it the "*body*" mentioned a few times before, or is it the "few clusters of cosmic matter" which Fohat has gathered together? Under what guidance does Fohat act in these cases? What is the process by which a globe passes into Pralaya? Does it do so *in situ* so to speak, that is to say, still remaining part of a planetary chain and maintaining its proper position in relation to the other globes? Does the dissociation by means of heat play any part in the passage of a globe into Pralaya?

Mme. Blavatsky: Well, I answer here, all this has reference to disrupted atoms from forms becoming Arūpa, that is to say, formless—from forms becoming formless. It has no reference to a special thing or some phenomenon here. It refers simply to the disruption of atoms, and once that they return to their primordial element, then Fohat begins again to turn them into use, that is to say, the vital electricity.

The President: To build them up into their aggregations.

Mme. Blavatsky: Certainly just the same as anyone does here. The atoms fly off, and half becomes a cabbage and so on.

The President: Until that combination is built up. It is no conscious force in itself. It requires Fohat to combine it.

Mme. Blavatsky: It requires Fohat to put it into form, to give it a number, a geometrical aspect, a colour, a sound; all these that it should acquire consciousness.

The President: I think that explains it.

Mr. A. Keightley: Then, question 11. In the passage of a globe into Pralaya, does it remain "in situ," i.e. still being part of a planetary chain, and maintaining its proper position in relation to the other globes? Does the dissociation by means of heat play any part in the passage of a globe into Pralaya?

Mme. Blavatsky: I think this is in *Esoteric Buddhism*, and it is explained there in the obscuration of the planets. Of course, when one of the globes of a planetary chain goes into obscuration, heat retires from it—it remains statu quo. It is just like the sleeping beauty: it remains so, until it is awakened by a kiss. It is like a frozen paralyzed thing, it remains as it is. There is no disruption, but there is no correlation going on, no renovation of atoms, no life.

Mr. Kingsland: And does it pass through the stage in which the mind is now?

Mme. Blavatsky: No, no; it will return again when its time comes, because, mind you, there is the planetary chain in every globe. One after the other passes into obscuration.

Mr. A. Keightley: Is that period of obscuration really and genuinely what is ordinarily meant by Pralaya?

Mme. Blavatsky: It is the Pralaya of the globe, but the globe above us will go on into activity.

Mr. A. Keightley: Is it a Pralaya of the globe, or is it a Pralaya only of the things upon the globe?

Mme. Blavatsky: No, it is a Pralaya of the globe, when it goes into obscuration——Pralaya of everything, of every atom.

Mr. A. Keightley: Take, for instance, the earth at the present moment, supposing this member of this particular chain went into obscuration. At the present moment it probably is visible to Mars. We will say, would the earth still continue to be visible?

Mme. Blavatsky: Certainly, it would continue to be visible. It would be just like the moon. You think the moon is a dead planet, because it has no more trees and that. It is a soulless planet, dead spiritually, but not dead—well, if you please, do not speak to me about it. It is a thing that Sinnett received on his fingers for asking too many questions. I know you are all dangerous fellows.

Mr. Kingsland: When our earth goes into Pralaya, it will become like the moon.

Mme. Blavatsky: I think it has become like the moon already. We are all lunatics, everyone of us here; mankind has become a perfect lunatic.

Mr. A. Keightley: Statement to question 12. In Sloka 11 the sons are spoken of as dissociating and scattering, and this appears to be opposed to the action of returning to their mother's bosom at the end of the "Great Day." Does the dissociating and scattering refer to the formation of the globes from the universally diffused *world stuff*? In other words, emerging from a state of Pralaya? What is meant by the expanding and contracting through their own selves and hearts, and how is this connected with the last line of the Sloka: "they embrace infinitude"?

Mme. Blavatsky: That has been answered. The dissociating and scattering refers to Nitya Pralaya in general. I explained to you what Nitya Pralaya is, so you may explain it in your turn. You brought it to me the other day. I explained to you what it was. It is an eternal and perpetual Pralaya which took place ever since the worlds were created, ever since there was something on the globes. It is going on always, and ever will be going on.

The President: It is death, simply—death in the sense of change.

Mme. Blavatsky: We are all of us in Nitya Pralaya. None of us has got the atoms that he or she had on entering the room an hour ago, and in an hour more, we will all be entirely changed.

Mr. A. Keightley: It is atomic change and nothing else.

Mme. Blavatsky: Yes. Nothing else. All the change is Nitya Pralaya.

Mr. A. Keightley: Question 13. What is meant by the expanding and contracting "through their own selves and hearts," and how is this connected with the last line of the Sloka: "they embrace infinitude?"

Mme. Blavatsky: It is just an Eastern metaphor in figurative language, meaning that which was already said—through their own inherent force imprisoned and each striving collectively to join in the universal forces, "embraces infinitude." This is, I think, very clear.

Mr. A. Keightley: Question 14. What is the relation between density and the "weight" of which you spoke last Thursday as the first quality manifested in matter?

Mme. Blavatsky: Density even in its first degree has a film, imparts weight. I believe one cannot exist without the other. If there is density, there is weight, certainly; that is the relation. Now 15.

Mr. A. Keightley: Question 15. What is the relation between electricity and (a) physical magnetism, (b) animal magnetism, and (c) hypnotism?

Mme. Blavatsky: I think this is a very long question, and we had better postpone it. One can be applied to the physical things, and the other is a thing which you could not apply. You could not apply hypnotism to this box, but you could apply electricity to it. The relation between them is that electricity is the mother of all these on the plane of manifestation, and Fohat is the father of all. Electricity is the mother of all the forces in mental and physical phenomena. First of all, and on what you call phenomenal matter, neither can act on a mineral or chemical element without Fohat, who turns about and acts upon the molecules, and the molecular cells of your brains. I think that is quite enough.

(Here the proceedings closed.)

10.
The Theosophical Society.
Meeting of the Blavatsky Lodge
17 Lansdowne Road, Holland Park, W.
Thursday, March 14, 1889.

Mr. Kingsland in the Chair

Mr. A. Keightley: Stanza 4, Sloka 1.

Mr. B. Keightley: (Reads the passage from *The Secret Doctrine*.)

Mr. A. Keightley: Question 1. Are the "Sons of the Fire" the subdivisions of the third Logos, or are they subdivisions of the Universal Mind? Are these two synonymous?

Mme. Blavatsky: You mean to say that you understand that the "Sons of the Fire" are simply a hierarchy of angels, or what?

Mr. A. Keightley: I understand that the "Sons of the Fire" are the various hierarchies comprised in the subdivision of the third Logos.

Mme. Blavatsky: The modern "Sons of the Fire," that is to say, those of the Fifth Race and sub-race, are called so simply because by their wisdom they belong to the hierarchies, which are nearer to it, of the "divine sons of the fire mists," the highest planetary Chohans or angels, but the "sons of the fire mists" who are spoken of here in the Stanza as addressing the "sons of the earth," {are} the royal king's instructors, who incarnated on this earth to teach nascent humanity. They belong as kings to the divine dynasties of which every ancient nation—India, Chaldea, Egypt, Homeric Greece, etc.—has preserved the tradition in some form or another. The subdivisions of the second Logos are unknown quantities, my dear sir, and those of the first or unmanifested Logos never existed except as a unity.

Mr. A. Keightley: My question was the third Logos.

Mme. Blavatsky: What is it you ask?

Mr. A. Keightley: I say, are these subdivisions of the third Logos?

Mme. Blavatsky: Certainly; they must be, because the subdivisions of the second Logos are unknown quantities. Those of the first never existed except as a unity, therefore, they must be necessarily of the third; they cannot be anything else. It is the first manifested point.

Mr. A. Keightley: Then what relation have they to the universal mind?

Mme. Blavatsky: What relation have they? Which ones?

Mr. A. Keightley: These hierarchies.

Mme. Blavatsky: They belong to the hierarchies that I have been explaining to you many, many times, beginning by the "fire Chohans," and the "fire angels," then the "ether angels," the "air angels," the "water angels," and the "earthly angels." The seven lower Sephiroth are the earthly to the seven hierarchies of the seven elements, of which five you know, and two you don't.

Mr. Kingsland: It would appear from what you say there, they also correspond to the races?

Mme. Blavatsky: Most assuredly, they correspond to the divine dynasties. Where would be the intellectual races with brains and thought if it were not for these hierarchies who incarnated it?

Mr. A. Keightley: Then the "Sons of the Fire" are these divine instructors?

Mme. Blavatsky: In this sense they are. They are king's instructors—those divine dynasties that the Chaldeans and the Egyptians and the Hindus have thus taken; even to the Greeks they are divine dynasties.

Mr. A. Keightley: Then so far as human beings are concerned, the "Sons of the Fire" are the highest incarnated on earth, as the "sons of the fire mists" are the highest in the celestial sphere.

Mme. Blavatsky: Yes, but they are also the "Sons of the fire mists," as the Hierophants were called in the days of old.

Mr. A. Keightley: Are not they and the "divine dynasties" almost identical? That is to say, they must have been in connection; they were king initiates.

Mme. Blavatsky: Yes, and they were moreover [ ], all of them; they were incarnations. So the occult doctrine teaches of those celestial hierarchies who came and incarnated in man, that they were the highest of those. You see the most puzzling thing before an audience that has been brought up in the belief that for every baby that is born there is a soul, immediately produced by God, and this is a thing which is extremely puzzling: nobody seems to take in that philosophical idea that nothing can come out of nothing, not even the breath of God, at least not of an anthropomorphic God. Of a deity, of course, I understand, because everything is breath, divine essence; but I mean this God that comes and breathes over a child that is born, even a child of sin, this is a thing which is most puzzling.

Mr. A. Keightley: I think the great difficulty in that case is to realize that the underlying soul is one, as distinct from the separated bodies.

Mme. Blavatsky: How is it distinguished? It cannot be distinguished {from} that underlying soul, because it permeates every atom of the human body, and everything in the universe. There is not an atom of mud that is not permeated by the divine soul. If it were otherwise, it would not be infinite, you must have it infinite or you cannot admit the other thing.

Mr. A. Keightley: That is the difficulty—the idea of the individuality as compared with the one underlying reality.

Mme. Blavatsky: Can you tell me about this lamp? This fire in it, is it an individual fire?

Mr. A. Keightley: So far, yes. Certainly, I should say so.

Mme. Blavatsky: Certainly, it is not. It is individual so long as it is in the lamp and it is confined to a vessel; but if you take it from there, it is not in any way any other fire than the one universal fire which is on earth—at least in our solar system. This you may bet your bottom dollar upon, there is no other. Mind you, I don't say it is of the same essence, it is of the same, though in another form, just the same for the souls and for the monads.

Mr. A. Keightley: There I get the analogy, but the difficulty in all distinctions is to disabuse one's mind of the idea that that is a separate piece of fire.

Mme. Blavatsky: He who wants to be an occultist has not to separate himself from anything in this world, and the moment he separates himself from any vessel of dishonour, he cannot belong to any vessel of honour; it is a perfect impossibility. You must either think of yourself as an infinitesimal something, not even individual, but a part of the one whole; or you are illusions, you are nobodies, and you will go out like breaths and leave no trace behind you. You are separate, so far as illusions are concerned. You are distinct bodies, every one of you, and you are marching about in masks furnished to you by "Maya." Can you claim one single atom in your bodies which is your own? Can you stop a set of atoms? You do not pay even the slightest attention to them. What are you? Is it your own intellect or soul, or spirit? Everything from the spirit down to the last of the atoms is a part of the whole. It is a link. You break one and then everything goes into annihilation. A link cannot be broken, it is impossible.

Mr. B. Keightley: You see, you get a series of vehicles increasing in grossness, so to speak, as you proceed from spirit into matter, so that with each step downward you get more and more the sense of separateness developed, until you get lower down. And yet that cannot exist, because if there was a real and complete separation between any two human beings they would not be able to understand or communicate with each other in any sort of way.

Mr. A. Keightley: Certainly; I am not arguing against the fact.

Mr. B. Keightley: But I am only putting that forward as a fact.

Mr. A. Keightley: Question 2: Are the "Sons of the Earth" simply human beings? If not, what?

Mme. Blavatsky: This question has just been answered. It is covered by the first answer.

Mr. A. Keightley: Then there is the passage: "The Fire, the Flame, the Day, this bright fortnight, the six months of the Northern Solstice departing (dying) in these, those who know the Brahman (yogis) go to Brahman," etc, p. 86.

Mme. Blavatsky: It is from the *Anugita*.[1]

Mr. A. Keightley: Question 3. Will you give an explanation of these terms? What is the meaning of the sentence?

Mme. Blavatsky: The meaning is given plainly enough in the commentary of *The Secret Doctrine*. If you did not pay attention to it, you tell me and I will try to explain it to you more fully. Will you read this thing?

Mr. B. Keightley: (After reading from *The Secret Doctrine*.) And then you go on to speak about the different hierarchies, but you do not explain the statement in the quotation, that those departing at that period would go to Brahman, or in the other case would go to the [ ] {lunar light}.

Mme. Blavatsky: It means that the "devotees" are divided into two broad classes, those who reach Nirvana, and either accept or don't accept it (Because they have the option of remaining on earth, at least in the atmosphere of doing good, or they have the option of going selfishly to plunge themselves into Nirvana and not caring for the world.), and those who do not do so and have not reached

---

1 Mme. Blavatsky misquotes. *The Secret Doctrine*, I:86 correctly attributes this quote to *The Bhagavad-Gita*, Chapter VIII. See W.Q. Judge's rendition, pp. 61-62.

Nirvana. Now the first ones will never be reborn in this {Mahakalpa} or the hundred years of the age of Brahmâ—and which means 15 figures; and those who don't reach Nirvana on earth, as Buddha and others did. It is all symbolical and metaphorical and easy enough to understand. I suppose "the Fire, the Flame, the Day, the bright fortnight of the moon" are all symbols of the highest absolute deity; those who had any such state of absolute purity as this symbol shows to be go to Brahman, that is to say, they have a right to {Moksha}. On the other hand, Smoke, Night, dark fortnight, etc. are all symbolical of matter and of ignorance, and those who die in such state of incomplete purification must of course be reborn. Only the homogeneous or pure and unalloyed spirit can become spirit and go to Brahman. It is as plain as can be that these are nothing but metaphors.

Mr. A. Keightley: Then what is the meaning of saying they are the highest deities or names of various deities?

Mme. Blavatsky: Because the hierarchies belonging to such are there connected correspondentially with the dark fortnight and the bright fortnight and the others that you read. Besides, I say it all pretends to esotericism. I never heard esotericism talked on a Thursday night before.

Mr. A. Keightley: It is a sort of transcendental astrology.

Mme. Blavatsky: It is para-metaphysics. Now question 4.

Mr. A. Keightley: You have already answered that. Question 4. What is the distinction between the yogis who do not return and the "devotees" who do return?

Mme. Blavatsky: Such is the distinction of the yogis who do not return on this earth—oh, I have answered this.

Mr. A. Keightley: Question 5.

Mr. B. Keightley: (Reads Sloka 2.)

Mr. A. Keightley: Then there are the two quotations in the commentary which follow: "The First Primordial are the highest beings on the scale of Existence." "The Primordial proceed from Father-Mother."[2] Question 5. Is Father-Mother here synonymous with the third Logos and not with Svabhavat in Darkness, as before, since it is now manifested and differentiated existence, "whereas the other manifested Quarternary and the seven proceed from the Mother alone"?

Mme. Blavatsky: Now you have put there two questions, to which I will give you two answers. The first primordial seven are born from the third Logos. This is before it is differentiated into the mother, when it becomes pure primordial matter in its first primitive essence—father, mother, potentially. All this is explained very plainly in the comment (a) of Sloka 2. Read it over, every word is explained there.

Mr. B. Keightley: (Reads passage from *Secret Doctrine*.)

Mme. Blavatsky: Now I will tell you. You asked what is synonymous there.

Mr. A. Keightley: Is Father-Mother here synonymous with the third Logos and not with Svabhavat in Darkness, as before, since it has now manifested and differentiated existence, "whereas the other manifested Quaternary and the seven proceed from the mother alone"?

Mme. Blavatsky: It is synonymous now with the third Logos, and Svabhavat is light, or manifestation. It is called both; it is perfectly interchangeable, as it was synonymous earlier with darkness, there it is Svabhavat in light, and in darkness the "first primordial" are always to be understood as the rays of the third Logos, not otherwise. They are the direct emanations of the secret [ ], because we reckon twice over. Father-Mother, Parabrahm, Mulaprakriti, the eternal ideal, the dual ideal potency in our mind and the Logos born from it are eternal. It is simply the difference between the existence—or simply

---

2 *The Secret Doctrine*, I:88.

the idea *in esse* and the idea *in actu*. I thought I had explained it perfectly well there.

Mr. B. Keightley: But one wants to come back, to know whether he understands it correctly.

Mme. Blavatsky: I thought you understood it correctly. Now, 6 is a continuation of this.

Mr. A. Keightley: Yes; question 6. What is Mother and what is Father in this sentence?

Mme. Blavatsky: Mother becomes the immaculate Mother only when differentiation is complete, otherwise there would be no such qualification. No one would speak, for instance, of pure spirit as an immaculate something, for it cannot be otherwise. Immaculate spirit becomes simply matter, so the immaculate mother shows to you that where qualification is possible, it is matter and it is lower; therefore the mother is the immaculate matter which begins the hierarchy. That will end by humanity and man, because it must begin by something which Father-Mother cannot be. They are in the beginning ideally potential; then in potentiality it becomes mother alone, because what is mother? Take the etymology of the word, and you will find it is simply matter, and this matter is the primordial matter which is alone, and after that, of course, the immaculate mother. The idea of the immaculate mother comes from that, because the spirit is invisible.

Mr. A. Keightley: Then one gets rather into difficulties in trying to understand the thing, because here you have the third Logos, which is Father-Mother in manifestation, isn't it?

Mme. Blavatsky: You will have time, if you please, to be confused and perplexed. You will find something more difficult, yet they are all interchangeable. Now, you see, it is just the same as though you were to take to task a chemist because he would show to you some compound or chemical preparation, and he would give you this name, and then he would call something by another name; but they are all one and all different. This is a thing you have to learn. It is the order of proceeding. You cannot go further because you would simply cobweb your head with perfectly useless things, unless you want to become a metaphysical Vedantin and go and give lectures upon it. I tell you, you will only confuse yourself and nothing more.

Mr. A. Keightley: My only object is to find out what is meant.

Mme. Blavatsky: What are you? You think you are—you are not at all. It is conceit. You are a part of humanity, though you are Archibald Keightley; and what is humanity? Humanity is a part of thousands of millions of humanity that passed away. It is a piece of dirt, nothing else. And what is the world? It is a little speck of dirt in the Universe. You cannot come and have this spirit of separateness—though you be an Englishman and a Conservative.

Mr. A. Keightley: When one is an illusion one wants to understand one's relation.

Mme. Blavatsky: An illusion is an illusion. If you thought you understood it, you would be perfectly disenchanted.

Mr. A. Keightley: Sloka 3, page 91. Question 7. It is on page 91 that the sentence occurs. (Reads.) Can you explain to us the principle of permutation by which 13514 becomes 31415? Page 92 {91}.

Mme. Blavatsky: I tell you everything is possible to God, and that if it is his sweet will that 2 and 2 should make 5 you know he will do it in a moment.

Mr. B. Keightley: (Reads passage from *The Secret Doctrine*.)

Mme. Blavatsky: As I said in my comment, we are not concerned at present with the process, which means that it cannot be given exoterically and publicly. That is said in so many words before on the page that you have just read the Sloka from, yet I don't mind explaining a little more, which I will do as much as I can. The set of figures must have the same meaning as the various cycles and ages of the first born, the 15 figures. 311, a great many more or less, and I don't know what. Never mind. I will try to give it to you and make you understand. Now, the Rabbis called the circle (What we call Parabrahm.) Achod {Ehad}, the One or Ein Soph. On the lower plane of the fourth it becomes Adam Kadmon, the manifested seven and the unmanifested ten, or the complete Sephirothal tree, which are the three and the seven lower ones, and the synthesis which makes the perfect ten. The Sephiroth, therefore, are the same as the Elohim. Now, the name of the latter written in Hebrew [ ] {Alhim} is composed of five letters. These letters or their values in numerals being placed upon a circle can be shifted or transmuted at will, as they could not be, were they applied to any other geometrical figure. The circle is endless and has neither beginning nor end. Now, the literal Kabalah is divided into three parts, as all know, or methods, the third of which is called Temurah, or the permutation. According to certain rules, one letter is replaced by another. The Kabbalistic alphabet is divided into two equal parts, each letter or numeral of one corresponding to the same number or letter in the sister half. It is a difficult process, and by changing alternately the letters one from the other, there are about, some say, 22 combinations. I have heard there are far more than that. In one case there are 22; there are four more in other combinations within combinations, at least as my Rabbi {said?}. Now if you make a circle in such a way (If I had a table, I would just draw it here.), if you make the circle, the perfect circle, and inscribe within these letters, A L H E or I and M, Elohim, and take their numerical values, it will yield to you either 13514 (I left out something.) Read this whichever way you like, and you may read it as 13514 or 31415, which is the value of the astronomical pi or the constant qualificient {coefficient} number, value, circumference of a circle whose diameter is one. That is a very plain thing in astronomy, that is to say, the five males-females or the ten (Because each one of them is a male-female and it makes five.) are ten resolving themselves into one. Not only can the numbers be replaced at will by the Temurah, but the Sephiroth, being synonymous with the Elohim, and of the 10 words or [ ] {D-BRIM or Dabarim}. These are all found inscribed numerically in the circle. Look at this for instance: there is the circle, which is the one, and there is the line, the straight line, the perpendicular line, which is the line of the first Logos. Then if you make another, and if you draw this line, this will be the plane of matter where will be the second Logos, and then there is the third. They are the seven creations. Nobody has ever remarked it, because they take literally every word of the Kabalah, and they take literally every word of the Bible. Whose fault is that? It is perfectly well defined, and I promised to show to you my answer to prove it. It is the same thing, but nobody has read it to the present day. They have taken it positively, literally, the circle and its dividing line and the prototype of ten, the sacred number—that is to say, infinite or passive unmanifested, and the infinite active or the Logos. The numerals of the Dabarim, the Sephiroth, which are in Hebrew Sephir, which means cipher or figures, are all inscribed within the two, and yield the values of their names. It all comes out anagrammatically, and so it does with all the Sanskrit names. You may take the circle, and if you put all the letters in Hebrew, of course, of the Sephiroth, Elohim, or our Dhyan-Chohans or of the Builders, anything, it will just give to you the same thing always. It will come out the pi. Why? Because those digits, or the small figures, if you take out, of course, the noughts they are subservient to the circumference and the diameter to the one in the circle. This is very plain; but how extraordinary it is that they should have adopted for the astronomical thing such a thing as that, which if you translate them, they make Elohim. If you translate it (Not as we take it, geometrically.), it gives the number and the names of the Dhyan-Chohans, their real secret esoteric name, with all of them. But only, instead of putting in letters and numerals as the Hebrews do, we put them in geometrical figures, and it comes to the same—a line, a triangle, a [ ], and a cube, 1234—until it comes to the digits 9 and 10, the three higher ones, and the seven lower ones. So, do you understand it now?

Mr. B. Keightley: I suppose the actual transformation is one of those anagrammatical transformations, in the way which the order of the digits has been shifted here.

Mme. Blavatsky: Dr Westcott has done it very nicely here.[3] Now you should take this, because you can see it very nicely.

Mr. Gardner: When you say it represents the name of the Dhyan-Chohans, do you mean to say the names in Sanskrit?

Mme. Blavatsky: Also in Sanskrit just the same, because it all comes from India through Chaldea.

Mr. Gardner: You mean the numerical value of the name.

Mme. Blavatsky: All the numbers are the same. You take it in Greek, and it will give you the same value, because it has been adapted so cunningly, so ingeniously, that it is impossible to do it better. If you are inclined to believe that the Patriarchs and the Jews were the first ones, then of course you are welcome to do it. I keep to my own views, and I am for the Hindus, being a true blue heathen myself, I am for the Hindus.

Mr. A. Keightley: Question 8. Will you give some explanation concerning the various hierarchies mentioned here? The terms are frequently used later on, and explanation in contrast as here would be very useful.

Mme. Blavatsky: I believe I have done so now quite enough. I have given it quite enough. You pass on to 9, because you are very fond of repeating the same questions over and over again.

Mr. A. Keightley: Sloka 4, page 95.

Mr. B. Keightley: (Reads passage from *The Secret Doctrine*.)

Mr. A. Keightley: Question 9. "What is the connection between the life-winds and the senses, and the connection of the intelligences with the latter?"

---

3 In the Preface to his *Numbers: Their Occult Powers and Mystic Virtue*, published by the Theosophical Publishing Society in 1890, William Wynn Westcott mentions that the manuscript had been in circulation among "students of mystic lore and occult meanings" for some time.

Mme. Blavatsky: There—a question to answer for one woman alone! Life-winds, or the various modes of in-breathing and out-breathing and changing thereby the polarity of one's object and state, and consciousness, and principles and so on is all esoteric, of course, but what can I tell you more? It being esoteric, the connection between the intelligences—and I suppose by the intelligences, you mean the Dhyan-Chohans—and the senses is all given in the Esoteric Instructions, numbers 1 and 2, if you know what that means. It is all given, the correspondencies. Now, why should you come and make me speak here of things that are perfectly explained? I don't know.

Mr. A. Keightley: Because it is elucidation of points in *The Secret Doctrine*.

Mr. B. Keightley: One point is that in the *Theosophist* the life-winds have been explained not as breath at all but as forces operating in the body, having nothing to do, apparently, with the actual in and out breathing.

Mme. Blavatsky: I never heard that the *Theosophist* was anything but an exoteric exposition of things. You won't find in the *Theosophist* [ ], and he who thinks that the [ ] can perform miracles, and find a yogi, will find himself very much mistaken indeed, because here, where they will call a thing, perhaps, a table, it will mean a kind of juice of a plant; and when he says put your right leg in such a posture, it means you have to turn your cheek or your eye to a certain star. It is perfectly all blind and nothing else. You have to take yogi theosophy and give it word for word, and he who relies upon it will make a sore yogi, I can assure you.

Mr. A. Keightley: Now 10. What is the meaning of "The Sparks of the Seven are subject to and servants of the first, second, third, fourth, fifth, and sixth, and the seventh of the Seven"? Page 95 {93}.

Mme. Blavatsky: I have explained it to you. The sparks mean here sparks or monads or the higher intelligences as much as the human sparks, or monads, or the higher intelligences. It means just as I told you. It can be applied on the plane below or the plane above;

it relates to the circle and the digits I have just shown you. It is the equivalent to saying in mathematical astronomy that the figures 31415 are all subject to the circumference and diameter, as I told you, of a circle. Think over it and I suppose you will see it. It is no use going over the old ground again; they are all subjects, that is what it means. And in the same way, all these hierarchies are subject to the circle which represents the symbol I. It is the symbol I of the absolute infinite circle; that is all.

Mr. A. Keightley: Now 11. Why is Sarasvati (The Goddess of Speech.) also called the goddess of Esoteric Wisdom? If the explanation lies in the meaning of the word Logos, why is there a distinction between the immovable mind and movable speech? Is mind equivalent to Mahat, or to the higher or lower Manas?

Mme. Blavatsky: Because and for the same reason that Logos or word is called incarnate wisdom in the Holy Bible, in the Book of God. "Light shining in darkness," also. Is it so? The distinction lies between the immovable or eternal immutable all, and the movable speech or Logos, that is to say, the periodical and the manifested. The Logos is not an eternal, only a [   ]. It becomes manifested only in the Manavantaric periods periodically; therefore it cannot be referred to as the one eternal or the immovable, for he is very much moveable, but moves from the subjective and the unknown. Mind is an abstraction. It can relate to the Universal or the individual Mind, to the Mahat or the higher human Manas, because that which is desire or instinctive impulse in the lower Manas becomes thought in the higher, and consciousness. The former finds expression in acts, the latter in words. Do you understand? Therefore, even in your laws the assault is more severely punished than mere thought. That is a very unpoetical simile, but still it will open your eyes. This is again food for thought to the wise. Do you understand the difference? It is a perfect impossibility not to. You find it in the fourth gospel in the first chapters, which are Platonic and esoteric.

Mr. A. Keightley: Then does this mean that there is a further meaning to that allegory that you put there, to speech and mind going and having a dispute?

Mme. Blavatsky: Yes, it is from *Anugita* again. Certainly it is, and the Brahmin gave the definition and shows what it is, and he reconciles them.

Mr. A. Keightley: He says neither is superior to the other; but speech having been uttered, and going and asking the question was rare also.

Mme. Blavatsky: And he snubs very prettily the speech.

Mr. A. Keightley: And then he talks about moveable and immoveable speech.

Mme. Blavatsky: Yes, it is purely esoteric, all this. Now 12.

Mr. A. Keightley: Page 92. We know that "God geometrizes," but, seeing that there is no personal God, will you explain why the process of formation should be by dots, lines, triangles, cubes, and why a cube should then expand into a sphere? Finally, why, when the sphere leaves the static state, the inherent force of Breath sets it whirling.

Mme. Blavatsky: Certainly. There is God standing here simply (As with Plato.) for the plural forces or rays emanating from the one and the Absolute; therefore, law is meant here. We say here law geometrizes, but in the day of Plato, "οἱ πολλοί"[4] would not certainly have understood, and therefore they used the word God. Why it should be so, I cannot tell certainly, because the Absolute did not unfortunately take my counsel; or perhaps, as I was part of him, if I had not been such a lazy woman, I might have heard. But I didn't, so how can I tell you such a thing as that? I don't think anyone in any book of wisdom would tell you such a thing as that. Now for instance, where you speak about the cubes and lines, and triangles: if you forget what you have learned in the simple, elemental physics, you just observe the snowflakes, the only things besides crystals

---

4 Greek: *hoi polloi*, the masses.

which show you all the geometrical aspects existing in Nature. This you certainly cannot contradict. Look at the water, if you would observe [ ] that is one thing you can do; and if you open any book of Tyndall you will find it. Now, heat affects the atomic particles of matter in a liquid state. What is heat, but the modification of the particles? It is a physical, or perhaps a mechanical law, that particles which are in motion of themselves become spheroidal. This is law, from a globe or planet down to a drop of rain; as soon as motion stops, the spheroidal shape alters and becomes a flat drop. But if it is passing through all the previous forms, that is to say, as soon as action ceases, as Tyndall teaches you, the drop becomes invariably an equilateral triangle, a hexagon, then cubes or squares coming out of the ends of the hexagon. You will see the six-pointed plane you see immediately forming cubes, and all kinds of things like that. In a lecture of his—something on ice, on the formation of particles in the ice, if I remember right—Tyndall, having observed the breaking up of ice particles in a large mass of ice through which he passed heat rays by electricity, assures us that the first or primary shape the particles assume is always triangular or pyramidal. Then they become cubical, and finally assume the form of hexagons, etc., etc.; I could not tell you where it is, but I know I know it, because it is just the thing that is taught in the occult doctrine. It is a law, and certainly there is no mistake about it—a law in Nature. Or take a snowflake, you find all these geometrical shapes in it.

Mr. Kingsland: Then as to that experiment of breaking up the piece of ice with a ray of heat. Can you tell us how it is that in examination through the reflection on a screen you see vegetable forms, the forms of ferns and plants?

Mme. Blavatsky: Most assuredly. They only show their astral bodies, which are preparing to form plants and all that. Ice is a species of matter which contains all the prototypes of matter in its future forms. It would not be seen there if you observed it on the surface, but when it comes to their forces and everything which will be, then you find that one ring throws off the ring that will become the future ring. This is all one link into another. I am very glad you know this experiment.

Mr. Kingsland: Yes, but it requires something else besides water to make these forms. He takes a large block of ice, and throws a very powerful ray on this ice and onto a screen, and this ray dissolves through, and on the screen you see these ferns and plumes.

Mme. Blavatsky: Don't you see triangles, hexagons, and cubes, and you see the ferns and plants, because it throws off the astral bodies—that which is contending in those particles of ice, because ice is matter? You see, if you think about it, you remember that ferns, that that class of plants, particularly ferns, that you most commonly see on a screen are to a large extent built up of geometrical figures. It is in Nature. It is impossible otherwise. Law geometrizes or God geometrizes. Why could we not call Law God, or vice versa? It is just the same.

Mr. B. Keightley: The fact of the matter being that these geometrical figures or mathematical figures are a part of the human law of thought, because they exist in the universal mind from which they proceed, and of which human mind is itself a reflection, a microcosm, I suppose.

Mme. Blavatsky: Now, 13.

Mr. A. Keightley: Sloka 5, page 99. Do numbers and geometrical figures represent to human consciousness the laws of action in the Divine Mind?

Mme. Blavatsky: They do, most assuredly. How can it be otherwise? There is no chance evolution of forms, nor is there any so-called abnormal appearance or cosmic phenomenon due to haphazard circumstances, but is always a stray something on our earth, either at its beginning or its end (Not of the earth, but of its phenomena.) For instance, meteors. Now, what are meteors? What does science say about them, that they fall from the Moon or the Sun, or what?

Mr. B. Keightley: One of two hypotheses. One is that they are the fragments of a broken-up planet, and the other is that these rings of matter from which the planets are supposed to be formed, on the hypothesis of Laplace, instead of the ring forming a single planet, owing to various circumstances, the matter consolidates into comparatively small lumps, and the meteor streams are the tracks of these rings of more or less diffuse matter.

Mme. Blavatsky: Of course, because the breath is always at work; even during Pralaya it never stops—that breath that I call motion. Perhaps during Pralaya it produces no results because there is no one to see those results. And if there were they would see results perfectly unexpected and which their finite intellect would not comprehend, surely. We call this very proudly Pralaya, but we do not know what we are talking about. We say there is nothing worth blowing for that breath.

Mr. Kingsland: Can't you tell us something more about meteors?

Mme. Blavatsky: Perhaps I may tell you at the end here. I think I have been writing at the end about it.

Mr. A. Keightley: Sloka 5, page 99.

Mr. B. Keightley: Which is (Reads passage from *Secret Doctrine*.)

Mr. A. Keightley: Astronomically, is there an explanation of Martanda's rejection?[5]

Mme. Blavatsky: I do not believe that there is. Astronomers can hardly look beyond their direct mathematical calculations, let alone what takes place in or around our Sun at the beginning of his young life. The Sun is several Manvantaras older than all these planets. His rejection means that when bodies or planets begin to form from his rays or his magnetic rays, or heat, then that attraction had to be stopped, for otherwise he would have swallowed back all his progeny, like Saturn is fabled to have done. I do not mean by progeny that

---

5 The Sun in Vedic mythology. In *The Secret Doctrine*, I:99, it is referred to as the "One Rejected."

all the planets were thrown out from the Sun; it is simply under his rays that they grow. Aditi is the ever-equilibrizing Mother Nature, or Space, on the purely spiritual and subjective plane; she is the Sakti, the female power or potency of the fecundating spirit, and it is for her to regulate the behavior of the Sons born in her bosom. The allegory is a very suggestive one. Now, if you turn to question 15, I will tell you what these things mean.

Mr. A. Keightley: Were all the planets in our solar system first comets and then suns?

Mme. Blavatsky: They were not comets, certainly, nor planets in our solar system, but comets in space in the beginning. They began life as wanderers over the face of the infinite kosmos. They detached themselves from the common storehouse of already prepared material ready for use, which is the Milky Way, for the Milky Way is nothing more nor less than that World-stuff, all the rest in space being crude material as yet. Now let me explain to you this. This Milky Way is just the prepared material ready for use. Whereas all the other that we do not see, which consists in these clouds of particles that we can never see any of the atoms of, that is the crude material not prepared yet.

Mr. A. Keightley: Then the process of formation is going on at the present time from the Milky Way.

Mme. Blavatsky: Positively, and having set on their long journey, those comets first settled in life where their conditions were prepared for them by Fohat. That is to say, where the conditions of equilibrizing and polarity were and beginning actually to form themselves into suns, each of them (Mind you, in space, not in our solar system, it didn't exist then.) then, each sun, when its Pralaya arrived, disrupted into millions and billions of fragments. Each of those fragments rolled to and fro in space, collecting fresh materials as it rolled on like an avalanche does until it was stopped by the laws of attraction and repulsion and its own weight (Why it should be weight, I do not know; I simply translate you what is said in the occult books.), and became a planet. After having disrupted, each fragment became a planet in our or some other system—beyond our telescopes, of course. The fragments of our Sun will be just such planets after our solar Pralaya. He was a comet once upon a time, at the beginning of Brahmâ's age—not day, don't confuse; then he fixed himself where we see or perhaps, rather, ought to see him in London. When he dies he will burst asunder, and his atoms will be whirled in space, eons upon eons, as though {those} of comets and meteors until each is caught up in the vortex of the two forces and placed in some higher and better system. Now, this is a thing which I told you last Thursday, when I was telling you about these two forces acting, the imprisoned and the free forces, that which produced the thing. And this you have to learn the correspondences of and how it acts—that it begins, for instance, by colour and goes on to sound and so and so—I need not detail. When it reaches the earth, when the two forces begin to act, and everything, it is just the same; as it is above so it is below, and as it is below so it is above. Let us hope that the astronomers of the future systems will be more fitted to appreciate Nature than {they} do now. Thus, the Sun will live in his children as a parent—as each one of us will live in his children (If we have any, of course.) This will show to those of you who are prepared to accept the occult teachings that the modern astronomers who have brought out that hypothesis to which they refer as the Nebula Theory have begun by the wrong end. Had they said that the future planets or planetary systems will be the fragments shot out from the body of our Sun, they would be right; as it is they are wrong. Moreover, when the day comes, the semblance or reflection of the Sun's ray, therefore, will first of all fall off like a veil from the true Sun—for no mortal will see it, because every being with eyes will become blind. It is an impossibility to see the real Sun, because there would not be such a thing as an eye left in the world, and everything would be burnt in a moment. This reflection or veil is a kind of safeguard of nature, and a very wise one; take it off, disperse this veil for one second, and all the planets in the system—everything—would be reduced to a handful of ashes. Because, take the Sun's rays and explain to me—you will speak about reverberation and all that—why is it that you catch the most terrible sunstrokes when there is the most foggy weather? Of course, on the physical plane I know what you will say.

Mr. B. Keightley: I do not think anybody does know or has properly explained that.

Mme. Blavatsky: Those able men of science will say it is the most ignorant thing in the world, but you will see it is a thousand times more probable and logical than to accept those 397,000 hypotheses which are only born to die, and which do not dovetail and do not cover the whole ground; and this, as I show to you, if you work out the system, you will find it covers the whole ground. This is a known fact. Now, gentleman, you may ask me any questions you like.

Mr. B. Keightley: As you have traced the stages of comet and sun and then the fragments of the Sun becoming planets, when the planets have lived their life and die, is that their final dispersion?

Mme. Blavatsky: We will bury them and write a magnificent epitaph, and we will ask George Washington Childs[6] in Philadelphia to prepare some verses.

Mr. A. Keightley: Then practically, the planets in the solar system are very much older than the Sun itself?

Mr. Kingsland: It is the opposite way.

Mme. Blavatsky: It is the Sun which is a great deal older, because the Sun is the Sun yet. When it becomes disrupted you just go and put together the figures.

Mr. A. Keightley: I understood you to say that the planets in this particular system are fragments of suns that had previously existed.

Mme. Blavatsky: They have been suns; they have been disrupted, and every fragment of such a disrupted sun has become a planet.

Mr. Kingsland: That Sun might have belonged to any other system far away.

---

6 A reference to George William Childs, American publisher, 1829-1894.

Mme. Blavatsky: There are millions and millions of systems. What is the use of your talking about this little horizon?

Mr. Kingsland: Do you say this earth of which this is composed came originally from the Milky Way?

Mme. Blavatsky: But mind you, you know what it is: there was the focus, that was prepared material, and it was in the Milky Way; and when it throws off its principles, it comes and animates, so to say, one of those things from the ready material.

Mr. A. Keightley: And these are the results of building on the imperishable centres.

Mme. Blavatsky: Yes, on the Laya centres.

Mr. Kingsland: Then is that Milky Way, as astronomers suppose, so far outside the limits of the solar system, or is that only an appearance? The astronomers suppose that the Milky Way lies far beyond the distance of the furthest fixed stars that we can see; is that actually the case, or is that a deceptive appearance?

Mme. Blavatsky: My idea is it is a deceptive appearance; it is very deceptive, because this thing that we see, it is only because it is at a distance that we see it, but this thing actually exists everywhere, in the atmosphere and everywhere. It is not that there is a particular thing at such and such a distance, so many miles away; it is perfect nonsense, because it is everywhere, though only at a certain distance we see it.

Mr. Kingsland: If you take only a foot section you do not see it.

Mme. Blavatsky: Just that. It is the same with every bit. This is what we call the prepared world-stuff which is ready for use, which has been differentiated and redifferentiated and combed out and everything has been done to it. And the other is simply everything that is otherwise, and the space which is between this inter-Milky Way space is nothing but ready material.

Mr. Kingsland: Can you tell us why they should appear more or less in the shape of a ring, instead of all round with equal density?

Mme. Blavatsky: I suppose there must be some reason. It must take absolutely some geometrical figure and space. You know, this is why with Pythagoras, geometry was the first sacred science which had to be studied and known before one could join the Pythagorean school; they had to study geometry and music, first of all. Now they ask, why music? Because of the sounds, you understand, the correspondences, that is why. You go and read the sacred science and you will find they had to know, among other things, mathematics, geometry and music. They had to know all these.

Mr. Kingsland: We want something more about the meteors.

Mme. Blavatsky: They ask me as though I were first cousin to the meteors, or the mother-in-law, or something like that.

Mr. Kingsland: I thought you had something more about it in your notes.

Mme. Blavatsky: I do not want any notes; I know what you are going to say without notes. It is only a few "happy thoughts" I book there.

Mr. Kingsland: I want to know what is the occult explanation of the meteors.

Mme. Blavatsky: Why, didn't I explain to you enough? Who is it that is dissatisfied?

Mr. B. Keightley: Are the meteors these fragments streaming through space, or what are they?

Mme. Blavatsky: In my humble opinion, I do not make much difference between a comet and a meteor. A meteor is something which is a dead comet, or something like that.

Mr. Kingsland: Are we right in supposing the meteors get their incandescence by coming into contact with our atmosphere?

Mr. B. Keightley: Well, there is one of the things: meteors have no tails.

Mme. Blavatsky: They are corpses.

Mr. Kingsland: What makes them incandescent?

Mme. Blavatsky: It is the nature of the beast, I suppose.

Mr. B. Keightley: We only see them when they come very close to the earth.

Mme. Blavatsky: You tell me why the comets are the cheekiest people you ever met with. They always cheek the Sun and snub him; they wag their tails against the Sun in all defiance of gravity, and the poor Sun stops and looks there in amazement and cannot help it. You tell me that, you gentlemen physicists and men of science.

Mr. A. Keightley: Perhaps it is a tone of contempt.

Mme. Blavatsky: They will penetrate right through in the most terrible way, and go into his drawing room and bedroom and come out of the kitchen and then go and wag their tails in defiance of all gravity. And the men of science will come and say: "Gravity! It cannot be; it is an immutable law." Is it? I am glad to hear it.

Mr. B. Keightley: What is the explanation of this extremely light-minded behavior?

Mme. Blavatsky: You make their acquaintance and ask them. I have no right to give out their secrets. It only puts there is no gravity, there is no such attraction and repulsion.

Mr. A. Keightley: Why should the tail be repelled?

Mme. Blavatsky: Because the Sun is not congenial to the tail. It has got quite enough of its own electricity and its own magnetic heat and doesn't want to spoil its complexion.

Mr. A. Keightley: You speak in *The Secret Doctrine* of the mysterious planet in connection with the moon. Does the moon act to that

10. MEETING MARCH 14, 1889

planet as a kind of veil in the same way as the things of the Sun?

Mme. Blavatsky: I think there is something—not behind the Moon, because the Moon is not motionless as the Sun, the Sun is always on the same spot—but the moon has not got such an electric thing. The moon has only magnetic power over the earth.

Mr. A. Keightley: I thought it might be an analogy.

Mr. B. Keightley: The moon has its own independent orbit; it doesn't cover any one point of space constantly.

Mme. Blavatsky: There are some planets, or something (I do not know what.) they do not pay much attention to, because it is not their time yet to appear. They may appear.

Mr. Kingsland: Between Mercury and the Sun?

Mme. Blavatsky: Oh, it is surely the planet between Mercury and the Sun. It was the beginning of the Fourth Race and then it went off. Just the same as if you take the Pleiades; it was seen very well once, and now it is seen no more. You can hardly see it in the telescopes, but it {Maia} was a bright one and a chief one, the nurse of [ ] {Arcas}.

Mr. Gardner: That was the seven Pleiades.

Mme. Blavatsky: They say it is because she married below her station and she was ashamed to show herself. They say it in the Greek mythology, that she made a *mésalliance*; she was a kind of Princess Louise, she married one of her subjects.[7] But these Pleiades are the most occult constellations that exist.

Mr. Gardner: More than Mercury?

Mme. Blavatsky: Oh, more. They are connected with nearly all the aristocracy. They are very occult, because they are connected with all

---

7 A reference to the marriage of Louise, 1848-1939, fourth daughter and sixth child of Queen Victoria, to John Douglas Sutherland Campbell, Marquis of Lorne, in 1871, considered beneath her station.

the Rishis, too; they have an interchange of thought with the Rishis.

Mr. Hall: "The sweet influence of the Pleiades."[8]

Mme. Blavatsky: If you read those allegories of the Hindus in the astronomy books, you see they had secrets and knowledge which really the moderns cannot think of approaching.

Mr. Gardner: Which old books do you refer to?

Mr. Keightley: The Puranas.

Mme. Blavatsky: Even the Puranas. But you read the old astronomical books.

Mr. A. Keightley: Then about the Sun following slowly after the planets, turning upon itself, the actual revolution of the Sun itself.

Mme. Blavatsky: Now, there is a thing! This is the most extraordinary thing, how they knew this. See what Bailly says about that.[9] There is not one second's difference if it is so, it is as the Hindus give it, because it is so mathematically correct; they have remarked it and they said because such and such constellations were in conjunction, and so on.

Mr. Hall: Why do we only see one side of the moon?

Mme. Blavatsky: Because she doesn't want to show the other; because perhaps she has not combed her hair. I can only tell you what I have learnt, I can't invent.

Mr. A. Keightley: You don't tell us all you know.

Mme. Blavatsky: I do not see why I should; we should have nothing for next Thursday.

Mr. Gardner: You were saying something about the Rishis of the

---

8 Job 38:31, "Canst thou bind the sweet influences of Pleiades, or loose the bands of Orion?"
9 Jean Sylvain Bailly, French astronomer, 1736-1793, whose *Traité De L'Astronomie Indienne Et Orientale*, 1787, is cited in *The Secret Doctrine*.

Ursa Major.

Mme. Blavatsky: The seven stars, and they are married. The Rishis are the husbands of the Pleiades.

Mr. Gardner: But which one made the *mésalliance*? (Loud laughter.)

Mme. Blavatsky: The one which hides herself.

Mr. A. Keightley: Gardner, you must not talk celestial scandal!

Mme. Blavatsky: It was Electra. (Qy. Should this not be Merope? B deB.)[10] {Added to text}.

Mr. Gardner: Is *he* the one?

Mme. Blavatsky: It was a *she*! What an infidel! Well, I think you ladies and gentlemen can all talk now, and I will faithfully answer your questions.

The proceedings here closed.

---

10 Both Electra and Merope are among the seven sisters known as the Pleiades.

11.
Theosophical Society.
Meeting of the Blavatsky Lodge
17 Lansdowne Road, Holland Park
Thursday, March 21, 1889.

Mr. Harbottle in the Chair

Mr. A. Keightley: Stanza 4, Sloka 6. "Then the Second Seven, who are the Lipika produced by the three (Word, Voice, and Spirit.)" Question 1. Can you explain to us the relation of the Lipika, the "Second Seven," to the "Primordial Seven," and to the first "Sacred Four"?

Mme. Blavatsky: I think it is rather a difficult thing to do. I think that if I explain to you, who know very little of the Sanskrit books, that which you have access to—for instance, these various systems of the Gnostics that you can easily get in the British Museum—you would understand it better. Now, I have taken from one something just to show to you this difference, and make you understand it better. If you study the Gnostic system of the first centuries of Christianity, from that of Simon Magus[1] down to the highest and noblest systems—the Valentinians[2]—you will comprehend better the relation you want me to explain. All these systems are derived from the East. That which we call the Primordial Seven and the Second Seven are called by Simon Magus, for instance, the Æons. The Valentinians call them the Æons, and many others, the primeval—the second and the third series of Syzygies,[3] I think it is—it is a Greek name. They are

---

1 First century A.D., Samaritan gnostic and thaumaturgist, whose system included a series of divine emanations.
2 Followers of the second century gnostic teacher, Valentinus.
3 Male-female pairs of Æons, or divine emanations.

graduated emanations ever descending lower and lower into matter from that primordial principle that is called fire. Simon Magus calls it fire and we call it Svabhavat, as behind that fire the manifested, the Silent Deity, stands with him as with us—that which is, was and ever will be. Therefore, take this fire, as he calls it, and that will be the root from which all these various powers and hierarchies descend. Therefore, since his doctrine is almost one with our cosmogony (And that you don't seem to see to this day, the philosophy or process of emanation.), permit me to quote to you the words of Simon Magus, as quoted from his work by the author of *Philosophumena*. He says: "From the permanent stability and personified immutability, fire and this manifested principle, which immutability does not preclude activity, as the second form is endowed with intelligence and reason, who are (Mahat), it (The fire.) passed from potentiality of action to action itself. From those series of evolutions were formed six beings, or the emanations from the infinite potency they were formed in Syzygies. That is to say, they are radiated out of the flame two by two, one being the active and the other the passive principle." Then Simon named Nous and [ ] {Epinoia}, or spirit and thought, and many others; and Logismos and Fumesis {Enthumêsis}, reasoning and reflection. Now, Simon shows the relation you want to know by saying as follows: "In each of the six primitive beings, the Infinite potency was in its totality, but it was there in potentiality only, not innate. It had to be established therein through an image, that of paradigm, in order that it should appear in all its essence, virtue, grandeur, and effects; for only then could it become like unto the parent potency, infinite and eternal. If on the contrary it was not conformed by or through the image, that potentiality could never become potency or pass into action but was lost for lack of use, as it happens to a man who, having an aptitude for grammar or geometry, does not exercise it; it gets lost for him just as if he never had it" (Page 250.)[4] Now, one of these, which he calls Nous, spirit,

---

4 The page number refers to the edition of *Philosophumena or Refutatio Omnium Haeresium ("The Refutation of all Heresies")*, believed to be by the schismatic St. Hippolytus, a third century bishop of Rome, translated from Greek into Latin by Patrice Cruice and published in Paris in 1860, where the passage appears.

and the other are one, he says, and inseparable. The system is too long and too complicated to give it here. Suffice it to say that he shows that whether his Æons belong to the superior, middle or lower world, they are all one except in material density, which determines their outward manifestation and the results produced and the real essence which is from their mutual relations, which are established from eternity, as he says, by immutable laws. The same, therefore, for the Lipika and the Second Seven or the Primordial Seven, whatever name we may give them for the sake of our own comprehension, which seems to necessitate a name or label in each case to enable us to recognize one from the other. Now, this first, second, third or primordial seven or Lipika is all one; therefore, how can I tell you what relation they are in? When once they emanate from one plane onto another it will be just the same, the repetition—as it is above so it will be below. That is the only relation. They are all simply differentiated in matter in density, but not in qualities. And the same qualities descend unto the last plane, which is our plane, and which shows man endowed just with the same potentiality, if he knows how to develop it as the highest Dhyan-Chohan. I quote it just on purpose to show you, because you can go and read it. In the British Museum you have the book, and there are many things which really will show to you that our doctrine is as old as can be. It is perfectly the occult doctrine in many things. Of course, it changes its name and all kinds of things; but it gives a very good definition of the nature and essence of these Æons only. For instance, he gives six of them, that is to say, six pairs of each—the seventh being that four which descends from one plane to another.[5]

Mr. A. Keightley: Then practically, the synthesis is on the plane above.

Mme. Blavatsky: Yes, just that.

The President: Then really these sevens are all identical, except that

---

5 The published *Transactions*, p. 148, gives this passage as: "In the hierarchies of Æons, Simon gives three pairs of two each, the seventh being the fourth which descends from one plane to another."

they are manifest on different planes, so that the Lipika are the same things as the Primordial Seven, except that the Primordial Seven are not manifest, they are the potentiality of manifestation.

Mme. Blavatsky: They are the first, but they are four, mind you, and have proceeded from Mahat, as I will show you. The Lipika are those who, in the Kabalah, are called the four recording angels. In India they call them the four Maharajahs, those who record every thought and deed of man. It is the book of life, as St. John calls it in Revelation.

The President: But they are called the seven in that passage, I think, of *The Secret Doctrine*. But that really means that the four are on the plane of the second seven. It does not mean that they are precisely the second seven.

Mme. Blavatsky: Just so. And the seven are simply seventy times seven; it is the seven hierarchies, the seven various degrees. And at the four corners of the world, these Lipikas are posted just to put down on the superior Astral Light the record of all our actions, deeds, words and everything.

The President: On the lowest plane of all, they are the cardinal points.

Mme. Blavatsky: They are directly connected with Karma, and they are connected with what the Christians call the Last Day of Judgment. And in the East it is called the Day after Maha-Manvantara, when they come all to receive what is called in Sinnett's *Esoteric Buddhism* the Judgment.

Mr. A. Keightley: "The Day Be With Us," isn't it?

Mme. Blavatsky: Yes, when everything becomes one, but with every Manvantara they become more and more, the Absolute becomes more and more, not only is it absolute intelligence, absolute consciousness and everything (Because on our plane it is non-consciousness, non-being.), but everyone will feel himself more; still every individuality knows itself. This may be a mysterious thing, but I tell you that which we are taught. Very often we are confronted with the statement: "you talk about Nirvana. What is Nirvana? It is an extinction, it is just like a flame that is blown out from the candle; there remains nothing. Nirvana—'the flame out'." I had how many times to have disputes and discussions about that. I said it is not that at all. It is that every particle of matter, of that which may have form in our conception or be conditioned or limited, everything disappears to make room for one homogeneity, and for the one absolute spirit. But this spirit is not at all; it is non-consciousness for us, but it is absolute consciousness there.

Mr. A. Keightley: Question 2. What relation have the Lipika to Mahat?

Mme. Blavatsky: That relation, that the Lipika are a division of the four degrees taken from the septenates that emanated from Mahat. This is what we have been talking about. The latter is as Simon Magus's four, the Mahat, the secret and the manifested or the divine ideation made to witness for itself in the subjective universe through the subjective forms we see upon it. You may call it evolution or creation or whatever you like. What other relation can they have, except that of being wheels within wheels? They are workers on their own plane. If you ask me what relation the Lipika have with humanity, with men, then I have just told you what it was: they are the recorders.

Mr. A. Keightley: Then the Lipika are on the same plane as Mahat.

Mme. Blavatsky: They are the sons of Mahat, as they call them. Certainly, they are immediately under the absolute plane of divine ideation, but even that is a very risky thing to say, because immediately it suggests to you that it is like a staircase, and there are stories in the house, one below and the other above. But it is not so at all; it would be a very erroneous conception. It is everywhere and nowhere, just as when we were speaking about the circle and the point and circumference and all that, because it is not a thing above or below, and the right or the left; it is as I have been explaining many times, something which is—well, it may be in one place and yet they are the seven planes, they are states, and being states other than ours, of course they are invisible and perfectly incomprehensible to us, and each state does not know the people of the other state.

The President: But still, it would not be right to describe them as being on the same plane as Mahat.

Mme. Blavatsky: Certainly not.

The President: Mahat is the synthesis of the plane above the Lipika.

Mme. Blavatsky: Certainly, and the Lipika are in the middle of the plane on the four quarters, that is to say, the higher ether or the higher Astral Light and the lower Akasa. Akasa certainly goes beyond the seventh.

The President: Can you tell us exactly how they would correspond with the archetypal worlds of the Kabalists? Is it between that and the next?

Mme. Blavatsky: The Kabalists have only four worlds and we have seven, because they leave out entirely the three upper ones and begin counting simply the archetypal world, which is the highest Astral Light, just the four, there it is; but the others are left in silence, and they are not spoken about.

The President: The Lipika really are on the plane which is above the archetypal world.

Mme. Blavatsky: Together they are on that plane, because their world begins where our globe A begins. And if you take *The Secret Doctrine*, you find there the division of the four planes; you see four planes; it begins there just above our sphere. Their archetypal world goes down, they have got only four worlds.

Mr. B. Keightley: That places, so to speak, the Lipika in relation to the kabalistic conception and to the evolution perfectly. They are on the highest plane corresponding to the highest plane of our chain of globes.

Mme. Blavatsky: What is the use of talking a language no one would understand and cannot even conceive of?

Mr. A. Keightley: Question 3. What is the difference made here between Word, Voice and Spirit?

Mme. Blavatsky: The same as between Atman, Buddhi and Manas. In one sense, spirit emanates from the unknown darkness into the mystery of which none of us can penetrate. That spirit—call it the Spirit of God that moves on the face of the waters, if you like, or primordial substance—the spirit mirrors itself in these waters and produces thereby the first flutter of differentiation in the homogeneousness of primordial matter. This is the voice, the first flutter of differentiated matter, if you like, in this sense manifestation number one, and from that voice emanates the word or Logos, that is to say, the definite and objective expression of that which has hitherto remained in the depths of the concealed thought. Of course we cannot begin here about colours and sounds and all that, but I tell you kabalistically, and kabalistically you will find that. And mind you the one that mirrors itself in space is the third Logos; they call it the unknown.

Mr. A. Keightley: Then speaking there as you spoke, the Logos there is the subdivided seven Logoi.

Mme. Blavatsky: Yes.

Mr. A. Keightley: And the voice is the synthesis of the Logos?

Mme. Blavatsky: It is just like saying, as we say in the esoteric thing, the colour, the sound, and numbers. Well, the Logoi ought to stand for numbers, then, in this sense, or the numbers will come after that when they divide the hierarchies.

Mr. Gardner: What stands for the colour?

Mme. Blavatsky: Well, you try to dream of it.

Mr. A. Keightley: Sloka 6 continued, etc. "The rejected Son is One, the 'Son-Suns' are countless." Question 4. Is this sentence to be understood in the light of the explanations given on page 99 (c)? And if so, why is the "Rejected One" mentioned again here in connection with the "Second Seven"?

Mme. Blavatsky: I have been reading the whole page, and I don't know what you mean. Where do I speak of the second seven? Unless it is the planets that you mean, in which case it would not be the second seven, it would by the seventy-seventh seven, because they are on the material plane.

Mr. B. Keightley: It is in this stanza. The stanza speaks of the second seven, and then goes on in the next sentence to speak of the "Rejected One," and you have been speaking about the "Rejected One" in an earlier part of the stanza.

Mme. Blavatsky: But you forget I have been skipping an innumerable number of times not only lines, but whole stanzas. You know perfectly well I have given you only about twelve in the first and about 42 in the second.

Mr. B. Keightley: The thing is to find out whether there has been a gap there.

Mme. Blavatsky: Certainly you will find gaps. I just try to explain as much as I can. It says there the Son is one and the "Sons-Suns" are many. It does not mean our Sun. It means the Spiritual Sun. You read it there.

Mr. A. Keightley: Is the Spiritual Sun also the Rejected One?

Mme. Blavatsky: No, no, no. I say here it is said somewhere there that the Son and the "Son-Suns" are countless.

Mr. A. Keightley: It is the "Rejected One."

Mme. Blavatsky: But it is this "Rejected One"; they are not the "Son-Suns." I don't call the planets the "Son-Suns." I speak in general. The Spiritual Sun is one, but the "Son-Suns" are countless, and it does not refer at all to the planets.

Mr. A. Keightley: Then has not it an equal application to the planets as well?

Mme. Blavatsky: It may be something like that, but they are not any more suns now. They were suns. In other places I speak about this. I have read it very well.

Mr. B. Keightley: It was in the stanza, that quotation; that is what puzzled me about it.

Mme. Blavatsky: Oh yes. You will be puzzled more than once, you know.

Mr. A. Keightley: Stanza 5, Sloka 1. "The Primordial Seven, the first Seven Breaths of the Dragon of Wisdom, produce in their turn from their holy circumgyrating Breaths the Fiery Whirlwind." Question 5: Can you explain in any way the necessity of each entity in becoming divine to pass through matter to self-experience?

Mme. Blavatsky: Well perhaps a sufficient reason might be found for it in the very nature of your question. This progress to a Divine state is but the first step, from our earth, at least, to Divine absorption. Now, the latter means that each entity will become Absoluteness when it reaches it—that is to say, that which contains all, and therefore every earthly experience, including the very strange question which is now offered (Because, really, it is a very strange question.) How could that Absoluteness become one, unless it contained every experience—that is to say, every stage and state of mind on the scale or ladder of collective experiences of beings? When you answer this, then I shall be able to proceed. Now answer me, how is it possible that Absoluteness, once that you reach it, there should be one single experience that would not be contained in it, including even the question that you put to me? It must be there.

Mr. A. Keightley: But it was there before.

Mme. Blavatsky: It was there in [　], as Simon Magus would say, it was in Divine ideation, when in Divine ideation it comes into Absoluteness. Divine ideation is not Absoluteness, it is the first manifestation of Absoluteness, and is Absolute. It is not the Absoluteness.

Mr. A. Keightley: Then the whole process of one Maha-Manvantara, that Divine ideation, after the previous Maha-Pralaya, shall become Absoluteness to again emanate another Divine ideation?

Mme. Blavatsky: Most assuredly, because we all change. With every Maha-Manvantara we become entirely different, and everything becomes different. We cannot say we will be a little better, or have more rosy cheeks, or longer noses. We shall be entirely something we cannot conceive of. We are that which we are only in this Manvantara, which lasts some trillions and trillions of years. That is the teaching, at least. I don't know anything about what we shall become. Therefore, I only know what we are now.

Mr. A. Keightley: That introduces a curious idea, that the Absolute of one Maha-Manvantara is different from the Absolute following it.

Mme. Blavatsky: Not at all. It is the same Absolute, only from this Absoluteness there are things which have been and things which are, but have not yet been, you understand, that which was is in that; that which will be is not yet, but it is still, it exists, but has not returned into Absoluteness. I don't see how you cannot understand it?

Mr. A. Keightley: That sounds as if there was in the Absolute a series of paradigms.

Mme. Blavatsky: It is on our manifested plane that I speak to you, about the Mahat which is born. Mahat has a beginning in the beginning of a Manvantara, therefore it must have an end. I speak to you about Divine ideation, not in its Absoluteness before manifestation, but the first flutter of manifestation, the first differentiated, when this Mahat is born of Brahmâ, as they say in the *Vishnu Purana*. Now, that is quite a different thing. Absoluteness does not differentiate the one never-to-be-known ideation. We speak now on the plane of manifestation at every Manvantara.

Mr. Kingsland: Then Mahat is ever becoming, but never does become the Absolute.

Mme. Blavatsky: The Mahat is the Absolute of our Manvantara, if you like to say so. Perhaps you will find a better expression. I don't say that I am Herbert Spencer, to come and invent new words, I simply try to tell you as I understand it.

The President: It is an Absolute which is not an Absolute. It is an Absolute which is limited.

Mme. Blavatsky: The Absolute cannot be limited.

The President: I know it cannot, really; at the same time, it is not the Absolute Absolute: there is that behind which contains the past, present, and future.

Mme. Blavatsky: That which they call fire, which is deity, from Simon Magus to the last, and we say in our philosophy it is this which was, is, and will be; and yet this which was, is and will be, is yet, has a beginning in every Manvantara before emanation begins. Now, every Æon becomes also, and is called in its turn that which was, is, and will be. So you take *Philosophumena*, you read the definition given by Simon Magus. Then take a better thing, take Valentinus, who was one of the highest philosophers, and one who explained it the best. You will see he calls it that which is, was, and will be. Every Æon will thus have a beginning, and an end, therefore, they are all emanations of the Absolute; they are not themselves Absolute.

Mr. Kingsland: Then in what sense do they become the Absolute?

Mme. Blavatsky: We are the Absolute, too. The spirit in us becomes the Absolute, but it is on its pilgrimage, it is this circumgyration.

Mr. Kingsland: In what sense do they become Absolute? Because it would appear from that in the next Manvantara, they have to pass to an experience.

Mme. Blavatsky: Because you cannot have anything which does not contain the Absolute. If it did not contain the Absolute it could not be anything and could not exist. There is not an atom in this world that has not got the Absolute in it.

Mr. Kingsland: When you speak of the Absolute in that sense, you don't mean the rootless root.

Mme. Blavatsky: I do mean it.

Mr. Kingsland: But this Mahat becomes the rootless root.

Mme. Blavatsky: Mahat is but a name which people have invented to show the emanation of a certain Manvantara in the Divine ideation. Now, we must call it Absoluteness, we cannot call it anything else, because the philosophy of such terms is not very easy.

Mr. Kingsland: What is it that has to evolve?

Mme. Blavatsky: The illusion and nothing more, and that illusion more or less illusionary.

Mr. Kingsland: Then that has no relation to the Absolute.

Mme. Blavatsky: I beg your pardon, it has. It is because the Absolute evolves one thing, and we with our finite and little brains see another thing. We are not only colour-blind, we are truth-blind, and we are everything-blind, and we must take these things as they present themselves, but it is not the Absolute.

Mr. B. Keightley: Did you ever think out, Kingsland, the mathematical point of a limit?

Mme. Blavatsky: What is a mathematical point? Does it exist? Is there such an animal in nature as a mathematical point? You see, we are obliged to use such expressions. How can you come and—well I cannot invent a phraseology—how can you express that which is inexpressible?

Mr. Kingsland: Well, of course, to our finite minds it is, we admit that, but we try to elucidate that one point. What is it that evolves?

Mme. Blavatsky: A Vedantin would tell you that it is an illusion, a Maha-Maya. That is why they call it illusion, because it lasts but a "wink of the eye," though it may last millions of years for us. What is there in Eternity which has a beginning and an end which is of consequence? It is expressed in the Bible that a thousand years is as a "wink of the eye" to the Lord, but I say it is perfect nonsense to speak of thousands of years. You speak of trillions and even higher than that, and then you won't be nearer the truth. Eternity is eternity, it cannot be divided, so as to say: half eternity and quarter of eternity, for then it cannot be eternity.

Mr. A. Keightley: Question 6. Are the atoms—in the occult sense of the term—eternal and indestructible, like the Monads of Leibniz, or are they dissolved during Pralaya?

Mme. Blavatsky: Now look at this question, if you please. This proves that the atoms are in your conceptions somethings, when there is no such thing in this world as atoms, except as mathematical points, as I say. The atoms, whether representing the Monads of Leibniz or the eternal and indestructible mathematical points of substance which our occult doctrine teaches, can neither be dissolved during Pralaya nor re-form during Manvantara. The atoms do not exist as appreciable quantities of matter on any plane. They are mathematical points of unknown quantity here. And whatever they are or may be on the seventh plane, each is and must be logically an absolute universe in itself, reflecting other universes and yet it is not matter and it is not spirit. Now, will you understand this? This is to say that which is Mahat or divine ideation, a sum total, and is a conceived fraction. Now when I speak of fraction, please don't allow your materialistic conceptions to imagine that Absolute can be divided into parts or pieces. The Absolute is everywhere, even in the smallest molecules of matter. It can neither be pressed into the infinitesimal part, nor enlarged into a limitless cosmos; it is both. And so much the worse for us who have not enough of the metaphysical element to understand the explanation. How could Brahmâ be called, Anu for instance—an atom—if it was not something of the kind that I tried to explain to you? If it could be conditioned or limited by space or time or anything? The atom is and is not. The atom is the mathematical point, the potentiality in space; and there is not, I suppose, a space in this world that is not an atom. If you call it molecule, it is a different thing. But if you speak about the atoms of Democritus[6] it is a different thing. Maybe he has been giving it in a very materialistic way, but if you speak about the atom, that which we call Anu, then certainly they have no substance that we know of.

Dr. Williams: Then what would you say was the ultimate constitution of the ordinary gases, like hydrogen and oxygen?

Mme. Blavatsky: Everything is an atom, but what are these atoms? We cannot see them, we cannot smell them or divide them; atoms are something science has accepted simply as hypothesis.

Dr. Williams: Most of them are detected by some one or other of the senses, if you admit that the gases do exist in the atomic form.

Mme. Blavatsky: Yes, if you call them molecules—the molecules that you have not yet come to, that Crookes has tried to divide and subdivide and he could not catch them, because every one of them might be divided ad infinitum—but when that becomes homogeneous, then you find these molecules become atoms. They may be the atoms of Democritus or somebody else, but they are not the atoms of esoteric science. It is quite a different thing.

Mr. A. Keightley: Question 7. In Occultism, are the true atoms conceived of as "particles" or as something nearer to what we may call "Vortex-Atoms"?

Mme. Blavatsky: I know nothing of "Vortex-Atoms," first laughed at by science when they were talked of by [ ] {Helmholtz?}; and now, it appears, Sir W. Thomson accepts them. If you mean those of Sir William Thomson, I don't know anything at all about them. Pass to 8.

---

6 Fourth century B.C. philosopher, known for his atomic theory of the universe.

Mr. A. Keightley: Sloka 2. "They make of him the messenger of their will. The Dzyu becomes Fohat; the Swift Son of the Divine sons, whose sons are the Lipika, runs circular errands." Question 8. Does this mean that the Lipika are the Sons of Fohat, or are they the Sons of the Primordial Seven?

Mme. Blavatsky: This means that they are the Sons of Fohat, as a personification of Mahat, the Manasaputras or "sons of the universal intelligences," and it means that the Lipika are the Sons of the "Primordial Seven." Whether the Lipikas' marriage certificate is illegal will be next asked, I suppose. I would not wonder, because, for instance, what can I answer you to this? They are the sons; they cannot be the Sons, it is simply an expression used. "The Sons of Fohat" means just as the sons of Lipika, it is simply one coming down from above to below, and that is all.

Mr. A. Keightley: Sloka 3. "He is their guiding spirit and leader. When he commences work he separates the sparks of the lower kingdom (*mineral atoms*) that float and thrill with joy in their radiant dwellings (*gaseous clouds*), and forms therewith the germs of wheels…" Question 9. What is meant by the "mineral atoms" spoken of here? For the stanza seems to refer to a period before even the "Wheels" were formed or placed.

Mme. Blavatsky: It means that which is to become in this Manavantara; and the "mineral atoms," that which was set apart for it in eternity; that is what it means and nothing else. You see, if the writers of the stanza were not born out of time they would learn to express themselves better; but really, I think it is impossible to satisfy you and to give you all these explanations. Now, those who wrote the stanzas wrote them just as they would write them in those times; they are perfectly philosophical, but if you come and ask every little thing, and want it to be expressed in Macaulean English,[7] it cannot be done.

---

7 A reference to Thomas Babington Macaulay, English writer and politician, 1800-1859, whose literary style was considered exemplary.

Mr. Kingsland: Have not those "mineral atoms" been through a previous state of evolution in a previous Manvantara?

Mme. Blavatsky: Most assuredly, nothing is lost, and they have been in thousands and millions of forms.

Mr. Kingsland: In this Manvantara they have reached the mineral kingdom.

Mme. Blavatsky: Yes, and they have been modeled and remodeled in the furnace of nature for millions and millions of years.

Mr. Kingsland: Can you tell us what will be the next stage of those "mineral atoms" in the next Manvantara?

Mme. Blavatsky: No, I don't know anything at all about them.

Mr. Kingsland: Will they remain as "mineral atoms" all through Manvantara?

Mme. Blavatsky: I don't know, they have got to evolute like everything else, to something else.

Mr. B. Keightley: I wish we could get at anything like a definite conception of what is meant in occultism by the term, atom.

Mr. A. Keightley: Question 10. Commentary (a). Do the six stages of consolidation here mentioned refer to six stages of matter on each plane?

Mme. Blavatsky: Yes they do, I suppose so. I wish you would meet on Tuesdays and try to ask some questions which should not be always going round and round the same thing. I believe all these questions I must have answered dozens and dozens of times. You all present the same questions in other forms, and it is an eternal squirrel's work around the wheel. Now, if you go over what has been written, you will see it is so. It is impossible, if we want to have it from all aspects, we must have hundreds and hundreds of volumes.

Mr. B. Keightley: There is that question we have been on the verge of a number of times, as to the true conception from the point of view of esoteric philosophy of atoms. It really lies at the root of a great deal of the difficulties. That is what I thought we should have spent most of the time over, because it is a very wide subject.

Mr. Kingsland: What distinction is there from the occult standpoint between an atom and a molecule?

Mme. Blavatsky: I have told you, and I cannot say anymore. Molecule you know, and atom you don't know. I cannot say anything more than what I have said.

Here the proceedings closed.

12.
The Theosophical Society.
Meeting of the Blavatsky Lodge
17 Lansdowne Road, Holland Park, W.
Thursday, March 28, 1889.

Mr. Kingsland in the Chair

Mr. A. Keightley: On page 101, line 18, it is stated that the Sun is merely the elder brother of the planets—but on page 103 it is stated that the planets were all comets and suns in their origin, and would therefore appear to be older than the Sun. What is therefore the real meaning of these statements?

Mme. Blavatsky: So far as our planetary system is concerned, the Sun is the oldest member in it. His place was fixed—as is seen by the language of the stanzas—at a very early period of the Manvantara, but the planets reached their places at a much later period. These planets {were?} dethroned suns, comets, etc. Each of them was at some time the central star, the sun in its own system, but of a lower order than this one, and in a previous Manvantara. In the same way so will our Sun become a planet in another Manvantara, only and also in another and higher system than ours. First he will be broken into innumerable fragments, which will form comets and meteors; these will be scattered through space to be ultimately drawn together by the Fohatic affinity. Well, any questions?

Mr. Kingsland: Then what becomes of the planets in this planetary chain? Are they absorbed in the Sun?

Mme. Blavatsky: No, they are not.

Mr. A. Keightley: Then what will become of the physical basis of these planets?

Mme. Blavatsky: What do you mean by "They will be absorbed in the Sun"? They are not thrown out of the Sun. Occultism teaches there is no such thing as that. Why, it is the modern theory of science that the planets are thrown off from the Sun. They were never thrown off—and then they will be absorbed again in the Sun. They will be disintegrated in the Manvantara. They will scatter into fragments and go into some higher life, into a higher system.

Mr. A. Keightley: Will the solid bodies of the planets in our system disintegrate into small fragments?

Mme. Blavatsky: Just the same as the earth—of course they will.

Mr. B. Keightley: You say somewhere, in speaking of the Moon, that the other planets have also had satellites, which stood to them as the Moon stands to the earth, but they faded out or disappeared altogether.

Mme. Blavatsky: Some of them on the secondary plane. I told you many times that there were seven sacred planets in occultism, and that these seven sacred planets had nothing to do with us. There are seven, two of which or three of which are not known yet, and I suppose will never be known, because two of them will never appear; they have disappeared since that time. I told you the Sun was not a planet, because it was a central star. Our earth is not, because we are living on it; it is a planet for others, but not for us; but it was the star which is seen between Mercury and the Sun. I don't know whether it is this one which the astronomers have seen.

Mr. B. Keightley: But when the Moon finally disappears it is not, so to speak, broken up violently according to the modern scientific idea, but rather disintegrates slowly, following the analogy of the human body.

Mme. Blavatsky: If the Pralaya does not catch it; but if the Pralaya sets in, then there is an end of it.

Mr. A. Keightley: Is it exactly as if it had a charge of dynamite inside and all burst up into fragments.

Mme. Blavatsky: Everything goes into space, and there is all the material of which one world is composed—not the world, the earth only, but the planetary system. All this, of course, will go into chaos again and begin its wanderings in space until it reforms in another Manvantara, a higher world, and the Sun itself will be even nothing but a planet in some higher world.

Mr. Kingsland: But not necessarily the integral parts of it as it now stands. Then how near is that expression in *Esoteric Buddhism*, that particles of matter greatly lose their force of cohesion?

Mme. Blavatsky: I suppose it is speaking about the temporary Pralayas.

Mr. Kingsland: Just as we have a tidal wave which becomes an earthquake, because the particles lose their force of cohesion and disintegrates in that way.

Mme. Blavatsky: I don't remember it. I mean to say as I don't think that the Pralaya is meant.

Mr. Kingsland: In what way does the material go off into space?

Mme. Blavatsky: It scatters, I suppose.

Mr. Kingsland: By reason of their losing their force of cohesion?

Mr. B. Keightley: That, of course, is due from the violent explosion, so to speak, which disintegrates the Sun at the end of the solar Manvantara. It is a different process. Is that so, HPB?

Mme. Blavatsky: I suppose so. Now the next.

Mr. A. Keightley: Can you also add to this by explaining what you state in *SD* as to the behavior of comets to the Sun?

Mme. Blavatsky: Well, the behavior of comets to the Sun is caused by the difference in density of the head and the tail. If science did not insist so dogmatically on its pretended laws of gravity, it would accept our explanation, which satisfies every condition. That is to say that we do not believe in the law of gravity as it is, but in attraction and repulsion, and if it is once accepted, then we should find it leaves no gaps and it explains many things that are not to be explained now on the hypothesis of science. Postulate instead of gravity the twin forces of attraction and repulsion, and many phenomena will be explained. In this case the Sun exerts a very much more powerful influence of attraction upon the head of the comet, which is approximately solid, than it does upon the tail of the comet, which though enormous in size is a phenomenon of vision, not of our perception. Consequently, it is perfectly that that which is most attracted will always be nearest to the Sun. You know what we spoke about, that the comets act most impudently towards the Sun, and that instead of following the law of gravity they turn tail and go off making faces at the Sun.

Mr. Kingsland: And actually flap their tails in the face of the Sun.

Mr. A. Keightley: They almost stare him out of countenance.

Mme. Blavatsky: Just in the same fashion, a man endeavoring with bladders upon his feet to walk upon the water will be drowned—his legs, which are necessarily the heaviest, will be buoyed up by the bladders. In addition to this is the fact that the tail of the comet is so attenuous, corresponding to the soul or spirit of gas, that it approaches in condition to the radiant robes of the Sun. Hence there is also a repulsive force exerted upon the tail of the comet by reason of the somewhat smaller polarities. Now you understand what I mean by this. You see, I don't know what the men of science say about the matter of the comet's tails. I know it is not matter, and it cannot be called matter. It is not matter that falls under the perceptive faculties, so to say, of the men of science here; they could not, if they had a bit of it, do anything with it. It is perfectly impossible. It is the spirit or the soul of gases, if that expression can be allowed. Certainly it is dreadfully unscientific, and all those who have been brought up in scientific reverence, of course, will be much shocked. Many will be; but I don't teach it out of my head. I teach simply that which the occult sciences teach. It remains now to be proved who is right, ancient wisdom or modern wisdom. It is a duel between them.

Mr. B. Keightley: A rather daring representative of modern wisdom suggested the idea that the tail of the comet is not matter at all, but is an optical illusion, produced in some way (Which he did not attempt to explain.) by some electrical action of the solid nucleus of the comet—

Mme. Blavatsky: Whoever he is, he is a very wise man, because it is almost what we say. It is a phenomenon of vision.

Mr. B. Keightley: Upon the matter through which the head of the comet was traveling, and its direction, was dependent upon some other things that I do not exactly remember.

Mme. Blavatsky: It is not quite so, because there is something; but it is not matter.

Mr. B. Keightley: But then, that is it. The difficulty of the explanation is in this: supposing, however, ethereally, and then you suppose the matter of the comet's tail to be the velocity with which it travels when, for instance, it approaches the Sun—and the tail is streaming away from the Sun—the body of the head of the comet reaches a point there, and the tail must move with enormous velocity, something too much to be expressed by figures.

Mr. Kingsland: Like a ray of light flashed round your eyes.

Mr. B. Keightley: Just as if you flashed a ray of light through a mirror.

Mme. Blavatsky: Not to the velocity or vibrations of the violet ray of which we spoke the other day.

Mr. B. Keightley: That is our vibrations in an actual transference of matter.

Mme. Blavatsky: How does motion manifest itself—the eternal motion, the in-breathing and the out-breathing which never will begin and never had an end? Those vibrations are certainly one of the causes of that manifestation of the motion in its various phases.

Mr. ———: How should we take the tail of the comet as visible, if it does not consist of matter?

Mme. Blavatsky: How would you say if you were shown a kind of thing—how do you explain those things the astronomers show—a shadow? It is not tangible and yet you see it; it is a reflection.

Mr. B. Keightley: How do you see the image of the Moon and the star?

Mme. Blavatsky: There is one thing occultism teaches and it is this, that there is not a single body in that part of the universe which is or which may be perceived by astronomy under the strongest telescope that is not a reflection. There is not a single planet which they see, really, as a planet. It is simply a reflection, neither is the Sun seen. It is simply the reflection and the screen, a veil thrown over it; and so it is the same with the planets. They may go and speculate till Doom's Day and say they see canals and they see mountains and rivers and all kinds of things, but all this is optical illusion, nothing else; nothing but reflections, because the real ones are not seen.

Mr. Kingsland: But to have a reflection you must have something which is reflected from it and that must in every case be matter.

Mme. Blavatsky: Most assuredly. Everything is matter.

Mr. Kingsland: Then is the tail of the comet matter in that sense?

Mme. Blavatsky: No, because the tail of the comet is rather a reflection thrown off. There is the enormous size of it, and this is more of optical illusion than anything else.

Mr. Kingsland: Is it not self-luminous?

Mme. Blavatsky: It is not.

Mr. A. Keightley: What is the relation of the tail of the comet to the nucleus?

Mme. Blavatsky: Oh, don't ask me this. I am not a man of science, and I could not come and tell you this. I cannot go and invent. You wise men of the West ought to tell me what it is. And once you tell me the cause, I will proceed and give you a little more. I suppose you astronomers ought to know better.

Mr. A. Keightley: I don't see that.

Mme. Blavatsky: Then I am not ashamed to say I don't know, either. I am glad they confess they don't know. There are, however, a few things they say they don't know.

Mr. Atkinson: Is not the relation rather like that of a ship traveling through the water, leaving a luminous trail behind her?

Mme. Blavatsky: That is a very good suggestion. It leaves a luminous trail because this friction produces it. This is a very good suggestion.

Mr. Kingsland: Then the tail of the comet does not always correspond with its orbit?

Mr. B. Keightley: This has brought back to my mind the suggestion I was speaking about before, that the luminous appearance caused by attraction in the other is owing to some peculiarity in the action of the Sun upon the waves, upon the vibrations so produced. They are so affected by the Sun that they appear to us to be an extension of the line which joins the nucleus of the comet at any moment; but the detailed explanation of that I do not know.

Mr. Atkinson: The head of the comet, the nucleus of the comet, acts simply like a lens; and where the tail is curved it is simply due to refraction through the nucleus.

Mr. B. Keightley: Refracted through the nucleus and forming a long tail; really refracted from fire particles of matter.

Mr. Atkinson: Round the substance of the Sun.

Mr. A. Keightley: Stanza 5, Sloka 1. "The Fiery Whirlwind." Question 2. On page 107, the "Fiery wind" is stated to be the kosmic dust, etc., and in this sense one would understand it to be the nebula—is this correct?

Mme. Blavatsky: Kosmic dust and nebula are one. We say the reason why there seem to be aggregations, which we call nebula, is that in those regions the force of affinity is at work on the formation of the future suns, planets and worlds. What you call nebula is not only in the region known as the Milky Way, but it is everywhere. Didn't I tell you last time that it was in this room and everywhere? It is 'round dust here in the streets of London as much as it is beyond the most distant and visible stars. It is universal stuff, called world stuff by some astronomers. To illustrate my meaning by physical examples, we don't see the dust in the air of a room at ordinary times, but supposing that the floor is swept so as to largely increase the amount flying in the air; it becomes at once visible, forms itself into clouds according to the currents of air, etcetera. Now pass a beam of sunlight into a dark room through a shutter, and the whole of the room is at once alive with the movements of the dust. In exactly the same way as the dust moves, and is collected by the currents of air in the room, so is the kosmic dust moved and collected by the Fohatic currents of affinity and attraction in the higher space, until it appears at the distance from us as the nebula with which science is familiar. Truly these calculations are described as the fiery whirling wind, and why you should object to the name I don't know. It is just the name which fits it the best: "fiery whirlwinds."

Mr. Kingsland: The reason why that question was put is that Fohat is called a little later on, the "fiery whirlwind."

Mme. Blavatsky: Yes sir, and so it is explained here. Fohat may be called anything you like.

Mr. B. Keightley: There is one point you might ask there, Kingsland, as to whether the kosmic dust when undergoing the process of collection is self-luminous, or like the dust you are comparing it to, by virtue of the light.

Mme. Blavatsky: By virtue of all your respective Mayas and nothing else. Because there is nothing luminous except the sun. All is borrowed light, and it is by virtue of the optical illusion and Maya.

Mr. B. Keightley: I thought that was the case, because it has been proved possible to photograph the nebulæ. Consequently, if that is the case, they must be visible, I should think, by reflected light, not by dark light.

Mr. A. Keightley: On page 108, Fohat is called the "fiery whirlwind" (As mentioned in the previous sloka.), and is referred to as the vehicle of the Primordial Seven. In what sense is Fohat identical with the fiery whirlwind of Sloka 1?

Mme. Blavatsky: Fohat is everything, he is the life principle, the vital air we breathe. He is in all the elements. Fohat is the symbol of the root of manifestation, and as such is necessarily the fiery whirlwind in synthesis. Fohat, in short, is the root and soul of motion. What do we call Fohat? It is not entity. It is called an entity. Fohat is not a gentleman of means or a young man of beauty or anything of the kind. Fohat is simply a force in nature. We may use, as the ancients did, all kinds of euhemerization, but it does not mean Fohat. It is anything, really. Fohat you have in your blood, every one of you. Fohat is the primal motor of everything, from the beginning of the Manvantara. That is what we are taught.

Mr. Kingsland: Then Fohat is a generic term, like Dhyan-Chohan.

Mme. Blavatsky: No. Without Fohat, the Dhyan-Chohan would not be much, anyway, for it is the cohesive force of everything; and it is the vivifying force and the force of vital action. Will somebody help me and give me a better word?

Mr. B. Keightley: You express that very well. You say somewhere in *The Secret Doctrine*, you say, actually, that Fohat is, and you say it is an entity, of which our electricity is the emanation.

Mme. Blavatsky: Is the universe that you see an entity, since it is?

Mr. A. Keightley: Do you see the universe?

Mme. Blavatsky: Well, that which you see, never mind; is it an entity or not? What is an entity, will you tell me? Something that is. Will you give me the etymology and definition of entity, before you criticize?

Mr. B. Keightley: Yes. Strictly and etymologically, it means something which is.

Mme. Blavatsky: Well, then what have you got to protest for? If Fohat is not, it is no use speaking about him or it or whatever it is. And if Fohat is, I call it entity—and why should I not? Invent some other words I may use. I am blessed if there are words enough in the English language to express the quarter or the millionth part of the ideas that are given in the occult teachings. The English language is inadequate. I don't say there is another better, because they are all in the same predicament.

Mr. B. Keightley: That is why we raise these questions.

Mme. Blavatsky: The Sanskrit language is a thousand times richer than the English language, and yet Sanskrit is full of symbols and figures of speech. Why? Because human language has not grown to say that which is in the human mind. The human mind is far more developed than the language. Thought, I mean.

Mr. Atkinson: Is Fohat in the Chinese represented by two Chinese syllables?

Mme. Blavatsky: It is from those parts something I have been asking many times. Fo means brilliant.

Mr. Atkinson: I know the root and the character of the Chinese syllable "Fo." If you could get the Chinese characters, I could turn it up in the Chinese dictionary.

Mme. Blavatsky: And in the Japanese, too. I don't think it is a real word, because some of them call it Fohat.

Mr. Atkinson: It would be "Ho" in Japanese. And it would represent the idea of "Ho," as "Ho" was a [ ] part of the phoenix. If it is the same as the Chinese, I mean. It becomes "Ho" in Japanese, and then becomes the "Ho" of the phoenix, as part of the compound name of the phoenix.

Mme. Blavatsky: Fohat is also a relation to the cycles, because the intensity of this vital force changes with every cycle.

Mr. Atkinson: It is in the celestial cosmogony of China. It is in the celestial beginning and the cosmogenesis.

Mme. Blavatsky: I wish you would look somewhere where you could find it, because I have been looking for it in India.

Mr. Atkinson: If you will only give me the Chinese characters, I will find it at once.

Mme. Blavatsky: I have got it somewhere, but not in the Chinese.

Mr. A. Keightley: Question 4. What are the sparks (atoms) which Fohat joins together?

Mme. Blavatsky: The particles of the Fiery World stuff, or dust of which we just spoke, nothing else.

Mr. B. Keightley: You might ask about what is really meant by the epithet "Fiery," if it is not the idea of being self-luminous.

Mme. Blavatsky: Oh, don't be so very dogmatic, for I cannot tell you anything, I am a poor, ignorant old woman, I cannot say anything at all. I cannot come and invent for you whether it is self-luminous or non-luminous. I don't care, I have not been at its birth, and I tell you I don't know.

Mr. B. Keightley: If you would explain it in any degree—the sense in which the word "fiery" is used—it would be helpful.

Mr. Kingsland: It is purely occult there.

Mme. Blavatsky: Fiery is fiery because it is not watery.

Mr. B. Keightley: Exactly, I see.

Mme. Blavatsky: Do you!

Mr. A. Keightley: Question 5. Are we to regard the atoms as purely metaphysical conceptions, even on the lowest material plane?

Mme. Blavatsky: I have just explained this very point. Now let me, if you please, remind you of what I read last Thursday, because I see I read one day, and then the following Thursday you forget it. This is what we said on Thursday: "The atoms, whether as representing Monads of Leibniz or the eternal, indestructible mathematical points of substance, can neither be dissolved during Pralaya nor reformed during Manvantara. The atoms do not exist as appreciable quantities of matter on any plane." When they come here they are not atoms, they are erroneously called atoms, "they are mathematical points of unknown quantity here, and whatever they are or may be on the seventh plane, each is and must be logically, as Leibniz says, an Absolute universe in itself, reflecting other universes. This is to say that each is Mahat or Divine Ideation," etc, etc. This I need not read any more, because I told you last time.

Mr. Kingsland: Just before, you speak of the atoms Fohat joined together as particles of the atoms of cosmic dust.

Mme. Blavatsky: Have patience and it will be here explained to you. Those atoms that we speak about do not exist, at least for us. They are simply mathematical points. There is not a man of science who can come and say to you that he saw the atoms or that he traced them, or that he smelt them or touched them or anything; it is a perfect impossibility. Now, what they call atoms they will find out are not atoms. If they ever find out, in I don't know how many thousand years, a little bit of homogeneous molecule or elements, they will be very happy. To this day they don't find a single speck or element, they have I suppose between sixty and seventy elements, and have they ever found molecules that are homogeneous? I do not think they have. Did they, Mr. Atkinson?

Mr. Atkinson: I think not.

Mme. Blavatsky: Very well, then; what is the use of calling them atoms and putting false noses on things, simply to confuse and perplex the mind? Why should we call elements that which are not elements and may be divided ad infinitum, and yet the chemist won't know what it is? They will come and mount on stilts and say we know everything. Elements, what are elements? There is one element, and it is the most tremendous conceit of modern science, such as I have never heard or read the like of in my days. They dogmatize and do everything, it appears. I am not at all learned, I have never studied; what I know is simply what I had to read in relation to the book that I had to write, but I say that, really, they give names which are positively ridiculous; they have no sense. Why should they go and call elements that which does not exist? And why should they go and pitch into the ancients about the four elements, speaking of earth, air, water and fire, saying we were all ignorant fools when our modern men of science act a thousand times more foolishly? They had not a *raison d'être* except only their fancy and whim. Now, do somebody take the part of the men of science. What silence! Well, 6.

Mr. A. Keightley: In what sense is electricity atomic?

Mme. Blavatsky: Electricity as an effect at work must certainly be atomic. Nothing that exhibits energy is non-atomic, or can be. Atoms confined to our world system are not what they are in space, or mathematical points. These latter are certainly metaphysical abstractions, and can only be considered in such terms; but what we know as atoms on this plane are gradations of substance, very attenuated. This will be easily understood by those who think over the occult axiom which tells us that spirit is matter, and matter spirit, and both one. Those who study esoteric philosophy will understand this better than those who do not. Now spirit does not become suddenly a lump of matter, any more than vapor becomes suddenly a lump of ice. To use again an illustration: the clairvoyant who can distinguish always, will see an occult atomic effect in any energetic, intense feeling in man or animal—such, for instance, as anger, fear, joy, etc. But these things are non-atomic to our sensuous perception. And if they are not such, how can science explain, for instance, the effects produced on persons and animals by various patients in their neighborhood? If, for instance, anger, love, joy or anything, any passion expresses in the most intense way, if that were not atomic, how is it that it produces effects not only on men, but in animals? How is it that the man who is very reserved and won't show his anger, and will be perfectly calm in his bearing and his features, won't show his passion or anything, yet you feel that this man is terribly hurt, and that he is angry or that he is rejoiced? Don't you feel it, is it through your eyes you see it; and how is it sometimes anger affects a person in the most terrible way, though it is not even directed against that person? This may seem a foolish question; but I ask you, how can anything be felt without it being an energy—atomic—I mean atomic in the occult sense, not in your sense of being molecular?

Mr. Kingsland: As I understand you, then, you say it is atomic as soon as a primordial substance begins to differentiate. Then you call it atomic.

Mme. Blavatsky: No, I called it atomic, perhaps before, because what I call atoms are the whole on the unmanifested plane. It would be mathematical points as soon as it is on the manifested plane. You cannot call it atoms; you call it world stuff, or anything you like. You have a definite idea of the word molecules, and therefore I cannot use that word.

Mr. B. Keightley: Material particles, you might say.

Mme. Blavatsky: Let it be material particles—the infinitesimal, but they have size.

Mr. Kingsland: We have got altogether out of the metaphysical conception.

Mme. Blavatsky: I don't want to do that, because on the physical plane your men of science are a great deal wiser than our metaphysical teachers, assuredly. They know all on the external plane. Now, whether they know as well that which underlies, I doubt.

Mr. B. Keightley: Now, on that analogy of anger, you call it atomic; it is more of a vibration?

Mme. Blavatsky: Vibration of what? What is that which vibrates spirit?

Mr. B. Keightley: That is what I want to get at.

Mme. Blavatsky: Nothingness vibrates. If there is something to vibrate, it is something.

Mr. Kingsland: And that must be atomic.

Mme. Blavatsky: Most assuredly. Now listen to the end. Another illustration. How would science have explained twenty years ago the contagion of disease? Now they have found out bacteria and bacilli, one of the most attenuated forms of matter, but atomic still. In another twenty years, perhaps they will discover the contagion of mental passions. Some people call it magnetism, a mesmeric power. Speaking of a lecturer, they say he electrifies his audience; we say that this electrification is purely atomic. The clairvoyant whose senses are opened in advance to the physiological, psychic condition of his age will perceive the stream of atoms proceeding from the lecturer to the audience, which will be coloured in various hues, according to his inner condition, and assuming different hues as it comes in contact with the various individuals in the audience, according {to} inner conditions and temperament. Do you see? Now, you will see a preacher who will be preaching most intensely about something; he will be preaching something, and he will be electrifying. They say Spurgeon produces a most extraordinary effect upon his hearers. Now, take the Salvation Army. Once that there are hundreds of thousands of them who will begin dancing and emanating all kinds of emotionalisms and everything, do you suppose it is not atomic? It sets the people crazy, it is infectious, it psychologizes them, it makes them lose all power over themselves, and they are obliged to think as General Booth,[1] once that they become perfectly under the influence, and they will give money, and believe in Jesus or anything you like. If General Booth went and preached instead of Jesus, H.P. Blavatsky once, everyone would believe in me, everyone would be a Blavatskyite. I can assure you he has the power, it is simply because it is a magnetic power. I wish I were friends with him. It is a good idea of making him preach me, and they would all come and believe in me.

Mr. Kingsland: Somebody must volunteer to become a General Booth.

Mr. ———: Then you hold that this atomic energy which emanates from the preacher has the same power upon all persons he addresses.

Mme. Blavatsky: Oh no, there is a great difference, some won't be affected at all. Now, some of us will go there and laugh. He could not affect us, because we have not got the temperament of others to be affected by his preaching. Those it would affect in an extraordinary way, and especially sensitive people.

Mr. Kingsland: And then they in their turns psychologize the others.

Mme. Blavatsky: It is an immense inter-psychology all around.

Mr. B. Keightley: You get a very good analogy from a lot of tuning forks varying in key. If you struck one it would be taken up by the whole mass, and get at last a whole volume of sound.

Mr. ———: Is that so? I think not.

Mr. B. Keightley: I think there is something of that kind, or how do you get a reverberation?

Mr. ———: One tuning fork will strike its octave.

---

1 William Booth, English Methodist preacher, 1829-1912, who founded the Salvation Army in 1865 and became its first "General."

Mr. B. Keightley: But I am supposing the other forks are on the same key.

Mr. ——: Oh, yes.

Mr. B. Keightley: I was thinking of the intensification of the sound, for instance as a sounding board intensifies. You put a tuning fork onto a sounding box, the sound becomes much louder.

Mr. A. Keightley: Stanza 5, Sloka 3, p. 118. In speaking of the six directions of space, is the term direction used in its ordinary sense, or does it mean here a property or attribute of space?

Mme. Blavatsky: Simply figuratively, it means the macrocosm is divided in occult philosophy, just as the microcosm, that is to say, into six principles, synthesized by the seventh, and space here is not limited to any particular area.

Mr. A. Keightley: Then space is used in its widest metaphysical sense.

Mme. Blavatsky: In its widest metaphysical sense. I would speak manifested. Every time I say space without the word manifested, it means in its widest metaphysical sense; if I want to speak about space in this universe, I would say manifested space, or something like that, just to make some qualification.

Mr. A. Keightley: Question 8. Are the six directions the six rays of the Logos?

Mme. Blavatsky: Just as I have explained, just the same.

Mr. A. Keightley: Question 9, Sloka 4: "Fohat traces spiral lines to unite the six to the seventh." Is there any special meaning in the word spiral, and is spiral action specially connected with Fohat?

Mme. Blavatsky: It is. Now in order that the neutral line, or zero point as Mr. Crookes calls it, and the centrifugal and centripetal must be made to run spirally, otherwise they would be entirely neutralized. I don't know how otherwise to call it, the neutral point can be destroyed. Now, see, if you please, in this volume, Gods, Monads, and Atoms, page 550, where the Caduceus of Mercury is represented.[2] Now, anyone who wants to know the explanation, let them read it. This spiral is represented in the Caduceus of Mercury. If you have a central point or a central line, for instance, like that (drawing), this must be the central line. As soon as you touch it, anything that is differentiated becomes undifferentiated again, and falls into the perfect Absolute. Then certainly, you must have the spirals go in such a way. One force goes in such a way (illustrating), and this is the Caduceus of Mercury which produces those miracles and marvels in the hands of [ ]. You look at this, and you will see that the healing powers and everything, that is what it means. And now Mr. Crookes finds—he speaks about number 8, perhaps you read it—he speaks about number 8, that he has found out that these forces go like that and make the figure 8, and the middle line is the central line. Therefore, there we are perfectly at one with ordinary science, of which I feel very proud. This is page 550.

Mr. A. Keightley: Then does that mean that by reason of a centrifugal and centripetal force, any force affected by that force must move in a spiral line?

Mme. Blavatsky: I believe it is a law that everything proceeds spirally, it never goes in straight lines. Science says something about gravity that goes on direct lines.

Mr. B. Keightley: That is one of the points I wanted to ask.

Mme. Blavatsky: I would never believe it. I can't give you my reasons, but I, knowing occultism, say it is impossible. There is nothing in this world that can proceed otherwise than in spirals, or on such things as that, but never in the direct line, never.

Mr. B. Keightley: Then the same thing would be true as to the conception of the action of the two forces of attraction and repulsion. You would not think of them as acting in direct lines, but always in

---

2 "Gods, Monads and Atoms", is the chapter heading in *The Secret Doctrine*, I:610, but HPB also refers to it on p. 549. The Caduceus is represented on p. 550.

spirals. I don't mean to say the effect, but as an abstract conception.

Mme. Blavatsky: Not only as an abstract conception, but I think you will find it in physical science that they must act something like that. They cannot act on direct lines.

Mr. B. Keightley: That is the effect they produce.

Mme. Blavatsky: Now look at the pranks that electricity plays with you. Put it on a sounding board. Does it do every straight line? A straight line is a thing unknown in the laws of Nature. Because that is why Pythagoras never would admit the straight line or number 2—because he says number 2 is not a creature that ought to exist in the Universe. We know the point which is not a point, but the point which is everywhere and nowhere, because it is absolute and universal, or it is the Triad or the Trinity.

Mr. B. Keightley: This is where the scientific idea comes in. They say the effects would be spiral. I think I would ask Mr. Kingsland if he agrees with this. The scientists would conceive as an abstract conception of the centripetal and centrifugal as acting in straight lines, combining together that would produce the spiral action—even in the abstract conception. I should think that occultism would stick to the spiral idea, if considered as abstractions.

Mr. Kingsland: They would not be conceived of as straight lines, and the two combined would produce the spiral.

Mr. B. Keightley: The abstract idea is, of course, the force acting in a straight line.

Mr. Kingsland: Oh, I see. In that sense, it is.

Mr. B. Keightley: Or any of the forces acting in a straight line. Suppose a force occupying a given point. It would be conceived to act upon any other point situated anywhere else in the room along the straight line joining the two points.

Mr. Kingsland: That is, for mathematical purposes.

Mme. Blavatsky: Whether for that or for anything else, I don't believe in it. That is all.

Mr. A. Keightley: Question 10. "If Fohat is the uniting power, while at the same time differentiation is going on, what is the disintegrating force which is at work; or is Fohat bipolar, i.e., does he produce both attraction and repulsion?"

Mme. Blavatsky: He does. I would like you to find me, as I said before, anything in this world that would not produce this bipolar action. Everything in creation is bipolar. Is there anyone very religious in the room, because I have to talk about personal God? Who of you is very religious?

Mr. ———: I am.

Mme. Blavatsky: You are not, I never would believe it, that is a blank denial. I want to say even your personal God is shown one moment infinite, and all kindness and mercy, the Creator and Preserver, and at another moment one of infinite anger, the destroyer and the annihilator. All this is bipolar, all this cannot be without, and if you take the God of your conception to be such a bipolar being, then how there can be any force, or anything that is not, I don't know. You cannot have a force absolutely good or absolutely bad, there is no such thing in Nature, therefore they must be bipolar. You take a little speck of something you will find the two poles in it, the negative and the positive.

Mr. A. Keightley: Then does that mean to say that the action of Fohat on any substance is alternately first one, and then the other— first constructive, and then destructive?

Mme. Blavatsky: I told you that. Take the trinity of the Hindus. There is Brahmâ the Creator, Vishnu the Preserver, Shiva the Destroyer, and all the three are one; and if you can conceive of one without the two others, then there remains no God but the flapdoodle, not good for anything. That which you call destruction is simply renovation, it is simply that. Well, I have explained it to you so many times: there is no such thing as Death, there is transformation. Now, if you sow a seed, as St. Paul says, in order—I forget how he says it.

Mr. B. Keightley: "In order that the seed may bear fruit it must fall into the ground and die."³

Mme. Blavatsky: Yes, that is perfectly true, that is to say, it must be transformed, it will not die, because there is no such thing as anything that is destructible, because it simply passes into something else. This even science has discovered 20 or 30 years, it is the conservation of energy, and this is the greatest truth and the greatest thing they have discovered; really, the greatest truth that they ever will, because this is the law on which everything is based. The whole of occultism it is that nothing is lost and everything transformed. They found it 20 or 30 years ago. I advise you to take the books which existed 4 or 500 years ago, and there the conservation of energy is positively proven, because, it is said plainly. Or look in the *Anugita*, where it is said that nothing is lost, that Vishnu transforms himself and becomes [ ] in humanity, but it will become always Vishnu; that every atom becomes something else, but it is still the sole atom, it is still the same thing. I cannot repeat it, because I have not got a good memory, but if you read the several pages, I am sure you will find that the conservation of the energy is perfectly well described there, three of four hundred years ago. Let it be 100 years before science, I am perfectly satisfied it is proven that they knew it, and that they know it now. I don't care whether it was many thousand years old. We speak about the manuscripts.

Mr. A. Keightley: Then is the idea of Vishnu, the Preserver in that Trinity, is that the idea of the conservation of energy?

Mme. Blavatsky: It is. He preserves everything, but he can preserve nothing without Shiva. Remember that Shiva must come and transform one thing into another, and he is, so to say, the helper of

---

3 Probably John 12:24, "Verily, verily, I say unto you, Except a corn of wheat fall into the ground and die, it abideth alone: but if it die, it bringeth forth much fruit."

Vishnu, and every time that Vishnu is left in the lurch, as is shown in the Puranas, they call Shiva to his help, and it is Vishnu he must come and help to transform one thing into another.

Mr. B. Keightley: And if I remember aright, Brahmâ is always appealing to Vishnu for help.

Mme. Blavatsky: He cannot move or do anything without Vishnu. You may say what you like, but it is highly philosophical, I assure you.

Mr. A. Keightley: Sloka 4, continued. "They (the Lipika) say: 'This is good.'" Question 11. What special meaning is this phrase of the Lipikas intended to convey?

Mme. Blavatsky: Why should not the Lipikas say this is good, when the Lord God in the first chapter of Genesis says it is good several times? And if he can say it, why cannot the Lipika say it?

Mr. B. Keightley: Certainly they can. It is not an objection. It shows that phrase has some special meaning, or it would {not} appear both in the old source from which you have taken the stanza and the Bible of the Jews. And the question is what is the special meaning?

Mme. Blavatsky: In the Bible, you know, there is as much philosophy as anything else, though half of it was thrown out. If you could have the whole Elohistic chapters you would see, if you please, what the philosophy is; but out of perhaps fourteen there remain now only one and a half, or something.

Mr. B. Keightley: The question is, what is the meaning?

Mme. Blavatsky: That this is good. What meaning do you want more? If it were bad they would not say a word, but they would proceed to correct their mistake and create it better.

Mr. Kingsland: But they might find out their mistake afterwards.

Mme. Blavatsky: Well, so did God also find his mistake afterwards, because he repented that he made man. Even a God repents, so why should not a Dhyan-Chohan?

Mr. Kingsland: Then it is only good, relatively?

Mr. A. Keightley: Is the "Chhaya-loka"—explained here as the shadowy world of primal form, or the intellectual—the same as what is called in the diagram on page 200 {of *The Secret Doctrine*} as the "Archetypal World"? Or is it what is there called the intellectual or creative world?

Mme. Blavatsky: The Archetypal World and the intellectual world; and of that, you can see in the Kabalah, it shows four planes. Take Mathers' *Kabalah*,[4] there it is shown. Don't show it to me. I know it by heart. The Archetypal World may be compared to the thought of man {that} precedes action; this is the kind of individual Manas in the light of the universal intelligence. The artist conceives his idea first of all, before he begins to work, but before he can paint his picture he has to gather and prepare his materials in accordance with the plans that are in his mind. He stretches his canvas and grinds his colours. This is on the intellectual or creative world. Then he roughly sketches his idea on the canvas, and this may be compared to the presentment in the substantial or affirmative {formative} world. If you will follow there, you will see what I mean. He fills in all the details and the picture is ready. In the physical aspect there, they are the four planes. So it is in nature. I do not speak about the three higher, because they cannot be expressed in human language. The universal mind is above what they call the Divine ideation. This is a thing which cannot be expressed, but this Divine ideation falls, so to say, from the beginning; and when I say from the beginning, it means there is no beginning and no end; and the light of it will fall on the Archetypal World where are the antetypes or prototypes of everything; there would be nothing, not even this old carpet, if there

---

4 *Kabbala Denudata: The Kabbalah Unveiled, containing the following books of the Zohar. 1. The book of concealed mystery. 2. The greater holy assembly. 3. The lesser holy assembly.* Translated into English from the Latin version of Knorr von Rosenroth, and collated with the original Chaldee and Hebrew text, by S. L. MacGregor Mathers. London: George Redway, 1887.

was not an antetype or prototype. You understand my idea?

Miss Kenealy: Yes, I think that is very clear.

Mr. A. Keightley: Stanza 5, Sloka 5. Question 13. What are the influences proceeding from the four quarters of the world? Why are some, such as that from the East, injurious to life?

Mme. Blavatsky: Because it is; and do not ask me any more questions. They have been asking me a thousand times. It means North and East are good, West and South are bad. West is bad because the Egyptians and the Hindus and all the Chaldeans and the Phoenicians and everyone had the idea that the Devil came from the West; why it should be, I don't know, because it is the presentment of western civilization in the present century. The Devil comes from the West in the Egyptian sacred books, in the Chaldean, in the Phoenician; in all he comes from the West. And everything that is good comes from the East, because the Sun is the regenerator and comes every day at the appointed time; and the Sun is our creator and friend and everything.

Mr. A. Keightley: If the evil influence is supposed to come from the West, and if the East is supposed to be good merely because the Sun, which is the regenerator, appears from there, what is the meaning of the Sun disappearing in the West? Is there any connection there? Is it merely an absence of good, or an actual presence of evil?

Mme. Blavatsky: It appears there, from whence comes darkness.

Mr. A. Keightley: But darkness does not come from the West.

Mme. Blavatsky: No, but light disappears in it, and therefore I suppose they made it bad, but they must have had some other occult influences. There is not a country that did not have West in their abomination positively, so that you must be mighty proud, all of you!

Mr. B. Keightley: Yet the islands of the blessed were always supposed to be in the West.

Mme. Blavatsky: Geographically; but it is quite a different thing really. Just as it speaks of the east wind in London, and he asks me how is it the east wind is the most pernicious wind, and all good comes from the East. I say it is geographically. It may be so in your little island, but it is not so in space universal.

Mr. A. Keightley: Then what is the meaning of it in space?

Mme. Blavatsky: In space there is neither East, West, North, or South, if you take infinite space; but if you take a limited space, nature has so ordained it that everything evil comes from the West.

Mr. A. Keightley: Take the solar system. What is the meaning of it?

Mme. Blavatsky: I don't know.

Mr. A. Keightley: Then what are the four corners?

Mme. Blavatsky: It is flapdoodle, because there are no corners in that which is spherical.

Mr. B. Keightley: I am afraid, Arch, your cross-examination won't bring you much.

Mme. Blavatsky: I am not afraid of cross-examination, to tell you the truth.

Mr. A. Keightley: What is the meaning of the evil influence coming from the East {West}?

Mme. Blavatsky: Because evil influences are illnesses, and it appears they thought the Devil lived there.

Mr. A. Keightley: Why should it be the West and the South which are bad?

Mme. Blavatsky: From the South Pole come all the evils of the world; that is why you are not allowed to go to the South Pole, it is evil. To the North Pole you are not allowed to go because it is the land of the Gods. And if you went there you would be desecrated. Seriously speaking, there is some magnetism, something magnetic coming from the South and the West, that is a very bad magnetism, the magnetism of the emanations of the earth. It depends on the earth. Now, let us speak of the earth. Why is it that the Hindus tell you to sleep in a certain way, with your heads so and so, that the magnetism should pass through you in a certain direction? I have read several men {of} science who say that it is not at all a foolish idea. There is such a thing as terrestrial magnetism. When you have calculated where it comes from, then you will see there is some philosophy in the way the evil influences come from the West and the good ones from the East.

Mr. A. Keightley: But supposing, for instance, you placed your body in the direct currents of magnetism, which are supposed to proceed from the magnetic pole in the North? That is not in the actual axis of the earth.

Mme. Blavatsky: I never said it was. What do you want to know? What are you driving at?

Mr. A. Keightley: I wanted to find out where these magnetic bad influences come from, with regard to the earth.

Mme. Blavatsky: When you are older you will know more; you need not come and burden your young brain with that, because you could not retain it, and it would become like a sieve and it would run through.

Mr. Atkinson: Is it magnetic North, or the geographical North?

Mme. Blavatsky: No, magnetic.

Mr. Atkinson: Because they are opposite to the other.

Mme. Blavatsky: I tell you more. I have just had the honour of telling you we don't believe in anything going in straight lines. Now, if you put 2 + 2 together, you will see what I mean; it does not go in straight lines. Therefore, you may say what you like, but unless you know occultism and all the points and everything you cannot know from where it comes and what is meant by it. There is simply the statement that it comes from such and such a thing. It is not meant for those who have {not} learnt occultism and who do not know there remained so many points into which the occultists divide the earth. And whilst you do not know it, how can you know how it passes, when it always goes either in a diagonal line or like that, in spirals, and never in a straight line? Therefore, it is extremely difficult to answer it; it is impossible.

Mr. A. Keightley: Then there is some special relation to the currents meant by the words East and West.

Mme. Blavatsky: Maybe there is, and maybe there is not. This is the sort of thing I am subjected to each Thursday. They will come and cross-examine me and pump out everything they can till Doomsday. I cannot say more than what I know.

Mr. A. Keightley: But you don't say all you do know.

Mme. Blavatsky: That is a different thing; you have no right to ask it.

Mr. A. Keightley: Question 14. Have the four Maharajahs and the four elements a special terrestrial application, as well as a kosmic one?

Mme. Blavatsky: Except in karma, nothing at all. The four Maharajahs produce karmic effects, certainly, because there the Lipika Maharajah is a title they have, simply.

Mr. A. Keightley: What is the meaning of the four elements, then?

Mme. Blavatsky: In what respect?

Mr. A. Keightley: As related to those four Maharajahs.

Mme. Blavatsky: I don't know what you are talking about. I didn't see the last question. I don't understand what you mean.

Mr. A. Keightley: We had better ask another time.

Mme. Blavatsky: I told you to take out the 15th.

Mr. A. Keightley: That is all there is, then.

Mme. Blavatsky: I think that my fate or my karma is to live all my life surrounded by points of interrogation. Sometimes I have the nightmare, and it seems to me I am surrounded by points of negation.

Mr. ———: Points of admiration, I hope, as well.

Mr. A. Keightley: Well, you should not convert yourself into such a perpetual conundrum.

Mme. Blavatsky: I am a very simple-minded old woman. I come here and offer to teach you what I can. You accept, very well; I cannot teach you more than I can, you know.

Miss Kenealy: You say so much we want to know.

Mme. Blavatsky: You all are discreet. It is this immediately in the house {sic}, I am sorry Dr. Williams is not here. He puts questions beautifully.

Miss Kenealy: I think you are rather hard on us all.

Mme. Blavatsky: In the first place, you ask sometimes questions that trespass on forbidden ground. What is the use of my telling you one thing, and then shutting the door in your face? It will only be vexation of spirit, and it won't teach you much. And I cannot say certain things. I tell all that is permitted me to give. It may be very foolish, very exclusive, very selfish. You may think what you like; I have not made the rules, I never made the laws. I have not so received it, nor shall I so impart. What I promised not to reveal I cannot, it is impossible.

Miss Kenealy: You know so much that what is very simple to you is often very hard to us.

Mme. Blavatsky: You see, you always continue to ask things that really I cannot give fully. So what is the use of saying it by bits?

Mr. Kingsland: We have a dim perception there is something behind, so we keep pegging away.

Mme. Blavatsky: You cannot complain, because you have the explanation of many things.

Mr. Kingsland: I am speaking now generally, for the company.

Here the proceedings terminated.

13.
The Theosophical Society
Meeting of the Blavatsky Lodge
17 Lansdowne Road, Holland Park, W.
Thursday, April 4, 1889

Mr. Kingsland in the Chair

S.D. page 129

Mr. A. Keightley: Stanza 5, Sloka 6, Commentary. Question 1. How do the "Recorders of the Karmic ledger" make an impassible barrier between the Personal Ego and the Impersonal Self?

Mme. Blavatsky: Now, it seems to me it is very easy to understand that. I think that whoever understands the real nature of Nirvana, or even of the Christian Kingdom of Heaven, where it is said no one marries or is given in marriage, etc., ought to see very well what is the meaning of it. Because, what is Rupa? What is "Personal"? It is always something objective or material, and how can it then pass there beyond the point where everything is formless and Arupa? I think it is not given in symbolical language, but quite plainly. Now, I ask you: who is it that goes into the state of Devachan? Is it spirit, spirit-soul, or the monad loaded with spiritual consciousness and intelligence, or is it the lower principles of the personal man? Which is it that goes? You know perfectly well that the "Personal" was the Kama-loka, therefore they cannot go even on this plane. The principles remain to fade out in time and Kama-loka. The Lipika is said to circumscribe within the egg—which is the magnetic aura or {of?} manifested kosmos—man, animal or any concrete object in the universe, or those objects which have form. It is an allegory, and is stated in allegorical language, this enchanted ring or circle. No such ring exists in nature, but there exists the plane of matter and spirit and consciousness. The Personal Self consists of a triangle in a square, man's seven principles, of which only the upper Triangle is left; it cannot pass beyond the plane of even the primitive differentiated matter. Every atom of the seven principles—even the refulgence of Atma-Buddhi, for refulgence is an attribute and related to absoluteness—every atom must remain outside the portal of Nirvana. Alone divine ideation—the consciousness, the bearer of Absolute memory, of its personalities now merged into the one impersonal—can cross the threshold of the Laya point, which lies at the very gate of manifestation, of the human soul and mind in which facts and events, past, present and future, were alike fixed during their joint pilgrimage. There remains, as it is said at the dawn of the great day, but that which is left of the various foods in a copper vessel when the latter is well washed out and dried. This is a quotation from the book. But if this is so at its dawn, what shall we say becomes of the same soul and mind during the great day itself? Why, that which remains of the said copper vessel when it is melted—the memory alone. (You understand there is an enormous difference between Devachan and the Great Day, or that plane which only is reached during the Maha-Pralaya after all the cycle of existence is done away with.) How is it possible, then, that anything personal should come into it? We are unable to represent to ourselves such an entirely formless, atomless consciousness. During ecstasy we can imagine something approximate to the fact. We say the subject in this state of Samadhi is beyond his everyday world of limits and conditions, and now all is one motionless day and state for him. The past and the future being all in his present, his spirit is freed from the trammels and changes of the body. The highest and most spiritual parts of his Manas only are united to his own particular monad, which, like the monad of Leibniz, reflects that and is the whole universe in itself. The yogi, we say, is become the partaker of the wisdom and omniscience of the universal mind; but can we say that of the mind when it crosses beyond the Laya point? If you can, gentlemen of Oxford and Cambridge, I cannot, for I cannot speak the language of the gods, and if I could you would not much understand me, I suppose. There is a question, and for the life of me

I cannot make out what you mean by it. Who put such a question? What does it mean—to draw the line between the personal and the impersonal? You all of you ought to know it.

Mr. Kingsland: Is the state of Nirvana beyond the Laya point?

Mme. Blavatsky: Most assuredly; why, the Laya point is simply only for the planes of matter. This is the Laya point, as we call it, which goes beyond the material manifestation.

Mr. Kingsland: You would not say Devachan was beyond the Laya point?

Mme. Blavatsky: Most assuredly not. Devachan is one thing, and "the Great Day Be-With-Us" is another, for it is not simply planetary Pralaya, it is universal Pralaya.

Mr. Kingsland: We are to call that Nirvana, are we not?

Mme. Blavatsky: No, it is para Nirvana; para, which means Meta.[1]

Mr. Kingsland: In the state of Samadhi, that is only Nirvana?

Mme. Blavatsky: It is simply Nirvana.

Mr. Kingsland: There is a certain amount of individuality attached to that.

Mme. Blavatsky: There is an individuality of spirit and soul, Atma-Buddhi.

Mr. Kingsland: You say the highest part of the Manas is assimilated with the Monad; you cannot say that of Nirvana.

Mme. Blavatsky: Most assuredly, you cannot. I explained it afterwards there, further on, because there are many places where you say things which I cannot make out. I cannot make out how you, who know all about the personal remains in Kama-loka, don't apply the same thing when you speak of the "Great Day Be-With-

---

1 The original has para- , but modern usage is pari-.

Us." I don't mean at all about our partial, short, little lives here. That is quite a different thing. You see, if I had some of those who put the questions to be there when I answer them, it would be a different thing.

Mr. A. Keightley: It is said here the esoteric meaning of the first sentence is that those who have been called Lipikas and the recorders make an impassable barrier between the personal ego and the impersonal self.

Mme. Blavatsky: Certainly.

Mr. B. Keightley: The phrase almost looks as if it were the line of demarcation and division between the four principles and the three. I think there is a question after that on that.

Mme. Blavatsky: I think you have a very erroneous opinion about the three principles or the upper triangle. You don't take into consideration, or make a difference, when we apply the seven principles on this plane as in man or in Devachan, or the same seven principles after the cycle of life is finished—which is a perfectly different thing, entirely different.

Mr. Kingsland: There is nothing in that Stanza to guide us to that.

Mme. Blavatsky: I could not write more than there is there.

Mr. B. Keightley: That is why these questions are asked.

Mme. Blavatsky: Don't you see very well that the Lipika, "the Great Day Be-With-Us," means when everything—when the cycle is finished? I am perfectly sure there must be some reference to it.

Mr. B. Keightley: That is plain; but then is there anything that can be spoken of as a "personal self" still remaining?

Mme. Blavatsky: I will tell you a thing which will settle the whole difficulty. This is what volume?

Mr. B. Keightley: The first.

Mme. Blavatsky: How is it called.

Mr. B. Keightley: Cosmogenesis.

Mme. Blavatsky: Then why should you make me speak of Anthropogenesis? The "personal self" is quite a different thing. This is a thing which has a relation, but no personal gods will have anything to do with it. It does not mean personal in the sense of our personality. It means objective individuality.

Mr. B. Keightley: Yes, but that is different from what the phrase would suggest.

Mr. A. Keightley: Question 2. Does "personal ego" here stand for the Upper Triad, Atma-Buddhi-Manas, or for the lower Quaternary?

Mme. Blavatsky: There it is. It would stand for all, if the principles of a still living man on Earth were meant; it stands for none in the case of the Lipika. It is said—I quote further—they circumscribe the triangle, the first one; the cube or quaternary, the second one; therefore all the seven contain in the triangle three, the quaternary or four within the circle. This is quite plain. No principles can cross the ring "pass not," only the memory of these in the eternal divine ideation, which ideation itself from something manifested becomes the Absolute on that "Day Be-With-Us." Therefore it is.

Mr. A. Keightley: Question 3. By "manifested plane of matter," do you here mean the four lower planes of the diagram on page 200, i.e., the four planes of the globes of our chain, or only the lowest of the four, that of our Earth?

Mme. Blavatsky: I mean what I say. Nothing manifested or having form or name or number can cross beyond the ring which divides the immutable {mutable} and the manifested from the ever-present and immutable. Now, do put this into your wise heads, my dear children. There is the difference between the immutable {mutable} and the manifested, and the ever-present and the immutable; and you cannot cross this line and you cannot—it is impossible—nothing that is within this domain can pass into the other, the beyond. It is impossible, at least in our philosophy; I don't know how it is in your conceptions, but in our philosophy, it is impossible. Where does our miserable atom of dirt, which gossipy conceit called the Earth, stand, once the Pralaya and universal destroyer and disappearance of the whole universe—the ideal as much as the physical—is concerned? How can I mean the Earth in one breath with absoluteness? Is it not said of the abstract elements on page 130 (Which, please, look up.) that even they, when they return into their primal element, or the one and secondless, can never cross beyond the Laya or zero point? Isn't it as plain as can be? Why do you torture me, then? There are seven meanings to every symbol. Astronomically, the ring "Pass-Not" means one thing, and metaphysically, quite another.

Mr. A. Keightley: You state here—you quote from the *Viśishtadvaita Catechism*[2] (Reads from *The Secret Doctrine*, page 132.) Question 4. Can you explain the esoteric meaning of the sentence: "Then it goes through a dark spot in the Sun"?

Mme. Blavatsky: Now, do you know what a Visishtadvaita is? They believe in a personal, in a personal God, and they are dualists. They are Vedantins, but they have got no right to the name of Vedantins. There are three sects among the Vedantins: the Dvaita dualists, the Visishtadvaita, which are more than dualists, and the Advaita, who are humanitarian, so to say, who believe only in one science. Therefore, I answer to this that you had better ask the [ ], because I don't understand what it means. The "dark spot in the Sun" must be on a par with the Angel standing on the Sun. I could never understand what was meant. I even took the trouble of writing to the Pundit himself,[3] and I commissioned Harte to ask him what it meant, and he could not tell me; so that what can I do?

Mr. B. Keightley: Then you cannot blame us for asking the question.

---

2 *A Catechism of the Viśishtadvaita Philosophy of Sri Ramanujacharya*, compiled by N. Bhashyacharya and S.E. Gopalacharlu. Madras: The Theosophical Society, 1888.
3 N. Bhashyacharya, Director of the Adyar Library of the Theosophical Society, who died in December 1889.

Mme. Blavatsky: I cannot, I don't know myself what it means. I have a dim idea, because for them the Sun is that Parabrahm; they don't know any better; and I do think, you know, that it means the heart of the Sun.

Mr. A. Keightley: Does it correspond at all with the point in the circle?

Mme. Blavatsky: I quote that simply to show the different systems in the Hindus. I don't blame you. I simply quote it to show what it says. Now comes a pretty question—number 5!

Mr. A. Keightley: Question 5, page 135. Can you tell us anything more as to the esoteric meaning of the 3,000 cycles of existence?

Mme. Blavatsky: Oh, immediately! Yes, of course! In the first place, I am not a mathematician—I say there it is perfectly impossible for me to go into figures. Secondly, you know perfectly well, as Mr. Sinnett has written already in his *Esoteric Buddhism*, that the powers that be and who have in their pockets the secret wisdom don't like to go into figures; they never do. The 3,000 cycles may mean any number of figures; it all depends upon the duration of each 3,000 cycles, which is, in short, the period of the whole Manvantara.

Mr. A. Keightley: Maha-Manvantara or minor?

Mme. Blavatsky: No, Manvantara; that is to say, when the seven rounds are accomplished.

Mr. A. Keightley: But is there any meaning attached to the idea of 3,000?

Mme. Blavatsky: I don't know; it may be.

Mr. A. Keightley: I am not asking the question numerically, but what is the idea?

Mme. Blavatsky: They say in many places 3,000; it has a Devachanic meaning, that is all. Every defunct who goes and crosses the Nile in the boat (You remember that ceremony.) is Osirified, he becomes his own spirit, and the spirit goes into the field of Aanroo. That is what it means.

Mr. A. Keightley: Question 6. Stanza 6, Sloka 1 (page 138). Can you further amplify this explanation as to the four kinds of Vach?

Mme. Blavatsky: In other words, can you analyze Subba Row's two lectures and once that it is published, to have all the blessed [ ] on my head. It is a quotation from his lectures in the [ ], he divides [ ] and speaks of four forms, as a Vedantin who lays stress on the four-faced Brahmâ, the one who manifests on our plane and who is identical with Tetragrammaton also; if not four-faced, then the four numbered. He divided Vach into seven parts, and speaks of the seven faces of our Avalokiteśvara, that is to say, the seven forces manifested in nature. Our Vach is the female Logos. Now read *Vishnu {Purana}*; and I need not ask you, because I know you have read this several times. Or again, in Manu, or in any other work in which Vach is mentioned, and you will find that Brahmâ had divided himself into two persons, male and female, and they created the seven Manus. Now this is the exoteric version of the esoteric, or that which I have taught you many times. We are Vedantin, so far that we maintain seven, Vach being the female aspect of the seven logos {i}. You must understand what it means. They are all androgynous. Even the first one, ethereal as he may be, might be made out of nothingness, but still he is androgynous—he has the feminine aspect in him, and because he emanates the second logos. Now the following question will give you more.

Mr. A. Keightley: Question 7. In speaking of the "Seven Sons of Light and Life" as being beyond the Laya centres, do you refer only to what may be termed the "relative" Laya centres which limit our solar system? For the term Laya centre seems usually to be used of the absolute limit of all differentiation.

Mme. Blavatsky: It is so, indeed, in the limit of differentiation in the manifested kosmos. What is meant may be absolute darkness for us, but certainly it can be neither differentiation nor Laya, as we conceive of them, in that beyond. When I speak of the "Seven Suns of Light and Life" as being beyond the Laya centres, it only means this: they are subject neither to Laya nor differentiation—during the cycle of their life, at any rate, which lasts a Maha-Manvantara. If you had only remembered the order in which the Dhyan-Chohans emanate, or theogony, which is there explained in many places, you would not have asked the question. I thought you knew by this time that logos number one radiated seven primeval rays, which are as one, and are called the septenary robe of destiny; and that from that one is ultimately born logos number three, whose seven rays become the kosmic builders and whose aggregate is Fohat. How, then, can the sons of Light and Life, the septenary robe of immutable destiny, be otherwise than beyond the Laya centres? It is just what I had the pleasure of explaining to our dear President, Mr. Kingsland. I think it is very conceivable, that. You cannot take Laya as referring to anything but matter, manifested matter, differentiation, even finite manifested differentiation, and beyond this Laya point, which is the Zero point of matter, is matter which never differentiates, and nothing. It is not that it is a question of heat or anything, it is simply the within—how shall we explain this—as I have been explaining to you many times. Everyone of them is endless, shoreless, limitless, and yet there are seven. Well, there is a riddle for you! If not a mathematical one, it is not a physical one, and yet I suppose everyone ought to try and conceive of that—that it is not a question of right, left, up, top, below, or beneath. It is simply a question of the state of matter or state of consciousness. Matter is everywhere, because matter and spirit are one, but the Laya point, or beyond the Laya point, you cannot call that matter nor spirit; it is neither matter nor spirit, it is both and nothing.

Mr. B. Keightley: Then, really, that looks as if the Laya point would divide the four planes which you may call more especially manifested— the planes of the globe and solar system, and so on— from the three upper planes of which we have been speaking.

Mme. Blavatsky: They do not. The three planes and the four are just in one Cosmos as the seven principles are in you; but it is simply this: if we cannot understand or realize that we have these three principles in us, such as the higher intelligences, or Manas, and Buddhi, the spiritual soul, and Atma, the soul that is the synthesis—if we cannot realize this, how can you pretend to go and conceive that which is perfectly inconceivable for human intellect, the three higher intelligences? That is why I only give the four, because they represent the planes on which our planetary chain is, but I can't go beyond, because it would be perfectly incomprehensible; and moreover my knowledge of the English language would not tell me, nor any language, for I could not explain it.

Mr. Kingsland: You must look upon the three higher principles as differentiations of the Absolute one, whereas beyond the Laya point you have no differentiation whatever.

Mme. Blavatsky: That is just what it is.

Mr. B. Keightley: But you have the seven hierarchies.

Mme. Blavatsky: You have no seven. All is one after that.

Mr. B. Keightley: It was seeing the phrase used—"the Seven Sons of Light."

Mme. Blavatsky: Never mind what we use; we have a language to say many things, and we cannot say more than what the philosophy has evolved. Try to understand it, if you please, that there are no differentiations, no spirit, nothing, it is the Absolute darkness for us. The highest Dhyan-Chohans could not tell you any more than could Mr. Herbert Spencer. It is a thing on which human intellect cannot speculate. It is perfectly ridiculous and absurd for us stupid men and women to go and speculate upon such a thing as that. When I speak of stupid men and women, I include all those who possess the highest intellects in the world.

Mr. Kingsland: At the same time, do you not speak relatively of a Laya point of matter beyond which there are {no} differentiations?

Mme. Blavatsky: No, no.

Mr. Kingsland: Relatively.

Mme. Blavatsky: Look here. Try to understand me. We have seven planes of matter. On each of these planes there are seven again, and each has its Laya point. When we are on our plane, there is a Laya point which is the seventh of our plane; but when you have gone beyond those seven planes or seven divine ideations, as they are called sometimes, then there is nothing. You cannot speculate, because there, where there is nothing to grasp at, you cannot conceive of it; it is a perfect impossibility.

Mr. Kingsland: That is exactly what I meant, that there are certain relative Laya points.

Mme. Blavatsky: Yes, but those that come from the first Logos are beyond any Laya point, because they do not belong yet to differentiated kosmos. They call it the septenary robe of destiny; I don't know why it is, but it is so. Mind you, though they are seven they are one; they are, so to say, the privations, the ideations of the seven that will be, of the second Logos—those that will be the seven from which will emanate the seven forces of nature. Please do ask me if you don't understand something, because I want to begin very seriously all these instructions.

Mr. A. Keightley: (Reads from *The Secret Doctrine*, page 138.) Question 8. Does Fohat stand in the same relation to the Hierarchy of Seven that Mayavi–rupa does to an adept, i.e., as the intelligent, formless, active thought power or energy?

Mme. Blavatsky: Whoever put the question has put an excellent definition. It is perfectly as you say. Who of you evolved this? Let me give him the laurel wreath.

Mr. B. Keightley: It was Arch.

Mme. Blavatsky: Well, for once I must pay you the compliment; it is perfectly well defined, it is the Mayavi–rupa. You cannot make a better illustration. (After a pause.) Now comes again a flapdoodle.

Mr. A. Keightley: Question 9. Sloka 3, page 140. After Maha-Pralaya or any of the lesser Pralayas, does "Matter" remain in *status quo* of progress, to re-emerge in Manvantara and take up differentiation and evolution at a corresponding point to where it was left at Pralaya?

Mme. Blavatsky: Matter remains *status quo*, that is to say, in the form it is found in at the hour of Pralaya, only with regard to the spheres or globes of our chain. Then the globe, going into obscuration (As Mr. Sinnett perfectly calls it, a name which has been given to him.), becomes, in the words of a Master, like a huge whale or mammoth caught in the masses of ice, and frozen. The moment Pralaya catches it, it remains *status quo*, everything. Even if a man happens not to be dead, he will remain just as he is. But now listen. Otherwise, and at the hour of any other Pralaya, save this planetary one in the solar Pralaya, for instance, when our Sun goes into sleep, the matter of that system which is to die and go out of existence is scattered in space to form other forms in other systems. Every atom or molecule of it has its Karma and its destiny, and everyone has worked out his way, unconsciously, or according to the little intelligence it has; or it will, if you please, go into other and higher systems when there begins the new Manvantara. But the planetary Manvantara is the only one where everything remains *status quo*. There are superb things in some Sanskrit books, the description of it: when the Pralaya is near, when you have to expect it, and all kinds of kosmic phenomena—most magnificent. I quote a passage of it, but it is a long thing of about 17 or 18 pages.

Mr. Gardner: Is it in the Purana?

Mme. Blavatsky: It is not in the Puranas; it is in a philosophical book by one of those Rishis. I have had it here, but I don't know what has been done with it. I had one of the great pundits to translate it for me word for word, and I was for about two weeks putting it down, because it is a magnificent thing. I wanted to have it in *The Theosophist*.

Mr. Gardner: Do animals exhibit any peculiarities?

Mme. Blavatsky: There are not many animals left. There are what they call the Śishta that remain, the seeds; they say they are great adepts who become Manu when the time comes, when the obscuration is ended and this wave of life again reaches that particular globe or planet, then they say they are the seed of life, the seed Manus.

Mr. Kingsland: Then the planet that is in obscuration will still be visible from other planets.

Mme. Blavatsky: Most assuredly, certainly; we see many dead planets.

Mr. Kingsland: The term obscuration gives us some idea, under the impression that in obscuration it would not be visible.

Mme. Blavatsky: It means from the standpoint of that which is on it, and not others.

A Lady: Is not the Moon in obscuration?

Mme. Blavatsky: No, it is not. The Moon is perfectly dead as a doornail.

Mr. Holt: Don't we understand obscuration by this paralytic condition?

Mme. Blavatsky: It is there that they are not asleep. "Not dead but sleeping."

Mr. Gardner: Suspended animation.

Mr. A. Keightley: There seem to be three stages then. There is obscuration, death, and dissolution.

Mme. Blavatsky: Yes.

Mr. A. Keightley: Progress towards destruction. There is the one you point out as the frozen state of paralysis; then there is the total death, like the Moon; finally the solar death, when the whole thing bursts up and goes on.

Mme. Blavatsky: But there are seven states, if you take not only planets but everything there is on them. Take sleep and take the trance state and take the yogi hibernation—for 40 or 50 days buried and then coming into life.

Mr. A. Keightley: Do the states of the planets correspond?

Mme. Blavatsky: Everything corresponds. There is nothing that happens to man that does not happen to everything else.

Mr. A. Keightley: Then what state does that sort of paralysis correspond to?

Mme. Blavatsky: Oh! This is not for you. Give your question. Don't you begin jumping.

Mr. Gardner: Can you tell us any of the planets that are in obscuration?

Mme. Blavatsky: We will tell you another day when you put the question. As the question is not there, I won't. Kindly learn a little more method.

Mr. B. Keightley: I think it is stated somewhere in *Esoteric Buddhism*. I think Mars is just emerging from obscuration and Venus is just passing into it. I don't remember exactly.

Mr. A. Keightley: Page 143. Can you give us a short sketch of "The Life and Adventures of an Atom?"

Mme. Blavatsky: That is the question I was expecting! "Can you give us a short sketch of the Life and Adventures of an Atom?" No, but I offer you two questions instead. Now you have to answer them. Which do you believe is larger, your body or that of the whole kosmos? You will say, of course, it is the kosmos.

Mr. A. Keightley: Well, wait a moment.

Mme. Blavatsky: And secondly, which of you has a greater number

13. MEETING APRIL 4, 1889

of atoms or molecules, you, or that kosmos? Choose.

Mr. Holt: I should say exactly the same number.

Mme. Blavatsky: Do you? And how about men who are smaller and men who are a great deal bigger?

Mr. Holt: It is a matter of the size of the atoms.

Mr. B. Keightley: No, the distance between the atoms, that is, from the scientific point of view.

Mme. Blavatsky: Oh! But we are anti-scientists here.

Mr. A. Keightley: A man is commensurate with the whole of the kosmos.

Mme. Blavatsky: I will tell you why I put this question. Now, supposing in view of the hopelessness of the task you offer me, and while I confess myself incapable of enlightening you with a sketch of the life and adventures of every atom, I seek to give you a biography of one of your personal atoms. Let us see now: am I generous and kind, that I consent to give you the life and adventures of only one?

Mr. A. Keightley: I asked for one.

Mme. Blavatsky: Now we will see if it is possible. How many years will it take me, do you think, to give you an accurate statement even about that one atom? For occult science teaches that from the moment of birth to that of death (And after death still more so.) every atom, or let us say particle, rather, alters with every seventh fraction of something far less than a second; that it shifts its place, and proteus-like travels incessantly in the same direction as the blood, externally and internally, night and day. Now you are 28, 29, or how old are you? Thirty, let us say. Then let us say, if you please, that I will take an atom of your body, and from the moment of your birth I will begin giving you the life and adventures of that blessed atom in all its transformations, in all its gyrations, in all its metempsychosis. How long will it take me, gentlemen mathematicians? Tell me how much.

Count and I will give it.

Mr. A. Keightley: Roughly, though; a short sketch.

Mme. Blavatsky: Go to bed!

Mr. Kingsland: If you ask a person to give a sketch of their life and history, you don't expect them to give the history of what they did every day of their time.

Mme. Blavatsky: An atom is not a man, an atom does not get into flirtations, and courtship and marriage, and pass through the Bankruptcy Court, and become a magistrate, and the Lord Mayor; nothing of the kind. An atom is a very well-behaved being, and what one atom does almost every other atom does. There are certain little variations, but it is nothing. But to come and tell you what I mean there, and give the life and adventures of an atom—which means, simply an impossibility. Because I said a chemist would be astounded and take it for the biggest nonsense for an alchemist to give him the life and adventures of an atom; and yet he comes and puts this question. Really and seriously, all of you, you must allow a margin, you must leave some possibility for a poor author to exercise his imagination.

Mr. Kingsland: We must have something to hang a discourse on.

Mme. Blavatsky: Oh, if it is only pegs you want, that is another thing.

Mr. B. Keightley: That question of atoms is consistently cropping up in *The Secret Doctrine*.

Mme. Blavatsky: It does, and I had the honour of telling you what I meant by atoms, that I used them in that sense of cosmogenesis. I said they were geometrical and mathematical points.

Mr. B. Keightley: Haven't you got something definite in your mind, when you write that?

Mme. Blavatsky: There are very many things I may have in my mind, and which I don't like to make public. There may be such.

Mr. Kingsland: I think Mr. Holt ought to tell us why he says there are the same number of atoms in the body as in Cosmos.

Mr. Holt: I was regarding the Earth and the solar system as but an atom; it was relatively. Each system might be regarded as but an atom of the whole Cosmos, just as we are but atoms of our permanent Earth with respect to our bodies.

Mr. Kingsland: Do you say every individual is an atom?

Mr. Holt: The mathematical idea of the atom is the least conceivable, not the least demonstrable—so that you see I am not begging the question. We may conceive the great and the small, and they are the same size in the noumenal. Are they not?

Mr. Kingsland: But when you compare the individual Cosmos, you are not working on that plane, you are working on the plane of manifestation.

Mr. Holt: I use it in that sense, but it was not until HPB gave us her definition of the atom that I thoroughly understood what was intended. If it is the mathematical atom, then I say just as many, I mean metaphysically.

Mr. B. Keightley: The peculiarity of the mathematical point definition is, it has not got a size at all, neither bigness or smallness.

Mr. Holt: Therefore, it may be all or it may be nothing, so that is really why I said the man has so many atoms.

Mme. Blavatsky: You said it simply kabalistically, as "the microcosm of the macrocosm."

Mr. A. Keightley: Question 11, footnote, {See *Secret Doctrine*, I:143†, implies} "Force is a state of matter." Are forces atomic and molecular, though supersensuous? The phrase used appears to imply Occultists make no distinction between force and matter. Is this the case? Please enlarge and explain.

Mme. Blavatsky: Still I say force as manifested on this plane is a state of matter. What would you call radiant matter, if not a state of matter? But the energy which produces the state of matter is perfectly the same as force. Call it force or energy, we consider it as a state of matter on this plane, for it cannot act without matter being present, and these two cannot be diverse. What force is on the other plane is quite a different thing, but I mean on this one, I say it is an electric state, that is what I say. Every force that is produced, to whatever it is applied, we call an electric force. It is a function of the whole universal electric ocean which acts. Do you understand my meaning?

Mr. Kingsland: Not thoroughly.

Mme. Blavatsky: As I don't know how science regards it this year, I am unable to make a comparison. I know how it regarded it last year, but it changes, you know, like an atom.

Mr. Holt: You admit of primordial substance, with the one absolute life moving or energizing in that substance?

Mme. Blavatsky: Most assuredly.

Mr. Holt: Then we may regard that as distinct ideal, but always co-existent and omnipresent.

Mme. Blavatsky: Certainly. I say that force on this plane is matter, a state of matter, at least; it has a function, a quality of matter—not of that matter on which it acts, but of the matter in general, of the Universal matter of the substance of the universal substance. Call it life, call it electricity, call it Fohat, call it whatever you like; it is always Fohat.

Mr. Holt: Would you then say that all cosmical force, as for instance planetary influence, is nothing else than the radiation of matter?

Mme. Blavatsky: It is the radiation of something, though for us it may not be matter, and we have no right to call it matter; yet it is matter on that plane, substance, call it if you like.

Mr. Holt: That would agree with the statement you made to me the other night, that everything is touch; thus, for instance, we might call light which is perceptible to the optic nerve, we might call it a force.

Mme. Blavatsky: I think it is more physical science, that wants to make the first one; but touch is something else than what is meant here. Who spoke to me about touch? I think Mr. Kingsland. One night here when we were talking about the first sense, which must be the touch.

Mr. Kingsland: Dr. Williams.

Mme. Blavatsky: But the way he explained it was not at all as we explain, it is touch, everything is touch. Taste and smell are touch, because everything must be touched in some way to produce or to put that particular sense into function or vibration, or whatever you call it—into activity, therefore, I say that force is certainly a state of matter, and what objections have you to what I say? In that question I mean.

Mr. A. Keightley: What I wanted to understand is this. Supposing we see, for instance, a matchbox. That is force manifested on this plane, isn't it? It represents force.

Mr. Holt: It is force taking form, perhaps.

Mr. A. Keightley: But it is force.

Mme. Blavatsky: Nothing can manifest itself without force.

Mr. B. Keightley: Crystallized force.

Mr. A. Keightley: It is force, in the static state.

Mme. Blavatsky: You should say better as the Buddhist philosophers say, the concatenation of force and effect. It is force.

Mr. B. Keightley: You see, the ordinary idea of force is that which changes or tends to change. The state of matter which moves matter, shortly.

Mme. Blavatsky: This is the inherent energy, the inherent motion, which tends to change, and not at all force. Force is everything, because you cannot produce the smallest little effect without the cause of it being some force used—intellectual, moral, physical, psychical, any way you like. And what is force? It is the incessant action of what we call the one life, the one motion, the great motion which never ceases, which always goes on in the universe.

Mr. Holt: Then you would say it was always moving in primordial matter?

Mme. Blavatsky: Always. Even during Pralaya it is going on. There is no one to see it, or take notice of it, of how many vibrations, but still it is.

Mr. Kingsland: Now, take light, for instance, and radiant heat. Is that an actual movement of particles of matter from the object which emits the light and heat to us?

Mme. Blavatsky: I don't know. You see, our ideas of light are quite different.

Mr. B. Keightley: Let us leave light out and deal with heat.

Mme. Blavatsky: You have your own preconceived ideas furnished you by science. You have science as the grand priest, the high priest and initiator of all your ideas. You are obliged and in honour bound to accept everything that the Royal College or Royal Fellows tell you. We, on the other hand, are, so to say, the ostracized ignoramuses, the occultists; we have our own ideas, our own science; therefore I, being one of the humblest and most ignorant of those ignoramuses, cannot come and base what I tell you and give you always illustrations from science, because I don't know anything about it.

Mr. B. Keightley: But I think what Kingsland is driving at is this: we have certain erroneous ideas put into our heads, and we are obliged to use the same language which is familiar to us.

Mme. Blavatsky: But if I don't know it?

Mr. B. Keightley: What I think he wanted to get at was, wanting you to explain as far as you could, the way in which occultism would teach about this communication of heat, for instance, from, say, a red hot lamp or anything that is hot.

Mme. Blavatsky: Just in the same way as colour or sound is produced or any force which becomes manifested and apparent. We teach it as all coming from the Dhyan-Chohans.

Mr. ———: Isn't it molecular, though?

Mme. Blavatsky: It may be; everything is molecular if you call molecular that it is something. Of course I know what you mean by molecular, even in science.

Mr. Kingsland: What I wanted to get at was this: science conceives of the transmission of light as a transmission through a certain medium. Supposing you have a long stick, and you hit one end of it without the stick as a whole moving—you have the transmission of the knock from one end to the other. There is nothing transferred from this end to the other end. We wish to know whether it is the same in the case of light, or whether there is actually a transfer of particles from the radiant object to us.

Mme. Blavatsky: I say there is transfer of particles.

Mr. Holt: Are they transmitted as light shines through glass? Do these transmitted particles pass through the glass?

Mme. Blavatsky: These particles can pass through anything. All these things are nothing to them. It is just the same as the spirit passing through a wall.

Mr. Holt: It does not partake of the nature of matter. It is matter, but on another plane.

Mr. Gardner: Although it manifests on this plane.

Mme. Blavatsky: It manifests—not in particles, because they are not particles in our sense, but they are rays, they are radiant energies. It is very difficult to explain. They are emanations or breaths. I am afraid you won't understand me.

Mr. B. Keightley: There was a great dispute that went on between somebody and Newton, who had this theory, the corpuscular theory; he formulated it. Then that has been superseded in the opinion of modern science by the [ ] theory of waves and vibrations along the stick.

Mme. Blavatsky: The corpuscular theory as it was presented by Newton, and the wave theory—the one that stands now through the ether that they were obliged to admit they took them from the ancients, however disagreeable it was for them—both of them are wrong. In both, according to occultism, there are right premises, and yet wrong conclusions. The thing is all muddled up both ways. It is excessively difficult, but perhaps in time we will come and coin words for things that you will have understood well; but until we have coined these words—upon my word, it seems almost hopeless to explain to you. For instance, I have had an idea perfectly clear and perfectly true to me; I know what it is. How can I explain it to you, even if I had at my command all the technical expressions used in physical science, and so on? I cannot, because there are not such expressions in existence.

Mr. Kingsland: No, but there are always analogies.

Mme. Blavatsky: But the analogy is very different for me. I am not at all of a scientific mind. I never learnt modern science in my life. All that I know is simply by reading, and sometimes not paying great attention to it. I know in some cases I had to learn, because I had to refute and I had to disprove it, but in general, I don't know; it does not interest me, because I know it is a flapdoodle, which will change tomorrow. Why should I go and cobweb my brain by learning all the lucubrations? Every day they invent something else, and on the following day you have to modify it or make away with it, or insult it in some way or other. I don't want to learn anything more, because one has the trouble of learning and unlearning. For you men of science who follow it, it is very easy—you remember the things you give up—but upon my word, I have too much of the occult theories that I have to learn and explain to you to go and bother myself with the physical science, which I hate.

Mr. Holt: May we pass on to the second part of that question, and ask whether this matter in its various forms is contactable on any plane, providing we have the requisite senses? And then I may supplement the question by: "Do we have the relative senses, even in the Nirvana?"

Mme. Blavatsky: Well, for the Nirvanic effect, certainly; but they call it Nirvanic. What does it mean? It means "a flame blown out"— Nir-vana, no more, nothing. It is like a wind that passes and blows out everything. There is an entire disappearance of everything like the matter we know of on earth, not only matter, but even of our attributes, functions, feelings, everything, nothing of the kind can go on in Nirvana. Therefore, they misunderstood the thing and they said it was annihilation, which is perfect nonsense.

Mr. Holt: But there is individual consciousness still retained, is there not?

Mme. Blavatsky: Not the individual consciousness of the present, but universal consciousness, in which the individual consciousness is a part. You see, it is quite a different thing, that. When you reach Nirvana you are the whole, the Absoluteness.

Mr. Gardner: But you are differentiated, all the same.

Mme. Blavatsky: Absolute differentiates? My goodness!

Mr. Holt: Then what is Paranirvana?

Mme. Blavatsky: Paranirvana differs from Nirvana because we are in the Absolute, which is just beyond the plane where differentiation begins. And Paranirvana is something which is beyond the Meta, of which you can know nothing. You come from Nirvana back into a new Maha-Manvantara, when there is Paranirvana. Then there is the end of all; and nobody has ever calculated what shall be afterwards. That is the whole difference, philosophically.

Mr. Holt: What is the Buddhist name of the state where individual consciousness first manifests itself, coming out of Nirvana, towards the plane of matter?

Mme. Blavatsky: I don't know what you mean.

Mr. Holt: You say that individual consciousness is annihilated, except as it is preserved in the Absolute. So far as individuality is concerned, the sons of the "I am" that is apart from the Absolute, that is annihilated in Nirvana?

Mme. Blavatsky: Certainly it is annihilated. The "I am that I am," that is to say, I am all, I am absolute. You are not then old {Holt}, but you are every blessed thing that there ever was, is, or will be; for what is it? You just make for yourself an idea of Absoluteness.

Mr. Holt: Does the identity merge itself into the Absolute?

Mme. Blavatsky: On our conceptions, it is no longer, but it is identity; it is a very abstruse metaphysical problem, this. You must understand this. If you conceive of deity as Absoluteness, or if you conceive of deity with attributes, then this deity cannot be infinite, it would be everlasting; it had a beginning and it had an end. Such are the Manvantaric Gods, those which are during the life cycle. The Absoluteness is that which is, to our minds, at least, immutable— which never had a beginning nor will ever have an end, which is omnipresent, which is absolute everything. And when we say of that Absoluteness that it is absolutely unconscious, absolutely without any desire, without any thought, it is because we mean and must mean that it is absolute consciousness, absolute desire, absolute love, absolute everything. Now you see how difficult is this thing to conceive. Those who have been brought up in a theology which limits and conditions everything, and makes and dwarfs everything that there is—the grandest things in the world—and those who, like the men of science, don't believe in anything but the limited and conditioned—they cannot conceive of anything which is not that. Therefore, occultism has to struggle with science and with more materialistic theologies yet, because the man of science holds to his department and he does his duty. He says: "I am incapable of understanding or believing; I am going to hold to that which my five senses show to me"; but the theologians who, at the same time claiming that God is infinite, God is endless, and God is absolute mercy and justice, gives to that absolute attributes, makes his God to be revengeful and make mistakes, repent that he has made man, do all kinds of things, and yet he will call him absolute and endless. This is where comes in this terrible, unphilosophical and illogical thing, which has neither head nor tail, which is a perfect, flat contradiction of everything. If you want to have it in a philosophical way, you have to take the Vendantin way of seeing things, but if you come to the theologians of the West, you are lost.

Mr. ——: Those are accommodations of truth.

Mme. Blavatsky: Not they, because you can do just the same as they do in India: they had to make accommodations for the minds of the poor Hindus, who are ignorant but there are no such contradictions. They say God. One will worship Vishnu, the other Shiva, the other anything you like, but they will never say these gods are endless and never had a beginning or an end. They will say the gods die, and Brahmâ at the end of Manvantara goes into Pralaya, and there remains only the one, to which they don't give a name, but they call "That," because, they say, "we cannot give it a name, it is that which ever was, is and will be and cannot not be." So you see how philosophical they are, much more philosophical than we are. I cannot understand even Herbert Spencer, speaking of the one deity and then calling it the "first cause" and calling it the "supreme cause." How is it possible?

Mr. ——: They are trying to comprehend things that are beyond the plane of their capacities.

Mme. Blavatsky: Most assuredly. That which is absolute, which is infinite, cannot have any attributes or anything; it is perfectly unphilosophical to speak of it in such a way as that. You cannot come and give any relations to that which is absolute, because the Absolute positively can have no relations and nothing to do with the conditioned; all this must be a thing entirely apart. When they ask me how is this, that this emanated, I say it emanates not at all, because if the supreme or the Heavenly father wants to emanate, it is simply because it is the Eternal law, the law of nights and days, as they speak of Brahmâ. There it is the breath, that principle, that law—and there is something which appears, the universe appears. I say it is a most magnificent and sublime conception of the Deity.

Mr. ——: The highest conceptions of the truth we have are not absolute truth. We can only take in what we are capable of taking in.

Mme. Blavatsky: That is why I say there is no one thing that is absolute and that we cannot speculate upon.

Mr. ——: And we are trying to talk about things about which we have no words.

Mme. Blavatsky: On this plane it may be speculation, but that which has no relation whatever to any ideas we have in our heads it is a perfect impossibility to speculate upon. That is why the Hindus call it "That"; they call it the one darkness, when it manifests in it but the rays. Then there is the manifestation and the creation, as they call it, the evolution of the world.

Mr. A. Keightley: Question 12. "Seven small wheels—one giving birth to the other." In view of the diagram on page 172 of Earth and Lunar chains, does this mean that globe A gives birth to globe B within our planetary Ring?

Mme. Blavatsky: It does most decidedly. One principle goes out after another from the dying planet and generates a globe, as each principle generates another, except the physical body; for both are the productions of the Lunar Kama-rupa. Now that which I mean to say is, it means our planetary chain. And in *Esoteric Buddhism*, you will find that this wave of life, as he calls it, as it passes on, and when one is formed, then the other begins forming; and then one goes into obscuration, and they go one after the other. They emanate, because, if you have to believe what the occult sciences teach, namely, that our Earth is a production of the Moon that is a little bit of mud—well, it is a question of preference. But if you have to believe the occult doctrine, then every principle goes one after the other. There comes the first principle, that lives {leaves} when the Moon begins dying, which produces globe A; then the other can produce globe B, and so on. It goes in a round, the middle one being the Lunar Kama-rupa, that is to say, the seat of material things.

Mr. B. Keightley: You see the diagram as it is drawn; you remember how it is, the two chains side by side. Then A projects its principles into A of the Earth chain, but the phrase used there in the commentary seems to suggest that instead of going that way, that A being established, then from A came the next planet on our chain B and A of its own plane.

Mme. Blavatsky: A produces A, B produces B, and so on.

Mr. B. Keightley: The words of the Stanza seem to suggest that A produces B.

Mme. Blavatsky: It must have been done by some of you six or seven editors.

Mr. B. Keightley: It is the words of the Stanzas, but there are no alterations made. It looks as if in English it meant each wheel of a succeeding wheel.

Mme. Blavatsky: Don't be so very fine. I may give it, and then you can change it if you like.

Mr. B. Keightley: It was only to find out whether anything wanted explaining.

Mme. Blavatsky: No; one wheel it means, one globe giving birth to the other.

Mr. B. Keightley: In two successive chains?

Mr. A. Keightley: Question 13, page 145. With reference to what was said last Thursday about nebulæ being collectively Fohatic affinity, what is the relation of a Laya centre to such nebulæ?

Mme. Blavatsky: Here comes Laya centre again. None whatever. A Laya point is a little absoluteness of its own and can have no relations to differentiated things, so far as I know. It is a state in a point, moreover. It is neither a point nor a triangle nor any geometrical figure at all. It is simply called the Laya point to show the Laya state. It is a state—Laya—and not at all anything that can be indicated by any geometrical figure whatever.

Mr. A. Keightley: Question 14, "…four and one Tsan (fraction) revealed—two and one half concealed…" Is there a distinctive separation into two parts of manifestation of the fifth element, corresponding to the separation of the Higher from Lower Manas?

Mme. Blavatsky: Yes there is. But you know this is a very abstruse question, in which you cannot go tonight. This is a thing which certainly it is, because if there is any analogy in nature it must be so; but we certainly cannot go into it tonight.

Mr. ———: Were the occultists aware that there were eight planets?

Mme. Blavatsky: They knew a great deal more. They simply speak about seven planets. They took the Earth and the Sun as substitutes, because they had planets of which our science now has vaguely and dimly an idea. There is one of the most sacred planets, the second one, which corresponded {to} that body which they take Mercury for. And it is the one between Mercury and the Sun.

Mr. ———: Is there one there?

Mme. Blavatsky: Most assuredly there is, and they searched for it, and they suspected it, and they cannot find it.

Mr. ———: That is to say, it is not visible to the physical sight.

Mme. Blavatsky: It is visible, but it is in its last obscuration. It will be seen from Mercury. It will be a moon, when there will be some other planet produced. There are figures for it.

Mr. Gardner: By what name was it known?

Mme. Blavatsky: Oh, you would like to know it! Ask your instructor. I don't know it, so I cannot tell you. They wanted to call it Vulcan; they say that they suspected. I don't know what some of them said; others deny it.

Mr. Gardner: When the eclipse came?

Mme. Blavatsky: They thought there was something. I don't think it is anything.

Mr. ———: Does that make it invisible, being in obscuration?

Mme. Blavatsky: It may come again, you understand, but it is in its last brightness. It is as the Moon was before, because the Moon was far less visible than it is now. Now it vampirizes the Earth, but before it didn't have to vampirize anything; and it was in its last degree of consumption.

Mr. Holt: I don't think its luminosity would have anything to do with its visibility to this Earth. The darker it were the better for us, because we should see it against the Sun's disc.

Mr. B. Keightley: But they do fancy they caught a glimpse of it during the eclipse.

Mr. Gardner: Do you say the Moon vampirizes on us?

Mme. Blavatsky: Certainly, it does. All the moons and all the parents vampirize on their children in this space.

Mr. Gardner: Saturn's moon and Jupiter's too?

Mme. Blavatsky: They are all the same; no altruism among them; It is the survival of the fittest in nature. It is only men who ought not to have this.

Mr. ——: Have you any theory as to the numerous minor planets?

Mr. B. Keightley: 178 or more of them. Planetoi {Planetoids?}, it is.

Mme. Blavatsky: There is not the smallest star that is not personified. You may believe how many when even exoterically they give 330 million of gods, and every one of these gods, is a star—a visible star or planet.

Mr. B. Keightley: And has a story.

Mme. Blavatsky: Now the astronomers have not got more than 60,000 stars.

Mr. B. Keightley: They have got some millions.

Mr. Holt: Taking the zodiac, 218,000,000.

Mme. Blavatsky: And the Hindus have 330,000,000, and every one of them has its history and its place and space.

Mr. Kingsland: Has its life and adventures.

Mme. Blavatsky: Yes; I bring it in, because every god is connected with a star, that is why. Oh, they knew all; I can assure you they are a wonderful people. Why is it that they knew perfectly, without any telescopes or instruments, the seven Pleiades—the seventh sister which now has disappeared, and you can hardly see it with the best telescope? And they knew it perfectly, and it had not disappeared in their day. Therefore calculate how many thousand years they must have had this astronomers' knowledge.

Mr. B. Keightley: Their tables for the Moon's motion, which have been absolutely proved to have been obtained by independent data, are more accurate than the very best modern tables.

Mme. Blavatsky: Surely, it is wonderful, and they have no telescopes. What had they? The most rudimentary things, yet see how they knew it, because in the temples and the hierophants, the twice-born, they had all the things a thousand times better than we have now; but they don't speak of it; it is gone. It was sacred with them. They did not make a speculation of it simply on the material plane, as they do here. It was their religion, their most sacred doctrine. Certainly they did not give it to the *hoi polloi*.

Mr. Holt: They would not have needed telescopes to see these things. Could not they have seen them astrally?

Mme. Blavatsky: In the Pleiades, they disappeared. You cannot see them now without a telescope.

Mr. Holt: It has its astral counterpart. It is double. Then they could see.

Mme. Blavatsky: They can see not only that, they had their seers, but they had astronomers likewise.

Mr. Gardner: They had their instruments, as well.

Mme. Blavatsky: They are what Proctor[4] writes about of the knowledge of the Chaldeans and the Egyptians.

Mr. Gardner: Did they have any force like Keely's force?

Mme. Blavatsky: That is not much. I suppose every yogi could produce Keely's force.

Mr. B. Keightley: There is not anything well-confirmed about this idea. I think it is flapdoodle. He might use it in some way to increase the power of perception, but I don't see how he can use his vibrating ether as a telescope. Somebody asserted that Keely could make use of his vibratory forces as a telescope.

Mr. A. Keightley: Hartmann[5] said he had seen it. He said that he could just be looking down the tube after reflecting this force or

---
4 R. A. Proctor, English astronomer, 1837-1888. HPB cites his *Myths and Marvels of Astronomy*, 1878, in *The Secret Doctrine*.
5 Franz Hartmann, German theosophist, author and physician, 1838-1912.

getting it in some way on to it, he could make a bacillus the size of an orange.

Mr. Gardner: What magnitude is that?

Mr. A. Keightley: I don't know how many thousandth parts of an inch it measures, I mean the microscope. If you can get Keely's power to magnify that sort of size, you can surely apply the same principle to a telescope.

Mr. B. Keightley: Yes, if you can do it.

Mr. Holt: I don't see the application of it.

Mr. A. Keightley: Hartmann said he had seen it.

Mme. Blavatsky: He says only one thing that has attracted your attention, and he says one thing which sounds very much like our theory, only he expresses it in other words. He says that the Sun is a dead planet. I say that it looks very much like that that we say. The Sun, nobody has ever seen; it is simply the shadow of the real Sun, which is perfectly invisible and certainly in this sense, you can call it dead. You have the rays of light, and the shadow is strong.

Mr. ———: It throws up enormous fountains of molten matter.

Mme. Blavatsky: He gives his reason for it, and I say that which occultism teaches. I say, it is not the Sun we see; we see the shadow, the screen, the phantom; the real Sun is not seen at all.

The proceedings here closed.

14.
Theosophical Society.
Meeting of the Blavatsky Lodge
17 Lansdowne Road, Holland Park, W.
Thursday, April 11, 1889.

Mr. Kingsland in the Chair.

Mr. B. Keightley: Page 143 {142}, line 7 of *The Secret Doctrine*, you say: "Neither Water, Air, Earth (Synonym for solids generally.) existed in their present form, representing the three states of matter alone recognized by Science; for all these are the productions already recombined by the atmospheres of globes completely formed—even to fire—so that in the first periods of the Earth's formation they were something quite *sui generis.* Now that the conditions and laws ruling our solar system are fully developed; and that the atmosphere of our Earth, as of every other globe, has become, so to say, a crucible of its own, Occult Science teaches that there is a perpetual exchange taking place in space of molecules, or of atoms rather, correlating, and thus changing their combining equivalents on every planet." Question 1 (a): This long sentence requires further elucidation. What, for instance, must we understand by "the productions already combined"? How recombined? How do the atmospheres of globes effect this recombination? Why "even to fire"? In what aspect are they *sui generis* in the first periods of the Earth's formation?

Mme. Blavatsky: Why do you ask such long questions? Can't you put them like that—you know, A, B, C, D—as you used to do before?

Mr. B. Keightley: Because it is really all referring to the same subject.

Mme. Blavatsky: I will answer about the productions. The

productions referred to are the differentiations of the primordial elements, water, air, fire, matter or earth, etcetera, which have all been very naturally combined in new forms in the atmosphere of the many globes they came in contact with—globes certainly anterior to our Earth by long eons of time. That is how they were recombined. How recombined, you ask? By the special crucible of each particular globe, recombined by heat, of course, by the internal fire latent in every form of every element, whether on this or the highest plane. Fire is spirit, the soul of things, whether in the form of Fohat or electricity or that magneto vital force which makes the plant grow. The term atmosphere in occultism does not mean the air we breathe; it applies to that Fohatic radiation or aura, which extends far beyond the limits of respirable air. This atmosphere is almost homogeneous, being the purest ether, or the seventh principle of that which on our Earth is the first or lowest principle, namely, breathable air. Well?

Mr. B. Keightley: Question 1 (b): How is the atmosphere of our Earth a crucible of its own?

Mme. Blavatsky: Between any two planets—say between the Earth and the Moon—there is a regular gradation of density and purity in the etheric atmosphere which lies between the two. It commences on a planet with the densely material air, which is the rupa, or body of ether, and is as opaque to the light of its higher principle as the body of man is to the light of the Divine Spirit. From that material darkness the etheric atmosphere shades off gradually, till it reaches a point of—say, the perfect brightness or luminosity. This is the Laya point, or line on our plane, of the atmosphere between two planets. It is the condition of Laya which preserves the due equilibrium between the planets and prevents them being precipitated one upon the other. Therefore, in occult science it is impossible for anything in the shape of a material body to pass from one planet to another. From the occult standpoint, the fallacy of the meteorite theory is great indeed. Now have you got any questions, if you understand that which I said?

Mr. Kingsland: It would almost appear from that first answer to that question that the chemical elements as we know them now have not been differentiated, so to speak, but they have gone through a lot of processes on other globes.

Mme. Blavatsky: Most assuredly. I believe these diagrams drawn by Crookes are very fine on this plane, but certainly they have no rapport at all, no relation to the first differentiation from primordial matter. This I have never regarded.

Mr. Kingsland: Our idea—or rather mine—has been that the chemical elements have been differentiated from the cosmic fire mists *in situ*, so to speak, on this globe.

Mme. Blavatsky: No, not on this globe; every one of them has passed. Matter is eternal, and all this whatever-it-is that goes and whirls about is once concerned with one globe, then with another body on this plane, on the other and so on, until it goes down to our plane, which is the lowest.

Mr. B. Keightley: So that all the matter that we know and perceive practically has passed through an endless series of combinations before it reaches our plane of perception state?

Mme. Blavatsky: Most assuredly, because you could never see it; you could never perceive or sense it.

Mr. B. Keightley: Even, for instance, when Thomas Vaughan[1] said: "no man had ever seen Earth," he was not speaking of earth in the sense of the primordial differentiation.

Mme. Blavatsky: He was speaking about here. "No man had seen Earth." Don't forget that—that it has to pass from the seventh or the highest to the lowest, which is our Earth, to the first. Why, our Earth was created—this planetary chain—milliards and milliards after others. This is one of the things; and you see how many millions they give in the occult science. If you look at their calculations of the yugas in the Manvantara and so on, why it makes the brains whirl,

---

1 Thomas Vaughan, Welsh philosopher and mystical writer, 1621-1666.

so to say, and get giddy to read those things.

Mr. Kingsland: On the last plane of all, take iron, for instance. Has that become iron on this globe, or was it iron before this globe?

Mme. Blavatsky: Take iron or take anything you like, it was, and all comes from, one and the same essence. One has become iron in reaching our globe, and another thing has become something else, and the third something else, and so on. But all these were the same thing. The essence of iron is no more than the purest ether.

Mr. Kingsland: But the material substance only became this on this globe?

Mme. Blavatsky: Yes, it can only be within our atmosphere; therefore, the occult sciences say, it is a perfect impossibility, the speculation of this science, that the meteorites fall sometimes from a planet, because they cannot pass the Laya point. There is the thing which begins: it is dense, it is as black as night in comparison; it is between the Moon and this Earth. It begins quite black, then grey, then lighter and lighter, and lighter, until it reaches the Laya point, and from the Laya point it begins to be darker and darker and darker, until it becomes as black as possible. Therefore, between every plane {planet?} there is the atmosphere and that which is beyond—not the breathable air, but the atmosphere; nobody breathed it, because you could not. If you went into a balloon you could not pass a certain point; there would be a certain stage where you would immediately die and be suffocated.

Mr. Kingsland: Then the "atmosphere" there is used in the purely occult sense, whereas, naturally, anyone reading it would take it as the ordinary atmosphere?

Mme. Blavatsky: I try to put in the words that everyone would understand. I did not use occult words there.

Mr. Gardner: Then we really see the stars through this atmosphere?

Mme. Blavatsky: But we don't see them as they are; it is a Maya, it is a regular Maya of vapors and things that prevent us seeing. It is all nothing but hallucination and illusion.

Mr. Gardner: Are not they really the distance off that the astronomers say?

Mme. Blavatsky: I don't believe in it.

Mr. Gardner: How about these meteoric signs?

Mme. Blavatsky: Have patience, and I will tell you. The meteors are, as a general rule, fragments of broken planets or comets. Once a planet is broken up, the Laya centres, which separate it from other planets, or the Laya line rather, I would say, disappears. It shifts its position so as to find itself between two planets which remain intact. You understand? You put our Earth, then there is a planet and then there is a third planet; the atmosphere begins dense here; it comes here, and there is the Laya between the line, and then it becomes dark here (illustrating). Then this is broken up, and immediately it goes and will form this between other planets, the next planet and the Earth.

Mr. Kingsland: It will spread out on the Laya point?

Mme. Blavatsky: It shifts its position so as to find itself between two planets which remain intact. The result is that some fragments of the broken planet remain in the old orbit of the destroyed planet. Thus, of course, when the Earth crosses the former orbit of that planet, any fragments that are brought within its attraction fall to the Earth as meteors. Did you understand, Mr. Old?

Mr. Old: I merely wish to ask whether this planetary disruption, which is the cause of cometary masses, is contrary to the general rule? It appears that the general rule is, in the formation of a body, gradually to transfer its vitality to another and thus to die out; but here we have a case where a planet coming between the equilibrating forces upon both sides goes into a state of disruption and splits up. This is contrary to the general rule, is it not?

Mme. Blavatsky: No, it is not. Because, the Moon it will happen to, as soon as it has nothing more—no force even to try to vampirise the Earth. The Moon will be just in that position; then it will be disrupted. It is most probable that the Earth will have some other moon, or we will go without, so that the poets will not be able to compose their pretty verses to their beloved, and everything will go on as usual.

Mr. Gardner: Some of the pieces of the Moon will come down on this Earth.

Mme. Blavatsky: I hope it will not come on my nose. I will be dead and gone by that time, though.

Mr. B. Keightley: As a rule, the cometary state of a planetary body is before it becomes a planet.

Mr. Old: Yes, but we are talking of the meteors now, not of the comets.

Mme. Blavatsky: You see, it differs so much from real, official science that really, a man of science, a physicist, or an astronomer, if he were here listening to us, would say we are all lunatics. But I teach you the occult doctrine, and I think it is on the whole—if you learn it from A to Z—you will find it is certainly worth the speculations of science, and that it gives far more rational explanations, and even fills up all the gaps and missing links.

Mr. B. Keightley: There is one point about the meteors. You find in meteorites exactly the same minerals, metals and so on that you find on Earth, and indistinguishable by any of the tests that chemistry, at any rate can apply, or spectroscope analysis.

Mme. Blavatsky: You will remember the passage from *The Secret Doctrine*, that a planet only breaks up after life has entirely left it, when it is even more dead than the Moon is now; that is to say, only after Seventh and last Round. Witness the Moon. Mind you, it is long eons after the Seventh Round; not directly. This accounts for the complete absence of any traces of life, or organic remains in the meteor; is it that that you want?

Mr. B. Keightley: You said a little while ago, in speaking about the elements, that they were so completely differentiated from any of our terrestrial elements. When a meteor falls to the Earth, you find it contains its constituents, the minerals and so on, and they are almost without exception the same as we find on Earth.

Mme. Blavatsky: Most assuredly, because as soon as they get on the atmosphere they change, and there is a kind of correlation, transformation—say what you like. This is what the Master taught Mr. Sinnett, of all these things. As soon as it comes, it goes beyond our atmosphere; it comes within the advantages of our atmosphere, and this atmosphere is a crucible—to which you just objected—because it changes everything that comes within it.

Mr. Old: When a planet is disrupted—and you say part of it may remain in the same orbit after the other planet died—does it continue to revolve round in just the same way as the original planet did, this fragment that remains?

Mme. Blavatsky: Yes, it has a motion of its own, but I don't think it dies; it falls in a kind of chaotic whirl.

Mr. Gardner: Supposing, for example, Jupiter was to come within the orbit of this disrupted meteor, that would leave a certain portion of it, the same as it does here.

Mme. Blavatsky: What applies to our planet applies to every planet.

Mr. Gardner: Would they have the same chemical combination?

Mme. Blavatsky: This I don't know. I cannot tell you what I don't know.

Mr. B. Keightley: The point raised before was that the elements—the substance of the matter—differed from one planet and the other.

Mme. Blavatsky: They will be remodeled according to the atmosphere.

Mr. Gardner: It does not change very quickly through the Laya point.

Mme. Blavatsky: Through the Laya point they cannot go; it is impossible. That is why I say that this theory, "that Mars fell down from some planet," is from the standpoint of occultism perfectly untenable, for it cannot pass the Laya point. If it did, it would be dissolved, it would exist no more; in the Laya point it cannot move, it is a negation of all movement.

Mr. Gardner: I cannot see that. You have potash and lime, and so on.

Mr. B. Keightley: Why should not they perform in the Earth's atmosphere?

Mme. Blavatsky: There is the occult student (Mr. B. Keightley), ask him.

Mr. B. Keightley: If you take a mineral out of a smelting furnace, you find all sorts of chemical combinations, lime and all sorts of things formed there, which are formed out of other substances which have been exposed to violent heat. Well, you get combinations, all sorts of combinations, formed out of what are to us unknown elements.

Mr. Gardner: You get different metals in these meteorites.

Mr. B. Keightley: Which enter into the material of the Earth. It is not a pot made of fire-clay, you know. It has the function of a crucible.

Mr. Hall: Then these meteors may be said to have in them certain potentialities, which, when they come within the crucible of this Earth, produce the metals that we know?

Mr. B. Keightley: Precisely. At least, that is the way I understand that.

Mr. Gardner: Then, if they get into the crucible of another planet?

Mr. B. Keightley: They would form others.

Mme. Blavatsky: There is something I took from the first question. "In what aspects are elements *sui generis?*" I answer, first, because no one period resembles the other, and secondly, because the First Round of every chain differs entirely from the subsequent {that} will appear subsequently. There is a greater difference between the First and Second Rounds of a Manvantara than between any two subsequent rounds. Then question (b) is: "How is the atmosphere of our Earth a crucible of its own?" That has already been answered as far as it can be done, so that this settles the first question.

Mr. Keightley: Had you anything more about the meteors which you have not read?

Mme. Blavatsky: No, I have read everything about the meteors; I just answered as much as there was there.

Mr. Hall: Will you give any explanation of the reason why there is so much more difference between the first and second Manvantara?

Mme. Blavatsky: No, I won't, because it will take us till tomorrow morning.

Mr. B. Keightley: It comes into the thing we go into about the Moon later on. Question 2. (a) Can you give us any instance of the atoms correlating and thus changing their combining equivalents? (b) What is meant by "combining equivalents," in this sense?

Mme. Blavatsky: I use the word "atoms" here not in the occult sense, but in that given to it by physical science, which speaks of an atom of iron, of hydrogen, and so on. *The Secret Doctrine* is not an occult book, as I told you, but a printed work for the public. What is meant by the terms "correlating," or "molecules changing their combining equivalents," is that the relations between what science calls atoms and molecules of our elements differ from planet to planet; therefore "b" in question 2 is also answered. That is all I can tell you. Has anyone to ask any questions—some of the physicists? Mr. Williams, have you nothing to say? Mr. Williams does not.

Mr. Williams: No, thank you, I have no questions to ask. I thought you were speaking of the other Mr. Williams, the doctor.

Mr. B. Keightley: Question 3. Page 143, line 10. Can you explain at all what is meant by "a current of efflux"?

Mme. Blavatsky: Which means that I am sat upon for using the word efflux.

Mr. B. Keightley: No, no, you are asked to explain what you mean.

Mme. Blavatsky: In physical science a current of efflux is a current of matter on one and the same plane, whatever its attraction. In occult science a current of efflux means a current passing from one plane to another, whether higher or lower. This efflux is not an objective movement in our third dimensional space, but a change of state from space without to space within, or vice-versa. Do you understand that? You see, in occult language it means quite a different thing.

Mr. Kingsland: It is change in differentiation.

Mme. Blavatsky: It is change from one plane to another.

Mr. B. Keightley: Question 4. Is the Laya centre that condition of primordial substance at which, or in which, Absolute Motion takes the specific name of Fohat? Or is Fohat the sum of the seven radical forces, in the same sense that Mahat is the sum of the seven intelligences of the Manvantara, called the "Seven Sons"?

Mme. Blavatsky: The Laya centre of primordial substance has everything else the side of it, or is the reflection of Absolute Motion, which adjective implies that it is equally Absolute rest or Non-Motion. In occult philosophy the Absolute can have no attributes; therefore the adjective, Absolute, permits of no nouns. Fohat is the collective radiation of the Seven Sons, but the Seven Sons are themselves the third degree of manifestation. Fohat is not the synthesis or the sum of the seven radical forces, but their collective radiation. That which has a right to the name, or the synthesis of the sum of seven radical forces, is the second Logos, considered as the unity of the seven Logoi, or the seven primordial rays, which we call the Seven Sons. Mahat, in its turn, is a reflection on a higher plane of the divine ideation; on a lower one, Mahat corresponds to the higher Manas in man, and divine ideation is Buddhi. One is the mind, whether of cosmos or man, the cosmic and human soul; the other the spiritual soul in the universe, the macrocosm of man, its microcosm. Now, ask questions about that, because I see you do not understand that, Mr. Old.

Mr. Old: I had conceived, from my reading of *The Secret Doctrine*, the idea that Fohat stood in the same relation to the seven radical forces as Mahat did to the seven Rishis or Logoi.

Mme. Blavatsky: So it does on this plane, but on the others not, because I say to you that Fohat is simply not the synthesis, he is the collective radiation of the seven—what we call Builders, but on the higher plane, Fohat is no more that. He is also a collective radiation, not of the Builders, but of the Seven Sons of Mahat. What is Mahat? It is the intelligent—how shall I say—reflection of what we call divine ideation, that which Plato calls divine ideation, just in the same sense, because Plato gives the purely esoteric oriental doctrine. So you understand, now, the difference. If you ask a question, you must always ask whether it is on this plane or any other, because on every plane it changes, it alters its name, its functions and everything; that is why it is so difficult for someone who does not know the things.

Mr. Old: It was understanding that which made me ask the leading question: Is it at the Laya point of this sphere that Fohat is called Fohat, or is it called so on any higher plane?

Mme. Blavatsky: It is so called everywhere. About the Laya point, I am going to answer you here.

Mr. Old: There is something else attached to that.

Mme. Blavatsky: It is question 5.

Mr. B. Keightley: Question 5. Why are the Laya centres called "imperishable" (page 145)? For if the Laya centres are "conditions," they must, as such, perish in passing into the conditionless—as in the Mahapralaya—must they not? Are they so called only in relationships to any given Manvantara?

Mme. Blavatsky: You see, there is again a mistaken notion, not a mistake, but a mistaken notion about the thing. The Laya centres are imperishable and eternal, because they are no manifestation, but simply rents in the veil of Maya, or manifestation. Do you understand? The Laya centres are that which are no reflection, but the reality, the one Absolute substance, so to say, which has all the negative qualities and none of the positive, which is Absolute all, the Absoluteness; therefore it is the Laya point.

Mr. Old: It is merely a relative matter as to how you use this.

Mme. Blavatsky: Now, mind you, everything has a Laya point. If you want the Laya point in this matchbox you will find it. There is nothing in this world that has not got its polarity and its seven principles, from the highest to the central one, which is the Laya point. Not that it is somewhere inside, within, but, as I say to you, everything has so many degrees. If you take the thinnest thing that you can conceive of, say the cobweb, it will have its seven planes. You see the one that is visible, which answers to our perceptions, which is sensed by us; and the second, which will be less sensed, and so on, until you do not see anything, and the last one will be the Laya point. It is not a thing that one is without and larger and the other is within and smaller, it is simply the degree of density and of state of the substance, of the universal substance.

Mr. Old: Yes, I understand now, thank you.

Mme. Blavatsky: The Laya *centres* are not conditions *per se* any more than the Absolute is a condition; but it is said of objects, subjects, men and things that they pass into the Laya-like condition. You see, much depends also on the way. In some places it ought to have been written more explicitly. The universe, strictly speaking, doesn't emerge or re-emerge from or into the Absolute Laya, which is only another name for the Absoluteness of Parabrahm, after [ ] or

Manvantara, but it is reflected in you from the eternal root on the now differentiated substance. You see what I mean.

Mr. Old: But it was reading the sentence where you tried to explain what the "Laya centres" was. You said it is not any point at all, but a condition, and therefore you qualified it with the idea opposed to the conditionless. I quote the passage.

Mme. Blavatsky: I must say I had too many editors for it. Now, I have remarked a mistake today, that it is said there "it is thrown into the Laya." You cannot throw anything *into* the Laya; I ought to have said "*onto*" the Laya—around the Laya, you understand. There are many such things that there may be. I am not English and I do not perceive immediately the mistake; and afterwards when I read it with a little more attention, I see there is something which might have been expressed better. You know very well under what difficult conditions I wrote this book. I asked two or three there and they helped me; they had to type it out. You had better put a mark for the second edition, "onto" and not "into."

Mr. Old: We shan't complain so long as it draws forth so much intelligent instruction. Even mistakes give rise to intelligent interest.

Mme. Blavatsky: My dear ladies and gentlemen, if I knew English, I would hold meetings. I have not got the talent for the gab. If I could only put into Olcott's head that which I know, or have his eloquence (Because he speaks beautifully.), I could do something.

Mr. B. Keightley: You might take each chapter of *The Secret Doctrine* as it stands and make a volume of it, and not go further than explain the things you say in good English. Question 6. In what sense are the seven sons of Fohat also his seven brothers (page 145)?

Mme. Blavatsky: There we come to a most metaphysical thing; that is a thing I want you to remember well, now. I will tell you better than that, that the sons of Fohat are not only his brothers; they are his aunts, his grandmothers, his mothers-in-law, everything, because I am going to prove to you what it is; why they use this phraseology in the Oriental metaphor, in the Oriental philosophy. In that sense they were sons, brothers, fathers, mothers, etc., only in our evanescent and personal states on this Earth and plane. In our origin we are all one essence, therefore at once fathers, mothers, sons, brothers, what you like. Thus we find in Indian, Egyptian, and other cosmogonies that wives of gods, such as Isis and Aditi and others, called their mothers and daughters. Take the Egyptian cosmogony, or pantheon; you will see that Isis is called the Mother of Horus, the wife; she is the mother of Osiris, the wife and sister and everything. That is just the reason why, because they are all and everything. You understand it is only on this plane that we assume personalities and play our parts in this world of Maya and become something to somebody else; there we are all one.

Mr. Old: But don't you think when you use a qualificative term like "sons," you immediately set this said Fohat in relation to some other part of itself?

Mme. Blavatsky: Most assuredly; and I will give you the explanation. I have given you a rather lengthy thing about Fohat.

Mr. B. Keightley: Question 7. Can you explain more fully what is intended by the expression "Fohat is forced to be born again time after time whenever any two of his son-brothers engage in too close contact, whether an embrace or a fight"?

Mme. Blavatsky: Now remember what I have given you two Thursdays ago, about the two forces, the two opposite forces, and what I told you about the centripetal and centrifugal forces. Now I am going to explain to you. Fohat is the symbol of universal, unpolarized electricity, you understand, his sons being the seven radicals of electro-magnetism, which are polarized forces. Electricity on this plane of visible Fohat is thus their brother of his sons, but relatively to that he is non-polarized, since he contains them all, and therefore he is their father. Now is this sufficiently explained to you?

Mr. Kingsland: It is all a question of the aspect in which you look at it.

Mme. Blavatsky: The Fohatic brothers are everywhere, one in each kingdom of nature. Now, take a piece of glass. To produce electricity you have to rub it with an animal or vegetable product. Then two of Fohat's sons are brought into close contact, and their father, Fohat, becomes now their son, because he is generated by them. Is not it so? He is the father on another plane, or in another aspect, and when you come to that friction business—take anything you like—then where electricity is generated, he becomes their son.

Mr. Old: Then Fohat is really not only electricity.

Mme. Blavatsky: He is unpolarized electricity, universal; it is the radiation of the seven highest Logoi of those seven rays that come from the second Logos, as we call it, or this manifestation that comes from the never-manifested.

Mr. B. Keightley: The more I think about it, the more I think that the English word which best translates the word Fohat is Energy.

Mme. Blavatsky: Energy is everything.

Mr. B. Keightley: So is Fohat.

Mme. Blavatsky: In the Kabalah you have grand expressions. I have never met a good Kabalist that wouldn't understand the real philosophical things.

Mr. Hall: Why not call Fohat the agent?

Mme. Blavatsky: Because you are an insurance agent we must call him agent! Why not call him prime minister? I won't, I have too much respect for Fohat.

Mr. B. Keightley: Fohat is all force, he is the causer, the mover, the radiator, everything. The only expression we have in English with anything like such a wide range is Energy.

Mr. Hall: Energy is what you might call the unapplied force. He is the applier of Energy.

Mme. Blavatsky: My dear sir, I will kick this thing and it will be energy that I use. Is it Fohat? Not at all. If I rub it, it will produce Fohat. You can't call that energy which applies to many other things. Energy is simply a force used. The word, Fohat, is the only one I have found.

Mr. Kingsland: Call it unpolarized electricity.

Mme. Blavatsky: Yes, but it means also the self-moving and that which forces to move; the brightness or the radiancy that moves and moves everything. This is the real, long translation of the word, Fohat.

Mr. Hall: Activity.

Mme. Blavatsky: Activity! No, your European languages will never express that which is expressed in Sanskrit.

Mr. Old: Five simple letters convey a great deal to you, but to us it is far from expressive under the name of Fohat.

Mme. Blavatsky: I explained it to Mr. Sinnett seven years ago. Rome was not built in one day. You have got to learn. There are thousands and thousands of things there, but if I were to come and speak in relation to these two forms there would be ten volumes and nobody would buy it, and they would put me into a lunatic asylum.

Mr. Keightley: You say here—speaking of the death and rebirth of planetary chains—you describe at the end of the Seventh Round on a planetary chain how the planets die, one after the other, and their principles and energies are thrown out from the dying planet and thrown upon a Laya centre, and then proceed to evolve round that Laya centre a new planetary chain. And you give, as an instance, that the Earth proceeds, so to speak, from the Moon in that way—that the Earth is the child of the Moon. The question asked is this: Question 8, page 155. Under what law may we account for the production by the Moon of a child (the Earth) much greater in point of size than its parent?

Mme. Blavatsky: I have seen sons that were six-footers from very small parents. This is nothing. But it is not the question. What do you want to know?

Mr. B. Keightley: Is it that in the transfer of the astral principles from the material body of the Moon to that Laya centre which becomes the Earth there is produced a falling in upon itself of the gross matter of the lunar body? And if so, may we say that the life-current, passing from the Laya centre of the parent to that of the offspring, contains the potentiality which is afterwards manifested in the development of the child-orb?

Mme. Blavatsky: The materials of the Earth were there in undifferentiated condition, for substance is eternal. There was never a moment when they were not a substance, the materials of which the Earth now is created, the whole chain; there was never a time when it was not. They were only awakened by the Moon's principles when one after the other they were transferred from the Moon to the nascent Earth when its turn came in the awakening of the chain. The phrase would run better in *The Secret Doctrine*, where it is said, all this, "the Moon's principles are sent out *onto*," instead of "*into*" the Laya centre, because a Laya centre is just as I told you, not differentiated, though everything around it can be differentiated. The Laya centre is the Atma, in this case, of the body that forms. The Moon shrinks after the loss of her principles as the dead body of a man shrinks after its vital and other principles have quitted it, and as it is so, the occultists say that, of course, the life current of the parent carries with it a potentiality of all that will be developed in the new planet. In the Moon there are no more principles, there is a kind of—how shall I say it? It is ridiculous to say vegetable—the life planet. There is a kind of a shadowy life. That is to say, you just think about a body in a trance condition: some of those bodies that are for 20, 30, or 40 days and live. There is the kind of life going on, but everything is dead to all appearances. Only there is something in the body that keeps up the vitality, and if certain substances are brought in contact with that body, that body will absorb it notwithstanding, by osmosis. You can perfume a body which is in such a condition as that. If you go and burn incense then the body for many hours afterwards will smell, which shows it absorbs. Now a thing which is perfectly dead will not, it will absorb nothing. Therefore, the Moon in the same way is said to vampirise. Now look at the terrible illnesses that are produced through the Moon. Look at the effects produced when you are in the Red Sea. Not a single sailor is allowed, when it is full moon, to sleep on deck without covered head, because he is sure to have his face paralyzed and burnt. I have seen two cases like that. I have seen a man become perfectly insane, and he kept so for five or six months; simply moonstruck during the passage in the Red Sea.

Mr. Gardner: Is there no remedy to obviate that? Is there nothing in nature?

Mme. Blavatsky: Certainly Nature herself will perhaps restore her equilibrium. The doctors don't know anything. The yogis have a plant, the moonplant. They will use it and of course restore the man. I have seen the Lascars,[2] but then you must go to a yogi who knows it, a European doctor will not know anything at all.

Mr. Hall: Then the Moon is cataleptic?

Mme. Blavatsky: It is something like that. It is very wicked.

Mr. ——: Is that a sort of reactory effect it has?

Mme. Blavatsky: See what an effect it has on vegetation. It has an enormous effect. There is not a plant, not a body in heaven that exchanges so much, or interchanges effects so much as the Moon and the Earth. There are not two such planets. It is always interchanging, that is going on, and there the Laya point won't prevent it; it is quite a different thing. This is a most occult thing.

Mr. ——: But the Earth in the end has greater power over the Moon than the Moon over the Earth.

Mme. Blavatsky: Certainly, because the Earth is a moving thing, and

---

2 Indian workers on British ships, usually recruited from Bengal or Assam.

the Moon is a dead one, or is dying—it is in a cataleptic condition.

Mr. ——: Does that apply to other planets, as well?

Mme. Blavatsky: Just the same. As above, so below, at least on the same plane to everything visible—stars and suns, and fixed stars and planets and everything.

Mr. Old: I might just mention that with respect to that vampirizing influence that the Moon has upon the Earth, it is strange that just those principles, or rather those elements, which it lacks, it most powerfully attracts from the Earth, for instance, the atmosphere and water. It has plenty of dense matter, of course, but has little influence upon the dense objects of this Earth, far less than the solar influence. But upon the water and upon all fluids in the human system, it is known to have a most powerful effect; and hence the determination of the fluids, the humors to the head in the case of lunatics, and in the case of those who are moonstruck.

Mme. Blavatsky: But it is a most extraordinary thing in the occult science. I have been putting the question several times to the Masters, I have asked: "How is it possible, if these meteors cannot pass or anything, how is it that the influences pass the Laya point?" They say it is quite a different thing. The conditions are given by the radiation of the moonlight, which shows to you that it passes with its seventh principle, and not with the first—not with the bodily elements of the principles, but with the seventh, you understand.

Mr. B. Keightley: And therefore passes through the Laya point in the same order.

Mr. Gardner: Then its first principles do pass through it eventually?

Mr. B. Keightley: No, no. The influence passes, not the matter; you may call it matter, in the same sense that everything is matter.

Mr. Kingsland: In the same sense that one magnet affects another, there is nothing {that} passes between them materially.

Mme. Blavatsky: You can put between two magnets a dead wall, a glass wall for instance, an iron wall, and yet it will pass. Put any wall you like it will pass, and it does not prevent it.

Mr. B. Keightley: Did you ever see a very curious experiment showing the presence of something, whatever you can call it, between the poles of a magnet? If you get a copper disc, so arranged that it is between the poles of a powerful electro-magnet, and there is no electricity passing, therefore, it is not a magnet, it is just a plain piece of iron. You can make the disc revolve as fast as you please; the disc feels as if it were passing through butter, and it will become heated red hot, if you force it to revolve between the poles of the magnet, just as if there were actually matter between. Don't you know that?

Mr. Kingsland: I think a very good illustration of the Laya point, a practical illustration, would be that common experiment of scattering iron filings over a glass plate under which you have two poles of a magnet. The filings arrange themselves in circles; there is a certain influence circling round the one and the other. They separate, as it were, they won't coalesce; you see distinct dividing lines; that would illustrate the Laya point between the two planets.

Mme. Blavatsky: That is a good illustration.

Mr. B. Keightley: What is there between the poles of a magnet in an experiment of that kind? Can you answer that question?

Mme. Blavatsky: Don't you ask me, if you please, things which pretend to your physical science, because I have told you hundreds of times I don't know anything. I don't say I feel proud of it, but I feel perfectly indifferent.

Mr. B. Keightley: I can say with perfect confidence you can answer, if you like. Question 9: From what source does the Earth draw its active vital principle in order to persevere in its own line of physical development, and at the same time to meet the vampirizing demands of its lunar parent?

Mme. Blavatsky: It draws its life from the universal and all-pervading ocean of life and also from the Sun, the great life giver. The child receives its first stroke of life from the mother, but once born, it grows and develops by assimilating life from everywhere around it. The child could not grow and live, did it depend only on the incipient life principle which it derives from the mother. It receives a certain thing; she starts him in life with a little capital, and then he goes and makes speculations himself. Doesn't everything live? We live in the ocean of vitality. It is only the men of science who will tell you that life is not at all an entity, or something separate, but simply a certain combination of organs. Oh, heavens! There is Allan Grant {Grant Allen}[3]! I wish you could see this new book of his, *Force and Energy*,[4] and the flapdoodle that the man says about the birth of the first man, and how he was born from the Earth, and some gasses and other things. Why, it beats anything I have ever heard in my life. The *Pall Mall* {*Gazette*}[5] laughs at him in the most extraordinary way. You ought to go and get his book.

Mr. Kingsland: I think that is a point that ought to be enforced a little more. There is rather a tendency to suppose the Earth became fully formed by the influence from the Moon.

Mme. Blavatsky: It received its principles, my dear sir; it is not said as you say. Once that it was started and was born, so to say, then it began to live; just the same as a child, it receives its first vital principle from the mother. Once it is born, it has to receive its influence and to be taken into the air and be promenaded. It takes its life from everything, from the air it breathes, and the food it eats.

Mr. Kingsland: It shows that the person who put that question seemed to think that the Earth ought not to be bigger than the Moon.

Mme. Blavatsky: No, I suppose he wanted to elicit an answer. No. The size is nothing.

---

3 Grant Allen, Canadian born writer on science and popular novelist, 1848-1899.
4 *Force and Energy: a Theory of Dynamics*, London: Longmans, Green and Co., 1888.
5 London evening paper, edited at the time by William T. Stead.

Mr. Hall: Even the child before it is born, isn't it nourished by outside influences?

Mme. Blavatsky: It is what I said, but I am not going to speak about this question now. Why should I?

Mr. B. Keightley: Question 10. Page 155, line 7. As suggested by the analogy of the planets with man, does the female ovum constitute a Laya centre, and the fructifying male element correspond to the energy and principles thrown out by a dying planet?

Mme. Blavatsky: There is a Laya centre in the ovum, as in everything else, but the ovum itself represents only the undifferentiated matter surrounding this point, and the male germ corresponds to the vital principle of the dying planet. As above, so below, again; the Laya point is there, and it remains. The Laya point cannot be touched, but it is the matter around it. The Laya point, for instance, is there, where the principles of the Moon will migrate or pass; transfer this from a planet that is dying, it goes and falls into another, just like a woman who has a child and dies. Just in the same way the planet will transfer its principles, but it is not *into* the Laya centre, but on the matter which is around that. The Laya centre is not seen, it is there. It is again my fault to have said *into* instead of *onto* it. It is very difficult.

Mr. B. Keightley: Onto would not express the thing.

Mr. Kingsland: Around.

Mme. Blavatsky: Around means that the Laya centre is smaller, and it is not. There's again a difficulty. It is not, as I told you, like a Chinese nest—that one is smaller than the other and another still smaller. It is not that. It is all one.

Mr. Kingsland: It is the metaphysical point in the circle.

Mme. Blavatsky: It is simply the degree—the same thing on another state of consciousness, on another plane.

Mr. B. Keightley: Now the eleventh. You say a bit further on, speaking about the Moon and the satellites and so on—you explained this. Question 11, page 165. Can you give us any further explanations as to the meaning of a planet's two or more satellites?

Mme. Blavatsky: Well, I am going to answer you that which will make you, not laugh, but think I have avoided the question. Now, really and indeed I cannot answer any better than what is. Prepare to laugh, if you like—because, I suppose, one planet has more magnetic attraction than the others. Just as a medium will attract spooks, which become his satellites, according to the degree of his mediumistic powers, so a planet may, besides its parent when the parent is not dead and faded out, have similar parasites attached to it. They are what I call poor relatives, the genteel hangers-on. I cannot tell you anything else, because it depends on the magnetic attractions. There are those planets that will attract more, and those that do not attract so many. Now the Earth has got only one, because the Earth is not capable of attracting anything. There is too much sin on it, and fibs. Mars is a powerful fellow, and he has more.

Mr. Gardner: Saturn has seven.

Mme. Blavatsky: He may have as many as he likes. He would have more if the law permitted, but it doesn't.

Mr. Keightley: Then the other question is practically the same. Question 12. Can you give us any explanation as to why Mars has two satellites, to which it has no right?

Mme. Blavatsky: It is the same thing, ditto. I tell you, what can I answer you? Will you give me an explanation why England has, besides India, Burma? She has no right to India any more than to Burma, and yet she has them. Can you give me an explanation? Or why Russia has Poland and Siberia, and she has no right to them?

Mr. B. Keightley: They happened to be handy and she took them.

Mme. Blavatsky: Might is right. And so it is in this world. A planet which is stronger will have more satellites and more things.

Mr. Kingsland: Are all these satellites in a similar condition to the Moon? Are they all dead?

Mme. Blavatsky: Not all. Some are more alive, some are ready to die. The Moon is dead, because she has passed her principles; the others appear to us moons, but they are simply forming something.

Mr. ———: What are the rings of the planet Saturn?

Mme. Blavatsky: It is nothing objective—at least, objective it is; it is nothing solid.

Mr. Gardner: Is it gassy?

Mme. Blavatsky: I suppose it is; I could not tell you what I have not learned.

Mr. B. Keightley: More optical.

Mme. Blavatsky: I don't believe they exist at all. It is all Maya. Mars is a fiery, strong planet which attracts to itself more than the others do. Once we accept the occult statement, it is easy to account for the rest. What is difficult and almost impossible is to make a European trained in physical science see that the occult sciences are far more logical and satisfactory than the former. Well, have you got anything else to ask?

Mr. Old: I should like to have asked, without intruding on time, whether these other satellites attached to the different planets are in the same relationship to these centres—that is to say, when they serve as satellites, as our Moon is to the other?

Mme. Blavatsky: I think they are the same, but not that they have any influence. I think they are fed by some planets, but they do not give out the interchange of influences on the Moon.

Mr. Old: They are not fading, the planets?

Mme. Blavatsky: No; it is only those who are parents, so long as they are not dislocated and disrupted, that have such influence. But the others, as far as I remember, are fed, so to say, on meteors. That is why I spoke about the power of the parents.

Mr. Old: It would be illogical to say that any one planet had half a dozen parents.

Mr. B. Keightley: Two are quite enough for any respectable planet.

Mme. Blavatsky: Quite enough!

Mr. Old: The case is different, then, with regard to the Moon, which is not only our satellite, but our parent.

Mme. Blavatsky: Yes, it is.

Mr. Gardner: Is that the only case in which we have them in a dual capacity? Are some of Jupiter's moons?

Mme. Blavatsky: Most assuredly. One of them is a parent. Now, it depends on the priority of the planets; it depends on their age. Some of the planets' fathers and mothers died long ago, as with Venus, and faded out entirely, in the case of one of them. It is said it was one of the sacred planets that disappeared, and this was the mother or father of the Moon. I am not sure—either the Moon or Venus; I think it is the Moon. This is a thing that I did not learn, since it doesn't exist. I was very anxious simply to learn about the existent.

Mr. Gardner: How about that other planet between Mercury and the Sun?

Mme. Blavatsky: Ask Tyndall or Huxley. Proctor is dead—well, somebody else.

Mr. Gardner: Is the parent dead of Mercury?

Mme. Blavatsky: I don't know. I know one thing, that there is a very funny thing in the *Path* which I think you had better read to them, and then we will just talk about it. There is something that is said from the Purana. Where he gets it from I cannot understand. "The

Origin of the Planet, Mercury" it is called. It is in this month's *Path*.[6]

Mr. B. Keightley: Having read the extract referred to, the proceedings shortly afterwards closed.

---

6 The extract, "Origin of Planet Mercury," is in the *Path*, Volume IV, April 1889, p. 6, under the subject heading "Culled from Aryan Science."

15.
The Theosophical Society.
Report of Proceedings,
held at Blavatsky Lodge,
April 18, 1889.

Mr. Kingsland in the Chair.

Mr. B. Keightley: Question 1 (a). In connection with the seven *relative* Laya points, are we to conceive of matter existing *simultaneously* on all the seven planes, or does it pass through the seven Laya centres from one state to another, actually? Or only relatively to our perceptions, or to the perceptions of beings on the other planes?

Mme. Blavatsky: During Maha-Pralaya there are no planes of matter, of course, since nothing exists. For the absolute Laya point is infinite. It cannot be. Who put that question?

Mr. Kingsland: I did.

Mme. Blavatsky: During Manvantara the seven planes of matter emanate, the one from the other in a regular order and succession, and embraces very naturally untold series of eons, with the exception of Manvantaric deities—a mystery, if you please. The beings on other planes must come down in the natural order of evolution, and to our plane, someday. All beings begin and end at the Laya point. Happy those who merge into it (I wish to goodness I was one of them!), for they will have no rebirth during that Manvantara. They begin on the highest plane and descend in regular sequence from plane to plane, the planes of all being *pari passu* with their descent. And let us add these planes of divine substance and consciousness are but the creations of these very beings. Now do you understand, from the first or highest, to the seventh or lowest state of consciousness?

It is the divine being, the macrocosm, which ends in the man form, which is the creation of the corresponding plane of the microcosm, for the whole universe of matter is, as philosophy teaches, but an illusory reflection—as you know. Now, are there any questions to this?

Mr. Kingsland: There is another question relating to the same thing.

Mr. B. Keightley: Yes. Question 1 (b). For instance, take a piece of iron, this is perceived by us on this plane as iron. Is it perceived by a consciousness acting on other planes as something else than iron, or is it absolutely non-perceptible?

Mme. Blavatsky: Now, how can it be? Most assuredly, there cannot be the same piece of iron for every plane; otherwise, why should we not perceive as easily beings from every other plane, and they us? I mean the globes of the planetary chains. Or why should the globes of our chain be concealed from us? The usual way of measuring the spiritual development of an adept among the disciples is to ask what plane of consciousness or perception he has reached; and this perception embraces the physical as well as the spiritual. This is the thing when you want to know what degree an adept belongs to, how far he has developed; what plane of perception is his. That is a kind of Masonic formula; but how can we see a piece of iron in the same way?

Mr. Kingsland: Not in the same way, but in a different way. What I wanted to elucidate was in reference to Laya centres, which we had before. You stated there are seven relative Laya centres—that is to say, corresponding to the transition from one plane to the other.

Mme. Blavatsky: So there are, on every one of the seven planes, only, of course, the Laya centre is Laya in accordance with the perception of that plane; that is to say that our plane being the grossest, the Laya point which exists for us would perhaps, be there no Laya point at all, and would be something a great deal more gross and perceptible. The Laya point is, of course, more refined on the following plane, and so on.

Mr. Kingsland: Then we may say that on the next plane, for instance, the iron is non-existent.

Mme. Blavatsky: Absolutely non-existent in the shape in which we see it here, because their perception is quite a different kind of perception. No comparison can be established.

Mr. Kingsland: But is it not perceived as something else?

Mme. Blavatsky: It may be, but I cannot tell you what.

Mr. B. Keightley: It would be translated into the terms of our consciousness.

Mme. Blavatsky: Matter is matter, and substance is substance, but it takes such various forms that certainly, that which would appear iron to us, may appear gooseberry jam on the other plane.

Mr. B. Keightley: It must exist on every plane, because we know the smallest atom existed on every one of the seven planes.

Mme. Blavatsky: But it exists in an atomic scattered condition. Once that you suppose a thing may fall from one planet to another, passing through the atmosphere of our Earth, it would change chemically all its constituent parts. It would become quite a different thing. It would become a thing of this plane; in fact, we could not see it if it didn't.

Mr. Kingsland: In fact, it exists, as substance but not as matter.

Mme. Blavatsky: Perfectly. And not as a definite form, or the definite form that it takes on our plane; it is quite a different story.

Mr. B. Keightley: Question 2. On page 150, it is stated that "each atom has seven planes of being or existence." Are we right in supposing that each corresponds with one of the seven globes of a planetary chain?

Mme. Blavatsky: No sir, most assuredly not. These seven globes are on four planes only, as you know.

Mr. B. Keightley: Question 3. In connection with this, how is it that in the diagram on page 153, the seven globes are represented as existing on only four planes?

Mme. Blavatsky: There you are, because the triangle, the quaternary or square are the symbols of {the} microcosm, or man. The globes are seven, but out of seven there are three pairs, or what the Gnostics call Syzygies, the couples, male and female—positive and negative, respectively. Our globe lies solitary on the fourth, or seventh, or first plane—just as you like to give the numbers; combines in itself the material by dual nature. The form of the globe of our planetary chain corresponds exactly to the esoteric diagrams of the principles, as every esotericist here knows—of the human principles, I mean. Atman stands for the triangle, remember, and the physical man for, firstly, the globe; secondly, the quaternary; and, finally, the pentagon, the five-pointed star. You must try to find out the eternal riddle of the Sphinx, without being blinded for it like Oedipus. Do you see what I mean by it, why it is so, why the seven are on the four planes?

Mr. Kingsland: Simply because they correspond to the quaternary in that respect.

Mme. Blavatsky: First there is our Earth, then comes the second plane, and there, too, they are couples; then come two again, and then two again—six in all.

Mr. Yates:[1] Are these the material, astral, sidereal planes of the diagrams?

Mme. Blavatsky: Yes; call them what names you like, I know it is. Ours is the lowest plane; then comes the more ethereal, and more ethereal, and still more ethereal, until no human conception can conceive of the three planes. And therefore we leave them alone, because it is perfectly ridiculous with our finite intellects to try to understand and unriddle the infinite. It is quite enough to take what

---

1 So spelled in the transcription, but it could be the Irish poet, William Butler Yeats, 1865-1939, who was in London at the time, especially because of his later questions about William Blake, whose poems he was to edit a few years later.

the seers can see.

Mr. Yates: Are not the seven planets that exist only on four planes, a microcosmic representation of the whole seven?

Mme. Blavatsky: They are, most assuredly, they are. Now, if you take the principles of man in a diagram, you see just the same thing as that; you see the physical body of man; then comes the vehicle of light and life; then comes the Manas and the Kama-rupa—the lower Manas, I mean—then comes the higher Manas, and Buddhi-Atman. I speak for you who know better, not for those who are exoteric, but for all those who have studied esoterically. You know Atman is not a principle in fact.

Mr. Yates: There was a sense, then, in which the seven planets were represented as existing upon the seven planes.

Mme. Blavatsky: They exist on four planes.

Mr. Yates: Do they correspond to the seven planes?

Mme. Blavatsky: Yes, but still it is four and seven.

Mr. Yates: I was simply trying to get that clear, that they did not exist—

Mme. Blavatsky: The globes pretend to matter, to form, and to shape, and there is nothing that exists on the third, remember, or higher planes that can have form or shape: they may have it, but not according to our conceptions. It does not exist in Nature, there are not any such things, as though you would put staircases, or ladders, or rungs. All this is metaphysical, and all this is symbolical; but still, to come and to try to precisely give a form, shape, to that which we cannot understand, is perfect nonsense.

Mr. Yates: The whole seven correspond to the seven planets, not only four.

Mme. Blavatsky: They do.

Mr. Kingsland: I put that question in order to elucidate that point a little more. It is stated that these planets did correspond to the states of matter.

Mme. Blavatsky: Seven states of consciousness, yes, and not to the seven states of perception.

Mr. Yates: You have again confused me. Though they do not exist on the plane, yet they correspond?

Mme. Blavatsky: In the first place, we cannot think with our lower four states of consciousness. We can hardly begin perceiving them with the fourth, and then come the others; therefore it is a perfect impossibility. You cannot see with your physical eyes, you cannot see with the state of consciousness which is located in the [ ], can you? You cannot, till you come to the upper Manas, to the fifth, so to say; then you can perceive them, but not with the lower Manas, or the Kama-rupa, or any of those principles, because these are purely physical—

Mr. B. Keightley: And pertain entirely and exclusively to the Earth, in fact.

Mme. Blavatsky: Certainly.

Mr. B. Keightley: Question 4. "What is the relation of these four planes to the seven states of matter?"

Mme. Blavatsky: None, except that each of the four planes has its own seven states of matter, that is all. For instance, it seems to me that all these questions are the same, under various forms. If they are made under the impression that the seven states of universal substance are identical with the planes of the globes in our chain, then I answer, it is not so. I don't know, you see, what your thoughts are. They are correspondential, but not consubstantial; the one belongs to a tiny solar system still denser in the degree of their materiality; the others are universal. It is our system which is still denser.

Mr. B. Keightley: Question 5, page 172, footnote. "Can you give us any idea of the states of consciousness corresponding to the various Pralayas: viz. between two globes, between two Rounds, and after seven Rounds?"

Mme. Blavatsky: There I am asked to deliver the keys of esoteric philosophy in about five seconds, on two pages, and on a Thursday! Now suppose we first studied thoroughly the nature of the Pralayas on our present plane, and within the limits of our present states of consciousness. How can one understand anything about states of consciousness without the limits of purely physical consciousness, when even the latter is in a state of most chaotic confusion as to itself and its own capacities? Don't you think we are often trying to mimic those frogs who wanted to become bulls, and they "busted up"? I don't want to bust up; I know I can go and speculate upon things that are within the possibility; but how can we? Sometimes they make such questions that positively I open my mouth and say: "Really now, what is that?" I look at them about 4 o'clock, and I say, "What can I answer?" So I leave them to the grace of God. This is very flattering, you know, because it shows you think I know more than I do. I cannot speak about things which it is impossible to speculate upon.

Mr. B. Keightley: (Reads from *The Secret Doctrine*.) "The Monadic hosts may be roughly divided into three classes," etc. Question 6, page 174. "Do the highest class of Monads, which attain the human stage on globe A in the First Round, appear at once in the human stage on that globe in the Second Round, or do they have to pass through any lower forms?"

Mme. Blavatsky: I cannot answer anything more than what I said in *The Secret Doctrine*. Pass on to question 7. Then I have something for you.

Mr. B. Keightley: Question 7, page 174. "Does the first class of Monads here mentioned consist of those who attained adeptship on the Lunar chain, or simply of the intellectually developed races of that chain?"

Mme. Blavatsky: How can anyone know whether there are adepts on the Moon? If there were adepts, they would call themselves lunatics, that is a fact! I ask you if it is possible? How can we know that? How can I answer you, so as to satisfy you? Now listen well to this, because it is very important. Of all the mysterious globes in our present Manvantara, the Moon is the most mysterious—not in relation to her physical formation, but to her psychic and spiritual functions. Now, do you remember, any one of you who read *Five Years of Theosophy*,[2] that there are some questions by an Englishman, and how poor Mr. Sinnett was snubbed for this moon question? So never touch questions of this kind. There are many mysteries that they don't want to speak about; it is the most mysterious of all. The Moon is our sidereal power of silence and the Venetian Piombi[3] thrown into one. Better never ask anything about the Moon, except that which relates to its half-dead body. Now pass to the eighth, because there is a continuation.

Mr. B. Keightley: Question 8. "What law is it that determines to which of the three classes named, a particular Monad will belong?"

Mme. Blavatsky: I suppose Karmic law, of course. What law is it which determines whether a child will be born the eldest son of a lord, and thus grab all the family estates, or as a penniless younger son having to take refuge in a family living, or to try to make money out of Jesus, as they generally do? Karma, of course. Yet very often the younger sons inherit all the brains of the family, whilst the former are but brainless bags of money. Therefore there is no law except Karmic law. What law can it be? It is simply an accident brought on by past incarnation; by merit or demerit, who knows? There are so many thousands of things. We see the most terrible injustice done in

---

2 *Five Years of Theosophy: Mystical, Philosophical, Theosophical, Historical, and Scientific Essays Selected from "The Theosophist,"* was published in London in 1885; though no name is given we know that it was edited by Mohini Chatterjee. The Englishman referred to was Frederick W.H. Myers. The article referenced is probably "Some Inquiries Suggested By Mr. Sinnett's *Esoteric Buddhism.*", p. 230.
3 The dreaded prison cells in the Palace of the Doges in Venice; among those held there was Giordano Bruno.

this of birth. You see men who ought really to be on thrones, and we see them starving miserably, and we see them kicked, and we see the biggest fools, and they are royalty and dukes and all kinds of things. Look at our emperors. Look at the Russian emperors. Oh, Lord! They were nice fools, all of them.

Mr. Yates: How far does the collective Karma control the individual beyond his own actions? Can an individual receive results he does not deserve, which are forced upon him by the Karma of the race?

Mme. Blavatsky: I suppose I do understand you, but it seems to me that the Karma of everyone and everything affects you just the same. You may be an excellent man and not deserve to have the measles, but if you go near a person who has it, you may have it, too.

Mr. Yates: How far the Karma of another may affect it is what I wished to know.

Mme. Blavatsky: You cannot touch pitch without being black. You cannot come into rapport with a person that can give you some disease without catching it. You will be rewarded for that injustice and the other man may not be punished, because it is not his fault. You see, the Karma is a question of such difficulty; it is such an abstruse thing that if we begin talking about Karma, we must not ask other questions. It is too abstruse, Karma.

Mr. Mead: Then that question with regard to the first Monads that come in?

Mme. Blavatsky: You will find it there.

Mr. B. Keightley: There are some questions on that subject. Keep your question clear in your head to the end, and if it is not answered then, you might mention it. Question 9 (a). Will a Monad belonging to one particular class always belong to that class?

Mme. Blavatsky: Certainly not. How can it be that? Because, if nature were stationary and never moved, it would be a different thing; but how can it be in this case? Because, there would be neither progress nor Karma nor anything, if it were such a thing as that.

Mr. Mead: I suppose that question means, would a Monad go on evolving in its own class?

Mr. B. Keightley: That, I think, is a fair question—whether a Monad in its evolution would remain together with the other Monads that formed the same class, or is it free to get ahead of the others or drop behind them?

Mr. Kingsland: Only during one cycle.

Mr. B. Keightley: If not, what law determines his rate of evolution, or the length of time he remains in that class?

Mme. Blavatsky: Again, Karma. I cannot answer you anything more. His own actions and previous existence; the collective existences of nations and races, of persons that are around—of everything.

Mr. B. Keightley: Question 10, page 175. Can you explain what is meant by the Monad's "skipping two planes and getting direct into the third"?

Mme. Blavatsky: The Monad, though meaning strictly one, is in its manifestation always Trinitarian—being one only in Nirvana. When it is in its Laya state every ancient philosophy proves it to be so. Now remember the Monad of Pythagoras having to descend and form the first triangle, after which it subsides again and disappears in darkness and silence. Take, for instance, the Kabalistic Sephirothal tree; you find that first it forms the triangle; just the same in the Pythagorean [ ] {Tetraktis?}; it produces the triangle and then leaves it to do the further business. So it is in the Kabalah, just in the same way; there is the first, Kether, Chochmah, and Binah; or the crown, wisdom, and understanding. Wisdom and understanding are on the same horizontal plane. It cannot be otherwise than Trinitarian. How can Monad manifest, unless it is Trinitarian and capable of acting only on the third plane, as the second and the first are too spiritual to be regarded in our perceptions as planes of any activity? Take the human septenary. Atma alone is nothing; it is not only not a breath, but it is simply an idea, nothing, because it is absoluteness; it is the essence of Ain Soph or Parabrahm; Buddhi is its vehicle, and yet Buddhi, even in conjunction with Atma, is still nothing on this plane. In Sankhya philosophy, Buddhi {Atma} is represented by Purusha, who has no legs; he has to mount on the shoulders of Prakriti, which is Buddhi, who has legs but no head, to form a manifested Monad with the potentiality of becoming rational and self-conscious. This is a most beautiful allegory, showing Purusha, who cannot walk; who, having no legs, is obliged to mount on the shoulders of Prakriti, and therefore the two produce a rational being.

Mr. Yates: Does the allegory refer to the silent one?

Mme. Blavatsky: It is Prakriti that gives the legs. Therefore it is said that the Monad skips the first two planes and gets direct into the plane of mentality.

Mr. Kingsland: Skips the two highest planes, that is. I think the question has been put on the supposition that it was kept to the two lower planes.

Mr. B. Keightley: No, it was the meaning of the phrase—why two higher planes are used. That is all in the questions about the Monad.

Mr. Mead: "Further, when globe A of the new chain is ready," etc. (Reads from *The Secret Doctrine*.)

Mme. Blavatsky: We will come to that further on. It comes here.

Mr. B. Keightley: Question 11, page 176, last paragraph. Can you name the "ten stages" here referred to? And what stage do you call "the first really manward stage"?

Mme. Blavatsky: I can. I name the first really manward stage when the Third Race, being at the threshold of the Fourth, the racial stage, as it is called, becomes a potential septenary through the incarnation in it of the Manas, or sense of wisdom. Hence with the three sub-elemental, or the sub-mineral kingdoms, we have certainly ten, all the ten that are mentioned there. Man is a septenary; arrived at the end of the Third Race, entering upon the Fourth, he is potentially septenary. The fifth yet is not quite developed in us; it will be because we are only on the Fifth Race, and with every race there is one higher and higher that develops, but still it is potentially a septenary, and this, with the others, we say are ten.

Mr. Yates: The fifth, you say. Is that counting from above or below? You say it is not yet fully developed.

Mme. Blavatsky: It is the Manas.

Mr. B. Keightley: Page 181: "It now becomes plain that there exists in nature," etc. (Reads from *The Secret Doctrine*.) Question 12. Does the fully developed man embody the perfection of each of the three schemes of evolution? Please enlarge on this idea.

Mme. Blavatsky: Certainly, for a perfect man has to be: 1, perfect in physical form, as regards the organism and health; 2, perfect intellectually; and 3, perfect spiritually. At any rate, he must have all the schemes of evolution sufficiently represented to produce perfect equilibrium. An absolutely healthy man, full of vitality, but deficient in intellectual powers, is an animal, not a man. A perfectly spiritual man with a sick limb, or weak body, is no man, but a spirit imprisoned, looking out of the window. A perfectly healthy, intellectual, well-developed man, without corresponding spiritual consciousness, is—his intellect not withstanding—an empty shell, and nothing more. If all three qualities are present, so as to produce equilibrium, the man himself will be a perfect man, on his particular plane, I mean—meaning by the latter not the universal planes, but his own personal or individual plane of the septenary scale of perfection. Do I explain it to you sufficiently well, this?

Mr. Kingsland: Yes.

Mr. B. Keightley: For each man, so to speak, as an individual, will have seven planes of activity, or seven degrees. Well, he may be perfect on one plane. He is a perfect man on that plane, but if, in his development, he has not reached one of the higher planes, he is not on that plane at the time you are considering.

Mr. Mead: I understand this about the harmony.

Mr. B. Keightley: You can take that perfect equilibrium on the plane in which a man happens to be, for the time being.

Mme. Blavatsky: Let me read to you, again, this thing.[4] A perfect man is not. He can be a perfect man on the first and the second and the third plane; it is a degree of perfectibility. Now, what I say is, that to make a perfect man, he is to be: 1, perfect in physical form, as regards his organism and health; 2, perfect intellectually; 3, perfect spiritually. All these must be equilibrized. At any rate, he must have all these three schemes of evolution sufficiently represented to produce perfect equilibrium. An absolutely healthy man, full of vitality, but deficient in intellectual powers, is an animal, as I say, not a man. A perfectly spiritual man with a sick limb and a weak body is not a man, but a spirit imprisoned, looking out of the window—an unfortunate spirit. A perfectly healthy and intellectual, well-developed man, without the corresponding spiritual consciousness, is (His intellect notwithstanding.) an empty shell and nothing more. If one of these things, there is no equilibrium, if all these three qualities are present so as to produce equilibrium, the man himself will be a perfect man on his particular plane—I mean. Meaning by the latter, not the universal planes, but his own personal or individual plane of the septenary scale of perfection. Now that is very easily understood.

Mr. Mead: I understood it perfectly up to the last.

Mme. Blavatsky: Why, look here—we have seven planes of perfection, everyone individually; every man has seven states of consciousness. A man may be, if he have all these three equilibrized in him, a perfect man in his own plane. If he is still more so, he will be a perfect man on the second, and then on the third and fourth, and so on.

Mr. Mead: I understand.

---

4 HPB is probably reading from her notes.

Mr. Yates: These three things—intellectual, physical, and spiritual—of course correspond to three of the four planes quarternary, do they not? Which, then, will the fourth be?

Mr. B. Keightley: Those three are taken as representing the body, soul, and spirit.

Mme. Blavatsky: You mix up the planes in the most terrible way. We spoke about the four planes of the globes—of the seven globes.

Mr. Yates: This is my difficulty. Of course, I see perfectly plainly that a man must have a triple harmony; I am not confusing it in that way. I know the triple harmony applies to each separately. That triple harmony itself, does it not correspond to the three planes of the four. In Blake's[5] system it does.

Mr. B. Keightley: How can it? Because the spiritual is the highest, the intellectual is the Manasic, and the physical is the lower.

Mr. Yates: But Blake has it in his.

Mme. Blavatsky: I don't know anything about Blake. I never read a single word about him. I am sorry, you know, that we disagree with him.

Mr. Yates: He considers it is the fourth plane which is higher.

Mme. Blavatsky: I speak about the Eastern system.

Mr. B. Keightley: Question 13, page 182. Do the "Sishta," the Seed-Humanity, remain on a globe during its Pralaya, while the rest of humanity has passed on to the next globe?

Mme. Blavatsky: The esoteric books say they do, and esoteric philosophy corroborates it. Otherwise, the Monads—or egos rather—would have to recommence again, in the same Round, every time they reached a new globe, the same process of evolution through the lower kingdoms as they did only on the First Round. Let us not misunderstand the thing. I mean by egos only those first

---

5 William Blake, English poet, and illustrator, 1757-1827.

class {of} Monads which reached the human stage of globe A and become Lunar Pitris on the fourth, and those later arrivals who reached the human stage before the middle of the Fourth Round; all the egos of the Third and Fourth Races, I mean, and not any others. Because after the Fourth Race—after the middle of the Fourth Race, there stops everything; there are no more Monads coming for this Manvantara. These are the younger sons we have just been speaking about. You said that Mr. Sinnett was interested in the Sishta. You came out very cunningly, you remember, with that "Noah's ark theory," as you call it.

Mr. B. Keightley: Question 14. Is the suggestion correct that, even during the depths of Pralaya, life remains *active* around the North Pole—the Land of the Gods?

Mme. Blavatsky: If you mean the Planetary Pralaya, then I say, "yes," esoteric science teaches us so; but not in every Pralaya. I mean that while one globe is in obscuration it remains, but when there is the whole chain certainly it does not; because they are all dissipated then.

Mr. Yates: Does esoteric philosophy imply that, as the Greeks believed, Mount Meru is inhabited at this moment?

Mme. Blavatsky: We see in the esoteric philosophy there is a Meru. What the Indians mean by the Meru is one thing, and what the Greeks mean is another. They call it the thigh, and they said that Bacchus was born in India, because he was born out of the thigh of his Father Jupiter; he is the Motherless, and that is Miros, which means the thigh in Greek;[6] therefore, being born on Mount Meru, he was an Indian.

Mr. Yates: I know nothing of the Indian at all, so I think I must be right. They suppose a region existed in the North Pole inhabited by a blameless people.

---

6 A similar etymology is given in the *Caves and Jungles of Hindostan*, Collected Writings edition, p. 609, where she follows E. Pococke's *India in Greece*, 1856, p. 266.

Mme. Blavatsky: Blameless people! Why, it is the gods. You read it in *The Secret Doctrine*, and you will find it all. You read it in the second volume. In the second volume I have got all that—the Eternal Land, the one Finite {infinite?} that never goes down.

Mr. Yates: Is it meant to be actually, physically located in the North Pole?

Mme. Blavatsky: We won't talk about it; it will take us into too high metaphysics.

Mr. B. Keightley: Question 15. Can you tell us anything more about the Sishta?

Mme. Blavatsky: The Sishtas are the highest adepts which happen to be on a globe when Pralaya reaches it. They sacrifice themselves for universal human good and cosmic purposes, too esoteric to discuss now. Let it be known only that they are the living and now objective Nirmanakayas—that is to say, that when the hour of the Pralaya strikes, some of the highest adepts, whether living objectively or subjectively, become the voluntary custodians of the sleeping planet. When it is morning dawn then these Terrene Pitris play the same parts as the Lunar Pitris did in the Fourth Round (That is to say, when there is the dawn for the globe.) They surrender or give their three lower principles as a ready, prepared vehicle for the incoming egos of the new round; then only are their Monads reached. They have done their duty and won a long, long rest. They will remain in Nirvanic bliss until the Manvantara of the successor in this planetary chain, until the dawn strikes for the successor {in} this chain. The successor will be the two globes on our plane above which will unite and form the androgynous earth of the new chain. For then the two uppermost globes will have descended to the plane which is now below them. Another planet shooting its principles into the Laya of the empty place will give birth to a globe which will replace one of these two, and still another to replace the second. There is certainly a mystery, and raison d'être of which mystery it is too early for us to know anything. Nor will the principles of the Earth be lost. As the egos, I mean, are incarnated on Earth, so are the principles of egos or departed globes incarnated in sidereal space. As above so below. As with the Moon, so with the Earth; and as with Father, so with Son. These are immutable lines of nature. Now, this is a thing I tell you perfectly new to you.

Mr. Kingsland: That is the most interesting thing we have had for a long while.

Mme. Blavatsky: I had very many interesting things for you.

Mr. Sinnett: I should like afterwards to see what passed before I arrived.

Mme. Blavatsky: I will read it again. It is very difficult to tell much more about it, because it is such a vast, but such a mysterious thing, that.

Mr. Sinnett: The point there is about the reincarnation of the Earth principle.

Mme. Blavatsky: Well, listen again. The Sishtas are the highest adepts which happen to be on a globe when Pralaya reaches it. Now, those who will be the highest are the voluntary—how shall I say—self-immolators or self-sacrificers. Do you remember what I say in *The Secret Doctrine*? They sacrifice themselves for human good, and cosmic purposes, too esoteric to discuss now. Let it be known only that they are the living and now objective Nirmanakayas. You know what that means? Nirmanakayas means, for instance, you become a great adept. You don't want to live any more, but you are not selfish enough to go into Nirvana (Because it is selfish: you will benefit no one by it but yourselves, and this selfishness is to be avoided.); therefore, instead of going into Devachan (You cannot go into Devachan, because it is yet an illusion for an adept; for mortals as we are, but not for a high adept.), therefore he leaves his body, and lives in all his six principles. Wherever he lives, of course, it is subjectively and in space; but he lives and helps humanity, and sometimes he will inspire people, or communicate with them, and so on. I know several cases like that. Very rarely of course, but it is because they do not generally go for individuals; but they will protect a nation, or protect a community, or something like that, and help as much as Karma permits them. That is to say that when the hour of the Pralaya strikes, some of the highest adepts, whether living objectively or subjectively, as Nirmanakayas become the voluntary custodians of the sleeping planet, etc. (Reads as before.) The Moon gives its principles; so will every planet do it. It goes with a great harmonious succession. There is not a single gap in Nature.

Mr. B. Keightley: From that it would follow, I think, that there are no Sishta until the Fourth Round. Until after the Fourth Round, really.

Mme. Blavatsky: Active Sishta, those that have to act, certainly, because man begins only on the Fourth Round. There are in the Third Round all kinds of astral shapes and things that we cannot speak about, or know anything about. The regular men, as we know them, begin on this round only. I don't suppose there were any adepts there before. I don't know. An adept has a definite meaning for us—it is on this plane, and that which is within our conception. How can we know they are adepts there?

Mr. B. Keightley: It again brings out into prominence the great importance which the Fourth Round plays.

Mme. Blavatsky: The Fourth Round is the adjustor; it adjusts all the things and brings matter and spirit into equilibrium. It is that which in the middle of the Fourth Round makes everything settled, and already, instead of spirit falling into matter, it is matter which begins to evolve into spirit.

Mr. B. Keightley: Question 16, page 184. What are we to understand by the phrase, "astral human forms (Or the highest elementals.)" in the following: Monads of the anthropoids, "the highest mammals after man…will be liberated and pass into the astral human forms (Or the highest elementals.) of the Sixth and Seventh Races, and then into the lowest human forms in the Fifth Round."

Mme. Blavatsky: By the time the Sixth Race comes on the scene, all the animal egos now inhabiting the highest anthropoid forms will have been liberated and will exist. Some exist now in sidereal spaces in astral human forms, as I say. This is what I call here the highest elementals—they have not been human yet. These will incarnate in the lowest men of the Sixth Race.[7] The young men of the Darwinians truly have dreamed dreams, and their old men seen visions, for their founder must have caught from the astral a glimpse of that which will be; and forthwith dragging it down to his own material plane, he made of it that which has been in his own imagination. This is the most curious thing, and I don't think it is Darwin; I think it is Haeckel who took the astral forms. The Master says himself there were gigantic astral forms in the Third Round. They were like gigantic apes, but they were not speaking of the dumb animals—they were men, ape-like, from which individuals evolved the apes. Millions and millions of years after, when there came the reversion to the primal type again, they produced the monsters for which they fell.

Mr. B. Keightley: What happens to the anthropoids is, when they die, they remain as semi-human elementals until the Sixth Race begins to come.

Mme. Blavatsky: They are not yet human, because they were not human.

Mr. B. Keightley: The elementals that will be human.

Mme. Blavatsky: Just as the egos of men are their past elementals.

Mr. Kingsland: But that is not in the Sixth Race, it is in the Sixth Round.

Mme. Blavatsky: There will be a few already in the Sixth Race. Like the chimpanzees, they do not come from space, but these are already imprisoned.

---

7 The MS continues with crossed out "or Seventh Race, I am not sure, it may be, but I don't think so."

Mr. Kingsland: You don't call them human Monads, yet.

Mme. Blavatsky: They are semi-human, because they are due to that Fourth Race. Do you suppose, really, that they are men? It is all very fine to listen to our missionaries, who say all the savages are our brothers. They are not. They have the potentiality; the mineral has the potentiality, but the savages are not—especially some of those who died out—they are not the same as we are.

Mr. Kingsland: Then they will come in at the Sixth Race?

Mme. Blavatsky: Yes. What I say is, that not a single Monad will come any more from space, so to say, unless it is here: that all that which had the time to settle in some of the higher shapes, till the middle of the Fourth Race, these will remain on this Earth till the end of the Manvantara, but certainly not afterwards. If you go and believe this absurd thing, that for every child that is born, there is a new soul breathed and created—that I cannot understand at all.

Mr. Kingsland: Then as a matter of fact, the Monads of some of the anthropoids are sufficiently near the human point to come within the Sixth Race.

Mr. B. Keightley: The exception is expressly made here, and insisted upon. I speak of the class of Monads that one expresses as emphasized.

Mr. Yates: The population of the world is unchanging.

Mme. Blavatsky: The Monads are unchanging in the middle of the Fourth Race.

Mr. B. Keightley: You may have any number of Monads in Devachan, and so on.

Mme. Blavatsky: It is unchanging. Otherwise, there would be no Karmic possibility of adjustment.

Mr. Yates: Take any time in the history of the world, and contrast it with any other period of 3,000 years. There must, of course, be variations; but still, go back—according to that theory, the population of the world was then the same as it is now.

Mme. Blavatsky: You don't know anything at all about population. What it was, and what I have learned, is that the population was almost twice as great as the one we have now—nearly twice as great. There was not a corner on the globe that was not populated, and that is why sometimes it must come, that some of you must be drowned. Look at China; it is the most providential occurrences, those tidal waves.

Mr. B. Keightley: And everywhere in the Atlantean times was twice as populated as China is now.

Mme. Blavatsky: Not twice; a great deal more than it is now. I remember one thing: there was a time when Africa was all inhabited (In times after that, when it had emerged from the ocean.) And now, why, how many parts of Africa are inhabited? I suppose not a twentieth part. You cannot call those savages inhabitants, those that Stanley[8] has been meeting with.

Mr. B. Keightley: A very sparse population ever, at that. But Yates' point is a curious one.

Mme. Blavatsky: They say the continents were greater. Look at the continent that went from India to Australia. It was one continent unbroken, and now it is all seas and seas.

Mr. B. Keightley: What I want to get at is, look at the population of the Earth now: The population of the Earth then was very much greater. It follows that a large number of the Monads which were then on Earth at the Atlantean period, incarnated, are still in Devachan.

Mr. Sinnett: I don't think it necessarily follows. Assume for the moment that a Devachanic period was 200 years, instead of 2,000. The change from a condition of things in which there were simply 200 years spent, to a condition in which you have 2,000 spent, would

---

8 Henry Stanley, born John Rowlands, Welsh journalist and explorer, 1841-1904, who had gained fame for his locating the Scottish missionary David Livingstone in Africa. At the time of HPB's reference, Stanley was in the Congo.

reduce the population to a tenth of what it was, without giving any Monad a period of longer than 2,000 years.

Mr. Kingsland: That is to say, the general period then was shorter than the general period is now.

Mr. Yates: That explains that so many of the greatest nations of the world have been very small in number.

Mme. Blavatsky: We had last time a very interesting thing about the planets, and I think Dr Berridge[9] was very much interested. It was all about planets and stars and astronomy in their astronomical bearing.

Mr. Sinnett: Taking the chimpanzees, the chimpanzee monad would be a more advanced creature than some of the human savages, for he belongs to the Fourth Race, and the savages belong to others.

Mme. Blavatsky: If you took the savage and brought him up as a chimpanzee, he would develop intellect just as much as a chimpanzee. It is because they remain there, entirely shut out from all civilization or anything to see, that they are ignorant. And the chimpanzee, when we take him, he sees the world, he lives in cultured localities, and so on, and becomes very intelligent; so would the poor savage be. Mind you, the savages will be more intelligent in the Sixth Race than these are now. I don't think we shall have one soon remaining from the old race; they are all dying out. I mean the direct ones, such as the flat-headed Australians were.

Mr. Sinnett: Some of the Chinese are a very early race.

Mme. Blavatsky: Some, but they are in the mountains. They are not really Chinese; they are extraordinary creatures.

Mr. Yates: There was that curious tribe in Southern India. In *Isis Unveiled* you have something about them.

---

9 Edmund (Edward?) William Berridge, homeopathic physician, 1843-1923. He joined the Hermetic Order of the Golden Dawn in May 1889.

Mme. Blavatsky: I say that the Todas[10] were the most mysterious race in all India, and I say what I said in *Isis Unveiled*, because there were three men who assured me of the same. I knew that they were that, and they assured me of it. They had lived years with them. They are very dirty, if you like, but they look like Grecian gods. It is about 70 years ago that they were discovered, and in these 70 years they found six or seven hundred of them. They are now the same number. They never vary; notwithstanding the panthers and the tigers and the leopards, they never lose a single buffalo. The buffalos of others will be stolen every night, especially by the leopards, but never one of their cattle. They have not got arms, they have not got even a knife. They sit there with a little thing like a kind of wand in their hands. I have watched them for years, when I was there with Mrs. Morgan.[11] They are the most extraordinary people you ever saw, and there is not a bit of the Indian in them. You see the round Dravidian race, and the flat-nosed, and all kinds of types; this type is the most pure type that you can find. They are tall; they have got most regular features, most handsome; and their women are ugly. Did you see them, Mr. Sinnett? Now, the missionaries did everything in creation to try and convert one, they never converted a single one.

Mr. B. Keightley: Don't you say that their wives are taken from the Dravidian tribes?

Mme. Blavatsky: No one knows what it is. Sometimes there are women that come there that are not of that tribe. A missionary went there, and he prided himself that he was the first one to have learnt the language of the Todas. He remained with them 18 or 20 years. When he came out he began talking with a Toda and he said,

---

10 The Todas are a pastoral people living in the Nilgiri, or Blue, Hills of Tamilnadu in South India. Their culture is centered around the raising of dairy-buffaloes. HPB writes about this mysterious tribe in *Isis Unveiled*, II:614-616, and devotes one of her Russian travel tales to them in *The Enigmatical Tribes of the Blue Hills*.
11 Ellen H. Morgan, who with her husband, Maj.-Gen. Henry Morgan, had founded a theosophical branch in Ootacamund, a popular hill station in the Nilgiris. HPB was their guest in the summer of 1883. A short record by Mrs. Morgan, "Witchcraft on the Nilgiris," detailing her experiences there is included in *Five Years of Theosophy*, p. 76.

"Where have you learnt [ ]? Isn't it the [ ] language?" Now, they don't work, they don't sow, they do nothing whatever, except have buffalos, live on milk and cheese, and so on. It is the Badagas[12] who are their voluntary tributaries; they bring them everything, corn and the first fruits of the Earth, etc. They do everything for them. They serve them just as priests would serve the gods, if the gods came on Earth. They are afraid of them, those Mulakurumbas;[13] and they are the most vile race of dwarfs that you can meet with. They are the embodiment of fiendish cunning. Ask Mrs. Morgan and General Morgan, who lived for years there. It is something awful, their black magic. They will do the most atrocious things. Mrs. Morgan lost about 23 men in one month, the best of her laborers and workmen. One would come and point out a man, yet never approach him; and in a few days he would be a dead man. There was a commissioner who never believed in them. The [ ] {Mulakurumbas} are fearfully afraid of the Todas; when they see them they will run away; they are just like a frog under the look of certain serpents; it is something terrible. Now Mrs. Bachelor,[14] whom we went with, speaks all these languages beautifully; and we went with Mrs. Morgan, and we passed days there. I have watched them, and it is something extraordinary. They don't pay any attention to you. With the long hair they have, they look like Roman senators in togas. For a painter, it is the most beautiful thing in the world; such grace and dignity—well, they look like gods.

A Lady: Are they great magicians?

Mme. Blavatsky: They say they are good men, and that the [ ] {Mulakurumbas} are mortally afraid of them.

The Lady: They have superior magic then?

Mme. Blavatsky: They have the most extraordinary power. There was 30 years ago a terrible lawsuit there. There were [ ] {Mulakurumbas}

---

12 Largest tribal group in the Nilgiri Hills. HPB in *Enigmatical Tribes* describes them as the vassals and worshippers of the Todas.
13 Dwarf tribe in the Nilgiris.
14 Rhoda Bachelor, daughter of Maj.-Gen. and Mrs. Morgan.

who had done such awful things that the [ ] {Badagas} went and made a conspiracy to burn them, and they roasted them in their village. And it was said that they could not burn their houses unless there was a Toda present. The legend goes that they brought a Toda with them, though they swore always that they never did that, because I don't think in 70 years there was one Toda who was ever imprisoned, except on the testimony of one of these women. I have read all the things General Morgan gave me. This Toda disappeared, and nobody knew where he was gone to, and that was the only Toda who was in prison. You may put millions of money, coins and everything in their way—they never were known to take a thing. You never saw such honesty as they have.

Mr. B. Keightley: Are they intellectually intelligent?

Mme. Blavatsky: General Morgan said to me: "They are very intellectual." Claud Vincent says they are amazingly intellectual, that they will talk on everything; but their dignity and manner and way is something extraordinary.

Mr. B. Keightley: I think you hinted somewhere that they are really of Greek descent?

Mme. Blavatsky: No, they are of Lanka descent, not Greek. They have got their own things. I have written all these legends that they gave me themselves, and what I heard of all these I have written in Russian.[15] They say by the calculation of the Moon it comes to something like 22 thousand years that they came on the hills, the blue hills of the gods, and that their forefathers were in the service of Rama. This is their story, and that they come from Lanka; but it was not what it is now. It was enormous. It was a part of the continent of the Atlanteans when it sunk, but they are the most mysterious race. I wish you had an opportunity to see them, what handsome men, all with long, beautiful wavy hair, even their old men.

Mr. Sinnett: Do they speak other languages besides their own?

---

15 *The Enigmatical Tribes of the Blue Hills of India*, published in the *Russian Messenger* of Moscow in 1884/85.

Mme. Blavatsky: They speak [ ]. Nobody in the world would know their rites, that they have—some of the rites, that they perform in their crypts, that they do in every one of their little houses, which are just like beehives, with a little door where they must come out bending. They have their buffaloes there, and among the buffaloes there is a leader with the silver bells, and one of them has golden bells, and he is a superb animal; but tell me how it is that never a tiger or leopard touches them? This is a thing Webster told me. His father was one of the first to go there 70 years ago, when it was discovered. A man who was in trouble a few years ago in Madras—he was on the Council of the Governor together with Webster there, and his father was one of the first who went there, so he has enormous narratives of them. He was born there, and he has been telling me many things. And he says never was there a case known that one of their cattle was carried away. But these Badagas number about 10,000; the Mulakurumba are many thousands; but they {the Todas} never vary between 600 and 700.

Mr. Sinnett: Do they come under the operation of the census?

Mme. Blavatsky: They are nomadic people. But how can you call them nomadic, when they go from one place to another and they have their own chief priests—those that are set apart, and who never marry, and who have got some ceremonies for the burials and the cremation, such customs as nobody knows of, entirely *sui generis*—and they say their forefathers served Rama, and went to Lanka, and after that were rewarded for services rendered to Rama. When [ ] was killed, they sent them there to take possession of the blue hills of the gods. And they say even the most curious thing, that the Government tried to coax from them—and they would not give—a kind of stone. Morgan tells me he saw it several times in his youth, and it was all with the most extraordinary characters. Nobody had the key to it, and this was the thing given to them by Rama and others.

Mr. B. Keightley: Will they go on living and living there until something happens?

Mme. Blavatsky: I know this man was the only one. When they roasted about 40 men, they said they had to have the Toda to preside over the operation, or else they could do nothing. They hung a good many of those Badagas; but that single Toda that was there disappeared. Speak [ ] of the curious nations, I can assure you, that there are nations that are very little known in India. Those who served them are the Badagas, and the others are the Mulakurumba. Mrs. Morgan knows all about them, and they like her very much, and they treat her to magnificent milk and buffalo cream, and so on. Very rarely they eat meat; they don't do anything; they are kept and served by the Badagas, who work for them perfectly voluntarily.

Mr. Kingsland: Do they practice some kind of yoga?

Mme. Blavatsky: No, they don't, not apparently. I never heard of one. I know they have got their men who know a good deal—I suppose they are priests. I conversed with some of them, but only through an interpreter. I don't know their language. Two of them always looked at me with a kind of grin and with a good-natured smile, and I returned the compliment. And when I went away they gave me a kind of a petrified fig, and he said, "Keep this because it is a good thing if you ever have fever," and so on. I lost it.

Here the proceedings closed.

16.
Theosophical Society.
Meeting of the Blavatsky Lodge
17 Lansdowne Road, Holland Park, W.
April 25, 1889.

Mr. Kingsland in the Chair

Mr. B. Keightley: Question 1. Why should rotation cease on a dead planet?

Mme. Blavatsky: Because the life of a body as a whole is nothing but motion, a reflection of that one life which is called in *The Secret Doctrine* absolute motion. When a man dies his body as a whole ceases to move, although the individual activity of its cells, and ultimately of its molecules, increases enormously. This is proved by the rapid and violent changes that take place in a decomposing corpse. In the same way when a planet dies, its rotatory motion about its own axis ceases, though its activity in its constituent particles is increased rather than diminished. Now, if I am asked if the Moon moves—it is in relation to the Moon that this is asked—if I am asked why the Moon moves in an orbit round the earth, I reply that this is caused by the vampirizing action of the Moon upon the earth—not as science teaches, owing to an attraction exerted by the earth upon the Moon, but rather the reverse: the Moon is so saturated with the magneto, vital emanation of the earth that she is carried along by it like an over-full sponge in a current of water. It is not the water that attracts the sponge in the case, but the sponge is carried along by the stream in its own movement. Does this explain satisfactorily, or did you want to know something very occult?

Mr. Kingsland: No, I only wanted to know why the mass of the Moon should cease to rotate as a mass of matter when the principles had left it—what was the relation between the principles having left it and the mass of the matter of the Moon ceasing to move.

Mme. Blavatsky: It did not cease to move; it moves.

Mr. Kingsland: But, as a whole, on its own axis.

Mme. Blavatsky: Because it cannot move, because the spirit is fled, because the principles are gone; so how can it move?

Mr. B. Keightley: I think you are answered by the analogy.

Mr. Kingsland: It is only removing the difficulty one step further.

Mr. B. Keightley: When a man is dead, when his principles have left him, the body as a whole does not move.

Mr. Kingsland: That is to say, that a man is walking consciously.

Mme. Blavatsky: It is not consciously that they move. They don't know what they are about. Take an idiot, a complete idiot: he will be moving and running and grinning and jumping, but he will not know what he is about.

Mr. Kingsland: Then it is purely internal force.

Mme. Blavatsky: It is simply vital impulse.

Mr. B. Keightley: The scientific idea of the thing is that it is a purely mechanical movement, because the large mass of matter having once been set spinning, there is no friction and nothing to stop it.

Mme. Blavatsky: Don't speak to me about science, because science and I are on cool terms.

Mr. Kingsland: The astronomical idea is that there is friction.

Mr. B. Keightley: Well, it is so slow that no calculation has found any trace of it.

Mr. Kingsland: They have found traces of it.

Mr. B. Keightley: It is supposed to take 300,000,000 of years to make the difference of ½ hour.

Mr. Mead: Are you right in saying the Moon does not move at all? Doesn't it revolve once?

Mr. B. Keightley: Not on its own axis; I don't think there is any rotation of the Moon about its own axis.

Mme. Blavatsky: It rotates (revolves) because it vampirizes and is carried away.

Mr. B. Keightley: Swept along, so to speak, in the current.

Mme. Blavatsky: It vampirizes—not by conscious action, but there is a kind of dead matter, which by its own inherent attribute or quality attracts.

Mr. B. Keightley: You cannot say a sponge absorbs water consciously, but it absorbs.

Mme. Blavatsky: Yes, it is carried up by the current.

Mr. Mead: In another way that is rather analogous, because it does rotate for some time—for instance, near the rocks.

Mme. Blavatsky: There are no rocks in space.

Mr. Kingsland: That gives us rather a different idea as to the planetary motion—the planets revolving by means of their own inherent force. If anything revolves in that way it must have something to revolve against, so to speak.

Mme. Blavatsky: One is a satellite, and the other an independent entity.

Mr. Kingsland: I mean to say it must be able to pull itself round by something, unless it is set going at the beginning, and goes on until it gradually stops by means of friction or some force acting upon it from outside. A man cannot lift himself by his own waistbelt, and you can hardly conceive of a planet revolving, and continuing to revolve, by means of its own axis.

Mr. B. Keightley: Has it ever occurred to you that the Laya centre is really, if you come to follow it out, the idea of rotatory motion, the centre of a vortex.

Mme. Blavatsky: It is.

Mr. Kingsland: This Laya centre does not correspond to the centre of the planet.

Mr. B. Keightley: There is a Laya centre, it is not in three-dimensional space, of course, but it must be the centre of the planet.

Mme. Blavatsky: The Laya centre is the Atman, so to say, the spirit of the Atman.

Mr. Kingsland: It is not a mathematical centre of a circle.

Mr. Old: There must be such a mathematical centre, I think, must there not?

Mr. B. Keightley: It must be the centre of rotation of the earth, that is to say, if you locate it anywhere, then of course the Laya centre is not a point in our three dimensional space.

Mme. Blavatsky: It is out of space and time, the real Laya centre.

Mr. Ingram: Each atom of the whole world has it own Laya centre?

Mme. Blavatsky: It has.

Mr. B. Keightley: Each body as a whole is formed of such particles.

Mr. Kingsland: Do the globes revolve in virtue of the circulation of their principles?

Mme. Blavatsky: I believe so; I could not tell you with certainty.

Mr. Kingsland: Take the analogy of a globe of some kind of substance—metal, or anything you like, immersed in water; that globe could not revolve in the water if it were only exercising an internal force, but if it emitted something that acted against the water, then it could cause it to revolve.

Mr. B. Keightley: All the planets are exercising attractive and repulsive forces upon each other.

Mr. Mead: In the present state of affairs, it would be impossible to introduce any internal power to make it revolve, it would be outside all experience. Take the case of a sphere revolving in water. You could not introduce an internal rotary motion into such a sphere.

Mr. Kingsland: The sphere as a whole could rotate if you had some gas which emanated from it. That is the conception I want to get at.

Mr. Old: We have such cases in mechanics where a body revolves for a long time after the cause of its revolution has ceased, as for instance the flywheel of a large piece of machinery. Or take the ordinary peg-top of our youth. After the first lash, after it is delivered from its cause of motion, it goes on manifesting that cause for a long time after the immediate cause has ceased. It seems to have a mediate cause in itself, a potency to retain the same motion.

Mr. Kingsland: That does not correspond to the planets; they are continually revolving in virtue of an inherent force. When the Pralaya comes, the planet will continue to revolve for some considerable time after its principles had left it.

Mme. Blavatsky: When the real Pralaya comes, the planets won't exist at all, because they will all disintegrate and fly asunder.

Mr. Old: And in the case of the Moon, which is considered as a satellite to us, it has a Pralaya, you know, its individual planetary Pralaya. And it has ceased to have any axcedal {axial} motion. The Moon has ceased to have such a motion on account of those principles having discharged themselves.

Mr. Kingsland: What is it—what are those principles, and what is the action that causes a life planet to revolve?

Mme. Blavatsky: I suppose the light, but there is a great difference between planets and the moon; the Moon is a dead planet.

Mr. Kingsland: And that is why it has ceased to revolve.

Mme. Blavatsky: It has ceased to revolve, and therefore it is carried on by induced motion, so to say, from that emanation from the Earth.

Mr. B. Keightley: It is swept along in a current of the Earth, in fact.

Mme. Blavatsky: Yes, where the Earth goes it will go. That is what I understood. As far as I remember what I have learnt, it is so.

Mr. Old: There is the ordinary circulation of the interplanetary plenum. Is that taken into consideration by you, Mr. Kingsland, in your thoughts?

Mr. Kingsland: That is what I want to get at and elucidate.

Mme. Blavatsky: Do you mean that there is nothing but stillness in space? Why there is a tremendous hurricane of all kinds of rotary motions going on, even outside of any visible planets, or existing planets, because all these currents of air are always in motion; there is the eternal breath which never ceases.

Mr. B. Keightley: You have not got an empty place full of a sort of semi-rigid jelly.

Mme. Blavatsky: Certainly not. It is all alive with all kinds of currents and counter-currents, and wheels within wheels and rotary motion, and so on. This is that which certainly may help to solve the difficulty.

Mr. Ingram: In some part of *The Secret Doctrine* it is treated of at length, the genesis of rotary motion, and the different scientific hypotheses.

Mr. B. Keightley: In the first volume, I think it is.

Mr. Mead: Is not the original rotary motion part of the original life of a planet? And doesn't it gradually decrease?

Mme. Blavatsky: Certainly, but this has nothing to do with the first impulse which is given to that which goes on and becomes a comet, and after a comet it becomes all kinds of things. The first thing is given to that particle which starts by Fohat.

Mr. B. Keightley: Fohat says, he collects the fiery dust and forms them into boards {balls}.

Mme. Blavatsky: And this Fohatic force is outside the planets, not only inside, as I explained in the case of centripetal and centrifugal forces—space is full of that.

Mr. B. Keightley: You always have that element which must apply equally to man as to everything else, the two forms: the internal force, which is limited and confined, so to speak, which is always seeking to free itself; and then the free force outside, which is again acting upon the body all the time, and, as it were, in correlating with the confined force. That, of course, would tend to produce a rotative motion.

Mr. Ingram: Then there are forces at work now, producing the rotary motion of the Earth?

Mr. B. Keightley: Well, of course—not solely because of the rotation must be kept up. Clearly we know, if we take the analogy and follow it out strictly, that a human being does not go on living and moving and expending energy simply in virtue of the life impulse which he receives from his parents, but he grows, and is nourished and takes in food and assimilates it and keeps up his strength in that way. And some process analogous to that must take place in the case of a planet.

Mme. Blavatsky: Certainly. I cannot tell you anything more, because I don't know anything about science.

Mr. Kingsland: I think there is something in *Lucifer* this month which bears upon that by Keely about the magnetic circulation of the Earth.¹ Has the rotation of the Earth anything to do with these magnetic currents that are always circling around it?

Mme. Blavatsky: Most assuredly.

Mr. Kingsland: And these currents cease when the Earth is dead?

Mme. Blavatsky: They won't cease, but the Earth won't be able to feel them any more because there will be no receptive hold upon them. They never cease; they are always going on, but the Earth cannot receive any more. Just the same if you have a hurricane, and it comes to Lansdowne Road,² and if you have got a dead cat there, the dead cat will be swept away. But once it touches it when it is dead, it cannot do anything.

Mr. Mead: And the Moon is unresponsive to these forces?

Mme. Blavatsky: No, because I have just explained why the Moon moves.

Mr. B. Keightley: The Moon is unresponsive to these forces, to the magnetic currents, but the Moon is swept on, carrying on a sort of vampirized life through absorption from the Earth.

Mr. Mead: It does not receive whatever it has of motion from the influences from the Earth.

Mme. Blavatsky: It is not entirely dead. It is paralyzed. It has no more its principles; they are gone.

Mr. B. Keightley: It is dead, but not corrupted yet.

Mme. Blavatsky: Therefore, there is the motion, but not its particles. Sometimes the motion is so great in a dead body that you will find it

---

1 *Lucifer* (the Lightbringer) was the name of the journal started by Mme. Blavatsky in London in September 1887. The article referred to is in the April 1889 issue, pp. 137-140, "Comments of John Worrell Keely on Dr. Schimmel's Lecture: 'The Unity of Forces'" by C.J.B-M. (Clara Jessup Bloomfield-Moore, a great supporter of Keely.)

2 17 Lansdowne Road in London was the location of the Blavatsky Lodge where HPB was domiciled.

turned; and then some will say: "the man was not dead," and came to himself—which is nothing at all but the work of the disintegrating forces.

Mr. B. Keightley: Question 2, page 171, last paragraph. What are the seven classes of monads here mentioned? Are they simply the mineral, vegetable, animal, etc? Can you give them seven distinctive names by which we may refer to them afterwards in the order of their appearance on a chain of globes?

Mme. Blavatsky: The seven classes here referred to are the seven classes of Lunar Pitris or fathers, all of which have reached the human stage of development on the lunar chain. They are therefore not the monads, or rather elementals, of the seven kingdoms of nature, but are the subdivisions of what we may term the lunar mankind—the (lunar lunatics). Of course, when they first arrive on the Earth chain they are very nearly in an undifferentiated condition, and as they descend into matter they differentiate even more and more, till at last they form seven distinctly marked types or classes. Therefore, how can we give them distinct names when these names indicate their attributes, and these are perpetually changing? They may be described by the names of the seven lower Sephiroth of the Kabalah, or by the seven Amshapends of Zoroaster; but this is only in their primitive differentiation from homogeneity. Every time they are transformed they go down lower on the hierarchy, or higher; they change names.

Mr. Kingsland: These human monads, lunar monads, have to pass through the mineral kingdom, have they not?

Mme. Blavatsky: Yes, on the globe A.

Mr. B. Keightley: On globe 2.

Mr. Kingsland: On the whole of the first round?

Mme. Blavatsky: Yes. They don't pass anymore on globe B; it is only the latest arrivals. Still, there are some monads, and they will be those who will come. And at the threshold of the Fourth Round and the fourth globe, which is ours, they are perfectly ready, and after that, having evolved their astral images, and so on—which are those images which become men, hereafter—they merge into that mankind. It is they themselves; it is not that they create, like the Lord God out of nothing, but it is simply that they evolve their Chhayas, and little by little they evolve into it.

Mr. Kingsland: Take the first class of Lunar Pitris. They have to go through the first round on our planetary chain, in one of the elemental kingdoms.

Mr. B. Keightley: No, they go through the three elemental kingdoms—mineral, animal, vegetable kingdoms—up to the human stage, and just enter it on globe A. Then they repeat the same process on globe B, on globe C, D and all round through the first round. The second class of monads arriving from the Lunar chain are a stage behind. They don't reach the human stage, they stop one stage short of that all through the first round; the third class of monads, a stage still later, and so on. So that if you take the Second Round, the first class have reached the human stage already, but the remaining classes each have one or more stages to complete in that round or subsequent rounds.

Mr. Kingsland: It is rather difficult to follow.

Mr. B. Keightley: That is the way it seems to be stated here.

Mr. Mead: But if all these seven classes of Lunar Pitris had reached a man stage on the Lunar chain, had they—all the seven classes—reached a human stage, so to speak?

Mme. Blavatsky: The human stage on the Moon is far inferior to that of the Earth, because every time that the principles of a plane go to form another plane, it is always on a higher scale.

Mr. Ingram: But they had, all of them, reached that stage, but they differed from themselves in order of merit.

Mme. Blavatsky: You don't think that the principles shot from the Moon in one day created the whole chain? It certainly required millions and millions of years to do such a thing as that. Once that globe A was ready, then the Lunar Pitris of the globe A passed into it. Then the others remained yet there during the time that the second, B, was produced; then the principles began shooting out from globe B of the Lunar chain, on to our earthly chain, and then the second ones came in. During the first round, when it comes to the last globe, then only it is that you can say the whole lunar chain is at an end, you understand, that it is dead, as it is now. But to the last moment they come.

Mr. B. Keightley: You say in *The Secret Doctrine* that only when the first or highest class of the monads leave the last globe of the lunar chain, that is the moment of death of the first globe.

Mme. Blavatsky: That is what I say. It is all explained there.

Mr. Mead: Yes, but I don't understand it.

Mme. Blavatsky: What don't you understand there?

Mr. Mead: The first class on the lunar chain have passed off the whole of the lunar planetary chain into a Laya centre, have not they?

Mme. Blavatsky: I beg your pardon; the monads go when the globes are ready.

Mr. B. Keightley: The monads are not the principles of the globe.

Mr. Old: Is it stated how long since the Moon ceased to give off monads to the Earth?

Mme. Blavatsky: I could not tell you. You are a mathematician: reckon. I cannot tell you, because they don't give the correct figures at all; they say simply it is 300,000,000 of years since life appeared on this Earth, and there they stop. I speak to you about the Hindu chronology, and then they leave you to whistle and infer for yourselves. They won't give it to you. Mr. Sinnett tried it several times and he met a Chinese wall. You must go by the Brahmanical calculation, and it gives a Manvantara of fifteen figures. It gives it to you certainly quite correctly. It is given in the second volume. Everything is given—how long it is since the universe was evolved; how long it is that such and such a thing happened; how many years the Manvantara consisted of, and the Pralaya, and when the Manu period was. It is 18,000,000 of years—that is to say, 18,000,000 of years is given to the appearance of the real man, and not the Chhaya. It begins, therefore, in the Fourth Round—or rather, in the middle of the Fourth {Third, see *S.D.* I:46} Race. This is when they begin their 18,000,000 of years, so you may count. Our Fifth Race is a million of years; take into consideration, if you please, that there are several kinds of Pralaya, that Pralaya is not only that which you think, when everything is dissolved and disappears. There are several kinds of Pralayas, and unless you learn all these, it is very easy for you in reading the *Vishnu Purana* to take one Pralaya for another. And they don't go to the trouble of qualifying the Pralayas, and they let you lose yourselves as much as you like. That was always a game of the priests.

Mr. ———: With regard to the first class of the Lunar Pitris, directly it leaves the seventh globe, does it incarnate?

Mr. B. Keightley: No, it passes into Nirvana.

Mme. Blavatsky: And then it comes in time for the Second Round, because between every life and evolution there is a temporary Pralaya between them—an obscuration—and then take into consideration that after every round there is the same period, the same duration, that lasted, for instance, for the Manvantaric day of the chain. It will be the same Pralaya, you understand: the night will be as long as the day. Mind you, I don't speak about the cosmic days; I speak simply about the days of the chain.

Mr. B. Keightley: That is to say, between the going to sleep of the last planet-chain, and the re-awakening, you have the time of the awakening of the whole chain.

Mme. Blavatsky: If you are a mathematician you can go and

do it very easily. For instance, if you take a given period of time approximately, and be guided by the Hindu chronology, you can do it. They say to you that 12,000 human years and 12,000 divine years make quite a difference, and they give you a proportion of how much more it is. There are divine years and human years and Manvantara years and all kinds of years. So if you are a good mathematician, you won't be lost in it.

Mr. ——: The first class goes on through the different kingdoms right up to the human stage, and following after the steps come other classes in such a way that when the first class leaves the first globe A, the seventh class appears on the first globe and passes on.

Mr. B. Keightley: Passes into the interplanetary.

Mr. ——: Do they all follow it and go into the two planets?

Mme. Blavatsky: Yes, but now comes algebra—that the duration of the lunar days and nights are in proportion a great deal shorter than those of the Earth, and that during, for instance, four and a half rounds, the whole seven come. That is a very great thing: the whole seven have the time to have their Pralayas, so that of the four rounds there is not a single Monad that can come. Every one of us is a Monad of the true blue stock; there is not a single Monad that has come since then. It is only, you see, the pious people who teach that God breathed a soul into every baby that appears. We say: "Fiddlesticks!"

Mr. Mead: These seven classes incarnated, we have said. When the first class leaves the globe A, does the sixth class—or rather, will the next one after it, the second class, which has reached the sixth kingdom, stop short of the human stage, because that class does not go into the human stage till the Second Round? Therefore, it leaves that planet and goes into the Pralaya or the animal kingdom.

Mme. Blavatsky: It seems to me, if my recollection is right, that the first class of Pitris, those who become the Lunar Pitris, have passed through all the kingdoms on globe A, and they don't pass through all the kingdoms on globe B.

Mr. B. Keightley: You are mistaken in your recollection.

Mr. Mead: If that is so, and they being the pioneers, when they incarnate they—being the first, into what kingdom do they go straight away? Into the human kingdom?

Mme. Blavatsky: That is what you have got to read. I have simply written and tried, without a single mistake, to give that which is in *The Secret Doctrine*. But when it comes to those calculations, after a time I don't want to remember it, even.

Mr. Kingsland: There is one point which is making a little confusion all through. The first class comes over from the lunar chain to globe A and they are followed by the second, third, fourth, and so on. Now, are all those seven classes on globe A at the same time, before the first class goes on to globe B?

Mr. B. Keightley: What is stated here is this, in this paragraph which we are just passing. (Reads from *The Secret Doctrine*.)

Mr. Kingsland: Has that first class been all round the chain by this time?

Mme. Blavatsky: No. It must be placed so that he who would like to know the time and calculate, would have to take into consideration the greater shortness of the Pralayas and of the Nirvanic state of the lunar classes. That is what you have to do.

Mr. Kingsland: You see, from that statement, class one are leaving globe A just when class seven are coming onto it; therefore, in the meantime, two, three, four, five and six are all on globe A.

Mr. B. Keightley: But, you see, when the Pralaya comes, as far as I can understand from this, the development of the several kingdoms is stopped short at the point they have reached for that time, and then they have to go on all round the chain.

Mr. Mead: I want to know if it is at the moment of that Pralaya when the last monad of the first class is passed on.

Mr. B. Keightley: That is not stated.

Mr. Kingsland: Does that obscuration come before all the classes have passed on globe B?

Mme. Blavatsky: No. There are those who remain, the last ones, and then they come after that, because they have only just come in, and it must be timed in such a way that the seven come into the space of the rotation or formation of the first globe, of the future humanity. Till the Fourth Round they are not really humans.

Mr. B. Keightley: This is what seems to be implied here, that the development of the other classes, as it were, reaches a point when the obscuration sets in in which they cannot go any further. On that globe the hour of the obscuration has struck, and they are developed on that globe and everything is stopped. Then they have to go on to globe B and repeat the process, and so on all round the chain.

Mr. Kingsland: We ought to have a board with seven rows and seven heads, as they have in the schools.

Mme. Blavatsky: And what good would it do to you? It would be loss of time, and nothing else.

Mr. Kingsland: My difficulty is to see how it is that a half of these do not come in in time to reach the human stage. Isn't that your difficulty, Mead?

Mr. Mead: No, I understand that. My difficulty is when this Pralaya, this obscuration, overtakes it. When does it?

Mr. B. Keightley: It comes at a moment, and then all these Monads who are cycling have to leave that planet.

Mr. Mead: In a rush?

Mr. B. Keightley: At that moment, apparently.

Mme. Blavatsky: It is so timed that they all enter into their Nirvanic state, their time of rest, between the two planets. Nature does not make mistakes in this case.

Mr. B. Keightley: Her timepieces do not require cleaning, you know.

Mme. Blavatsky: You see, in mathematics, I was never a Newton in my life.

Mr. Mead: If this first class goes through all the kingdoms up to man, the second class will have been worked up once with the first class, so that the seventh class coming in, it will have been six times differentiated by the six classes that have gone before.

Mr. B. Keightley: So that it is able to work up by degrees. That is how it is that all the seven classes reach the human stage of the Fourth Round.

Mr. Ingram: Have we been Lunar Pitris?

Mme. Blavatsky: We are the Lunar Pitris.

Mr. Ingram: Then we are talking of ourselves when we are talking of these?

Mme. Blavatsky: It is "we," if you please, but we do not remember it. To think that we have been angels and have become—what—such pumpkins, knowing nothing at all! To think we have been ornamented with beautiful wings and pinions, and where are they? Gentlemen, you are very much addicted to questioning, and you really ought not to pry into the mysteries of God!

Mr. B. Keightley: Question 3, page 172. What are the seven principles of the globes which are transferred one after the other to the globes of the new chain?

Mme. Blavatsky: Each globe has seven principles which are correlative with the seven principles in man; but this must not be understood to mean that the seven principles are represented by the Monads which are performing their cyclic pilgrimages through the seven kingdoms of nature. For example, the seventh or highest principle of the planet is not the Monads which have reached the human stage of development, but the planet as a whole has its own seven principles, as any other body has. To make it clear. The Earth has its physical or material body, its astral body, its life principle, its animal nature, its instincts, or lower Manas, its higher intelligence which it imparts to and shares with some of the animals, its Buddhi, composed of the gnomes, or earth elementals, and its Atman, represented by an intelligence called the spirit of the Earth, which some Kabbalists have identified with Jehovah. This latter belief was a dogma with the Valentinians and the Ophites, who said that the God of the Jews was simply the spirit of the Earth. You will find this if you read the Valentinians. They all say that the God was the spirit of the last terrestrial plane which created this, and then you can read the corrections that are there, with this Bahak-Zivo, and Fetahil and so on. Did you ever read this? It is the most interesting thing in the world, only, unfortunately, it is not translated and you can only get it in Latin. It is one of the oldest gospels, and one of the most interesting.[3]

Mr. Mead: Would you mind reading that again? Not the explanations of the principles, but the last principles of the Earth upwards.

Mme. Blavatsky: (Reads again, "The earth has its physical," etc., etc.)

Mr. Kingsland: Then what we have been calling the planetary spirits in the previous discussions are simply the Atman of each of the planets?

Mme. Blavatsky: Some of them. Because they are again divided into seven. This is the great mysterious number of this Manvantara, so you had better not mix up too many things, because you will be terribly confused, that is sure.

Mr. Kingsland: Then are we to understand that the Monads,

---

3 Clearly, the reference is to *Codex Nazaræus*. See *The Secret Doctrine*, I:194-196, and *Theosophical Glossary*, pp. 86-87.

although independent of these seven principles, are necessary for the completion, so to speak, of the animal life of the planet?

Mme. Blavatsky: Certainly.

Mr. Kingsland: Of the individual animal life of the globe or planet?

Mme. Blavatsky: You mean the elementals which precede the other kingdoms?

Mr. Kingsland: I mean the Monads in their whole career.

Mme. Blavatsky: Certainly, they are necessary.

Mr. Mead: Wouldn't it be convenient to give some name to these three sub-kingdoms?

Mme. Blavatsky: Call them Smith or Brown or anything you like, because I am not going to bother myself. They called me by a pet name when I was young, but they would not call me by that now, I have changed.

Mr. Kingsland: Can you tell us at all in what way the seven human principles are necessary for the completion of these seven principles?

Mme. Blavatsky: Because it is a link. Because every one of them radiates something which corresponds in some other principle, in anything, in any being. If you break one link, the whole goes to nothing.

Mr. Kingsland: But they are not identical.

Mr. B. Keightley: As far as I gathered, as far as I inferred, it was that the development of the earth, of the principles of the earth, is assisted and carried on, or very largely assisted by the development of humanity after it has once made its appearance on a globe.

Mme. Blavatsky: Most assuredly, because the sins of humanity affect the earth, and the joys of humanity affect the earth. And you will see that when humanity is at its worst, then they will have neither harvest nor anything growing, and the earth will be in perfect sterility and despair.

Mr. B. Keightley: You must have this intimate connection between man and the earth, or else you would have no relation at all.

Mme. Blavatsky: The ancients were wise when they called the earth the mother of man.

Mr. Kingsland: What is the difference between the mineral kingdom before these Monads have come over from the other chain and after?

Mr. B. Keightley: Greater perfection.

Mme. Blavatsky: Everything grows. That which we see now certainly has not existed at the beginning of the round; and that which was at the beginning of the round did not exist and was entirely different at the third round, and so on. As we go on, when we reach the point at the Fourth Round, then everything is adjusted. There is a totally complete adjustment of matter and spirit. And then, till that point we were falling into matter, but from that point, once it is reached, it is matter that goes and ascends into spirit.

Mr. ———: Has not the worst point of human life been passed, yet?

Mme. Blavatsky: I do not know, physically. I say we will have worse days than we have had yet, because we have been sinning so much.

Mr. ———: Then we have not reached the lowest point, yet?

Mme. Blavatsky: We have not reached the lowest point.

Mr. B. Keightley: The greater the responsibility, the heavier the sin. While we were falling into matter, and while the spiritual consciousness was entirely obscured by matter, we had not anything like the responsibility that we have now, not in the same way. Because now we passed that point to a considerable extent, and we are beginning to become more spiritualized. With that comes at the same time a possibility of much more far-reaching sin or breach of the law, which would be very much farther reaching in its effects, and something more serious.

Mme. Blavatsky: This is perfectly logical and comprehensible.

Mr. Ingram: Isn't there, at the same time, on the other side, a greater acquiescence and obedience to law, as against the disobedience? Isn't there a larger part of mankind that obeys the law and whose accumulated Karma neutralizes the bad Karma of the others?

Mme. Blavatsky: I do not know. I do not think so. Nothing can neutralize the bad Karma of individuals. Collectively there may be some equilibrium, but I am afraid it is all the wrong way. You see, evil predominates everywhere. It is not good. Go where you like, you find there is not a thing that is done that is not done with selfish motives and so as to benefit all one's self, or nation, or individual, and that the others would be the losers thereby. It is something terrible when you come to look at the present state of business, of life, and of civilization. This civilization is the cancer of humanity; it will be the ruin of humanity in the way it is conducted. I do not say civilization as it ought to be. It is the most gigantic development of selfishness that ever was known. And I can assure you that the Fifth Race will go out with a great flourish of trumpets, which will be other than the trumpets of the war cry.

Mr. Ingram: Is the selfishness greater now than it was in the Fourth Race?

Mme. Blavatsky: A thousand times worse, because they are just descending into spirit {sic}, and they cling to matter with the utmost desperation, that is why.

Mr. B. Keightley: Question 4. Are these principles all transferred from each of the globes of the lunar chain to the earth chain, and the latter made complete in all the seven principles of each of the seven globes, *before* the *Monads* emerge from the Nirvana into which they pass after leaving the lunar chain? Or does the evolution of the new chain, as regards the transfer of the principles and the evolution of the Monads, proceed *pari passu*?

Mme. Blavatsky: The question is answered in *The Secret Doctrine*, so why should you ask? Of course the principles of the globe of the lunar chain are all transferred, each septenary, to its corresponding globe of the earth chain. And the earth chain globes have attained their full septenary constitution before the first Monads make their appearance on globe A. From that time onwards the evolution of the globes and the Monads proceed *pari passu*, not before.

Mr. B. Keightley: That is to say, each globe in its turn has attained its full septenary constitution before any Monads make their appearance on it.

Mr. Kingsland: But that is only the starting point of the evolution of the globe; it is not the obtaining of these seven principles, but something further beyond.

Mr. B. Keightley: The child attains his full septenary constitution at the age of seven years, but you can't say the evolution of the man is complete.

Mme. Blavatsky: You can't say the evolution is complete, ever. It is complete only an instant before the final Pralaya. Nature is always evolving, always transforming itself and going higher and higher and higher. Once Nature stops it is death, it is stagnation.

Mr. Kingsland: In what does the evolution of the globes consist, apart from the evolution of the Monads?

Mme. Blavatsky: In its own external evolution and everything.

Mr. B. Keightley: It has got to form itself into a globe. Of course, it has to be done up to a certain point, so there is a complete septenary.

Mme. Blavatsky: The evolution must proceed.

Mr. B. Keightley: Question 5. "Nature, the physical evolutionary power." What does "Nature" represent?

Mme. Blavatsky: "Nature, the physical evolutionary power," stands here for all the forces which are innate in the four lower Kosmic principles, or the Kosmic quaternary. For Kosmos has got its seven principles, as we have—e.g., my hand in conjunction with my brain makes signs on this paper which convey an intelligible meaning (I am not sure of it, though!). But if my brain were partially paralyzed, as has been observed in certain cases of disease, my hand may still, by sheer force of habit, make signs on this paper, or pretend to write, but these signs would convey no meaning whatever. In the latter case, only the lower quaternary or physical evolutionary power is acting. This, I suppose, answers sufficiently. That is what I mean by it.

Mr. B. Keightley: Question 6. What class or classes of intelligences are included here under the term "Nature"?

Mme. Blavatsky: The four lower classes or principles, as I have just said. There is no need to repeat it.

Mr. B. Keightley: Question 7. "The Chhayas of the Lunar Pitris." What is a Chhaya?

Mme. Blavatsky: Did I not tell you 29,000 times, Chhaya is a Sanskrit word, meaning shadow, or image, or what we call astral body? [ ] {Sañjña},[4] the wife of Surya, the Sun, becoming tired of the too ardent love of her husband, left him her handmaiden, Chhaya, that is to say, her own astral image, or body, and took herself off to the jungles to become a yogi. So runs the tradition. Somehow or other, as *Vishnu Purana* narrates, the Sun, deceived by the likeness, managed to have two children from this astral body—so it is stated in *Vishnu Purana*—and that is the origin of Chhaya, the astral body.

Mr. B. Keightley: Question 8. Has a planet an individuality as a man has an Ego?

Mme. Blavatsky: It has. Its ruling spirit, or governor, as it is called in *Pimander*,[5] is self-conscious. Any questions to that?

Mr. Kingsland: That has been partially answered before.

---

4 *The Secret Doctrine* II:174 supplies the name and story.
5 Also known as *Pœmandres*, *Pœmander* or *Poimandres*, the title of one of the books in the *Corpus Hermeticum*, often used to refer to the entire collection.

Mr. B. Keightley: Question 9. Is there any analogy between the Monad of man and the vital essence of a planet?

Mme. Blavatsky: You do offer very funny questions! Certainly not. There is an analogy—I would call it a perfect correspondence—between the Monad of a man and the ruling spirit or governor of a spirit {planet}. But the vital essence of that planet corresponds to the vital essence of man, therefore to the Kama-rupa. For Prana (or life) has, strictly speaking, two vehicles, as Manas is double: Linga-sarira, or astral body, is the vehicle of the life principle, or spirit life; while Kama-rupa is the vehicle of the physical or material essence. In other words, the three higher principles of the septenary of Prana reside in the astral body, while the four lower principles have their seat in Kama-rupa. You have learnt something new tonight, because I discovered, to my great surprise, that Mr. Bert Keightley did not know what I meant, that Kama-rupa was the vehicle of the life essence and that there was a difference between it and Prana, which has seven principles. Therefore, as Kama-rupa is the vehicle of the grossest of that form, that Prana the astral body has got is a vehicle of the spirit of the life principle, because it is connected with the higher principles of the triad and not with the quaternary.

Mr. Kingsland: That is certainly a new idea.

Mme. Blavatsky: I did not know it was a new idea at all.

Mr. B. Keightley: Nobody had ever stated it in any theosophical work.

Mme. Blavatsky: My dear sirs, I say to all you, "Not guilty," who do not live in the house; but those who live in the house and from morning to night speak and live and have their being in occultism ought to know it. I absolve everyone who does not live here, but not Mr. Bertram Keightley, because he ought to know.

Mr. Kingsland: It has not been done in any published work so far.

Mme. Blavatsky: My dear sir, it was said to Mr. Sinnett before he wrote *Esoteric Buddhism* (Whether he put it there, I don't know.), but it is a thing which is an axiom, and it has been put, I am perfectly sure, in *The Theosophist*—that there is not a thing in nature which has not got its two poles and its seven principles. That is one of the fundamental axioms of the occult sciences and the esoteric doctrines, that every blessed thing has its seven principles and its polarity.

Mr. Kingsland: If you can divide each principle into seven you get 49, which is confusing.

Mr. ———: And then divide each of those 49 into seven.

Mr. Mead: One understands that everything is subdivisible into sevens like that, but that Prana principle having two vehicles is difficult to follow.

Mme. Blavatsky: Prana in man has two vehicles because there is a spiritual life and there is a material, physical life. Now, that which is in the Kama-rupa is the grossest sub-principle, so to say, and all that, but that which is in the astral body is the pure spiritual life. Now, if you do not understand this, how will you understand the 49 fires of occultism? If you don't understand them, you are simply a flapdoodle, and he who wants to be a flapdoodle, let him neglect the 49 fires. That is all I can tell you. The astral body being the shadow or the image of man is in direct communication with the higher principles, whereas Kama-rupa is the animal. It is the seat of everything animal.

Mr. B. Keightley: If you look at the diagram of the planet in the human principles which is given a few pages back, you will find you get exactly the explanation of the two vehicles.

Mme. Blavatsky: You cannot expect me to give everything; something must be left to the intuition and to human intelligence. If I had written everything I would have had to make 25 volumes and it would not have been enough. I told you hundreds of times, stick to analogy here.

Mr. B. Keightley: If you look at page 153 {of volume 1 of *The Secret Doctrine*}, you get it. That diagram gives the key if you make that substitution, if you put it in its proper order.

Mme. Blavatsky: I have remarked you must not number them. The number "one" is that principle which is predominant in man. Now, if you happen to have your fourth principle predominant, it will be the first. They want to have everything put straight for them. They won't shake their own brains.

Mr. B. Keightley: Question 10, page 192: "The holy youths refused to multiply…" If these "sons" could once refuse to inhabit the Chhaya-rupas, why could they not continue to refuse? And what was the necessity which finally compelled them to incarnate in even less pure rupas?

Mme. Blavatsky: Because they were not independent Englishmen, but simply poor celestial beings, and they were not as obstinate as your nation is. And what prevented them was Karma. Not a single word more can I say. Let us not forget that there is a limit to the freedom of action of every differentiated being in the whole universe. Karma, being the absolute adjusting law, whether in heaven or on earth, says to the proud waves: "So far shalt thou go and no farther." If it says this to the waves, it says it to the angels, and anything you like. It is Karma, and they cannot go against Karma. It is the whole thing. They may kick as much as they like, but they have to do it. Instead of pure and wholesome bodies, they had to enter into defiled bodies.

Mr. Mead: Then free will is always circumscribed?

Mr. ———: Did these beings that refused to incarnate know they were doing wrong?

Mme. Blavatsky: I suppose they did, but it was disagreeable to imprison themselves into those bodies once more, and they delayed and delayed. And if you read *The Secret Doctrine*, you will see what occurred.

Mr. ———: How did the law of Karma act on them?

Mme. Blavatsky: It acts on everything that is differentiated under the Sun—not our Sun, but the spiritual Sun.

Mr. B. Keightley: All these classes and hierarchies of divine beings are these evolutions of previous Manvantaras, and they have an infinite line of Karma behind them.

Mme. Blavatsky: They do not come created by anything or make a simultaneous appearance with the universe.

Mr. B. Keightley: Question 11, page 193: You say that the Jewish Kabbalists argue "that no Spirit could belong to the divine hierarchy unless Ruach (Spirit) was united to Nephesh (living soul)." That is to say that "it is necessary for each ego to attain full self-consciousness as a human, i.e., conscious being."

Mme. Blavatsky: They do belong to the divine hierarchy, because they had been men in the preceding Manvantara. Now, whether it was on this earth or on other earths, I do not know; never mind they were men or human beings. I do not know whether they had two arms and two legs and a head, but they were Manus—thinking beings. As the sons of divine hierarchy, which will represent divine creators in the Manvantara to come, will be those men of this earth who will have attained the highest perfection, everyone of us, ladies and gentlemen, has before him or her a chance. If we behave well we will become, every one of us, one of these gentlemen—the Kumaras, they call them, the youths. Perhaps they too will in their turn hesitate to inhabit very unsavory bodies and be imprisoned in them; but they will have to do it in order to atone for the unpaid bills of the total of their past existence. Every one of us has to act according to law and Karmic law.

Mr. B. Keightley: Question 12 (Originally question 14.), page 194: "Bahak-Zivo…is ignorant of Orcus." What does "Orcus" symbolize? You say in *The Secret Doctrine* that it is the "rebellious angels," those who refuse to create, that are the intellectual saviors of mankind, and you prove that the fall through pride is only a theological libel on these, our true deliverers from ignorance. Yet what you have just said in answer to question 10 seems to imply this latter view. Please explain.

Mme. Blavatsky: It is true they have fallen in one sense, but not through pride; only through unwillingness to imprison themselves, as I have just said, in finite and limited form. But this is quite a different thing from what the theologians say. They aver these angels sought to become gods and dethrone gods, which is an absurdity. We say they were gods whom the law of evolution compelled to descend into matter, that is to say, to fall, but instead of submitting quietly to the law and incarnating at the proper time, they delayed until man had brutalized himself in his ignorance, and thus defiled themselves and the bodies which the law compelled them to inhabit. Theologians now speak of a hell into which they were hurled; and the occultists say the hell means simply the human body, and there is no other hell than earth. The fact that Christ and so many other solar gods—Hercules, etc.—descended into hell is an allegory pointing to just such imprisonment in the physical body. They are certainly our saviors, because without them we would be simply senseless animals. Therefore, what the theologians say is a perfect libel. They speak of angels who wanted to become gods.

Mr. ———: Is there no limit to the cycle of necessity after the egos attained the state Nirvana? Is there a possibility of having to go through succeeding rounds?

Mme. Blavatsky: The universe that they will inhabit will be immeasurably higher than the one they have inhabited, and therefore it is one more step to perfection—more and more and more.

Mr. B. Keightley: One question that suggests: When there is one more step to perfection, does it mean to carry with it the idea that as it is analogous to this universe, so, on the higher universe, there will be pleasure and pain?

Mme. Blavatsky: As the Absolute has never taken me into his confidence (For which perhaps he is to be blamed.), I cannot answer such questions as that.

Mr. B. Keightley: The question is whether pleasure and pain are really limited to our plane of consciousness.

Mme. Blavatsky: I would ask you, if you please, what is pleasure and pain? Is it an eternal entity, or eternal entities?

Mr. B. Keightley: Why I put the question was this. For instance, we know there is differentiation—

Mme. Blavatsky: We know there is differentiation? We *understand* there is differentiation and are very proud of it, but whether there will be a differentiation of the same kind or another in other Manvantaras, this remains a secret. Even between the Absolute and the Logos.

Mr. Kingsland: Isn't it possible that during another Manvantara everything may be arranged into nines or sixes, instead of sevens?

Mme. Blavatsky: It may be in the following Manvantara that two and two may not make four any longer, but it may make twelve. Something will happen we cannot expect.

Mr. —— Has there ever been number one evolved?

Mme. Blavatsky: Number one would be a difficult thing. It does not yield to any combination, it is unity. We must have two, at least, and two will never make a figure. Two is a despised number. Despised by the Pythagoreans. They were two straight lines, which started from nowhere, and did not know where they went to. Two we must not take, also.

Mr. ——: Then three is the lowest number?

Mme. Blavatsky: It is the first one from which you can make anything. You cannot make of one anything, or of two. One is unity. It may be endless and infinite.

Mr. ——: That is all from the point of view of the seven?

Mr. ——: Unless it is a circle.

Mme. Blavatsky: The circle, if you please, is "the," the root of number one, which is no number.

Mr. B. Keightley: You speak a good deal about various Gnostic systems; there are one or two points that wanted clearing up a little. Question 13, page 194: If Fetahil, as stated later, represents the host of the Lunar Pitris who created a senseless man, and if he is "a still purer spirit" than Bahak-Zivo, what does the latter correspond to?

Mme. Blavatsky: The Nazarene business is not at all plain, and is full of metaphor, chiefly directed against the God of the Jews, and their opponents. Therefore it is so mixed up that nobody will know which is which. He is represented sometimes as a higher spirit, and sometimes as a lower. Bahak-Zivo corresponds sometimes to Christ, and sometimes to other things. I have been bringing this in, not at all that you should come and ask me to learn it, because everyone can go and read it in the original, who reads Latin. But why I have quoted it here is, to show that in every system, high or low, the "Secret Doctrine" was repeated, and there were things which were all based on truth. But you need not go out of your way to make me teach you the Nazarene system.

Mr. B. Keightley: Question 14, page 194: "Bahak-Zivo…is ignorant of Orcus." What does "Orcus" symbolize?

Mme. Blavatsky: Orcus symbolizes many things: Death, Hell; it symbolizes what the Buddhists would call Mara—many, many things. Orcus is a place of Darkness and Desolation, and since Bahak-Zivo was not acquainted with Orcus, that is to say, with the corresponding contrasted pole of life, he could not create beings, because he could not make a finite being. It is just the same as the thing which Siva throws out, which is more necessary than the Prince of Denmark to "Hamlet."

Mr. B. Keightley: That is all in the questions.

Mr. Old: I was trying to evolve that idea which was generated with me, which you call wisdom. A thought did strike me a short time ago, that was in respect to the numerical basis of a Manvantara, or order of creation. There was the number seven as the root basis of this Manvantara. Do you speak of our limited Manvantara, or the Maha-Manvantara?

Mme. Blavatsky: Of all the Manvantaras that the Hindus speak about. Maybe it is of the solar system only.

Mr. Old: You speak of it in *The Secret Doctrine* as the root number of nature.

Mme. Blavatsky: In this Manvantara.

Mr. Old: You say in another Manvantara we may have five.

Mme. Blavatsky: Most assuredly we may, because Nature changes entirely in her manifestations and forms. Now go and see, if you please, and ask medicine, ask botany—you find in every department the septenary everywhere. Even the diseases can be septenary, 7, 14, 21, and so on. Here is a doctor; he will tell you everything is in seven. Take the flakes of snow, you will find in it the septenary number. You find six little spots, and a seventh in the middle. You take a drop of water, it splashes, and becomes a pentagon, and a six-pointed star. See what Tyndall writes about it. Once we had a discussion about it. There is not a thing where you can escape it. All this goes by the weeks of the Moon, weeks by septenates and everything.

Mr. Old: Of course that is quite true, but our scope of observation is so limited, that it is tied down to this plane.

Mme. Blavatsky: Then extend it. Try to see it with your third eye, and don't look only with your two eyes. And try also to think with your spiritual brain.

Mr. Old: I want to identify myself with somebody or some Monad outside our solar system altogether.

Mme. Blavatsky: You cannot fail to identify yourself because *it* will identify you if you don't. Every one of us, we were before and will be afterwards—not in our personalities, but in our higher selves. We may defy those selves as much as we like, yet they remain immortal. We cannot get rid of them, but they can get rid of us. Every and each consciousness of ours will feel it, and will see that it is entirely linked to it. It cannot be separated.

Mr. Old: Then the number of changes in mere units for the basic number would be seven. 2 you do not count, 1 is Absolute, 2 is nothing, and you have 3, 4, 5, 6, 7, 8, and 9 as possibilities, that is to say, you have 7 possibilities.

Mme. Blavatsky: But the 7 are the principal forces in Nature. The 7 are all the 7 planets, the 7 planes of consciousness. It is the great mystery number. Take the Kabalah; you know yourself how the name is written, even the name of Tetragrammaton. If you put it in the Jewish letters, you make of it 3 and 4. Out of these, the 4 represent the 7 lower Sephiroth, and the 3, the 3 higher Sephiroth. If you add Shekhinah and Ain-Soph, you will have 9, not the 12, because the 3 are apart. Even the year is divided, because it divides itself naturally. Everything is divided into that.

Mr. Old: Then the term Nature—does that apply to everything in the solar system, or right away to infinity?

Mme. Blavatsky: It occurs in our solar system. At all events, I can't say to anything outside of it, and you won't find high adepts who will tell you much outside of the solar system.

Mr. B. Keightley: You said just now number 7 is found in the solar year. I don't see quite how it comes in. It does not divide into 365.

Mme. Blavatsky: Ask Old, he'll tell you.

Mr. Old: There was a difference. It was a matter of 360, the difference between 360 lunar, and 370 solar—that is to say, reckoning by digits or the degrees in the zodiac, apparent degrees—mathematical degrees, I should say. And the difference between these two was 365, which gives a solar circle roughly.

Mme. Blavatsky: Very roughly, because in the tropical year it won't agree.

Mr. B. Keightley: The true solar year is 365 and a quarter, about, and a fraction less than a quarter; but then I don't think that divides into 7.

Mr. Old: No, certainly not. Not unless we proceed to minutes or seconds. I don't know how it would work out then.

Mr. B. Keightley: I don't see the 7.

Mr. Old: I will try and work it out.

Mme. Blavatsky: You will have 7 always, because 7 Manvantaras go in that, and the 7 in the tropical year, and the 7 in the solar year and the cycles. Well if you reckon or calculate you will see that the cycles come to number 7. They are septenates, the cycles, that is sure.

Mr. ——: Just now, madam, you were speaking of the word Nature as applying only to the solar system. Do you mean the planetary chain?

Mme. Blavatsky: No, the whole of the system.

Mr. ——: Then surely it includes the other ever-invisible planet.

Mr. B. Keightley: Certainly I think so.

Mr. ——: That is divisible by 7. 365 days, 4 hours, 49 minutes, 49 seconds.

Mr. Old: The latest calculation is 365 days, 5 hours, making nearly 6 hours. And if you add one leap day, you get beyond this, so that in about 213 years you would require to drop a day.

Mme. Blavatsky: That shows that you have got to calculate as the Hindus do, because they calculate, and sometimes they drop out, and sometimes they bring in. They always bring them into sevens. Look at their old astronomical works, the buildings in Benares, and in the old cities, they are all worked on that system. They were most curious machines for their buildings, instruments, and so on. The chief constellations are all septenaries. The seven Pleiades and the Great Bear and everywhere are all seven. When I come to think about this blessed Sabbath and the seventh day and rest that is taken bodily from the periods, the Manvantaric periods, the seven races and so on, I say they don't understand it. That is the day of rest, that is to say, the Pralaya. They come and they make in this blessed England a regular Pralaya on the Sundays, so that everyone is ready to go and cut off his head and die; because to begin with the ancient Jews did not have a week at all, they did not have names for days of the week. They had only one, it was the seventh day they knew, and nothing else. They were calculating by the Moon, the lunar calculation.

Mr. Old: How far back do the Jews' days date? We have 300 B.C., we have the seven days of the week given according to the planets. I suppose it would be a period quite anterior to that you refer to?

Mme. Blavatsky: They never had a week.

Mr. Old: Was it the Assyrians?

Mme. Blavatsky: The Chaldeans had. The Athenian week was ten days, the Roman eight days. It was only the Hindus who had seven days, and had a planetary name for each day of the week, and it is from the Hindus that it comes. They went and began calculating, and took the names of the solar angels, which belong to the solar calculation, and they shoved them and stuck them on the weeks which belong to the lunar calculations, so they made a mess of it. It is a terrible mess in astronomy; they have mixed up the colours, the metals, they have mixed up everything, as you know yourself.

Proceedings closed.

17.
Theosophical Society.
Blavatsky Lodge, May 2, 1889.
Meeting at 17 Lansdowne Road, Holland Park, W.

Mr. Kingsland in the Chair

Mr. B. Keightley: You quoted this passage: "And there was war in heaven." etc. (Reads from *The Secret Doctrine*.) Question 1. "Michael and his angels fought against the Dragon and his angels" (page 194). What is the "Dragon," exactly?

Mme. Blavatsky: The "Dragon" is so many things, my beloved brethren, that my answer depends on what you mean by the question. In which of the seven symbolical meanings do you want me to explain it? If your answer refers to Revelation, then I cannot answer it, as I would have to tread on forbidden grounds—not because I am a Christian—St. John's Revelation is not a Christian work, but is simply the Christianized form of prophecy, which is universal—and I can assure you it is one of the most occult things for anyone who understands it. Now, astronomically, of course, in one sense—for there are several—the "Dragon" is the Moon producing an eclipse over the Sun. This you all know, and astrologists more than any anyone else. Mystically, in general, it is matter or the lower self. It was called the "Dragon" over which the Sun's spirit, or the higher self, triumphed during the trials of initiation. Now the third meaning, also an occult meaning, is in *The Secret Doctrine*, and in connection with the allegorical "fall." The "Dragon" symbolized the sons of wisdom incarnating in humanity, and thus hurled into the Hell of matter, which is our bodies, because there is no Hell outside of our own dear persons here. It is humanity, and on this Earth, that is Hell, and nowhere else. Four, in esoterical allegorical history the "Dragon" represents the secret wisdom which was obscured and driven from the field by the dead letter of dogma in ritualism; while five, Christian theology has availed itself of all these Pagan legends to build up the dogma of "Satan," the foremost pillar of the Christian religious scheme, because if there were not devils there would be no Christian religion. Take away the Devil, and what will remain? Why should Christ come to have saved, and who would he have saved? So that the Devil really is the great prop of Christianity, and so you must, everyone of you who feels like it, have a great reverence for the Devil. This is my advice to you all; I do not suppose any of you will accept it.

Mr. B. Keightley: Then further on you compare the cosmogony of the old Gnostics with that of the "Secret Doctrine," and you speak about the "Seven Stellars." Question 2, page 195: The "Seven Stellars," being the product of the Astral Light and blind Matter, must be evil. Is, then, the influence of the seven planets all evil as far as man is concerned?

Mme. Blavatsky: I do not think so. Why should you go and insult the poor planets? The term planets here does not refer to the seven sacred planets at all, but means simply they are planetary bodies within our system. If the expression is erroneous or leads to any equivocation, in the second edition you have only to make a mark there and change it. But this is what it means. The seven bad Stellars are the progeny of Saturn and the Moon. That is to say, corruptness in the Nazarenes representing in one sense blind, frantic matter ever devouring its own progeny, is identical with Saturn; while [ ], the mother of that [ ], in the Nazarenes is the Moon, at the same time that she is the lower Astral Light. Some mystics assert that these seven bad Stellars are represented by seven moons, though there are eight. There is an old Coptic legend which related how the mother, or the Moon, after her union and junction with her son, Saturn, in order to prevent him from devouring his own children cast him down on to the earth, where they became the seven capital sons. It is they who are credited with the building of everything material on the Earth. Even western astrologers are familiar with the evil effects of the junction of Saturn with the Moon. Now, Mr. Old, tell us something about that. In what way is it bad?

Mr. Old: It has so many renderings, and the influences are so various, it depends entirely upon the radical tendency to take that particular form of evil—as for instance, the corrupt tendencies at birth, which you understand is nothing less than the Karmic horoscope. If the tendency were towards martial or inflammatory evils and diseases and rash precipitous forms of mind, then of course they would not come in the same degree under the influence of Saturn. But if you were predisposed to melancholia and so catch cold and so suffer all those evils which arise out of adjustion {adjustment} and contraction, frigidity, then you would come remarkably under the influence of Saturn at the time of this junction and according to the position in your own Karmic Map, then you would suffer accordingly. So that you see it depends entirely upon the angular distance with respect to the space of the birth, and then also the sign of the zodiac from which it transpires.

Mme. Blavatsky: In astrology I believe there are many good things, only somehow or other they do not reckon as we do. Of course it comes to the same results; but there is a difference.

Mr. B. Keightley: Saturn is regarded in astrology as the most evil-producing of all the planets.

Mr. Old: Certainly, and at the same time, you know, it has been said that the origin of the name is [ ], the pure fire. So that he has a reverse aspect also; whereas he is the great evil, he is also the great good, in this sense.

Mme. Blavatsky: Just like the Hindu Shiva, he is destructive because he is the regenerative power; because a seed cannot come to life unless it first perishes, he destroys only to regenerate.

Mr. Old: I noticed that particularly when you spoke of the

Dragons—that is to say, the [ ], the eighth sign of the zodiac,[1] which corresponds to the eighth house of death; and you know eight is a very bad number.

Mr. B. Keightley: Well! It is all matter, matter, matter.

Mr. Old: And while you said that, I have no doubt they also noticed it was also the symbol of archaic wisdom.

Mme. Blavatsky: Well, the "Dragons" are, which I will give you here by and by—all the "Dragons" were the emblems. They called the sons of the "Dragons," the initiates. In China, also where the "Dragon" is the symbol of power and the symbol of the Imperial family, the "Dragons" are considered very high beings. It is an allegory.

Mr. Old: I suppose the New Testament assertion is a Gnostic assertion? (Quotes from the Testament. Mem., I could not catch the quotation - BdB.)

Mme. Blavatsky: Most assuredly.

Mr. B. Keightley: Question 3, page 199: "The older wheels rotated downward and upward..." Does the expression "rotated downward and upward" refer to the outbreathing, which occupies the first half of any Manvantara, and the "inbreathing," which takes place in its second half? Or does it refer to the direction of the rotation which takes place about the Laya centres, upon which the wheels are formed?

Mme. Blavatsky: It refers to neither and to both and so much more, which I cannot give out now. You will have to wait for it. Have patience a little.

Mr. B. Keightley: Question 4. You say that man must awaken the three "seats" to life and activity. Do you mean by this phrase that the three "seats" have no life and activity on their own planes, i.e. *per se*, or, merely, that our human consciousness on this plane must be awakened to perceive and reflect their activity?

---

1 Scorpio.

Mme. Blavatsky: It refers to what is said in *The Secret Doctrine*, and very plainly; whatever the three higher "seats" in cosmos may be, the three corresponding higher "seats" in man—whether we call them states or seats of consciousness, or principles—have to be awakened before they can be attuned to the three higher planes in cosmos. And once they are so attuned, the knowledge will {reveal} sufficiently what their sources and *fons et origo* are. It is knowledge enough. Besides which, *The Secret Doctrine* teems with this. And I am not going to answer things that *The Secret Doctrine* explains. If you who put the questions do not choose to read *The Secret Doctrine*, I am not going to repeat it like a poll parrot, because it is perfectly useless asking me questions that are impossible of explanation. Ask me questions that are dark then I am perfectly ready and at your service, but not to say things which have been a great deal better put in *The Secret Doctrine* than I can give you.

Mr. Old: You see, HPB, I had some little hand in formulating that question. You see, it leaves us in the dark to a certain extent; because, although perhaps reference is found and full information given elsewhere, still in confining ourselves to respectable limits for one evening it did not give me the idea that there was any activity *per se*.

Mme. Blavatsky: Where? In the human "seats," or the cosmic "seats"?

Mr. Old: In the human, because you speak of that being awakened.

Mme. Blavatsky: Certainly, there are none; but once that they are awakened, they must be attuned to the seats of the cosmic planes, or else I can assure you it won't produce good results, because the man will become a Frankenstein Jr.—everything that is horrid. For those are the rare cases when the higher powers are awakened and put to bad use by matter, which is so intensely stronger that it forces a man into the worst of vices and black magic and therefore he ends in Avichi. These are the rare cases that are spoken about in *Esoteric Buddhism*.

Mr. B. Keightley: It is what Sinnett calls "evil spirituality."

Mr. Old: Does the elevation of the spiritual consciousness precede or come after the awakening? Or is it the cause of the awakening?

Mme. Blavatsky: The cause of awakening depends a good deal upon the higher Manas, and how it perceives the universe, and how it can discern right from the wrong—for the man has the faculty in him of discerning, really, that which is wrong universally (I do not mean about Mrs. Grundy's code of honour.) Then he can attune his seats with those on the higher cosmic plane. And then he becomes at one with Nature; he becomes a co-worker with Nature, he helps Nature, and therefore Nature helps him. But, gentlemen, unfortunately, the three—excepting persons who lead very high lives—this certainly don't awaken. There is the higher Manas, the intelligence in man in the physical brain. We see plenty of intellectual men, but they are nothing but—they are higher intellectual animals. They have no spirituality in them.

Mr. Old: Would not you rather say then it is the men, the individuals, who don't awaken to the existence of these three higher principles—not the principles which awaken?

Mme. Blavatsky: I never said the cosmic seats have to be awakened. Perhaps it is badly put; it is the fault of the editors. You see, I don't understand the value of the English language, and I had about six or seven editors, and they have made a nice mess of it. For me it is perfectly written. Now, if I happen to have written it in such a way as to lead into error, it is the right thing to make a sign or mark and correct it in the second edition.

Mr. B. Keightley: I think it is to a certain extent expressed, because she says here: it remains with him to attune the three higher states in himself, but before he can attune these states he must awaken the "seats" to life and activity.[2]

Mme. Blavatsky: It is not the "seats" at all in cosmos. It is just the same as if you told me that a mosquito could influence the

---

2 *The Secret Doctrine*, I:199.

Himalayas.

Mr. Old: You mean to say their correspondences on this plane have to be awakened.

Mme. Blavatsky: Most assuredly.

Mr. Kingsland: If you said, instead of "seats," "sense" or "principles," there would be no confusion. I don't think seats is quite a good word.

Mme. Blavatsky: Why don't you put it for the second or third edition.

Mr. Kingsland: Even "sense" would be a better word than "seats."

Mr. B. Keightley: It is the occult words.

Mme. Blavatsky: "Seats" means vehicles.

Mr. B. Keightley: It is put in converted commas.

Mr. Old: We are quite right in saying that whether we know it or not, these three principles—Atman, Buddhi, and Buddhi-Manas—all have activity on their own planes.

Mme. Blavatsky: They have, but not with respect to man. They don't influence, so to say, the lower quaternary, which is the personal man. They have certainly their activity, but it does not influence, and therefore the lower quaternary remains the animal, the personality, that is for eating and drinking, and selfishness and money-making, and political things and so on. I wish them joy.

Mr. B. Keightley: Question 5, page 200: In the diagram, Hod and Netzah are figured as lying on two planes at once, which is not the case for the corresponding "globes" in the eastern system. Is this intentional?

Mme. Blavatsky: It is done not intentionally, but because it was a thing of necessity. We live in a three-dimensional space, and a certain limited set of geometrical figures are given to us. The Hod and Netzah are not on two planes at once; but as a sphere cannot be well put astride on a straight line otherwise than by seeming on two planes, how could I do it? The diagram could not be done otherwise, if the orthodox Kabalistic arrangement had to be retained at all. I tried to retain it, and I could not do otherwise. Mind you, I take the seven lower Sephiroth, I do not take the whole ten. I leave others, as I don't mention them here. They put the whole ten on four planes: the archetypal world, the intellectual, and so on; I could not do it because we have a thing of seven, therefore I had to come and cram these in. Moreover, remembering that the Sephiroth letter is on four planes, and composed of ten Sephiroth and in the Kabalah, how could one arrange the thing otherwise, when only the seven lower Sephiroth were used? The Chaldean Kabalah, moreover, the Book of Numbers, agrees perfectly with the eastern arrangement, and disagrees with the present orthodox Kabalah in its diagrams. This is no fault of *The Secret Doctrine*. Now, look here: I had a rabbi who had the real Book of Numbers—and there is another; I have only seen two in my life, and I don't think there exist more. He had fragments of the Chaldean Kabalah. With that, when I came to take notes (I had large books.), when I came to compare with the Rosenroth translation,[3] I saw they had changed it in the most wonderful way. How can you have the Kabalah of [ ], when the Kabalah was entirely lost in the thirteenth century? Moses de Leon, who is accused of forgery—which is perfect nonsense—took all he could find.[4] What did he do? He had, as so many links were missing, and so many things were lost, to go to the eastern Christians, and to the Chaldean Gnostics to ask them to help, since they had their own Kabalah. And the result is, you find more of Christian eternity—the Virgin Mary, Joseph, etc.—than the wisdom of the old [ ]. That is the result. Now, in the Chaldean Kabalah, in the Book of Numbers, you have the wisdom of the Hebrew initiates, but you have not got it in this; they have been so interfering with it, that Mr. Isaac Myer

---

3 Christian Knorr von Rosenroth, Christian kabbalist, 1631-1689, known for his Latin translation of Hebrew texts, *Kabbala Denudata*, three of which were rendered into English by S.L. Mathers in 1887.
4 Spanish rabbi and kabbalist, 1250-1305, who published the Zohar, which was attributed to the second century A.D. rabbi, Shimon bar Yohai.

may say what he likes, and Mr. Mathers also; I say there is more flapdoodle than truth. There is a thing just as Isaac Myer says; did you hear about him, Mr. Cobb,[5] of Mr. Isaac Myer, who wrote the *Qabbalah*?[6]

Mr. Cobb: I did not.

Mme. Blavatsky: He writes perfectly truly that the Kabalah written there is one of the eleventh century, which is written by Ben Judah.[7] They thought the man an Arabic philosopher. Very well, he has these things perfectly. Many of his fragments are perfectly Kabalistic, and just the same as the Chaldean Kabalah; whereas you don't find it, if you compare it with the other. I say it is more than that.

Mr. Mead: These Chaldean Gnostics, are they the Gnostics of [ ]?

Mme. Blavatsky: Yes, they had dogma enough to throw everything into confusion, and that is why you find now that by the methods, by these Gemara,[8] you can do anything you like; you can find in the Kabalah Washington and the President of the United States: you can find anything in the Kabalah.

Mr. Kingsland: Are there any more questions with reference to this diagram?

Mr. B. Keightley: There is a question relating to the note to the diagram. Question 6. (Note to diagram.) Can you define more clearly the term "Cosmic Consciousness"?

Mme. Blavatsky: It is an easy question, this. "Cosmic Consciousness" has been defined hundreds of times in *The Secret Doctrine* as the

---

5 John Storer Cobb, 1842-1904, one of the original Councilors of the Theosophical Society from its New York days.
6 Isaac Myer of Philadelphia, 1836-1902, whose 1888 *Qabbalah* HPB cites in *The Secret Doctrine*.
7 Solomon ibn Gabirol.
8 Gemara is that part of the Talmud dealing with rabbinical law; perhaps Gematria, which deals with the relationships between words and their numerical values, is meant here.

collective or aggregate consciousness of those Dhyanis, or Dhyan-Chohans, called the builders of the universe, physical and spiritual, or that which the Masons call—making a plurality of unity—the architects or the G.A.O.T.U.,[9] so that the Cosmic Consciousness will come after.

Mr. Kingsland: There is a question which I had here.

Mr. Keightley: Page 199, last paragraph. You have spoken of "these seven planes (which) correspond to the seven states of (human) consciousness in man," and in the note {on page 200}, the second note to the diagram, you say "the seven states of human consciousness pertain to quite another question." Speaking of the diagram you say, "these are the four lower planes of Cosmic Consciousness…the seven states of human consciousness pertain to quite another question." These two quotations appear to contradict each other. What then is the connection between the seven planes as given in the diagram, and the seven states of consciousness? And what is the "other question"?

Mme. Blavatsky: Ah! But you see, you want me to give you three volumes, and I cannot give it to you. Remember only one thing, that the seven states of consciousness in man are not only states of consciousness as Herbert Spencer understands it, but also the feeling, the consciousness of the ego. For instance, I am smoking a cigarette, and I am pitching into you, and so on. There are many states of consciousness. Those states of which I speak belong to one order, and others to another. I don't mean to say they are not the same, but there is an infinite gradation in all of them. Now, there are the higher states of metaphysical consciousness. Can you compare it with the consciousness I have of having taken a cigarette, and smoking it?

Mr. Kingsland: What is the order of those states of consciousness, which refer to those seven planes? It will all come in analogy. If you read it afterwards, you will find it all dovetails.

Mr. B. Keightley: I don't know whether this is legitimate, but it

---

[9] Great Architect of the Universe.

is what struck me. The seven states of human consciousness are practically seven states of consciousness on the terrestrial plane.

Mme. Blavatsky: There is a consciousness while we sleep—during sleep, and a consciousness while we are awake. There is a consciousness when we look mechanically at something. There is one consciousness {that} takes in external objects, and the other goes wool-gathering. There are many degrees of consciousness; you cannot go and call consciousness all one.

Mr. B. Keightley: Yet get to this, the seven planes of Cosmic Consciousness.

Mme. Blavatsky: There is consciousness that I am positively in India with this lamp, and here I am in the North Pole.

Mr. B. Keightley: I think there is where the distinction lies, that the seven human states are analogous to the seven cosmic states, but they cover a very much smaller range.

Mr. Kingsland: The fact of the matter is, there are seven states of consciousness on each of the seven planes.

Mme. Blavatsky: You remember what Cobb said the other day. He began to give us the mathematical series that never ended. There was some seventh question that I got mad over, and which has been asked hundreds of times. I said this has been stated very clearly in *The Secret Doctrine*, and I refuse to answer questions that have been already in previous writings, and are in *The Secret Doctrine*, and have been stated on Thursdays. I refuse to pass time on Thursday nights in more repetition.

Mr. B. Keightley: Well, question 8. Question 8, page 200: In occultism, are the terms "seed" and "atom" synonymous?

Mme. Blavatsky: There, there! Isn't that the same thing?

Mr. B. Keightley: You give a hint there as to the question we have been hunting after a good deal: the real meaning of the word "atom."

Mme. Blavatsky: You are the most inquisitive people I ever met. If it were not your unmentionables that protect you, you would all be Mother Eves, every one of you! You are the most inquisitive people I ever saw in my life, and you are the most impertinent. You cannot come and ask one thing after another, Tuesday after Monday, Wednesday after Tuesday, and so on. You want to jump from Monday to Saturday and from Saturday to Halifax. Upon my word, I have no patience.

Mr. B. Keightley: Question 9, page 201: Can you give us some more definite idea—e.g., an analogy on the physical plane—of what is meant here by "Cosmic Desire" which "evolves into absolute Light"?

Mme. Blavatsky: Now there is a question for a modest young woman. The answer is found even in Hesiod's cosmogony. What is the use of attempting to learn occultism and eastern esoteric philosophy, if one is not acquainted with the exoteric classics? The reply to this is stated in *The Secret Doctrine*. Now I am going to examine you. Have you read Hesiod's cosmogony, Old?

Mr. Old: No.

Mme. Blavatsky: Have the goodness to go to the British Museum, and read it. Mr. Cobb has read it. If you have not read it, what {can} I do? Nevertheless, I will attempt to explain it again in a few words. Take Hesiod, and try and understand what he says, and better still, [ ] Phoenician cosmogony. There you will find that what [ ] calls pure force is the principle of creation. It is identical with Brahmā's will to create, which you have read many times in the *Vishnu Purana*. In the primitive world cosmogonies, Chaos is not what it became later on, or that on which the Spirit of God moved on the waters. It is not the [ ] of Ovid, matter in its inert and confused or chaotic state. Chaos was space, according to Aristotle, gaping space or the void—χινω,[10] and after Hesiod, Chaos is absolutely limitless, it is the dark shoreless cloud of vapors, which gives birth to the universe.

---

10 χινω (*chino*) does not relate to the discussion; probably κενόν (*kenon*), Greek for vacuum or void, was meant.

Now, if you remember that the first of the three primordial elements at the first flutter of differentiation were and are with Hesiod, Chaos, and, with Eros, elements that were never conceived (As they were co-existent potentiality in all eternity.), you will perhaps understand that which I say, that no more than primordial Venus was Eros—that which both became in later ages. Now Eros means simply human love, and worse; but then it meant the most solemn metaphysical and divine thing. Eros was not at the beginning the wily God of Love and passion with wings and arrows to wound the hearts of sentimental ninnies with. There were no such fools, nor yet men enough; but he who is now God of human love was simply an abstract idea, and image of the Divine creative force—that universal force of attraction which causes particles to congregate, combine, and correlate, and to produce a triad. Well, that creative force is our Fohat, who neither creates, nor does he produce anything *per se* and by himself, but in virtue of his action, elements, as well as beings, seek to unite in polarity; from which unison results life. Remember that in the first cosmogony out of Chaos are born Erebus and Nox, primordial and already differentiated darkness divided into two principles, male and female, from which two emanate the other two, Aether and [ ] {Hemera}, in the light of the superior regions and that inferior or terrestrial atmosphere. Light is born of darkness number two, darkness on the differentiated plane, and that darkness begets light under the influence of creative love, or that which is called there "cosmic desire"; or again Fohat, the electric creative principles which make of all one, and which produces the three, the correlation.

Mr. B. Keightley: What you have said there is very good, and it is a great deal more than you have said anywhere in *The Secret Doctrine*.

Mme. Blavatsky: But I thought you stood there over me when I was writing.

Mr. Mead: Eros was always first-born of the Gods.

Mme. Blavatsky: Eros is the first-born—he is not the first-born, he is coeval. Chaos, Eros and [ ] {Gaia} are coeval, therefore none of these three elements are conceived, they are simply co-existent in eternity; only at the moment of differentiation they manifest themselves, that is to say, out of the subjective and the non-being comes being, and then after that they begin to come on each other and react. This is the polarity, this electrical force, to which belongs our blood and life and anything. It is life, in short. This is cosmic desire.

Mr. Mead: Cupid is simply the lower aspect.

Mme. Blavatsky: Take Hesiod's cosmogony, and see the enormous difference there is between what Hesiod says and what later on the mythologies have invented. Even a few hundred years before our era, then it was a most sublime thing, and pretended to the mysteries, and now they made of it—I don't know what.

Mr. ——: How can Gaia be said to be coeval?

Mme. Blavatsky: Ask Hesiod; take him by the beard.

Mr. B. Keightley: It means the abstract.

Mme. Blavatsky: The female portion in Chaos.

Mr. Mead: The Earth that no one has seen.

Mr. Old: There was just that word "absolute" that I have not, and if they made it in connection with that, this absolute appears to be the effect of cosmic desire. Well now, the idea of the absolute as we postulate it—

Mme. Blavatsky: Why do you use the word absolute?

Mr. B. Keightley: It evolves into absolute light.

Mme. Blavatsky: On the manifested plane; if we take it metaphysically again, I say the Christians can make it into perfect light. When I say "Absolute" I quote it or underline it. But when I put absolute, I just use the expression as perfect.

Mr. B. Keightley: Absolute light of the manifested plane.

Mr. Old: But Eros, or Lucifer, any one aspect, is that light?

Mme. Blavatsky: Certainly it is.

Mr. B. Keightley: Then you go on to say this: "now light without any shadow would be absolute light," etc. (Reads from *The Secret Doctrine*. {I:201}) Question 10. The idea of "Fire" has usually been associated in mystic writings with *Spirit* rather than *Matter*. Can you tell us why you associate it here with the latter?

Mme. Blavatsky: Because I am not a mystic writer, and I try to make you understand things a little less misty than they are, and you instead in thanking me, criticize me. The physical, or the material and finite universe, is the shadow thrown upon the screen or illusion or Maya by eternal light, or the universal fire. It symbolizes with every nation the creative deity. Primordial matter is not our dense matter, but spirit; hence the spirit of creative fire, or heat, or cosmic desire again. How can you dissociate fire from matter, any more than spirit from matter? Can you do it, when the latter spirit or matter is materialized spirit, and spirit is potentially matter? That is what we say in occultism. If mystic writings held less to poetry and fantastic imagery, and a little more to plain statement of fact, they would be less misty, and those who study them more positive than they are now about the real end of things. Fire is spirit and fire is matter, and if a particle of the London slush can be found without the two qualities, fire and spirit, then mankind had better accept at once the anthropomorphic idea of the Church Fathers, and the dead letter of the Bible, and not its philosophy. You cannot come and say what the mystic writers could write in those days, when for every truth it was said there was immediately an inquisition, and so many cardinals to burn and roast you. Now you won't find mystic writers; now it is time to state plain facts, because there is no one to burn them any more—except after death.

Mr. B. Keightley: In this little extract from the commentaries, speaking about the world germs and so on, you say (Reads from *The Secret Doctrine*.) Question 11. It is said that "the older (bodies) attract the younger, while others repel them." What are these "others" here spoken of, and why should it be the *older* bodies that attract?

Mme. Blavatsky: I suppose they are wiser, less green than others. On this I can say no more than is given in *The Secret Doctrine*. There is such a thing as attraction and repulsion, and in occultism it stands in the place of gravity, the scientific teachings about which we reject. This belongs to occult physics, before the turn of which comes for us on Thursday evenings the twentieth century must have dawned. I give you everything I can give; don't you ask me for more.

Mr. Old: Then I suppose occultism recognizes an attraction which has no relation to bulk. It overthrows the accepted Western idea.

Mme. Blavatsky: If I have one thing well in my memory it is the 20, 30, perhaps 100 conversations we had with Mr. Cobb, sitting there. When it came out here with the fourth-dimensional space—which was ridiculous, because the fourth-dimensional space, taken simply, means the fall of matter through matter, the impenetrability of matter—and we had many conversations; and he knows perfectly well in occultism no one believes in this gravity question. We believe attraction and repulsion. Is it not so, Mr. Cobb?

Mr. Cobb: I believe it is so.

Mme. Blavatsky: You remember what conversations we had in New York? And you were the first one who said it.

Mr. Cobb: I do not know about that, I am sure.

Mme. Blavatsky: You said always it was attraction and repulsion.

Mr. Cobb: I did not know I was the first, at all.

Mme. Blavatsky: Well, it is the old occult axiom.

Mr. B. Keightley: Question 12, page 202: In these pages you distinctly state that, even in the higher phases of cosmic evolution, there rages a "struggle for existence." Now it is on this struggle for existence, regarded as a universal law, that the materialists base their justification of human selfishness. We would therefore ask: (a) Where does this "struggle" for existence" cease: (1) in reference to the cosmos; (2) as regards humanity? (b) How is it that this cosmic law is suspended by that of altruism in the case of human beings?

Mme. Blavatsky: The struggle for existence rages universally in sidereal as in terrene spaces. This is the first fundamental law in nature, the visible effects of which materialistic science has called correlation of physical forces in matter. But this applies only and solely to differentiated matter; it has nothing to do with individual or even personal units, which ought to be, if they are not, guided by the higher laws of the upper triad and not by the instinctual impulses acting on the plane of the lower quarternary. The struggle for existence begins with the physical molecules and ends with those animals which are quite irrational. This is therefore no justification for human selfishness, as man is an animal on a higher plane of being and consciousness than is the animal. The man is a higher animal and on a higher plane of consciousness than the animal; even the most abject savage is. I answer with regard to physical cosmos; the struggle will come {to an end?} only with the coming of Pralaya. With respect to its living and conscious beings, however, the [ ] ceases to operate at that human stage where consciousness and reason make their appearance. It is in man alone that the higher divine triad may be fully active, but this triad is trinity in unity, and unity or homogeneity characterizes the plane of its action. In the four lower planes of cosmos, on the contrary, it is the law of diversity and heterogeneity which reign supreme. Hence those beings who are endowed with the higher triad come under its laws, not under those of the lower quaternary, which act only upon those beings, atoms or things in which rationality is still an underdeveloped potentiality. Therefore, since true law of being is unity, the higher self in him, it follows that the individual human being can only attain his complete and perfect development by acting in perfect unity, that is to say harmony, with all other men. Now (b). The struggle for existence which exists today among men proves only that firstly, man has not yet fully emerged from his savage animal condition, his Manas not yet being fully developed in this our Fourth Round, for it will be only in the fifth; and secondly, that the great men of learning who proclaim selfishness as the great law of human life are, their learning and intellect notwithstanding, not on a much higher plane themselves. In other words, these learned gentlemen are still animals. Whoever wants to go and tell them, let them. What have you got to say? Are you going to take up the defense of the men of learning—of the F.R.S.'s[11] and so on?

Mr. Kingsland: There is a question of mine that rather bears upon that, if I might read it.

Mme. Blavatsky: Do please.

Mr. Kingsland: Is it the case that no human being, adept, or initiate can progress during the present round beyond what humanity will be at the close of the Seventh Race, or can they progress as far as what humanity will be at the close of the Seventh *Round*? Is there not some limit beyond which they cannot progress as individuals, but must wait for the development of humanity as a whole?

Mme. Blavatsky: Assuredly, the Seventh *Round*. They cannot—the greatest adepts cannot. When I say the word adepts in the plural, it is too bumptious. I have heard of one only, or two—one at the beginning of each age that may progress and be in that state in which man will be in the Seventh Round; beyond that they cannot. No one can go beyond his Manvantara, not the highest adepts.

Mr. Kingsland: Then that is really the basis of everyone helping humanity. It is really helping themselves?

Mme. Blavatsky: Most assuredly. It is the most logical thing and the plainest in the world. People will not understand that by hurting their neighbors they hurt themselves. If it is not now, it will be in another incarnation. Of course if you don't believe in it, it is another thing. But if you believe in it, it will be so, because if I hurt this finger the whole of my body will feel it. I may neglect it, but it may come

---

11 Fellows of the Royal Society, England's oldest scientific body, founded in 1662.

in five years, because not the smallest little things remain without effects. Our universe is a concatenation of causes and effects. There is not the smallest thing that we can do to our brothers or neighbors—or even persons—that we won't suffer for, and the whole humanity also. It is just the same when you disturb an enormous pool of water; if you disturb but in one place, then every drop of water in that pool will feel it; there will be reaction. I say that this selfishness of races, of individuals; of diversity of religion; of everything, this is the great curse not only of the nineteenth century, but it will last so long as we do not change or become a little better than we are. But this humanity here, nothing can be compared with. No imagination can create devils in hell as bad and as wicked as humanity is on the whole. Every race hates the other. One race goes and spits on the other; another says: "I am the one." It is something terrible to look at. Man, instead of becoming better spiritually every day, becomes worse and worse and worse. This selfishness that you think—"everything for me"—it is a thing which hurts you first and most; this will be proven to you logically as 2 and 2 make 4; it cannot fail to do so. When they come and speak to me about a struggle, I say, the materialists go and say: "The struggle for existence is the great law; therefore let us go and annex a country, as the Russians go and annex places"; but you begin by putting stuff in your guns and shooting out of them at these unfortunate people—as they did last year in Burma, where about 200 were shot. That is the brotherly love; and they call themselves Christians. Good Heavens! Why, they are devils, all of them! They are not human beings, all those who go and make war and kill people and hurt everyone.

Mr. Old: But apart from any efforts that we may make either individually or as a race, is there not a law in the human universe which prescribes our making a certain advance? Is there no law which limits our advance during a certain age?

Mme. Blavatsky: There are certain boundaries; you cannot go further. Nobody expects you to become omniscient gods all at once, or angels and the kindest men; but there are limits, that the more civilization progresses the more man becomes wicked and selfish and the more it is the poor who suffer on account of the rich. The misery and the suffering never was greater on this Earth than it is in the nineteenth century, which is the accursed age among all ages.

Mr. Hall: I suppose there will be a reaction?

Mme. Blavatsky: And the reaction will be a terrible one. Look at the socialists. It is the highest and the noble-minded; notwithstanding their efforts, it is the anarchism that is produced. And when the time comes that the people starve wholesale everywhere, I can assure you there is no law that will be able to impede the movement.

Mr. Hall: Do you think it will ever come?

Mme. Blavatsky: You have great faith in your 10,000 policemen. Fortunately the time has not come yet. If they go on as they do it is something terrible. I don't mean England alone. Show to me the country where people are not starving. With every new invention that comes, there are several who become millionaires, and in proportion there are so many thousands who starve. That seems to be the law.

Mr. Hall: I should not think the reaction will be quite so severe as that. It will be met through legislation.

Mme. Blavatsky: I invite you to read my editorial in *Lucifer*.[12] I have poured all my heart there, and I can assure you I did not pay them compliments. They may abuse me as much as they like. For me and for every Theosophist there ought to be no distinction between races, colour, creed, ideas or anything.

A Lady: There ought to be.

Mme. Blavatsky: But there is, unfortunately. Look at the Anglo-Indians;[13] look at the supreme contempt they show for the Hindus

---

12 "Our Cycle and the Next," *Lucifer*, Vol. 4, May 1889, p. 177. See also *Theosophical Articles by H. P. Blavatsky*, Vol. I, p. 367.
13 The term in HPB's day meant the British domiciled in India; it has come to mean those in India of British and Indian parentage.

who are intellectually and spiritually a thousand times higher than we are. "Inferior race." Inferior for what? Why, Englishmen were not even in the state of molecules in space when India was old with wisdom, and they come and speak about the Hindus being an inferior race! Now this is that pride of which it is spoken in the Bible, and I verily believe all you English say you were the fallen angels. Every one of you are devils from your wickedness.

Mr. Kingsland: Is it not possible for the different races to incarnate in another race? May we not have been Indians on previous incarnations?

Mme. Blavatsky: Yes; or you would not be as you are. You are sure to be, all of you who are so proud—I tell Sinnett every day that I see him, he is sure to be an outcast in India for his sins. And he does not like it at all.

Mr. B. Keightley: Question 13, page 204: The nuclei of cosmic matter after generation take elliptic and parabolic courses. The former, owing to their inferior velocity, are generally absorbed by suns, whereas the latter escape absorption by their greater velocity. Can any explanation be given of this original difference of velocity, on which the whole future evolution of the "nucleus" depends?

Mme. Blavatsky: The velocity with which a nucleus starts on its sidereal career depends in the first place upon the "hour" of its birth. By hour I mean the stage or period of the universal life cycle at which it starts upon its life pilgrimage. Of these stages there are seven to which the Brahmins refer as the seven creations, and which in Genesis are called the six but ought to be called the seven days of creation. Now, if you ask me why the seven days and not the six, I answer because the seventh day which is described in Genesis as the day of rest really represents the seventh stage of creation. It is not one of full rest or inactivity, but simply represents that period when everything has been harmonized and came into equilibrium, and when the evolutionary impulse has slackened down to a uniform rate of motion and everything assumed an orderly and uninterrupted and regular course, as is exhibited to us in the regular succession of years, seasons, months, weeks, days, etc. All those chaotic forces which have been in their impulse struggling for life came down and settled; and there is the first day of rest when everything went in the orderly way. This is what I mean. Now, the seventh day, really, taking it occultly, means the seventh Manvantara; that is, the day when everything has evolved in this life cycle, and everything will come to a point and everyone will be as good as the other, and there will be no more backbiting and no more hitting of each other's noses, and we will be decent people, then. The Pralaya is the seventh day. The Pralaya is called generally the evening of the day of the Seventh Round; and then it will last as long as the whole. If you go and read the old rabbinical books and all those things of Babylonia, you will find the idea stated perfectly well. Why is it that the Sadducees did not believe as the Pharisees did? Because they were learned occultists and kabalists; they observed Sabbath, but they understood what the meaning of Sabbath was perfectly philosophically. Because look at this Babylonian treatise and you find that it means the seventh period and that it means—well, it is a perfectly astronomical thing, but it is just what the Brahmins called the seventh creation, as it is seventh day and nothing else.

Mr. Kingsland: In Genesis it says the evening and morning were the seventh day.

Mme. Blavatsky: It is the Manvantaric dawn and Pralaya, as well.

Mr. Kingsland: Just the same as we count the day as the day and the night.

Mr. B. Keightley: Have you not got something more?

Mme. Blavatsky: The creative impulse has settled down to quiet family life for a time. Consequently, the initial velocity of the nucleus depends upon the place it occupies in the series of descending generations from the primordial mother or matter. Mother and matter are the same, and now some dark disciples who know what I mean may explain further. There is one (Pointing to Mr. B Keightley.)

who has learned enough to have forgotten half of it, but I would like to know if he has forgotten the other half.

Mr. B. Keightley: What that means is this: if you take the very beginning of the Manvantara, you get from the descendants of primordial matter the first animated cosmic nuclei; then after that they pass through their Manvantara, and they become, first comets, then suns and then planets; then they die and their principles are transferred to a fresh Laya centre, which are like the children of the first generation. Then they pass through their series of evolutions and are reborn again as the grandchildren, and so on through innumerable generations.

Mme. Blavatsky: You had better to have also about the mother-in-law!

Mr. B. Keightley: In each of these stages the impulse, as it were, gradually diminishes to a certain extent so that the velocity with which the Laya centre or cosmic nucleus starts on its career is diminished.

Mr. Mead: What was puzzling there was the elliptical and the parabolic orbit.

Mr. B. Keightley: Many comets have elliptical orbits. It is simply a question of the velocity, as it is stated here. Entirely a question of the initial velocity with which a nucleus starts. There are comets which have both elliptical and parabolic orbits.

Mme. Blavatsky: In the beginning there is always the impulse, and it goes quicker.

Mr. B. Keightley: There are several comets the return periods of which are well-known. They expect them back at certain periods, and look out for them. They have very elongated elliptical orbits of enormous concentricity. Other comets have arrived in parabolic orbits, and we shall never have the pleasure of seeing them again; they are gone. Look at any map of the Sun.

Mme. Blavatsky: I would like them to understand why the impulse is greater at the beginning and then slackens—because it sets into respectable form, and there are laws; and periodically it goes on seasons and years and so on which it did not before; therefore it slackens. The motion is always there.

Mr. B. Keightley: "'The abodes of Fohat are many,' it is said," etc. (Reads from *The Secret Doctrine.* {I:204}) Question 14. "The ancients made the polar circles seven instead of two." Are we to assign four of these to the North Pole, and three to the South; or are the seven lokas counted from the equator, north and south?

Mme. Blavatsky: If I were you I would, every one of you, go and ask to become a critic in *The Saturday Review*,[14] because you are so crotchety. I now say this is not my fault, but as the proverb says: "seven cooks spoil the broth," so I had seven editors. I wrote and wrote and they took it and corrected; and so, if you please, there would be no mistakes. And the result is that they have allowed to pass such flapdoodles and corrected some that were well written, only "to better the English," and they have made a flapdoodle of it. And this is one of the flapdoodles, because it is not in this way that it ought to read. The sentence should be: "The ancients counted seven circles and at each pole" instead of one at each—instead of two; or to have said: "at every pole there is one"; but the Brahmins have counted seven at each.

Mr. Kingsland: Counting from the equator?

Mme. Blavatsky: The seven circles which are the seven steps of Meru are the seven below—are the seven hells, as they call them.

Mr. Mead: The seven silver ones down, and the seven golden ones up.

Mr. B. Keightley: They divide the twenty-eight degrees from the Pole to the Arctic Circle into seven sets, each four degrees apart,

---

14 *The Saturday Review of politics, literature, science, and art* was a weekly London newspaper published until 1938.

which is not the whole space from the equator to the pole. From 0° to 28° latitude, that space is divided into seven circles, each four degrees apart.

Mr. Kingsland: I understood HPB to say from the equator.

Mme. Blavatsky: The seven in the north and the seven in the south; not at the equator, at the poles.

Mr. B. Keightley: I will tell you where the expression is derived from. She is really referring to speculations by a man named Mackay.[15] Where you speak about Mackay is another place in *The Secret Doctrine.*

Mme. Blavatsky: It is written in such a way that it leads to entirely another thing. Modern science gives one ring, or pole, and the Brahmins gave seven to the top and seven to the South Pole. The southern pole represented the seven Arakas in Patala; but their idea of hell was not our idea. There it was a place of rejoicing. When [ ] went to hell he said he never had a more pleasant time, just like one going now to the Paris Exhibition;[16] and he learned his wisdom, his astronomy there from Sesha, the serpent of eternity on which Vishnu sleeps; and that serpent gave him hospitality and taught him astronomy magnificently. That is where you ought to go and learn.

Mr. Old: I want to know something about the division of the globe by the Hindus. Do they count five of our degrees to one of theirs, making 72 degrees instead of 360? Are you counting from the equator to the pole according to our degrees?

Mr. B. Keightley: Yes. You know the present Arctic Circle is 28 degrees. That space they divide into spaces of four degrees each; this

---

15 Sampson Arnold Mackey, 1765-1843, was a Norwich shoemaker with a passion for astronomy and mythology who self-published the results of his studies in his books and pamphlets. The work HPB refers to in *The Secret Doctrine,* II:362 fn.* and 431 fn.*, is his *The Mythological Astronomy of the Ancients Demonstrated,* 1822-24.
16 The Exposition Universelle of 1889 was held in Paris, France, from May 6, to October 31, 1889. The Eiffel Tower served as the entrance arch to the Fair.

is according to Arnold Mackey.

Mme. Blavatsky: But Mackey is perfectly wrong there. He is only right about the seven. But this fourteen is a flapdoodle, because he takes fourteen Manus, and these Manus have nothing to do with it. It is the seven steps of Meru.

Mr. B. Keightley: Mead has an idea in his head that these are counted from the equator. They are counted from the Pole.

Mme. Blavatsky: It is the land of bliss—and after that, when Asia was entirely formed, the last races of the Third Race, those that separated into males and females.

Mr. Kingsland: It was at that time the North Pole.

Mme. Blavatsky: It was simply the Meru, the land of bliss, the land of the gods, and you find references to this in Hesiod, where Apollo is said to go to Eternal Light and Eternal Day. It was tropical country then. Where Greenland is now you had palm trees, laurels, and I don't know what.

Mr. B. Keightley: Remember this, Kingsland, that the axis of the Earth relatively to the Earth {Sun} is fixed; it has the inclination to the ecliptic.

Mr. Kingsland: The inclination you thought [ ] the tropics.

Mme. Blavatsky: All this changes twice every tropical year; everything is shifted, if you please. Every 12,500 or 12,600 years it changes.

Mr. Mead: Twice every tropical year, do you say?

Mme. Blavatsky: Yes, sir. Every 12,500 or 12,600 years.

Mr. Kingsland: Does this change take place gradually?

Mme. Blavatsky: Gradually! To what do you attribute the fact that the seas more and more encroach upon the earth? All this is that action. That there are continents that are sinking and the sea that is rising.

Mr. Kingsland: That is why we always get spring a month later.

Mme. Blavatsky: Twelve thousand years ago, the Earth was not as it is now.

Mr. Kingsland: I think twelve years ago it was not, either.

Mme. Blavatsky: Now it goes very rapidly. And it is time it should go and rest and give room to something better.

Mr. Mead: How much does this angle change by?

Mme. Blavatsky: This I could not tell you. I am not learned enough.

Mr. B. Keightley: Four degrees, I think, every sidereal year of 25,000 years.

Mme. Blavatsky: Old has studied it well.

Mr. Old: I gave it as well as I could in the [ ]. What Mackey says would agree, because there are 28 degrees to be divided.

Mr. B. Keightley: Question 15. "As soon as a nucleus of primordial substance in the Laya state is informed by the freed principles of a just deceased sidereal body, it becomes a comet, then a sun, then a world." Is the term "sidereal body" used in a general sense, as applying to all bodies in cosmos, or technically, to distinguish it from a planetary body?

Mme. Blavatsky: I use the term "sidereal body" in a general sense, as applying to bodies in cosmos in general. I do not give it any technical or special signification.

Mr. B. Keightley: Then page 205 you have a very important note about the stages in the evolution of the cosmic bodies (Reads from *Secret Doctrine*.) Question 16, page 205, note. In the order of evolution of globes with respect to their material transformation, does the Laya state correspond to (1); the cometary to (4); the solar to (5)? If so, to what do (2) and (6) correspond?

Mme. Blavatsky: Now, look here. You just answer me a question frankly and sincerely, as I would to a mother-in-law. Do you ask me these things because it is so obscurely put in *The Secret Doctrine*, or is it that you want to pump me out?

Mr. B. Keightley: It is for this reason, to make quite certain that we get a right basis of correspondence and analogies to go upon. Because if we get that wrong, we shall go making mistakes all through.

Mme. Blavatsky: You corroborate that statement, Mr. President?

Mr. Kingsland: I think so.

Mr. B. Keightley: If we once get a wrong idea, we continue to go wrong.

Mme. Blavatsky: It seems to me you want to pump me out.

Mr. Old: You don't suspect us of wanting to know anything, do you?

Mme. Blavatsky: Yes! I do. Well, the Laya state corresponds to the atomic or ethereal, and the solar to germinal and the fiery.

Mr. B. Keightley: That being so, what do the second and the sixth and seventh, that is to say, the aeriform and the radiant or gaseous—well, that first.

Mme. Blavatsky: The aeriform or gaseous transformation does not write a distinct stage in the cosmic evolution; but, rather, a link connecting the homogeneous with the nebulæ or curd-like stage, a correlation of one into the other.

Mr. Mead: That is what you call matter in a critical state.

Mme. Blavatsky: Yes, sir. The fourfold vapor represents the stages through which the Earth has past {passed} to reach its present condition. The earth is materialized vapor, as ice is materialized steam. The seventh or depending stage describes the stage the Earth will reach at the end of the Seventh Round. Then men will depend on no other sustenance than their own divine natures. There will be no need of food or drink; they will have no more clubs or lawn tennis, or anything. The principles of the Earth will have almost entirely left her physical body, save the upper triad, just as this Moon had done at the close of the lunar Manvantara; and its principles will be ready to shoot, each in its turn, on to a new Laya centre to form a new globe, which will {be} the Earth's Septenary Only Begotten Son. Do you want to know anything more? You are the biggest pumpers I have seen in my life. My notes are at an end, and I open my brains to you, and you may ask what you like.

Mr. Hall: Will this new earth be constructed and worked on the same principles as the old one?

Mme. Blavatsky: Behave yourself, Hall. We had a very great philosopher in Russia, some of whose aphorisms and axioms I have been translating for Bert's gratification, and he is called [ ] {Kozma Prutkov}. Well, [ ] {Prutkov} has got a magnificent aphorism, and he says: "Plug thy fountain, if thou hast one, because even the fountain needs a little rest."[17] That is one of the best things I have read. So I wonder when anyone of you will know when to plug your fountains and to give a little bit of rest?

Mr. Kingsland: They rest for six days; they are only open on Thursdays.

Mr. Hall: It is always leaking at other times.

Mr. Kingsland: I have got one question that has not been asked. It would appear from analogy that there should be seven chains of planets (Each consisting of seven planets—total 49.) in which humanity develops, the lunar chain being one, and our Earth chain another. Is this so, and is our chain the fourth in the series, lunar chain being the third?

Mme. Blavatsky: It may be. I am not sure of it, but I would not destroy your illusions.

---

17 Kozma Prutkov, Russian fiction writer, 1803-1863, whose aphorisms were popular in the mid 19th century.

A Lady: I thought it was good to destroy illusions.

Mme. Blavatsky: Yes, because everything is illusion on this plane of existence. I have been thinking myself about this.

Mr. Kingsland: Are the seven sacred planets, the planets which correspond to our Earth, in the above-named seven chains?

Mme. Blavatsky: No, I don't think so. Really, I do not know. There are very few things that I know, really.

Mr. Hall: What is the meaning in the fable of Jason going to fetch the Golden Fleece, and his having to sow the Dragon's teeth?

Mme. Blavatsky: What does he mean?

Mr. B. Keightley: You know, the fable of Jason and the Argonauts. One of the labors he has to undertake is to sow Dragon's teeth. First of all he has to plow the ground with fiery bulls; then, having plowed the ground, he sows the Dragon's teeth from which grow a crop of armed men.

Mr. Mead: Cadmus does the same.

Mr. B. Keightley: Hall wants to know what the interpretation is.

Mme. Blavatsky: Exercise your own imagination. You know what a "Dragon" is; I told you just now.

Mr. Hall: It was in connection with that, that I asked the question.

Mme. Blavatsky: I don't know. I could not tell you.

Mr. Hall: Is it a symbol of initiation?

Mme. Blavatsky: I have plugged my fountain. It may be.

Mr. Mead: The armed men that spring up from the teeth Cadmus sows all fall to fighting one another.

Mr. Hall: That is only because he tricks them.

Mr. Mead: They straight away fall to work to fight one another.

Mr. B. Keightley: He throws an enchanted helmet among them.

Mme. Blavatsky: I have been on that spot,[18] and if you want an interpretation of it, there are again seven legends, each relating to one of the keys.

Mr. Mead: Simon gave one in the ———

Mme. Blavatsky: Take the alchemical, if you please, in connection with the expedition of the Argonauts. All alchemy is there, if you could only understand it; the philosopher's stone and everything is in that expedition of the Argonauts, there in the Golden Fleece.

Mr. Hall: I wish I could understand why Jason deserts the deer {Medea?}.[19]

Mme. Blavatsky: If we begin about these allegories, we will never end.

The proceedings here closed.

---

18 Colchis, the modern Black Sea coast of Georgia.
19 An example of the dangers inherent in the stenographer's report. The person taking it down heard "the deer" but obviously "Medea" was meant.

18.
Meeting May 9, 1889
Transcription missing.

19.
Theosophical Society.
Meeting of the Blavatsky Lodge
Held at 17 Lansdowne Road, Holland Park
May 16, 1889.

{W. Kingsland in the Chair}

Mr. B. Keightley: This is an attempt to put forth in plain and simple language the principal ideas of Theosophy, what we believe in and what we don't believe in, in the form of question and answer between a Mystic and an Enquirer. It is just divided into sections—fourteen sections—each of which again is subdivided under headings—not numbers—but headings with titles, just to indicate the subjects that are dealt with. The whole idea of the thing is to make it practical, simple and straightforward, and not very metaphysical or abstruse. It is more of the nature of a popular book.

Mme. Blavatsky: You see, the people ask such extraordinary questions. Anyone who speaks of Theosophy will ask you if you are a Buddhist. Theosophy is not a religion, it is not a sect, and nobody is forced to believe or not believe. A Theosophist may belong to any religion, and to no religion, if he likes. What does it matter? He may be a very good man and justify his name of Theosophist more than anyone else; but people will not take this in their heads, they will come and say all of them that we are esoteric Buddhists, without understanding what esoteric Buddhism means. So it is time to give them answers to the most simple questions as to what we believe and don't believe, and this thing is one of the chapters. Of course, it is impossible to read the others, but I have taken one of them—for instance, "Theosophical Duties"—and I want everyone to suggest what will be the needed thing. What questions are the most necessary? All of you go about, and you ought to know what it is that which the public misunderstands the most, what is that which will do the most good; because it is something terrible, the misconceptions that are in the world about Theosophy. They do not seem to know what Theosophy is.

Mr. B. Keightley: I think the best plan would be that as I read it, anybody who has suggestions to make should stop me—because they will not be able to follow me, otherwise. The section, as a whole, is called "What is Practical Theosophy," and the first subdivision is on "Duty" (Reads from manuscript.)[1]

Mr. Williams: Is it proposed that this should be circulated about?

Mr. B. Keightley: This is part of a book that HPB has written.

Mme. Blavatsky: I will finish it in a day or two. It has been announced yesterday, *The Key to Theosophy*. Everyone complains that *The Secret Doctrine* is so abstruse and difficult, that we will give this and perhaps they will say this one is too difficult. I don't know what to say. I am putting all the questions I have had over and over again; therefore, I am answering these.

A Lady: I think that is most useful.

Mme. Blavatsky: But now we must have suggestions, if there is anything more to say; because, when it goes to press we cannot put anything more, and we have to explain as much as we can all that Theosophy is and is not. Afterwards, people may come and say, why didn't you put this and that? And then it will be too late.

Mr. Old: There is a statement that the attainment of freedom of individual progress and eventual happiness can only be attained by life experience. Might this not be logically proven without going very far into words?

Mme. Blavatsky: How would you do it?

---

1 Published as Section XII in *The Key to Theosophy*, London, 1889.

Mr. Old: You need a logical necessity. It is a bare statement, and not satisfactory, perhaps, to the inquirer. It has to be shown how individual happiness—which, in the altruistic sense, of course, is based in the happiness of the whole body, of which that ego is only an atom—it has to be shown how this happiness can be attained only by life experience. For myself, I should first go to show that the earth plane upon which we live—or perhaps, this would be entering rather deeply into the matter—by showing this earth is the ultimate of spiritual action, it is that plane on which action ceases and reaction commences, and therefore the dual action is only manifest here. That is to say, the descending and ascending, and therefore it is the only point at which evolution can take place. There is a decided motion or progress of spirit towards matter from the standpoint of the spiritual planes; that is, they are all downward, and there is—or, as HPB puts it in *The Secret Doctrine*—the angel has desired to be man, and man desired to become an angel. You can quite see what I mean, perhaps? The personality, the incarnating ego, is the only point of differentiation—of individual differentiation—at which mankind are interblended; and, therefore, co-mingle and produce individual evolutions.

Mme. Blavatsky: Would you put this there?

Mr. Old: Do not put my words.

Mme. Blavatsky: We avoid putting metaphysics. This is the complaint of everyone, that they don't understand half or two thirds in *The Secret Doctrine*. What I have tried to avoid was metaphysics in this little book, because if you do put metaphysics it will confuse them, and they won't understand anything, and there will be complaints again. These things, as I put them, are as plain as can be.

Mr. Kingsland: I think you want a little more connection.

Mr. B. Keightley: Your statement is open to this objection: on the three planets preceding our own, there must be evolution of some kind. You must be careful not to land yourself in subsequent [ ].

Mr. Kingsland: What he said is very valuable, but does not touch that point in reference to the question which has been asked, it is in reference to incarnation. The questioner may grant all that, and then say: "well, the man has passed through his earthly life into another plane."

Mr. B. Keightley: The drift of the question is this: a man finds no satisfaction or peace as the result of his life. He has left[2] unsatisfied, then he asks, where is the necessity for reincarnation, if you don't attain peace during one life? Then the answer is, because it is only attainable by a series of life experiences.

Mr. Kingsland: That is the point Old wants to prove.

Mr. Old: I was a bit too metaphysical, perhaps.

Mr. Williams: It would be a good thing to give examples of lives that have not shown any experience.

Mme. Blavatsky: I do not think I have ever met a truly happy man. To everyone life is a burden, there is something they cannot find—any interior satisfaction, or peace of mind. I have never met one man yet who was perfectly satisfied.

Mr. B. Keightley: The conclusion to be drawn from that would seem to be that no permanent satisfaction is possible in material life.

Mme. Blavatsky: If evolution progresses in such a way as that, then they will most certainly go *pari passu* with physical evolution; and what matters it, now that we have all the joys and blessings of civilization? They come and say to us: Christianity has softened the customs. I say, did it? Why, the more civilized a country is, the more cant it has, and the more miserable are the people. Look at England. Where is there more wealth, and every blessing in the world? If they only thought a little bit about the people! Where is there more misery than in England?

Mr. B. Keightley: That is not a direct answer to this question; your

---

2 The original has "lived," which was changed to "left".

assertion is perfectly general here, that the final goal, or peace, can only be reached through life experiences. That applies broadly all round, whether you speak about a civilized country or a Buddhist country. Then you want to give a general answer.

Mme. Blavatsky: I do not answer it on the paper. As we speak now, it is quite a different thing. I simply answer to that: there is no man that is satisfied; because, civilization brings outward blessings, but that civilization shows there is every day more and more immorality, corruption, and selfishness. And what does selfishness lead to? It leads to the thing that half of mankind have become: the Cains of the others, which are the Abels.

Mr. B. Keightley: Would you say you have found amongst the Buddhists, people who would say they were perfectly happy?

Mme. Blavatsky: Perfectly, they die with as great serenity as they get up in the morning.

Mr. B. Keightley: But are they happy?

Mme. Blavatsky: I never saw happier people than in Ceylon where they don't believe in god or soul. They believe in incarnation simply. They don't think anything of the previous man passes into this. They are perfectly incapable of talking metaphysics; and, yet, see the effect it produces upon them. Every man is taught that whatever he does he will be either punished or rewarded for. Whatever the cause he produces, it will have the same effects; therefore, he knows if he does something bad, he will have bad results; if he does anything good, then good results will ensue from it, whether it is in this life or another. Now, look here! You just ask every one of yourselves—you have all been little boys—is it not a thing, that when you know you have deserved something, that you don't murmur as you would otherwise? You don't feel this terrible feeling of injustice. Don't you know that, every one of you?

Mr. B. Keightley: That is absolutely and entirely true.

Mme. Blavatsky: You may swear at it and be angry, but you will say I have done it. This is the only thing that can lead people to happiness. I don't know what you are driving at now.

Mr. B. Keightley: What Old is after is the purely general statement here: that the goal of peace is only to be attained by life experience.

Mr. Old: Might I have another try? I think it might be done on the *ad absurdum* principle, by proving that happiness cannot be attained elsewhere. For instance: a person dies; he hopes to go to heaven. Ask him his definition of heaven. He says: "the place of happiness." Ask him what "happiness" is; he says: "it is a relative thing." (Happiness, I suppose, in heaven would be to have everything you want, and nothing you don't want.) Consequently, it is nothing else than an expression or full realization of Kama, desire, of individual desire. Can this be a condition of progress?

Mme. Blavatsky: Even Devachan is a state of exalted selfishness, but this is finite. It is not as theology says, that because a man has been "goody-goody" he will be given a golden harp and be very happy for eternity; there is no logic in it. A man says very well, if I only believe what I am told, I may have the golden harp and sit—I don't know what they do there; I think, recline on the soft clouds! This is the most absurd thing in the world. A man is taught thus to believe: that, do what he may, if he only believes that because another man has been put to death on his account, his sins are pardoned to him. I say it is the most pernicious doctrine in the world. It forces every man to lose self-esteem and self-reliance. It makes him lose sight of this terrible injustice, that because I may go and steal cherries another will be flogged for me. This is an absurdity.

Mr. Old: Moral responsibility is lost sight of.

Mme. Blavatsky: However, I want you to hear to the end, and after he has read all this, then we will have a general conversation, because I want you to see if anything is forgotten.

Mr. B. Keightley: The second section is on "Self-sacrifice." (Reads.)

Mr. Old: That section is very beautiful.

A Lady: I don't think there is anything to be added to it.

Mme. Blavatsky: Did I make it comprehensive enough?

A Lady: Perfectly clear.

Mr. Johnson:[3] I thought the attack on the Roman Catholics was rather severe, Madam, to single them particularly.

Mme. Blavatsky: The priests are self-sacrificing. It is not against any particular priest, but such a pernicious system.

Mr. Kingsland: Say simply missionaries, not Roman Catholic missionaries.

Mr. Old: Call them Christian missionaries.

Mr. Kingsland: I think you are quite right not to single out one particular sect.

Mme. Blavatsky: Were there any Christian missionaries who were killed in China?

Mr. Old: Any amount of them.

Mme. Blavatsky: This Damien, I tell you I was going to start for a collection among we Theosophists just to send him, and the poor man dies.[4] I just got some shillings, and he died. Let him be any religion, such a man is the highest Theosophist possible. I am perfectly sure the Roman Catholic Church will not recognize it. They recognize Labro, who for forty years allowed himself to be devoured

---

3 The identity of this individual is not apparent. We print it as it is given, noting that there were members of the London Lodge named Johnson, but it could also be a misprint for Charles Johnston (1867-1931), who had married HPB's niece in October 1888, and left for India at the end of that month to join the Civil Service there.
4 Father Damien (Jozef De Veuster), 1840-1889, a Roman Catholic priest from Belgium, devoted his life to ministering to the leper colony on the Hawaiian island of Molokai. He eventually contracted the disease and died there on April 15, 1889. He was canonized a saint in 2009.

by vermin.⁵ I say it is positively ridiculous. They make a saint of this Labro, and the unfortunate Damien they won't make anything of. You won't find a Jain who does not lie in the sun and allow vermin to come upon him, because they say: "They are our younger brothers." They allow all the vermin to come upon them, fleas, and all the less comely animals.

Mr. B. Keightley: It is carrying the point too far.

Mme. Blavatsky: We have Jains among our Theosophists in India, and they plead to me, saying it is a very sinful thing that I permitted our Malay to kill cobras. But, I say I am not going to allow the cobras to sting.

Mr. Kingsland: Better a dead cobra than a dead Theosophist.

Mme. Blavatsky: He says: why don't you throw some powder? He wants me to throw salt on his tail. They could not pardon me, and many of them left because I had two or three cobras killed.

Countess Wachtmeister: Mr. Johnson thought you had taken the Jains' advice when we saw all the cockroaches about here.

Mr. B. Keightley: I am afraid that is illegal; that would not stand before law.

Mme. Blavatsky: We laugh at this, but really it is a most sublime thing—because they are so sincere, they would not breathe. They wear those things so as not to breathe the air and swallow those unfortunate insects, those animalculae; and they sweep as they go along not to walk by chance on some insect. It appears ridiculous; but, really, if you analyze the thing, it is the most sublime thing. They

---

5 The transcription gives the spelling as Laboreaux. Probably Saint Benedict Joseph Labré, 1748-1783, known for his subsistence living. He was canonized in 1881. The glossary attached to the second edition of *The Key to Theosophy* describes him as "Labro, St. A Roman Saint solemnly beatified a few years ago. His great holiness consisted in sitting at one of the gates of Rome night and day for forty years, and remaining unwashed through the whole of that time, the result of which was that he was eaten by vermin to his bones." He is cited on pp. 239 and 259 of that book.

do it with the greatest discomfort in the world, and they believe in it.

Mr. Kingsland: The principal thing is to force out how Altruism, like everything else, can be abused. And the only question for us to decide is whether that is pointed out forcibly enough, or whether anybody can suggest a more forcible illustration.

A Lady: I think it is the most forcible you can find.

Mr. Kingsland: I don't know anything about Labro, but the majority of people won't know.

Mme. Blavatsky: He is the last saint who was beatified. For forty years he was sitting on the Piazza di Spagna.[6]

A Lady: I read a piece in the American newspaper about him. A Nonconformist was calling him over the coals so cruelly because he was not a Protestant, because he was a Catholic, and would not recognize his work.

Mme. Blavatsky: You see how these Christians love each other? Just as much as Theosophists love each other.

A Lady: As much as you love the Roman Catholic.

Mme. Blavatsky: I speak against the system, not against the Roman Catholics. I say, pitch into systems but don't touch personalities. We have quite enough to do with pitching into systems, because systems are abominable.

Mr. B. Keightley: Then this is on "Charity" (Reads.)

Mr. Kingsland: I think it is better to eliminate all reference to any special sect or creed whatever, and I should eliminate Spurgeon's name.

Mme. Blavatsky: Oh Lord! I must not, because it is a personality, but I do despise the fellow. Very well, we will take out "Spurgeon" and put simply "Fashionable Preacher." Now I have made two

---

6 A square in Rome.

concessions. I have taken out for Mr. Johnson the "Catholic," and for you, "Spurgeon."

Mr. Old: Someone will ask you to take out Buddha's name, presently.

Mme. Blavatsky: "The Most Popular Preacher."

Mr. Kingsland: I think if you refer to the "Asbestos Soul," everyone will know who it means.

Mr. Keightley: "Theosophy for the Masses." (Reads.) Then the last is: "How Members Can Help the Society."

Mme. Blavatsky: This is where you have to give your suggestions.

Mr. B. Keightley: (Reads.)

Mme. Blavatsky: Give us suggestions what to put more, because I put only that which comes into my head, and I may forget hundreds of things which you Theosophists ought to think about, and see what could be added. Mr. Cobbold[7] came too late, and did not hear the beginning.

Mr. Kingsland: Mr. Cobbold as a practical Theosophist will give us his views.

Mme. Blavatsky: What can Theosophists do?

Countess Wachtmeister: Theosophists should try and not backbite their neighbors.

Mr. Old: I think there is a negative aspect to action, HPB I was thinking the same as yourself, Countess. I thought there was a negative side to Theosophical duty—what the Theosophist should *not* do; that is to say, he should not create any obstructions—which very often he does, unconsciously through ignorance, or consciously through spleen.

---

7 Arthur Westhrop Cobbold, a member of London Lodge of the T.S. since 1887.

Mme. Blavatsky: Personality is the curse in the Theosophical Society, as it is everywhere.

Countess Wachtmeister: I don't think it is put strongly enough there, that every evil springs from personality, and that personality is the great curse.

Mme. Blavatsky: You have not heard the whole thing. This is only a chapter, and I have eleven more.

Countess Wachtmeister: The first duty of a Theosophist is to try and forget his personality.

Mme. Blavatsky: Exactly. How few do it. You just make a footnote, and mark it there. Are not these Buddhist precepts beautiful! I can assure you, if I one day translate them, you will say they are splendid.

Mr. Old: They are very poetical.

Mme. Blavatsky: And written so beautifully.

A Lady: They are indeed sublime.

Mr. Johnson: It says there that "attacks made on the Society should be defended by any means in one's power." I think that is rather loose.

Mme. Blavatsky: We cannot oblige anyone to do anything. We cannot create penances.

Countess Wachtmeister: I think Mr. Johnson meant "legitimate means," that is what he meant.

Mr. Kingsland: Not in the doctrine of the Jesuits.

Mme. Blavatsky: Now, gentlemen, please, some more.

Countess Wachtmeister: You put down your negative points, that Mr. Old was just saying, of what Theosophists should not do. That is later on in the book.

Mme. Blavatsky: I have covered all the tenets of Theosophy. I have spoken about Karma and Devachan and the states of afterlife—not that we are obliged to believe in it, but only Theosophists who study Occultism believe in it. This is what I have been putting. A Theosophist may believe in anything he likes.

Mr. B. Keightley: Another thing which has been slightly touched upon is a thing which I have very often been asked, whether vegetarianism is a tenet of the Theosophical Society, and whether abstention from alcoholism, and so on?

Countess Wachtmeister: And then, also, you should distinctly state that Theosophy has nothing to do with Spiritualism.

Mr. B. Keightley: That is stated.

Mr. Kingsland: I think, in reference to this objection, this must be fully answered. He thinks all the literature is not of much practical value. I think I would point out that right thinking is the basis of right acting, and we are not a Charity Organization Society to merely alleviate misery on the surface. Each one does that as much as he can. We believe that by promulgating these doctrines that that will in time naturally work out on the physical plane.

Mme. Blavatsky: I say literature will reach ten thousands, where all the money we can get will reach one hundred.

Mr. Kingsland: The Charity Organization, and even legislation, is only working on the surface of things.

Mme. Blavatsky: We don't take any concern in politics, because what is the use of making political reforms with men who are not yet reformed? Let them be Conservative or Liberal, it is six of one, and half dozen of the other.

Mr. Johnson: Theosophy cannot be preached to a man who has an empty stomach.

Mme. Blavatsky: Among Theosophists there are far more with hardly filled stomachs, and yet they try to do what they can. I know many of them who have hardly money enough to get food.

Countess Wachtmeister: They would starve in India to enable them to join the Theosophical Society. On joining formerly they had to pay a certain fee. Some of these Hindus have starved themselves for a week, so as to enable them to join the Theosophical Society. They have done it, not only once or twice, but again and again.

Mme. Blavatsky: What I want to put are the rules of the Theosophical Society at the end—rules and so on. A selection, of course.

Mr. Kingsland: You mean the objects?

Mme. Blavatsky: No, the rules as they are in India.

Mr. B. Keightley: Only a selection.

Mme. Blavatsky: Then to give how many branches we have and their names, and everything.

A Lady: I think that would make a very good impression, the immense number of people that have joined the Society, and the number of branches.

Mme. Blavatsky: You see, we have one-hundred and seventy-three branches, but in India alone there are one-hundred and twenty-nine or one-hundred and thirty. Now, in America we have about twenty-four, and six which are forming; here, we have six or seven branches in England. It is growing very rapidly, and really, there are as many Theosophists who don't know what the Theosophical Society is as there are outsiders.

Mr. Johnson: I think that book will do splendid work for the cause.

Mr. Kingsland: Most undoubtedly.

Mr. ——: What is the Theosophical Society good for? Well, we might say to promote Altruism, the answer to that would be. A Christian has done the same thing, taught the same thing.

Mme. Blavatsky: They speak a good deal of it in Christianity, but they act mightily little.

Mr. ———: And that puts a stop to progress.

Mme. Blavatsky: These people would be just as good Buddhists.

Mr. Old: It is the best thing they know of.

Mr. B. Keightley: They all go in for this fallacy, that their idea of helping other people is almost in all cases confined to the physical. They don't try to give them actual moral stamina; it is always, "your sins have been wiped out and washed in the blood of Jesus," and so on.

A Lady: They teach them sectarianism.

Mr. B. Keightley: They teach them hardly anything which has any basis in it.

Mr. Old: The man who trained the fleas to do tricks did a good deal more than Labre, because the one only educates the physical idea——

Countess Wachtmeister: And the other develops the intelligences.

Mr. Old: It shows there is a ray of intelligence in the smaller parts of humanity.

Mme. Blavatsky: The Roman Catholic Church did not have that superb contempt for animals always that it has now, saying they have no souls. Read the *Golden Legend*:[8] you will see any number of wolves who have been converted, a dragon who had some sore in his eye, and some saint drew it out of his eye, and he immediately shed tears and became a Christian. It is a fact—animals of all kinds, wolves, dragons, and hyenas.

Mr. B. Keightley: There is the story of St Francis's preaching to the animals.

---

8 *Legenda Sanctorum* (*Readings of the Saints*), popularly known as *Legenda Aurea*, was compiled by Jacobus de Voragine, Archbishop of Genoa, about 1260.

A Lady: And the Jackdaw of Rheims became a saint.[9]

Mr. Kingsland: When the ban was removed.

Mr. Old: I have seen a more Christian spirit in some faithful dogs, than I have seen in man.

Mme. Blavatsky: They are the most respectful fellows I have ever met with, under any circumstance they will remain faithful.

A Lady: Even with a master as bad as Bill Sykes.[10]

Mr. Old: Martin Tupper[11] says: "What if they cannot rise so high? They can't fall so far." Which is quite true.

Mme. Blavatsky: What are we to do more? Because there are two sections more, representing 30 or 40 pages.

Mr. Old: I think something might be said as to what constitutes happiness.

Mme. Blavatsky: With me, to sit and never move.

Mr. Kingsland: And never have anyone asking questions.

Mme. Blavatsky: This young creature sitting here cannot live without air, and air kills me.[12]

Mr. Old: That is not happiness. I think a person who has suffered physically, intense tortures, may still be happy.

Mme. Blavatsky: One man is very fond of money.

Mr. Old: It depends where the individual consciousness happens to be gravitating for the time being. If it is in the body, physical

---

9 The tale of "The Jackdaw of Rheims" was known to Victorians through the poem of Richard Harris Barham (1788-1845) published in 1837. In it a crow gains religion and is eventually made a saint. It was included in the popular collection, *The Ingoldsby Legends,* written under his pen-name Thomas Ingoldsby.
10 A violent character in Charles Dickens' novel *Oliver Twist.*
11 Martin Farquhar Tupper, English writer, 1810-1889.
12 Mme. Blavatsky had a dislike of drafts and kept her rooms sealed and heated.

ailments cause misery, but otherwise he would still be happy.

Mr. B. Keightley: There is a certain amount of truth in the old saying: "What philosopher was ever able to bear the toothache?"

Mme. Blavatsky: Now what are you going to do with this Burgoyne, who writes a book against us?[13] It shows to you the perseverance with which they act against the "Theosophical Society." I have just received this. Burgoyne as a young man, Mr. Johnson will tell you about him, was two and a half years away for some swindling.

Mr. Johnson: He had to quit the country. He victimized me; he was two years in Bradford Gaol.

Mme. Blavatsky: I have got a portrait of him that was sent from Scotland Yard, and he has got on the handcuffs; and there he was taken before {he} was handcuffed, where he appears very smiling, and there he appears with handcuffs—well, he doesn't smile—and this is the bright and shining light of esotericism in America.

Mr. Johnson: I know perfectly well he is an enemy of the Society, and especially about you.

Mr. Kingsland: How long is it since he was in England?

Mr. Johnson: Three and a half years ago.

Countess Wachtmeister: He had to leave the country quickly.

Mr. Kingsland: For the country's good.

Countess Wachtmeister: The police said it would be the greatest swindle England had ever known. They were collecting money to purchase land out in America, and the whole thing was a bubble, and

---

13 Thomas H. Burgoyne, alias of Thomas Henry Dalton, 1855-1894. He had been imprisoned in Leeds, England, in 1883, on fraud, and fled to the U.S., eventually settling in California where he died. HPB's ire was directed at him because of his connection with the Hermetic Brotherhood of Luxor, an occult organization that she considered a swindle. He published his major work, *The Light of Egypt*, in 1889.

they went off to America with all they had collected. They intended to swindle the Theosophist out of his land, and not pay for it.

Mr. Old: I think the best thing the "Theosophist" can do is to prepare a counterblast.

Countess Wachtmeister: There are numbers of people who lost money.

Mme. Blavatsky: But this is a *Religio-Philosophical Journal*.[14] It is the same paper that for years and years has been putting in letters about my habitual drunkenness. You know, they said that I habitually every morning danced on a tightrope for an hour—I never even tasted liquor in my life, because I hate it: there is no virtue in it at all.

Mr. Kingsland: I would like a few suggestions as to letting Theosophists know as to these scandalous things: for instance, there are the monthly papers, there will be some notice of it in these journals, but all Theosophists do not take these journals.

Mr. B. Keightley: There is this objection to be raised against it, that you only advertise a book of that nature.

Countess Wachtmeister: Yes, everybody goes and purchases it. I think the best plan is to take no notice.

Mr. B. Keightley: The thing that will be done, if Judge is wise, is to simply not to refer to the book, but show up Burgoyne as a fraud.

Mme. Blavatsky: Then, if there are the same laws in America as here, you told me the more a statement is true, the more it is libelous, and he may bring an action against Judge.[15] It seems if you speak the truth you are taken up as a confederate. You are always nicely situated.

Mr. Old: I think if Judge were to just write to some of the local

---

14 Chicago weekly Spiritualist journal.
15 William Q. Judge, 1851-1896, General Secretary of the American Section of the T.S. and editor of the New York *Path*.

papers and make a thorough exposé of the man, and just conclude by saying he proposes to publish a book—which will be his book—you could still mention the book, and everybody would fly at it, but they would know how to take the contents in the face of these facts.

Mr. B. Keightley: I don't think anybody will take any notice of the book.

Mr. Kingsland: Unless any paper puffs it up; then we should write a counterblast.

Mr. Old: I think the great question in America today is, what is a Theosophist? Here is this man and that man, all pseudo-theosophists, who claim to be *the* Theosophists, representative members of a society which does not exist, but which nevertheless is Theosophical. I don't wonder at all at the Americans raising the question, what is a Theosophist?

Mme. Blavatsky: Hiram Butler founded the Esoteric Society, and allowed people to believe he was a Theosophist.[16] Now he has been pounced upon by the police for all kinds of very queer-looking tricks, and he had to run away from Boston, and he went to California.

Countess Wachtmeister: I think all Theosophists ought to protest when they see anything of the kind.

Mr. B. Keightley: They say some astrologers used to say that the stars ruled human destinies and were active agents in controlling human destinies. Others put it that that was not the case, but that there was a sympathetic relationship between human beings and the stars, so that they moved parallel to each other; that you can predict the conditions under which a human being would find himself from

16 Hiram Erastus Butler, 1841-1916, American occultist who started the Esoteric Society in Boston in the 1880s. He moved it to California where he died. Judge reviewed his career in *The Path,* March 1889, "Occultism for Barter: Esoteric Colleges and False Prophets," and a long letter from HPB exposing Butler was published in the *Boston Daily Globe,* Mar. 8, 1889. The April 1889 issue of *Lucifer* reprinted a notice from the *Los Angeles Times* captioned "The Boston Frauds and Delusions."

the stellar aspects, but it was not inferred that there was any cause of relationship between them. Those are, broadly speaking, the two different views put forward by the astrologer. The old one is the orthodox.

Mr. Old: There is almost a third class of thinkers on this question, that is those who believe in the planetary spirits—you know, that there are legions under them who directly influence the minds of us, the thoughts, desires, and actions of individuals. But my own personal opinion is—and also that which seems to me to be reflected dimly in the Hindu works on the subject, in both North and South Hindustan—that there is a relationship between the terrestrial body, of which man's body is but a differentiation, and the material bodies of all the planets. There is also a sympathy between his astral body, and the whole astral plane to which he belongs, in which—or of which, I might say—and the astral principles animating the planetary bodies. Themselves are the composites, that is, that the astral bodies of planets and of men all enter into and are integral parts of the universal astral plane. Material atoms either collectively or individually make up the material universe; so with respect to the individual or collective astral. Now, it would appear that the life current, called by the Hindus Prana, radiates, permeates, acts and moves in this astral plane, and that it is in passing through this astral that it becomes stranded, as it were, and thrown off, just as a ray of light.

Mr. B. Keightley: Reflected?

Mr. Old: Well, I don't mean that exactly; spread out, I mean, into its different parts or principles.

A Lady: Refracted?

Mr. Old: And this severance of the one Pranic ray causes the different aspects of life. Thus we might have a single ray of light coming from the sun entering the earth, and, as you know, immediately stranded off into so many other rays—refraction is the word, of course. So it is with the universal life, which has no particular reference to our visible sun, which is in the material universe, and is part of it, although it is the most sublimated kind of matter; but it is with respect to the Pranic plane, that is to say, the plane above the astral plane. Then they say that the various astral planets corresponding to the material planets receive the rays of the sun and reflect to the earth, first of all to the astral plane, then precipitated on the plane on {where?} the astral planets receive the life rays of the sun. I am speaking of the sun on the Pranic plane, and the astral planets receive these rays and reflect them to the astral body of this earth, which is in the astral plane, and thence they are precipitated on to the earth, and so into individuals. Now as every person is born [ ] {of?}, as it is said, well through the astral plane, it hence follows that the moment of birth is that time when the individual existence commences, and the person is brought under an individual law, and in the general law which controls the revolution of the planets, both in the astral plane and in the physical plane. And I believe myself that planets only exert an influence upon us through the astral plane itself—that is to say, that it is not the material planet, Saturn, Jupiter, Mars, or any other—which affects us, except physically. But we know they do affect us in our desires; for it can be without a doubt predicated that at any particular time a person will be actuated by desires which are, to a certain extent, foreign to the general tenor of that person's life. If that can be done—and it certainly can—that at certain times people shall be moved by influences not generally a characteristic of theirs, then we can refer these, of course, to a plane which is certainly higher than the material plane. And therefore these forces—not being physical forces, but psychic forces acting on the psychic plane on the individual and of nature—must necessarily originate in the psychical plane. That is to say, in a plane higher, at least, than the physical plane. And thus its seems there is a necessity for planets existing in planes higher than the material plane, and yet corresponding to the material planes which are visible to us on this physical plane. I think you will see that necessity yourself, because life in itself is homogenous. It has but one quality and that is life; it is only when it becomes refracted or differentiated that it has a quality, that it can be said to have any particular quality. The modifications of life, hence, would be what constitute individual life, very much like, of course, the colours on the prism: they are all light, but it is the aggregate of all degrees of colours, all tones in equal proportions, that would make up the white. It is when one predominates that the white becomes tinged with a tone or a distinct colour. Thus, if more pink were in the aggregate, then the white would be no longer white but it would be pink; so, whatever principle happens to be in excess in an individual, so that person is called either Saturnian, Jovian, Marsian etc. I am speaking, of course, of the ultimate effects of planetary influences upon individuals and how it would operate.

Mme. Blavatsky: Occult astrology says that, just as you explain it, but that colours having, each of them, a particular tendency or a faculty of impressing one way or the other what ray that individual will be, so are his passions or desires affected. It is the colour of the ray that impresses. For instance, if such a colour comes {from} Saturn or Venus, if he happens to be born under this planet, then certainly every time that a certain colour—by passing through this astral plane that you have been talking about, and passing through other certain things—assumes a certain colour, this colour it is which affects the individual mentally, and psychically, and spiritually, and all kinds of ways. Is it like that?

Mr. Old: Yes. Of course, we know that we individually are impervious to certain colours. Thus, some people show an instinctive liking for this colour, and a distinct hatred for the other; at any rate, they feel a psychic influence arising from the presence of these colours.

A Lady: What do colour-blind people feel, a psychic influence?

Mme. Blavatsky: No. It happens to be a colour which is of a planet which is perfectly contrary to theirs.

Mr. Old: They would feel it on a psychic plane.

Mr. B. Keightley: All that colour-blind means is that there is something wrong with the physically registering apparatus. A man cannot be occultly colour-blind.

Mme. Blavatsky: This is the keynote of Occultism, to know the true relation of sounds, colours, and numbers. There are so many. There are seven rays, but what are they? They have got seventy-seven thousand times seven, all kinds of combinations; it takes a lifetime to learn them, and you cannot do it by registering all these in your physical memory. It is a perfect impossibility. You have to use your intuition, and your psychic memory, the memory of your ego, of the astral. You have to register it on your astral form.

Mr. Cross: It appears to me the books you circulate on astrology are rather written above the heads of the people. As an outsider, I can tell you that really, the people who want to know about Theosophy want to know the first steps, rather than these advanced theories. These are very well for your own Society; but, if these books which come out from time to time are supposed to spread the doctrine, I don't think, speaking from experience, that they really do so much good. They come out along with the others.

Countess Wachtmeister: Could not you give us a series of questions, such as outsiders ask themselves?

Mr. Cross: I should like to know why the person who so very clearly answers the questions so clearly is called a mystic.

Mme. Blavatsky: There you are. Mr. Keightley wanted "Mystic." I said put "Q" and "A." I wanted to put "Theosophist," but that is such a name which is arrogant.

Mr. Kingsland: Put "Teacher."

Mme. Blavatsky: No! No! No! It is worse, yet.

Mr. Cross: That is really the objection that outsiders have, that it is vague. Does not the use of the word "Mystic" go to build up that idea?

Mr. B. Keightley: You are perfectly correct.

Mme. Blavatsky: What name would you suggest?

Mr. Cross: Why won't you put your own name?

Mme. Blavatsky: "H.P.B." stinks in the nostrils already.

Mr. Cross: But people look to you as the kind of oracle of the movement.

Mme. Blavatsky: There is my name there already; everyone would know I have written this. But I would like throughout the book not to put so many times my name. I know that "Mystic" was not good. Now please give me some good advice.

Mr. B. Keightley: "Q" and "A" as an alternative would be good.

Mr. Cross: I suppose there is an objection to using "Theosophist"?

Countess Wachtmeister: Explain what Theosophist is, HPB.

Mme. Blavatsky: It is very arrogant, because "Theosophist" we call men who are really holy, saintly men, whoever they be, whatever nation they belong to, or whatever religion. Now, I don't think myself holy, good, or even learned enough to call myself a "Theosophist."

Mr. Cross: If you are not a Theosophist, who are the Theosophists? Are we going to do away with the term Theosophist, simply because nobody can live up to the ideal? "Theosophist" is an ideal, not what he really is, the same as Christian might be.

Mme. Blavatsky: I think "Theosophist" is better than "Mystic." They will only say it is very mystic. Let it be "Theosophist."

Mr. Cross: I feel I am not competent to speak, not knowing enough.

Mr. Kingsland: Then you can just give us advice.

Mme. Blavatsky: We are so immersed in this Theosophical Society business that we cannot see things as those who surround us can. The heads of outsiders are a great deal clearer.

Mr. Cross: It would be better if you could have a line drawn—a more definite line—between Occultism and Theosophy.

Mme. Blavatsky: We have it, a very great line. I am going to {have} a chapter on the difference between Occultism and Theosophy. Theosophist may be any member of a Theosophical Society. They may study or not as they like; it obliges to nothing; you have not to change your religion, or give up anything. But those who study Occultism, who study esoteric Theosophy, those have, of course, to believe. They must have one belief. Certainly Theosophy and Occultism are different, for an Occultist must be a Theosophist if he would not be a black magician, but you may be a Theosophist without being an Occultist.

Mr. Cross: But why do you bring out these books together? Now, I got hold of a book called *The Higher Science*; that did me a great deal of good. Another time I had a book called *The Black Art*, and it was something I knew nothing about.

Mme. Blavatsky: If you know about the light side, you must know the dark side. If you know anything about night, you must know what day is.

Mr. Cross: You are handicapping yourself before the British public by bringing these things together, because we know that astrology in the ordinary man is a good deal connected with fraud. No doubt there is a great deal of truth in these old sciences, but you are really doing yourself harm. You are handicapping yourself, so to speak.

Mr. Kingsland: You cannot help that, because Theosophy is based upon Occultism. Occultism is the theoretical study of the laws upon which Theosophy as an exoteric thing is based.

Mme. Blavatsky: And the laws of nature.

Mr. Kingsland: You must have some law to which you can point as the reason for your Theosophical tenets, and that is Occultism. It is necessary for those who are the leaders in the movement to have this in our knowledge, so that they may meet the opponents of Theosophy on all planes, on the intellectual as well as on others.

Mr. Cross: Then pray let us have it in plain terms. We want no such scientific terms, we want everything clearly defined.

Countess Wachtmeister: Learning Theosophy is not like going to a schoolmaster. Learning Theosophy is by developing your intuition; it is not like having your lesson, just made easy. What Theosophy really is, is the development of the inner man.

Mr. Cross: True. But before you know anything about composition you must learn grammar. What I say is we should know something about the more simple things.

Mme. Blavatsky: I have tried to put it in as simple language as I could. Everyone throws it at my head; the outside public certainly does not. I took it into my head to write this *Key to Theosophy*; two weeks ago I began it, and I am finishing it; it will be about 250 pages.

Mr. Cross: Let us have books on astrology, by all means. Let us have books on Occultism, but begin at the ABC.

Mr. Kingsland: There are ABC theosophical books. We are sending out books which are both ABC and the most metaphysical books.

Countess Wachtmeister: There are so very different minds.

Mr. Kingsland: If a man wants only the ABC of Theosophy, a Theosophist will tell him: "what you want is such and such a book." Another man comes and says I want to find the scriptural basis of things; there is *The Secret Doctrine* for him. The only practical way is for a man to go to a Theosophist.

Mme. Blavatsky: Theosophy is a very easy thing if you happen to meet a Theosophist who can give you an exposition of it clearly, well, so as to make you understand; but sometimes you happen to meet a Theosophist who will appall you with all kinds of metaphysical terms. Now, for instance, for myself I speak very indifferent English, but still I am accustomed to use Theosophical terms that every Theosophist will understand, but other people will look at me and take me for a lunatic; for us it is perfectly comprehensible, and you must understand that a person accustomed to talk a certain language cannot come and speak to children. Take a mathematician: he could not. It is extremely difficult for a Theosophist to come and speak plainly to those who have never heard of Theosophy, and therefore, there is the difficulty. I wrote *The Secret Doctrine*. It seems to me every word is comprehensible; many of our Theosophists understand it, and that which they cannot they come to me about and I explain to them. Every Thursday I explained that which was not clear enough. But look at those newspapers; they don't understand it, they say it is all bosh.

Mr. ——: You must not take any notice of what the *Telegraph* says.

Mme. Blavatsky: Now, has *The Saturday Review* even given a single word?

Mr. ——: You must take into consideration it is their business.

Mme. Blavatsky: What, to sit on every book that appears?

Mr. ——: It is not a fair criticism, and you must not take it as such. If you write anything new in music or art they sit on it, because they like a thing that they know; that is why music is so popular, because it is like so very many other things.

Mr. Kingsland: Mr. Cross's contention is perfectly valid; but it seems to me there is a remedy for it. It is not supposed you could select what you could best read, but you will find that you will want to read these very books that you are now condemning.

Mr. Cross: I want a book that will tell me what to read.

Mr. Kingsland: Only someone who has been over the ground can help you.

20.
Theosophical Society.
Meeting of the Blavatsky Lodge
Held at 17 Lansdowne Road, Holland Park, W.
Thursday, May 30, 1889.

W. Kingsland Esq., in the Chair

Mr. Old: The first question this evening is: *Jiva* is sometimes used as synonymous with *Prana*, or simply "life"; but it appears also to be used in the plural as synonymous with the Monads, and in some other senses in the Commentary onscrofula this and the following sloka. Please throw a little more light on the meaning of the word "Jivas" in *The Secret Doctrine*.

Mme. Blavatsky: Well, I said many times that there are six schools of philosophy in India; each school has its own terms, and uses them sometimes in a different sense. What a Vedantin of the Vishishtadvaita sect will call "Jiva," that, for instance, the Advaita, also belonging to the Vedantin school, will say is a great heresy, because they call "Jiva" "One," which cannot be plural—that is to say, which is Parabrahm; it is the one universal principle. Therefore, it is very difficult to know which to use, and you must know in the light of what philosophy you use it, otherwise there will always be confusion. "Jiva" is really the incarnating ego, the fifth principle, in our school, in the esoteric school.

Mr. Kingsland: Jivas in the plural are very often used for the Monads.

Mme. Blavatsky: No, you cannot use Monad, because Monad is one thing and Jiva is another. If you take Atma-Buddhi-Manas, then, it will be another thing; but, if you use them in distinction, it is impossible to say that, because Monad is Atma, what is Monad?

Mr. Kingsland: It appears often to be used there in the same sense.

Mme. Blavatsky: The Monad is from Greek, "One," the unit, whatever it is; if we call it Monad, it is simply because it is with Buddhi; and that Atma in reality is not a unit, but the one universal principle, and it is simply a ray. That which uses Buddhi as a vehicle is that ray of that universal principle, therefore, in reality it is Buddhi which is the Monad, the one unit.

Mr. Kingsland: The Monad. But it is used in reference to the Monad in the lower forms of life.

Mme. Blavatsky: That is a different thing. Leibniz uses it in quite a different way.

Mr. Kingsland: But, is not it used there in the same sense as in *The Secret Doctrine*?

Mme. Blavatsky: The Monad is that which incarnated in {the} Chhaya, in the image, in the first image projected by the Lunar Pitris; but, it is perfectly senseless, because it has not got the cementing link, so to say, the Manas which comes after that, one comes in the First Race, and the other in the Third, so you see the difference.

Mr. Old: In reading through *The Secret Doctrine* I have been led to conclude that Jiva was always used in the sense of the individual life principle.

Mme. Blavatsky: You must pay attention to what part of the book it is used in, and when. For instance, if you see that I quote something there from some sectarian book, then it will be a different thing; or if I quote Leibniz, I will say the "Monads"; but I don't think you will find that it is used simply when I speak from my own philosophy, that I mix them up, because it is impossible to mix up the two.

Mr. Old: May we conclude, then, that Jiva is the individual expression, and Prana the universal?

Mme. Blavatsky: Prana is simply physical life, that in which animals and men and all the animal kingdom and the vegetable kingdom are; but Jiva can only be applied to the one universal principle, that is to say, the unknowable Parabrahm. Prana is the Sanskrit for the life principle. There are no "Pranas," for you cannot use it in the plural. Life is indivisible; but it is used sometimes as a synonym for Jiva, when Jiva is applied to the one life or the universal living essence—another term for the unknowable, yet self-manifesting and evident principle, the first emanation, or that which you ordinarily call the first Logos—not the second, the manifestation from the one universal.

Mr. Kingsland: Are not the Jivas synonymous with what are called the "Devourers," later on in the stanza?

Mme. Blavatsky: Every life has a Jiva in it. Every little insect has a Jiva. Every microbe, every speck of dust will have its Jiva, but that is a different thing. "Jivas" mean "the lives."

Mr. Kingsland: That is identical with Leibniz' idea of the Monads.

Mme. Blavatsky: Yes, well, but it is not that. It can be called the same. The Monads of Leibniz are quite a different thing. In one sense it is, because Leibniz calls the Monads, every atom; so there is a great difference.

Mr. Old: Whether your Monad has intelligence or not, of course it has a sentient intelligence of its own, peculiar to its degree.

Mme. Blavatsky: There is a great difference between Monad, a unit, like an atom, and a Monad which is an intelligent Monad. Such a one as reflects the whole universe is the Monad of Leibniz. One is on the plane of manifestation, and of gross matter, and the other is on the plane of pure spirituality. The two planes are quite different. You take the two, and at one end of the pole is pure spirit and at the other pole there is the gross matter. So you see you cannot mix it up. You must always see in what sense it is used. One is the Unknowable, as I say, and the other is what I have said. This is a mistake which is very often made.

Mr. Old: Question 2. You speak of the Unknowable. "Is the Unknowable of Occultism the same as the Unknowable of {Herbert} Spencer?"

Mme. Blavatsky: Well, that is just what I want to tell you, because there is a very great difference. It is not. Herbert Spencer's "Unknowable" is that which we Occultists would simply call the "unknown," or that first invisible and intangible, yet logically necessary, existing principle which some call the first cause. Now, the Unknowable of Herbert Spencer is that which he calls the first cause, and we would never call the first cause, but the first Logos. We do not call Parabrahm the first cause, because Parabrahm is the all-cause, the universal cause, or the causeless cause, which is quite a different thing. The first cause has a cause preceding it, and from which it emanates. The causeless cause has no cause, because it is the Absolute Cause itself. The Unknowable or Parabrahm of the Vedantin philosophy cannot manifest, since it is Absolute, hence the immutable; it can undergo no change whatever. To understand this Occult doctrine one would do well to study critically the quarrel between Harrison, the Positivist,[1] with Herbert Spencer, in regard to this term. Now, as I understand it, Unknowable, which to Harrison means Unknown—has anyone of you read this thing between Harrison and Herbert Spencer?

Mr. Burrows: Yes.

Mme. Blavatsky: So you know it then. You will tell me, if you please, if it is as I understand it. The "Unknowable" Harrison would replace by the word "Unknown." Neither Spencer nor Harrison makes this abstract doctrine any clearer by their discussion and coined terms, for both of them are right, and both are wrong. It is as if one insisted that the diurnal period of 24 hours should be termed day, and the other would insist upon calling it night; it is both a day and a night that make up in our perception that period, and one without the other would at once become meaningless. It is both the Unknowable

---

1 Frederic Harrison, British jurist and historian, 1831-1923, who publicized the Positivism of the French philosopher Auguste Comte in England.

and the Unknown. If then you blend together the Unknowable of Herbert Spencer and the Unknown of Harrison, the sum total will give you a relative idea of what we Occultists mean by the term, and why the words Jiva, Prana, Monad—the latter in its universal application of aggregate—are in reality all one; but yet on this plane of manifestation we are obliged to differentiate them and give a name to each and not mix them up. Now, Herbert Spencer thinks that the final aim and expression of the deific idea is an unconditioned and illimitable absoluteness, and he is right. For us there exists only one absolute certitude, viz. this: that the human spirit or consciousness finds itself constantly, uninterruptedly in the presence of infinite and eternal energy, whence emanates—or rather, radiates—all that which exists, or is. Is the idea of Herbert Spencer this?

Mr. Burrows: Yes, in the main.

Mme. Blavatsky: This is then the Unknowable, and this contains more than a simple negation. It is the confession of our human ignorance; but also the tacit or virtual admission that within man there is that which feels that energy which is the universal substance; it is fabric, so to speak. Now, Spencer repeats very often that Unknowable is that energy which manifests itself simultaneously in the universe, and in our consciousness, and that it is the highest existing reality, only concealed in the ever-changing progress of physical manifestation; and yet spirit for Herbert Spencer is simply the invisible cosmic cause of these phenomena. As I understand him he does not see in spirit anything more. He attributes to this essence, as we do, unity, homogeneity, and a limitless existence outside space and time, whose means of activity are universal laws. We say so, too, but we add that above that essence and plurality of the laws whose manifestations are only periodical, there is the one eternal law, the causeless cause, as we call it. Spencer places the Unknowable face to face with the abstract and the cosmic phenomena, and sees in this Unknowable the cause of the manifestation. The Positivist, on the other hand, while admitting the existence of a certain fundamental or basic energy, speaks, nevertheless, of the Unknowable as being simply a negative quantity, which is a contradiction in terms. Now, you understand the idea. One calls it the Unknowable, and the other the Unknown. It is positively a contradiction in terms, and both mean quite a different thing; and yet, the same thing. Because Herbert Spencer calls that which we would call the First Logos—or the first manifestation, the radiation from the eternal—he calls it the first cause; and then he speaks about the Unknowable. The other one speaks of the Unknown and wants to make of the Unknown the Parabrahm. You understand? But the Parabrahm {is} entirely unconsciousness, that is to say, a negative quantity, as he calls it. Now, what we Occultists say is that neither Spencer nor Harrison offers anything like a complete philosophy. The Unknowable or the Unknown could not exist for our perceptions, nor could our perceptions for it. It is the Unknown, or the Invisible manifesting the Logos, which we place face to face with every phenomenon—abstract, physical, psychic, mental, or spiritual—because the Unknown will always contain in itself some portion of the Unknowable, that is to say, some of the laws and manifestations which elude our perception for a time. On the other hand, Unknowable, being the sum of all that which owing to our finite intellectual organization may elude forever our perceptions, is the Parabrahm, or the causeless cause. Now, if I have succeeded in making myself understood, then I say if you study Spencer's Unknowable, and take Harrison's Unknown, instead of accepting either one or the other, seeing the necessary complements of each one life, then our one abstract Monad, and our one universal Prana, whose eternal, immutable, causeless cause is our Vedantic Parabrahm at one end of the line, and the great being, the human race or humanity at the other, then you will have the true idea of what the Occultists mean. You see it is this humanity and each unit in it which are, at one and the same time, the Unknowable, the Unknown, and the To-Be-Known. This is what Occultism says: as it is impossible for the human mind to know anything definite even of the unknown essence, so let us turn our whole attention to its highest manifestation on earth, mankind, and say as is said in John: "In it we live and move and have our being"—"Illo vivicuus movemur et sumus".[2]

Mr. Old: There is one point that I don't quite understand—perhaps it is not understandable—but that was that the Unknowable could not differentiate.

Mme. Blavatsky: I should say it could not, if it is the Absolute.

Mr. Old: But that Absolute, as the Absolute, is this, and that, and everything.

Mme. Blavatsky: Yes.

Mr. Old: Well, we are a differentiation, certainly; we are the being in that non-being. Humanity is the being, the one end of the line of life, and Parabrahm is at the other, and yet Parabrahm comprehends them both. He is not only the centre, but the radius and also the limitless circumference; it looks like a contradiction in terms.

Mme. Blavatsky: I will say, if you please, the Absolute cannot differentiate. You don't take the philosophical idea. You cannot say in philosophy that the Absolute differentiates, that the unconditioned has any relation whatever to the conditioned, or the finite; the infinite can have no relation to it. So you cannot, in thinking about cosmos, or the universe in its manifestations—perhaps you may use your argument—you cannot, if you talk pure philosophy and Vedantin philosophy, fix it up and say the Absolute can differentiate.

Mr. Old: Of course I see in the true idea of absolute being is lost in non-being.

Mme. Blavatsky: We say that Parabrahm is perfect, absolute unconsciousness. By saying that it is absolute unconsciousness, we say it is absolute consciousness. Now, can you imagine absolute consciousness? The Vedantins will. If it is absolute unconsciousness, it must be absolute consciousness; but, as it is absolute, it can have

---

2 Acts 17:28, "For in him we live, and move, and have our being—In ipso enim vivimus et movemur et sumus." Paul quotes Epimenides of Knossos (Crete), a 6th century BC semi-mythical seer and philosopher-poet.

no relation to the finite consciousness or to finite unconsciousness. Do try and understand that difference. You see those enormously difficult and abstruse ideas in the Occult philosophy.

Mr. Old: I think it is high reasoning, which our language scarcely portrays at all.

Mme. Blavatsky: Herbert Spencer has tried it, and made a mess of it, because he takes the Unknowable for a kind of transcendental first cause, which appears a little less than anthropomorphic. It is simply invisible, and he does not give it a personality. I don't think that he is at all a Vedantic philosopher.

Mr. Old: I believe that the pure idea can be conceived, but I do not think it can be expressed.

Mme. Blavatsky: Everyone must feel it, certainly. Let me tell you, and perhaps it will help you. The Unknowable, as absoluteness, is eternal, immutable; had neither beginning, nor will it have an end. The Unknowable, as a manifestation, is periodical. The one is immutable, outside of space and time; the other is finite, because it is periodical—that is why the Parabrahmic period or the Manvantaric period is separated or divided into days of Brahmâ and nights of Brahmâ. The days are the periods of activity, in which this periodical manifestation, or the Unknowable manifested, puts in an appearance; and the night of Brahmâ is a period when everything merges in this one non-entity. Now, when the age of Brahmâ has finished the hundred years—which are not our human hundred years, but which it takes about 17 or 18 figures to express, milliards and milliards, I think about 17 milliards {15 figures}[3]—then it is a period which will take as many years as it took years of activity. Do you understand this division? The Unknowable is always the absolute unknowable, the abstract unknowable, or what Harrison calls the negative quantity—which, for our perceptions, it may be.

Mr. Old: Then you might say that the unknown is, in reality, that

---

3 *The Secret Doctrine* I:36: [...] a Maha-Kalpa or the "Great Age"—100 years of Brahmâ—making a total of 311,040,000,000,000 of years.

which is to be known.

Mme. Blavatsky: The unknown cannot be; because the unknown has always some potentiality of the unknowable in it, whereas the unknowable cannot have such a potentiality.

Mr. Old: But I, like yourself, distinguish here between the words "unknown" and "unknowable." I should call Herbert Spencer's first cause "unknown."

Mme. Blavatsky: Harrison is perfectly right. But, don't you call it Unknowable, because that is what we call Parabrahm.

Mr. Kingsland: It is the difference between Brahmâ and Parabrahm.

Mr. Old: Question 3. In reference to the whole of paragraph (e), and to some points which were raised last Thursday, it would be as well to devote a little more time to the subject of reincarnation. And then there are several clauses which I think it would be well to read separately. Unfortunately, the paragraph is omitted.

Mr. Kingsland: "The fourth order are substantial entities, etc." (Reads paragraph e.) {*The Secret Doctrine* I:218}

Mr. Old: (a) For example, we have been accustomed to think of the "Imperishable Jivas," or "Monads," as the Atma-Buddhi-Manas (exoterically), and that this "Monad" incarnates at some period or other in the newly-born child—not, however, fully incarnating until seven years after birth.

Mme. Blavatsky: I told you that "Imperishable Monads" are not at all what you think. It is that which I have told you already, that the "Imperishable Jivas" are the incarnating individualities, not personalities; and they are not the Monads. The Monads take immediate possession of the astral images, the Chhaya of the Lunar Pitris; the Jivas or Manasaputra, only at the end of the Third Race. With the child it is just as it is with the First Race. The Monads, Atma-Buddhis, are said to have fully incarnated only when full consciousness is developed in the child mankind—that is to say, the Third Race—and so it is with the child unit, or man. Take always analogy, then you will find invariably the key to the occult explanation. As it is with the First Race to the Third Race, so it is with the child, because the child is microcosmos of the macrocosm, and it repeats, stage by stage, everything. The whole evolution of the universe is found in the evolution of the fetus and of the child. That is a well-known fact, which the Occultists ought to know, more or less.

Mr. Old: Then you say that the Monad does not incarnate.

Mme. Blavatsky: The Monad incarnates the Monad, so to say, of a shadow. It is not united, because Chhaya—or this image, the astral form—is not conscious of the presence of the Monad, because there is no Manasic element to appreciate or to be conscious of that Monad in it. Therefore, it is just as though he did not have it. So it is with the child.

Mr. Old: It is merely the vehicle of the individual life.

Mme. Blavatsky: Nothing else. But when the Manas comes, or the mind, then there is the union of all the principles, and all the principles appear all about between seven and eight years when the child becomes conscious.

Mr. Old: Manas is a connecting link. Then (b). It was suggested by Mr. Sinnett last Thursday, and also apparently by the paragraph before us, that the Monad is really necessary as a potentiality denominating, and being in fact the "germ" which causes the development of the entity from the germinal cell onwards. But can we really say that the Devachanic entity or upper triad has anything to do, as an entity, with the purely physical evolution of that form in which it will presently incarnate? Are not the four lower principles derived entirely from the parent and following broadly what we usually call heredity? And may we not say that this affects the four lower, but not the three higher principles?

Mme. Blavatsky: Now, I will try to answer you seriatim. Mr. Sinnett probably calls Monad that which we call the image, Chhaya, unless he misunderstood the teaching—which I don't think, because he understood it well. And I think you misunderstood Mr. Sinnett. He did not say this about the Monad, because it is the first thing that is taught, that the Monad does not come but at a certain stage of the life of the child—the Buddhi, especially.

Mr. Old: He has prescribed that seven years in his *Esoteric Buddhism*.

Mme. Blavatsky: The germinal cell contains the seed or astral form only. The father plants the seed in the soil of matter. This seed is like a flame without wick or fuel: it neither decreases nor increases, and whether he has one or a hundred children, each of these children will be like a rush candle[4] to which was imparted a light from the same inexhaustible flame. There is a thing which goes for millions and millions, from the time when mankind began. It all passes from father to son, from father to son, and so on. You understand the meaning, and certainly it cannot decrease.

Mr. Old: But for how many principles is the human parent responsible?

Mme. Blavatsky: I will tell you all this which is written here. The Monad overshadows the fetus only in the seventh month, and enters fully the child after he reaches consciousness. The Devachanic entity envelops, so to speak, the new entity, lights it up, but begins its process of assimilation only after the first ray of consciousness, say at seven or eight months, then it does not enter it, it begins to overshadow it, it is there, it is led by Karmic law to it, but it cannot enter immediately. It is perfect nonsense to say the child has a soul, and is a human being before it is born.

Mr. Kingsland: Then it is attracted by the astral shadow?

Mme. Blavatsky: Just in the same way.

Mr. Old: It is rather dangerous against the law of infanticide.

---

4 Candle made from rushes dipped in grease drippings.

Mme. Blavatsky: It cannot be taught to the masses and the people. But unfortunately the Hindus know it, and therefore they get rid of their children very easily. But this is certainly Karma. But whether the child has got a will or not, it is a human being, and there are other laws in the code of philosophy which prevent infanticide; that will always be a crime. From the parents the child receives only the astral and physical bodies and the Kama-rupa, the animal soul. It receives life from no one. It does not receive life from father or mother; it is born, and therefore it is in life. I ask you, do you receive the ocean? Can it be said that you receive the ocean when you bathe in it, or does the sponge receive it? You and the sponge have your being, and that ocean because you are in its waters. Now, suppose that the waters penetrated you entirely, that is life, the water. The child receives life from no one, the life is there, it is the universal principle. Of course, science will tell you it is nothing of the kind. It is nonsense, that life is not an entity. Life is just that deity of which we know nothing.

Mr. Old: You think the physical parents have the power of focusing this life and bringing it into distinct channels.

Mme. Blavatsky: The form is made which, as soon as it is born, receives, or as soon as it begins developing, receives life; just the same as you breathe air unconsciously. Nobody gives you the air that you breathe. Without air you would die, that is all.

Mr. Old: Then you really mean to say that the endowment of life is the result of certain physical development which has led up to that stage when the reception of life is a necessity.

Mme. Blavatsky: Most assuredly. You are born, you are formed to come into being, and you live because life is there. You are in life. When you die, it is not that life leaves you; you are in the life. It is you who leave the life, and not life that leaves you.

Mr. Kingsland: Life begins to function and manifest through you.

Mme. Blavatsky: And once that your organs are destroyed, it won't function. It is like the force in the clock. You wind it up; so long as it is wound up it will work, but once that this force is exhausted—not the force that made it—but once the thing has been wound up and runs down, there is an end of it, it cannot function, and this force cannot function where there are no conditions.

Mr. Kingsland: It is more like a tree moving about in the wind. You see the effect of the wind by the tree, but if you take away the tree, the wind is blowing past there, just the same.

Mme. Blavatsky: The three higher principles are the human trinity, the three in one. They do not come to the child from the parents. If somebody objects to this and asks: how about the heredity intellect and its absence? You know, as they said the other time when somebody here thought the heredity the all. I say it is perfect nonsense. Neither this heredity intellect or dullness rests with the higher ego or Manas at all. Their degrees are dependent upon our physical organism and brain, the size of which, by the bye, does not always go *pari passu* with the quality of the brain. Now, some persons will say: "He has got an enormous brain, and it shows the intellect." Not at all. I have been reading things in the medical books. The pig has a far larger brain than the man, and yet it is not quite so intellectual.

Mr. Old: They say the depth of convolutions, rather.

Mme. Blavatsky: No, they weigh the brain. Such a one has got so many ounces or pounds or tons. I say it is the quality, not the quantity. If the father or the mother were intellectual people, they will sometimes pass by inheritance an organism as theirs was to the child. Thence the son will have the same capacities of receiving into and reflecting in his physical brain the same amount of light from Manas or the mind principle. But how often do we find stupid sons of intellectual parents, and vice versa? This is not heredity. Do you understand this? The parents may give by heredity their organism, their convolutions, or whatever it is, the physical material, which will have the same capacity of reflecting the light from Manas as they had, therefore the child will be as intellectual; but Manas is not at all that. It is always the same, it is omniscient. It becomes dull or stupid only in its personalities and incarnations upon earth. You can't say of Manas that one ego is more intellectual than the other.

Mr. Kingsland: Does not one ego bring back more Manases from the Devachanic state than another?

Mme. Blavatsky: Not at all. One ego will have a better Karmic development than another, but it does not bring back at all. Once it is past its period of illusion in Devachan—when it is in Devachan or anything, it becomes the omniscient ego.

Mr. Kingsland: But that portion which we have always understood to be assimilating, is not that brought back again?

Mme. Blavatsky: It is, but in Devachan it is not itself. It is very difficult to explain; it reflects the human personality, because if it did not do that, it could not have the bliss that it has, because Devachan, after all, is an illusion, the Fool's Paradise.

Mr. Kingsland: But then that portion of Manas surely develops with every individual.

Mme. Blavatsky: It does, because the personality differs, but the Manas *per se* is the incarnating ego.

Mr. ———: Manifestation depends upon the perfection or the imperfection of the instrument.

A Lady: It would really be, then, from the parents you have a certain development or non-development of mechanism, and it is according to that the Manas is able to manifest itself in ordinary life, and that is where heredity will come in.

Mme. Blavatsky: The Manas is always the same. It is the stem, the eternal stem around which cling the personalities, so to say, those that come and go, and so on. It is called the Sutratma, the silver thread on which are strung those pearls as personalities—you know the expression—in its own inherent nature, or essence, it is omniscient, for it is part of the Divine Mind. But once that it has been brought to incarnate on earth, it takes up all the materiality and all the finite attributes, so to say, and the qualities of the personalities it incarnates in, and moreover, these personalities are subject to the {im?}perfections of the material form.

A Lady: Supposing during the human life, the spiritual nature has been developed up to a very considerable extent, and then death comes. When that Manas returns to a fresh incarnation, will the progress that has been made in the past life settle the type of humanity that it will then take up, so that its past life will carry it on further?

Mme. Blavatsky: Certainly, if the Karma was good, it will go higher and higher, and all the experiences of the past life will come in this life, because, when you find children who are not at all like their parents—no musicians in the family—and you see little boy phenomenons, Hofmann,[5] or some such things, this is a thing which comes from the previous life. It comes to him as easily as water to a duck.

Mr. ———: How does it happen that the mechanism he gets from his parents does not retard that? Because, if his parents are non-musical, then their mechanism, so far as regards music, must be stronger than his.

Mme. Blavatsky: It overpowers blind matter.

Mr. Kingsland: In many cases, I fancy it is retarded?

Mme. Blavatsky: Look at little, blind Tom, who is in America, a little nigger of four years, who is perfectly blind, and yet see the wonderful things that he does.[6]

A Lady: Would it be attracted, rather, towards the musical

---

5 Child prodigy, Josef Hofmann, 1876-1957, who played piano concerts at the age of 10, and was very much in the public eye in 1887 and 1888.
6 Thomas "Blind Tom" Wiggins, 1849-1908, born a blind slave in Georgia in the U.S., by the age of four he evinced a talent for playing the piano, for which he had no training, and was put on tour by his owner.

mechanism?

Mme. Blavatsky: Heredity is a Karmic effect, therefore, if an individuality has to incarnate in Karma in a person, then the frame will be given to him, which will give to him this musical mechanism.

A Lady: There will be a sort of affinity?

Mr. Old: And then has not an astral body the power of impressing its own image upon the gross matter supplied by the physical parents?

Mr. Kingsland: The other way about.

Mr. Old: The antitype which exists previous to the child's birth.

Mme. Blavatsky: This astral is nothing at all with the Manas that incarnates. This belongs to the lower matter, and this is given by the father and mother, by the parents, and around this astral then forms the physical child. But this astral is nothing to do with that. It is nothing to do with the ego, which is one and continuous, unbroken.

Mr. Old: The Monad, in incarnating, projects its shadow Chhaya.

Mme. Blavatsky: No, no, not at all.

Mr. Old: Does not it overshadow? It is said to overshadow the child.

Mme. Blavatsky: It overshadows the child that has its astral self in it, and its body. Then it begins overshadowing when the child is born, the Monad Buddhi, this immortal principle, gets into the child and overshadows it as soon as the child begins to be conscious—as conscious as a kitten, for instance, it is there already, but the Manas is called a different thing. The Manas is mind, that is why the child will never become intellectual before five or six years. It depends upon how precocious he is. Read in the second volume of *The Secret Doctrine* and see how the Lunar Pitris project their Chhayas, and having projected their Chhayas, this is the vehicle of the Monad.

Mr. Old: That is just what I understood, and it carries it towards the child—the as yet unintelligent child.

Mme. Blavatsky: I tell you again that till the Third Race, it does not link itself entirely.

Mr. Kingsland: It has nothing to do with the development of the germ, either physically or astrally, but it is attracted afterwards at a certain period to the already partly developed germ.

Mr. Old: How much of the individuality, then, shapes the organism?

Mr. Kingsland: That is the point I don't think has been quite elucidated yet. Where does the individuality of the reincarnating Monad come in?

Mme. Blavatsky: The individuality is the reincarnating ego, the Manas. Manas is a thing, it is Sutratma. The personality and individuality are quite different. You make the same thing out of personality and individuality.

Mr. Kingsland: Where does the musical quality come in? How does that belong to it?

Mme. Blavatsky: It belongs to it because every personality that passes gives a certain colour, and gives more and more and more to the incarnating ego; and then it remains, this talent for music, and it brings it back. Very well; all that remains on the individuality, on the ego being reincarnated, is brought back on earth, and therefore it is an inherent soul quality.

Mr. Kingsland: I understood you just now, the intellectuality does not depend upon Manas at all, but upon physical qualifications.

Mme. Blavatsky: Intellectuality and music are quite different things. I have known idiots who played beautifully. I said the parents did not give to the child anything but the form, and certainly there is the lower Manas and the higher Manas. If they made the form fit enough to receive this higher light, or to have untrammeled this light from the Manas, he will be intellectual. If the Kama-rupa, or the lower Manas, predominates too much, then he won't receive, because he will be dull. There will be no light coming from Manas.

Manas, itself, depends upon Buddhi.

Mr. Kingsland: Then, as a matter of fact, there is a large portion of everyone's Manas, that does not incarnate at all, that always remains undeveloped, unrepresented, in the present personality of the person.

Mme. Blavatsky: Remember that we are in the Fifth Race and only at the end of the Fifth Race will Manas be entirely developed, and we are yet on the Fourth Round only. I cannot tell you all that I would like to. There are three more rounds.

Mr. Kingsland: Take the case of the person who has got this inherent quality. Suppose he doesn't find the physical conditions?

Mme. Blavatsky: Then he won't be a musician. There is Karma that will always find that.

Mr. Kingsland: Surely the whole of your Karma does not find all the development. Where is it during the present incarnation?

Mme. Blavatsky: I can't understand what you mean.

Mr. Old: I can understand your question, because it was one that arose in my mind.

Mr. Kingsland: Instead of saying music or intellectuality, let us say the character. Isn't it the Manas or distinctive quality that gives character to the person?

Mme. Blavatsky: To give character to the person, do you mean that the Manas would have to change and become a different Manas every time? Where would be, if you please, the incarnating ego, the Sutratman?

Mr. Old: Then you think character is only an expression of mind?

Mme. Blavatsky: I only know one thing. Let us say this pair of spectacles is the Manas. It is always for ever eternally the same. Now, I put the spectacles in mud; something will remain on it of this mud. Then I will put them in jam, there will be some jam left. Then I will put it in something else. Every incarnation gives to the Manas some personality, and at the end of the Manvantaric round, that is to say, at the end of the cycles of incarnation, there will be the Manas with all the experiences it has acquired. For personality dies. It is only the secret of spirituality, of the spiritual qualities, of the eternal qualities, that will survive. You read *Esoteric Buddhism*, and *Esoteric Buddhism* is well-enough written. You read it, Dr Berridge, I can't explain it any better.

Mr. ——: Putting it into very bold English, supposing you always dropped them into jam?

Mme. Blavatsky: They will be very sweet then.

Mr. ——: Taking an analogy of jam and music—supposing it will be always music—Jozef Hofmann will have so much by and bye that it will be bound to come to the front.

Mme. Blavatsky: Certainly I like somebody who can speak plainly.

A Lady: He will also incarnate into a body in which the mechanism is likely to go towards music.

Mme. Blavatsky: I say that {in} the Karmic-sense heredity is governed by Karma, therefore, when the musical entity is to reincarnate, then certainly this law will take care that the body will be musical and fit for it—that they should not be born with stumps instead of fingers.

Mr. Old: You would say, really, that individual character is nothing else than expression of mind through different organisms, and that the organisms control the expression of character?

Mme. Blavatsky: For instance, you put some intelligence under blue glass, it will appear to you blue, or under red, and so on, it will go on like that.

Mr. Kingsland: If that is so, if Manas as we find it here depends upon the quality of the organism that it functions in, where does the development of Manas come in?

Mme. Blavatsky: It develops through the personality. Manas does not come to be happy and to be developed, Manas comes because it is too pure and being too pure, it has neither merit nor demerit. Therefore, it must come and suffer a little bit, and have the experience of everything that can be got in this cycle of imagination {incarnation?}, and therefore, the same experiences will make it fit to emerge {merge?} in the Absolute. It contains all the experiences in this blessed world, and the worlds that have been and will be.

Mr. Kingsland: It appears from that, that Manas is something that is to be, still qualified by the individual lives with no life.

Mme. Blavatsky: Most assuredly. In the *Key to Theosophy* I give all this. Read the *Key to Theosophy*. It will come out in two or three weeks. I think I answer every question there. It is extremely difficult for me, "unaccustomed as I am to public speaking," to come and explain this. Really, I want to say one thing, and I say quite a different thing—or you take it as such.

Mr. Old: The next paragraph clears it up, I think. Question 3 (c). According to this view, the "spiritual plasm" referred to in the paragraph in question is not the Devachanic Entity, though it is liable to be confounded with it.[7] There is, of course, a mystery within a mystery here, but it is very desirable that we should have a clear view of the matter, in connection with the more immediate derivation and evolution of the seven human principles.

Mme. Blavatsky: You see what I said. You are right, and Mr. Sinnett or somebody else spoke also of this heredity business as being an obstacle. Do you remember, Mr. Burrows, who spoke about it, that it was an obstacle?

Mr. Burrows: I don't remember.

Mme. Blavatsky: It is just that which enters into Karmic attributes. Heredity is governed by Karma, in short. Therefore, you see, Karma will take care to bring it into a musical physical body.

---

7 Spiritual plasm is mentioned in *The Secret Doctrine* I:219 and 224.

Mr. Old: Then we may say that the law of heredity applies to the four lower principles, and the law of Karma operates in the plane of the three higher.

Mme. Blavatsky: The law of heredity has nothing to do with life. Remember what you learn, if you please, apart from the Thursdays. Exoterically it is, not esoterically.

Mr. Old: (d) From what is said on page 224, line 10 et seq, the above view would appear to be supported, with the further addition that the parent is also responsible for Manas—perhaps we should say, some portion of Manas?

Mme. Blavatsky: Now, how can the parent be responsible for Manas? You will say next it is responsible for Atma.

Mr. Old: It is the animal mind we refer to, perhaps?

Mme. Blavatsky: It is the reflection from the higher mind. We say it is dual simply because on this plane the full Manas cannot manifest; and in relation to its lower Manas, it is just the same as Parabrahm's relation to the first Logos; it radiates. Very well, and the rest depends upon the more or less perfect organisms, on education, on environment, and on everything, on the vices that are inculcated; all these things that come, and are so many obstacles.

Mr. Kingsland: Then Manas stands there in the same way as Prana does in reference to the lower, to the life on the physical plane. It is universal, so to speak.

Mme. Blavatsky: The Manas is universal. These are distinct entities which incarnate, which in other Manvantaras have finished their cycle, and it is their time to incarnate in this cycle.

Mr. Kingsland: It says here the five lower principles in the four.

Mme. Blavatsky: It is not the five principles of the seven, it is the five principles of the lower principles. It is perfectly correctly said there. Man must have the fruition of all the five, it is said, and this fruition carries within it no responsibility to anyone. You look there on the page that you have been mentioning, page 224, line 20. You find there the phrase I have quoted: "Man must have the fruition of all the five", and this fruition carries with it no responsibility to anyone. How can the parents be responsible for Manas, where Manas is a defined and independent entity? The parents may in some way be karmically responsible for the physical organism of the child, but certainly not for Manas.

Mr. Kingsland: Not responsible for Manas any more than they are responsible for Prana.

Mme. Blavatsky: Most assuredly.

Mr. Old: Question 4 (page 233). Since each round, globe, etc., is under the guidance of a "Creator," "Builder," or "Watcher," can you tell us what part, if any, these Manus play in polity of nations on the terrestrial plane?

Mme. Blavatsky: None at all. The "Watchers" or "Builders" are commissioned by law to guide and animate, so to say, the elements of which our globe is composed; but they have no power to interfere with Karmic law, because they are not anthropomorphic gods. They are simply powers, cosmic powers, of which we have no ideas; not what you men of science and naturalists would call cosmic powers, but what we Occultists would call cosmic powers.

Mr. Old: Question 5. During the reign of one Manu or Race, have the other six any *direct* influence on human affairs?

Mme. Blavatsky: Well, I would say to you with the French. When the king dies they say: "The king is dead; long live the king!" How can the six Manus have anything to do with the Manus now? When an age or race has passed away, nothing that has caused the Nidanas, or the concatenation of causes of the previous, act on the new one. It is only the Karmic effects that develop. When Victoria dies, and you have your next royal—ninny, shall I say—shall the four Georges[8] have any direct influence on the forces of England? You see, I am a very great Republican.

Mr. Old: Question 6, page 238, Sloka 5: "Sacred Animals." Elsewhere you explain the term "Sacred Animals" as referring symbolically to the signs of the zodiac. How is this meaning of the term connected with the explanation given here of it as "the first shadow of physical man"?

Mme. Blavatsky: How many times shall I have to repeat that each symbol has a septenary significance? Did I tell you one, or twenty, or a hundred times, that everything has seven meanings? In astronomy, the "Sacred Animals" mean the zodiacal signs; in geology, they mean the globes, which are also the planets (Which may be taken astronomically.), or geologically, as worlds; in zoology, they are sacrificial animals; in anthropology it is physical man. It has, in every department, some meaning, just as you apply it.

Mr. Old: Question 7, page 250: It would be interesting to have a clearer definition of the three "waters"—"solid water," "liquid mist, watery," "third world-element water"; also, to know the order of the development of the senses in the races of the Fourth Round. We are in the Fourth Round, but Fifth Race, and therefore are developing a sense which cannot reach its full expansions till the Fifth Round: 1. Fire (sight); 2. Air (touch); 3 Water (taste); 4. Earth (smell); 5. Ether (sound); 6. Akasa (intuition); 7. Kundalini sense (includes all others).

Mme. Blavatsky: We are, for the first time, in this Fourth Round; and we are, for the first time, men. In the three previous Rounds we were mere intangible phantoms; then ethereal, fluidic creatures; then jelly-like animals; and only in the Fourth Race we have become real physical men, haven't we? Then, take the analogy, and look what I have written there, and go to bed. You must ask this question with

---

8 The "four Georges" refers to the monarchs of Great Britain who preceded Queen Victoria, who died January 21nd, 1901.

your initiation of the masters, not of me (See footnote on page 252.) You put me questions that are—well, extraordinary. All this is esoteric, but I don't mind telling you something of it. If you have air in seven states of density, why cannot you have water in such seven states of degree, and everything else, including fire? I ask you the question. Of course, if we represented and analyzed them, we shall find in each all the other elements, in one form or the other. Now, let us take earth, and we will find in it that we divide it into seven. We find in its lowest and most material end granite rock, the hardest that you can think of, which will become softer and softer as it passes through each of its states until it becomes mud, and what you would call simply dirty water. It will be matter, still. Now, in the rock, matter, or earth, you will find fire concealed, that is to say, it contains fire potentially, as it contains air and everything else. The same with air, which begins at the third stage above radiant matter, and ends with ether and Akasa, and so on. All this will show to you that, whether four or seven, these are called elements, are correlative, and each becomes a definite element only on our plane of perception and by one of its seven aspects, because that aspect which predominates over the others will give that qualifaction to that element. We call it water because that aspect is more developed than air, or fire; but, you will find all the seven in every element occultly, in reality, in their final essence, and on the plane of manifestation, they are all one element. And when they have achieved their cycle of evolution in the world of manifestation, this one disappears and they merge back into their primal cause, and from the one element they become no element again, absoluteness. I did not create the world. I cannot explain this to you; I must not.

Mr. Old: Question 8 (Page 260—end of second paragraph.) If our globe is in its Kama-rupic state, in what state was it during the First, Second, and Third Rounds?

Mme. Blavatsky: That is a modest man, and he asks very easy things, to which extremely easy answers can be given. Count from what you will, it is always the Kama-rupic state, since it is right in the middle.

From above or below it will become rupa. It is the middle thing; but, if we count from the races—for the evolution of the globes has to begin by the highest, or seventh—the second will correspond to the second, and so on. We call it Kama-rupic because there are no words to express the corresponding states. If from round we turn to races, it will be easier, and it is explained in *The Secret Doctrine*; everything is explained there, how with every race you acquire new facility. In the Fifth Race we have attained the highest intellectuality in this round; but in the Sixth Round or the Fifth Round, the Fifth Race will be a thousand times more intellectual yet. Take it all on analogy. Now, gentlemen, let us have questions, and I am ready to answer you.

Mr. Old: What is the meaning of the second plane mentioned here (page 262 note)?

Mme. Blavatsky: That is what I say. You ask me in three years that! Now, you had better ask questions, and we will make the conversation general.

(The proceedings then closed.)

21.
Theosophical Society.
Meeting of the Blavatsky Lodge
Held at 17 Lansdowne Road, Holland Park, W.
Thursday, June 6, 1889.

{W. Kingsland in the Chair}

Mr. Old: These are questions such as would come from a person beginning to search out Theosophical truth, and I thought myself that it would be a leader to the issue of this new book, *The Key to Theosophy*. I thought a consideration of some of the elementary questions would not only fill up a very pleasant evening, but, at the same time, would excite some interest in the book which is now approaching completion. They are mere elementary questions on Karma, Devachan, and Reincarnation; the How, When, and Where of Theosophy. Question 1. What is Karma?

Mme. Blavatsky: Am I really expected to answer this?

Mr. Old: You are.

Mme. Blavatsky: Karma is the law of retribution. Now, Mr. Bertram Keightley, go on.

Mr. B. Keightley: They would much rather listen to you than to me. However, Karma is, as HPB began to say, the law of retribution— that which is recognized by modern science as the law of cause and effect; but although that law is absolutely universal, the law of Karma is more frequently used in a narrower sense as applying more particularly to the law of cause and effect acting on the moral plane. Literally, it means simply action, and it expresses the idea that every action is productive of consequence, and so the chain of causation goes on infinitely; but, it is not simply that causes operate blindly, because in the Theosophical view the law of Karma is absolute intelligence; and it also has to be remembered that the law of Karma applies to the individual. It is not merely that a man performs certain actions.

Mme. Blavatsky: Stop. You say that the law of Karma is intelligent.

Mr. B. Keightley: I said "intelligence."

Mme. Blavatsky: I say it is not. It is neither intelligence nor non-intelligence.

Mr. B. Keightley: It is absolute intelligence.

Mme. Blavatsky: Because you will make of it immediately a personal god, and I protest against that. That is to say, that everything that falls under the sway or the influence of that ever-present law will have certain effects, as in the physical world there is a concatenation of causes and effects always. For instance, if I do like that, I will just hurt my hand; the pain I feel in my hand will be the effect of having done that; so it is in the world of moral causes, but you cannot and must not say it is intelligent or intelligence. Is it simply the absolute harmony, absolute—well, call it intelligence, wisdom, anything you like. There again I am stuck for a word.

Mr. B. Keightley: It is true to say it acts with intelligence.

Mme. Blavatsky: It does not act. It is our actions that act, and that awaken into all kinds of influences. Look here, if you say that Karma acts and you say it has intelligence, immediately you suggest the idea of a personal god. It is not so, because Karma does not see and Karma does not watch, and does not repent as the Lord God repented. Karma is a universal law, immutable and changeless.

Mr. B. Keightley: But you cannot conceive of a law which does not act.

Mme. Blavatsky: Well, I say it does not act; in my conception, it does not act. Well, Karma does not act any more than water drowns you.

Mr. B. Keightley: But water does drown you.

Mme. Blavatsky: Water does not drown you. You drown yourselves in the water. Don't go into the water and you won't get drowned.

Mr. Old: Is it possible to get outside the law of Karma, then?

Mme. Blavatsky: You cannot.

Mr. Old: The analogies scarcely fit.

Mme. Blavatsky: I beg your pardon. It does, as much as it can fit in this world of physical symbols, or whatever you may call them, because it is the way that you act. It is not because you act wickedly or sinfully, or with or without a motive, you produce an effect. You strike a note in the universal.

Mr. Ralph Sneyd: Is not ignorance the cause of all evil action?

Mme. Blavatsky: It is, but Karma does not take stock of it, does not concern itself whether you do it from ignorance or from too much learning. It is simply if you do a certain thing, so the effect will be on a similar line. For instance, you will strike one note, and you know perfectly well what will be the consequence of that note. That is why I simply wanted to stop Mr. Keightley, because he said it was intelligent and it acted. Certainly we must say that it acts; but, I want you at the same time to understand that in saying it acts, we use the same expression as if we said the sun is setting. The sun does not set at all.

Mr. Burrows: If our action is a note which we strike, that really is the echo of some previous note which has been struck somewhere in the universe.

Mme. Blavatsky: Certainly, it is not the first time that you struck this note. Whether you strike it in the ordinary way, or otherwise, it depends on that whether it will be flat, sharp or something else.

Mr. Kingsland: Karma is, so to speak, the absolute equilibrium; and however we act we disturb that equilibrium one way or another, and Karma adjusts.

Mr. B. Keightley: The analogy that dwells in my mind is this—it almost presents itself to me under this form: If we conceive ourselves as beings absolutely surrounded and penetrating everything in fluid of such a nature that every action we make in that fluid produces a series of vibrations which eventually react upon ourselves; if you imagine a body suspended in a perfect fluid, no movement is possible without disturbing the fluid. That sort of pressure pressing in upon you from all sides, that substance—if you like to call it that—is Karma, or rather, Karma describes the relation of that subject.

Mme. Blavatsky: There is simply one way of getting outside the influence of Karma; it is the yogis who do it only; it is by merging oneself more and more in the Laya state. That is to say, that you are just like in a vessel out of which air has been pumped—a perfect vacuum. In that vacuum, of course, you cannot go either left or right or any way; there is no point of attraction, and there you are. You understand the analogy?

Mrs. Besant: Then it would always be the striving after equilibrium?

Mme. Blavatsky: Certainly! Every action produces a Karmic effect on the spiritual plane, on the psychic, on the spiritual, and everything, and the only thing is to be in this neutral point where there is no differentiation, where there is no action.

Mr. Old: Then we understand Karma to be the law of equilibrium.

Mme. Blavatsky: It is perfect harmony and equilibrium.

Mr. B. Keightley: I think you want to add to it one thing. People get an idea very often that Karma only applies to bad actions. Karma is simply the action, the law of the consequence of action of all kinds, whether good or bad, and it is, entirely apart from that, the inevitable sequence of cause and effect. It will fall upon you whether the action is good or bad.

Mr. Sneyd: But would not you say that all that arose—every evil consequence which decreased happiness—arose from ignorance on the part of the conscious being that did the action? However learned a person may be, supposing he does an action which results in the decrease of his happiness, should not you say that action was caused by his ignorance in some respect?

Mme. Blavatsky: But ignorance won't save you from the effects of Karma.

Mr. Sneyd: Don't you think ignorance is the cause of bad Karma?

Mme. Blavatsky: It is.

Mr. Sneyd: And that knowledge is the cause of all good Karma? Supposing you did a thing and it increased your happiness; would not it be the reason of that would most likely be that you had done something with knowledge, as it were?

Mr. B. Keightley: I don't think so, because the effects produced by a given cause are not always of the same character. You see, a man who uses his knowledge to do good, to make good Karma for himself, acts fundamentally from a selfish motive, which is again a wrong motive, at the back of his good action.

Mr. Sneyd: Would not the reason be that he was ignorant in so far as he did not know the interest of one conscious being was the interest of all?

Mme. Blavatsky: Wait a moment, there is another question about Karma here.

Mr. Old: I thought it would not do to let each question go too far into the discussion, otherwise it might overlap some of the other questions. The second question is: How far does this law operate in this life, and how far in Devachan?

Mme. Blavatsky: In Devachan, it does not operate at all. It is the law of Karma which sends a man to Devachan with a programme already prepared beforehand, which program is the consequence of his suffering and of the miseries that he had in this world, and it is already there; it is cut and dried for him. Karma waits on the threshold of Devachan at the moment of reincarnation, and then it pounces upon the individual when he is rewarded. There is no punishment in the hereafter, in the other world, as you call it.

Mrs. Besant: It only works then, really, in this world?

Mme. Blavatsky: It is the hell, and the purgatory, and everything, and the paradise.

Mr. B. Keightley: The good effects are reaped in Devachan.

Mme. Blavatsky: Reaped for those who want a consolation, and want a rest, and bliss, and care for it; those who don't care for it won't have it.

Mr. Gardner: The fool's paradise.

Mme. Blavatsky: For instance, you are perfectly indifferent to everything.

Mr. Kingsland: There is a question which might be put with reference to very wicked people who don't go into Devachan.

Mme. Blavatsky: They are born almost immediately after a kind of sleep in which they won't have very nice dreams.

Mr. Kingsland: That is what I wanted to say.

Mme. Blavatsky: There is nothing, you see, like Devachan; there is Avichi, but that is quite a different thing.

Mr. Kingsland: In the state of Kamaloka.

Mme. Blavatsky: There it is no more the man, the entire man. He has been left and abandoned by one of his principles, he has no more of the Atma over him; he has simply his intelligence and his consciousness. That is why I say those creatures that you see in the séance rooms are so very dangerous. It is not the man, it is the shadow of the man, and his reflection; but with all the wickedness and with all the wicked influences, the utmost fear of all that which he has committed in this life. And certainly he will inoculate it in those present as though a living man came with the smallpox and gave it to you all. All this idea of spiritualism is perfectly ridiculous.

Mr. Old: Then Karma does not operate, or has no active operation, only a reflex operation, in Devachan?

Mme. Blavatsky: Merely sends a man into Devachan and stops on the threshold. Allegorically speaking, it waits when the man comes out of the state of bliss, during which he will be rewarded for all the unmerited suffering and all the things he had—for after all, a man is a very miserable creature. A man does not want to be born, and does not know he is born.

Mr. Burrows: Is there such a thing as unmerited suffering?

Mme. Blavatsky: If you suffer from causes you produce, it is merited; but very often you have sufferings through causes generated by other persons, of which you are not guilty at all.

Mrs. Besant: For instance, national Karma.

Mme. Blavatsky: Very often you suffer for things you have never committed, but you simply happen to fall under this current, and there you are. You suffer tremendously, and you suffer that which is not merited, and then you have to have an adequate bliss and reward for it.

Mr. B. Keightley: That is the personal Karma. The suffering man has a conscious personality—Mr. Smith or Mr. Brown, who is not aware he has committed any of these crimes, how shall we say? Take for instance now, this accident in America;[1] it will be a very good instance. Now, you could not suppose that all the people that have been drowned or have suffered in various ways, and all the children

---

1 The Johnstown Flood in Pennsylvania, May 31, 1889, killing over 2,000 in a matter of hours when the dam broke.

in that catastrophe, were all, as it were, brought under its influence by their personal Karma, so to speak, would you, HPB?

Mme. Blavatsky: No. It is just that, you know.

Mr. B. Keightley: There a dam bursts and these people are swept away.

Mr. Sneyd: Would not you say it was the result of a sort of ignorance on the part of those people being there and not knowing the train would come to a smash?

Mr. B. Keightley: Of course it is, in one sense.

Mr. Old: This is what you call diffused Karma. A person comes under it by virtue of being an atom of a body. He cannot have a law separate from the body to which he belongs.

Mr. B. Keightley: The distinction I drew between the personality and individuality of a man is of special importance, because as a personality he has not perhaps a responsibility for that; he is one of a race, and he suffers the Karma of the race.

Mr. Burrows: And then the justice comes in afterwards.

Mr. B. Keightley: Because he has suffered personally more than he has merited, he receives his reward in Devachan in the shape of a personal reward. Is not that so, HPB?

Mr. Old: Then our third question is: How far can this law of Karma be diverted, deferred, or prevented—diverted in the sense of turning off one track, onto another?

Mme. Blavatsky: You meddle with Karma, and then it will be just a thousand times worse. You can defer it and you can stop it for a while, but it will come always.

Mr. Old: You cannot prevent it, then?

Mme. Blavatsky: You cannot; it will become worse.

Mr. B. Keightley: Can you divert it in the sense of changing the character of its manifestation? Can you neutralize bad Karma by subsequent good action?

Mr. Old: Can an individual take on the Karma of half a dozen people?

Mme. Blavatsky: He cannot. No! Sir.

Mr. Kingsland: But you can make new Karma for half a dozen people.

Mme. Blavatsky: Yes, but you cannot *take* it any more than you can take the illness of a half a dozen persons. Now, if it is not Karmic, of course you may stop it—this thing which has been produced by someone else—but if it is Karmic, nothing will stop it.

Mr. Old: A person who alleviates suffering only generates good Karma for himself.

Mme. Blavatsky: He does temporary good to the persons, but the Karma must come in some other shape.

Mr. Old: Because I was wondering how far Karma was worked out, or worked off, in physical suffering.

Mme. Blavatsky: Who told you that? I don't know what you mean.

Mr. Old: Well, you know, some people suffer tremendously in this world, they undergo physical suffering. Well, I presume that is one of the effects comprehended under the law of Karma.

Mme. Blavatsky: Or perhaps the Karma of your parents.

Mr. Old: Well, that is a diversion of Karma.

Mme. Blavatsky: But you can't take it voluntarily. Your parents have been creating a bad Karma for you in the shape of heredity, disease, and therefore for this you are going to be rewarded in Devachan, and consoled for it, and your parents when they are incarnated will have to pay for it. For instance, there is one kind of Karma that nobody thinks of: it is for statesmen and kings and all the blessed autocrats. If they wanted to do any good, they ought to do the following: to have the strictest laws not to permit diseased persons, consumptive people, those with anything like insanity or scrofula[2] in them, to get married and to have children, because this is the greatest crime that can be. They have no right to do it, and this is the thing that brings the worst Karma, and changes whole populations. I know I was forty years ago in England, and I saw of every ten men, there were seven or eight who were magnificently and stoutly built. I come here now, if you please, and I see the population altered. Look at the army. You have no more of those men you had forty years ago, there are none, it is changing entirely. You see sometimes tall men, and that is all; but certainly it is not what it used to be.

Mr. B. Keightley: How far is it that the Karma of the reincarnating egos in those diseased and unhealthy bodies—how far does their Karma attract?

Mme. Blavatsky: I suppose it does attract them, but sometimes it does not. It is very difficult to come and tell you of these workings of Karma.

Mr. B. Keightley: It is one of the very great points.

Mr. Old: I want to know if it is any good alleviating suffering.

Mme. Blavatsky: It is good if you distribute suffering, so that you will have a little today and a little tomorrow. When you suffer terribly, you lose your head; but on the other hand, you get accustomed to suffering. Now, I don't remark my pains and aches, but if I had them all at once, I don't know what I would be.

Mr. Kingsland: Is there not all along the tendency to refer Karma too much to the physical plane? All we are making that mistake, I think.

Mme. Blavatsky: Surely.

---

2 A form of tuberculosis.

Mr. Kingsland: People are apt to imagine that you do an act, and that that act produces a certain effect in the next incarnation. Well that act, as an act on the physical plane, can only produce a physical result on the physical plane. What is carried over in the next incarnation, which becomes your Karma, is the effect which is produced in you. The state of consciousness, so to speak, in doing that act; it is not the act itself. The mere act of killing a man is a physical act on the physical plane, and won't result in Karma on the physical plane.

Mme. Blavatsky: But see the moral effect it produces—and that goes for a thousand times more than the physical act. The man that dies today, dies instead of dying two or three days later, but he may leave orphans. By the act of killing, the generations will be thrown entirely in a new track. They will be scattered, every one of them will go into other creations they never thought about; others will go into other parts. Physically it is nothing; only, the physical produces moral effects and results.

Mr. Sneyd: Supposing we say there is a man that is blind, and he runs in the way of a railway train, that train runs over him. Is not that the result of a sort of ignorance, or absence of knowledge and perceptions?

Mme. Blavatsky: Again this may be merited or unmerited, as the case may be.

Mr. Sneyd: Supposing we say that the driver stopped the train in time?

Mr. B. Keightley: The driver saw him and stopped the train?

Mr. Sneyd: How would it be then?

Mr. B. Keightley: It was the man's Karma to be saved.

Mr. Sneyd: You could not say that he was ignorant, then, to a certain extent?

Mr. B. Keightley: Oh yes. He was not saved by his own act, but by the act of somebody else.

Mr. Old: Question 4. How far does the general belief in Karma operate towards the acceptance of fatalism?

Mme. Blavatsky: If you are ignorant, you see fatalism.

Mrs. Besant: But the way it comes from outsiders sometimes is, that supposing you believe in these evils, why should you go against them?

Mme. Blavatsky: That is what the Easterners do. We don't do it, but the Eastern people do it.

Mr. B. Keightley: Is it right to do that?

Mme. Blavatsky: Not always. When it is done as the Muslim does it, it is bad, because it is crass fatalism.

Mr. B. Keightley: Take the people in Burma. They practically, until they were brought under the influence of Olcott and yourself, sat down under the state of things.

Mme. Blavatsky: They accepted it not on account of Karma, but on account of [ ].

Mr. B. Keightley: Well that is Karma in another form. It is really an important question, what is the right spirit to develop, to cultivate in yourself in reference to the action of Karma.

Mme. Blavatsky: To do your duty on this plane. Not to go and kick against Karma, any more than what a Christian will tell you—don't fly into the face of Providence, to a certain extent. But it {is} your duty when you see any evil to try and avoid it, not only for yourself—which would be very little—but for anyone else.

Mrs. Besant: And try to help other people out of it.

Mme. Blavatsky: Yes, more than you help yourself.

Mr. Burrows: Is not the true solution that we should separate "it" from humanity?

Mr. B. Keightley: Here you get this: Before the last 25 years, the population in India, broadly speaking, sat down and submitted to European rule and domination—I am speaking very broadly—but now what they do is to try and wake themselves up from their sloth and apathy, and to reorganize and to start a fresh current of activity in which the Theosophical Society has had a very large share. They are reacting, and are doing their best to react against the condition into which their past history in Karma had brought them. Is that right or is that wrong?

Mme. Blavatsky: It is right, because a life of inaction is worse than a life of action.

Mr. B. Keightley: If a man feels the impulse in himself, it is a part of the law working through him.

Mr. Old: It is like Bailey's definition, "Freewill in man is necessity in play."[3]

Mme. Blavatsky: Individually, there is free will, but once you take it collectively, there is no free will. It operates only with personalities. But speak of a nation or think of a nation, what kind of a free will has it? It is simply a dry leaf that is blown hither and thither, and sent by the wind everywhere. You have no right to sit and do nothing. You are obliged to be coworkers with Nature. But otherwise, as is said in the Apocalypse, "Nature will spew you out of the mouth."[4]

Mr. B. Keightley: The law of progress is as much a part of the law of Karma. The thing to get out of the idea of Karma is not the idea that you have to sit down and accept things as they are—though you should not resent things—but you should strive your level {best} to

---

3 Philip James Bailey, English poet, 1816-1902. The quote is from his 1839 poem *Festus* where the line reads: "Freewill is but necessity in play."
4 Revelation 3:16, "because thou art lukewarm...I will spew thee out of my mouth."

make those things right, without the feeling of bitter resentment.

Mr. Burrows: If we try to alter them now, it will be better in the future. It is not selfishness.

Mr. B. Keightley: Then that again is productive of evil.

Mrs. Besant: So that really you strive against the evil.

Mr. B. Keightley: Yes. Without resentment.

Mr. Burrows: That is a very important point, because the tendency now is get angry and bitter.

Mr. Sneyd: How do you say about free will? How can one prove there is such a thing, when everything is the result of cause and effect? I don't say that exactly. Well, I can see one thing, I suppose you the cause—the individual himself is the cause.

Mr. B. Keightley: Yes, the primary cause. The conditions under which he operates the Karma, so to speak, that is working out. As an individual, he is a cause.

Mr. Burrows: But would it be right to say that we can really create fresh causes?

Mme. Blavatsky: Most assuredly. Every one of you creates fresh causes from morning to night. That is where the free will comes in, because if there were no free will you would not create causes, you would simply be under the thrashing of this law.

Mr. B. Keightley: Under the blows of the law.

Mr. Gardner: The results of past Karma. If the actions are happening by accident, they are the result of past Karma.

Mme. Blavatsky: The accidents are commas and semicolons, that is all they are.

Mr. B. Keightley: Yes, the accidents are the punctuation of life.

Mr. Old: Things from which we measure off theories.

Mme. Blavatsky: Accidents are not things that are preordained, if you please.

Mr. Old: Then we branch off on to the subject of death.

Mme. Blavatsky: That is why we say we are our own punishers and rewarders and saviors.

Mr. Old: Then come questions on Devachan. It opens up with the orthodox question: What is Devachan—a state, a place, or both?

Mme. Blavatsky: A state. It is no more a place than your dreams.

Mr. Old: Has it any corresponding loka?

Mme. Blavatsky: No, it has not. We may be in Devachan, I can be in this chair, and you can be on yours. It is a state, not a locality.

Mr. B. Keightley: That is one of the things that strengthens its analogy to sleep.

Mme. Blavatsky: It is a dream—the most vivid, so vivid that even in this life there are dreams that sometimes you awaken and are not sure whether it was reality or not. You just imagine yourself a dream as vivid as life.

Mr. Kingsland: Now we think of an entity in Kamaloka, which is attracted at certain times to a séance room.

Mme. Blavatsky: They are not entities, they are reflections, they are spooks.

Mr. Kingsland: For the time being, they are to a certain extent individualized. We have been accustomed to talk of the Devachanic entity.

Mme. Blavatsky: Yes, because it is the three higher principles; but would you think of an entity of a personality? You would not call the reflection of a personality in the looking glass an entity.

Mrs. Besant: But the one in Devachan is the three higher principles.

Mme. Blavatsky: It is consciousness.

Mr. B. Keightley: The three higher principles, at any rate, have some sort of Upadhi, or basis. Where is the Upadhi of the three higher principles during the Devachanic period?

Mme. Blavatsky: Upadhi is the consciousness of it and nothing else. It is the Manas.

Mr. Old: Is there no form under which this Monad is identified?

Mme. Blavatsky: No form at all. It has a form in your own consciousness, and everything else that it sees are forms, created by the consciousness.

Mr. B. Keightley: Can you say that your thought is anywhere? That is the analogy.

Mr. Old: No, but you can embody it.

Mme. Blavatsky: No, you cannot.

Mr. B. Keightley: If the thought or Manas is the Upadhi of the Devachanic entity, then you can't say your thought is located anywhere.

Mme. Blavatsky: "Remembrance" will not express the thing. It is the recollection of your personality, the feeling of the ego, that you were the personal ego; and that is the Upadhi of Devachan. Because if you are Mr. Smith, Mr. Smith will be in Devachan as Mr. Smith and will have the little Smiths around him, if he loved them, and his Mrs. Smith and everything. Therefore the Upadhi is the consciousness of this personality for the time being. After it leaves Devachan, it is no more Mr. Brown.

Mrs. Besant: But would Mr. Smith be visible to a higher intelligence?

Mme. Blavatsky: Why should a higher intelligence look at him, what is there to see in the consciousness of another personality? The higher intelligence has got something better to do. What do you mean, Mrs. Besant, by higher intelligence—a Deva, a god?

Mrs. Besant: Yes, in all those higher instances.

Mme. Blavatsky: We are not concerned with them. During the Devachanic period the personality becomes, for the time being, so to say, merged in the individuality. It is immortal, for the time of the cycle of life and, so to say, the individuality plays the part of that personality that he or she was during the life period, and this is the Upadhi, this is the basis upon which the whole Devachanic experiences and thoughts of bliss go and act.

Mrs. Besant: Suppose we take it as a state of sleep. A bystander would see the person, but not the mind. Then if that body is gone, there is nothing left to see.

Mme. Blavatsky: Certainly that is what it is. It is consciousness, just that.

Mr. B. Keightley: I suppose you could only say it was the centre of consciousness in the Akasa?

Mme. Blavatsky: Now what has Akasa to do with it? Neither Akasa, nor ether, nor air has anything to do with it. It is simply a state of consciousness. It is a state, and not a locality.

Mr. Kingsland: But it is an individualized state of consciousness.

Mme. Blavatsky: Yes, for a person that is in a Devachanic condition. My Devachan won't be yours, and yours won't be mine. It is that a person dies and suddenly finds itself in Devachan, where the separation of the principles takes in a moment—or several days or weeks or months. All this depends upon the previous life of the personality, on the statement, on the degree of intellectuality, on the degree of everything.

Mr. Burrows: Then if Mr. Smith has Mrs. Smith there, it does not follow of necessity that Mrs. Smith has got Mr. Smith?

Mme. Blavatsky: Yes. If Mr. Smith loved her he would have Mrs. Smith, but if he did not, he won't even remember her.

Mr. Burrows: But suppose Mrs. Smith did not love him.

Mme. Blavatsky: That is another thing.

Mr. Burrows: He will have her, and she won't have him.

Mme. Blavatsky: It is that which we loved. In Devachan there is a perfect oblivion of everything that was disagreeable or that caused any pain, or of anything but an eternal bliss—which must be, by the way, exceedingly monotonous and stupid.

Mrs. Besant: It is really, then, the fruition of our desires.

Mme. Blavatsky: All the aspirations you had which were unsatisfied, all that which you could not have here through divers circumstances, you will have in Devachan. You will have all your desires realized, everything that you loved and could not have—perhaps that from which you are separated—but spiritually; nothing that pretends to the earth. For instance, if you had some vicious love or something like that, you will have nothing of the kind there.

Mr. Burrows: Supposing three or four people had the same desire.

Mme. Blavatsky: Every one of them will have it, so long as it is not vicious. Now, for instance, a man who drank himself to death will certainly not have his whiskey there.

Mrs. Besant: It is only Buddhi-Manas that goes.

Mme. Blavatsky: Atma is nothing; it is all absolute, and it cannot be said that it is this, that, or the other. It is simply that in which we are—not only that we live and breathe and have our being, but in the whole universe, and during the whole Manvantaric period. Therefore, Atma is said to have Buddhi for a vehicle, because Buddhi is already the first differentiation after the evolution of the universe; it is the first differentiation, and it is the Upadhi, so to say, of Atma. Then Buddhi is nothing, per se, but simply the first differentiation, and it is the consciousness in the universal consciousness, but it is non-consciousness in this world. On this plane of finite consciousness it is nothing, for it is infinite consciousness. Understand me, Atman cannot be called infinite consciousness. It is the one Absolute, which is conscious non-consciousness; it contains everything, the potentiality of all; therefore, it is nothing and all. It is Ain Soph, and it is the Parabrahm and so on; many names you can give it. It is "No Thing," you understand? Therefore, Buddhi being the first differentiation, the first ray, it is universal consciousness, and could not act on any one plane, especially on the terrestrial plane; and to be conscious of something, of somebody, it must have Manas, that is to say, the consciousness of this plane. If you read *The Secret Doctrine* you will see that men had nothing of the kind until the Manasaputra (The sons of the mind.) incarnated in the forms that were projected by the Lunar Pitris. There was nothing but matter, and the nothingness of Buddhi and Atma; therefore, they had to be cemented, so to say, between this Buddhi and themselves. They had to have this Manas, which is the finite consciousness of our plane of existence and their incarnating ego. This incarnating ego, which goes from one personality to another, collects the experiences of every life. After having collected all the experience of millions and millions of incarnations, then, when the Manvantaric period ceases, and this world goes into dissolution, this ego, having had all this experience, approaches more and more of the Absolute, and, at the end of I do not know how many Manvantaras, certainly it will become—before it merges into the one, it must have the experience. Then it approaches more and more and more that which is all and nothing. Finally it emerges. When we say that we speak about the state of Nirvana, that is nothing. It is Para-Nirvana that we are speaking about. Nirvana is simply a high Devachan.

Mr. Burrows: When does the memory come in of all the previous incarnations?

Mme. Blavatsky: To have a memory you have to live. You can have the memory of what? If you have never been anything, you cannot have a memory. You must have a memory of something.

Mr. Kingsland: Mr. Burrows asked at what point it came on.

Mme. Blavatsky: Every life is a peg on which you hang that memory.

Mr. Burrows: When does the universal memory come in?

Mme. Blavatsky: That is a thing which is during the whole Manvantara; it is the Mahat, as they call it. It is the universal intelligence, and all these incarnating egos are simply rays of that.

Mr. Keightley: When the ray has succeeded in merging itself into the universal mind, it then recovers the knowledge.

Mme. Blavatsky: When there is an end of all, there is the Maha-Pralaya—not what will come after our little earth is destroyed. Then Mahat itself disappears and is merged in Parabrahm, and is merged in the All.

Mr. Burrows: Then does reincarnation go on again in the higher plane?

Mme. Blavatsky: Yes. You see, the butterfly will never become the chrysalis and the grub again. It goes on, and nature never goes back, but always goes progressing higher and higher. It may become, for instance, mentally, and in its acts, a thousand times worse than it was before, but it will be higher on the plane of physical manifestation—physically.

Mr. Old: What gave me the opinion that the Devachan had some particular form and a place corresponding to its state was this. I think on page 235 {157}, Volume 1, where those tables are given and the scheme of the different schools of thought in the East, it says: Upadhi is a basis and in a corresponding system of philosophy it is translated by the word {kosha}, which means a sheath. That word is very confounding, especially when we see that opposite Manas. Thus: one of the Devachanic principles is put [ ], or [ ], the causal basis or sheath. You see, that is what gives one an incorrect opinion.

Mr. B. Keightley: Are not you confusing the idea of basis with the idea of form? They are not the same. For instance, the water you may consider the basis of something, but you could not say it has a form, *per se*.

Mme. Blavatsky: You consider gas the basis of something.

Mr. B. Keightley: Upadhi and form are not the same things.

Mr. Old: Has this monad a diffused consciousness into the whole universal Devachan? Has it a locus? Has it a distinct place? Has it a limitation?

Mme. Blavatsky: It has not. Consciousness has no limitation.

Mr. B. Keightley: How can it have, when three belong to the Arupa world?

Mme. Blavatsky: Of which two are nothing.

Mr. B. Keightley: I was quoting *The Secret Doctrine*.

Mme. Blavatsky: You take the three systems of philosophy {in *The Secret Doctrine*, I:157}, one of which shows what the Theosophists give, one what the [ ] {Taraka Raja Yoga} give, and the other what the Vedantins give; it is not at all that it corresponds. It corresponds to one as a sheath, and the other does not. It is only our [ ], or the occult system, because that is a thing which is confined to the three principles, and we are dividing it into seven principles, because it is a great deal easier to explain. The Vedantins have got five sheaths and the sixth, the Atma and the Buddhi, of which they don't speak at {all}, because what they mean by [ ] does not mean at all the Buddhi, but simply the astral form.

Mr. Old: The next question is: What determines the length of the Devachanic state?

Mme. Blavatsky: Your actions.

Mr. Old: In the previous life?

Mme. Blavatsky: In the previous life.

Mr. Old: It is not, then, the aggregate?

Mme. Blavatsky: It is not the aggregate, unless there is some surplus that has to be worked out.

Mr. Old: Then you consider that at the end of Devachan, we are quits?

Mme. Blavatsky: We are quits with that personality of Mr. Smith and Mr. Brown, and there is the end of it.

Mr. Gardner: Still, it is possible to spread it over a series of Devachans. For instance, Napoleon Bonaparte's Devachan—that would be spread over several.

Mme. Blavatsky: Yes. I think he will have a nice Karma for the people he has killed.

Mr. Old: It is such an accumulation of energy. It is quite an event to have a man like Bonaparte in the world, and in order to have reaction in the next life, it would be quite a different thing.

Mme. Blavatsky: I don't suppose he has much to do in Devachan. He was the most materialistic man that ever was. He had no Devachan. If he had a Devachan after his own mind he would have all you English and try that you should have one head, and cut it off.

Mr. Gardner: I suppose he was the embodiment of the nation?

Mme. Blavatsky: No.

Mr. Old: What seems to determine the length in my mind is the activity of the nature, the rate at which the monad runs.

Mme. Blavatsky: The intensity of your aspirations or desires, and the degree of your sufferings unmerited—those that you have not deserved directly, but through the Karma or the bad actions of somebody else—that is what determines it.

Mrs. Besant: The more desires you have, the longer you will be there?

Mme. Blavatsky: Yes. But if you have desires that were perfectly on the spiritual plane, then you are sure to be a spook.

Mr. Sneyd: When the individuality becomes merged in Parabrahm, then in that state, why do they call it the nothing, if it is the reality?

Mr. Old: It is not called nothing; it is *no thing*.

Mme. Blavatsky: It is the All.

Mr. Sneyd: But they only mean when they say nothing, no thing.

Mr. Old: Nothing is the wrong pronunciation; it is *no thing*.

Mr. Sneyd: It seems a contradiction.

Mme. Blavatsky: Ain Soph—No thing.

Mr. Sneyd: It is, really, I suppose, the state of intense happiness?

Mme. Blavatsky: That cannot be, unless you feel intense unhappiness—a contrast. Parabrahm is not to be either happy or unhappy, and does not feel, because feeling is a finite thing.

Mr. Sneyd: Then why should we wish for it?

Mme. Blavatsky: I suppose on account of our stupidity, which is great.

Mr. B. Keightley: Or because we have learned that you cannot have happiness apart from suffering. Why do you go in for differentiated existence? Why do you desire pleasure, or happiness? You desire by that very fact the corresponding pain or suffering, the two being differentiated aspects.

Mr. Old: Everything exists by relation of its own opposites.

Mr. Sneyd: For instance, I can go to a beautiful picture gallery.

Mme. Blavatsky: You won't have them in Devachan.

Mr. Kingsland: The more your mind is attuned to happiness, the more it is subject to the shock of discord; and the more intense your pains are in one direction, the more pleasure in another.

Mr. Sneyd: Why should we say that is Parabrahm?

Mr. B. Keightley: May I put this question to you? Can you imagine this condition as lasting permanently? Can you really suppose every desire that you conceive of, gratified? You will find it uncommonly slow when you try it on for about five minutes, because the very fact of having a desire produces suffering until it is fulfilled.

Mme. Blavatsky: To have a desire is already suffering, because it is something ungratified. The fact of desiring is suffering.

Mr. Sneyd: But you know you would have it soon, that there is something new coming, something coming on extra, as it were. You are satisfied with what you have got, but you are very glad of this extra.

Mr. Kingsland: You can go piling the extras up until there was nothing left of extras.

Mr. Old: Parabrahm is a state of absolute indifference.

Mme. Blavatsky: Please don't call Parabrahm happiness, because it is lowering to the idea of the happy god who sits and rejoices and something smells sweet to his nostrils.

Mr. B. Keightley: If you think about it you will see you cannot have one without the other, really and truly.

Mr. Sneyd: But why should we wish for it? Supposing we say it is absolute indifference. Why should we wish for it?

Mr. Kingsland: You think that over, and in the meanwhile we will go on.

Mr. Old: What is the impulse which determines the Devachanee to incarnate?

Mme. Blavatsky: It is Karma that makes him incarnate. He won't have more than he deserves; there is no impulse in him, but he dies out, his dream is at an end.

Mr. Old: When a man takes a meal, he satisfies his hunger. When the Devachanee has assimilated the experiences of his past existence, then there is reaction which takes place.

Mr. B. Keightley: I think that gives the impression on the mind that the Devachanee is actually desiring reincarnation, which is not the case.

Mr. Kingsland: He has no choice.

Mr. B. Keightley: If he did, you do away with one of the first great causes.

Mr. Old: But you must get rid of the sense of individual desire, because the monads have no such desire. Then how would you define that impulse?

Mme. Blavatsky: There is no impulse on the part of the Devachanee; it is no impulse at all. Karma takes him by the nape of his neck, and there is no impulse at all, just as when a policeman comes and takes yours.

Mr. B. Keightley: In which case, there is a strong impulse to take to your heels and run away.

Mr. Burrows: Does he know that he is going to be reincarnated at all?

Mme. Blavatsky: Well, it is a poetical expression.

Mr. Sneyd: I think you said it had no effect, in Devachan?

Mme. Blavatsky: There is no new effect produced. It has placed the Devachanee into the state of happiness; it gives him his fill of what he deserves and stands and whistles at the door. When that is finished, Karma takes him by the nape of the neck and puts him into the new body.

Mr. B. Keightley: Then you come to the question which Mr. Burrows raised—when the Devachanee knows he is reincarnated.

Mme. Blavatsky: You will see it in the *Key to Theosophy*. There are two moments when the reincarnating ego returns to its pristine omniscience, because, since it is Manasaputra (Meaning the son of wisdom or the universal intelligence.), it is omniscient—or it is at the moment of death, just at the moment when a man dies. When he is dead, he is dead, and it is finished, and he sees everything.

Mr. B. Keightley: He sees the life he is going to enter into.

Mme. Blavatsky: He is really himself and knows everything.

Mr. Gardner: Does he see his past lives?

Mme. Blavatsky: Most assuredly he does; it is what the Buddha saw.

Mr. B. Keightley: He does not forget, but the impression is not transferred.

Mme. Blavatsky: It cannot be transferred, because the instrument cannot receive it. Sometimes you have it, in moments of high vision. What is it, for instance, the states the sensitive persons have? It is simply by some circumstance, some physiological cause or reason or nervous condition. The faculties that were impeding the man to receive this light from his Manas, from his higher ego, are suddenly taken away.

Mr. B. Keightley: Occasionally the light is reflected upon our physical brain.

Mme. Blavatsky: It is like a cobweb. For a moment he says: that is what it is, because the ego is omniscience *per se*, not omniscience in the body. It is an extremely interesting thing, if only one could put it into language. If I had your gift of speech, I can assure you I would make all London Theosophists. It is one thing to be plain, because

I sit and explain, and another to say in one sweeping, magnificent phrase the whole thing. I have not got "the gift of the gab."

Mr. Old: Is it possible to escape Devachan, say from pure aversion to its useless inactivity?

Mme. Blavatsky: Most assuredly. Don't desire anything and you won't have Devachan. You will have nothing to hang your consciousness on. You will be asleep and snore and have no dreams.

Mr. Old: That is worse than ever. Let us dream out of preference.

Mme. Blavatsky: But there are persons who reach to such wisdom that once they are dead they are perfectly done with. I have taken off my dress and here I am. What am I going to do? Shall I go to sleep, and so on. And the person shall do as he likes.

Mr. Old: Could you predetermine those which should be your experience?

A Lady: Then you want another body.

Mme. Blavatsky: You live in your five principles.

Mrs. Besant: You keep on getting in your five principles.

Mme. Blavatsky: That is just what the adepts do; they have a perfect right to Nirvana, but they won't go; they think it is selfish to do so, and they won't go. They refuse the Nirvanic condition. That is just like Gautama did. He wants to be present, but he has no right to interfere with Karma.

Mr. Burrows: That would be the highest form of unselfishness.

Mme. Blavatsky: Most assuredly, because it is suffering. Every Nirmanakaya suffers, because it is terrible to be there, and see the misery and sufferings of people, and not to be able to help them.

Mrs. Besant: Still, you are a force for good.

Mme. Blavatsky: Most assuredly. This is the most glorious thing, and that is what they say that Buddha did and many of the adepts.

Mr. Old: It is called the great renunciation.

Mme. Blavatsky: Yes. Remember what I speak about with reference to the Silent Watcher. This has got a very profound occult meaning.

Mrs. Besant: That is the great sacrifice.

Mr. Sneyd: Is not Gautama now in Nirvana?

Mme. Blavatsky: The orthodox Buddhist will tell you he is, but he is not.

Mr. B. Keightley: Besides the Nirmanakayas, others escape. There are numerous cases of speedy reincarnation without Devachan.

Mme. Blavatsky: For instance, children who died before the age of reason. Immediately they are reincarnated. Persons who did not have a glimpse of spirituality in them. It is a degree of consciousness. If he is Gautama, of course he will have a kind of Devachan of his own, but there are children who have had no consciousness at all.

Mr. Burrows: What form will their incarnation take?

Mme. Blavatsky: A child who dies is but a mistake of nature, a failure.

Mr. Gardner: It is sometimes the same with parents.

Mme. Blavatsky: I don't think so.

Mrs. Besant: Suppose you had a very noble type who had not evolved sufficiently to refuse Nirvana. Would he be obliged to reincarnate? He who had not reached quite far enough to remain?

Mme. Blavatsky: An adept who has not even reached and who may not reach Nirvana may remain as Nirmanakaya. He may refuse the higher state of Devachan, simply if he reached that point of consciousness in which there is no illusion possible for him—that he knows too much.

Mr. Old: I thought perhaps there was a middle way.

Mme. Blavatsky: No sooner they are dead than there are some who step into another body where they can do good.

Mr. Burrows: And the more we eliminate desire the more we escape from Devachan?

Mme. Blavatsky: Certainly.

Mr. B. Keightley: The man I was thinking of was Dramar.[5] I think I heard you say he would incarnate very speedily.

Mr. Old: This is the last question on Devachan. Physical rest may be accomplished in the same and even less time than the period of wakeful consciousness and activity. Why then should Devachan extend to twenty or more times the short span of life?

Mme. Blavatsky: You had better ask Karma this question, for I cannot answer you.

Mr. Old: Is not there any theory then in the Vedanta philosophy?

Mme. Blavatsky: I teach you the occult philosophy. Really, I don't know; it is too difficult.

Mr. Old: Then we go on with questions on reincarnation. Can any reason be given for the necessity of reincarnation?

Mr. B. Keightley: The first great reason is, on no other hypothesis can you account for the inequalities of life—not only of condition and of circumstances under which a man is born, but inequalities in the actual inborn faculties and powers of the man himself, his mental powers, his moral force, his development in all respects—unless you have some antecedent existence. In the first place, whether you assume it to be on this earth or some other state, unless you assume some other existence for the man, it is impossible to account for the varying conditions of life, with any appearance of justice whatever.

---

5 Possibly Louis Dramard, 1848-1887, President of the Isis Lodge of the T.S. in Paris, France.

Mr. Burrows: You will never get your equilibrium.

Mr. B. Keightley: The great thing to my mind is, you don't account for the different stages of development in which the people are obviously born. If neither preexisted, how does that difference come in? I have always thought the fundamental idea of the Christian heaven was injustice in this respect. They say there the poor man, the man who has had little or no chances, is to be rewarded by heaven for the very little good he has done; the man who has had very little or no temptation owing to his low state of development. But a very highly developed man is exposed to much more temptation, yet he is to be weighed, so to speak, in the same scale as the other man.

Mr. Burrows: They take the other side of it though—they rather teach the poor that because of their suffering they are going to be rewarded by and bye. Of course, that is the pastoral idea.

Mr. B. Keightley: If you make an eternal idea, where is the proportion?

Mr. Sneyd: Supposing we say Parabrahm is a state of indifference. Do you think it is a state to be desired? Do you think a state which is not a happy state is a state we should desire?

Mme. Blavatsky: I can't understand this. How can you be happy, if you are not unhappy? You won't appreciate happiness unless you have the contrast. Happiness or unhappiness is a thing which is of very little moment indeed, which begins this moment and ends three moments afterwards. How can you have such transitory and such evanescent ideas, which can have no relation whatever to the {in}finite?

Mr. B. Keightley: Anyone who studies the facts of their own consciousness must have found his active, definite consciousness is neither happiness nor unhappiness.

Mr. Sneyd: Is it to be desired?

Mr. B. Keightley: It is eminently to be desired, because it is a great deal more permanent and useful condition than either happiness or unhappiness.

Mr. Sneyd: It is a quietude, a sort of peace.

Mr. B. Keightley: I should not call it quietude or peace. It is a thing for which we have not got any very good expressions in the English language.

Mr. Old: How do you account for the association of persons on this earth plane as an apparent result of reincarnation?

Mr. B. Keightley: Karma.

Mr. Old: Then we may always presume that we have met before.

Mme. Blavatsky: You may.

Mrs. Besant: And does the mental condition influence that at all? Supposing people have reached something of the same mental state, will there be a tendency, then?

Mme. Blavatsky: Don't you always experience when you meet a person for the first time whether you like that person, whether you are drawn towards him or have an antipathy? Even the dogs have their sympathies and their antipathies. It must be some reason, some cause.

Mr. Old: It must have been a past cause, if you have not met before. Then can a person of strong will, by a persistent effort, determine the conditions of the next incarnation?

Mme. Blavatsky: You go, my dear sir, into the domain of the adept, into the region of creation.

Mr. Old: That is the only person who has the strong will?

Mme. Blavatsky: Of course, desire has a great deal to do with it. An intense desire creates the circumstances, and creates the conditions.

Mr. Old: Then the last question is: "How far do the psychic, mental, and spiritual attainments of the past incarnations advantage the ego in its new life?"

Mme. Blavatsky: There is always the reflection that if you worked you cannot become an adept in one life. It is impossible. You must have begun desire for adeptship and for knowledge many, many previous incarnations before, because you may have a great desire for it, and you may be born in a man whose circumstances and conditions make him forget that and lose sight of that desire. You will be incarnated ten times, and then these desires and longings for knowledge come in. Then again you go perhaps to a life where it cannot be gratified. There are no conditions to develop this thing, and then you become all that which you had in the previous life, and it all comes in the present life.

Mr. B. Keightley: Until you go to several successive lives in which by effort the man has worked himself into a favorable condition.

22.
Theosophical Society.
Meeting of the Blavatsky Lodge
Held at 17 Lansdowne Road, Holland Park, W.
Thursday June 20, 1889.

Mr. Kingsland opened the proceedings by reading a paper on [ ]

Mme. Blavatsky: Now you have got to study for yourselves. The only thing I can give you is just to put the "Key" in your hands and say: "This opens this way, and this that way," and so on. You understand that whereas one person will understand well, another will understand less.

Mrs. Gordon: Because you must have the possibility of understanding transcendental ideas.

Mme. Blavatsky: No, it is not that. You have been many years in India and yet you have never taken any pleasure in those ancient religions; others have given their practice to the study of it. Now, if all these Orientalists were not such terrible materialists, with the knowledge they have—I speak about the Max Müllers, not the Sir Monier Williams,[1] because he has no more spirituality in him than this chair—but about him and others, they would understand perfectly; but they won't, they are materialists. Even that which they understand they would not accept; they would not permit themselves; but I don't see what there is that you don't understand. Mr. Kingsland, you have summarized it beautifully. What are all complaining of?

Mr. Old: That is a broad question, HPB

---
1 Monier Monier-Williams, English Orientalist, 1819-1899, professor of Sanskrit at Oxford University at the time.

Mme. Blavatsky: You will end by saying it is all flapdoodle, and that there is nothing to understand.

Mrs. Gordon: I don't think we can expect to understand it all.

Mme. Blavatsky: But these ladies and gentlemen who have been here Thursday after Thursday for, I suppose, a year, I don't see that you don't understand it. How is it possible?

Mrs. Gordon: You may accept things intellectually without saying you understand them. You may accept them as being true theories.

Mme. Blavatsky: Take it vice versa. Take it there are persons who feel it is a truth, and yet intellectually, on scientific grounds, they would not take it.

Mr. B. Keightley: Take the one point Kingsland touched on.

Mme. Blavatsky: You have to use your high faculty; intellect has nothing to do here. Materialistic science would step in.

Mrs. Gordon: It is a spiritual conception, as it were.

Mr. B. Keightley: Take that point you touched upon, Kingsland, for instance, how to conceive of the relation between these celestial hierarchies of Dhyan-Chohans and the physical forces, or what we call physical forces, if you like, with which we are ordinarily familiar. Of course, these physical forces, according to *The Secret Doctrine*, are the effects produced on the plane of Maya, the plane of objectivity, proceeding through or caused by these hierarchies; but the difficulty is how to understand, how to form to one's self a conception of what that means.

Mr. Kingsland: I confess I have not been able to form a conception. I have only got the general idea.

Mme. Blavatsky: Every hierarchy relates to some force in nature. There are seven fundamental forces in nature; there are seven hierarchies. Now, to come and say that I will undertake to explain to you every one of the seven, which may be subdivided ad infinitum, is impossible. In the first place, if I know what it means, I am not scientific enough to come and give you the correspondences in scientific terms. I only know that not only every hierarchy and the Dhyan-Chohans, but every one of those that have been mentioned, correspond; and it may be shown how they correspond to the forces in nature. That would necessitate ten volumes, not two.

Mr. B. Keightley: Take, for instance, this question: There is a well-known property of matter which is called chemical affinity, the combining power which varies from substance to substance; certain things you can take hold of and touch and our physical senses respond to them. How to conceive corresponding relations of things on the next plane above our own, to the next plane behind the objective plane? Because those combinations, I take it, in the objective plane—say, of oxygen and hydrogen to form water—can only take place because the things on the next plane behind ours are also related in some way which corresponds to the relation that we see in the physical substances of oxygen and hydrogen, and so on.

Mme. Blavatsky: To whom did you address this speech? To Mr. Kingsland, or me?

Mr. B. Keightley: To you and Mr. Kingsland.

Mme. Blavatsky: I did not hear half of what you said. I want a definite question, and I cannot afford to answer about two pages of uninterrupted speech. This may sound very pretty, but I want to have a definite question; otherwise, before you end, I forget what you began.

Mr. Kingsland: These forces, what we call natural forces, are simply emanations from one or other of these hierarchies; that is the term you use—"emanations."

Mme. Blavatsky: I have not any better word.

Mr. Kingsland: How can we dissociate that as an emanation from a hierarchy?

Mme. Blavatsky: With physical means, you cannot. Mr. Crookes has done the best he could, and certainly he is the greatest chemist in the whole world.

Mr. Kingsland: Bert has taken one particular thing, chemical affinity. How are we to connect that with an intelligent entity on a higher plane?

Mme. Blavatsky: Well, look here! If you are prepared to tell me that everything that shows some action is an action which has its laws, and a scientist may tell you beforehand how such and such a thing may become definite and fixed affinity; if you are prepared to tell me there are no intentions behind it, I will say alright. I say there is not the smallest thing in the universe—there is not the contact of two atoms, take any two things in nature—there is certainly an intelligence in them, behind them, and they act through intelligence, in intelligence, and we are all immersed in intelligence.

Mr. B. Keightley: That is what we believe is at the basis, but Kingsland's difficulty is how to think intellectually of the relation between that intelligence and the physical facts that we observe.

Mme. Blavatsky: To drop entirely your scientific and your inductive methods and become not a physician but a metaphysician, that is the only thing I can tell you. Once that you become instead of a metaphysician a physician, and take it from the standpoint of physical nature and mix up orthodox science, you will never arrive at anything.

Mr. B. Keightley: I don't think that is what Kingsland was doing.

Mme. Blavatsky: By knowing better than you do everything from the first beginning, from the first flutter of differentiation. Learn it just as I learned. I am not a scientific person at all. I am simply a metaphysician. I have been looking at it; I know it, I feel it in me, I see it before me. I could not put it in scientific terms, because I am not scientific enough; but I say that it is the easiest thing in the world to trace it if you begin by the beginning, but if you do as the men of science do, and begin by the tail, and by that which appears here on this plane of illusion, you will never arrive at anything.

Mr. Sargeant: It seems the question is very simple. If there is no correspondency between the seven hierarchies and the manifestations of these physical forces on the physical plane, then there can be no correspondency between cause and effect. We know effect proceeds from cause; and we should know that the seven manifestations on this physical plane must proceed from one of the hierarchies.

Mr. Kingsland: You can't always trace the effect to a theological cause.

Mme. Blavatsky: Shall I tell you a mistake, gentlemen, that you fall into? It is because you take independently all these causes that you want to call intelligent, that you take them one by one, instead of taking the whole. You cannot come and take this affinity. Let us take the Fohatic hierarchies, which are all for the electrical phenomena. You must take them in conjunction with all others, and take them as a whole; because, you see, science is perfectly right from its physical standpoint to say that they are blind forces of nature, because science does not see farther than its nose, and it does not permit itself to go farther than its plane of physical manifestations. But, if we go from the beginning, and if we imagine to ourselves this one life, this eternal, omnipresent homogeneity, that which underlies every phenomenon in nature—which underlies nature itself—which I won't call spirit, because it is far more than spirit (Spirit is something definite, in our language it has no name; it can have only existence in our perception, and then only when we are perfectly divorced from matter.)—but you have to take the whole thing and then proceed from the universals to the particulars. Otherwise you cannot grasp the thing. It is impossible. You have to skip many things, or to embrace it in a general sense, and then begin it in the first manifestation that you can; otherwise, you cannot make to yourself a clear representation. To me it is as clear and intelligible as can be. It may be because I am an innocent fool, but it has never presented to me any difficulty.

Mr. Sargeant: Is it because ladies and gentlemen must first seek the kingdom of heaven?

Mme. Blavatsky: I don't know, but it is quite on a different plane.

Mr. Sargeant: That would be from universals to particulars.

Mme. Blavatsky: If there is anything like a middle heaven, then it must be in the clouds, represented by those seraphs with the golden harps. That is what I understand by the kingdom of heaven.

Mr. Sargeant: Unfortunately, *that* in twelve hours time will be the kingdom of hell, because it will be below.

Mr. Old: It is not the general law that causes do proceed into effects that we wish to know.

Mr. Sargeant: Call it a fortuitous combination of circumstances.

Mr. B. Keightley: What Old was after was that here are a lot of effects; well, when we talk about the higher intellectual hierarchies, they are only represented to us by words, at the present moment.

Mme. Blavatsky: They cannot be represented by words, they must be represented by the feeling of intuition. If they are represented by words, you have nothing, you have a flapdoodle. You have to represent them to yourselves in your intellectual perception, in your spiritual perception. It is impossible. It is with your higher self that you must understand, and not with your brains and intellectual perceptions, which are all sensuous perceptions, and will not help you. You have to reach to that point when you feel yourself one with the whole, and perfectly inseparable from it—from the one and the eternal, which has no end and no beginning. Otherwise, it is impossible.

Mrs. Gordon: The higher consciousness.

Mme. Blavatsky: Well, the higher consciousness. Maybe I speak to you Greek and Hebrew, but to me it is perfectly clear, and I don't know how to explain it better.

Mr. B. Keightley: The thing has to be understood by direct consciousness, the direct contact—your consciousness having been attuned to the universal consciousness. Then you are in direct contact with those hierarchies, and you perceive them or sense them.

Mme. Blavatsky: Why should not you put yourself as these hierarchies?

Mr. Kingsland: Which in fact you are.

Mrs. Gordon: Then we have a dual consciousness. The higher consciousness, it is, that we must cultivate, and in some way bring it en rapport with our inner consciousness. That is what, of course, the men in India do—they bring their higher consciousness into outer consciousness.

Mr. Sargeant: Are not all higher truths which can be perceived through the universe perceived through the automatic flow of thought?

Mme. Blavatsky: I don't think so. I don't believe it.

Mr. Sargeant: It is a thought of which we are partially conscious on the higher plane, but not on the lower plane.

Mr. Kingsland: But what is that but the intuition? You are only giving it another name. It is intuition, is it not?

Mr. Sargeant: I don't think we can call it so. We may intuitively know a thing without understanding it.

Mme. Blavatsky: You may intuitively know a thing without being able to give it expression, but you must understand it. You understand it in your spiritual understanding, but very likely you cannot give it an expression, because the European languages cannot convey it; not even Sanskrit, which is certainly a thousand times richer. These are things you have to use your soul language for, as it is called—the inner perception and the unspoken language.

Mr. Sargeant: May we not intuitively know that a certain cause will yield a certain effect, without knowing the way in which that effect will be yielded?

Mme. Blavatsky: Certainly there is not the smallest effect that can be produced without a cause, and certainly if there is an effect there must be a cause.

Mr. Sargeant: Then intuition can exist with partial knowledge?

Mr. Old: I don't think you can call that the inner aspect of Manas or the mind, because, you see, we identify the faculty of intuition with Buddhi, which is a separate principle.

Mme. Blavatsky: Not quite; it is Manas that you have to identify first.

Mr. Kingsland: It is the essence of all your reincarnations.

Mr. Old: Manas is?

Mr. Kingsland: No, intuition is.

Mme. Blavatsky: It passes through the incarnating ego.

Mr. B. Keightley: If you had Buddhi by itself, without any conjunction with Manas on this plane, you would have no intuition at all.

Mme. Blavatsky: The mission of Buddhi is simply to shadow divine light on Manas, otherwise Manas will be always falling into the Karmic {Kamic} principle, into the principle of matter; it will become the lower Manas, and act as the lower Manas or mind. But the incarnating ego is certainly the mind, the Manas.

Mr. B. Keightley: And intuition is the recollection.

Mme. Blavatsky: Of all the past accumulated experiences.

Mr. Old: But they would be sublimated.

Mr. Kingsland: How is it that one man's intuition will make a

Theosophist of him, and another man's will make a Roman Catholic of him?

Mr. Sargeant: Because a Roman Catholic is a Theosophist. It must necessarily be so, if Theosophy embodies all the wisdoms of known religions. All the Roman Catholics are really Theosophists.

Mme. Blavatsky: So far, I know only of one real Theosophist among the Roman Catholics: it was poor Father Damien. But not at all because he was a Roman Catholic, but because he was a real Christ-like man.

Mr. Old: Don't you claim St Aloysius[2] as such?

Mme. Blavatsky: Fanaticism we cannot believe in, and we must not believe in. We say there is truth in everything, for it is impossible a thing should exist without having some leaven of truth.

Mr. Sargeant: And consequently there is Theosophy in everything, even in fanaticism.

Mr. B. Keightley: Fanaticism is the negation of the first principle of Theosophy, which is universalism.

Mme. Blavatsky: Fanaticism is nothing but concentrated selfishness and vanity. A man says: "I believe in it, and therefore it must be so. I am *the* one wise man and everyone else must be a fool." He who is a fanatic shuts himself out of the universal truth. He simply sticks to a little thing like a fly sticks to one of those medicated papers. It is just that and nothing else.

Mr. Sargeant: What about Peter the Hermit,[3] whose fierce preaching stirred up the whole of Europe? Was he a Theosophist?

Mme. Blavatsky: Not a bit of it. He was an anti-Theosophist. He forced people to make fools of themselves and led them to death,

---

2 Saint Aloysius (Luigi) Gonzaga, Italian Jesuit, 1568-1591, who gave up his inheritance and died working with the sick.
3 Late eleventh century priest who instigated the People's Crusade that traveled from Germany to Jerusalem.

and made them ridiculous to posterity. He represented to them the goose as the Holy Ghost.

Mr. Sargeant: And yet with the views these people came back with from the Holy Land, Christianity became something grand. Our ancestors never knew the principle of toleration on the battlefield until Saladin taught them.[4]

Mme. Blavatsky: There was more Theosophy in Saladin than there ever was in Peter the Hermit. Perhaps you will say Louis XI[5] was also a Theosophist. You are a paradoxalist.

Mr. Kingsland: It is a universalist. But then you must make a distinction in terms.

Mr. Sargeant: There is no distinction in spirit.

Mr. B. Keightley: But you see, we are not in the spirit, but in the flesh.

Mr. Sargeant: The great error of today is that man imagines he is a body possessed of a spirit, instead of a spirit possessed of a body.

Mme. Blavatsky: My dear Sargeant, you would appear to me the embodiment of wisdom, if you spoke in a way that I could hear.

Mr. Sargeant: If it is that I speak low, it is because of those internal breathings.

Mme. Blavatsky: You are a humbug! Perhaps he will say there is real Theosophy in humbug.

Mr. B. Keightley: Perhaps I might quote the lines of Olcott: "There's a spirit above, and a spirit below; A spirit of love, and a spirit of woe; The spirit above is the spirit divine; The spirit below is the spirit of wine!"

---

4 Twelfth century Sultan of Egypt who led the Muslim resistance to the Crusades. He gained a lasting reputation as a chivalrous knight for his treatment of prisoners.
5 Louis XI, 1423-1483, King of France from 1461 to 1483.

Mr. Sargeant: And yet the "spirit of wine" is only an expression of the "spirit divine." If you read your esoterical works, you will see what affinities there were between these things.

Mme. Blavatsky: Now this man's intuition tells him you are trying to humbug me; he does not understand English, and yet his intuition tells him that. You are trying to tease me, he says.

Mr. Old: I wanted to say I didn't think I was agreeable to the proposition. But unconscious thought, cerebration—no, ratiocination—not the physical action which is called cerebration, but the higher, the metaphysical correspondence—this unconscious thought is not in itself intuition, because, reasoning from analogies, we have these two things represented on the lowest plane which we can apply to every one of the seven principles. There is in nerves—the automatic arc of nerves and the influential arc of nerves—the voluntary and involuntary. Exactly the same with the vital process; there is the voluntary and involuntary. There are functions over which we have voluntary control, and there are those over which we have none, except in strange, complex cases like Captain Townsend and others who are able to control the vital processes as well as the muscles. Seeing there is the unconscious and the conscious, the dark and the light side of every bifacial monad, might we not argue that there is the conscious and the unconscious cerebration, both identified with Manas? Because I have seen instances precipitated in the form of automatic writing where a person has been holding a conversation on one subject and writing on another.

Mr. Kingsland: Supposing we say that intuition is the unconscious action?

Mr. Old: I wish to say it is not.

Mr. Kingsland: You take the unconscious vital action, for instance. The action goes on without your will. How does that come about? Is not that the accumulation of numerous past experiences?

Mr. Sargeant: No.

Mr. Kingsland: What is it, then?

Mr. Sargeant: It is simply owing to the action of a universal flood on nerves which are termed involuntary. They affect these nerves in such a manner that they restore any equilibrium which has been lost.

Mr. Kingsland: How does it arise that we have certain physical functions? You are simply tracing it back. I say those functions develop through innumerable ages by means of evolution; these things act through the Kama-rupa experience of past action.

Mr. Sargeant: You don't mean that the past experiences are the very causes that set these influences at work?

Mr. Kingsland: I don't. I carry that analogy up to what Old says about the conscious and the unconscious ratiocination. I say that the unconscious is simply that same result. By analogy you can put it in the same way: that your intuition is the result of all the past stages you have gone through in the stages of consciousness—in fact, your evolution.

Mr. B. Keightley: I think it works out from the known experience of the training of the muscles. You learn to do certain very complicated muscular actions at first with great pain and difficulty, such as writing. Gradually the thing becomes automatic; you do it without thinking of the different steps. You think of the sense you are going to express, and you do not think of the individual movement of your hand.

Mr. Kingsland: There is nothing you can do at the present moment but what is the result of your past experiences.

Mr. Old: I can trace it in what the physicists call inhibited action. If one gets into the way of nursing his thumb in his pocket, it is a strange thing how this will become habitual. First of all, it is generally voluntary, but it becomes a habit, and it is then called an inhibited action. And the seat of the cerebral forces is the [ ] {cerebrum}; it is supposed to be the lieutenant of the thinking brain. Then, when you have decided to walk home, you don't have to think of putting more than the first foot foremost; the rest follow. What I wish to say is this: I find some difficulty in tracing this inhabited {inhibited} action which has once been voluntary action. How can you say that vital action was ever inhibited, was ever involuntary? If you can prove that each pulsation of the aorta of the heart was controlled voluntarily, then you prove the case.

Mr. Kingsland: Your present physical body is the result of several influences which can be traced back to a previous incarnation.

Mr. Keightley: The point is this: whether, for instance, the involuntary action of the muscles—as in the beating of the heart—is the result of evolution. I contend it is the result of the evolution of the molecules forming the heart.

Mr. Old: But not of conscious experiences.

Mr. Kingsland: Not in your present lifetime.

Mr. Old: I merely wish to show, reasoning by analogy, just as there was the conscious and unconscious action of the physical body, and there were conscious and unconscious systems of nervation and so forth on the physical plane, so there was in every principle this conscious and unconscious, this dark and light side.

Mme. Blavatsky: I think you confuse the material things with the spiritual.

Mr. Old: We know every one of those principles has a manifesting and an unmanifesting side.

Mme. Blavatsky: If you speak of one of the acquired habits, as nursing your thumb, it is a different thing. It is not a thing which is natural and normal. The beating of the heart is a thing which pretends to the physical, the habits of men. This has nothing to do with acquired things.

Mr. Kingsland: It has nothing to do with the acquired habits in this incarnation. But you can trace back the beating of your heart, which takes place automatically; you can trace that back to the evolution, where it was first.

Mme. Blavatsky: Certainly.

Mr. Old: I cannot go so far as that.

Mr. Kingsland: Suppose we take your analogy?

Mr. Old: Reasoning from this by analogy, on this line I wanted to show that there would be conscious and unconscious thought, both identified with and peculiar to the Manas.

Mr. Kingsland: Very well, let us say that. Then I say that the conscious thought you are going through now is your present intellectuation.

Mr. Old: We have already identified intuition with Buddhi. Now you wish to identify Buddhi with the higher aspect of Manas.

Mr. B. Keightley: You are taking that from Sinnett, Old.

Mr. Old: Is not Buddhi the sixth principle, and is not intuition the sixth sense?

Mme. Blavatsky: You argue on the line of what? Do you bring the thing as it is given to you in the esoteric instructions, or the exoteric? There is the difference, you know what I mean. Exoterically, there is another thing. Of course, the Buddhi will be the sixth, for the Buddhi is quite a different thing, exoterically. The Buddhi, per se, has nothing to do with any qualification of anything; it is simply the vehicle of Atman, of spirit; and spirit is nothing; it cannot be said it is something; it is that which has neither beginning nor end; it is the *one thing*.

Mr. B. Keightley: Old's identification of the Buddhi's intuition is derived from Sinnett's *Esoteric Buddhism*.

Mme. Blavatsky: That is certainly not esoteric.

Mr. Kingsland: You cannot identify Buddhi with intuition, because intuition, after all, is only the intellectual process of the very highest order.

Mr. Old: I understand there are two facets to Buddhi?

Mme. Blavatsky: One thing you may say about Buddhi. Intuition is in Manas for the more or less light shed on it by Buddhi, whether it is assimilated much or little with Buddhi.

Mr. Kingsland: It must pass through Manas. It is derived from Manas.

Mr. Old: Ultimately it is from the brain; it can flow down. The brain is the instrument of thought.

Mme. Blavatsky: My poor Old! I never thought you were as materialistic as you are.

Mr. Old: You have put me off the track by asking me the question whether I was speaking esoterically or exoterically. I was talking on my ground, and you told me to get off.

Mme. Blavatsky: Was I wrong?

Mr. Old: No, you were right.

Mme. Blavatsky: There are esotericists here, and exotericists. The esotericists will be terribly confused if we speak in this way, and the exotericists still more.

Mr. Old: I ought not to have mooted it.

Mme. Blavatsky: Buddhi by itself can neither have intuition, nor non-intuition, nor anything; it is simply the cementing link, so to say, between the higher spirit and Manas. What goes into Devachan? What reincarnates? It is certainly the ego, the Manas, the higher portion of Manas. Once in Devachan we call it the eternity, but it has no eternity at all, because Buddhi and Atma are nothing but obstructions, in the strict sense of the word. It is the reincarnating Manas that goes; and therefore intuition belongs to Manas, because it brings it through all the reincarnations that it passed through. All this is more or less defined through the amount of light shed on Manas by Buddhi, but so far as regards this life. You understand? Because the intuition is one. You have learned enough about that, Mrs. Gordon.

Mr. Old: What is your distinction, Kingsland, between unconscious cerebration and intuition?

Mr. Kingsland: Unconscious cerebration is a thing belonging purely to the physical plane, and the other thing is different.

Mr. Old: So is unconscious thought, then?

Mr. Kingsland: Take the extreme case of the lad who could solve the most difficult mathematical problems that were given him immediately without any reference to figures at all. That you will say was a purely intellectual process. He must have had it in previous times; he had assimilated that knowledge at some time or other, and it was owing to certain combinations of astral influences that he was able to make use of that information, for the time being, in that rapid manner. His physical senses overclouded this, in time.

Mr. Sargeant: That is the product of unconscious thought.

Mme. Blavatsky: Unconscious cerebration is something that was suggested to the brain unconsciously to yourselves, though perhaps you heard it or saw it and had no remembrance of it; and there it comes out. But, intuition is a different thing.

Mr. B. Keightley: I don't think such a term as "unconscious thought" can mean anything.

Mr. Sargeant: Then "unconscious cerebration"?

Mr. B. Keightley: "Unconscious thought"—what meaning can you attach to the phrase?

Mr. Old: Call it ideation, if you like.

Mr. B. Keightley: It is conscious enough on the right plane.

Mr. Old: There is nothing unconscious, as a matter of fact. Because, if you only identify your consciousness for the time being with that plane, you would be perfectly conscious you were so engaged; therefore, I think the term is a bad one, and I only wish to use it relatively, in contradistinction to relative thought.

Mrs. Gordon: It seems to me that the experiments that have been made in regard to hypnotism show that there is this higher consciousness which may be brought forward occasionally under exceptional circumstances—that is, with exceptional natures. It is not everyone in whom it can be developed. Don't you think so, Madame? I am speaking of the latent soul. The other half which is not unconscious can be, as it were, more or less exhibited under some forms of hypnotism, in which the higher self becomes clairvoyant, and the other faculties always develop.

Mme. Blavatsky: Don't you use the term "higher self." That is the Atman.

Mr. B. Keightley: Say the higher ego. In most cases, that consciousness or ego refers to the personality in the third person speaking, for instance, of the name.

Mr. Kingsland: I take it in this way: that we have stored up, so to speak, in our Manas an enormous amount of experience that we have passed through in past incarnations, and we are not able by certain reasons of our physical constitution to assimilate and give expression to all that in our present lifetime, but the act of making use of your intuition is simply the act of getting at this storehouse that you have already in your Manas, and what it is that clouds our intuition is our connection with {the} physical plane, and if we can get rid of that, we can make use of our intuition.

Mme. Blavatsky: It is the amount of weeds and parasites that we have collected in our life which makes us positively fools.

Mrs. Gordon: You always see children much more intuitive than adults. Children have the intuition much more prominent than we who live in the world and are more of the world, and our minds are exercised in connection with worldly things.

Mr. Kingsland: I think that also is the case.

Mrs. Gordon: I have seen it myself, among friends of my own. They had a sixth sense, as I may say. They lived in another atmosphere altogether, you see.

Mr. Kingsland: There are a great many cases in which that is brought forward—abnormal cases, such as I have mentioned. Take the case of Josef Hofmann, the young pianist. Where does his musical knowledge come from? It is nothing but intuition. He is able to give expression to that on the physical plane through his physical body.

Mrs. Gordon: Of course the child has not learned it intellectually. He has not brain enough to do it. He has brought it with him.

Mr. Kingsland: The basis of all our actions is simply intuition.

Mme. Blavatsky: Is it your Buddhi, Old, that made you what you are?

Mr. Old: It is my Atma.

Mme. Blavatsky: You have got no Atma, distinct from others.

Mr. Old: There is the divine spark in me.

Mme. Blavatsky: It is not yours; it is common property. It is your ego, and your incarnating ego. It is that which you were in past lives that makes you what you are, a young man of 25 that has such a wonderful capacity of grasping all these things.

Mr. Old: There are certain things—as, for instance, these abstract meditations—which are not the result of experience. What experience, what self-consciousness have I when I am in Devachan? I have no relative consciousness except my own that forms the creation in my own mind.

Mr. Kingsland: And yet you believe that Devachan is the result of your experiences that you have passed through in your previous life.

Mr. Old: Certainly. But there are other abstract problems which are thinkable and cognizable by me which it is perhaps impossible to formulate, but which I can feel; and I say that these laws, this consciousness, belongs to Atma. It is related to Manas by its vehicle Buddhi, and therein this absolute consciousness is, to a certain extent, capable of being appreciated by the Manas, the monad.

Mme. Blavatsky: You are a heretic, because you speak entirely against not only the occult philosophy, but against the Vedantin philosophy.

Mr. Kingsland: Does Atma accumulate experiences?

Mr. Old: No! But you have got hold of the idea that it is only accumulated experience that we know.

Mr. Kingsland: It is only accumulated experience which is our intuition.

Mme. Blavatsky: How can you give experience to that which is absolute? How is it possible to fall into such a philosophical error as that? The Atma no more belongs to you than to this lamp; it is common property.

Mr. Old: Every higher self is, so to speak, the manifested end of a ray.

Mme. Blavatsky: It is not; it is the Manas itself.

Mr. Old: There is the individual logos, as well as the universal logos.

Mme. Blavatsky: Not at all. It is simply that Atma and Buddhi cannot be predicated as having anything to do with a man, except that man is immersed in them; so long as he lives he is overshadowed by these two; but it is no more the property of that than of anything else.

Mr. Old: This is identifying Atman with Jiva.

Mme. Blavatsky: I beg a thousand pardons. Jiva and Atma are one, only Jiva is this end, and Atma at the highest end; but you cannot make the difference in England. It would have a meaning for the Sanskrit, but not in the European languages, or any of them, because there is but one essence in the universe, and this has neither beginning nor end, and the various shadows or rays of that absoluteness during the period of differentiation, this is that which makes it the final essence of everything, and of man.

Mr. Old: Then would you say that all this which is written of Nirvana of Brahmâ, of Para-Nirvana, of Para-Brahm, is the result of experience?

Mr. Kingsland: All that you can understand of it, that is the result of experience.

Mr. Old: I take it as the result of intuition.

Mme. Blavatsky: It is simply a symbol expressed in the best language in which man is capable of expressing it, that is all.

Mr. B. Keightley: Try to formulate your idea more clearly by explaining what kind of meditation you refer to, because I think you will find that the very highest meditation you can conceive of is really Manasic, and nothing more. Manas and experience are not synonymous.

Mr. Old: Kingsland wishes to identify intuition with experience. According to Kingsland, intuition is one aspect of Manas.

Mme. Blavatsky: Look here, you Europeans ought never to have been given the seven principles. Well, perhaps in a hundred years you will understand it. It would be a thousand times better to hold to the old methods, those that I have held to in *Isis Unveiled*, and to speak about triple man: spirit, soul, and matter; then you would not fall into the heresies, in such heresies as you do. Why do we divide this into seven parts or aspects? Because ours is the highest philosophy. But, for the general mortal, certainly it is a great deal easier to understand if they say man is triple: he has got spirit, soul, and matter. What is spirit? Spirit then becomes the ego. Soul is simply the Nephesh, the living soul of every animal, that is to say, the lower Jiva, and matter is his physical body. Now, we, having divided it, as all esoteric philosophies divide it, have simply confused the European mind, because it has not been trained in that direction. It is too early for them, and there are very few men who will really understand the seven divisions. And, therefore, we are called lunatics or frauds—one of the two—and nobody will understand what we mean. I say it is a thousand times better not to understand it, and not to go and speak about this septenary number, and simply take it on the old ground of spirit, soul and matter. There would be no heresy, then.

Mr. Kingsland: It has been broached abroad now, this seven principle, and we have to clear our ideas of it.

Mme. Blavatsky: You must never say: "my Atma"; you have no Atma; this idea is the curse of the world; it has produced this tremendous selfishness, this egotism [ ] we say "we are," "*my* Atma," "*my* Buddhi". Who are you? You are nobodies; you are something today, and tomorrow you are not. Even that disappears at the end of the Manvantara in the one.

Mr. B. Keightley: To go back to what Kingsland was saying. Intuition as we know it is defined in this way: the memory, the action or the reflection on our lower plane of the hierarchies. It is not the higher aspect of the hierarchies, nor does it exhaust the Manas.

Mme. Blavatsky: The incarnating principle simply. It is not something that is an individual or entity. It is simply the highest mind.

Mr. Old: That incarnating ego consists of what?

Mme. Blavatsky: What do you want it to consist of? Plums, or oranges, or what?

Mr. Old: How do you formulate it? Do you say it is Atma-Buddhi?

Mme. Blavatsky: I say it is Atma-Buddhi, certainly. Because, in every incarnation, it is under the direct ray of Buddhi, if he wants to assimilate. If he does not want to, it is his look out; his personality will drop out. It is only in the case which assimilates Buddhi that it really lives throughout, and will belong to that string of personality which forms consciousness after the Manvantara is at an end—the direct, immortal ray.

Mr. Old: I thought I was quite right in saying Buddhi was a ray from Atma; it is that vehicle.

Mme. Blavatsky: You would not call this lamp a ray of the flame that burns in it, would you?

Mr. Old: Certainly not.

Mme. Blavatsky: That is Buddhi, if you please—the vehicle. It is not a ray; it is only that through which that ray passes. It is the agent of that light that it throws on Buddhi. How is that we read in all those books about Nirvana and Atma, when they say: "Does Parabrahm exist? It does not. Then Parabrahm is not. Yes it is, but it does not exist."

Mr. Old: You say the incarnating ego consists of Buddhi-Manas, or rather Atma-Buddhi.

Mme. Blavatsky: It consists only of itself.

Mr. Kingsland: In the aspect in which we are discussing, it is simply the assimilation of the higher Manas.

Mr. Old: What assimilates it?

Mme. Blavatsky: Consciousness. It is universal consciousness, which falling into matter becomes personal consciousness in its last manifestation on earth. And when it gets rid of all the matter that impedes it, when it becomes more and more pure, and finally it reaches its highest manifestation, or whatever you call it, then it gradually falls into the universal consciousness; it is again reabsorbed into universal consciousness. That is what Manas is. But as it falls lower and lower, it would be nothing but a material entity—I don't mean material physically, but material de facto, nothing but a bundle of nothing—if it were not under the ray of this Atma-Buddhi. But Atma-Buddhi certainly does not follow the reincarnating ego. Simply, once it is reincarnated, they are again in the region of the universe in which there is Atma and Buddhi, therefore, we say that Atma and Buddhi exist in every man.

Mr. Old: It is a contradiction between the undifferentiated Atman and Buddhi.

Mme. Blavatsky: It is simply that Atma is beyond the seventh plane. Buddhi is one of the planes; you understand that. Therefore, if Atma, which is beyond the seventh plane, falls on the ego through seven planes, it will fall a great deal weaker. You understand what I mean? It depends on our ego to draw it immediately on itself, or to have a kind of wall between it and the other planes. This depends on the degree of assimilation. I don't know if you understand my meaning.

Mr. B. Keightley: Yes, you put it very well.

Mme. Blavatsky: Well, it is extremely difficult to do so, because those who don't understand what I mean by planes will not understand me. It has seven degrees of spirit-matter, and certainly it depends on the force or degree, the intensity with which it assimilates, and if it is too opaque, and too dull, then certainly it won't reach it.

Mr. B. Keightley: I don't know whether you ever studied that problem, Old, the definition of liberation. There is always that rather puzzling explanation: "the soul is neither bound, nor is it ever liberated." It is a very intricate problem, which has never been really satisfactorily explained.

Mme. Blavatsky: What do you take Purusha to be on this plane? Which of the principles? To which of the principles does it belong?

Mr. B. Keightley: They talk about Purusha mounting on the shoulders of Prakriti.

Mme. Blavatsky: Prakriti is simply a body, and therefore the body would be a perfectly blind animal if Pursha were not there; and Purusha without the body could not manifest. Purusha emanates from Brahmâ, and from [ ], or from [ ], whatever school he belonged to.

Mr. B. Keightley: I could show passages in which Purusha is not taken in that sense, but in the higher sense.

Mme. Blavatsky: If you speak about mind, Purusha corresponds with the ego. If you take it in the universal sense, then it corresponds to the universal soul, to the Anima Mundi.

Mr. Kingsland: I think you might look at it in this light: by analogy, it is exactly the same as the way in which we require to postulate for the descending scale of manifestation—first the manifesting spirit, then the first Logos, and then the second. Isn't it the same?

Mr. Old: Who is your first Logos in this case?

Mr. Kingsland: It is Buddhi, and the second is Manas.

Mr. Old: A short time ago I ventured the remark that Buddhi was the Logos, and I was told that I was incorrect.

Mr. B. Keightley: You spoke of an individual Logos.

Mr. Old: Of an individual ray—because Atma has to radiate in order to function any particular—

Mme. Blavatsky: Atma has to radiate! It cannot radiate anything. Atma, if you take it of the third Logos, then yes, but not Atma in the universal sense of Parabrahm.

Mr. Old: We are not teaching Parabrahm here. If we entered Parabrahm, or if we entered into the consideration of Parabrahm, here would come in that intuition which I speak of.

Mme. Blavatsky: I thought I knew pretty well the philosophy, and I don't think I know it. I never said that Atma or Parabrahm could radiate. If you take it in the sense of the third Logos, then I admit it radiates.

Mr. Kingsland: Correspondentially, Atma is Parabrahm.

Mr. Old: There is a source of confusion to an occidental mind; just the same with your juxtaposition of the two words Jiva and Prana, which throws everybody into confusion. I mean to say, your repetition of the language.

Mr. B. Keightley: The juxtaposition was sensed, and nobody ever took it up.

Mme. Blavatsky: The Brahmins have given it to us, and they all fell on me as to why I permitted Sinnett to do this. Sinnett never asked me my permission, and I did not know until *Esoteric Buddhism* came out. It is not my fault.

Mr. Old: Oh! No; only, in some parts of *The Secret Doctrine* it is difficult to tell if Jiva is to be taken on the noumenal plane or on the phenomenal.

Mme. Blavatsky: When you speak about the objective things then it is Jiva. (At least it is Prana.) When you speak about the universal life, then it is Jiva. In some schools of philosophy they call it Jiva; the Vedantins will call it Jiva; the Sankhya will never call it that, and the six schools are entirely distinct. That which the Vedantins call Jiva, others will call Prana, and vice versa.

Mr. Old: One conceives of abstract ideas apart from the formula. The formula is the matter of experience; it belongs to Manas.

Mr. B. Keightley: Don't you conceive that it is the Manas which conceives the abstract ideas? Because, how do they exist, otherwise?

Mr. Kingsland: You cannot conceive of abstract ideas without the experience. That is just my point.

Mr. Old: Who was Hermes?

Mme. Blavatsky: If you mix up the Greek gods with the philosophy, then we are lost.

Mr. Old: I will bear it.

Mr. Kingsland: But our brains won't.

Mme. Blavatsky: Let us leave in quietude all these analogies.

Mr. Old: But this is our only key.

Mr. B. Keightley: Your argument is open to this reply. If abstract ideas can only be received in virtue of experience, how do you ever get your chain started?

Mr. Kingsland: By the first emanation. When you first emanate from the Absolute, it is when you begin your cycle of experiences.

Mme. Blavatsky: There is a potentiality of everything: past, present, and future.

Mr. Old: That is better. This is not experience.

Mme. Blavatsky: If you take the present Manavantara for the only one, then, of course, granted you are right.

Mr. Old: This is making two square walls meet, that the past, present, and future are comprehended in the now. It is a matter of experience. There are the future Manvantaras.

Mme. Blavatsky: What do you make of the past Manvantaras? If you were in the first, you would be right.

Mr. Old: You have no individual consciousness, in Parabrahm, in which you enter at the Maha-pralaya. I mean in Nirvana.

Mme. Blavatsky: You don't understand what Nirvana is. It is absolute consciousness.

Mr. Old: There is no individual consciousness. How do we know anything about Nirvana?

Mr. Kingsland: Do you believe that the future Manvantara will be an improvement upon the present one, or not?

Mr. Old: Yes! I do, because my experience has told me from what little I have seen that the law of nature is progression.

Mr. Kingsland: Is not that the same as saying it is experience?

Mr. Old: Plus analogy.

Mr. Kingsland: I am drawing the analogy now. I say you can carry it not only from your past life to the present, but from the past Manvantara to the next Manvantara.

Mr. B. Keightley: If you ever read Froude,[6] he talks about the faculty of apprehending abstract ideas. HPB, answer this, if you can, from the point of view of exotericism. Is the apprehension of highest abstract ideas the function of Manas, or of Buddhi?

Mme. Blavatsky: Buddhi can have the apprehension of nothing.

Mr. B. Keightley: There you are answered, Old.

Mr. Old: Yes! Certainly.

Mme. Blavatsky: If we argue or discuss about the universe we had better leave the first two things—Parabrahm, and the first Logos, call it; and when we speak of men, let us remember that it is a perfect analogy—that that which we call Parabrahm in the first Logos is in man, Atma, and Buddhi. Then as we begin by the third or second Logos, so we must begin by Manas, because there it is where the point of differentiation begins, otherwise you are lost. You will only make confusion, otherwise.

Mr. Old: It is having to keep parallel texts before you all the time. Knowing certain teachings on the one side of the book, and trying to keep them parallel.

---

6 Probably James Anthony Froude, English writer, 1818-1894, whose multivolume biography of Thomas Carlyle had just been completed.

Mme. Blavatsky: He will come and reproach us that he knows too much.

Mr. Old: I refer to esoteric teaching.

Mme. Blavatsky: Most assuredly; therefore, every time you put this question, I say, do go to bed, let us talk of something else; let us talk about exoteric subjects, of which we can discuss as much as you like, but the others—well, it is very difficult to speak of that which we had better keep silent about.

Appendix 1

[In the transcription of the meeting of January 10, 1889, page 4 is missing. An edited version of what it may have contained is supplied from pp. 5-6 of the original 1890 printed edition of *The Transactions of the Blavatsky Lodge* below. See also *Transactions*, pp. 4-5, The Theosophy Company, Los Angles, California, 1923.]

Q. What, then, are the seven layers of Space, for in the "Proem" we read about the "Seven-Skinned Mother-Father"?

A. Plato and Hermes Trismegistus would have regarded this as the *Divine Thought,* and Aristotle would have viewed this "Mother-Father" as the "privation" of matter. It is that which will become the seven planes of being, commencing with the spiritual and passing through the psychic to the material plane. The seven planes of thought or the seven states of consciousness correspond to these planes. All these septenaries are symbolized by the seven "Skins."

Q. The divine ideas in the Divine Mind? But the Divine Mind is not yet.

A. The Divine Mind *is,* and must be, before differentiation takes place. It is called the divine Ideation, which is eternal in its Potentiality and periodical in its Potency, when it becomes *Mahat, Anima Mundi* or Universal Soul. But remember that, however you name it, each of these conceptions has its most metaphysical, most material, and also intermediate aspects.

Q. What is the meaning of the term "Ever invisible robes"?

A. It is, of course, as every allegory in the Eastern philosophies, a figurative expression. Perhaps it may be the hypothetical Protyle that Professor Crookes is in search of, but which can certainly never be found on this our earth or plane. It is the non-differentiated substance or spiritual matter.

Appendix 2

[The "Appendix on Dreams," first published in the original *Transactions of the Blavatsky Lodge*, is included here as a convenience to the reader. The meetings upon which it is based probably occurred December 20 and 27, 1888, and complete the series of discussions HPB held with her students through June, 1889. See also *Transactions*, pages 59-79, The Theosophy Company.]

DREAMS.

Q. What are the "principles" which are active during dreams?

A. The "principles" active during ordinary dreams—which ought to be distinguished from real dreams, and called idle visions—are *Kama,* the seat of the personal Ego and of desire awakened into chaotic activity by the slumbering reminiscences of the lower Manas.

Q. What is the "lower Manas"?

A. It is usually called the animal soul (the *Nephesh* of the Hebrew Kabalists). It is the ray which emanates from the Higher Manas or permanent EGO, and is that "principle" which forms the human mind—in animals instinct, for animals also dream.[1] The combined action of Kama and the "animal soul," however, are purely mechanical. It is instinct, not reason, which is active in them. During the sleep of the body they receive and send out mechanically electric shocks to and from various nerve-centres. The brain is hardly impressed by them, and memory stores them, of course, without order or sequence. On waking these impressions gradually fade out, as does every fleeting shadow that has no basic or substantial reality underlying it. The retentive faculty of the brain, however, may register and preserve them if they are only impressed strongly enough. But, as a rule, our memory registers only the fugitive and distorted impressions which the brain receives at the moment of awakening. This aspect of "dreams" however, has been sufficiently observed and is described correctly enough in modern physiological and biological works, as

---

1 The word dream means really "to slumber"—the latter function being called in Russian "*dreamatj.*"—ED.

such human dreams do not differ much from those of the animals. That which is entirely *terra incognita* for Science is the real dreams and experiences of the higher EGO, which are also called dreams, but ought not to be so termed, or else the term for the other sleeping "visions" changed.

Q. How do these differ?

A. The nature and functions of real dreams cannot be understood unless we admit the existence of an immortal Ego in mortal man, independent of the physical body, for the subject becomes quite unintelligible unless we believe—that which is a fact—that during sleep there remains only an animated form of clay, whose powers of independent thinking are utterly paralyzed.

But if we admit the existence of a higher or permanent *Ego* in us—which Ego must not be confused with what we call the "Higher Self," we can comprehend that what we often regard as dreams, generally accepted as idle fancies, are, in truth, stray pages torn out from the life and experiences of the *inner* man, and the dim recollection of which at the moment of awakening becomes more or less distorted by our physical memory. The latter catches mechanically a few impressions of the thoughts, facts witnessed, and deeds performed by the *inner* man during its hours of complete freedom. For our *Ego* lives its own separate life within its prison of clay whenever it becomes free from the trammels of matter, *i.e.*, during the sleep of the physical man. This Ego it is which is the actor, the real man, the true human self. But the physical man cannot feel or be conscious during dreams; for the personality, the outer man, with its brain and thinking apparatus, are paralyzed more or less completely.

We might well compare the real Ego to a prisoner, and the physical personality to the gaoler of his prison. If the gaoler falls asleep, the prisoner escapes, or, at least, passes outside the walls of his prison. The gaoler is half asleep, and looks nodding all the time out of a window, through which he can catch only occasional glimpses of his prisoner, as he would a kind of shadow moving in front of it. But what can he perceive, and what can he know of the real actions, and especially the thoughts, of his charge?

Q. Do not the thoughts of the one impress themselves upon the other?

A. Not during sleep, at all events; for the real Ego does not think as his evanescent and temporary personality does. During the waking hours the thoughts and Voice of the Higher Ego do or do not reach his gaoler— the physical man, for they are the *Voice of his Conscience,* but during his sleep they are absolutely the "Voice in the desert." In the thoughts of the *real* man, or the immortal "Individuality," the pictures and visions of the Past and Future are as the Present; nor are his thoughts like ours, subjective pictures in our cerebration, but living acts and deeds, present actualities. They are realities, even as they were when speech expressed in sounds did not exist; when thoughts were things and men did not need to express them in speeches; for they instantly realized themselves in action by the power of *Kriya-Sakti,* that mysterious power which transforms instantaneously ideas into visible forms, and these were as objective to the "man" of the early *third* Race as objects of sight are now to us.

Q. How, then, does Esoteric Philosophy account for the transmission of even a few fragments of those thoughts of the Ego to our physical memory which it sometimes retains?

A. All such are reflected on the brain of the sleeper, like outside shadows on the canvas walls of a tent, which the occupier sees as he wakes. Then the man thinks that he has dreamed all that, and feels as though *he* had lived through something, while in reality it is the *thought-actions* of the true Ego which he has dimly perceived. As he becomes fully awake, his recollections become with every minute more distorted, and mingle with the images projected from the physical brain, under the action of the stimulus which causes the sleeper to awaken. These recollections, by the power of association, set in motion various trains of ideas.

Q. It is difficult to see how the Ego can be acting during the night things which have taken place long ago. Was it not stated that dreams are not subjective?

A. How can they be subjective when the dream state is itself for us, and on our plane, at any rate, a subjective one? To the dreamer (the Ego), on his own plane, the things on that plane are as objective to him as our acts are to us.

Q. What are the senses which act in dreams?

A. The senses of the sleeper receive occasional shocks, and are awakened into mechanical action; what he hears and sees are, as has been said, a distorted reflection of the thoughts of the Ego. The latter is highly spiritual, and is linked very closely with the higher principles, Buddhi and Atma. These higher principles are entirely inactive on our plane, and the higher Ego (*Manas*) itself is more or less dormant during the waking of the physical man. This is especially the case with persons of very materialistic mind. So dormant are the Spiritual faculties, because the Ego is so trammelled by matter, that *It* can hardly give all its attention to the man's actions, even should the latter commit sins for which that Ego—when reunited with its *lower* Manas—will have to suffer conjointly in the future. It is, as I said, the impressions projected into the physical man by this Ego which constitute what we call "conscience"; and in proportion as the Personality, the lower Soul (or *Manas*), unites itself to its higher consciousness, or Ego, does the action of the latter upon the life of mortal man become more marked.

Q. This Ego, then, is the "Higher Ego"?

A. Yes; it is the higher Manas illuminated by Buddhi; the principle of self-consciousness, the "I-am-I," in short. It is the Karana-Sarira, the immortal man, which passes from one incarnation to another.

Q. Is the "register" or "tablet of memory" for the true dream-state different from that of waking life?

A. Since dreams are in reality the actions of the Ego during physical sleep, they are, of course, recorded on their own plane and produce their appropriate effects on this one. But it must be always remembered that dreams in general, and as we know them, are simply our waking and hazy recollections of these facts.

It often happens, indeed, that we have no recollection of having dreamt at all, but later in the day the remembrance of the dream will suddenly flash upon us. Of this there are many causes. It is analogous to what sometimes happens to every one of us. Often a sensation, a smell, even a casual noise, or a sound, brings instantaneously to our mind long-forgotten events, scenes and persons. Something of what was seen, done, or thought by the "night-performer," the Ego, impressed itself at that time on the physical brain, but was not brought into the conscious, waking memory, owing to some physical condition or obstacle. This impression is registered on the brain in its appropriate cell or nerve centre, but owing to some accidental circumstance it "hangs fire," so to say, till something gives it the needed impulse. Then the brain slips it off immediately into the conscious memory of the waking man; for as soon as the conditions required are supplied, that particular centre starts forthwith into activity, and does the work which it had to do, but was hindered at the time from completing.

Q. How does this process take place?

A. There is a sort of conscious telegraphic communication going on incessantly, day and night, between the physical brain and the inner man. The brain is such a complex thing, both physically and metaphysically, that it is like a tree whose bark you can remove layer by layer, each layer being different from all the others, and each having its own special work, function, and properties.

Q. What distinguishes the "dreaming" memory and imagination from those of waking consciousness?

A. During sleep the physical memory and imagination are of course passive, because the dreamer is asleep: his brain is asleep, his memory is asleep, all his functions are dormant and at rest. It is only when they are stimulated, as I told you, that they are aroused. Thus the consciousness of the sleeper is not active, but passive. The inner man, however, the real Ego, acts independently during the sleep of the body; but it is doubtful if any of us—unless thoroughly acquainted with the physiology of occultism—could understand the nature of its action.

Q. What relation have the Astral Light and Akâsa to memory?

A. The former is the "tablet of the memory" of the animal man, the latter of the spiritual Ego. The "dreams" of the Ego, as much as the acts of the physical man, are all recorded, since both are actions based on causes and producing results. Our "dreams," being simply the waking state and actions of the true Self, must be, of course, recorded somewhere. Read "Karmic Visions" in *Lucifer,** and note the description of the real Ego, sitting as a spectator of the life of the hero, and perhaps something will strike you.

Q. What, in reality, is the Astral Light?

A. As the Esoteric Philosophy teaches us, the *Astral Light* is simply the dregs of *Akâsa* or the Universal Ideation in its metaphysical sense. Though invisible, it is yet, so to speak, the phosphorescent radiation of the latter, and is the medium between it and man's thought-faculties. It is these which pollute the Astral Light, and make it what it is—the storehouse of all human and especially psychic iniquities. In its primordial genesis, the astral light as a radiation is quite pure, though the lower it descends approaching our terrestrial sphere, the more it differentiates, and becomes as a result impure in its very constitution. But man helps considerably to this pollution, and gives it back its essence far worse than when he received it.

Q. Can you explain to us how it is related to man, and its action

---

* Reprinted in *H. P. Blavatsky Theosophical Articles* I:382. The Theosophy Company.

in dream-life?

A. Differentiation in the physical world is infinite. Universal ideation—or *Mahat*, if you like it—sends its homogeneous radiation into the heterogeneous world, and this reaches the human or *personal* mind through the Astral Light.

Q. But do not our minds receive their illuminations direct from the Higher Manas through the Lower? And is not the former the pure emanation of divine Ideation—the "*Manasa-Putras*," which incarnated in men?

A. They are. Individual *Manasa-Putras* or the Kumaras are the direct radiations of the divine Ideation—"individual" in the sense of later differentiation, owing to numberless incarnations. In sum they are the collective aggregation of that Ideation, become on our plane, or from our point of view, *Mahat,* as the Dhyan-Chohans are in their aggregate the Word or "Logos" in the formation of the World. Were the Personalities (Lower Manas or the *physical* minds) to be inspired and illumined solely by their higher *alter Egos* there would be little sin in this world. But they are not; and getting entangled in the meshes of the Astral Light, they separate themselves more and more from their parent Egos. Read and study what Eliphas Lévi says of the Astral Light, which he calls Satan and the Great Serpent. The Astral Light has been taken too literally to mean some sort of a second blue sky. This imaginary space, however, on which are impressed the countless images of all that ever was, is, and will be, is but a too sad reality. It becomes in, and for, man—if at all psychic—and who is not?—a tempting Demon, his "evil angel," and the inspirer of all our worst deeds. It acts on the will of even the sleeping man, through visions impressed upon his slumbering brain (which visions must not be confused with the "dreams"), and these germs bear their fruit when he awakes.

Q. What is the part played by Will in dreams?

A. The will of the outer man, our volition, is of course dormant and inactive during dreams; but a certain bent can be given to the slumbering will during its inactivity, and certain after-results developed by the mutual inter-action—produced almost mechanically—through union between two or more "principles" into one, so that they will act in perfect harmony, without any friction or a single false note, when awake. But this is one of the dodges of "black magic," and when used for good purposes belongs to the training of an Occultist. One must be far advanced on the "path" to have a will which can act consciously during his physical sleep, or act on the will of another person during the sleep of the latter, *e.g.*, to control his dreams, and thus control his actions when awake.

Q. We are taught that a man can unite all his "principles" into one—what does this mean?

A. When an adept succeeds in doing this he is a *Jivanmukta:* he is no more of this earth virtually, and becomes a Nirvanee, who can go into *Samadhi* at will. Adepts are generally classed by the number of "principles" they have under their perfect control, for that which we call will has its seat in the higher EGO, and the latter, when it is rid of its sin-laden personality, is divine and pure.

Q. What part does Karma play in dreams? In India they say that every man receives the reward or punishment of all his acts, both in the waking and the dream state.

A. If they say so, it is because they have preserved in all their purity and remembered the traditions of their forefathers. They know that the Self is the *real* Ego, and that it lives and acts, though on a different plane. The external life is a "dream" to this Ego, while the inner life, or the life on what we call the dream plane, is the real life for it. And so the Hindus (the profane, of course) say that Karma is generous, and rewards the real man in dreams as well as it does the false personality in physical life.

Q. What is the difference, "karmically," between the two?

A. The physical animal man is as little responsible as a dog or a mouse. For the bodily form all is over with the death of the body. But the real SELF, that which emanated its own shadow, or the lower thinking personality, that enacted and pulled the wires during the life of the physical automaton, will have to suffer conjointly with its *factotum and alter ego* in its next incarnation.

Q. But the two, the higher and the lower, Manas are one, are they not?

A. They are, and yet they are not—and that is the great mystery. The Higher Manas or EGO is essentially divine, and therefore pure; no stain can pollute it, as no punishment can reach it, *per se*, the more so since it is innocent of, and takes no part in, the deliberate transactions of its Lower Ego. Yet by the very fact that, though dual and during life the Higher is distinct from the Lower, "the Father and Son" *are one*, and because that in reuniting with the parent Ego, the Lower Soul fastens upon and impresses upon it all its bad as well as good actions—both have to suffer, the Higher Ego, though innocent and without blemish, has to bear the punishment of the misdeeds committed by the *lower* Self together with it in their future incarnation. The whole doctrine of atonement is built upon this old esoteric tenet; for the Higher Ego is the antitype of that which is on this earth the type, namely the personality. It is, for those who understand it, the old Vedic story of Visvakarman over again, practically demonstrated. Visvakarman, the all-seeing Father-God, who is beyond the comprehension of mortals, ends, as son of Bhuvana, the holy Spirit, *by sacrificing himself to himself*, to save the worlds. The mystic name of the "Higher Ego" is, in the Indian philosophy, *Kshetrajna*, or "embodied Spirit," that which knows or informs *kshetra*, "the body." Etymologize the name, and you will find in it the term *aja*, "first-born," and also the "lamb." All this is very suggestive, and volumes might be written upon the pregenetic and postgenetic development of type and antitype—of Christ-*Kshetrajna*, the "God-Man," the First-born, symbolized as the "lamb." The *Secret Doctrine* shows that the Manasa-Putras or incarnating EGOS have taken upon themselves, voluntarily and knowingly, the burden of all the future sins of their future personalities. Thence it is easy to see that it is neither Mr. A. nor Mr. B., nor any of the personalities that periodically clothe the Self-Sacrificing EGO, which are the real Sufferers, but verily the innocent *Christos* within us. Hence the mystic Hindus say that the Eternal Self, or the Ego (the one in three and three in one), is the "Charioteer" or driver; the personalities are the temporary and evanescent passengers; while the horses are the animal passions of man. It is, then, true to say that when we remain deaf to the Voice of our Conscience, we crucify the Christos within us. But let us return to dreams.

Q. Are so-called prophetic dreams a sign that the dreamer has strong clairvoyant faculties?

A. It may be said, in the case of persons who have truly prophetic dreams, that it is because their physical brains and memory are in closer relation and sympathy with their "Higher Ego" than in the generality of men. The Ego-Self has more facilities for impressing upon the physical shell and memory that which is of importance to such persons than it has in the case of other less gifted persons. Remember that the only God man comes in contact with is his own God, called Spirit, Soul and Mind, or Consciousness, and these three are one.

But there are weeds that must be destroyed in order that a plant may grow. We must die, said St. Paul, that we may live again. It is through destruction that we may improve, and the three powers, the preserving, the creating and the destroying, are only so many aspects of the divine spark within man.

Q. Do Adepts dream?

A. No advanced Adept dreams. An adept is one who has obtained mastery over his four lower principles, including his body, and does not, therefore, let flesh have its own way. He simply paralyzes his lower Self during Sleep, and becomes perfectly free. A dream, as we understand it, is an illusion. Shall an adept, then, dream when he has rid himself of every other illusion? In his sleep he simply lives on another and more real plane.

Q. Are there people who have never dreamed?

A. There is no such man in the world so far as I am aware. All dream more or less; only with most, dreams vanish suddenly upon waking. This depends on the more or less receptive condition of the brain ganglia. Unspiritual men, and those who do not exercise their imaginative faculties, or those whom manual labour has exhausted, so that the ganglia do not act even mechanically during rest, dream rarely, if ever, with any coherence.

Q. What is the difference between the dreams of men and those of beasts?

A. The dream state is common not only to all men, but also to all animals, of course, from the highest mammalia to the smallest birds, and even insects. Every being endowed with a physical brain, or organs approximating thereto, must dream. Every animal, large or small, has, more or less, physical senses; and though these senses are dulled during sleep, memory will still, so to say, act mechanically, reproducing past sensations. That dogs and horses and cattle dream we all know, and so also do canaries, but such dreams are, I think, merely physiological. Like the last embers of a dying fire, with its spasmodic flare and occasional flames, so acts the brain in falling asleep. Dreams are not, as Dryden says, "interludes which fancy makes," for such can only refer to physiological dreams provoked by indigestion, or some idea or event which has impressed itself upon the active brain during waking hours.

Q. What, then, is the process of going to sleep?

A. This is partially explained by Physiology. It is said by Occultism to be the periodical and regulated exhaustion of the nervous centres, and especially of the sensory ganglia of the brain, which refuse to act any longer on this plane, and, if they would not become unfit for work, are compelled to recuperate their strength on another plane or *Upadhi*. First comes the *Svapna*, or dreaming state, and this leads to that of *Shushupti*. Now it must be remembered that our senses are all dual, and act according to the plane of consciousness on which the thinking entity energises. Physical sleep affords the greatest facility for its action on the various planes; at the same time it is a necessity, in order that the senses may recuperate and obtain a new lease of life for the *Jagrata*, or waking state, from the *Svapna* and *Shushupti*. According to *Raj Yoga*, *Turya* is the highest state. As a man exhausted by one state of the life fluid seeks another; as, for example, when exhausted by the hot air he refreshes himself with cool water; so sleep is the shady nook in the sunlit valley of life.

Sleep is a sign that waking life has become too strong for the physical organism, and that the force of the life current must be broken by changing the waking for the sleeping state. Ask a good clairvoyant to describe the aura of a person just refreshed by sleep, and that of another just before going to sleep. The former will be seen bathed in rhythmical vibrations of life currents—golden, blue, and rosy; these are the electrical waves of Life. The latter is, as it were, in a mist of intense golden-orange hue, composed of atoms whirling with an almost incredible spasmodic rapidity, showing that the person begins to be too strongly saturated with Life; the life essence is too strong for his physical organs, and he must seek relief in the shadowy side of that essence, which side is the dream element, or physical sleep, one of the states of consciousness.

Q. But what is a dream?

A. That depends on the meaning of the term. You may "dream," or, as we say, sleep visions, awake or asleep. If the Astral Light is collected in a cup or metal vessel by will-power, and the eyes fixed on some point in it with a strong will to see, a waking vision or "dream" is the result, if the person is at all sensitive. The reflections in the Astral Light are seen better with closed eyes, and, in sleep, still more distinctly. From a lucid state, vision becomes trans-lucid;

from normal organic consciousness it rises to a transcendental state of consciousness.

Q. To what causes are dreams chiefly due?

A. There are many kinds of dreams, as we all know. Leaving the "digestion dream" aside, there are brain dreams and memory dreams, mechanical and conscious visions. Dreams of warning and premonition require the active co-operation of the inner Ego. They are also often due to the conscious or unconscious co-operation of the brains of two living persons, or of their two Egos.

Q. What is it that dreams, then?

A. Generally the physical brain of the personal Ego, the seat of memory, radiating and throwing off sparks like the dying embers of a fire. The memory of the Sleeper is like an Æolian seven-stringed harp; and his state of mind may be compared to the wind that sweeps over the chords. The corresponding string of the harp will respond to that one of the seven states of mental activity in which the sleeper was before falling asleep. If it is a gentle breeze the harp will be affected but little; if a hurricane, the vibrations will be proportionately powerful. If the personal Ego is in touch with its higher principles and the veils of the higher planes are drawn aside, all is well; if on the contrary it is of a materialistic animal nature, there will be probably no dreams; or if the memory by chance catch the breath of a "wind" from a higher plane, seeing that it will be impressed through the sensory ganglia of the cerebellum, and not by the direct agency of the spiritual Ego, it will receive pictures and sounds so distorted and inharmonious that even a Devachanic vision would appear a nightmare or grotesque caricature. Therefore there is no simple answer to the question "What is it that dreams?" for it depends entirely on each individual what principle will be the chief motor in dreams, and whether they will be remembered or forgotten.

Q. Is the apparent objectivity in a dream really objective or subjective?

A. If it is admitted to be apparent, then of course it is subjective. The question should rather be, to whom or what are the pictures or representations in dreams either objective or subjective? To the physical man, the *dreamer*, all he sees with his eyes shut, and in or through his mind, is of course subjective. But to the *Seer* within the physical dreamer, that Seer himself being subjective to our material senses, all he sees is as objective as he is himself to himself and to others like himself. Materialists will probably laugh, and say that we make of a man a whole family of entities, but this is not so. Occultism teaches that physical man is one, but the thinking man septenary, thinking, acting, feeling, and living on seven different states of being or planes of consciousness, and that for all these states and planes the permanent Ego (not the false personality) has a distinct set of senses.

Q. Can these different senses be distinguished?

A. Not unless you are an Adept or highly-trained Chela, thoroughly acquainted with these different states. Sciences, such as biology, physiology, and even psychology (of the Maudsley, Bain, and Herbert Spencer schools), do not touch on this subject. Science teaches us about the phenomena of volition, sensation, intellect, and instinct, and says that these are all manifested through the nervous centres, the most important of which is our brain. She will speak of the peculiar agent or substance through which these phenomena take place as the vascular and fibrous tissues, and explain their relation to one another, dividing the ganglionic centres into motor, sensory and sympathetic, but will never breathe one word of the mysterious agency of intellect itself, or of the mind and its functions.

Now, it frequently happens that we are conscious and know that we are dreaming; this is a very good proof that man is a multiple being on the thought plane; so that not only is the Ego, or thinking man, Proteus, a multiform, ever-changing entity, but he is also, so to speak, capable of separating himself on the mind or dream plane into two or more entities; and on the plane of illusion which follows us to the threshold of Nirvâna, he is like Ain-Soph talking to Ain-Soph, holding a dialogue with himself and speaking through, about, and to himself. And this is the mystery of the inscrutable Deity in the *Zohar*, as in the Hindu philosophies; it is the same in the Kabala, Puranas, Vedantic metaphysics, or even in the so-called Christian mystery of the Godhead and Trinity. Man is the microcosm of the macrocosm; the god on earth is built on the pattern of the god in nature. But the universal consciousness of the real Ego transcends a millionfold the self-consciousness of the personal or false Ego.

Q. Is that which is termed "unconscious cerebration" during sleep a mechanical process of the physical brain, or is it a conscious operation of the Ego, the result of which only is impressed on the ordinary consciousness?

A. It is the latter; for is it possible to remember in our conscious state what took place while our brain worked unconsciously? This is apparently a contradiction in terms.

Q. How does it happen that persons who have never seen mountains in nature often see them distinctly in sleep, and are able to note their features?

A. Most probably because they have seen pictures of mountains; otherwise it is somebody or something in us which has previously seen them.

Q. What is the cause of that experience in dreams in which the dreamer seems to be ever striving after something, but never attaining it?

A. It is because the physical self and its memory are shut out of the possibility of knowing what the real Ego does. The dreamer only catches faint glimpses of the doings of the Ego, whose actions produce the so-called dream on the physical man, but is unable to follow it consecutively. A delirious patient, on recovery, bears the same relation to the nurse who watched and tended him in his illness as the physical man to his real Ego. The Ego acts as consciously within and without him as the nurse acts in tending and watching over the sick man. But neither the patient after leaving his sick bed, nor the dreamer on awaking, will be able to remember anything except in snatches and glimpses.

Q. How does sleep differ from death?

A. There is an analogy certainly, but a very great difference between the two. In sleep there is a connection, weak though it may be, between the lower and higher mind of man, and the latter is more or less reflected into the former, however much its rays may be distorted. But once the body is dead, the body of illusion, *Mayavi Rupa*, becomes Kama Rupa, or the animal soul, and is left to its own devices. Therefore, there is as much difference between the spook and man as there is between a gross material, animal but sober mortal, and a man incapably drunk and unable to distinguish the most prominent surroundings; between a person shut up in a perfectly dark room and one in a room lighted, however imperfectly, by some light or other.

The lower principles are like wild beasts, and the higher Manas is the rational man who tames or subdues them more or less successfully. But once the animal gets free from the master who held it in subjection; no sooner has it ceased to hear his voice and see him than it starts off again to the jungle and its ancient den. It takes, however, some time for an animal to return to its original and natural state, but these lower principles or "spook" return instantly, and no sooner has the higher Triad entered the Devachanic state than the lower Duad rebecomes that which it was from the beginning, a principle endued with purely animal instincts, made happier still by the great change.

Q. What is the condition of the *Linga Sarira*, or plastic body, during dreams?

A. The condition of the Plastic form is to sleep with its body, unless projected by some powerful desire generated in the higher Manas. In dreams it plays no active part, but on the contrary is entirely passive, being the involuntarily half-sleepy witness of the experiences through which the higher principles are passing.

Q. Under what circumstances is this wraith seen?

A. Sometimes, in cases of illness or very strong passion on the part of the person seen or the person who sees; the possibility is mutual. A sick person especially just before death, is very likely to see in dream, or vision, those whom he loves and is continually thinking of, and so also is a person awake, but intensely thinking of a person who is asleep at the time.

Q. Can a Magician summon such a dreaming entity and have intercourse with it?

A. In black Magic it is no rare thing to evoke the "spirit" of a sleeping person; the sorcerer may then learn from the apparition any secret he chooses, and the sleeper be quite ignorant of what is occurring. Under such circumstances that which appears is the *Mayavi rupa*; but there is always a danger that the memory of the living man will preserve the recollections of the evocation and remember it as a vivid dream. If it is not, however, at a great distance, the Double or *Linga Sarira* may be evoked, but this can neither speak nor give information, and there is always the possibility of the sleeper being killed through this forced separation. Many sudden deaths in sleep have thus occurred, and the world been no wiser.

Q. Can there be any connection between a dreamer and an entity in "*Kama Loka*"?

A. The dreamer of an entity in *Kama Loka* would probably bring upon himself a nightmare, or would run the risk of becoming "possessed" by the "spook" so attracted, if he happened to be a medium, or one who had made himself so passive during his waking hours that even his higher Self is now unable to protect him. This is why the mediumistic state of passivity is so dangerous, and in time renders the Higher Self entirely helpless to aid or even warn the sleeping or entranced person. Passivity paralyzes the connection between the lower and higher principles. It is very rare to find instances of mediums who, while remaining passive *at will*, for the purpose of communicating with some higher intelligence, some *exterraneous* spirit (not disembodied), will yet preserve sufficiently their personal will so as not to break off all connection with the higher Self.

Q. Can a dreamer be "en rapport" with an entity in Devachan?

A. The only possible means of communicating with Devachanees is during sleep by a dream or vision, or in trance state. No Devachanee can descend into our plane; it is for us— or rather our *inner Self*—to ascend to his.

Q. What is the state of mind of a drunkard during sleep?

A. It is no real sleep, but a heavy stupor; no physical rest, but worse than sleeplessness, and kills the drunkard as quickly. During such stupor, as also during the waking drunken state, everything turns and whirls round in the brain, producing in the imagination and fancy horrid and grotesque shapes in continual motion and convolutions.

Q. What is the cause of nightmare, and how is it that the dreams of persons suffering from advanced consumption are often pleasant?

A. The cause of the former is simply physiological. A nightmare arises from oppression and difficulty in breathing; and difficulty in breathing will always create such a feeling of oppression and produce a sensation of impending calamity. In the second case, dreams become pleasant because the consumptive grows daily severed from his material body, and more clairvoyant in proportion. As death approaches, the body wastes away and ceases to be an impediment or barrier between the brain of the physical man and his Higher Self.

Q. Is it a good thing to cultivate dreaming?

A. It is by cultivating the power of what is called "dreaming" that clairvoyance is developed.

Q. Are there any means of interpreting dreams—for instance, the interpretations given in dream-books?

A. None but the clairvoyant faculty and the spiritual intuition of the "interpreter." Every dreaming Ego differs from every other, as our physical bodies do. If everything in the universe has seven keys to its symbolism on the physical plane, how many keys may it not have on higher planes?

Q. Is there any way in which dreams may be classified?

A. We may roughly divide dreams also into seven classes, and subdivide these in turn. Thus, we would divide them into:

1. Prophetic dreams. These are impressed on our memory by the Higher Self, and are generally plain and clear: either a voice heard or the coming event foreseen.

2. Allegorical dreams, or hazy glimpses of realities caught by the brain and distorted by our fancy. These are generally only half true.

3. Dreams sent by adepts, good or bad, by mesmerisers, or by the thoughts of very powerful minds bent on making us do their will.

4. Retrospective; dreams of events belonging to past incarnations.

5. Warning dreams for others who are unable to be impressed themselves.

6. Confused dreams, the causes of which have been discussed above.

7. Dreams which are mere fancies and chaotic pictures, owing to digestion, some mental trouble, or such-like external cause.

Appendix 3

Blavatsky Lodge Meetings:
Participants in order of appearance

1. January 10, 1889: Bertram Keightley, HPB, Thomas B. Harbottle (President), William Kingsland, William Ashton Ellis, Dr. Williams, Mr. X, {Roger} Hall, Mr. —, Miss —, Mr. Duncan

2. January 17, 1889: Archibald Keightley, HPB, T.B. Harbottle (President), Dr. Williams, Bertram Keightley, William Kingsland, G.R.S. Mead, {Roger} Hall

3. January 24, 1889: Archibald Keightley, HPB, Bertram Keightley, William Kingsland, Col. Chowne, Bulaki Rama, F.L. Gardner, {Roger} Hall, Dr. Williams, A Lady

4. January 31, 1889: Archibald Keightley, HPB, William Kingsland, T.B. Harbottle (Chairman), F.L. Gardner, Bertram Keightley, Mrs. Williams, Bulaki Rama, Dr. Williams

5. February 7, 1889: Archibald Keightley, HPB, T.B. Harbottle (President), Bertram Keightley, William Kingsland, Mr. Forsyth, A Lady, Mr. —, F.L. Gardner

6. February 14, 1889: Archibald Keightley, HPB, Bertram Keightley, William Kingsland (Chairman), Mr. W. Scott-Elliot, Dr. Williams, {Roger} Hall, Miss Kenealy

7. February 21, 1889: Bertram Keightley, HPB, William Kingsland, T.B. Harbottle (President), {Roger} Hall, F.L. Gardner, Eduoard Coulomb, Mr. Johnston {Charles Johnston?}

8. February 28, 1889: Bertram Keightley, HPB, William Kingsland, T.B. Harbottle (President), F.L. Gardner, Mr. —, Mme. Tambaco, Dr. Williams, Alexander Fullerton

9. March 7, 1889: T.B. Harbottle (President), Archibald Keightley, HPB, William Kingsland, Bertram Keightley, Dr. Williams, Mr. Yates {W.B. Yeats?}

10. March 14, 1889: Archibald Keightley, Bertram Keightley, HPB, William Kingsland (Chairman), F.L. Gardner, {Roger} Hall

11. March 21, 1889: Archibald Keightley, HPB, T.B. Harbottle (President). Bertram Keightley. F.L. Gardner, William Kingsland, Dr. Williams

12. March 28, 1889: Archibald Keightley, HPB, William Kingsland (Chairman), Bertram Keightley, Mr. ——, Mr. Atkinson, Miss Kenealy

13. April 4, 1889: Archibald Keightley, HPB, William Kingsland (Chairman), Bertram Keightley, F.L. Gardner, A Lady, Mr. {Robert B.?} Holt, Mr. ——

14. April 11, 1889: Bertram Keightley, HPB, William Kingsland (Chairman), F.L. Gardner, W.R. Old, {Roger} Hall, Dr. Williams, Mr. ——

15. April 18, 1889: Bertram Keightley, HPB, William Kingsland (Chairman), Yates {W.B. Yeats?}, G.R.S. Mead, A.P. Sinnett, A Lady

16. April 25, 1889: Bertram Keightley, HPB, William Kingsland (Chairman), G.R.S. Mead, W.R. Old, Mr. {Charles?} Ingram, Mr. ——

17. May 2, 1880: Bertram Keightley, HPB, W.R. Old, William Kingsland (Chairman), {John Storer} Cobb, G.R.S. Mead, Mr. ——, {Roger} Hall, A Lady

18. May 9, 1889: Transcription missing.

19. May 16, 1889: Bertram Keightley, HPB, Dr. Williams, A Lady, W.R. Old, William Kingsland (Chairman), Mr. Johnson {Johnston?}, Mr. ——, Countess Wachtmeister, Mr. Cross

May 23, 1889. No record of a meeting being held.

20. May 30, 1889: W.R. Old, HPB, William Kingsland (Chairman), Herbert Burrows, Mr. ——, A Lady

21. June 6, 1889: W.R. Old, HPB, Bertram Keightley, Ralph Sneyd, William Kingsland (Chairman), Herbert Burrows, Annie Besant, F.L. Gardner, A Lady

June 13, 1889. No record of a meeting being held.

22. June 20, 1889: HPB, Mrs. Alice Gordon, W.R. Old, Bertram Keightley, William Kingsland (Chairman), Mr. Sargeant

Alphabetical list of participants at the Blavatsky Lodge meetings: the number after the name indicates the number of the attended meeting.
No record for meeting: 18. May 9, 1889; May 23, 1889 and June 13, 1889.

Miss --:	1
Mr. --:	1, 5, 8, 12, 13, 14, 16, 17, 19, 20
Mr. Atkinson:	12
Annie Besant:	21
Herbert Burrows:	20, 21
Col. Chowne:	3
{John Storer} Cobb:	17
Eduoard Coulomb:	7
Mr. Cross:	19
Mr. Duncan:	1
William Ashton Ellis:	1
Mr. Forsyth:	5
Alexander Fullerton:	8
F.L. Gardner:	3, 4, 5, 7, 8, 10, 11, 13, 14, 21
Mrs. Alice Gordon:	22
{Roger} Hall:	1, 2, 3, 6, 7, 10, 14, 17
Thomas B. Harbottle:	1, 2, 4, 5, 7, 8, 9, 11
Mr. {Robert B.?} Holt:	13
Mr. {Charles?} Ingram:	16
Mr. Johnston {Charles Johnston?}:	7 - 19
Archibald Keightley:	1, 2, 3, 4, 5, 6, 9, 10, 11, 12, 13
Bertram Keightley:	Every meeting, except meeting 20
Miss Kenealy:	6, 12
William Kingsland:	Every meeting
A Lady:	3, 5, 13, 15, 17, 19, 20, 21
G.R.S. Mead:	2, 15, 16, 17
W.R. Old:	14, 16, 17, 19, 20, 21, 22
Bulaki Rama:	3, 4
Mr. Sargeant:	22
Mr. W. Scott-Elliot:	6
A.P. Sinnett:	15
Ralph Sneyd:	21
Mme. Tambaco:	8
Countess Wachtmeister:	19
Dr. Williams:	1, 2, 3, 4, 6, 8, 9, 11, 14, 19
Mrs. Williams:	4
Mr. X:	1
Mr. Yates {W.B. Yeats?}:	9, 15

Appendix 4

The Secret Doctrine
A Paper read before the Blavatsky Lodge of the T.S.
by William Kingsland, President

In the course of our systematic study of *The Secret Doctrine,* which we have now pursued for nearly six months, we have arrived at the conclusion of the stanzas of the first volume. It would be well to pause and ask ourselves what is the net gain which we have derived? In what respects are our ideas altered or modified, what have we learnt which is new, and how much do we recognize the value of the book?

It has been no easy matter to form a clear and concise idea of the *modus operandi* of cosmogenesis as set forth in the stanzas and the accompanying commentary. They do not profess to do more than lift the corner of the veil. Large numbers of intermediate slokas we are told are omitted, and certain occult keys, which it is not yet permitted to make public, are withheld. Those who are members of the Esoteric Section of the T.S. have a better chance of understanding the matter than the ordinary reader, but since numbers who have attended our Thursday evening meetings are not Esotericists, it has been impossible to treat the matter from any but an exoteric standpoint.

In order to present an abstract principle in anything like a comprehensible manner, it is necessary that it should be represented in some form having reference to our ordinary methods of intellectual apprehension, and our ordinary states of consciousness. Some kind of *form* is indispensable for the conceptions which arise out of our present state of consciousness, and the one great fallacy which we should constantly guard against, is the mistaking of the form for the reality, the effect for the cause. It is this self same illusion of form, Maya, which is the great deceiver, the great tempter. It deceives our physical senses and our intellectual faculties. It is the cause of all the illusive forms of superstition and religion which have prevailed in all ages. Let not the student of *The Secret Doctrine* fall under the same illusion, and mistake the form which is there presented for the principles which underlie the form, or materialize into a dogma the priceless treasure of wisdom and knowledge therein contained.

I know that some have come to grief over the various celestial Hierarchies of Dhyāni-Chohans, being totally unable to connect these with the physical forces with which they are familiar, or to see any connection whatever between them and the physical universe. Perhaps if they will dematerialize their ideas of celestial beings, disconnect them from all preconceived ideas of Angels and Archangels derived from Biblical fairy tales, instilled into their youthful minds—not an easy matter, by the way—and give free play to their intuition, they will be able to surmount what at present appears to them such a formidable obstacle.

The mysteries of Parabrahman have been touched upon more than once, and it has been pointed out that this term is not used to designate either a *God* or a *machine*, but as a purely metaphysical abstraction—albeit the one reality, the *absolute*. Nevertheless *Parabrahman* appears to have been a very hard nut for some to crack, as also the first and second *Logos*, Brahma and *Brahmā, Fohat,* and a host of other *personified* forces. We can hardly be surprised if the casual and superficial reader should be lost in the vast pantheon of *The Secret Doctrine,* and should fly for comparative intellectual safety to the orthodox doctrine of the trinity.

But let us not, as students of *The Secret Doctrine,* be hasty in forming either our conceptions or our conclusions. We must bear in mind that we are dealing with the imaginative powers of the Eastern mind, and with the deepest and most subtle of metaphysical and philosophical systems. Let us try and understand *The Secret Doctrine* in its materialized form, and then, when we have mastered the form, we may be the better able to understand what that form represents.

Setting aside now all concrete ideas having reference to the form in which the teachings are moulded, I imagine that those who have followed closely the course of instructions, cannot have failed to have grasped some general principles of the utmost importance. They cannot have failed to have obtained such a broad and comprehensive view of the law of *evolution,* of the essential unity and oneness of nature—including in that term both the visible and the invisible universe—and of the law of correspondences and analogy, such as could not have been obtained by them by the study of half the scientific books in the world.

Science prides itself upon its generalizations, such as the law of the conservation of energy and the doctrine of evolution, and these two doctrines have certainly been responsible, more than everything else that science has done, for the breaking down of the narrow and superstitious conceptions of the government of the universe by the personal fiat of a Biblical Jehovah.

But *The Secret Doctrine* carries these generalizations immeasurably further than even science itself has yet ventured to do. *The Secret Doctrine*, in fact, proceeds by an opposite method to that of science. The methods of science are *inductive*, proceeding from particulars to universals; the method of *The Secret Doctrine* is deductive, proceeding from universals to particulars. Now each of these methods has its own particular application and value. Implicit faith should not be placed in either the one or the other, but each should be used in a legitimate way. Science ignores altogether the deductive method. Her generalizations and theories are built upon a vast mass of accumulated facts, which scientific men are ever adding to, while at the same time they endeavor to piece them together so as to form a connected whole. The generalizations of science are the result of numbers of isolated observations and experiments. It may fall to the lot of some one man to enunciate some particular law of nature, which he is therefore said to have discovered, and which is labeled with his name; but it is seldom the case that the discovery is due to his own unaided and original observations. He is indebted to numberless other experimenters, it may be to a line of research which has been carried on for centuries, but it has fallen to the lot of this particular individual to crown the efforts of others by the enunciation of a law which binds together and shows the essential relation of phenomena, which have hitherto appeared to be isolated and arbitrary.

But we may well doubt whether science by means of the inductive method can ever teach us anything respecting the deeper problems of our consciousness, can ever reach such generalizations and principles as are to be found in *The Secret Doctrine*. Science refuses to deal with metaphysics, or even with such physics as psychical phenomena, and we certainly cannot, as individuals, afford to wait until science shall have seen fit to offer a solution of certain problems with which we are more immediately acquainted. Let us recognize the value of inductive science in its own proper sphere, but meanwhile let us also use the deductive method, and see whether we cannot arrive at general principles without having to spend our lives in accumulating innumerable facts, or in labeling with learned names the minutest subdivisions of every insect or plant which we can meet with in the remotest corners of the globe.

If we push back our enquiries respecting the phenomenal universe, and the causes which are operating to produce the effects which we see around us, we very soon reach a point where physics cannot help us, and where we must resort to metaphysics and abstract ideas. We cannot employ the inductive method here, for we have exhausted our knowledge of facts. We stand before the great ocean of the unknown, that strange illusion which we call time and space. What is to be our guide here; how does *The Secret Doctrine* help us?

By analogy. By showing us the past, the present and the future, contained in the highest possible metaphysical abstraction, in the *Absolute* or *Parabrahman,* and then proceeding downwards through the various manifestations in time and space of this one absolute reality—always by analogy, and in lines that never vary in principle—until we reach those finite manifestations which constitute our present physical universe, and our human consciousness.

Analogy is the great law of *The Secret Doctrine.* As above, so below. The microcosm is a reflection of the macrocosm. These occult axioms are to be found elsewhere, but in no other book are they so exemplified, or worked out in such detail, or made to cover such a vast area as in *The Secret Doctrine.* Truly this is a key which is worth having, a universal key with which we can unlock one by one every mystery of our being. We must first of all learn to grasp firmly this principle of analogy, and if we do this I imagine that we shall soon discover its value in every department of those regions which we are endeavoring to penetrate.

And now we stand face to face with the greatest question of all. Thus far we have been dealing with cosmogenesis, and have only incidentally touched on the deeper problems of life and consciousness. Stanza VII opens with these words: "Behold the beginning of sentient formless life." "Formless life!" What can we apprehend of life without form? And yet as we read and reread the stanza it impresses us with a sublimity of philosophic thought which surely is nowhere else to be found.

It presents itself to our mind like a ray of the one Divine Life itself flashed into the darkness of our materiality; or like the lightning in the blackness of the night it suddenly illumines the earth, enabling us to discern the outlines of our surroundings—then leaves us in deeper darkness.

What is this deep mystery of Life, these countless myriads of lives "the beams and the sparks of one moon reflected in the running waves of all the rivers of earth?"

Tell us, oh, Sphinx, of the three letters and the nine! Tell us—lest the insatiable desire to know which you have instilled into our minds pursue you as *Nemesis* through countless reincarnations.

What is life, mind, consciousness, man? Are not all these conglomerated, collected, distributed, permutated, annihilated, in the stanza before us, till our brain becomes a fiery whirlwind, and our reason sinks into the deep waters of space. We stand before the mystery of Life; we catch a glimpse of the awful depths of our own being, and those heights to scale which we must become—Gods! We stand for a moment on the verge of that infinite consciousness where there is neither great nor small, being or non-being, time or space, light or darkness, sound or silence.

The stanza reads like the great diapason tone of nature; it swells into a harmony that seems the very source of our being. Who but a great musician or magician can analyse these tones, or fit them to the scale of our earth-bound consciousness. Let us pause and listen, if perchance we may attune our minds to the divine harmony, and carry some portion of it with us into our daily life. Truly our task has been no light one thus far, but with the strength we have gained we will still push forward, and master these deeper secrets of life by which alone we can hope to free ourselves from the great illusion.

Originally published in HPB's magazine, *Lucifer*, 4: 23 (July, 1889): 416-20

Index

Words are transcribed as used in the original manuscript, and follow the usage of H. P. Blavatsky and most writers of her time.

A

Abel *(Heb.)*
  as female marries Cain, 149-150
Absolute
  compared to Absoluteness, 73, 331-332, 394
  conditionless, 39, 396, 412
  defined as reality, 150
  devas rays of, 103
  difficult to conceive, 394
  as eternal darkness, 272
  as eternal law, 396
  Felix on temple for, 162
  First Cause is not, 70
  identity annihilated in, 394
  immutable, 67-68
  indivisible, 335
  infinite or unlimited, 198, 269-270, 332-335, 396
  Logos cannot perceive, 4
  manifest, or not, 214, 272-274
  Maya not aspect of, 49
  motion, 457
  must always be, 33, 62, 270, 272
  neither desire nor thought in, 22-23, 73
  no consciousness for, 73, 270-271, 273-274
  no prayer to, 103
  not manifest, 49
  omnipresent, 116, 335
  One and only One, 118, 642
  no attributes for, 67, 73, 150, 396, 412
  no truth is, 396
  Parabrahman is not, 68
  radiation from, not emanation, 154, 156-157
  ray from, in everyone, 104, 333
  as rootless root, 334
  roots of all latent in, 272
  science cannot perceive, 273, 274
  Seers conscious of, 272-273
  Spencer on unknowable, 124, 126-127, 270, 552-553
  is That of Hindus, 396
  transcends human consciousness, 270-271, 273-274, 642-643
  a unity, 198
Absoluteness
  awakens from dormancy, 271
  divine mind or ideation and, 158, 271, 331-333
  immutable and omnipresent, 394, 552, 553
  IT is, 73
  manvantaric emanations &, 332-335, 632
  is Nirvana, 393, 632
  omnipresent, 331-332
  not a cause, 70
  Parabrahman is, 68, 552, 553
  a relative term, 214
  Spencer on unknowable as, 553-554, 556
Acorn
  phenomenal germ becomes, 165

Acts
  quote applies to Unknowable, 554-555&fn
Adept(s)
  degree depends on, plane of perception, 430
  Devachan an illusion for, 445, 601-602
  great, as seed Manus, 383
  highest, may become sishtas, 444, 445
  many lives needed to become, 606
  may remain as Nirmanakayas, 602-603
  progress limited, 508
  protect nations, 445-446
  refuse Nirvana, 601-602
  self-sacrifice of, 445-446
  use thoughts not language, 182
Aditi *(Sk.)*
  in Hindu cosmogony, 416
  as shakti or space, 313
  Vedic term for Mulaprakriti, 4
Æon(s) *(Gk.)*
  emanations of Absolute, 333
  emanations of primordial fire, 323-324, 325
  meanings of, 10-11, 323-326
  Primordial Seven, 323-326
Aether *(Gk.)*
  Erebus & Nox emanate, 503
  Ether and, cp., 259
Ah-hi *(Sensar)* **(Ahi)** *(Sk.)*
  absolute vs. cosmic ideation and, 33
  exist no more, 37
  are forces not men, 38
  highest Dhyanis 28
  human stage and, 36-38
  intelligent forces, 27
  Manasa-Dhyanis and, 43
  manifestation of the Law, 29
  no free will of, 38
  planes & correspondences of, 35
  proceed from unity, 40
  universal mind and, 27-28, 30-34
  were not, 32, 34
Ain-Soph *(Heb.) see also* **Atma(n)**
  absolute consciousness, 50
  endless duration, 10
  is IT or negative or zero, 2
  no attributes, 2
  Parabrahman is, 10, 50, 71, 439
  perfectly unknown, 61
  Vishnu as, 61
Akasha (Akasa) *(Sk.)*
  Astral Light and, 157-158, 328
  Buddhi proceeds from, 42
  first production of, or Chaos, 21
  grossest form is ether, 202
  homogeneous, 260
  Logos is attribute of, 72
  as middle is dual, 258
  rootless root of Nature, 260
Alaya *(Sk.)*
  as Anima Mundi, 134
  Logos as male aspect of, 134
  meaning of, 108-109
Allen, Grant
  popular novelist on science, 423
  ——— *Force and Energy* HPB calls, 'flapdoodle', 423
Amber
  latent electricity of, 244, 248
  molecular effect of rubbing, 238-239, 243-244
  white ants react to 239-240
Amshapends *(Zend)*
  as seven classes of monads, 465
Analogy(ies)
  'as above so below', 200
  better than theory, 200
  comparisons and, 194
  correspondences and, 398
  depends on planes perceived, 194
  invariable law of, 9
  an occult axiom, 642

universal key, 642-643
Anarchism
notwithstanding socialists efforts 510
Andromeda Nebula
not a star cluster, 225
Angel(s)
allegory of solar gods and, 483
fall into matter or hell, 483
rebellious, of theology, 482-483
seven hierarchies of, & elements 296
Anger
is atomic, 354-355
effects on men & animals, 354
Anima Mundi *(Lat.)*
is Jivatma or Soul of the World, 109, 635
Logos is male aspect of, 134
Purusha and, 630
universal soul, 630
Animal(s)
few, during Pralaya, 382-383
Golden Legend about, 536
mind of, 16-18, 57
Saint Francis preached to, 536-537
seven meanings to 'sacred', 571
treatment of, by Church, 536-537
Ant(s)
come from lower sphere, 241, 242
intellect of, 16
perceptive power of, 241-242, 243
Anthropoids
liberated at Sixth Race, 446-447
semi-human elementals, 447
some in sidereal spaces now, 447
Anu *(Sk.)*
as atom or name of Brahmā, 208, 264-265
Anugita *(Sk.)*
conservation of energy in, 361
speech & mind allegory in, 308-309
worth reading, 85&fn
Apes
better than men, 93
will become men in Sixth Race, 446-447
Archetypal World
in Kabalah has four planes, 363
prototypes of all in, 363
Ariadne's Thread
as Fohat, 227&fn
Aristotle
chaos is space for, 502
poor method of, 73, 118-119
privation of matter of, 3, 165, 635
Arnold, Edwin
——— *The Light of Asia*, 46&fn
Arupa *(Sk.)*
Astral Light and, plane, 164
existence on, plane, 77-78
rupa cp. to formless, 371
Aryasanga
two men with same name, 46&fn
Astral Body
overshadowed by Monad, 564-565
parents give, to child, 560, 564
Astral Light
Akasha and, 157, 328
on four lower planes only, 158, 163, 328
generic term, 157
great deceiver & illusion, 147, 157-158, 159, 171
handwriting, 170-171, 182
ideas drawn from, 187, 188-189
infernal aspect of ether, 260
lies between Tetragrammaton and Reality, 150
is periodic, 158-159
prototypes of forms and, 164-165, 181
Astral Plane
deceptive, 41
life currents and, 541
physical forms and, 165
planetary colors and, 543
Pranic plane above, 542

prediction and, 167
Astrologer(s)
  Hindu, on pranic influences, 541-542
  views on stars ruling man, 540-541
Astrology
  basic Theosophy preferred over, 544
  Hindu, on planetary influences, 541-542
  occult, and planetary colors, 543
  popular views on, 544
  sacred animals as zodiac signs, 571
Atma(n) *(Sk.)* see also **Ain Soph**
  is Absoluteness, 439, 626
  Ah-hi and, 35
  beyond seventh plane, 629
  Buddhi as vehicle of, 592-593
  is conscious non-consciousness, 593
  corresponds to Parabrahman, 3, 439, 630, 631
  defined, 109, 592-593
  fire corresponds to, 248
  Higher Self is, 623
  Jiva and, are one, 625-626
  as Laya center, 419, 460
  Nirvana and, 628
  no, in séance rooms, 580
  no personal, but common property, 624-625, 627
  not a principle, 433
  is nothing, 592
  radiation and, 630
  ray of universal principle, 550
  spirit of Earth and, 473
  is synthesis soul, 380
  vehicle is Buddhi, 439, 530, 620
Atma-Buddhi *(Sk.)*
  cannot pass to Nirvana, 373, 373
  Devachan and, 621
  fully conscious with Manas, 558, 564, 620-621, 627
  goes to Devachan, 371-373, 375
  incarnating ego and, 628-629

  individuality of, 372-373
  immortal principle, 564
  as Monad incarnated in Third Race, 557-558
  Parabrahman, First Logos and, 633
  ray from, and Manas, 628-629
  refulgence of, & Absoluteness, 372
  Vedantins' five sheaths ignore, 595
Atma-Buddhi-Manas *(Sk.)*
  completes incarnating ego, 593
  differentiations of Absolute, 380
  Manasaputra and, 593
  not hereditary, 561
  occult system & seven-fold sheaths, 595
  Spirit, Voice, Word and, 329
Atmosphere
  of earth a crucible, 404, 405, 409
  etheric gradations of, 404
  of globes alter elements, 403-405, 409, 431
  not air but aura in occultism, 404
Atom(s) see also **Mineral Atom(s)**
  alterations of, 293, 385-387
  as Anu, a germ 264, 336
  chemical elements and, 208, 352-353
  of Democritus, 336
  exists as substance not matter, 431
  indestructible, 133, 298, 335-336, 352
  inherent powers of, 267, 268
  man compared to, 268, 298, 384-387
  of man and kosmos, 384-385
  as mathematical point, 201, 335-336, 352-353, 386-387
  microcosm of macrocosm, 387
  molecule cp. to, 203-209, 336, 339, 352
  as monads of Leibniz, 335
  not our own, 298
  not to be found, 6, 201, 336, 386-387
  occult, is not chemical, 203-208,

209-210, 264-265, 336, 339, 352-353
  primordial, transformed by Fohat, 290-291
  real, not on this plane, 201-202
  reflect other universes, 352
  scattering of, 292, 382, 431
  on seven planes of being, 431
  seventh principle of molecule, 203-205
  sponge simile and, 268
  turned into vital electricity, 290
  universe in itself, 267-268
  unmanifested plane, 352-355
Atomic
  Dalton and, theory 9
  passion as, 354-355
Attribute(s) *see also* **Absolute; Infinite; It; Parabrahm(an)**
  disappear in Nirvana, 393
  eternal-egg and, 181
  First Logos lacks, of desire, 74
  Mulaprakriti is an, 71
  nature of deity and, 394-396
  no, for Alaya, 108
  no, for circle, 20
  no, for 'Darkness', 60
  one, of Akasa, 72
  only finite can have, 39
  Reality has no, 150
  refulgence is an, 372
Aura *(Gr., Lat.) see also* **Atmosphere**
  Lipika & magnetic, of kosmos, 371
Axiom
  analogy, key to *The Secret Doctrine*, 642
  Occult, 200, 232, 642
  scientific, & theory, 8, 203-204

B

Bachelor, Rhoda
  daughter of Morgans in S. India, 452fn
  knew tribal languages, 452
Baconian Method
  a poor choice, 119, 121
Bacteria
  is attenuated atomic matter, 355
Badagas
  burning & hanging of, 454-455
  fear the Mulakurumbas, 452, 453-454
  lawsuit regarding, 453
  worshippers & vassals of Todas, 452&fn, 454, 455
Bahak-Zivo (Bahak-Ziwa) *(Gnos.)*
  could not create beings, 473, 482, 485
Bailey, Philip James
  English poet on free will, 587&fn
Bailly, Jean Sylvain
  French astronomer, 320fn
  shows Hindus correct, 320&fn
Barham, Richard H.
  poem by, on saintly crow, 537&fn
Being(s)
  Be-ness is not, 23
  emerge & end of Laya point, 429
  finite, causes of terrestrial plane, 67
  planes emanate from conscious, 429-430
  planes of, and non-being, 197-198
  seven planes of, 3
Bellamy, Edward
  writes story for *Harper's*, 88&fn
Be-ness
  absolute and immutable, 27
  Laya and, 109
  is Parabrahman, 71
  translates Sat, 23, 27
Berridge, Edward W.
  homeopathic physician, 450fn
Bhagavad-Gita *(Sk.)*
  on departure of souls, 299&fn-300
  metaphors of bright & dark fortnight

in, 300
Bhashyacharya, N.
Adyar Library director, 376fn
Bhu *(Sk.)*
meaning of, 138
Bible
Aeon use in, 10
Elohistic influences in, 362
Gnostics on God of, 160
on gods & God, 103
on Light, 156
on Logos, 308
on void, 60
Binah *(Heb.)*
a female intelligence, 102
Keter, Chokhmah and, 129, 131, 438
or Mahat, 144
part of manifested Logos, 129, 131
as understanding, 438
Black Magic
killing from dream state is, 78
of dwarf tribe, 452
three 'seats' and, 495
Blake, William
English poet & artist, 442fn
had system of planes, 442
Blavatsky, Helena P. *see also* **Stanza(s)**
criticizes science, 119, 125, 392-393, 422-423, 610-611
gives keys to study, 607
healing fig given to, by Todas, 455
how ideas come to, 186-187
Jains left, because of killing cobras, 530
on *Lucifer* editorial of, 510&fn
a metaphysician, 610
never drank, 539
never met a truly happy man, 526
'no gift of the gab', 600-601
not qualified as Theosophist, 545
not permitted to reveal all, 368, 435, 436, 506
prefers silence on esoteric subjects, 634
says study exoteric classics, 502
on skepticism of students 608, 610
urges going beyond intellect, 608, 610, 612
wanted *Pistis Sophia* translated, 160
—— *The Enigmatical Tribes of the Blue Hills* about the Todas, 451fn, 452fn, 453fn
—— *Isis Unveiled* on mysterious Todas, 450-451&fn
triple man in, 626
—— *The Key to Theosophy* on basic beliefs & principal ideas, 523, 534
dialogue format, 523
metaphysics avoided in, 525
personal criticism avoided in, 531-532
plan & purpose of, 523-524
Roman Catholicism attacked in, 529, 531
rules of T.S. in, 535
section on self sacrifice, 528-530
what to call Blavatsky in, 544-546
—— *The Secret Doctrine* 157, 178, 201
analogy is great law of, 642
applies to solar system & earth, 136
basics of, must be grasped, 640-641, 642
Celestial Hierarchies and, 640
considered difficult, 524, 525, 547-548, 639-640
five Buddhas mentioned in, 100
misprint in, 146
newspaper criticism of, 548
on Manu, 172
second volume on life on Earth, 136
sublime thought in, 643
third and fourth volumes, 102
vast pantheon of forces in, 640
Blavatsky Lodge
on meetings at, 162

participants at, 636-638
Blind
associates sound with color, 89, 543
spirit, as well as color, 136-137
Blind Will
Absolute and, 74
of Schopenhauer, not a stupid idea, 68
Bliss
Devachan a state of, 25, 562, 580-581, 591-592
eightfold path and, 47
Meru the land of, 516
no, for Absolute, 38-39
of Non-Being, 110
Pitris and nirvanic, 444
seven ways to, are faculties, 45
Booth, William
persuasive powers of, 355-356
Salvation Army founder, 356fn
Brahma (Brahmâ) *(Sk.)*
Age of, & causes of existence, 67, 556
Age of, and Parabrahman, 70, 556
aspect of Vishnu, 61
as "atom" or anu, 203, 208, 264-265, 335
as breath, 396
creative power, 133
Creator of Hindu trinity, 360, 502
Day of, has latent qualities, 271
depends on Vishnu, 362
differentiation of, 155, 271
during pralaya, 103, 265, 395
female aspect of, 2
Fohat and, one thing, 135
four-faced, in Vedanta, 378
as germ of unknown darkness, 261, 264-265
Golden Egg and, 20, 201
karmic law rules, 167
law of days & nights as, 396
Mahat born of, 332
not prominent in Vedas, 61

Parabrahm higher than, 100
part of manifested Logos, 129
Sephirothal tree and, 129
seven Manus and, 105-106, 378
Swayambhu and, 138
Sun and Age of, 314
vehicle of, 237
Brahman *(Sk.)*
symbols of those who go to, 299-300
Brahmins
postulate 7 creations, 271
Brain *see also* **Cerebrum; Cerebellum**
cerebrum & cerebellum of, 41, 51-58
consciousness and, 43-44
sponge-like, capture ideas, 187-188
unconscious cerebration and, 617-619, 622-623
Brotherhood
HPB article mentions, 510&fn
no distinctions in, 510-511
Buddha(s) *see also* **Dhyani-Buddhas**
called Pho in China, 138
five mentioned in *S.D.*, 100
Gautama, a Manushi, 101
humans all will become, 101, 102
life of, by Arnold, 46fn
on Nirvana, 14-15, 23, 69
past lives seen by, 600
refused Nirvana, 601-602
Supreme, or [Vajrasattva], 100&fn
Buddhi *(Sk.)*
Ah-hi and, 35
allegory of, as purusha & prakriti, 439
cementing link, 621
corresponds to Eternal Parent, 3
divine light of, on Manas, 614
intuition and, 620-621
of man and cosmic, 42
monadic evolution and, 439
not a ray, 628
universal consciousness, 593
as vehicle of Atma, 593, 620-621,

626-629
Buddhism
  four truths of, 46-47, 59-60
  reincarnation belief in, 527
Buddhists
  happiest & most serene people, 527
Budha *(Sk.)*
  means wisdom, 138
Builders *see also* **Kosmocratores**
  animate elements of globe, 570
  celestial masons, 570
  defined, 99, 111-112
  Fohat and seven, 138
  karma of lower plane, 166
  lower worlds, 163
  many classes of, 95, 99, 176
  not anthropomorphic gods, 570
Burgoyne, Thomas H.
  alias of swindler, 538&fn, 539
Butler, Hiram
  American pseudo-occultist, 540&fn

C

Caduceus *(Gr.)*
  healing power of, 358
  of Mercury, 357-358
Cain or *Kayn (Heb.)*
  Abel as female aspect of, 149-150
Carlyle, Thomas
  Froude wrote biography of, 633fn
  on mankind, 40
  ———— *Sartor Resartus* quotes Goethe, 261fn
Catholic(s), Roman *see also* **Church**
  had animal converts, 536-537&fn
  HPB against, system not persons, 531
  HPB tries not to hurt feelings of, 116
  pagans source of, rites, 161
Cause *see also* **Karma**
  causeless, 70-71, 73-74, 553, 554
  First, not the Absolute, 70-71, 122
  law of, and effect, 574, 577, 578
  Parabrahman is not a, 68, 552
  Supreme, 30
Centripetal *see also* **Force**
  and centrifugal force, 65-66, 70, 275, 276, 278, 289, 357-358, 416, 463
Cerebellum *(Lat.)*
  Instinctual, 41, 52, 57
  sleeps while cerebrum awake, 41, 51
Cerebrum *(Lat.)*
  cerebellum lost in functions of, 55
  polishes ideas, 56
Chain *see* **Earth Chain; Planetary Chain**
Chaldean(s)
  cosmogony, 6-7, 155
  Devil from the West say, 364
  'divine dynasties' of, 296
  Kabalah differs from orthodox, 498-499
  knew astronomy, 401
  seven day week of, 489
Chaos *(Gr.)*
  absolutely limitless, 502-503
  Akasa is, 21
  Brahmā's will is, 502
  coeval with Eros & Gaia, 503-504
  creative principle of ancients, 502
  darkness term for, 80
  intelligences from sun of, 163
  as space or void, 60, 237, 502
  as waters of space, 157-158, 180
Chemistry
  a limited science, 203-207
Chhaya(s) *(Sk.)*
  evolved into men, 176-177, 466, 478, 557-558
  Hindu legend about, 478&fn
  Karma of those, who refused 481
  meaning of, 176-177

Monads develop, of Lunar Pitris, 557-558
Child(ren)
diseased parents should not bear, 583-584
Father gives, germinal cell, 559
genius as recollection in, 622
immediate rebirth, cases of, 602
Monad enters, at 7 or 8 years, 558-559
Monad overshadows fetus of, 559
more intuitive than adults, 623-624
parents give, lower principles, 560-561, 564-565
Chimpanzee
monad, 447, 450
savage cp. to, 450
China
Buddha called Pho in, 138
dragon as emblem of power, 494
early race in, isolated, 450
Chokhmah *(Heb.)*
Binah and, 102, 129, 131, 144, 438
as Wisdom, 144, 438
Christ
descended into Hell, 483
HPB never goes against, 161
symbolic mysteries of, 116, 140, 161-162
Christian(s)
early, had no churches, 162
on eternity, 11
Fathers, 160-161
Revelation not a, work, 491
Christianity
animals respected in, 536
cross symbolism of, 145
disfigured everything, 161
foremost dogma of, 492
moral failings of, 526-527
sectarianism of, 536
Sun and early, 215
Church(es)

curse of, cant, 162
early Christian, 161-162, 214-217
pagan rites copied by, 161, 216
symbolism of, communion, 216
transubstantiation of, has some truth, 116
Circle(s) *see also* **Point**
absolute infinite symbol, 308
astronomical pi of, 304, 308
first form imaginable, 262
geometrical & numerical meanings, 304-305, 308
germ as point in, 193, 264
no attributes for, 20
not a being, 263
as Parabrahman, 304
planetary motion and, 278
point in, is unmanifested Logos, 20-21, 129-131
is root of number one, 484
seven, and poles, 514
sphere or, 264
squaring the, 143, 264
a triangle in objective world, 265
Civilization
Devil as Western, 364
corruption & misery of, 476, 509-510, 526-527
raises intelligence of chimps, 450
Clairvoyants
perceive atomic effects of emotions, 353-354
senses and types of, 56, 81-82, 86-87, 89
Clement of Alexandria
early leader of Christians, 161fn
Clock
analogy of, 67-68, 80
Codex Nazaræus *(Lat.)*
on Bahak-Zivo in Gnostic gospel, 473, 485
legend about Bahak-Zivo, Fetahil & Orcus, 473, 482, 485

Cold
 effect of extreme, 282
Color(s)
 Absolute has no, 150
 Fohat and, 291
 no distinctions of, race etc. for Theosophist, 510
 occult astrology and, 543-544
 pain and, 91-92
 personality, individuality, 565
 planes each have own, 241
 point in circle has no, 130
 of prism, 40, 90-91, 140, 194, 213
 reality has no, 150
 sound and, 89-91, 314, 329
Comet(s)
 defy gravity, 234, 318, 344-345
 on luminous tail of, 346-347
 on matter of tail of, 344-46
 meteors are fragments of, 407
 optical illusion of, 345, 346
 orbits and momentum of, 513-514
 planets were, 313
 radiant robes of Sun and, 344
 repelled by Sun, 345, 513
 stage is first in Manvantara, 513
 Sun was a, 314
 Sun will become a, 254
Consciousness
 Absolute, is not, 23, 28, 32, 34
 Absolute has no, 73, 108
 Absoluteness and, 394
 animal cp. to human, 16, 19
 on awakening higher 'seats' of, 495, 496-497
 on beginning of, 20-21
 collective, of Dhyanis as cosmic, 500
 cosmic, defined, 499-500
 development of higher, 612-613
 divine, 159, 429-430
 in dreams, 25, 42
 as faculty of mind or soul, 43-45
 inherent in man, 119, 429

 measuring Adept, 430
 must be attuned to cosmic planes, 495-497
 Nirvana and individual, 393-394
 perception differs from, 434
 planes of, created, 429-430
 purification of, 628
 'Robes' invisible to, 3-4
 seven states of human, 500-501
 sleeping and waking, 55-58, 501
 spiritual, not intellectual needed, 496
 of time, 21-22, 25, 42
 Universal becomes personal, 628
 is unlimited, 21, 501, 595, 628
Conservation
 in *Anugita*, 361
 of energy an occult truth, 361
 as transformation, 360-361
Contagion
 of disease, 355
 of mental passions, 355
 worst Karma of, from parents, 583-584
Continent(s)
 Lanka part of Atlantis, 453
 once greater than now, 449
 sink as axis shifts, 516-517
Cooper-Oakley, Isabel
 English Theosophist, 222fn
 HPB's companion to India, 222&fn
Cosmic Desire
 evolves into absolute Light, 502-505
 Fohat as, 503
Cosmic Dust
 affect Sun's spectra, 255
 optical illusions caused by, 256
Cosmic Matter *see* **Matter**
Cosmic Mind *see* **Mind**
Cosmic Plane *see* **Plane**
Cosmocratores *(Gr.) see also* **Builders**
 astral light and, 176
 builders, 99, 110, 111-112, 138
 Dhyani-Buddhas and, 176

Cosmogony(ies)
Chaldean, used term 'hyle', 6-7
first, of Hesiod, 503-504
Isis in Egyptian, 416
no Parabrahm in Hindu, 2
Phoenician, cp. to Brahmanical, 502
Simon Magus, similar to theosophic, 324
of world on Logos, 155
Coulomb, Edouard,
———— *Parabrahm*
Mead translates, in *Theosophical Siftings*, 199fn
pamphlet transl. from *Le Lotus*, 199&fn.
Creation(s)
bad word for there is no, 29
of Brahmins & *Genesis* cp., 511-512
Brahmins postulate seven, 271
everything in, is bipolar, 360
evolution is better word than, 272, 327
idea of existence and, 23
of Kabbalists & Occultists, 512
principle of, 502
self, of elementals, 179
seven, 305, 511, 512
seventh day of, meaning, 512
Crookes, William
great man of science, 250-251
greatest chemist, 610
protyle and, 5, 6, 7, 8, 63, 206-208, 635
search for elements and, 207-208, 251, 609-610
on spiral forces & number 8, 357-358
on zero point, 357
Cross
as cube unfolded, 145
symbolism of, 145
Crystal(ized)
geometrical aspects of, 309

immaculate medium, 140
matter is, ether or spirit, 202, 247
producing, as nutrition, 246
Cube
as base of tetraktys, 143-145
geometric code and, 305, 309-310, 375
Kepler's Third law and, 278
in Pythagorean geometry, 142-143
Curds
as first differentiation, 223-224
Milky Way, 223-224
Current(s)
of efflux in Occultism, 412
Fohatic, 348
hurricane of, in space, 462
life, of parent, 419
magnetic, of earth, 463-464
of national Karma, 581
rapport with thought, 187
Cycle(s)
Age or Day of Brahma, 70, 271
Astral Light changes with every, 158
day & night, 9, 512
of dying, 299-300
of existence not revealed, 377
Fohat changes with every, 351
Hindu, 467-469
Manas and, of incarnation, 566-567, 569
Manvantaric, 37&fn
meaning of, 303-304, 377
of necessity after Nirvana, 483
as septenates, 486-487, 488-489
of seven eternities, 9-10, 512
sidereal year, 517
of sinking continents, 516-517
universal life, 511
velocity of, changes, 513, 514
waking & sleeping, 51-57

D

Dalton, John
noted for atomic theory, 9
Damien, Father (Jozef De Veuster)
Christ-like man, 615
sainted priest to lepers, 529&fn-530
Dangma *(Tib.)*
eye of, 75-76
term used in stanza, 108
Dark(ness)
as Absoluteness, 60-61, 194, 237, 272
bright fortnight deaths and, 300
Builders in Unknown, 110
as chaos, 237
as duration, 227
Ever, defined, 130
Fire of Deity, 227
fortnight symbolism, 300
Hindu That and, 396
light and, cp. 80, 227
male & female, 503
negative state of nature, 232
Orcus a place of, 485
Pythagoras on, and Monad, 129, 151
quality of ether or force, 258, 269
radiates Light, 129, 194-195, 233
space & bright space, 236
spirit emanates from, 329
swan of eternity, 237
Third Logos and, 301
vehicle of Brahmā, 237, 261
when Kosmos had no form, 237
Darwin, Charles
astral glimpse of future by, 447
Haeckel as intuitive, 447
scientific intuition and, 121-122
Day(s)
'Be With Us' as Day of Judgement, 326
night and, cycle, 9, 13
Nights &, of Brahma, 556
of week in various cultures, 489
Death
for body only, 44-45
occult view on, 245
Orcus as, 485
sleep cp. to, 384
soul free at, 44-45
stages of, 383-384
as transformation, 360, 383-384
Deductive Method *see also* **Inductive Method**
universals to particulars is, 118-120, 123-124, 126, 170, 611-612, 641
Plato's method, 73
Deity
as Absoluteness, 394
fire as, 227, 232-233, 333
Life is, 560
seven-voweled, 240
Silent, 324
space as, 3, 13, 64, 75
sublime conception of, 396, 643
symbols of, 300, 505
Demiurgi *(Gk.)*
builders or masons, 64
Democritus
atomic theory of, 336
philosopher, 336fn
Desha *(Sk.)*
ten divinities of space, 64
Desire(s)
Absolute has no, 22-23, 73, 394
becomes thought in higher Manas, 308
in dreams, 78
to exist & 'cause' of Universe, 66-67, 73
Fohat or Life and Cosmic, 503-504
intense, and next life conditions, 605-606
intense, lengthens Devachan, 596-597
no, means no Devachan, 601, 603

primordial matter and Cosmic, 505
spiritual, realized in Devachan, 592
is suffering, 598
Destruction
is renovation, 360
Deva(s) *(Sk.)*
or celestial beings, 95
higher, as Dhyani-Buddhas, 100
as highest Dhyani-Chohans, 169
humanity in Seventh Round becomes, 101
Devachan (bDe-ba-can) *(Tib.)*
change of time in, population, 449-450
a dream, 589, 592
Egyptian cycle of, 377
as exalted selfishness, 528
field of Aanroo, 377
Fools Paradise, 562, 580
heaven compared to, 528
how to escape, 601, 603
illusion for Adept, 445
individualized state of consciousness, 591-592, 595
Karma and time in, 603, 624
Karma sends one to, 579-580
no idea of time in, 25, 589, 621
no karma created in, 579-582
monad or spirit-soul only enters, 370, 374-375
Nirvana a high, 593
not the 'Great Day', 372, 373-374
previous life and, 624-625
reward in, for diseases from parents, 583
sleep compared to, 591
soul not limited in, 45
speedy rebirth without, 602
a temporary state, 25, 45, 542, 589-591, 595-596
unmerited suffering and, 596
wicked people have no, 580, 596
Devachanee *(Devachani)*

blissful state of, 25, 45, 589, 591, 595-600
consciousness of 3 higher principles in, 589-590
not conscious of time, 24-25, 589
Osirified, 377
on reincarnation of, 599-603, 621
time in Devachan for, 596
Devil
came from West, 364-365
humans worst sort of, 509
pillar of Christian religion, 492
Dhyani(s) *(Sk.)*
Ah-hi as highest, 28
a generic name, 102
Dhyani-Buddhas *(Sk.)*
destiny of, 100-101
distinct class of celestial beings, 95, 98, 100, 102
divine freewill and, 276
endless hierarchy of, 176
a hierarchy of spirit, 98, 100-102
on higher plane than Manus, 174
not Manus, 176
once were human, 101
as ruler or supervisor, 175
seven classes esoterically, 100, 102, 176
Seventh Round incarnation, 101-102
Dhyan(i)-Chohans [Chohan *(Tib.)*]
celestial beings, 95, 158
color or sound manifested by, 391
Cosmic Consciousness and, 499-500
dematerialize ideas about, 640
on emanation of, 379
finite beings, 198, 380
generic name, 95, 99-100, 102-103, 168, 169
highest know only our solar system, 198
man's potential same as, 325
not Dhyani-Buddhas, 168
pre-human 100-101, 158

reflect Divine Mind into all Kingdoms, 166-169, 289
related to Mahat, 158, 167
relation to Fohat, 290, 349
secret names in geometry, 305-306
will dissolve in time, 198

Differentiation
beginning of, 270-272
light & darkness of matter, 60, 210-211, 269, 270-272, 429, 430-431
not all Manvantaras have same, 484
of planes from conscious beings, 429-430
sexless on first plane, 140, 155
in space, 60, 140, 193, 210
as 'war in heaven', 210-211

Directions, Four
influences described, 364-365
occult meanings, 365-367

Disease(s)
can be septenary, 486
karma of, 437, 583-584
of mental passions, 355

Divine
dynasties of King instructors, 295-297
free will, 276
hierarchies and Third Logos, 296-297
as inherent force, 275

Divine Ideation *see also* **Ideation; Mahat**
Absoluteness is not, 331-332
alone enters Nirvana, 373, 374, 375
Astral Light a reflection of, 157-159
bearer of Absolute memory, 372, 375
is Buddhi, 413
first flutter of manifestation, 271, 332-333
Lipika and, 327
Plato on, 413
Potency and Potentiality of, 635
universal mind above, 363

Divine Mind *see also* **Mind**
Absoluteness and, 158
aspects of, 135
Fohat represents, 290
Mahat and, 20, 635
Manas part of, 562
numbers & geometrical forms in, 311

Divine Thought
of arupa world, 164-166
Astral Light distorts, 164-165
becomes seven planes, 271, 635
everything exists in, 158
Fohatic impress of, 134
Plato called, eternal idea, 271
prototypes of forms in, 164, 271

Dogma
danger of making, of teachings, 639-640

Dragon
in Christian prophecy, 491
dogma about Satan as, 492
Initiates as sons of, 494
mystic & occult meanings of, 491-492, 494
Primordial Seven and, of Wisdom, 331

Dramard, Louis
T.S. lodge President, 603&fn

Dream(s)
cerebellum active in, 41, 51-54, 55-57
consciousness of brain in, 51-54, 55-56, 58
deeper conceptions in, 263
Devachan a vivid, 589
dreamless sleep and, 77, 79
Karma can be generated by, 78-79
no conception of time in, 22, 25, 42
reconstruction of, 54

Du Prel, Baron Carl
experiments in consciousness, 56
German philosopher, 56fn

Duration *see also* **Eternity**
'Eternity' is not, 10

Logos and Time, 153-156, 158
Time compared with, 12-14, 21-22, 24, 42, 153-156, 227
Duty(ies)
alotted, for cells even, 175
to help others, 586
of Manu, 172
of Terrene Pitris, 444
of true Theosophist, 523, 524, 532-533
Dzyu *(Tib.)*
becomes Fohat, 337

E

Earth
atmosphere a crucible, 408-409
changes elements of meteors, 409, 410
Dhyani-Buddhas will incarnate on, 101-102
element, 112-113, 181, 376, 404-405
Gnostics on builders of, 160
is Hell, 483
lunar kama-rupa and, 396, 397, 419-420
magnetic currents and, 464
Malkuth or, 43, 114, 150
Manu is beginning of, 172-173
is materialized vapor, 518
meteors attracted to, 407, 409
Milky Way matter differs from our, 223-224
moon is parent of, 176, 230, 397, 418-419, 475
moon swept in, current, 462
moon's effect on, 318-319, 399, 404, 408, 419-420, 423
not a sacred planet, 95, 96, 518-519, 520
planetary spirit of, not very high, 98-99
principles of, 473
protyle not on, 3
ocean of vitality around, 422-423
rotary motion and, 462-464
solar ceremonies and, 216
soul needs, and water, 181
spirit of, is Jehovah, 473
stages of material transformation, 517-518
sterility of, due to man, 474
Sun and, as substitutes, 398
transfers principles in Seventh Round, 519
is very young planet, 230
Earth Chain
dawn of new, 444
formed later than other chains, 404, 405
globes developed before monads arrive, 476-477
on globes of, development, 465-467, 517-518
higher globes of, non-molecular, 202, 518-519
manvantaric change for, 342, 404-406, 444-445
moon transfers principles to, 418-419, 465-477
obscuration of, 292
Planetary Spirit rules, 95
produced from dying moon, 396-397, 418-419
Rounds or rings of, 396-397
six companion globes of, 95-96
three highest planes not part of, 148
East
good comes from, 364
Egg *see also* **Ovum**
Brahmā born in golden, 20
Eternal, 133-134, 181
golden, has seven skins, 20
hen &, analogy for Causeless Cause, 72, 270

Luminous, same as Radiant Essence, 200
is magnetic aura, 371
Mundane, periodical, 134
point is germ in Mundane, 129-131, 132, 134
Solar, 131
triangle in Mundane, manifested Logos, 129, 130-131
Universal, beyond terrestrial, 131, 133
Universal, indestructible, 133
Virgin, is differentiated, 181

Ego(s) *see also* **Incarnating Ego**
of child conscious at 7 or 8 years, 558-559
Devachan and 45, 562, 590-591, 592
freed at death, 44-45
individuality is reincarnating, 565
karmic development of, 562
Manas is incarnating, 562, 564-565, 593
Manas reflected by, and intellect, 561
is Manasic not astral, 564
Manvantaric period of, 593
of men, once elementals, 447
must reincarnate, 45
omniscient at two points, 562, 600
overshadowed by Atma-Buddhi, 625, 628-629
as rays of Mahat, 594

Egyptian(s)
on creative Logos, 155
Devil came from West, 364
divine dynasties of, 296
on, Isis & other gods, 416
knew astronomy, 401
Space and Neith of, 1-2

Egyptologist(s)
search for Great Pyramid chambers, 219-222

Ehyeh asher Ehyeh *(Heb.)*
"I am that I am," 23

Eightfold Path
is seven ways to bliss, 47

Electricity
is atomic, 353
an entity, 238-239
Fohat and, 135, 240, 290, 293-294, 349, 388, 404, 416-417
is not Fohat, 238, 240
life and, 138-139, 293
a modified condition of one force, 268-269
molecular principle, 238, 239, 243
mother of all forces, 293-294
never acts in straight line, 359
occult axiom concerning, 232
real furnace of solar system and, 254
Sun's forces not common, 227-228
unpolarized, rays from Second Logos, 417

Element(s)
all, have 7 states of density, 571-572
on chemical combinations of, 409-411
chemical, of science, 205-209, 352-353
on correlation of, 112-118, 241, 247, 403-406, 409-410, 411, 572
as deities, 258, 259
fifth, yet to be, 258, 261
Kosmic, are beyond solar system, 178
meteors and, 421
not elementals, 178-179
nomenclature of, 8
One, in nature, 112-115, 117-118, 223, 572
primordial, vary on every plane, 241, 404-405, 572
recombine on globe chain, 404
related to races, 258, 261
of science, 8, 115, 241,
seven, in Occultism, 180, 571-572
three higher, unknown, 115
three primordial, 503-504

universal, as noumena of terrestrial, 178, 353
water as, 178, 179, 180
Elemental(s)
animate plant kingdom, 168
astral prototypes and, 169
Buddhi of Earth and, 473
danger to mediums, 179
elements are not, 178-179
evolve into animals etc., 169, 447
intelligent forces, 179
man's relation to, 169-170
matter issues types of, 179
as nature spirits, 179
seven classes of monads and, 465
Sixth Race and highest, 446-447
three sub, kingdoms, 439
Elohim *(Heb.)*
defined, 149
numerical meaning, 304-305
Sephirot same as, 304
Emanation(s)
Æons are, of Absolute, 333
Ah-hi and, 28
bad, of Astral, 41
of Earth saturates Moon, 457, 462
of electricity, 349
First Cause as unconscious, 70
First Logos and, 551
Fohat an, 240
Gnostic system of, 323-324
magnetism of Earth, 365-366
no, from Absolute, 1, 154
of primordial principle, 323-324
and radiation, 156-157
of Seventh Round, 101
Energy(ies) *see also* **Force(s)**
conservation of, 361
as electric force, 388
Fohat and, 417-418
as rays or breath, 392
as state of matter, 388
English

diseased parents weaken, nation, 583-584
injustice of, in India, 510-511
language limited, 11, 24, 31, 39, 70, 147-148, 156
Stanzas cannot be expressed in Macaulean, 337
universities, 87
Episcopal Church(es)
rites of, pagan in origin, 161, 162
Eros *(Gr.)*
degraded into Cupid, 503-504
as Divine creative force, 503
or Lucifer as light, 505
Esoteric Instructions
correspondences in, 307
on pursuit of, 273
Esoteric Section
includes Masons, 151-152
instruction for members of, 273&fn
Eternal(ly)
Absoluteness is, 556
Æons not, 10
causeless cause is one, Law, 553
Divine ideation is & is not, 375, 635
Duration is, 22, 154
Ever-Darkness is, 130, 194
gods are periodical not, 135
idea of Plato, 271
invisible deity is, 75
Law of periodicity, 396
Laya centres are, 414
light or universal fire, 505
Manas is, stem, 562
Matri-Padma is, 134
matter or substance is, 405, 419
motion is, fire, 232
Nitya Pralaya is, 292-293
no, male or female principles, 132
one essence, 12
One Life is, 611
Parabrahm is, 70
primordial matter is, 272

rotation of 'world-stuff', 229
Space is, 193
war in heaven going on, 210
Eternal Parent
Boundless Space, 1-3, 60
Parabrahman and, 1-3
Eternity(ies)
Ancients had no, 10-12
Duration and, 10-12, 15, 335
Duration is one real, 13
Great Breath in, 140, 345-346, 462
illusion of, 335
Pralaya and, 10
serpent of, 515
Seven, 1, 9, 11
Seventh, 154
swan of, 237
three elements coexist in, 503-504
Ether
Akasha and, 157, 258-259, 261
Akasha's lowest form, 202-203
Astral light of Kabbalist, 260
between planes, 404
born of motion, 232
celestial fire and, 259
as dual, 258-259
future Manvantara state, 202
gradations of density & purity, 404, 406
Keely's force as, 248, 249
midway in subjective universe, 258, 260
in motion is heat, 232
not accepted by science, 249
only molecular in gross matter, 202
of science, 202, 258-259, 260-261
is universal, 258
universal flame and, 117-118
we are crystallized, 202
European(s)
mind not ready for seven-fold division, 627
not trained in metaphysics, 170, 426

poor languages, 5, 11, 39, 418, 613, 626
Evolution
aeriform transformation and, 518
Ah-hi begin work of, 28
Astral Light and, 159
Buddhi and, 592-593
complete only at final Pralaya, 477
involution and, 275
Manu and, of humanity, 172-173
no chance, of forms, 311
nuclei velocity and, 511-512
rate of, and karmic law, 438
sequence of globe, 572-573
struggle for existence and, 506-507
three schemes of, & perfect man, 440-441
of universe like that of fetus, 558
Eye(s)
of Dangma, 75-76,
as physical sense, 86, 159
real Sun cannot be seen by, 314
sight and sound, 85-87
spiritual, 77

F

Fanaticism
danger of, 615
egotism & vanity of, 615
Fatalism
in East & Muslim, 586-587
Karma is not, 586-589
Father
anthropomorphized by West, 65
concealed, as unmanifested Logos, 2-3
fire stands for, 266
Father-God
as unmanifested Logos, 2-3, 2
Father-Mother
relates to solar & objective universe, 37-38

seven-skinned, 2, 20
Son and, are One, 61-63, 65
-Son is manifested Logos, 2-3
symbolized, 2, 20, 21, 37, 65, 257, 266
synonymous with Third Logos, 301
Fawcett, Edward Douglas
English metaphysical journalist, 35fn
helped with *S.D.*, 35&fn, 75
Felix, Minucius *see* **Minucius Felix**
Fetahil (Phetahil) *(Gnos.)*
represents Lunar Pitris, 485
Fire(s) *see also* **Element(s), Sons of Fire**
Atma corresponds to, on seventh plane, 248
ether and, 180, 232
is ether born of motion, 232
father of light, 227
as Fohat, electricity or vital force, 404
forty-nine, of Kosmos, 226-227, 480
Gnostic hierarchies emanate from, 323, 324
of Life, 117, 226, 232-233, 266, 298
most mystic element, 226, 227, 233
occult meaning, 40, 117, 226-227, 232-233, 247-248, 266
shoreless sea of, 237
solar, 227
as spirit matter, 236, 505
Sun is not furnace of system but, 254
symbol of deity, 300, 333
universal deity, 232, 233, 298, 505
will become Pho, 248
worshippers and, 233
First Cause *see* **Cause**
First Logos *see* **Logos**
Five Years of Theosophy
Mrs. Morgan writes on witchcraft in, 451fn
Sinnett question on moon ignored in, 436&fn
Flame(s)

father's seed like a, 559
Nirvana and, 327, 393
one, of life, 117
rays from, 40
seven rays and, of beings, 110
Simon Magus on, 324
on Spirit of the, 240-241
of Sun are nerves of system, 231, 254
symbol of deity, 300
Flammarion, Camille
French astronomer, 282fn
Sinnett quotes, 282
Flea Circuses
display animal intelligence, 17&fn
Flower(s)
Sun, considered pious, 168
Fohat ('pho-ba) *(Tib.)*
abodes of, 514
aspect of Divine Mind, 135, 138, 289-290
bipolar & dual action of, 360, 463
changes every Manvantara, 351
cohesive force, 349
collective radiation of 7 sons, 412, 416-417
as cosmic force, 280, 286, 288, 289, 290-291, 463
creates and destroys, 360
an entity, 135, 238, 349-350
etymology, 138-139
as Fiery Whirlwind, 348, 349, 351
Fohatic principle and, 135
as formless thought power, 381
joins atoms or sparks, 351
as knot-tie-er, 251, 252
a later manifestation, 64, 134-135, 158
Laya point and, 413, 418
life principle, 349
not electricity, 238, 240, 293-294
not exactly energy, 417-418
potency of being or Sat, 139
real 'translation' of, 418

relation to Hierarchy, 381, 611
root and soul of motion, 349
runs circular errands, 337
seven sub-logoi and, 240, 381, 412-413
sons of, and, 412, 413, 415-416, 417
spiral action of, 357-358
swift Son of the Divine sons, 337
synthesis of primordial seven, 135-136, 349, 412
term used many ways, 64, 135
thread of primordial light, 227, 230
universal force, 289, 416-417
universal matter and, 388-389
unpolarized electricity, 416, 417, 418

Force(s) *see also* **Energy**
all, move in spirals, 358
of Divine Mind, 135
dual nature of, 268-269, 275, 281, 286, 387-388, 463
electrical nature of, 387
expansion and contraction, 275-276
free, or will, 281, 288-289
imprisoned or inherent, 269, 275, 276, 281, 286-287, 293, 463
is matter on our plane, 387-389
never acts in straight line, 359-360
noumenal & phenomenal, 39-40, 165
occultism on, 269-270, 358-359, 387-390
persistence of, 287
of renovation in destruction, 360, 383
science on extra-cosmic, 280, 287
seven, of Nature, 111
or Shakti of Divine, 135
source of physical, 164, 165, 286-287
as transformation, 360-361, 387-389
unity of, 283
universal, 269-270, 388-390
universal, not a conscious, 281, 288, 289, 293

"unknowable", of Spencer, 287

Foreign Words
Blavatsky tries to avoid, 11, 24
some, don't translate into English, 24, 39, 156

Form(s)
cannot express formless, 71, 372
disrupted atoms go from, to formless, 290
as germ in acorn has many, 165
prototypes of, 165
Reality has no, 150
Void has no, 60&fn

Formless
Ah-hi are, 37
first body of man was, 177
Fohat as, thought power, 381
Monad and, worlds, 195
universe as, space, 192

Four *see also* **Tetragrammaton**
in cube, 142-143
as material plane, 145
noble truths, 47
in plane square, 143, 144, 145
in pyramid, 142-143, 144, 145
in Pythagorean geometry, 142-143
as sacred number, 144-145
squaring circle, 143
as tetraktys, 143, 144, 151

Free Will
Ah-hi has no, 38
conscious or unconscious, 617-619
Karma and, 586-589
man has, 38
plants have, 168

Frog
according to science, 126

Froude, James Anthony
biographer of Carlyle, 633fn

Fullerton, Alexander
American Theosophist, 248&fn
views on Keely, 248

G

Gaia (Gæa) *(Gr.)*
female aspect of Chaos, 504
G.A.O.T.U.
or Grand Architect of the Universe, 99-100, 500
Universal Mind and, 100
Gas
comet's tail and, 344
flammable hydrogen, 235
perception of occult element in, 116-117
Gautama Buddha *see* **Buddha**
Genesis
'days' of, 511-12
on light, 156&fn
Lipika saying and, 362
Tetragrammaton in, 149
on the void, 60&fn, 237
Geometry
occult Pythagorean, 142, 143-145, 309-310
of Plato, 309
sacred science, 317
Germ(s)
as eternal abstract Space, 192
as First Logos, 193
noumenal and phenomenal, 165
physical, in Astral Light, 165
as point in circle, 193
as point is everywhere, 133
potency in Mundane Egg, 128-134
in primordial triangle, 191, 192
prototype in, 165
Second Logos and, 130
triangle as, 131
German
on, term sein, 24
Globe(s) *see also* **Earth Chain**
atmosphere of, alter elements, 404-405
birth of new, 444-445, 517-519
Builders of, cannot interfere with Karma, 570
correspond to principles, 432
during Pralaya, 291-292, 382, 444
each, has 7 principles, 472-474
on egos of departed, 445
evolution of, 517-519
fire of highest, 233
germinal & fiery stages of, 518
kama-rupic state of our, 572-573
Lipika and, A, 328
little Manvantara of, 176
obscuration of, 382, 383
of our & other chains concealed, 430
our, not of universal substance, 434
passage of life-wave forms, 396-398
Planetary Spirit watches over, 95, 100-103
Sacred Animals and, 571
seven, on four planes, 431-432
Sishta remain on, during Pralaya, 442-446
three pairs out of seven, 7, 432
Gnostic(s) *(Gr.) see also* **Codex Nazaræus**; **Kabbalist(s)**
Chaldean, and Kabbalistic code, 499&fn
cosmogony on 'Seven Stellars', 492
on middle space, 160
Pistis Sophia a, text, 160fn
on Sophia Achamoth as builders, 160
system cp. to Sanskrit, 323-324
God(s) *see also* **Theogony(ies)**
androgynous, 259
anthropomorphized, 199, 297, 395
Apollo & Bacchus Sun, 216
of Bible, 60, 149, 160, 199, 237, 308, 362
born through immaculate source, 139-141
destroyer, highest of three, 105
Dhyan-Chohans more than personal, 198

in Egyptian & Indian cosmogonies, 416
Eros first-born of, 503
ether and two aspects of, 259
every, linked to star or planet, 400
fallen angels as, 483
fire as, 232
first self-conscious, 227
idolatry limits, 103, 104
impersonal, 103, 269-270, 281, 288-289, 309, 576
on Jewish, 473, 485
land of, 516
Law or, geometrizes, 311
as Lawgiver, 215, 309
manvantaric, not infinite, 394
are many, 103-104, 400-401
not immortal, 135, 395
ocean churned by, 209-211
personal, 360, 376
planetary spirit a kind of, 95
Platonic meaning of, 309
prayers to, 103-104
as rays emanating from Absolute, 309
repented he made man, 362
sky & sun as, 215
soul of baby and, 469
on spirit of, 329, 502
tribal worship of, 103
under karmic law, 166-167
war of, and asuras, 211
within, 104

Goethe, Johann Wolfgang von
Faust on roaring loom of time, 261

Golden Egg
Brahmā born in, 20, 201
of the world, 20
radiant essence or Luminous, 200-201

Gonzaga, St. Aloysius
Italian Jesuit, 615&fn

Gospel
fourth, Platonic, 308

light as first term in, 158

Gravity
another force than, 268
astronomical view of, 277, 278
as attraction & repulsion, 234, 344, 506
comets defy, 234, 343-345
not immutable law, 318
occult, not Newtonian, 234, 505-506
planetary motion and, 278, 279

Great Breath
always in motion, 312
ceaseless, 10
motion during Pralaya, 10, 312
thrills through Space, 140

Greek
language and words, 5, 10-11
no word for eternity in, 10-11

Greenland
once tropical, 516

'Grundy, Mrs.'
as public opinion, 88

H

Haeckel, Ernst
astral forms glimpsed by, 447
German biologist, 268fn
on matter, 268

Hall, Fitzedward
editor & Orientalist, 254&fn

Hamadryads *(Gk.)*
as spirits of trees, 167

Hamilton, Sir William
Scot metaphysician, 8&fn, 43

Happiness
of Devachan, 599
faith in karma gives, 527-528
Parabrahma has no, 598
suffering needed for, 39, 597, 604

Harper's Magazine
story on castaway, 88

Harrison, Frederic
English Positivist, 552fn
Spencer &, debate on 'Unknowable', 552-553
on 'Unknown' of, 552-554, 556-557
Harte, Richard
helped with *S.D.*, 112
Hartmann, Eduard von
German philosopher, 120fn, 121
Hartmann, Franz
undines seem real to, 179
on Keely's force magnifying objects, 401
wrote on creatures of elements, 179fn
Hearing *see* **Sense(s)**
Heart
beating of, and evolution, 619
once not automatic, 619
Sun has invisible, of system, 231
Heat
atoms disrupted by, 290
as centers of force, 281, 283-285
Fohat and, 290-291
as matter in motion, 283-84
occultism on, 283-284, 290, 291
Heaven *see also* **War in Heaven**
biblical view of, 210, 215
in cosmogonical allegory, 211
differentiation as war in, 210-211
fall of man from, 210
Sophia Achamoth on middle, 160
Sun as Most High in, 215
Hebrew
on Alhim, 304
anagrammatic terms in, 305
'I am' of, Jehovah, 23
numerical values of, 217
symbolic, mistranslated, 149
wisdom of, initiates, 498
Helioscope
colors reduced by, 90-91
Hell
descent of Christ, Hercules *et al* into, 483, 485
as human body, 483, 491
Helmholtz, Hermann von
German physicist, 228&fn
Hen and egg
analogy, 72
Hercules *(Lat.) (Herakles) (Gr.)*
descent into hell allegory of, 483
Heredity
of child and race, 583-584
higher principles not from, 561
intellect and 561
a Karmic effect, 563-564, 568-569
Hermes Trismegistus *(Gr.)*
on Divine Thought, 635
Herschel, William
astronomer, 96fn
planet discovery by, 96-97
Hesiod *(Gr.)*
on Chaos, Eros & Gaia, 503
on Chaos as birth of universe, 502-504
on land of the gods, 516
Hierarchy(ies)
of celestial, incarnated, 297, 482
celestial, of Dhyani-Chohans, 608-609
correspond to forces in nature, 608, 609
creators in future Manvantara, 482-483
of fire Chohans, 296
intuition only can perceive, 612-613, 640
Kumaras as sons of Divine, 482
seven, of 7 elements, 296, 608-609
Hierophants (Hierophantes) *(Gr.)*
as Sons of the fire mists, 297
Hinayana *(Sk.)*
Buddhist precepts and, school, 46-47
Hindu(s)
astronomical knowledge of, 400, 488-489

chronology of Manvantara, 467-469, 488-489
correct about the Sun, 320
cosmogony, 2, 4, 20-21, 488
language disfigured, 5
on Maya, 49
not inferior, 510-511
Pleiades seen by, 400, 401
poem on Pralaya, 10
schools vary, 4-5, 20-21
seven day week of, 467-468
tables of moon's motion accurate, 400
Trinity of, is one 360-361

Hippolytus, St.
——— *Philosophumena*
Gnostic ideas of Simon Magus, 324&fn

Hofmann, Josef
musical prodigy, 563fn, 567, 624

Holy Ghost
Mary and, 140

Horus *((Eg.)*
Isis and, 416
as Second Logos, 155

Humanity(ies)
all, becomes Devas or Buddhas, 101, 102, 169
angels incarnate in, 216, 491
bodies of, are Hell, 491
born from Manu, 172, 176
ever perfecting, 6
Fifth Race civilization as cancer of, 476
on first, 177
higher principles of, not hereditary, 561
Lipikas and, 327
lowest point not reached yet, 475-476
Nirmanakayas help, 445-446
is Parabrahm, 554
separateness and, 303
sins & joys of, affect Earth, 474

on Sishta or Seed, 442-443
teachers of nascent, 295
wickedness of, 476, 509

Huxley, Thomas Henry
dogmatic scientist, 127-128
English biologist, 58&fn
hypothetical science of, 120, 125, 127, 128

Hydrogen
chemical analysis of, 112-115
occult correspondences, 113-115
protyle as pre-, 6

Hyle *(Gk.)*
protyle derived from word, 6-7
as root of matter, 7

Hylo-Idealism
distorted views of, 7, 14

Hypnotism
can kill, 79
transubstantiation and, 116

I

"I am that I am"
Ehyeh asher Ehyeh (Heb.), 23

Ibn Gabirol, Solomon
Chaldean Kabalah and, 499
wrote as 'Ben Judah', 499

Ice
element perceived as, 112

Idea(s)
on eternal, or Divine Thought, 271, 635
man has, animals do not, 57
no, of time in Devachan, 25
precipitate into thought, 185
rejection of personal god, 103-104
thoughts cp. to, 184-186
training needed for metaphysical, 170

Ideation *see also* **Divine Ideation;**
Mahat
cosmic mind differs from universal, 30-31, 33

during Pralaya, 27-28
self, worthless, 159
Idolatry
objections to, 103-104
Illusion *see also* **Maya**
Astral Light an, 158-159
Nirvana is, 50
reality is, 50
of separateness, 298, 303
Immaculate conception
139, 140-141
Inaction
life of, worse than action, 587
Inanimate
no such thing as, or inorganic, 244-245, 246
Incarnating Ego(s)
Ah-Hi and, 37&fn
is Atma & Buddhi, 627-629
collects experiences, 593
is Jiva or fifth principle, 549
mind or Manas is, 562, 565, 593, 614, 621, 628-629
India(n)
contempt for 'inferior races' of, 510-511
cosmogony on Second Logos, 155
Inductive Method *see also* **Deductive Method**
examples of, 641
HPB urges students to drop, 73, 610
science relies on, 641-642
Infanticide
always a crime, 560
Hindus misuse of, 559-560
Infinite
no attributes for, 15
space as, 14-15
Inorganic
nothing, in this world, 245, 246-247
Intellect(s)
ant has more, 18

as brain conceptions, 15
limitations of, 15-16, 68, 71, 198, 257, 272, 612
lower principles and, 145
man endowed with, 216
other, on our plane, 16
rely on, of ancient sages, 119
states of consciousness, 16
train the, 73
Intelligence(s)
animal & insect, 16-17, 18-19
in atoms, 276
Devachan and, 371
differentiation evolves, 179
human, 15-16, 18
in Kabalah, 102, 144
Karma is absolute, 576
Lipika & universal, 337
in plants, 168
of Spirit of the Earth, 473
three higher, 379-380
universal, and Manas, 363, 600
Universe immersed in, 610
Intuition
facts in flashes of, 121-122
in Manas, 620-621
not unconscious cerebration, 622
as recollection, 614
scientific, 121-122
as spiritual understanding, 612, 613
students must develop, 612-613, 640
'Invisible that is'
eternal, present deity, 75
Iron
differs on every plane, 430, 431
essence of, 406
molecular structure alters, 205-206
not an element, 205-208
Ishwara (Iswara) *(Sk.)*
not highest Logos, 20
Subba Row's view of, 20
Isis *(Gr.)* (Issa) *(Eg.)*
Osiris and, 155, 416

Second Logos as, 155
wife and mother, 416
IT
  Absoluteness is, 73
  forces emanating from, 69
  Nirvana is, 393
  no attributes for, 73
  nothing proceeds from, 1, 73
  Parabrahman as, 2
  perpetual motion in, 69

J

Jacob
  twelve sons of, & zodiac, 217-218
Jadoo *(Hindi)*
  conjurer's magic, 78
Jains *(Sk.)*
  Indian Theosophists, 530
  plead for life of cobras, 530
  sublime harmlessness of, 530-531
Jason
  and Argonauts fable, 520-521
  Golden Fleece alchemy and, 521
Jehovah *(Heb..)*
  Binah in Kabalah, 102
  as Cain, 149, 150
  Earth spirit is, 473
  God is not, 149-150
  Hebrew mistranslation of, 149
Jesus *see also* **Christ**
  blasphemy of, 141, 162
  Church cant about, 162
Jew(s) *see also* **Kabalah**
  calculate days by moon, 489
  Gabirol very great man, 123
  never had a 'week', 489
  Ophites on God of, 473
Jiva(s) *(Sk.)*
  Atma and, are one, 625-626
  as incarnating ego, 549
  incarnating individualities, 557
  fifth principle in E.S., 549

Indian schools vary on, 549
'lives' are, 551
not Monads, 557
not personalities, 557
as One life, 109, 551
one Universal principle, 551
not Monad, 549-551
Prana compared to, 550-551, 631
Jivatma *(Sk.)*
  Anima Mundi, 109
  pervades everywhere, 110, 201
  Universal Soul, 109, 201
Jod-he-vah (Yod-he-va) *(Heb.) see also*
Jehovah
  or man, 149
Johnstown Flood
  dam break as collective Karma, 581-582
  as unmerited suffering, 581
Joshua
  paraphrased, 104&fn
Judge, William Q.
  Bhagavad-Gita of, cited, 299
  defends T.S., 540&fn
  edited *Path* magazine, 539fn
Jupiter *(Lat.)*
  dual capacity of, moons, 427
  Earth compared to, 99

K

Kabalah (Kabbalah) *(Heb.)*
  Ain-Soph as Boundless in, 2, 50
  anagrammatic values in, 305
  Angelic names in, 107
  Book of Numbers as real, 498
  Chaldean, has Eastern system, 498
  on four recording angels, 326
  Gnostic view of, 160
  of de Leon & Rosenroth cp. 498-499
  on Logos, 329
  on Malkuth, 43
  mathematical key to, 139&fn, 144,

145, 217-219
  numerical value of man in, 217
  only 7 lower Sephiroth used, 498
  permutations in, 304-305
  S.D. explains, 123
  on Sephiroth, 107-108, 465
  Tetragrammaton in, 144-145, 147-152
  three methods to interpret, 304
  on Torah, 2
  Triad as 3 higher planes, 102, 144
  triune monad of, 438
  worlds of, cp. to occult, 328
  zodiac signs as sons of Jacob, 217-218
Kabalists (Kabbalists)
  on Astral Light, 157
  Gnostics on text of, 160
  Occultists agree with, 51, 123
  on Ruach & Nephesh, 482
  Skinner as extraordinary, 218
Kala *(Sk.)*
  as periodical time, 155-156
Kalahansa (or Hamsa) *(Sk.)*
  dark swan of eternity, 237
Kama-loka (Kamaloka) *(Sk.)*
  attracted to séance room, 589
  danger of spiritualism and, 580-581
  lower principles fade out in, 371-372
  only man's shadow, 580-581
  of personal ego, 371, 373
  reflections or spooks in, 589
Kama-rupa (Kamarupa) *(Sk.)*
  of objects disturbed, 238, 240, 244
Kant, Immanuel
  agrees with occult views, 247
  not dogmatic, 247
Karma *(Sk.)*
  accidents not preordained, 588-589
  Adepts' help limited by, 446
  adjusts equilibrium, 578, 588
  affinities & heredity, 564
  apparent injustice and, 437
  astrological influences in, 493

  as cause & effect on moral plane, 574, 577, 578, 585, 588
  collective, 437, 581-582, 585, 587
  defined as action, 575-576, 578
  in dreams, 77-79
  from previous Manvantaras, 482
  gods under law of, 166
  heredity and, 583-584
  ignorance of, no excuse, 579
  incarnation caused by, 599-600
  law of retributive, 436-437, 575-579
  Nidanas and, 48
  no, created in Devachan, 579-582
  not fatalism, 586-589
  planes of action, 77-78, 575-576, 578, 584-585
  rate of evolution determined by, 438
  of refusing Chhayas, 481-482
  resumes after Devachan, 581
  suffering and, 581-585, 586
  taking, of another not possible, 583
  universal Law, 436-437, 575-577
  unmerited, 437, 581-583, 585, 596
  worse if deferred, 582-583
  worst, is giving diseases to children, 583-584
  yogis can avoid, 578
Keely, John Worrell
  discovered new energy, 248fn
  on etheric force as magnifier, 401-402
  inter-etheric ideas of, 248-249, 281, 401-402
  Lucifer article of, 463-364&fn
  on magnetic circulation of earth, 463-464
  neither occultist nor scientist, 248
  on Unity of forces, 463-464&fn
  yogis produce same force, 401
Kepler, Johannes
  German astronomer, 274fn
  on gravity as conflict of forces, 278-279
  laws of, 274, 277, 278-279

occultism and Third law of, 278-279
Kether (Keter) *(Heb.)*
  Chokhmah & Binah, 129, 131, 144, 438
  is Crown, 438
  point in Mundane Egg, 131
  in Sephirothal tree, 129, 131, 438
  Tetragrammaton and, 144
Khedive
  Egyptian ruler's title, 220fn
  HPB knew father & son Pashas, 220
Kosmic
  builders and Third Logos, 379
  dust and nebula same, 348
  quaternary, 477
  nebula is everywhere, 348
  not solar system, is infinite, 178
  phenomena as 'animated geometry', 232
  water as first, element, 178, 179
Kosmocratores *(Gr.)* see
Cosmocratores
Krishna *(Sk.)*
  as Hindu god, 104
Kuan (shih) yin (Kwan-(Shai-)Yin *(Chin.)*
  dual primordial deities, 235, 236
  symbolized by fire & water, 235
Kumara(s) *(Sk.)*
  as intellectual saviors, 482-483
  men can become, 482
  as 'rebellious angels', 482-483

L

Labre, St.
  devoured by vermin, 529-530&fn, 531
Language(s)
  in Adept-chela communication, 182
  on coining of, terms, 5
  of 'deaf & dumb', 183
  'from' vs. 'through', 140-141
  human, is poor, 70
  Sanskrit cp. to modern, 613
  soul, is unspoken, 613
  of Thought, 182, 183, 184
  words as symbols, 183-184
Lanka
  once part of Atlantis, 453
  Todas came from, 453
Laplace, Pierre-Simon
  French mathematician, 228&fn
  meteor theory of, 312
  planetary formation theories of, 229
  probability theory of, 228-229
  similarities to Occult theory, 230, 312
Latin
  Pistis Sophia in, 160
Law(s) *see also* **Kepler**
  Æons and immutable, 325
  against infanticide, 560
  against sick couples bearing children, 583-584
  Ah-hi and, 27, 38
  of analogy, 9, 136
  comets go against, 234
  of conservation of energy, 361
  Devachanic entity & Karmic, 559-560
  of diversity, 507
  Dyaus the, giver, 215
  of evolution and gods, 483
  Fohat has one, 281, 288-289
  geometrizes, 309-311
  gods all under karmic, 166-167
  Karma the absolute, 481, 482, 575-580
  no straight line in, of Nature, 359
  occultists do not believe in, of gravity, 343-344
  one eternal, 553
  of Nature, 309, 310, 311, 507, 546
  of periodical manifestation, 29, 80, 396

planetary spirit to watch, 101
of spiral motion, 358
Watchers commissioned by, 570
Laya *(Sk.)*
Alaya and, 108-109
Atman as, center, 460
center unseen & untouched, 424
centers and heat, 281
centers eternal and imperishable, 414, 460
centers undifferentiated, 419, 424
correspondences, 517-519
cosmic matter and, condition, 12, 424, 517-519
Father-Mother and, 63-64
First Logos and, 153
Karma, yogis and, state, 578
meaning, 7, 63, 264, 398, 414-415, 438
protyle and, 3, 5
rents in veil of Maya, 414
shoreless, limitless beyond, 379
state corresponds to atomic or ethereal, 518
a state not a figure, 398, 414, 415, 430-431
zero point and, 7, 63, 264, 271, 376, 379
Laya Point(s)
absolute memory only passes, 372-373
as absolute rest or non-motion, 412
between two planets, 422
differ from plane to plane, 430-431
each atom has a, 460
at gate of manifestation, 372-373, 424
infinite as absolute, 429
meteors and, 407, 408, 409-410
Nirvana and, 372-373
no differentiation beyond, 380-381, 414, 415, 419, 424
not matter or spirit, 379

only for planes of matter, 373
in ovum, 424
preserves equilibrium between planets, 404
as reflection of absolute motion, 412
septenary 'robe of destiny' and, 381
in seven planes of matter, 381, 429-430
at universal pralaya, 372-373
Levi, Eliphas
laughed at people, 151-152
pen name, 143&fn
Lewins, Dr. Robert
Hylo-Idealist, 7&fn
Leibniz, Gottfried
on atoms & monads, 133, 267
German polymath, 133fn
on monads of, 133, 267, 550, 551
——— *Monadologie* on ultimate unit, 133fn
Life *see also* **One Life**
electricity and, are one, 138-139
Fohat as, essence, 138-139
formless, a sublime notion, 643
Maha-manvantaric cycle of, & Light, 379
myriads of, and lives, 643
mystery of, 643
not endowed by parents, 560
reflection of One Life, 457, 643
septenary robe of 7 Sons of Light &, 379
a universal principle, 560, 643
Life-Wave
emanates its principles, 397
planetary passage of, 397
Life-Winds
esoteric correspondences, 307
intelligences, senses and, 306-307
Light *see also* **Life**
controls all nature, 232
darkness and, 60-61, 80-81, 227
first Divine, is radiation, 156, 227,

232
Logos and, 61
as radiant energies, 391-392
scale of vibrations and, 90
seven Sons of – and Life, 378-379
as time, 227
as transfer of particles, 391
wave & corpuscular theories of –
wrong, 392
Line(s)
no straight, in Occultism, 358-360, 366
in Pythagorean geometry, 142-144
Lipika *(Sk.)*
as four Maharajahs, 326
God in *Genesis* cp. to, 362
Gnostic Æons cp. to, 323-327
as Great Day Be With Us, 374-375
Karma and, 326
kosmos magnetic aura and, 371
Maharajahs, 367
on plane above ours, 328
Primordial Seven related to, 325-326, 337
as Recording Angels, 326, 327, 371, 374
'ring pass not' and, 375
as Sons of Fohat, 337
Sons of Mahat, 327, 337
Liquid(s)
solid & gas, 116-117
Logoi *(Gk.)*
Fohat and, 240
or highest Dhyanis, 28
as numbers, 329
seven, 110, 329
unity of seven, & Second Logos, 412-413, 417
Logos *(Gk.)*
Divine Thought or, 134
First and Second, cp., 194, 295, 308, 381
First, radiated seven primeval rays, 379
First, unmanifested, 2-3, 20-21, 61, 64, 129-131, 151, 155, 194, 233, 237, 295-296, 379
geometrical symbols of, 304-305
Logoi and, 329
male aspect of Alaya, 134
manifested, as triangle, 129-131
as movable speech, 308
no desire in First, 74
Second, manifested, 2-3, 20-21, 64, 130, 154-156, 295, 308, 381, 412-413
sees Mulaprakriti as veil, 4, 130
seven rays from manifested, 131
sons of the fire mists and, 295-296
as spirit of God, 237
Subba Row on, 378
Third, and subdivisions, 295-297, 379
Third, radiates 630
three, and Oeaohoo the younger, 235-236
unmanifested, as point in circle, 20-21, 129, 131
unmanifested, or First Cause, 70-71
Vach is female, 378
voice emanates, 329
Looking Glass
simile, 145, 159
Lotus
bud simile, 153, 155
as Matri-Padma, 129, 134
Lubbock, Sir John
16&fn
Lucifer *(Lat.)*
HPB editorial in, 510&fn
Kingsland article from, 639-643
Pistis Sophia translated in, 160fn
rites of ritualism in, 161&fn
Lucretius *(Lat.)*
cited, 125&fn
Lunar Pitris *(Sk.)*

Monads develop Chhayas of, 557-558
Monads from Moon Chain, 176, 465-468, 469-472
project Chhayas of men, 176-177, 466
seven distinct classes, 465-466, 469-472

M

Macaulay, Thomas B.
English writer, 337fn
Mackey, Sampson Arnold
——— *Mythological Astronomy of the Ancients Demonstrated* corrected by HPB 515-516
Macrocosm
man is microcosm of, 77, 268, 387, 413, 430, 558, 642
Manvantaric dawn and, 36
mind as microcosm of, 124, 268
seven principles in, 357
Magnet(s)
electro-, poles experiment, 422
Laya point illustrated by poles of, 422
Magnetism
atomic contagion of, 355
electricity and, 293-294, 422
a mesmeric power, 355
of preachers, 355-356
Salvation Army use of, 355
of South & North, 365-366
of Sun, 227-228
terrestrial, 366
terrestrial, aided by Sun, 422-423
tuning fork analogy of mass, 356
Maha Pralaya (Maha-Pralaya) *(Sk.)*
after cycle of existence, 372
at 'Great Day', 372-373
missing stanzas and, 137
new Maha-Manvantara after, 199
for whole Universe? 199

Maharajahs, Four
meaning of, 367
Mahat *(Sk.)*
absolute & universal, 308
Absolute of our Manvantara, 332-334
or Binah, 144
corresponds to Manas, 3, 363, 413
is differentiated consciousness, 158
Divine ideation and, 327, 352, 363, 413, 635
ever becoming, 332-333
Fohat and 7 sons of, 413
Fohat comes from, 138
in Gnostic system, cp., 324, 326, 327
higher human Manas, 308
Lipika as emanations from, 327, 328
Logos and, 20
Manasaputras linked to, 337
merges into All at Mahapralaya, 594
reflected in atoms, 352
seven prakriti come from, 4, 42
universal mind or intelligence, 43, 363, 594, 635
Malkuth (Malkut) *(Heb.)*
Bride of Heavenly Man, 43, 108
Tetragrammaton is, 150
Man(kind)
arrived at end of Third Race, 439-440
astral shapes and Third Round, 446
astrology and destiny of, 540-541
Atma & Buddhi cp. to First Logos, 633
begins at Fourth Round, 446, 468, 469-471, 507-508, 571
in Blake's system, 442
can alter Karma, 582-583, 586, 587-589
child's development mirrors Third Race, 557-558
at close of Seventh Round, 518-519
compared to animal, 18-19, 507-508
compared to atom, 268

consciousness in seven states, 441, 500-501
dwells in Divine World also, 169
equilibrium of a perfect, 440-441
evil predominates, 476
evolution of, until final Pralaya, 477
in Fifth Race now, 440
happiness for, not in material living, 526-527
highest manifestation of unknown essence, 554-555
immersed in Atma-Buddhi, 625
limit to spiritual progress of, 508
Manas and lower principles of, 569-570
Manu creates, 172
many consciousness states in, 500-501
as microcosm, 268, 430
needs to be co-worker with Nature, 496
new facility for each race of, 573
peace of mind as goal for, 526-528
perfect animal, 18-19, 507
potential septenary with manas, 439-440
principles of, as shadows, 169, 626
propagation of, from Chhayas, 176-177, 466, 478
responsibility increases in Fourth Round, 475-476
seven planes of perfection for, 441
seven-fold in E.S. philosophy, 626
sins and joys of, affect Earth, 474-475
Spirit of, becomes Absolute, 333
stage reached by Third & Fourth Race, 439-440, 443, 468, 469-471, 557-558
struggle for existence and, 507-508
ten stages of, 439
in three previous Rounds, 571
threefold evolution & perfect man, 440-441

triple division, 626-627
triple harmony needed by, 440-442
two vehicles of prana in, 479-480
universal consciousness and, 628-629

Manas *(Sk.)*
abstract ideas function of, 633
awakened, unifies all principles, 558, 559
carries spiritual qualities, 566-567
cosmic planes and, 35-36, 363, 496
developed fully at end of Fifth Race, 566
discerning faculty of higher, 496
Divine Mind reflected in Man, 562-563
dual only on this plane, 569
during sleep, 41-42
incarnating Ego is, 628
incarnation of in Third Race, 439-440
intuition belongs to, 620-621, 626
link to Divine Monad, 281
Mahat corresponds to, 3, 363
not fully developed yet, 440
omniscient as a principle, 561
parents not responsible for, 569-570
personality and, 566-567
spiritual consciousness and, 496
as Sutratman, 562, 565, 566
Third Logos and, 633
thought and, 620
is universal, 569
vehicle of Buddhi, 42-43

Manas, Higher
Buddhi sheds light on, 614, 620-621
desire becomes thought in, 308
moments of higher vision from, 600-601
is reincarnating ego, 621-623, 628
storehouse of past experiences, 622-623
vehicle of Buddhi, 628

Manas, Lower

desire impulse of, 308
Earth has, 473
kama-rupa or, 433-434, 565
Manas radiates toward, 569
mission of Buddhi and, 614
reflection from higher mind, 569
Manasa-Dhyanis *(Sk.)*
are Ah-hi, 43
Manasaputra(s) *(Sk.)*
Ah-hi and, 37-38
linked to Mahat, 337
Son of Wisdom, 600
Manasa-Rupa *(Sk.)*
Ah-hi and, 37
Manifestation(s)
of cosmic mind, 30
'Darkness' is opposite of, 60-61
Divine ideation is first, 332-333
Fohat is a, 64, 135, 294
on illusion of, 237, 270-273, 426, 429-430
of Law, 29
Laya centers no, 414
Mahat the third, 20
mind is, universal mind is not, 33
of Monad, 438
Mother Goddess is first, 2
Mundane Egg and, 133-134
no, for Absolute, 49
non-, and, 213-214, 270, 271-274
planes of, 213, 270-274, 429-430
Svabhavat is, 301
symbol of root or first, 144, 349
Manu(s) *(Sk.)*
Brahmā, Rishi or, 105-106
contains all forms, 172
creates humanity, 172
derivation of term, 172
differentiation and, 173-174, 175, 210, 378
duty to watch over planet & rounds, 105, 172
each Manvantara has a, 172, 173

former, no direct action on present, 570
fourteen, in minor Manvantara, 177, 210
mankind issues from, 172-173, 175
men in prior Manvantaras, 482
Root and Seed, 172, 177, 210
Seven, 105, 172, 378
unity of consciousness, 172-174, 175
on universal plane, 173
Manushi Buddha *see* **Buddha**
Manvantara(s) *(Sk.)*
absolute mind and, 27-28
Absoluteness & change in, 332-334, 632-633
Ah-hi and, 36-37
Alaya and end of, 109
analogous to waking state, 12
Astral Light changes with, 158
between two Manus, 177
comet stage is first in, 513
cosmic ideation only during, 33
days and nights of, 9, 468
deities free of rebirth during a, 429
Dhyani-Buddhas from previous, 100
ethers alters in future, 202-203
evolution & dawn of, 36, 210, 230, 265, 632-633
in Hindu chronologies, 467-469
immutable cause of, 67-68
invisible deity and past, 75
length not revealed, 177-178, 467-468
Luminous Sons of, dawning, 110
Manas at end of, 566-567
Milky Way begins at dawn of, 230
minor and major, 177, 377, 382-383
planetary cp. with solar, 382
potentiality of past, present & future, 632-633
Pralaya at Seventh Round and, 512-513
seven as root basis of this, 485-486

seven kinds of, 178
seven periods of, 9, 468, 473
seven planes of matter emanate in, 429
seven rounds equal our, 176, 177, 377, 465-471
spiritual progress limited to this, 508
Sun becomes a comet in next, 254
war in heaven and, 210
Marcion
a Gnostic, 160
Mariette-Bey, Auguste
French Egyptologist, 222fn
pyramid's alchemical secrets known by, 222
Mars *(Lat.)*
a fiery, strong planet, 425-426
Mercury &, not part of Earth Chain, 112
Martanda (Marttanda) *(Sk.) see* **Sun**
Maspero, Gaston
alchemical materials found by, 222
director of Boulaq museum, 222
French Egyptologist in Cairo, 221-222
T.S. member who found secret chambers, 222
Massey, Thomas Gerald
poet & writer, 66&fn
Materialism
worse now than in Fourth Race, 476
Mathematics *see also* **Geometry**
only exact science, 92
Blavatsky weak in, 139-140
Mathers, Samuel Liddell MacGregor
a founder of Hermetic Order, 160fn
Pistis Sophia and, 160&fn
────── *Kabbala Denudata: The Kabbalah Unveiled* part of *Zohar* in, 363fn
shows four planes, 363, 498
translated from Latin, 498fn
Matri-Padma *(Sk.)*

First Logos and, 134
Matter *see also* **Substance**
in aeriform or gaseous state, 518
contraction of primordial, 266-267, 292
cosmic, needs rest, 12
differentiations of, 405, 429-431
dreamless sleep and, 77
crystallized spirit, 247
during Pralaya, 382
is eternal, 405
ether crystallized, 202
evolve into spirit in Fourth Round, 446, 475
force and, 269, 343
an illusory reflection, 430
inter-molecular states of, 249, 405
light first flutter in undifferentiated, 80
is materialized spirit, 505
Mundane Egg and, 132-133
on primordial, 388
primordial, the mother, 266, 354
protyle and, 5-6
pure, is pure Spirit, 257
radiant & cool, 225-226
ring 'Pass-Not' for, 375-376
on seven planes of, 429-430
spirit and, are one, 353
Spirit and, as opposites, 257-258
squaring circle and, 143, 264
symbols of ignorance and, 300
triangle and, 144, 264-265
Maya *(Sk.)*
Astral Light is, 148
cause of misery, 45
of finite universe, 505
great deceiver, 639
illusion, 47-50, 236, 298, 639-640, 643
Maha-, of eternity, 334-335
manifestation is, 50
Nirvana is a, 14, 50, 69

veil of, 236
Mayavi-rupa *(Sk.)*
 Fohat and, 381
Mazzaroth (Mazarot) *(Heb.)*
 Job mentions, 9&fn
Mead, G.R.S.
 translates *Parabrahm* pamphlet, 199fn.
Meditation(s)
 thoughts and, 185
Medium(s)
 astral handwriting and, 182
 blinded by astral matter, 250
 danger to, 179
Memory
 dreams and, 53-54
 of previous lives, 593-594
 universal, and Mahat, 594
Mercury
 hides sacred planet, 398-399
 origin of, 428
 parent moon of, 427-428
Meru *(Sk.)*
 eternal land of the Gods, 444, 516
 Greek & Indian meanings for, 443, 516
Metaphysics
 theory a term of, 8
 training needed to understand, 170, 610-611
Meteor(ites)
 atmosphere of earth changes, 409
 as corpses, 318
 feed some planets, 426-427
 Fohat and flaming, 255-256
 hypotheses about, 311-312, 404, 406
 Laplace theory in, 312
 Laya points and, 406-407, 409-410
 occult explanation, 317-318, 406-407
Methodist Churches
 some, try to catch Jesus, 141
Microcosm *see also* **Macrocosm**
 mind is, & means to macrocosm, 124, 268
Milky Way
 another state of matter, 224-225, 253
 Earth originally from, 316
 inexhaustible & invisible immensity, 252-253
 nebular theory about, 225
 portions only seen, 253
 relates to Laya centers, 316
 as World-stuff, 224-225, 252, 313, 316
Mind *see also* **Manas**; **Soul**; **Universal Mind**
 aspects of Divine, 135, 635
 consciousness is faculty of, 43
 contagion of, passions, 355
 Cosmic, defined, 30
 as higher human Manas, 308
 higher not instinctual, 41
 Mahat is Divine, 20, 635
 a manifestation, 33
 synonym for soul, 43
 waking and sleeping, 41-42, 51
Mineral Atom(s)
 evolved in prior Manvantara, 338, 475
 as 'germs of wheels', 337-338
 greater perfection of, on this Chain, 475
 next stage for, unknown, 338
Minucius Felix *(Lat.)*
 ——— *Octavius* on why we have no temples, 162&fn
Molecule(s)
 atoms and, differ between planets, 411
 atoms cp. to, 202-208, 352-353
 composed of many other, 204
 on lowest plane, 214
 only of our globe, 202
 seventh principle of each, an atom, 203, 204-205

in transfer of light, heat & sound, 391

Monad(s) *(Gr.)*
of anthropoids, 446-447, 448
astral images evolved by, 466, 557-558
is Buddhi as vehicle of Atma, 549-550
can evolve beyond his class, 437-438
descent of Pythagorean & Kabbalistic, 438
differentiate on Earth Chain, 465-467
higher Manas and, 372, 373, 558
incarnated fully in Third Race, 557-558
independent of the principles, 473-475
karmic law determines class of, 436, 438
in Laya state is One, 438
of Leibniz, 133, 267, 550-551
liberation of, 447
Manas linked to Divine, 281
meaning, 550
never-manifested, of Pythagoras, 129, 151
no more, coming in this Manvantara, 443, 448
not Jivas, 549, 557
only one in Nirvana, 438
overshadows fetus, 559
passage through kingdoms, 437-438, 465-466, 469-474
potentiality of semi-human, 447-448
reflects universe, 372
of 'savages' return in Sixth Race, 447-448
seven classes of Lunar Pitris are, 465-467, 470-472
third plane action of, 438-439
three classes of, mentioned in *S.D.*, 435

on transfer of, from Moon to Earth, 465-470
triangular path of, 195-196
trinitarian, 438
unchanging in mid Fourth Race, 448

Monier-Williams, Monier
Oxford Sanskrit professor, 607&fn

Monotheism
worship of one god, 103

Moon(s)
affects vegetation, 420
danger of sleeping under Full, 420, 421
disintegrates slowly, 342, 408
as dragon in Sun's eclipse, 491
dual capacity of our, 427
dying, principles form Earth Chain, 397, 465-475
ends with Pralaya, 342, 461
information on, beings not given, 436
long dead cp. to planets, 95, 383, 462
lunar mankind, 465-467
magnetic effect on Earth, 319, 404, 408, 422, 423
man stage on, inferior to same on Earth, 466
most mysterious of globes, 436
mystery planet and, 318-319
not dead planet, 292, 457, 464-465
not in obscuration, 383, 462-465
our, already old, 230
planets' magnetism & number of, 425
planets will become, 230, 292
principles of dying, form new chains, 446
on rotary motion of, 457-465
seventh principle of, and Laya point, 421
shows only one side, 320
some, both parents & satellites, 427
a soulless planet, 292

substitute for Herschel, 97
tables of Hindus on, 400
vampirize their children, 399-400, 420, 457, 459, 464
will lose its hold on Earth, 408
Morgan, Ellen H.
co-founded T.S. branch in So. India, 451fn
wrote "Witchcraft on the Nilgiris," 451fn
Morgan, Maj.-Gen. Henry
Ootacamund T.S. co-founded by, 451fn
saw sacred stone given to Todas by Rama, 454
Moses *(Heb.)*
on making a living soul, 181
Moses de Leon
Spanish rabbi & Kabbalist, 498fn
Zohar edited by, 498fn
Mother
immaculate, begins hierarchy, 302
meanings of Father, Son and, 62-65
as primordial matter, 301
on swelling of, 153-155
synonym of matter, 132
Mother Goddess
Father god and, 2
Motion *see also* **Fohat**
on Absolute, 457
'Breath' as, 312
inherent, is ceaseless, 390, 457-465, 513-514
manifestation of fire, 232
of moon & planets, 457-465
occult axiom on, 232
root and soul of, 349
vibrations as cause of, 345-346
Mulakurumbas
afraid of Todas, 452, 454
vile dwarf tribe, 452, 454
Mulaprakriti *(Sk.)*
Akasa is, 260

defined, 2-4
Logos sees veil of, 68, 130
as primordial matter, 71
Muller, Friederich Max
editor of *Sacred* Books series, 24&fn, 85&fn
terrible materialist, 607
Mundane Egg *see* **Egg**
Music
in Pythagorean school, 317
talent an inherent quality, 565, 567
talent for, not hereditary, 563-564, 565
Myer, Isaac
——— *Qabbalah*, 123fn
on Ben Judah as perfect Kabbalist, 499
HPB cites, in *S.D.*, 499&fn
Myers, Frederick
questioned Adepts, 436fn
Mystery(ies)
hint on death of, schools, 120
of Life & Consciousness, 643

N

Nagas *(Sk.)*
allegory of war in heaven and, 211
Nagasena *(Sk.)*
on Nirvana, 23, 270
Name(s)
anagrammatical meanings, 107, 304-306
Kabbalistic value of, for man, 217
transformations, 217, 304-305
Narayana *(Sk.)*
Ishwara not, 20
as unmanifested Logos, 20
Nature
all, has elemental spirits, 167, 169
always evolving, 477
is bipolar, 360
essential unity of, 640-641

forces of, as emanations of Hierarchy, 609-610
geometrical aspects in, 309-310
intelligence in, 610
kosmic quaternary and, 477-478
Laws of, 309, 310, 311
man obliged to work with, 587
no straight lines in, 359
not a single gap in, 446
seven forces in, 111, 232, 257, 608, 609
seven is root number of, 486-487
two poles & seven principles of, 479-480

Nebulæ (Nebula) *(Lat.)*
Fohat and, 280, 348
no relation to Laya centers, 398
a stage in cosmic evolution, 518
theory of science, 314

Nefesh *(Heb.)*
dual nature, 181
jivatma and, 201
Kabbalists on, as living soul, 482

Neith *(Eg.)*
Parabrahman and Egyptian, 1-2

Neros(es) or Naros *(Heb., Chald., Gr.)*
cycle of time, 10&fn

Neuralgia
color and, 91-92

Newton, Sir Isaac
on attraction of particles, 267
intuition of, 122
laws of, 274, 277, 279

Nidana(s) *(Sk.)*
a cause of misery, 45, 47
causes of existence, 66-67
finite cause of past ages, 67, 570
Maya awakens, 48-49

Nirmanakaya(s) *(Sk.) see also* **Adept(s)**
every, suffers, 601
great sacrifice of, 445, 601
inspire & communicate with some, 446

lives subjectively to help mankind, 445-446
Nirvanic bliss delayed for, 444
as sisthas aid humanity & cosmos, 445
as sisthas and Terrene Pitris, 444
voluntary custodians of sleeping planet, 446

Nirvana *(Sk.)*
as absolute consciousness, 327, 393-394, 632
after 'Great Day', 372-373
Brahman and, 300
cycle of necessity and, 483
defined, 393
egos attaining, still must return, 483
fate of not reaching, 300
great renunciation of Gautama, 601-602
is but does not exist, 270
is Maya, 14, 50, 69
not annihilation, 393-394
not Pari-Nirvana, 373
Parinirvana cp. to, 393-394, 626
postponed for sisthas, 444
refusal of, by some, 299-300, 444, 445, 602
selfish state, 445
as universal consciousness, 393

Nirvanee (Nirvani)
Ego and, 44, 326-327

Nitya Pralaya *(Sk.)*
all change is, 293
our atoms are in, 293
as perpetual change, 292-293

Noumenal
Absoluteness and, space, 158
all merges into, at Pralaya, 12
Jiva and, 631
phenomenal and, 39-40, 165
universe lacks space & time, 14

Number(s)
circle as root of, 484

of Dhyan-Chohans, 305
eight as bad astrologically, 494
as entities, 211-212, 304-305
figure 8 as spiral, 358
occult value of, 212-213, 305, 358
One, as unity, 484
permutation of, 303-306
Pythagoras avoided, two, 359, 484
as signs & symbols, 211-212
ten as perfect, 213

O

Occult Science
on ether, 258, 259
materialistic Science cp. to, 262
study nature to penetrate, 200, 204, 309-310, 311, 544

Occult Societies
Esoteric Section and, 152

Occultism
on 'atmosphere', 404
atoms of, 133, 201, 298
differs from Theosophy, 534, 545-547
everything transformed in, 361
first axiom in, 200
geometrical proofs in, 279
gravity not believed in, 506
HPB teaches, 65, 108, 262, 358
intuition must be used in, 544, 547
keynote of, 544
metaphysical books & basic, 547-548
seven rays & combinations in, 544
seven sacred planets in, 342
on source of everything, 269
spirit & matter one in, 257-258, 505
struggles with science & some theologies, 395
telescope reveals only reflections says, 346

Occultist(s)
'fire' as used by, 232-233

have own science, 390
on Hell, 483
learned, on Kepler's laws, 278-279
must be Theosophist, 546
non-separateness of, 298, 533, 546
Prana's spectrum of, 554
one force of, has differing names, 268-269
West's hunting of, 120

Ocean
churning of, in Hindu allegory, 209-211
of Life, 200-201
universal differentiation &, 209-210

Oeaohoo
emanation of Fohat, 240
defined, 240
not to be talked about, 240
veil lifted by, the younger, 236

Olcott, Henry Steel
a pious Buddhist, 47
on spirit, 616
——— *A Buddhist Catechism*, 47fn, 59&fn

One
life & electricity are, 139
point or, 20-21, 129-131, 142, 144-145, 151

One Life *see also* **Life**
ceaseless motion of, 390
energizes substance, 388
eternal homogeneity, 611
force as action of, 390
Jivatma as, 201
Life a reflection of, 457
Ocean of Life is, 201
as Paramatma, 201
Root as potency in, 201

Orcus *(Gr.)*
as Death, Hell or Mara, 485

Organic
everything that changes is, 247
and 'inorganic', 246-247

Ormuzd *(Zend)*
is "I am", 23
Osiris *(Eg.)*
Isis and, 155, 416
Ovid *(Lat.)*
Chaos as matter for, 502
Ovum *(Lat.) see also* **Egg**
correspondences, 424
Oxygen
quality & intensity of, 112-115
universal flame and, 117

P

Pagan(s)
Church uses ideas of, mob, 161
rites adopted by Church, 216
Parabrahm
Edouard Coulomb author of, 199fn
pamphlet on Parabrahman, 199
Parabrahm(an) *(Sk.)*
absolute unconsciousness, 554, 555-556
Absoluteness or, 68, 70, 72
or Ain Soph, 10, 50, 71, 597
is All, 69, 72, 116, 597
is but does not exist, 628
Atman corresponds to, 3, 633
is Be-ness not a thing, 71, 597, 628
beyond conception, 1, 110, 628
causeless cause, 70, 73, 552, 554
discussion on nature of, 68-72
endless duration of, 10
as Ever Darkness, 130, 193
First Logos and, 633
First Logos cannot see, 68
or It, 2, 73
Jiva applied to, 551
Mulaprakriti and, 2, 71
not a cause, 68, 70-71, 72
not happiness, 597-598
not the Absolute, 68, 71
not veil behind veil, 72

as nothingness, 72
Sat is, 72
Paramatma *(Sk.)*
Supreme Soul, 201
Paranishpanna (Parinishpanna) *(Sk.)*
66
Parent(s)
diseased, should not bear children, 583-584
Karma of, for giving disease to child, 583
only, lowest principles given to child, 560-561, 564, 565, 570
Paranirvana (Parinirvana) *(Sk.)*
differs from Nirvana, 373, 393-394, 593
Maha-manvantara and, 394
Particles
in motion become spheroidal, 310
scattered at Pralaya, 342-343
Tyndall experiment with water, 310
Pasha, Ishmail
as mystic Khedive, 220
Pasha, Tewfik
not a mystic, 220&fn
stopped pyramid research, 219-220
Path Magazine
exposes Butler in, 540fn
Judge editor of, 539fn
on 'origin of planet Mercury', 428&fn
Pentagon *(Gr.)*
five-pointed, equals man, 217
transformed into six, 142
Perfection
increasing, always, 483, 507-508
Kumara life may await, now, 482
threefold, of man, 440-441
Permutation
of numbers & letters, 303-306
principle not for public, 303
or Temurah in Kabalah, 304
Perpetuum Mobile *(Lat.)*
Great Breath as, 10, 312

Personal Self
differs from personality, 375
impersonal self vs., 371-375
as triangle in square, 371-372, 375
Personality
in Devachan, 591
duty to forget, 533
everywhere, is the curse, 533
incarnating ego goes from, to, 593
individuality differs from, 565
is lower quaternary, 497
Manas touched by, each life, 566-567
is objective individuality, 375, 565
suffering of, helps Manas, 567-568
Peter the Hermit
led Peoples' Crusade, 615&fn, 616
Petrie, William Flinders
English Egyptologist, 219fn
pyramid measurements of, 219
Phallic Symbol
cross as, 145
Pharisees
prayer of, *vs.* Jesus, 162
Pho *(Turanian)*
meanings of, 138-139
Physiology
parents give, to child, 560-561, 564-565
on senses, 84-86
Pi
numerical & geometrical value of, 304
Pistis Sophia *(Gr.) see also* **Sophia**
Gnostic text in *Lucifer*, 160&fn
Pitris *(Sk.) see also* **Lunar Pitris**
as Manus, the forefathers, 175-176
progenitors of mankind, 175, 177
Plane(s)
of being and non-being, 197-198, 213-214
Cosmic, 163, 379-380
creations of conscious beings, 429-430

of divine substance and consciousness, 429-430
each, has own colors, sounds, etc., 241, 544
each, has 7 states of matter not substance, 434, 544
every, a reflection of another, 136, 542-544
of globe and solar system, 379-380
higher & lower, than ours, 16-17, 241, 284, 285, 396-397, 542-544
inhabitants of other, 241
infinite number of, 198
lowest, of chemical molecule, 214
of manifestation, 271-274, 379-380, 396-397
only four, manifested, 148, 432, 379-380
our lowest, most material & dense, 432, 434
passage of Life-Wave through, 397
point becomes the, 265
relate to seven principles, 433
senses vary on each, 285
seven, become 49 etc., 214, 544
seven, on each, 246
Seventh, of primordial matter, 5-6, 270-271, 272
unifying of, 284
upper, more ethereal, 432
Planet(s)
astrological, 96-97
bodies cannot pass from, to, 404
break up after Seventh Round, 408, 518-519
comets or suns once, 230, 313-314, 331, 341-343, 517
correspond to 7 states of consciousness, 434
dying, generate new, 396-397, 462-463, 519
elements remodeled by atmosphere, 409

equilibrium preserved by laya, 404
exist on four planes not seven, 433
fragmentation of, disrupted, 342, 409, 410
fragments go to higher system, 341-343
gives its principles at death, 446, 519
Herschel or Uranus, 96fn
on hidden, 319, 398-399
influence not all bad, 492
kosmic wanderers, 313-314
Laya centers and, 409, 407, 410, 519
numerous minor, 400
in obscuration still visible, 383
as reflections, 346
on rotation of, and moon, 457-465
seven sacred, and two secret, 95-97, 98, 342
Sun did not throw off, 341-342
Sun older than, 312
Sun will become, 343
two secret, and seven, 96-97, 398-399
vital essence of, cp. to kama-rupa of man, 479
as 'wheels' 396, 397-398
why some, have several moons, 425

Planetary Chain(s) *see also* **Earth Chain**
emanation of, 397, 518-519
exist on other planes, 202, 519-520
on four lower planes, 380, 434
manvantaric lives of, 341-342, 382
meaning of, vs. Planetary System, 111-112
matter of & planetary spirit, 95
obscuration of, 291-292, 382, 397, 443
passage of life-wave to, 397
pralaya and, 291-293, 382, 443
Sun does not absorb, 341-342

Planetary Spirit(s)
Builders a lower kind of, 99

Earth's, not very high, 98
Hindu astrology on, 541-543
influence man's destiny, 541-543
no relation to Sephirot, 106
one, for each globe, 102
only rule matter of globes, 95, 98-99
pralaya of, 101
ruling, is self-conscious, 478

Planetary System(s)
gravitation alone cannot explain, 268
mathematical proofs about, in *S.D.*, 279
millions of, 316
motion phenomena in, 277-279, 457-465
Pralaya and, 461
or solar system, 111-112
Sun oldest in our, 340

Plant(s)
ferns and, prototypes in ice, 310-311
free will in, 168
intelligence in, 167-168
sensitivity in, 167-168

Plato *(Gr.)*
on eternal idea or Divine Thought, 271, 635
deductive method of, 73, 120, 641
modern philosophers cp. to, 120, 635

Pleiades *(Gr.)*
all seven seen by ancient Hindus, 401
Electra & Merope of, 321
most occult constellation, 319-320
once hidden, 319, 321
Rishis connected with, 319-320

Poimandres *(Pimander) (Gr.)*
a book of *Corpus Hermeticum*, 478fn
on planetary spirit, 478

Point(s)
atoms as mathematical, 335
mathematic, an illusion, 334-335
Pythagorean geometry and, 142-145, 151
within circle, 20-21, 129-131, 151,

264-265
Pole(s)
Brahmins on, 514-517
evil magnetism from South, 365
good magnetism of North, 365-366
North, land of the gods, 365, 443
S.D. correction on, 514
seven Arakas in Patala, 515
seven circles at each, 514-515
seven steps of Meru at, 514-515
South, place of rejoicing for Hindus, 515
shifted at every tropical year, 516
Population(s)
Africa once had vast, 449
of China, 449
of world greater than now, 449
Potency *see also* **Potentiality**
of Aditi, 313
causeless cause will become, 71-72
dual ideal, 301
emanations from infinite, 324
Mundane Egg and, 133-134
periodical, of Divine Ideation, 635
of Pho, 139
Potentiality
Atman is, of all, 593
atom as, in space, 336
cosmic mind is, 30
early Stanzas refer to, 193
elements co-existent, 503
eternal, of Divine Ideation, 635
of fire, 324
of First Logos, 64
latent, radiates, 158
of manifested Monad, 439
potency and, 71, 134, 139, 201, 635
Primordial Seven a, 326
Sat is, of being, 139
sex and, 132
of space, 60
Prakriti(s) *(Sk.) see also* **Mulaprakriti**;
Purusha *(Sk.)*

Kwan-Yin and, 235
Malkuth or, 43
not primordial matter, 505
Purusha and, 439
Seven, from Mahat, 4, 42
Pralaya(s) *(Sk.) see also* **Nitya Pralaya**
Absolute during, 62
animals during, 383
consciousness in, unknowable, 435
earth's, not same as Solar, 230, 382
of globes & chain, 290, 291-293, 382, 468-470
Great Breath during, 10, 266-267, 312
impulse to manifest and, 74-75, 266-267, 382
of lunar classes, 470
Manvantara &, same length, 468
Manvantaric dawn and, 512
mind and, 27-28
motion ceaseless in, 390
Nitya, perpetual change, 292-293
planetary spirits have, 101
Rishi described, 382
seven periods of, 9, 468-471
as seventh day, 512
Universe disappears in, 12
Vishnu Purana names seven kinds of, 178, 254
Prana *(Sk.)*
compared to kama-rupa as life essence, 479
forty-nine fires and 480
in Hindu astrology, 541-542
Jiva compared to, 550-551
as life principle, 551
septenary nature of, 479, 480
sun rays carry, into astral plane, 542-543
two vehicles of, in man, 479-480
Primordial Beings
highest in existence, 301
seven, born from Third Logos, 303

Svabhavat and, 301
Primordial Substance *see also* **Substance**
  begins to differentiate, 3-4, 63, 329, 354, 388
  creative deity symbolism of, 505
  descendents of, as cosmic nuclei, 512-514, 517-518
  differentiation of, 354
  force always moving in, 388, 390, 412
  Mundane Egg as undifferentiated, 132-133
  not our dense matter, 505
  Protyle cp. to, 5-8
  radiation of cosmical force and, 388, 390
  reflection of absolute motion as Laya of, 412
  spirit of creative fire, 505
Principle(s) *see also* **Man(kind)**
  cosmogenic vs. anthropogenic, 375
  esoteric philosophies teach seven, 627
  Female & Male, 132, 144-145
  forty-nine fires and seven, 480
  on four lower, 145, 371, 374-375, 379-380
  in man differ in Devachan, 374-375
  no eternal male or female, 132
  or Pythagorean properties, 145
  in Sephirot, 213
  seven, in everything, 205, 213, 472, 473-474, 476-480
  seven, obscure to Europeans, 626-627
  seven, only aspects of the One, 66, 374
Prism
  color combinations, 90-91, 194, 213
  white ray divided by, 40, 140, 213
Privation of Matter *see also* **Prototype(s)**
  lower builders trace, 166

  prototype or, 165, 635
  seven planes and, 3
Proctor, R.A.
  English astronomer, 401fn
  ——— *Myths & Marvels of Astronomy*
  S.D. source cited, 401fn
  writes on knowledge of ancients, 401
Proserpine (Proserpina) *(Lat.)*
  mysteries of, 216
Protestant Church(es)
  rites of, from pagans, 161
Prototype(s)
  Archetypal World has all, 365
  astral, are shadows, 169
  Astral Light and, 157-159, 164-166, 181
  ice contains, 310
  of ten, 305
Protyle *(Gr.) see also* **Substance**
  Crookes coined term, 5&fn
  Greek root of, 6-7
  hypothetical, 635
  non-differentiated matter, 63
  not on this plane, 3
Puranas *(Sk.) see also* **Vishnu Purana**
  cited, 105, 176
  secret allegories of Hindus in, 320, 439, 629-630
Purusha *(Sk.)*
  is Anima Mundi, 630
  Prakriti and, allegory, 439, 629-630
Pyramid, Great
  chambers protected from discovery, 220-222
  coffers & niche in, 218-219
  iron door protects from Nile, 221
  on Kabbalistic measure as "man", 217
  Pythagorean geometry and, 142-145
  "Son" in occult symbolism, 217
  as temple of initiation, 219
Pythagoras *(Gr.)*
  denied straight line, 359
  geometry sacred science to, 317

never manifested Monad of, 129, 151
point as universal & absolute, 359
school studied math & music, 317
studied in India, 197
swore by holy Tetraktys, 151
triad and, 35, 359
triangle and, 64, 195-197, 359
as Yavanacharya Greek teacher, 197

Pythagorean(s)
contempt for digit 2, 144, 359
occult geometry of, 142, 359
seven properties in man, 145

Q

Qabbalah *see* **Kabalah; Myer, Isaac**

R

Race(s)
age of Fifth, 468
animal egos and Sixth, 447-448
early, in mountains of China, 450
elements develop with, 258, 260-261
Fifth, a cancer of humanity, 476
Fifth, high intellectuality, 573
first man-ward, 439-440
Fohat and First, 281
Fourth, becomes physical, 571
hierarchies correspond to, 296
Hindus a superior, 510-511
Manas develops in Fifth, 566
mankind changed in Sixth, 6
Monads in early, 557-558
Monads stop at Fourth, 442-443, 448
mysterious, of Todas, 451-455
planet disappears during Fourth, 319
selfishness of, 509
sex and Second, 177
Sixth & seventh, Buddhas to come, 100

'Sons of the Fire' of Fifth, 295
Third, and separation of sexes, 516

Radiant Essence
in Hindu allegory, 209-210
issues rays or breaths, 392, 541-542
non-atomic, 201
pre-cosmic state, 201, 276
radiant energies and, 392
seven inside & out, 213, 214
as shoreless ocean, 210

Radiation
emanation and cp., 156-157, 541-542
First Cause or Logos and, 70, 237, 554
Fohatic, 404, 411, 413, 417
no, from It, 1
primordial, 154, 225

Rama *(Sk.)*
gave sacred stone to Todas, 454
served by Todas in Lanka, 453, 454

Ramanujacharya, Sri *(Sk.)*
────── *Catechism of the Visishtadwaita Philosophy* on dark spot in the Sun, 376

Ray(s)
astral planets and Sun's life, 542
each, breaks into thousands, 167
of First Logos, 154
primordial seven, 110-111, 544
prismatic, issue from one, 40, 90-91, 213, 543
as Pythagorean Monad, 195
refraction of Sun's, 541-543
solitary expands into seven, 194-195, 197
white, & prismatic colors, 40, 91, 194-195, 213, 543

Red
color and pain, 91

Reincarnation
always progressing to higher planes, 594

attraction & antipathy explained by, 605
butterfly & chrysalis analogy, 594
each, adds spiritual qualities, 566-567
of ego & omniscience, 600
immediate, cases, 602-603
justice of, 603, 604
memory of past, 593-594, 596, 600
strong will can influence, 605

Religio-Philosophical Journal
Chicago Spiritualist journal, 539&fn

Religion(s)
any, or no, for Theosophist, 523, 545
cause of illusive forms of, 639-640
change of, not needed for T.S. member, 546
diversity of, a great curse, 509
early Christian, cp. with Church, 160-162
Gnostic, 160
immaculate conception in, 141
materialism in, 141, 161
of Paul had no rites or temples, 162
Roman Catholic, drew on Paganism, 161
theology disfigures, 160-161
Theosophy is not a, 523

Revelation
not a Christian work, 491
prophecy about Dragon, 491

Ring-Pass-Not
meanings, 375-376

Rishi(s) *(Sk.)*
on Great Breath, 10
Manus and, 105-106
seven 'husbands' of Pleiades, 320-321
of Ursa Major, 320-321

Rites
Church copied pagan, 161, 216
early Christians had no, 162

Ritualism
churches disfigured pagan, 161, 216
roots in Church & Masonry, 161&fn

roots of, 161, 217

Robes
Eternal Parent's Invisible, 1, 3-4, 6
laya condition of Eternal Parent, 3
as veil of Absolute, 4

Roman Catholic(s)
cant of, 163
immaculate conception, 140-141
pagan rites disfigured by, 161
on Virgin Mary, 140-141

Rootless Root
causality itself, 72, 201
Ocean of Life and, 201
remains One element, 223

Rosenroth, Christian Knorr von
Kabbalist & translator, 498fn

Rosicrucians
Astral Light known to, 157
on kosmical phenomena, 232
on One flame, 117
seven principles known to, 145

Rotation
genesis of motion and, 462-464
of planets and moon, 457-465
principles of globes and, 460, 461-462

Round(s)
on astral forms of Third, 447
Dhyani-Buddhas come in Seventh, 101, 102
Earth at end of Seventh, 518-519
First and Second, differ, 411
gigantic astrals in Third, 447
limit of progress during Fourth, 508
man appears in Fourth, 468, 471
Manus and, 177
Manus or Rishis watch over, 105
middle of Fourth, brings equilibrium, 443, 446, 475
Monads and, 176, 469
Pitris during, 444, 466-467
planets die after Seventh, 408
Pralaya and Seventh, 512

we are on Fourth, 566, 571
Row, T. Subba *see* **Subba Row, T.**
Rupa *(Sk.)*
    Arupa vs., 371
    fade out in kama-loka, 371, 373
    lower personal man, 371, 373

S

Sacred Books of the East
    Anugita part of, 85fn
Sacred Planet(s) *see* **Planet(s)**
Sacrifice
    great, of Buddha & Adepts, 602
    of Sishtas, 444-445
Sakti *(Sk.)*
    Fohat and, 135
Saladin *(Arab.)*
    chivalrous Muslim knight, 616&fn
Salvation Army
    infectious magnetism of, 355-356
Samadhi *(Sk.)*
    on state of, 372
Sankhya *(Sk.)*
    HPB does not teach, 65
Sanskrit
    dictionaries short on meaning, 138
    numerical meanings of, 305
    planet name not occult name, 97
    richer than European languages, 613
    secret names derived from, 305, 306
    superior to English, 39, 85
Sarasvati *(Sk.)*
    goddess of speech, 308
Sat *(Sk.)*
    abstract space or, 75
    or Be-ness, 23, 27
    is potentiality of being, 139
    synonyms of, 72
Satan *(Heb.)*
    dogma of Devil in Christianity and, 492
Saturn (Saturnus) *(Lat.)*
    bad & good influence of, 492-493
    destroys to regenerate, 493
    on rings of, 426
Savage(s)
    all, dying out, 450
    return in Sixth Race, 448
    more intelligent in Sixth Race, 450
Schopenhauer, Arthur
    'blind will' of, 74, 120
    German philosopher, 67&fn
    intuition of, 121
Science
    animal remembrance and, 17
    a conceit, 119, 125
    deductive method ignored by, 641
    HPB used to respect, 126
    mathematics only exact, 92
    mistaken to say 'inanimate' atoms, 244-245
    no extra-cosmic force says, 280
    pet theories upset, 8, 275, 277-278, 392-393, 395, 423
    speculates and guesses, 16, 115, 203
    of today is ignorance of tomorrow, 6, 203-204, 275, 277, 392-393
    visible only perceived by, 274, 395, 611
Seer(s)
    ages of, attest to ranges of Absolute, 272-273
    consciousness reaps positive concept, 273
    esoteric instructions & capacity of, 273-274
Selfishness
    becoming worse, 509-510
    civilization breeds, 526-527
    Devachan a state of, 528
    of fanaticism, 615
    gigantic, now in Fifth Race, 476
    of lower quaternary, 497
    Nirvana a state of, 445
    no justification for, 507-508

Sense(s)
of direction, 83
of hearing and sound, 83, 85-87
seven, 85
shifting of, 81-82, 389
of sight, 82-87, 389
sixth, 81-82, 620, 624
of smell, 87
of touch, 81-82, 85, 389
Separateness
warning against, 298, 303, 505-509, 510
Sephira *(Heb.)*
2, 131, 144
Sephiroth (Sephirot) *(Heb.)*
angelic hierarchy of, 106-108, 129
same as Elohim, 304
sephirothal tree and, 129
seven classes of lower, 465
seven lower & three higher, 106, 150, 151, 213
ten as perfect number in, 213
Seven *see also* **Principle(s)**; **Ray(s)**
degrees of spirit-matter, 629
first of, rays, 40
-fold man, 66, 625
great mystery root number, 473, 486-487, 488, 489, 544
layers of Space, 1fn, 3
planes as reflections, 28, 136, 433, 542-544, 626, 627-629
Prakriti and, planes, 42
rays and multiples of, 544
sacred planets, 96
in solar year, 487-489
why, eternities, 9-10
Seven Principles *see* **Principle(s)**
Seven-Skinned Eternal Mother-Father
as space, 1fn, 2, 3
undifferentiated, 2-3
Seven Stellars
Coptic legend about, 492

evil, progeny of Saturn & moon, 492-493
Shaivas (Saivas) *(Sk.)*
worship Siva, 104
Shiva (Siva) *(Sk.)*
compared to Saturn, 493
highest of three gods, 105
as transformer not destroyer, 105, 360-361
as Vishnu's helper, 361
Sloka (Shloka) *(Sk.)*
pronunciation, 64
Sidereal Body
in cosmos explained, 517
Sight *see* **Sense(s)**
Silent Watcher
great sacrifice, 602
Simon Magus *(Lat.)*
on Æons, 333
on divine emanations or Syzygies, 324, 325fn
on Nous and Epinoia, 324
Sinnett, Alfred P.
—— *Esoteric Buddhism* cited, 291, 326, 343, 384, 436fn, 479, 567, 620, 631
Buddhi & intuition in, 620
death of Chain and, 396-397
exact figures not in, 377
Flammarion quoted in, 282
on life wave, 397
on Monad contact with child, 558-559
on obscuration of Mars, 384
Sishta(s) *(Sk.)*
custodians of sleeping planet, 444
highest Adepts as Terrene Pitris, 444
objective Nirmanakayas, 444
future Nirvanic bliss for, 444
sacrifice themselves, 444
seed-humanity, 383-384
as seed Manus, 383
Six

schools of Indian philosophy, 4,
squares of cube, 145
Skinner, James Ralston
on Jehovah, 150
Mason & Kabbalist, 218
on numerical value of "man", 217-219
――― *Source of Measures* math of Kabbalist in, 139&fn, 217-219
possible errors in, 218-219
Sky
or Dyaus, 215
as heavenly abode, 215
Sleep
brain and, 41, 51-56, 58
consciousness and, 56-57
dreamless, 76-77
mind during, 40-41
Smyth, Charles Piazzi
Astronomer Royal, 218fn
on pyramid measurements by, 219, 219
Snowdon, Mount (Wales)
purity of water from, 114
Socialists
efforts can't prevent anarchism, 510
Socrates (*(Gr.)*
Plato superior sage to, 120
Solar System
danger from too much thinking beyond, 200, 518-519
Solid(s)
first formation of, 144
six concrete, 145
Solomon Ben Judah (Solomon Ibn Gabirol)
Jewish philosopher, 123&fn
Son
differentiated state of Father-Mother &, 62-63, 64-65
as manifested Logos, 2, 3, 65
potentiality of, in First Logos, 64
Universe as, of necessity, 66

Sons of Fire
as Divine Dynasties of instructors, 296
modern, are Fifth Race, 295
Third Logos as, 296
Sophia *(Gr.)* see also **Pistis Sophia**
Achamoth mother of evil, 160
Achamoth is Astral Light, 180-181
Æons and, or Primordial Seven, 323-325
Divine, of Gnostics, 160&fn
middle space as region of, 160
text on Divine, 160&fn
Soul *see also* **Alaya**; **Nefesh**
Atma Buddhi and, 380
child & animal, 560
divine, permeates all, 297
Fohat as, of motion, 349
freed after death, 44
language, 613
Manu & evolution of, 172
as Nephesh is dual, 181
no new, for each baby, 297, 469
overshadows fetus, 559
is part of whole, 298
permeates all, 297
as Spirit, 62
supreme, & manifested, 201, 413
synonym for mind, 43-44
in three-fold division of man, 626-627
universal, or Anima Mundi, 630, 635
Sound
attribute of Akasa, 72
as first sense, 85, 86-87
seeing, 86-87, 89-90
as speech, 88
touch related to, 85
vibration and, 89-90
Space
Aristotle on, 502
causality of, and time, 67-69, 153-155

dark & bright, 236
Duration & abstract, 13-15, 22, 24, 42, 154, 158
as Eternal Parent, 1, 3, 60, 155
First Logos outside, and time, 153-155, 192
full of Fohatic force, 463
no rocks in, 459
not still, 462
six directions of, synthesized in seventh, 357
struggle for existence in, 507
Universe wound up in, 67, 68
upper, is within, 236-237
Waters of, 157-158, 180-181, 193, 237
in widest metaphysical sense, 357, 365

Sparks
circle symbolism and, 308
monads, or higher intelligences, 307-308
of 'the Seven', 307-308

Speech
esoteric meanings in *Anugita*, 309
faculty of lower brain, 188
movable & immovable, 309
as precipitated thought, 184, 185

Spencer, Herbert
Absolute is 'First Cause' for, 70-71, 122
English philosopher, 35&fn, 120
on First Cause, 395
idea on evolution, 284&fn
as scientist, 66, 124-125, 126-127
"unknowable" of, 287

Spirals
all forces move in, 358

Spirit
becomes objective matter, 258
body opaque to, 404
crystallized, is matter, 247
of Earth, 473

female aspect of, 235
fire as solid, 236
of God, 237, 329, 502
individuality of, and soul, 373
Laya center &, of Atman, 460
man's, becomes the Absolute, 333
-matter a dual force, 269, 629
matter and, are one, 353, 379
matter and, part of same web, 257-258, 266, 298
matter now evolving to, 446, 475
Monad & ruling, of planet, 479
primordial matter is, 505
is potentially matter, 505
pure, is pure matter, 257
substance and, metaphor, 62-63, 629-630
tetraktys and, 144-145
as universal life or consciousness, 247, 269

Spirits, Planetary *see* **Planetary Spirits**

Spiritualist(s) *see also* **Medium(s)**
create elementals, 179
danger to, 179&fn

Spiritual(ity)
awakening depends on Higher Manas, 496
incarnations add, qualities, 566-567
not personality, 565
only, survives death, 565-567

Spurgeon, Charles Haddon
electrifying magnetic power of, 355-356
English Baptist preacher, 160&fn

Square *see also* **Cube**; **Tetragrammaton**
as base of pyramid, 142-145
represents matter, 143

Stanley, Henry
Livingstone and, 449fn
Welsh explorer & journalist, 449fn

Stanza(s) of Dzyan
first, negative, 193
interpreted on seven planes, 136, 137

lift only corner of veil, 639
many slokas of, omitted, 639
method of, 135-137
occult keys to, withheld, 639
second, positive 193-194
seven meanings in, 137
solar system focus of, 38, 136-137
some, skipped, 38, 111, 137
Stanza 1
Sloka 1: 1-12
Sloka 2: 12-25
Sloka 3: 27-45
Sloka 4: 45-60
Sloka 5: 60-66
Sloka 6: 66, 95
Sloka 7: 66-75
Sloka 8: 75-93
Sloka 9: 108-110
Stanza 2
Sloka 1: 110-112
Sloka 2: 112-117
Sloka 3: 129-134
Sloka 4: 134-137
Stanza 3
Sloka 1: 153-181
Sloka 2: 191-194
Sloka 3: 181, 194-200
Sloka 4: 200-216
Sloka 5: 223-226
Sloka 6: 226-235
Sloka 7: 235-240, 242-245
Sloka 8: 240-241
Sloka 10: 257-265
Sloka 11: 265-294
Stanza 4
Sloka 1: 295-301
Sloka 2: 301-303
Sloka 3: 303-306
Sloka 4: 306-311
Sloka 5: 311-321, 341-347
Sloka 6: 323-331
Stanza 5
Sloka 1: 331-336, 348-349

Sloka 2: 337, 349-357
Sloka 3: 337, 357
Sloka 4: 357-363
Sloka 5: 363-369
Sloka 6: 371-377
Stanza 6
Sloka 1: 378
Sloka 2: 378-381
Sloka 3: 382-412
Sloka 4: 414-418
Sloka 5: 481-494
Sloka 6: 494-519
Star(s)
astral counterparts of, 401
five-pointed, means man, 217
as gods in Hinduism, 400
Mayavic atmosphere of, 406-407
our Sun a central, 341, 349
as ruling or relating to destiny, 540-541
self-luminous, 349
Struggle for Existence
applies only to differentiated matter, 507
man can rise above, 507-508
scientific malady, 507-508
on sidereal & terrene space, 507
Subba Row, T.
on *Gita* and Logos, 19-20, 68
Hindu metaphysican, 19fn, 49
on Maya, 49-50
on Mulaprakriti, 68
questioned seven principles, 148-149
Subjective
Aditi on, plane, 313
aspects of physical, 114
circle in, world, 265
emanation of, 2
germ, 201
Logos moves from, 308
Mahat and, universe, 327
mother's touch contracts, 266
as noumenal, 14

Paramatma as, soul, 201
Substance *see also* **Matter**; **Primordial Substance**
  as abstract form, 132, 133
  Ah-hi lack, 37
  as body or Son, 62-63
  differentiated as Father-Mother, 2-3, 63
  Laya center of primordial, 412, 414
  nuclei of cosmic, after generation, 511, 512-513
  occult doctrine on eternal, 335, 352, 419
  pilgrimage in sidereal career, 511-512, 513-514
  primordial, or Spirit of God, 329
  seven days of creation and, 511-512
  seven states of, & globe planes, 434
  Spirit and, 62, 132-133, 353-355
  as tetrad or tetraktys, 132, 143-145
  velocity of descent into, 512-514
Suffering
  desiring is, 598
  Devachan and, 579-581, 596
  great, of 19th century, 510
  lessening, but not Karma of others, 583-585, 586-587
  of Nirmanakayas, 601
  no happiness without knowing, 39
Sun
  after Pralaya of, 253-254, 341-343, 382
  Apollo & Bacchus, gods, 216
  atmospheric effect on, 255-256
  becomes comet in next Manvantara, 254, 341-343
  comet's tail repelled by, 318
  dark spot in, 376
  as 'dead' planet, 402
  God as, of early Christians, 215
  heart of solar system, 231, 233, 253
  Hindus on revolving of, 320
  as knot of Fohat, 227-228, 230
  manvantaric fragmentation of, 341-342, 343, 382
  as Martanda, 312-313
  nothing luminous except, 349
  older than its planets, 312, 315, 341
  protects from rays of true, 314
  a reflection only, 227, 228, 231, 253-254, 402
  solar fires and, 228, 231
  solar pralaya and death of, 313-314, 315, 382
  'son-suns' are countless, 330
  spectroscope analysis of, 255
  spiritual, is the One, 330
  substitute for sacred planet, 398
  symbol, 215, 364
  true, no one has seen, 402
  vampirizes, 228, 318
  in Vedic myth, 312&fn
  Vishnu Purana on pralaya of, 254
Sunflower
  piety of, 168
Superficies
  of Pythagorean triangle, 142-144
Surya *(Sk.)*
  Hindu legends about, 320, 376, 478
Sutratman *(Sk.) see also* **Manas**
  links personalities, 562, 565
  like a silver thread, 562
Svabhavat *(Sk.)*
  androgynous, 3
  is light of manifestation, 301, 324
  root of the world, 110
Swayambhu *(Sk.)*
  meaning changes with accents, 138
  self-essence, self-existing, 138
Symbol(ism)
  in *Bhagavad Gita*, 300
  borrowed from physical science, 284
  circle, 265, 308
  cross, 145
  dragon, 491-492
  fire & water, 235, 505

Fohat, 349, 416, 494
lotus bud, 155
Manus, 177
microcosm, 432
Orcus, 485
in Pythagorean geometry, 142-145
Sanskrit is full of, 350
seven meanings to every, 211, 376, 571
of seven skins, 635
Space, 1fn
Sun, 215, 233, 320, 364, 376
triangle, 144, 265
wine & bread, 216
Syzygies *(Gk.)*
Gnostic term for Divine emanations, 323-325

T

Tamilnadu (South India)
Nilgiri Blue Hill tribes in, 451fn
Telang, Kashinath Trimbak
Anugita translated by, 85fn
Temple(s)
early Christians had no, 161-62
Temurah *(Heb.) see also* **Kabalah**
third method to Kabalah, 304
Tetrad *(Gr.)*
as base of pyramid, 145
transformed into cube, 143-144, 145
Tetragrammaton *(Gr.)*
Eliphas Levi on, 151-152
Kabbalistic & Pythagorean, 144-145, 146-152
is Malkhut, 150
as Second Logos, 147, 148-151, 152
Tetraktys not same as, 151
Tetraktys *(Gk.)*
on first, 132
not tetragrammaton, 151, 152
triangle becomes a, 143-145
Theogony(ies)

on cosmic builders, 163
Second Logos in all, 155
Theory *see also* **Deductive Method; Inductive Method**
axiom not, 8, 200
scientific use of word, 8-9, 203-204
Theosophical Society
altruism and, 535-536
on criticism of, 54
on defense of, 533, 539-540
Hindus starve to join, 535
not a charity organ, 534
not a sect, 531, 534
personality is curse of, 533
vegetarianism as tenet of, 534
The Theosophist
on exoteric matters only, 307
Five Years of Theosophy from, 436&fn
on Maya, 49
on sound being seen, 87-88&fn
yogi theosophy a blind in, 307
Theosophist(s) *see also* **Occultist(s)**
Blavatsky calls holy men only, 545
considered Buddhists by some, 523
dogmatism to be avoided by, 640
duties of, 532-533
Father Damien a great, 529
first duty of, 533
intuition must be used by, 640
many poor, 535
may believe anything, 534
may belong to any religion, 523, 533
need to grasp general principles, 640-641
not all, are Occultists, 546-547, 639
not concerned with miracles, 307
not concerned with politics, 534
pseudo-, in America, 540
term is an ideal, 545
Theosophical duties and, 523-524
true, defined, 545
use deductive method, 642
use of word, in *Key to Theosophy*, 544-

546
Theosophy
based on laws of nature & Occultism, 545-546
differs from Occultism, 545-546
first principle of, 615
not a religion or sect, 523, 531, 534
seven principles of, 145
not spiritualism, 534
not yoga, 307
practical, 523-525
tenets of, 534
what is, and what is not, needs clarifying, 524
Thomson, Sir William
changing hypotheses of, 120&fn, 250
extra mundane corpuscles of, 250
Thought *see also* **Divine Thought**
automatic action and, 618-619
both conscious & unconscious, 617-620
cannot be defined, 188
cerebration voluntary or involuntary, 617-619, 622-623
feeling cp. to, 190
Fohat as active, power, 381
language of, 182-185
meditation and, 185
speech and, 184-185, 189-190
sponge cp. to, 187
Three *see also* **Number(s)**
in Pythagorean geometry, 129, 142-145, 195, 359
as triangle falling into matter, 151
Tidal Wave(s)
as providential, 449
Time *see also* **Cycle(s)**
clock simile and, 67
consciousness and, 21-22
Devachani has no idea of, 25
dreamer knows no, 42
Duration and, 12-15, 21-22, 42, 153-155

Earth & Moon, 469
First Logos has no, 155
light as, 227
noumenal has no, 14
periodical cycle of, 156-157
Second Logos involves, 155-156
space and, 14-15, 67-68, 153-155
velocity and, 513-514
Todas
came from Atlantis & served Rama, 453, 454
Dravidian god-like pastoral tribe, 451&fn
mysterious race described in *Isis*, 451
powers of, 452-453
rites and crypts of, 454
served by dwarf tribes, 452
of South India, 450-451
Tohu-va-Bohu
chaos or darkness, 60
Torah *(Heb.)*
the Law, 2
Touch *see also* **Sense(s)**
as first sense, 389
Transformation
of consciousness, 496, 500-501
of elements, 112-115
Transubstantiation
occult view of, 116
Tree(s)
acorn as germ of Oak, 165-166
Karma in, 166
privation of Oak, 166
Triangle *see also* **Tetraktys**; **Upper Triad**
is first differentiation, 197, 264-265
first Ray forms, 196-197
first real figure, 144, 151
manifested Logos, 64, 129, 151
pyramid related to, 145
Pythagorean, 64, 129, 142-145, 195-197, 265, 359
seven principles and, 145

square, cube and, 142-143, 145
tetrad derived from, 142-145
Trinity *see also* **Brahmâ**; **Vishnu**; **Shiva**
of Hindus is one, 360
human, not inherited, 561
Shiva as 'destroyer' in, 360-361
Vishnu as 'Preserver' in, 361
Tropical Year *see* **Year**
Truth(s)
analogy gives key to, 642-643
axiom about, 204, 642
of exoteric Buddhism, 59-60
Four noble, of Buddhism, 46-47, 59
in Olcott's *A Buddhist Catechism*, 59&fn
Tupper, Martin
English writer, 537&fn
Turanian
Fohat compound term in, 138
Two *see also* **Number(s)**
in Pythagorean geometry, 142-143, 144, 145, 151
Tyndall, John
geometrical change in particles, 310
Irish physicist & lecturer, 127fn, 128
science outlook of, 127, 128
water experiments show occult law, 310-311

U

Universals and Particulars *see also* **Deductive Method**
Aristotelian views on, 123
intuition vs. reason in, 123-126
modern knowledge and, 122-124
scientific method and, 124-126, 641-642
syllogisms and, 124
Universal Mind *see also* **Mind**; **Mahat**
above Divine Ideation, 363, 635
Absolute, and, 27-28, 30-31
Ah-hi and, 27-29

always is yet never manifest, 34
darkness and, 61
Fohat reflection of, 138
time and, 22
Universe
causes of 66-67, 505, 635
as formless Space, 192, 237
immersed in intelligence, 610
manifestation of, 63, 66-67, 505, 626
not differentiated in early Stanzas, 192-193
one essence of, 626
a shadow cast by universal fire, 505
a shoreless sea of fire, 237
Son of Necessity, 66
Space synonymous, 193
as Space where, will be, 192
unmanifested in early Stanzas, 192-193
wound like a clock, 67
Unknowable
as absoluteness vs. manifestation, 556
debate on, & Unknown, 552-553
is First Logos of Occultists, 552, 554
Parabrahman is, 551, 552-556, 640
Upper Triad
Atma-Buddhi-Manas, 329, 375, 380
personal ego and, 375

V

Vach (Sk.)
androgynous, 378
Avalokiteshvara seven-faced, 378
Brahmā and, 155
esoteric and exoteric, 378
female Logos, 378
four-faced in Vedanta, 378
Second Logos as, 155
in *Vishnu Purana* etc., 378
Vacuum
Universal Mind cp. to, 28-29

vessel broken destroys, 28
Vaishnavas *(Sk.)*
  Vishnu as god of, 104
Valentinians
  on Æons & Syzygies, 323&fn
  dogma of, and Ophites regarding Jehovah, 473
Valentinus
  on Æons, 333
  Gnostic philosopher, 323fn, 333
Vaughan, Thomas
  Welsh mystic, 405fn
Veda(s) *(Sk.)*
  on Aditi, 4
  Parabrahman vs., 69
  Vishnu not prominent in, 61, 378
Vedanta *(Sk.)*
  defined, 4
  no philosophy higher, 74
  Occultism and, 65
  three sects of, 376
Vedantin(s)
  Absolute in view of, 71
  Jivatma as life of, 110
  on Mulaprakriti, 3, 4, 71
  stress four-faced Brahmā, 378
  three main sects of, 376
Vedder, Elihu
  illustrated *Rubaiyat*, 251
  Symbolist painter & knots of Fohat, 251
Veil
  of matter, 68, 600
  Mulaprakriti as, of Parabrahman, 68
Velocity
  changes with descent of cosmic nuclei, 512-514
Venus *(Lat.)*
  parent moons faded out, 427
Vibration(s)
  before manifestation in *S.D.*, 190-193
  as cause of motion, 345-346

color and sound, 89-90
  the point of unmanifested Logos, 192
  primordial radiation, 153-154, 156-157
  Seventh, and First Logos, 153-155
  wavelength measurement, 90-91
Vinegar
  intensity varies, 115
Virgin Mary
  Church makes, goddess, 141
  materialized, 141
Virgin Mother
  Jesus incarnation and, 141
  manifested Logos as, 154, 155
Vishnu *(Sk.)*
  Absolute or Ain Soph as, 61
  Brahma as aspect of, 61
  as Preserver, 105, 361-362
  transformation of, 361
  Vaishnavas worship, 104
Vishnu Purana *(Sk.)*
  Akasha in, 72
  on Brahmā, 378, 502
  Golden Egg in, 20-21&fn
  legend about Surya, 478
  Mahat in, 4, 20, 158
  names seven kinds of pralayas, 178
  philosophical allegories in, 254, 502
  on Rishis of Ursa Major, 320-321
  on solar pralaya, 254
  Vishnu as Absolute in, 61
'Visible that was'
  as past Manvantara, 75
Vision
  comet tail and, 344-345
  moments of high, 600
Visishtadwaita *(Sk.) see also*
Ramanujacharya
  catechism of, 376&fn
  dualists, 376
  personal God belief of, 376
  on Sun's dark spot, 376
Voice, The

as synthesis of Logos, 329
Voragine, Jacobus de, Archbishop
 compiled *Golden Legends*, 536fn
Vulcan (Vulcanus) *(Lat.)*
 intra-Mercurial planet, 96, 319, 342, 398-399
 one of secret planets, 96, 398-399
 science suspects, 398-399

W

Wallace, Alfred Russel
 open-minded naturalist, 127&fn
War in Heaven
 allegorical meaning, 210, 215, 491
 eternal, as differentiation, 210-211
 gods & asuras, 211
 human evolution and, 215-216
 theological view of, 210, 211, 215, 216, 491
Washington, George
 thought posture of, 185
Water
 element analyzed, 112, 113-114, 117, 178, 179, 235, 310-311
 female aspect of fire, 235, 236
 geometric shapes in, and ice, 310
 Kabbalistic terms for, 181
 occult intensity of, 114, 117
 in Occultism, 180-181, 235, 236, 310-311
 primordial fire in fluidic form, 235
 of space or chaos, 180-181
 stands for matter, 236
Web
 becomes radiant, 276
 centers of heat and, 276-277
 expansion of the, 266
 as primordial matter, 266
 spirit & matter at opposite ends of, 257
Weight
 as air or ether in primordial state, 233

density imparts, 293
 as gravity, 234
West
 ancients thought, bad, 364
 Devil comes from, 364
Westcott, William Wynn
 Freemason & Hermeticist, 152&fn
 ——— *Numbers, Their Occult Powers & Mystic Virtue* preface on transformations, 304&fn
Westerners
 confusion & speculations of, 10, 119-120, 123-128, 152
Wheel(s)
 Anupadaka as Great, 108
 Earth Chain and, 396-397
 as Fiery Whirlwind, 337, 348, 349, 351
 Fohat and, 337
 as rotation centers, 327, 494
 of time and space, 67
 within wheels, 327
Wilson, Horace Hayman
 English Orientalist, 21fn
 mistakes in *Vishnu Purana* translation, 254-255
Wiggins, Blind Tom
 slave pianist, 563&fn
Words
 abstract thought precedes, 184
 as symbols, 183-184, 188

Y

Yavanacharya *(Sk.) see* **Pythagoras**
Year
 Astral Light changes with tropical, 158-159
Yogi(s) *(Sk.)*
 buried in trance, 45
 karma can be avoided by, 578
 postures as blinds, 307
 on those, not returning to Earth, 300

Z

Zero
   as negative in Kabalah, 2
Zero-point
   as laya state, 7, 63
Zervana Akerne *(Pahlavi)*
   of Avesta as true 'eternity', 10&fn
Zodiac *(Gr.)*
   meaning of, signs, 217-218, 400, 487, 493-494
   signs as 'sacred animals', 571
Zollner, Johann
   scientist, 127&fn

CPSIA information can be obtained
at www.ICGtesting.com
Printed in the USA
LVOW11*2012060617
537156LV00001B/1/P